The Constitutional Law Dictionary

THE
CONSTITUTIONAL
LAW DICTIONARY

VOLUME 1:
INDIVIDUAL RIGHTS

Ralph C. Chandler
Richard A. Enslen
Peter G. Renstrom

ABC-Clio Information Services
Santa Barbara, California
Denver, Colorado
Oxford, England

This book is Smyth sewn and printed on acid-free paper to meet library specifications.

Library of Congress Cataloging in Publication Data

Chandler, Ralph C., 1934–
   The constitutional law dictionary.

   (Clio dictionaries in political science; #8)
   Includes index.
   1. Civil rights—United States—Terms and phrases.
2. Civil rights—United States—Cases. I. Enslen,
Richard A., 1931–   . II. Renstrom, Peter G., 1943–
III. Title. IV. Series.
KF4747.5.C52 1984   342.73   84–12320

ISBN 0-87436-031-5 (v. 1)   347.302

10 9 8 7 6 5 4 3 2 1

ABC-Clio Information Services
2040 Alameda Padre Serra, Box 4397
Santa Barbara, California 93103

Clio Press Ltd.
55 St. Thomas Street
Oxford, OX1 1JG, England

Manufactured in the United States of America

This book is dedicated to

ROGER CLARK CHANDLER
whose gentle spirit ministers
grace to his father

JOAN A. ENSLEN
whose support has given nourishment
to her husband

FRANKLIN and MILDRED RENSTROM
whose affection and encouragement
are ever present with their son

Clio Dictionaries in Political Science

SERIES STATEMENT

Language precision is the primary tool of every scientific discipline. That aphorism serves as the guideline for this series of political dictionaries. Although each book in the series relates to a specific topical or regional area in the discipline of political science, entries in the dictionaries also emphasize history, geography, economics, sociology, philosophy, and religion.

This dictionary series incorporates special features designed to help the reader overcome any language barriers that may impede a full understanding of the subject matter. For example, the concepts included in each volume were selected to complement the subject matter found in existing texts and other books. All but one volume utilize a subject-matter chapter arrangement that is most useful for classroom and study purposes.

Entries in all volumes include an up-to-date definition plus a paragraph of *Significance* in which the authors discuss and analyze each term's historical and current relevance. Most entries are also cross-referenced, providing the reader an opportunity to seek additional information related to the subject of inquiry. A comprehensive index, found in both hardcover and paperback editions, allows the reader to locate major entries and other concepts, events, and institutions discussed within these entries.

The political and social sciences suffer more than most disciplines from semantic confusion. This is attributable, *inter alia,* to the popularization of the language, and to the focus on many diverse foreign political and social systems. This dictionary series is dedicated to overcoming some of this confusion through careful writing of thorough, accurate definitions for the central concepts, institutions, and events that comprise the basic knowledge of each of the subject fields. New titles in the series will be issued periodically, including some in related social science disciplines.

—Jack C. Plano
Series Editor

ix

CONTENTS

A NOTE ON HOW TO USE THIS BOOK

The Constitutional Law Dictionary: Individual Rights focuses on concepts of constitutionalism, words and phrases common to American constitutional law, and leading case decisions rendered by the United States Supreme Court. Several techniques have been utilized to help the reader locate entries with ease.

The materials in Chapters 1 and 8 are arranged alphabetically. The terms in Chapter 1 develop the major elements of constitutionalism and provide the conceptual framework around which the other chapters are organized. Chapter 1 should be reviewed in its entirety for an understanding of the fundamental characteristics of constitutional law. Chapter 8 closely resembles a traditional dictionary. It contains definitions standing alone but also words and phrases that appear in other entries in the volume. The terms in Chapter 8 do not constitute an exhaustive listing of legal words and phrases, however. The closest this book comes to that kind of listing is the comprehensive Index.

Chapters 2–7 are organized around topical issues, with older cases preceding more recent ones. The reader may locate a case or concept in the area of interest by scanning the summary of entries at the beginning of each chapter. The summary has the page number of each entry.

A complete, alphabetical listing of all case entries and their respective page references is provided at the front of the book.

The reader can explore the implications of a topic by using the cross-references provided at the end of each definitional paragraph. The references point to related materials included in the same chapter or to relevant discussions in other chapters. Page numbers have been provided for all cross-references.

Finally, if the reader is unsure about which chapter to consult for a particular case or concept, he or she may consult the comprehensive Index at the end of the book. It includes every case or concept contained in the dictionary, either as a major entry or as a reference within an entry. Various permutations of entries are included in the Index to aid in the reader's search. All indexed terms include page numbers.

The authors have designed the format of the book to offer the student or general reader a variety of useful approaches to locating information. The book may be used as (1) a *dictionary* and *reference guide* to the language and major decisions of the United States Supreme Court in the field of individual rights; (2) a *study guide* for students enrolled in law school or in political science classes in colleges and universities; (3) a *handbook* for use by lawyers, police officers, and others entrusted with enforcement of the law and/or protection of individual rights; (4) a *supplement* to a textbook or a book of readings in the field of constitutional law; (5) a source of *review materials* for the attorney, judge, professor, or student of constitutional law; and (6) a *social science aid* for use in cognate fields, such as business and commercial law, economics, history, and sociology.

PREFACE

Precise language is a basic requirement of every intellectual discipline. This is particularly true in the field of law. We undertook to write *The Constitutional Law Dictionary: Individual Rights* in pursuit of clear and precise legal language.

The authors have tried to assemble a book that explicates the fundamental ideas of constitutionalism in general and American constitutional law in particular. The task involved the integration of many elements reflective of the multidimensional character of the subject matter. We hoped to reach both general readers and specific audiences of academics and practitioners. A major objective was to introduce students who might be considering a career in law to some of the operational concepts in the field. We also intended to reach the legal community, including lawyers who may find themselves removed by the circumstances of their lives from easy access to the essential elements of constitutional law.

The concepts, terms, and cases selected here represent our best judgment about how to advance the understanding of constitutional law in the area of individual rights. A large number of terms and cases could have been selected. We did not intend, however, that the book should be an exhaustive reference source. A number of such volumes already exist. Our selections were guided by such questions as: Does this term, concept, or case enhance the ability of the reader to communicate in the fundamental language of the field? Will the entry facilitate the reader's search for knowledge and understanding? Will the volume complement and supplement materials commonly used in courses in constitutional law? By limiting our dictionary to fundamental concepts, we believe a more thorough description and analysis has been made possible.

Two considerations were important in the selection of Supreme Court cases. One was that certain cases should be included because they are generally regarded as landmark cases. *Brown* v. *Board of*

Education is one such case. No discussion of the Equal Protection Clause can be complete without it. The second consideration was that we thought a conscious effort should be made to emphasize *recent* decisions, both to present the current thinking of the Court and to provide a sense of how the evolution of a particular line of cases has taken place. The Burger Court is therefore heavily represented. We thought it should be this way because of the extensive activity of the Burger Court in defining and redefining individual rights. Citations for 1983 cases are sometimes referred to within the text using references to the Lawyer's Editions of the United States Reports series. The obvious reason for this is that, at the time of publication of our book, the complete United States Reports series was not available from the publisher.

Although all dictionaries tend to resemble one another, *The Constitutional Law Dictionary: Individual Rights* has some unique features. First, entries have been selected to reflect the major issue areas of the field. The book has a subject-matter chapter format by which key cases are grouped for study and review purposes. This allows the dictionary to be used both in and out of class as a teaching and learning tool by professors, students, and practitioners. The chapters are linked through their subject matter to leading textbooks. A second unique feature is the inclusion of a paragraph of *Significance* following the definitional discussion. The authors have sought to provide historical perspective through this paragraph. We offer comments that underscore why we think the case is important. A third feature is the inclusion of cross-references that function as suggestions about how to seek additional information within the volume. Finally, the book incorporates a comprehensive Index to facilitate the location of entries.

We wish to acknowledge the large number of scholars who have contributed to the volume by their elaboration of the language of constitutional law. We are greatly indebted to them. We also wish to acknowledge with deep gratitude the intellectual stimulation of our students. We want to express our sincere appreciation for the inspiration provided by Professor Jack C. Plano, series editor of the ABC-Clio Political Dictionary Series. Professor Plano has spent many hours with our manuscript. There likely would never have been a *Constitutional Law Dictionary* without his years of labor in the development of the art of lexicography. A hearty thanks is extended to John Mausert-Mooney, Mary H. Schaafsma, and Angela G. LaVanway, who assisted substantially in the research undergirding the book. Finally, we offer special thanks to Dorothea Bradford Barr, our patient and extraordinarily skilled typist. These colleagues and friends made the enterprise possible. The authors accept full responsibility for errors. We invite readers to communicate with us about any aspect of the book.

—Ralph C. Chandler
Professor of Political Science
Western Michigan University

—Richard A. Enslen
United States District Judge
Western District of Michigan

—Peter G. Renstrom
Associate Professor of Political Science
Western Michigan University

ALPHABETICAL LIST OF CASE ENTRIES

The Constitutional Law Dictionary

1. Constitutionalism

Articles of Confederation   The first constitution of the United States of America. The Articles of Confederation governed the united colonies from 1781 until 1789, when they were superseded by the new federal Constitution. The drafting of the Articles of Confederation by the Second Continental Congress began on June 7, 1776, the same day the first formal motion was introduced to declare independence from Great Britain. The battles of Lexington and Concord in April had made it clear to all but the staunchest loyalists that a war of independence was inevitable. A formal government for the united colonies was needed, if only for military purposes. The Second Continental Congress rejected John Dickenson's first draft because it created too strong a central government. Congress approved Dickenson's second draft on November 15, 1777. The required ratification by all the states was not completed until Maryland's approval was given on March 1, 1781. Maryland's price of ratification was Virginia's agreement on a controversial western territories land question.

The general issue in congressional debate had been what kind of union was best for the thirteen colonies. Although there was a spectrum of opinion from monarchist to fervent state sovereignty, historians have distinguished two main groups in opposition to each other. The original Federalists wanted a weak central government. They were led in the Second Continental Congress by Thomas Burke and included Richard Henry Lee, John Witherspoon, and George Mason. Thomas Jefferson, Patrick Henry, and Thomas Paine were sympathetic to that position but were not present at the Congress. The Nationalists, called Federalists in the subsequent debate in the 1787 Constitution, wanted a strong central government. The Nationalists were led in the Second Continental Congress by John Dickenson and later by James Wilson. The party included John Adams, Charles Carroll, James Duane, Joseph Galloway, John Jay, James Madison, Gouverneur Morris, John Rutledge, and George Washington. A combination of hatred for the tyranny of the British government, strong patriotic feelings for individual states, distrust of politicians and rulers generally, and the self-interest of groups and regions won the day for the old Federalists.

In its thirteen articles, the final version of the Articles of Confederation laid out a loose confederation of sovereign states over which the central government had only the limited powers enumerated in the document. Since there was provision only for a weak executive and no judiciary, most of the powers of the central government were vested in the Congress. It was to meet at least every six months. Each state, represented by from two to seven persons elected and reimbursed by the state legislature, had just one vote in the Congress. Any important issue required the consent of nine states, and any amendment to the Articles had to be unanimous. When Congress was not in session, the daily business of the United States was to be conducted by a Committee of the States. The Committee was composed of one representative from each state, with one of the thirteen members elected president for a one-year term. The Articles also permitted the establishment of any necessary congressional committees. The government was soon run by the four committees regulating finance, the army, the navy, and foreign affairs.

The enumerated powers of Congress included the determination of each state's share of the confederation's common expenses, although Congress had no power actually to collect taxes or to compel individual states to do so. Congress was given procedural and moral authority to settle disputes between individual states, but it had no authority to enforce compliance with the settlements. Congress had the exclusive power to declare war and peace; conduct foreign diplomacy (except for commercial treaties that limited the rights of individual states to impose tariffs and embargoes); regulate currency, weights, and measures; run the postal service; appoint the highest officers in the army and navy; and set limits of size for the armies and navies of the individual states.

Three specific issues occupied much of the debate over the Articles. They were the formula of representation in the Congress, the formula for the sharing by the states of the confederacy's common debts, and jurisdiction over the lands west of the Alleghenies. Representation was finally set at one vote per state. The larger states' desire for representation in proportion to population was defeated. The more populous but underdeveloped southern states finally won the common-debt debate, with the stipulation that a state's share would be proportionate to the improved value of its land. On the western land question, Maryland's dogged refusal to ratify the Articles finally won the concession of the eight states with western land claims, especially Virginia. The jurisdiction of that land was turned over to Congress. The Articles of Confederation contained no bill of rights. Many anti-Nationalists would later criticize the Constitution of 1787 because it had the same defect. *See also* CONSTITUTIONAL-ISM, HISTORICAL DEVELOPMENT OF, p. 16; CONSTITUTION OF THE UNITED STATES OF AMERICA, p. 19; CONTINENTAL CONGRESS, p. 24.

Significance   The Articles of Confederation created the thirteen United States of America from thirteen British colonies and enabled the new government to survive both a war with Great Britain and the war's aftermath. The perennial question regarding the Articles has been whether they represented a noble but necessarily transitional form of government that was legitimately replaced by the 1787 Constitution, or whether they were the sole authentic governmental embodiment of the Declaration of Independence and the Revolution. In the latter view the Articles were illegitimately supplanted by the Constitution. Today historians admit that many of the alleged weaknesses of government under the Articles have been exaggerated. There is also general agreement that refusal to establish a stronger central government under the Articles was the reason for the confederation's inability to make individual states share the $60 million national debt after the Revolutionary War. The Articles were also the reason for the young nation's inability to overcome British, French, and Spanish interference with American commerce. Historian Merrill Jensen maintains that accounts of such weaknesses are based on the shoddy historical reports of John Fiske. Jensen argues that the supplanting of the Articles in 1787 reflected the conservatives' successful interruption of an internal sociopolitical revolution that had been the real inspiration for the external revolution against Great Britain. Whatever one's view of this historical debate, there can be little doubt that the centralization-decentralization issue has continued to be a prime source of disagreement throughout the history of the United States. From the debate over the Articles, through Jefferson's conversion from the old Federalist to the new Federalist position, through New England's strong states' rights position during the War of 1812 and the Webster-Calhoun debates before the Civil War, all the way to the debates over the New Deal and Ronald Reagan's New Federalism, the United States has continued to search for the proper balance between an adequate central government and the rights of states and individuals.

Bill of Rights   The enumeration of the rights of individuals legally protected against violation by government. The American Bill of Rights is found in the federal Constitution and its amendments, especially the first ten. The Bill of Rights is broader than the first ten amendments, with which it has traditionally been identified. The protection of many individual rights was included in the body of the original Constitution of 1787: (1) the prohibition of suspension of *habeas corpus* except in wars and rebellions and the prohibition of bills of attainder or *ex post facto* laws (Article 1, Section 9); (2) trial by jury for all crimes except impeachment (Article III, Section 2); (3) limitations concerning indictments, trials, and punishments of accused traitors (Article III, Section 3); and (4) the prohibition of religious tests for public officeholders (Article VI). Moreover, there are many personal rights protected by amendments subsequent to the first ten: (1) the prohibition of slavery (the Thirteenth Amendment, ratified 1865); (2) the prohibition of racial bars to voting rights (the Fifteenth Amendment, ratified 1870); (3) the prohibition of gender bars to voting rights (the Nineteenth Amendment, ratified 1920); (4) the right to drink alcohol (the Twenty-first Amendment, ratified 1933); (5) the prohibition of tax payment as a condition for voting (the Twenty-fourth Amendment, ratified 1964); and (6) the prohibition of age bars to voting rights for those over 18 years of age (the Twenty-sixth Amendment, ratified 1971). Although it does not enumerate any new personal rights, the Fourteenth Amendment (ratified 1868) played a crucial role in broadening the enforcement of all personal rights in American constitutionalism.

The first ten amendments themselves guarantee the following personal rights: (1) the freedom of religion, speech, press, assembly, and peaceful protest; (2) the right to bear arms in order to maintain a well-regulated militia; (3) freedom from having soldiers quartered in one's home; (4) freedom from search and seizure without probable cause; (5) the requirement of grand jury indictment for all but military crimes, freedom from double jeopardy and judicial self-incrimination, and the guarantee of legal due process, as well as just compensation for publicly appropriated private property; (6) the right to a speedy, public, and impartial trial, with the right to know the charge against one, the right to compel witnesses for the defense, and the right to have legal counsel; (7) the right to jury trial for civil matters concerning $20 or more, and the prohibition of judicial review of such trials except in accordance with civil law; (8) prohibition of excessive bails or fines and of cruel and unusual punishment; (9–10) of those rights not enumerated in the Constitution or its amendments, individuals enjoy all other rights except those delegated to the central government, reserved to individual states, or forbidden by the states.

The history of the federal Bill of Rights can be traced in five stages: (1) its British and philosophical antecedents; (2) early colonial enumerations of personal rights; (3) the bills of rights of states during the Revolutionary period; (4) the actual drafting of the federal Bill of Rights; and (5) the extension of federal enforcement of the Bill of Rights to prevent violations by the states. The two primary sources of the Bill of Rights were British statutory and common law on the one hand and natural law theory on the other. During the colonial period Americans stressed the protection of their rights by British law, especially as found in Magna Carta (1215), the Petition of Rights (1628), the Bill of Rights (1689), and as expounded in Blackstone's *Commentaries*. As the American desire for independence from Great

Britain increased, the colonists became more and more assertive of the natural law basis of their rights, especially as found in Locke, Montesquieu, and Beccaria. Many of the colonies adopted an enumeration of individual rights in their charters or in separate statutes. Maryland's Act for the Liberties of the People (1639) was the first. Rhode Island's charter (1663) was the first to allow broad religious freedom. The most developed charters were West New Jersey's Great Charter of Fundamentals (1676), the Pennsylvania Frame of Government (1683), the New York Charter of Liberties and Privileges (1683), and especially the Pennsylvania Charter of Privileges of 1701.

When the inevitability of the war for independence became clear, the Revolutionary leaders urged colonial legislatures to draft autonomous constitutions. Sensitive to governmental abuses in these documents, the legislatures sought guarantees for personal rights in the new state constitutions. The most influential document of this period was the Virginia Declaration of Rights (June 12, 1776), drafted by George Mason. Six other states followed Virginia's example in drafting a bill of rights separate from their new constitutions: Pennsylvania, Delaware, Maryland, and North Carolina in 1776, Massachusetts in 1780, and New Hampshire in 1784. New Jersey, Georgia, New York, and South Carolina drafted new constitutions between 1776 and 1778 with guarantees of personal rights embodied in the constitution itself rather than in a separate bill of rights. Only Connecticut and Rhode Island continued to operate under their colonial charters, which contained what they considered adequate provisions for individual rights. The Articles of Confederation (drafted 1777, ratified 1781) contained no individual rights guarantees either in the body of the document or in an appendix.

When the federal Constitution was drafted in 1787, it contained various guarantees in the body of the text but lacked a separate bill. The omission received more public criticism from opponents of ratification than did any other aspect of the Constitution. Among the proponents of ratification, Alexander Hamilton considered a separate bill of rights unnecessary because he said the states already had the power to protect individual rights. He believed an enumeration of rights to be dangerous because any listing might be considered exhaustive. Hamilton argued that social diversity and watchfulness were the ultimate guarantees of personal rights. Although James Madison originally agreed with Hamilton, he eventually came to support the drafting of a separate bill of rights. Madison was persuaded by his friend Thomas Jefferson and perhaps convinced by political necessity as well. Two months after Congress convened in 1789, Madison therefore proposed a federal bill of rights. He became the document's primary author, relying heavily on the Virginia Declaration of Rights and Jefferson's Virginia Statute for Establishing Religious Freedom. On September 25, 1789, Congress gave final approval to an American Bill of Rights containing twelve amendments. All but two were subsequently ratified by the states, Virginia completing the process on December 15, 1791.

The final phase in the development of the Bill of Rights came in the Reconstruction Era following the Civil War. The Thirteenth Amendment added to the content of the Bill of Rights, while the Fourteenth Amendment increased its scope. Until the Thirteenth Amendment, the Bill of Rights was understood to forbid only federal violations of personal rights. The Fourteenth Amendment required the federal government to ensure that individual states guaranteed individuals due process of law and equal protection of the laws in matters concerning life, liberty, or property. Still, it was not until the 1920s that the Supreme Court began to incorporate the specific rights contained in the federal Bill of Rights in decisions directly affecting the states. Eventually the position of Justice Benjamin N. Cardozo in *Palko* v. *Connecticut* (302 U.S. 319: 1937) prevailed: Although the Fourteenth Amendment does not incorporate the whole federal Bill of Rights, it does include all those federally guaranteed rights implicit in the concept of "ordered liberty." *See also* BLACKSTONE'S *COMMENTARIES,* p. 11; COMMON LAW, p. 13; *PALKO* v. *CONNECTICUT* (302 U.S. 319: 1937), p. 207.

Significance   If the ultimate purpose of constitutionalism is the protection of individual rights against the encroachments of government, the full fruit of any constitution is the enforcement of its bill of rights. Separation of powers and the specified rights of states within a federal system are the constitutional root, trunk, and branches meant to ensure the rights of persons. The key structural elements of a bill of rights are an enumeration of personal rights, a statement of the government's obligation to protect them, and effective provisions for their enforcement. Whether and how federal governments guarantee these elements determines the authenticity of their bills of rights. Great Britain, for example, has no single-document bill of rights, just as Great Britain has no written constitution. It does have a long tradition of protecting the rights of individual citizens, however, a tradition contained in centuries of common and statutory law such as the Bill of Rights Act of 1689. On the other hand, the Soviet Union's single-document constitution of 1936 has a highly developed bill of rights. But given the Communist party's unlimited power, the document does not have the enforcement provisions that would qualify it as an authentic bill of rights. For different reasons the United Nations

Universal Declaration of Human Rights of 1948 also lacks the enforcement provisions of a genuine bill of rights. How well does the American Bill of Rights meet the criteria of legitimacy? Its enumeration of rights was the most complete of its era, adding rights of speech, press, peaceful protest, and religion then unheard of in England. Yet the original Bill of Rights failed to abolish slavery despite the deep qualms of Jefferson and Washington. Today some would insist that the enumeration of the rights of American citizens should include the right to education, the right to be employed, and the Equal Rights Amendment. Implicit in such argumentation is the question of the grounds for including new rights in a bill of rights. Is the right to education a natural right? Are there utilitarian reasons for enumerating new rights such as employment? Does popular opinion suffice to establish the Equal Rights Amendment? Perhaps more crucial is the issue of effective provisions for enforcement. The Supreme Court has established itself as the ultimate guarantor of individual rights in the United States. While the institution of judicial review has generally worked well as a vehicle for the Court to monitor compliance with the Bill of Rights, there are glaring examples of the Court's willingness to sacrifice individual rights to the prevailing national *Zeitgeist* or to the will of the other two branches of government. In *Dred Scott* v. *Sandford* (19 How. 393: 1857), for example, the Court actually quoted the Fifth Amendment to oppose the abolition of slavery. In World War I the Court upheld federal convictions of persons who merely criticized the draft. In *Korematsu* v. *United States* (323 U.S. 214: 1944), the Court justified the federal government's indiscriminate internment of Japanese Americans during World War II. When the Supreme Court overturned state abortion laws in *Roe* v. *Wade* (410 U.S. 113: 1973), critics accused it of simply yielding to the social prejudices of the times. Such alleged or real weaknesses in the enforcement of the Bill of Rights have led political scientist Robert A. Dahl to repeat Alexander Hamilton's thesis that extraconstitutional mechanisms, especially a widespread grass roots sensitivity to justice, are far more important guarantees of human rights than are constitutional norms. Perhaps Dahl and Hamilton are correct. If they are not, however, and if a societal passion for justice is in fact a fragile if not a utopian idea, the Bill of Rights enforced through judicial review remains an irreplaceable protection for individual freedom in the United States.

Blackstone's *Commentaries*   An eighteenth-century compilation of English common law. Blackstone's *Commentaries on the Laws of England* was the most influential body of common law writing in the early modern era. Sir William Blackstone was born in 1723. He served one term as an elected member of Parliament, then was appointed Vinerian Professor of Law at Oxford University in 1758. His appointment was the first time anyone had been given an academic chair to teach English law exclusively, rather than English law as related to Roman law. Blackstone wrote the *Commentaries* between 1765 and 1769. In 1770 he became a judge in the Court of Common Pleas of England, and he died ten years later. Blackstone's *Commentaries* consist of four volumes totaling 2,000 pages. The volumes are entitled (1) *Of The Rights of Persons;* (2) *Of the Rights of Things;* (3) *Of Private Wrongs;* and (4) *Of Public Wrongs.* Blackstone believed that English common law could be discovered through the study of English history and that knowledge of the law should be made available to people at all levels of society, especially to members of Parliament. He said, for example, "How unbecoming must it appear for a member of the legislature to vote for a new law while being utterly ignorant of the old." Blackstone presented the law as the perfection of reason. His emphasis on logic and principle popularized his work, and he became something of an involuntary law reformer. Blackstone wrote that man's actions are subject to the laws of nature and that no human law could be considered valid if it contradicted the laws of nature. He said that common law is in fact a secondary law of nature with principles that are fixed and unchangeable. Blackstone opined about such specific ideas as a prisoner's right to counsel when his life is at stake. He said that no one should be forced to incriminate himself, or be tried twice for the same crime. He presented these kinds of concepts as maxims, or universal rules of nature. They were said to be simultaneously part of the law of nature and examples of the common law of England. No one successfully challenged Blackstone's legal theory or his reading of English history. *See also* BILL OF RIGHTS, p. 7; COMMON LAW, p. 13; MAGNA CARTA, p. 46.

Significance   Blackstone's *Commentaries* were decisive in the development of constitutional government both because they were the best law books of their time and because they appeared when the struggle between the American colonies and the British Crown was at its zenith. The legal theory of Blackstone largely shaped the political attitudes of the American colonists. They had long cherished elements of the common law of England, especially its forms of civil and criminal procedure. When the *Commentaries* were published, American lawyers made them popular and undertook to write American law in a manner similar to the language of the *Commentaries.* The idea that law is rule-permanent, uniform, and universal is a permanent legacy from Blackstone, as is the concept that law is an entity separate from society, which it in fact controls. Blackstone's maxims were affirmed by the inclusion of most of them in the American Bill of Rights. The First Amendment, for example, is an extension of Blackstone's discussion in Book IV, Chapter 11, where he adds to his discussion of freedom of the press, "If one publishes what is improper, mischievous, or illegal, he must take the consequences of his own temerity." The Fifth Amendment's holding that no person can be held to answer for a capital crime except by the indictment of a grand jury is taken almost verbatim from the *Commentaries.* The restriction against the taking of private property for public use without just compensation is an institutionalization of Blackstone's maxim that the possession of property is an inherent right of every man. Yet the American legal system also has unique characteristics not found in the *Commentaries.* In *Marbury* v. *Madison* (1 Cranch 137: 1803), for example, the Supreme Court broke with the English common law tradition, which maintained that judges or justices must remain interpreters of the law and never become makers of new law. The Court's claim of the right to declare acts of Congress unconstitutional was a radical departure from the basic conservatism of Blackstone. The *Commentaries* made their contribution to American constitutionalism primarily as textbooks for late eighteenth-century legal philosophy and as a comprehensive reference source for the writers of American state constitutions, the federal Constitution of 1787, and especially the Bill of Rights of 1789.

Common Law The tradition that a single body of law represents valid judicial interpretations of customary rules of action. Common law is a peculiarly English institution because it preserves and promulgates principles of law based on judicial decisions rather than on rules resulting from legislative enactments. France and Germany, in contrast, pursue a jurisprudential system founded on codified statutory law in the Roman tradition. Common law is judge-made law as opposed to statutory law. Soon after the Norman Conquest, in an attempt to establish and administer the King's Justice, Henry III authorized a circuit commission that charged circuit judges from the King's Bench with the responsibility of selecting the best of English county laws and transforming them into the common law of the kingdom. The process by which the justice of the king was defined, and his subjects controlled, created the common law. It was an astute and prudent sovereign who recognized the practical usefulness of adopting the best features of the county administration of justice, and who also was willing to chance that what was effective at the county level would also be effective throughout the realm. The circuit judges also sat on the royal courts at Westminster, where discussions shaped the rendering of local decisions and created the corpus of English common law. One law was made applicable to all disputes before the bar, set apart from ecclesiastical law and equity pleadings. Common law was therefore very much a statement of royal law as it was interpreted through the central royal courts. Those who found themselves pleading before a court on a common law issue were most often members of the aristocracy. Only infrequently were the lower classes affected by the principles of early English common law, for nonlandowners were governed by manor law.

The tradition of common law evolved in large part because the English legal profession strongly resisted the establishment of a statutory system. Students of law in England were trained more in the pragmatic applications of the law than they were in documentary systems of law enforcement. The legal profession was not so much interested in anticipating the adjudication of infractions of the law, such as those anticipated by statutory proscriptions, as it was in maintaining the precedent-setting value of actual controversies settled. This reliance on the value of precedent is perhaps the greatest legacy of the English common law system. Judges were placed in the position of either following the established precedent or distinguishing it, and in either case, they became the arbiters of the existing law. No decision was made unless an actual dispute existed. Much that was fundamental to common law was recorded only in the opinions rendered by judges.

From 1765 to 1769, Sir William Blackstone undertook the task of reducing to writing what he considered to be the essence of the common law. He said that common law was "nothing else but custom, arising from the universal agreement of the whole community," and that common law judges were "the depositories of the law—the living oracles who must decide all cases of doubt, and who are bound by an oath to decide according to the [precedent] law of the land." Blackstone's four-volume *Commentaries on the Laws of England* were not without their flaws and misrepresentations, however. Utilitarian philosopher Jeremy Bentham condemned them as worthless because they were not succinctly reasoned expositions of the law and could not, therefore, be scientifically accurate. Nonetheless, the *Commentaries* represented the first concerted attempt to commit to writing the evolving patterns of the common law. They served as a textbook and as a legal tool for students of law both in England and in the American colonies. The *Commentaries* became an indispensable guide in articulating the common law origins of both English and American jurisprudence. Another chronicler and advocate of the common law was Sir Edward Coke, the Chief Justice of the Royal Court. He reacted to Benthem's criticism of Blackstone by arguing that the common law was identical to natural law and was inherently the very embodiment of reason. *See also* BLACKSTONE'S *COMMENTARIES,* p. 11; ENGLISH CONSTITUTION, p. 27; SOCIAL CONTRACT, p. 61.

Significance   Common law in England represents the oldest corpus of jurisprudence administered by a central court and made applicable to an entire country. As originally conceived, it assigned powers to the king and clearly delineated the rights and privileges accruing to the king's subjects. Coke maintained that by the seventeenth century the common law also limited royal prerogatives. Chief Justice Coke said from the bench that "the king cannot create any offense by his prohibition or proclamation which was not an offense before." It is ironical that the impetus for the common law should have come from the king who would eventually be called to task for abuses of it. English common law found its way into the Constitution and the Bill of Rights of the United States. The framers were determined to maintain Blackstone's and Coke's legal theory in the new republic. It was in fact a reaction to English departures from the position of Blackstone and Coke that precipitated the events of the American Revolution. The federal Constitution is replete with barely disguised language from Blackstone, including that concerning indictment by a grand jury in the Fifth Amendment, trial by jury in the accused's vicinage in the Sixth Amendment, the prohibition against cruel and unusual punishment in the Eighth Amendment, the right to writs of *habeas corpus,* and the principle of stare decisis. Indeed, one of the fundamental doctrines of constitutionalism in the United States is its adherence to the tradition of stare decisis. Despite the fact that the United States is governed in the twentieth century by more and more statutory law, common law continues to be highly influential in American legal circles. The judiciary is concerned to remember its legacy. In *Bishop v. United States* (334 F. Supp. 415: 1971), the Supreme Court consciously deviated from a holding on strict statutory construction to credit once again the ultimate source of much of its decision making.

> The common law is generally described as those principles, usage, and rules of action applicable to the government and security of persons and property which do not rest for their authority upon any express and positive declaration of the will of the legislature.

Thus custom continues to be as important as statute in the definition of American legal standards.

Constitutionalism, Historical Development of   The growth of constitutional theory and practice through human history. The historical development of constitutionalism begins in a technical sense when the English term *constitution* was first used in its current political science context in the late seventeenth century. *Constitutionalism* was introduced in the mid-eighteenth century. The concept itself ante-dates use of either term, however. Political scientist Carl Friedrich notes six senses of the idea of constitutionalism. The first five of them are (1) philosophical, including Aristotle's definition of *politeia;* (2) structural, including the general organization of any actual govern-ment; (3) legal, including the basic law of a political entity; (4) documentary, including written constitutions; and (5) procedural, requiring more intricate amendment procedures for constitutions than for ordinary statutes. This entry traces the history of constitu-tionalism in its sixth sense, which Friedrich calls its modern and normative sense, including the theory and practice of effective, systematic, and institutionalized restraints on political and govern-mental power in order to prevent the violation of individual rights. Most constitutional scholars divide the history of constitutionalism into an ancient, a medieval, a modern, and a contemporary period.

The roots of modern constitutionalism, both its theory and prac-tice, stretch back to Greece, Rome, and the Judaeo-Christian reli-gions. Plato advanced the theory of constitutionalism by stressing that government must be guided by law (*nomos*). But he also insisted that the law-making power be concentrated in wise men. Aristotle distin-guished between a nation's basic governmental structure, its laws, and its changeable policies (*politeia*). He helped to clarify the fundamental and semipermanent nature of constitutions. Aristotle's description of the "mixed constitution" foreshadowed modern constitutionalism's separation of powers and its doctrine of the balance of power. Whatever their theories, however, Plato and Aristotle's Athens was not a constitutional democracy, if only because it denied women, foreigners, and slaves the rights of citizenship. The Roman stoics advanced constitutional theory by emphasizing the equality of all human beings, despite the widespread practice of slavery in Rome, and by formulating a natural law theory that would be further developed in the medieval period. The Roman jurists—notably the authors of the *Institutes,* the *Digests,* and the *Code of Justinian*—moved the practice of constitutionalism forward by giving "government by law" a written and codified foundation. Together with Roman natural law theory, the Judaeo-Christian belief in the inviolable dignity of the individual constituted the most important inspiration for modern constitutionalism. Less important roots are found in certain ancient tribal practices of the early Germans, such as the division of power between dual kings, and in the egalitarian temperament and social practices of the first residents of the British Isles.

Building on an ancient heritage, thinkers in the medieval period added important new dimensions to the developing theory of constitutional government. Canon lawyers, especially Gratian in his *Decrees,* underscored the importance of written and codified laws. Thomas Aquinas worked out a fully developed natural law theory, on the basis of which he subordinated all government to good law. The proponents of conciliarism, notably William of Ocham, Nicholas of Cusa, and Marsilius of Padua, were unsuccessful in replacing papal absolutism with a more participative form of church government, but they did develop an influential body of governmental theory based on the consent of the governed. Despite its authoritarian internal governmental practices, the church exercised considerable restraint on would-be absolute rulers in the secular realm. The church maintained a constitutionalism "from the outside" that broke down only with the Reformation. Medieval Europeans sponsored movements demanding charters of royal privileges. The best known of these charters, Magna Carta (1215), gave a new impulse to the development of common law in England. Henry de Bratton (d. 1268), also known as Bracton, completed a *Treatise on the Laws of England* that served as the most complete codification of English law until Blackstone's *Commentaries.* Another English author, John Fortescue (d. ca. 1479), developed a theory of legal restraints upon government based on the work of Thomas Aquinas.

A number of authors helped provide the theoretical transition from the medieval to the modern period. Richard Hooker (1553–1600) kept Aquinas's natural law theory alive and further developed the ideas of consent of the governed and social contract. The latter two traditions were elaborated fully by Johannes Althusius (1557–1638) and Hugo Grotius (1583–1645). The classical development of social contract theory was then achieved by Thomas Hobbes (1588–1679), John Locke (1632–1704), and Jean-Jacques Rousseau (1712–1778). Locke and the Baron de Montesquieu (1689–1755) also helped to define the doctrine of separation of powers. American writers such as Thomas Jefferson (1743–1826), Alexander Hamilton (1755–1804), and James Madison (1751–1836) wrote penetrating analyses of the American experiment in putting constitutionalism into practice. The modern development of constitutionalism came about as much through events as by the elaboration of ideas. The fragmentation of the church's secular influence through the Reformation removed the foremost obstacle to the royal absolutism that had begun in the fifteenth and sixteenth centuries. Yet the increasingly powerful commercial class, having outgrown its need for government-supported mercantilism, plotted to reduce the power of its former royal patrons. The first phase of constitutionalism in the modern period was England's development of a constitutsuperior monarchy. It began with Sir Edward Coke's successful defense of common law as superior to royal prerogative and subject only to Parliament. Gradually as the supremacy of Parliament was established Parliament itself became absolutist, until the role of the opposition and of regular popular elections was secured. Through all of these events, England never had a unitary constitutional document, except for Cromwell's short-lived *Instrument of Government* (1653). After England's constitutional monarchy, the next phase in the development of modern constitutionalism was the American Revolution and constitutional movement (1776–1789), which founded the first constitutional republic since Athens. The American Revolution began a widespread push to develop written constitutions throughout the civilized world. The American experiment was followed by the French Revolution (1789) and France's own constitutional experiments. The constitutional movement then spread to the other countries of Continental Europe. The final phase of modern constitutionalism was its democratization, beginning in the United States with Andrew Jackson and Abraham Lincoln and in Great Britain with the Reform Act of 1832.

The contemporary phase of constitutionalism includes five trends, all of which throw the future of constitutionalism into question. The first trend is the "negative revolutions" in France, Italy, and West Germany, where weakened forms of constitutionalism were adopted in reaction against a recent fascist past (Petain-Laval, Mussolini, and Hitler). All of the negative revolutions have failed to guarantee constitutional restraints on government power. The second trend is that toward supranational constitutionalism, as seen in the United Nations and especially in the European Common Market. Many constitutionalists see this as a positive and necessary development. They say that intranational constitutionalism is not secure without an international counterpart. The third trend is the generally unsuccessful attempt to constitutionalize emerging nations. Although virtually every new nation hastens to draft a constitution, the written document frequently lacks social institutionalization and is quickly set aside in times of crisis. The fourth trend is the appearance of constitutions in communist countries, which proclaim themselves to be both democratic and constitutional. Most constitutional lawyers say they are neither, while communist writers in turn consider many aspects of Western constitutionalism, such as the independent judiciary and the separation of powers, to be aberrations that pander to bourgeois individualism. The fifth trend is toward anarchy. Although anarchy is frequently overlooked as an alternative outcome to totalitarianism and constitutionalism, it continues to be a possible choice, if only by default. Anarchy has increased in the modern world, not only in the instability of emerging nations, but also in sociopolitical breakdowns in such developed nations as the United States, France, West Germany, and Italy during the 1960s and 1970s. *See also* CONSTITUTION OF THE UNITED STATES, p. 19; ENGLISH CONSTITUTION, p. 27; CARL FRIEDRICH, p. 34; REPUBLICANISM, p. 56.

Significance   The historical development of constitutionalism gives the reader an important sense of the contingency of the social institutions he or she may consider eternal and unchanging. Constitutionalism is neither an historical nor a logical necessity. Were it not for a very contingent historical sequence of ideas and events, it would not have arisen at all. Constitutionalism also embodies a practical and theoretically troublesome logical paradox—self-limiting absolute power—that its rival, unrestrained absolutism, neatly avoids. Constitutionalism's future direction is not at all clear. There are unresolved questions. Will greater socialization and centralization usher in new phases of constitutionalism, such as republicanism and democratization did in the past? Will international federalism and constitutionalism increase? What will be the effects of international federalism on intranational constitutionalism? It appears that constitutionalism's future is not guaranteed. In emerging countries it is frequently overwhelmed by totalitarian regimes. Traditional constitutional governments are frequently tempted to adopt unconstitutional measures to protect their constitutionalism. The first step in guaranteeing the future existence of constitutionalism is the development of consensus on whether and how it should exist. The consensus necessarily involves a reaffirmation of the inviolability of the individual person's rights and the basis for that inviolability, whether Judaeo-Christian religion, natural law, or some alternative ground of argument. It may also involve a realization that respect for the person does not necessarily imply unchecked individualism and that there may be important truths in the Marxist critique of Western institutions. Constitutionalism's continuing task is to achieve the proper balance between the rights of the community and the rights of the individual.

Constitution of the United States of America   The federal Constitution of the United States was completed by the Constitutional Convention on September 17, 1787. It was ratified by the requisite ninth state, New Hampshire, on June 21, 1788, and put into effect on

March 4, 1789. The document consists of a preamble of purpose, a body of articles, and a series of amendments. The body of articles regulates the following subjects: (I) the legislative branch; (II) the executive branch; (III) the judicial branch; (IV) the relation of the states to each other and to the central government, the admission of new states, and the regulation of territories; (V) the methods of amending the constitution; (VI) provisions for the national debt, the oath required of all state and federal officials to support the federal Constitution, laws, and treaties as "the supreme law of the land," and the prohibition of religious tests for officeholders; and (VII) provisions for ratification of the Constitution. Through 1983, 26 amendments, technically called "articles," had been ratified. Further, there is a "living Constitution" that includes developments and interpretations not included in the document itself.

The federal Constitution of 1787–1789 is really the second constitution of the United States. The first was the Articles of Confederation, drafted in 1777 and ratified in 1781. Because the Articles deprived the central government of any real power over the individual states, a host of problems arose concerning domestic and foreign commerce, the national debt, and internal and external security. Consensus developed that the central government had to have more power. After the successful Mount Vernon Convention to resolve commercial and boundary disputes between Virginia and Maryland in 1785, representatives from five states met at Annapolis in 1786 to discuss interstate trade conflicts. The Annapolis delegates soon abandoned their original purpose and instead called for a convention of all the states in Philadelphia to work out the measures "necessary to cement the Union of the United States." The Continental Congress gave its approval to the proposed meeting on the condition that the Philadelphia convention limit itself to amending the Articles of Confederation.

The Philadelphia convention met from May 25 to September 17, 1787. By the time of its adjournment, it bore the descriptive title Constitutional Convention, because it proposed not amendments to the Articles of Confederation but rather the constitution for a very different government. A total of 73 delegates were elected by the states to attend the Philadelphia convention, of whom 55 actually did attend, and 39 signed the finished document. Many of the delegates were widely read in political theory and had played leading roles in the drafting of their state constitutions. Since the convention's official secretary, William Jackson, kept such poor records, the best guides to the proceedings are the notes of Robert Yates and James Madison. George Washington was elected unanimously to the chair, but the dominant figure at the convention was Madison, later called the "Father of the Constitution." Although there was a wide range of opinion among the delegates, the combination of strong and moderate Nationalists far outnumbered the proponents of state sovereignty. The strong Nationalists included Washington, Madison, Benjamin Franklin, Alexander Hamilton, Rufus King, Gouverneur Morris, Edmund Randolph, John Rutledge, and James Wilson. The moderate Nationalists included Oliver Ellsworth, Eldbridge Gerry, George Mason, and Roger Sherman. Among the strong state sovereignty delegates were Gunning Bedford, John Lansing, William Peterson, and Robert Yates. Near the outset of the convention, Governor Edmund Randolph of Virginia presented the Virginia Plan, which proposed a strongly centralized parliamentary form of government. On June 15, William Patterson countered with the New Jersey Plan, which called for a somewhat stronger central government but stayed within the framework of the Articles of Confederation. The rest of the convention was devoted to working out compromises between these positions and conflicts related to them.

The first was the Connecticut Compromise, which attempted to balance the interests of small and large states. While representation in the House of Representatives would be set in proportion to population, thus favoring the large states, representation in the Senate was set at two for each state, thus favoring the smaller states. Another successful compromise guaranteed to the commercial North the federal protection of all trade, while to the agrarian South it guaranteed freedom from export taxes and the right to continue the slave trade until at least the year 1808. The nature and the method of election of the executive presented some of the convention's thorniest problems. The insistence of Madison, James Wilson, and Gouverneur Morris on a clear separation of powers defeated the proposal for a parliamentary executive and won approval for a presidential office. In a compromise between direct popular election, considered dangerously populist, and election by state legislatures, considered too great a concession to state sovereignty, the convention approved the election of the president by an electoral college. The Supremacy Clause of Article VI was introduced by the states' rights delegates as preferable to the proposed congressional veto power over state legislation. The states' rights group also successfully insisted on the powers of Congress being enumerated rather than broad and unspecified. To win this concession, however, they had to agree on the Necessary and Proper Clause (Article I, Section 8), which did in fact give Congress wide discretionary powers. The Constitution approved by the convention was a tremendous victory for those favoring a strong central government. The ensuing ratification debate, best preserved in the opposing viewpoints of *The Federalist* and Richard Henry Lee's *Letters of the Federal Farmer,* was long and furious. North Carolina and Rhode Island were the last two states to ratify, North Carolina in November of 1789, and Rhode Island in May of 1790.

The Constitution was never an inert document. Immediately it began to grow through amendments, interpretations, and other developments. Constitutional lawyer Paul Murphy has grouped the amendments into four historical phases: (1) early amendments (Amendments 1–12); (2) Reconstruction Era amendments (Amendments 13–15); (3) progressive era amendments (Amendments 16–19 and Amendment 21); and (4) later procedural amendments (Amendment 20 and Amendments 22–25). The Twenty-sixth Amendment and the attempts to pass an Equal Rights Amendment and a Right to Life Amendment reflect a new social reform phase of American constitutional history. The Constitution has also grown through interpretation. This includes presidential, congressional, and judicial interpretations, as well as the theories of influential statesmen. One example is President Madison's broad interpretation of the pocket veto, an interpretation that has persisted despite strong congressional opposition. Another example is the case of *Marbury* v. *Madison* (1 Cranch 137: 1803), in which the Supreme Court declared itself the final interpreter of constitutional matters, a claim that was generally accepted by the 1860s. The interpretations of the Supreme Court have rarely reflected a neutral reading of the Constitution, especially regarding such distinctions as strict versus broad construction of it. The Court has passed through various phases of interpretation: John Marshall's defense of federal supremacy and of inviolate property rights; Roger B. Taney's emphasis on community rights as a limitation on property rights; Salmon P. Chase's defense of local sovereignty against federal legislation; the return to Marshall's interpretation by Stephen J. Field, Joseph P. Bradley, and Melville W. Fuller; permission for broad federal regulation granted by the Court in the progressive era; and the property-oriented opposition to New Deal legislation that lasted until 1937, when the Court began to concentrate on guarantees of personal rights. The final way the Constitution has grown is vague to describe but fundamental in importance. It includes sociopolitical developments such as the two-party system and the aggrandized power of the presidential office. It embraces the changing economic and moral climate of the country as these factors influence the interpretation and enforcement of the documentary Constitution. As it allows for continuing citizen input, the Constitution becomes more and more a living document. *See also* ARTICLES

OF CONFEDERATION, p. 5; ENGLISH CONSTITUTION, p. 27; SEPARATION OF POWERS, p. 58; STATE CONSTITUTIONS, p. 62; VIRGINIA PLAN, p. 65.

Significance   The federal Constitution of the United States is the oldest documentary constitution in force in the modern world. Aside from its other merits, the Constitution's longevity has won widespread respect for it and frequent imitation of it on the part of other nations. It is held in near religious reverence by Americans. Still, the Constitution has faced severe criticisms, four of which are summarized here. The first, dating from the time of the Constitutional Convention, but also implicit in the works of modern historians, is that the convention itself was unconstitutional for two reasons. The convention exceeded the mandate given to it by the Continental Congress as well as the mandates the state legislatures had given their delegates, and it violated the amendment procedures defined in the Articles of Confederation. Constitutional lawyer Benjamin F. Wright has conceded the technical extralegality of the convention and its Constitution. He argues, however, that it was a necessary solution to the constitutional impasse created by the requirement of the Articles that the states be unanimous on any major question. Wright also maintains that the Constitution was far more democratic than either the Declaration of Independence or the Articles of Confederation. The Declaration had not been submitted to either the states or the people for approval. The Articles were drafted by the Continental Congress and ratified by the state legislatures, but none of the principals had been elected by the people for that purpose. The Constitution, by contrast, was drafted by delegates elected by their legislatures specifically for that purpose, was widely reported upon, was subjected to a long public debate, and was ratified by state convention selected by the people specifically for that purpose. The second criticism of the Constitution concerns the motives of the drafters. Historian Merrill Jensen argues that the new Constitution aborted the internal socioeconomic revolution that was the real inspiration of the external revolution against Great Britain. The new government's strong centralism protected the interests of the big land owners and merchants against the small landowners, tradesmen, and businessmen. Historian Charles A. Beard advanced a similar position in his seminal *An Economic Interpretation of the Constitution of the United States* (1913). The motivation of the framers remains a contested issue. The third criticism concerns the written document's omissions and ambiguities. Its fuzziness about the role of the Supreme Court in constitutional interpretation and about the implied powers of Congress caused decades of debate. The Constitution's initial omission of a bill of rights was soon corrected, but the new Bill of Rights refused to deal with the problem of slavery. The conflicts between the rights of the central government and state governments came to be fought not just in the halls of government but finally with great bloodshed on the battlefields of the Civil War. The final criticism concerns the interpretations and developments that have guided the growth of the living Constitution. The frontier and its disappearance, industrialization, immigration, the Great Depression, America's emergence as a major world power after two world wars, the civil-rights movement of the 1960s, and the tragedy of Vietnam are just some of the forces that have shaped the American character and thus the living Constitution. Some conservatives argue that the central government has become dangerously strong and expensive, that individual rights and enterprise are being stifled, and that the nation is degenerating into a welfare collectivity. Some liberals argue that the Constitution's provisions for procedural justice are often a cloak for the denial of substantive justice for the powerless and that the government is a pawn if not an accomplice of the domestic and foreign imperialism of American business. If there is substance to any of these criticisms, the Constitution is still an unfinished work. Each generation of Americans is required to provide new framers of the Constitution.

Continental Congress   The assembly serving as the collective voice and advisory forum for the thirteen colonies from 1774 until 1781, and then as the central government of the thirteen states from 1781 until 1789. The Continental Congress, whose official name was simply "Congress," is usually divided into four historical periods: (1) the First Continental Congress, September 5 to October 26, 1774; (2) the Second Continental Congress, May 10, 1775, to December 12, 1776; (3) the sessions from late December 1776 until the end of February 1781; and (4) the sessions under the Articles of Confederation, also called the Congress of the Confederation, from March 1, 1781, to March 4, 1789. On the latter date the Continental Congress was replaced by the three branches of the new federal government. The First Continental Congress met in Philadelphia's Carpenter's Hall at the urging of groups from Massachusetts, Virginia, New York City, Philadelphia, and Providence. Although the Congress had no legal status, its conveners were convinced that the colonies had to present a united front against the "Intolerable," or "Coercive," Acts passed by the British Parliament in 1774. Those acts, especially the Boston Port Act and the Massachusetts Government Act, threatened the commercial interests and the self-rule of the Massachusetts Bay

Colony and, by implication, of all the colonies. Fifty-six representatives from 12 colonies attended the First Continental Congress, Georgia alone refusing to participate. The main achievements of the first Congress were the Suffolk Resolves opposing the Intolerable Acts, the Declaration of Rights, and the establishment of the Continental Association. The Continental Association agreed on the nonimportation and nonconsumption of British goods and on the nonexportation of colonial goods to Great Britain. The Second Continental Congress met at the Statehouse in Philadelphia, later called Independence Hall. Planned by the first Congress in view of Great Britain's likely refusal to redress American grievances, the second Congress found its real urgency in the battles of Lexington and Concord, which had occurred just three weeks earlier. Twelve colonies were represented from the beginning, and Georgia finally sent representatives in the fall of 1775. Like its predecessor, the second Congress had no legal status. But it soon became the provisional government when hopes died for reconciliation with Great Britain. On June 7, 1776, Richard Henry Lee of Virginia presented a revolutionary dual motion: that the united colonies were and had the right to be independent states, and that Congress should draft articles of confederation for the new political entity. Events moved fast after that. On June 12, a drafting committee was established to write the Articles of Confederation. On June 15, George Washington was appointed Commander-in-Chief of the Army, although the Continental Army itself was not created until October 13. On July 2, Congress passed a resolution of independence. The resolution was formally announced to the colonies and the world two days later. From the end of its second session until early 1781, Congress met several times, focusing on the war and its aftermath. The Second Continental Congress also devoted a good deal of time to debating the Articles of Confederation. On November 15, 1777, the Articles were approved, and Congress referred them to the state legislatures for ratification. With the ratification of the Articles, Congress was reorganized according to the Articles' provisions and became the first central government of the United States. In fact the Articles created a very limited central government, little more than an instrument of state sovereignty. All governmental authority resided in the Congress. When it was not in session, the business of government was handled by a Committee of the States and the four congressional committees in charge of finance, the army, the navy, and foreign affairs. One of the main achievements of the Congress of the Confederation, the fourth phase of the Continental Congress, was the Northwest Ordinance (1787). This ordinance regulated the establishment of governments in the lands north of the Ohio River and west of the

Alleghenies and made provisions for the eventual statehood of those lands. The severe limitations on central power under the Articles hindered government from dealing with some of the other major issues of the day, such as the United States' mounting debt and poor foreign credit, growing disunity among the states, Shays' Rebellion (1786–1787), and commercial pressures from Britain, France, and Spain. A number of attempted amendments to the Articles that would have strengthened the central government were blocked by small and varying groups of states. Finally, a commercial convention in Annapolis (1786) issued a call for a major convention in Philadelphia in 1787 "to consider the exigencies of the Union." Congress cautiously endorsed the convention, with the proviso that it have the "sole and express purpose of revising the Articles of Confederation." Within four months, however, Philadelphia's Constitutional Convention had approved a federal Constitution that would replace the Continental Congress in 1789 with a new and stronger form of central government. *See also* ARTICLES OF CONFEDERATION, p. 5; NATURAL LAW AND NATURAL RIGHTS, p. 51; REPUBLICANISM, p. 56; SEPARATION OF POWERS, p. 58.

Significance   The Continental Congress was an attempt to unify the American colonies, but it was not the first attempt. As early as 1696 William Penn had formulated a plan for colonial unification. From 1643 through 1684, the Puritans of Connecticut, Massachusetts, New Haven, and Plymouth joined together in the United Colonies of New England, also called the New England Confederation, for their mutual defense and for the spread of their common religion. From 1686 through 1689, Great Britain grouped Massachusetts, Plymouth, Rhode Island, Connecticut, New Hampshire, Cornwall County in north Maine, and King's Province into the Dominion of New England, an administrative grouping the British hoped to replicate in the other colonies. In 1754, Benjamin Franklin proposed the Albany Plan, with "one general government" for all the colonies as its purpose. Great Britian rejected the plan because it undercut royal authority, and the colonies rejected it because it weakened each colony's independence. In 1765, representatives from nine colonies met in New York City for the Stamp Act Congress, whose collective protest helped force Great Britain's repeal of the Stamp Act. In the First Continental Congress, loyalist Joseph Galloway proposed a "General Council" that would have established a colonial branch of the British Parliament. Despite these precedents, the Continental Congress was unique because it included all the colonies and because its authority was totally indigenous. The Continental Congress provided the necessary transition from a loose grouping of British colonies to the United States of America.

English Constitution   The foremost example of a "living" constitution, drawing its authority not from a written document but from the promulgation of statutes, the evolving interpretations of common law, and faith in custom and convention. The English constitution represents an unbroken legal tradition reaching across 14 centuries. It is highly adaptive to political changes and conditions, and it provides a strong and effective system of governance because it depends on the application of logic by those charged with the constitution's interpretation. Stability depends on the commonsense interpretation of law by the monarch, Parliament, and the judiciary. The living constitution also relies heavily on the British people, assuming, for example, that in the event of a crisis that could threaten civil liberties, public outrage in opposition to the threat would preserve the common law. The English constitution recognizes at least three different sources of its authority: (1) statutes; (2) the common law; and (3) conventions.

Among the historic statutes and charters it considers important is Magna Carta. The Great Charter was the consequence of an attempt by English barons at Runnymede to articulate a constitutional basis for ensuring a balanced relationship between the sovereign and his subjects. Magna Carta is not unlike the American Declaration of Independence in that it serves as a focal point for the living tradition of a government. Several statutes spanning many centuries are also considered fundamental to the English constitutional tradition. The Statute of York of 1322 established the basis for the House of Commons. The Petition of Right of 1628 was passed to denounce the abuses of royal prerogatives by Charles I and to reassert intrinsic common law liberties. In fact many of the statutes that found their way into the tradition of the English constitution were designed to limit abuses of royal power, but at the same time to maintain recognition of the propriety of the monarchy. Another part of the constitutional tradition is the consequence of struggles for power between the Crown, Parliament, and the arbiters of the common law. A typical statute in this regard is one resulting from the Tudor reign of absolutism and the Revolution of 1688–1689: the Bill of Rights of 1689. This act assured the legislative authority of Parliament, forbade the Crown from imposing any tax or duty without the consent of Parliament, mandated the regular convening of Parliament, and incorporated and effected specific common law civil liberties. The Act of Settlement of 1701, as modified by the Abdication Act of 1936, altered the order of royal succession and mandated that the monarch be a member of the Church of England. The Act of Settlement also incorporated Protestant Scotland into Great Britain. By the beginning of the eighteenth century, the constitutional dynamic between the monarch and Parliament can be characterized as a kind of harmonic dissonance. This dissonance became the model for the system of checks and balances favored by the authors of the United States Constitution. What it meant in England was that the Crown had the power to dissolve Parliament at any time, while Parliament could bring the Crown's governing processes to a halt by refusing to legislate financial support and/or by disbanding the King's Army. It was understood by both institutions that such a constitutional deadlock would precipitate anarchy. Such a fundamental dislocation of English government was clearly unacceptable to either party, the Crown or Parliament. The Reform Act of 1832 is yet another historic statute in the tradition of the living English constitution. This act significantly altered the balance of power within Parliament. The assumption that the Lords would dominate both houses ended, and the franchise was extended to include greater numbers of British citizens. The Reform Act of 1832 was also significant in that it marked the beginning of parliamentary considerations of party rather than dependence on patronage as an instrument of royal prerogative. Important twentieth-century statutes are the Parliament Acts of 1911 and 1949, which delineate the relationships between the House of Lords and the House of Commons. The statutory basis of the English constitution also recognizes that the monarch must always respond positively to the cabinet because the cabinet represents the inherent power of Parliament. The cabinet in turn must depend on the support of the House of Commons. In such a system there is little room for the kinds of conflict frequently seen between the executive and legislative branches of government in the United States. Parliament is able to exercise supreme legal power in Great Britain. The potential abuses inherent in such power make Parliament constantly aware of the need for self-restraint. A constitutional principle in Great Britain is that no act of Parliament can be declared unconstitutional because only Parliament can repeal its own statutes. While the heritage of the English constitution supports the vesting of all legal authority in Parliament, at the same time it acknowledges that ultimate political authority rests with the people.

The English constitutional tradition also looks to the common law as a source of its authority. Indeed, the most important principles of the constitution are those decisions ordered and reported by the courts applying the principles of the common law. Most of the civil liberties and rights that inure to a British citizen are not to be found in statutes passed by Parliament. They are found rather in the corpus of the common law. Trial by jury and the writ of *habeas corpus* are but two of these constitutional rights that emanate from the heritage of the common law. Common law courts have been vigilant in protecting individual rights against arbitrary government actions. The English constitutional tradition rests on the public consciousness that Parliament will not defy the common law by passing legislation contrary to it.

The living constitution also relies on customs, conventions, and usages considered practical for the efficient operation of government that have no foundation in either statutory or common law. Ministers in the cabinet, for example, are expected to resign immediately after defeat in a general election. The Crown, at least since the reign of Queen Anne, will not refuse its assent to legislation passed in good faith by the House of Commons and the House of Lords. A prime minister will hold his or her office only so long as he or she retains the trust of a majority of the members of the House of Commons. Such customs and conventions form an unquestioned part of the consensus of English constitutionalism. *See also* BLACKSTONE'S *COMMENTARIES*, p. 11; COMMON LAW, p. 13; MAGNA CARTA, p. 46.

Significance   The English constitution is a "living" constitution because the people of Great Britain have never felt compelled to commit their governing agreements and processes to paper. The government of Great Britain is a remarkably stable system that has not undergone any significant upheaval in at least three centuries. It certainly has not experienced in recent times the kind of drama that concluded with the Constitution of the United States in 1789. The English Civil War of 1642–1649 was the last such national trauma in Great Britain. It resulted in the execution of Charles I, and it also produced the only written constitution Great Britain has ever had. An *Instrument of Government* was promulgated by Oliver Cromwell as self-appointed Lord Protector. By 1658, however, the *Instrument of Government* had disappeared. The English constitution is amended in a subtle process that is quite unlike the amendment procedure through which additions to the United States Constitution must pass. In England it is done simply by legislation and by decisions of the courts of common law. The maintenance of the United States Constitution relies on the Supreme Court as its ultimate arbiter, but the survival of the English constitution depends on the infrastructural governing processes of both executive and legislative apparatuses as well as on the political awareness and strength of those governed. To observe the evolution of the English constitution is to appreciate certain fundamental characteristics of English history. To understand fully the unwillingness of the English people to adopt a document into which they incorporate their constitutional precepts, one must appreciate the English penchant for tradition and the tradition's reliance on acts of Parliament to correct perceived inequities in the distribution of political power. The English people have reposited a great deal of faith in their governors, knowing their governors are prisoners of the common law and imperial custom.

Federalism   The theory and practice of joining several political entities into a larger political unity while preserving the basic political integrity of each entity. Federations and federal principles are found in many different kinds of organizations, such as labor unions (e.g., the American Federation of Labor–Congress of Industrial Organizations [AFL-CIO], church bodies (e.g., the World Council of Churches), and supranational political associations (e.g., the European Common Market). There is also an economic version of federalism called fiscal federalism, which claims superiority over both economic centralization and decentralization. But the term *federalism* is usually reserved for federations at the national political level. Strictly speaking, "federal government" refers to an overall system containing both central and state governments. Common usage, however, equates "federal government" with "central government." Political scientists generally have continued to affirm the classical problem of federalism as formulated in the sixteenth and seventeenth centuries: the proper balance between local sovereignty and the requirements of centralization. Some political unions remain weak because none of their members are willing to forego any of their sovereignty. Weak unions are commonly called associations, leagues, or confederations. Other political unions are so dominant that they destroy the real sovereignty of their members. These are empires and unitary states. Even though 17 countries claimed to have federal governments in the early 1980s, political scientists question the authenticity of many. Because of the dominance of the Russian Soviet Federated Socialist Republic, for example, the Union of Soviet Socialist Republics, the USSR, is more an empire than a federated state.

There were prototypes of federal states in the ancient and medieval world. Ancient Israel and the Delphic League were *amphictyonies*, or federations of tribes or cities united around a common religious center. The Achaean League (280–146 B.C.) was a defensive league of Greek cities. A number of medieval commercial towns joined in leagues for mutual assistance. In 1291, the Swiss cantons formed a defensive confederation that still exists today as the world's oldest uninterrupted federal government. A young federal system was growing in Aragon until Ferdinand and Isabella imposed a unitary system on the united kingdoms of Aragon and Castille. Reformation ecclesiology and the beginnings of national unification encouraged the growth of federal principles in Scotland, England, parts of France and Germany, and especially Switzerland and the Netherlands in the sixteenth century. These developments gave rise to the first theories of federalism by Jean Bodin, Hugh Grotius, Samuel Pufendorf, and Johannes Althusius. Since they viewed state sovereignty as absolute, these early writers on federalism tended to consider only looser forms of political union such as leagues and confederations. Federalist theory took a qualitative leap with the American Revolution. Alexander Hamilton, John Jay, and James Madison gave modern federalism its classical exposition in *The Federalist.* Federalism became the territorial version of the separation of powers and the bulwark of constitutional democracy. In contrast, the French Revolution's emphasis on the centralized rule of the majority left no room for federalism. Since the nineteenth century, federalism, or the use of federal principles, has grown in Europe, Latin America, and Asia. Important theoretical advances were made by J. K. Bluntschli and Otto von Gierke. In the twentieth century federalism has been used to create political unities out of hitherto independent cultural, political, and tribal groups, often in the wake of war or decolonialization. Such was the origin of the USSR, Yugoslavia, India, and many African nations. *See also* THE FEDERALIST, p. 32; REPUBLICANISM, p. 56; SEPARATION OF POWERS, p. 58.

Significance   Federalism is an essential element in constitutional democracy. Like the functional separation of powers (legislative, executive, and judicial), federalism's territorial separation of powers protects individual and local rights by discouraging the concentration of power in any individual or group. A number of issues continue to dominate both the practice and theory of federalism. Among them is the question of sovereignty. How can the constituent members of a federal union simultaneously keep their individual sovereignty intact and yet give a measure of it to a central government? Political scientist Carl Friedrich argues that sovereignty is a red herring because strict sovereignty, i.e., absolute independence, is a fiction in both personal and political life. Friedrich says the issue is not sovereignty versus unity but "autonomy in community." In this view the crucial question is not which powers a smaller unit decides to share or forego in order to join a larger community, but whether the smaller unit fully and freely participates in the decision. Others maintain that the classical attempt to distinguish various classifications of political centralization (e.g., leagues, confederations, and federal governments) incorrectly makes discrete categories out of what is really a continuous process. "Federalizing" is a common trait of all human life. While the balance between centralization and decentralization may shift back and forth, the overall tendency of personal and corporate life is toward more inclusive unions. Finally, not all political thinkers agree that federalism is absolutely essential for constitutional democracy. The "federalists" say it is, but the "pluralists" say it is not. Using the centralized government of Great Britain as an example, the pluralists argue that other forms of separation of powers can secure the foundations of constitutional democracy even in the absence of federalism. In *Constitutional Government and Democracy* (1968) Friedrich is not frightened by the prospect that "the pressures and exigencies of a compact and highly industrialized national economy may eventually force the United States to abandon federalism."

The Federalist   The title of the 1788 edition of a collection of essays by Alexander Hamilton, James Madison, and John Jay aimed at winning support for state ratification of the federal Constitution of 1787. *The Federalist* contained 85 essays in two volumes, all but the last 8 essays having previously appeared as letters in various New York newspapers between October 1787, and April 1788. Bearing the collective pen-name "Publius," reminiscent of republican Rome, the essays were begun by Hamilton, who soon enlisted the help of Madison and Jay. Hamilton also appealed to William Duer and Gouverneur Morris, but they were unable to oblige. Jay wrote only 5 essays, none of them exceptionally important. Hamilton and Madison wrote the remaining 80, usually alone but sometimes jointly, with Hamilton the author of the majority. Scholars still disagree about the authorship of a small number of the essays. Although he hoped the essays would influence the ratification process in other states as well, Hamilton's immediate concern was to convince his native state of New York. He had been the sole member of the New York delegation to the Constitutional Convention who supported the new document. The other two, Robert Yates and John Lansing, were avid supporters of New York's strong states' rights governor, George Clinton. Because of Clinton's great popularity, Hamilton knew that only a massive public education effort could win New York for the Constitution. As it turned out, New York's ratifying convention voted overwhelmingly against the Constitution and ratified it only after learning that one more than the necessary nine states had already done so.

There was general agreement among opponents of the proposed Constitution about its main defects. First, it violated the true federalism authorized by the Articles of Confederation and created a unitary and national government that usurped state sovereignty. Second, the federated states were territorially too large to be governed as a whole. Third, the proposed Constitution permitted the central government to maintain a peacetime army and navy, a power that could be easily abused. Fourth, the proposed Constitution did not include a bill of individual rights. Fifth, the separation of powers proposed in the new Constitution was not clear enough and thus was antidemocratic. In response to the first three objections, Hamilton and Madison conceded that the new Constitution did create an unprecedented form of federalism in which the central government had real sovereignty of its own and was not a mere instrument of the confederated states. Madison's Essay 39 contained the most comprehensive discussion of the new federalism, arguing that it in no way destroyed the sovereignty of the individual states. Hamilton and Madison insisted that a strong central government was necessary for the defense of the states against foreign and domestic foes, especially the British and Indians. A strong central government would also be necessary in resolving disputes among the states concerning boundaries, trade, and shares in the national debt. Finally, they held that while a "democracy" (a direct democracy) was not possible for such a large area, a "republic" (a representative democracy) was possible. Such a representative form of government was well suited to mitigate the destructive influence of the factions that typically plague democracies. The first 46 essays state and restate the necessity of a strong central government. *The Federalist* spent little time defending the omission of a bill of rights. Hamilton and Madison, like the other drafters of the Constitution, assumed that the case for individual rights was secure enough through the Declaration of Independence and the bills of rights of the individual states. Moreover, they were convinced that the bill of rights issue was a cover for the real issue, the reluctance of powerful groups to share or relinquish part of their sovereignty to a central government. The new Constitution was more democratic than most state constitutions, which still contained property requirements for voters and officeholders. Hamilton and Madison argued that the proposed separation of powers was adequate to ensure democracy. Madison explained how the bicameral legislature furthered that end, while Hamilton distinguished the roles played by the executive and the judiciary. In the course of this discussion, in Essays 78 and 81, Hamilton anticipated Marshall's *Marbury* v. *Madison* ruling of 1803, which established the Supreme Court as the ultimate interpreter of the Constitution and of the constitutionality of federal laws. Many individual essays of *The Federalist* have been the focus of scholarly interest, such as Madison's Essay 10, which some have claimed to be an anticipation of the Marxist theory of economic class struggle. The main purpose of the essays is quite clear, however. Their authors wanted to convince their fellow citizens that, if the United States were to survive and flourish, a stronger form of union was necessary and that form was aptly developed in the Constitution of 1787. *See also* CONSTITUTION OF THE UNITED STATES, p. 19; FEDERALISM, p. 30; SEPARATION OF POWERS, p. 58.

Significance   *The Federalist* is a political classic although it is in no sense a systematic treatise on government. It provides the best access we have to the original intent of the authors of the federal Constitution, the oldest unitary written constitution and the basis for the first modern federated republic. *The Federalist*'s primary authors, Hamilton and Madison, put aside their personal differences and the differences they had with a document crafted through compromise in Philadelphia, in order to defend it and win its ratification. Privately, both were for a more centralized government than was provided for by the Constitution. Hamilton later questioned whether the American version of democracy was acceptable to him. A sharp split between Hamilton and Madison did not occur until 1791, but even in their *Federalist* collaboration Hamilton could not win Madison over to his view on the supremacy of the Supreme Court. Still, both were so convinced of the value of the Constitution that they borrowed time from their busy lives to join forces in its defense. As with the other drafters of the Constitution, their underlying view of human nature was pessimistic. They were convinced that neither individuals nor the majority itself could be trusted with absolute power. In designing a government that had enough power to function as a modern state while dividing the functions of that power sufficiently to avoid tyranny, they gave birth to a new era of constitutionalism.

Carl Friedrich (b. 1901)   German-born American political scientist and contemporary scholar of constitutionalism. Carl Friedrich came to Harvard University as an undergraduate transfer student after World War I. After finishing his doctorate at Heidelberg, he returned to Harvard in 1926 and taught there until retiring in 1971. Some fifteen of Friedrich's published works deal with issues central to constitutionalism. The most important is *Constitutional Government and Democracy: Theory and Practice in Europe and America* (4th Ed., 1968), which has been translated into five foreign languages. His "Constitutions and Constitutionalism" in the *International Encyclopedia of the Social Sciences* (1968) summarized the main points of that seminal work. His *Transcendent Justice: the Religious Dimensions of*

Constitutionalism (1964) analyzes the religious roots of constitutionalism, especially in the Judaeo-Christian tradition. His most recent work is *Limited Government: A Comparison* (1974). Friedrich writes not only out of immense scholarly research but also out of rich practical experience in government. He helped train United States military government officers in postwar West Germany and served as a consultant for the restoration of constitutional democracy there. He also served as an adviser in setting up the Puerto Rican commonwealth and in writing the constitution of the Virgin Islands. Friedrich stresses the importance of functional definitions of constitutionalism, by which he means effectiveness of regularized restraints upon political and governmental powers. He has a very normative approach to constitutionalism, although his writing brims with historical and comparative analyses of governments. He ultimately measures them all by the purpose he sees as central to genuine constitutionalism, and that is the protection of individual rights against the tyranny of government. Friedrich maintains that a government must first be effective before it can be constitutional, arguing that a well-developed bureaucracy is central to any good government. To achieve its ultimate purpose, however, a constitutional government must allow for a division of power, functionally by separation of branches of government, and territorially through federalism. Friedrich says that not all democracies with a constitution are constitutionalist. The constitution of the Roman Republic before Christ, for example, was merely a facade for the aristocratic control of the Senate. The "people's democracy" found in the Union of Soviet Socialist Republics is a facade for the oligarchy of the Communist party. And an absolute democracy can be a facade for the tyranny of the majority.

Significance   Friedrich's analysis of constitutionalism follows closely that of earlier scholars, notably Charles McIlwain and Francis Wilmuth, but the notable difference in Friedrich's approach is that it is "functional-political." It is functional because it studies the actual workings of government, not just its legally mandated structure. It is political because it considers not just the governmental aspects of constitutionalism but also the effects of the political environment on constitutional practices. The reader of *Constitutional Government and Democracy* becomes aware that all the details packed into its 700 pages constitute a single thesis: that a country's living constitution is determined not only by the documentary constitution and its governmental structures but also by its political parties, lobbies, mass media, educational, military, and economic systems, and by its international relations. Friedrich says that federalism is best described as a *process,* which he calls "federalizing." Federalizing is the process of increasing the unity between several previously separate political entities, and Friedrich believes federalizing is the major constitutional trend of the modern world. The growing social and economic interdependence of the United States may eventually so unify the nation that its federal structure may become obsolete, says Friedrich. Since nations are independent only in a legal sense, world federalism can be expected to grow as well. Indeed, Friedrich considers world federalism a necessary safeguard for national constitutionalism. He declares sovereignty to be an illusion, since it overlooks the essential interdependence of persons and nations. Following his favorite "philosopher of freedom," Immanuel Kant, Friedrich focuses finally on the autonomy of constituent members of a political union. After carefully distinguishing planning, socialization, and socialism, Friedrich asserts that modern constitutional democracy is compatible with, and even requires, a high degree of planning and social control.

The Fundamental Orders of Connecticut (1639)   The basic laws for self-government adopted by the early settlers of Connecticut in 1639. The Fundamental Orders of Connecticut were the first constitution written in the Anglo-American world. In 1635, under the leadership of Roger Ludlow and the Puritan minister Thomas Hooker, inhabitants of several Massachusetts Bay towns set out to find more land in the Connecticut River Valley. There they founded the towns of Hartford, Wethersfield, and Windsor. The Massachusetts legislature, called the General Court, gave the Connecticut towns legitimacy by appointing eight commissioners to govern them from 1636 to 1638. The commissioners convened several sessions of a General Assembly, also called a General Court, between 1637 and 1638. Although there is no solid historical information about the precise origins of the Fundamental Orders, we know they were drafted in 1638 and approved on January 14, 1639. Most historians assume they were requested and approved by the local General Court and written by Roger Ludlow.

The document consists of a preamble and eleven "orders." The preamble portrays the document as setting up "an orderly and peaceful government established according to God," the purpose of which is "to maintain the peace and union of such a people." The document makes no mention of either the king or natural law requiring or authorizing the government. The only authority mentioned is "the word of God." The document itself derives its name from the opening words of each of the eleven orders: "It is ordered, sentenced, and decreed that. . . ." The orders outline the government of the confederated towns and of any towns that might later be allied with them. There were to be two General Assemblies each year, attended by four deputies elected from each town. One of the assemblies would be a Court of Elections, at which a governor and six magistrates would be elected. Governors and magistrates could hold office only in alternate years. There were no religious requirements for voting, but the governor had to belong to "an approved congregation." Should the governor and magistrates refuse to call a General Assembly at the required time, the freemen of the three towns retained the ultimate authority to do so. The Connecticut towns were governed by the Fundamental Orders from 1639 until 1662. The General Assemblies served as both legislature and judiciary. In 1645 the General Assemblies became bicameral, the deputies being distinguished from the magistrates. The governor had no vote, except in the case of a tie, and no veto. It soon became the custom for the governor and the deputy governor to alternate years of service as governor until, in 1660, the General Assembly amended the Fundamental Orders so that Governor John Winthrop, Jr., could be reelected indefinitely. There were two levels of suffrage: "freemen" and "admitted inhabitants." The freemen had the right to elect officials at all levels—governor, magistrates, deputies, and town officials. The admitted inhabitants, who lacked the required property holdings to be freemen but who were approved by a majority of the freemen, could vote for only deputies and town officials.

The Fundamental Orders had no legal standing with the king of England. When Charles II assumed the throne under the Restoration, John Winthrop, Jr., went to England and returned with a royal charter for Connecticut in 1662. Although the charter superseded the Fundamental Orders, it changed very little. The only major difference was that it barred approved inhabitants from voting for deputies. The citizens of Connecticut were so pleased with their charter, and with the Fundamental Orders upon which it was based, that they, along with Rhode Island, were the only colonies that did not draft new constitutions during the revolutionary period. Connecticut did not draft a new state constitution until 1818. *See also* MAYFLOWER COMPACT, p. 48; SOCIAL CONTRACT, p. 61; STATE CONSTITUTIONS, p. 62.

Significance   The Fundamental Orders of Connecticut paved the way for constitutionalism in the United States. Connecticut still proclaims on its automobile license plates that it is the "constitution state." American historian Benjamin F. Wright agrees with the citizens of Connecticut that the Fundamental Orders were the first constitution in America, but other historians such as Robert J. Taylor consider it an anachronism to call the Fundamental Orders a constitution. Taylor says constitutionalism was an idea that did not develop in America for several generations after 1639. The language of the document may indeed mark it more as a religious covenant than a political charter. Perhaps the same aspirations that grasped for Biblical foundations in seventeenth-century Hartford grasped for political foundations in eighteenth-century Philadelphia. If constitutionalism is more a process than an accomplishment, Connecticut's Fundamental Orders are one of the early mountain streams that would flow together to form a mighty torrent of constitutionalism a century later. An assessment of the Fundamental Orders would not be complete without some comment on the role of the Reverend Thomas Hooker, not to be confused with Richard Hooker, a near-contemporary philosopher of constitutionalism. Earlier historians have called Thomas Hooker "the father of American democracy," basing their opinion largely on his insistence in 1638 that a popularly elected assembly was best suited to conduct important public business. The context of his remarks was negotiations about the New England Confederation, not the Fundamental Orders of Connecticut. His democratic principles were less consistently applied to local government than they were to rhetoric about the theory of intercolonial cooperation. Modern historians are more modest in their claims for Hooker's role in the democratization of America.

Jurisprudence   The science of law. Jurisprudence has evolved to include the examination and classification of legal ideas, theories, and analyses based on lines of inquiry developed in anthropology, philosophy, politics, psychology, and sociology. Jurisprudence as a mode of thought has its genesis in Plato and Aristotle, neither of whom distinguished between legal and social theory. They said that without law there could be no polity. Later Roman writers summarized jurisprudence in the phrase, "Jurisprudentia est divinarum atque humanarum rerum notitia, justi atque injusti scientia," or "Jurisprudence is the knowledge of things divine and human, the science of what is right and what is wrong." Jurisprudence can be considered, therefore, the repository of thought and the body of sources from which the law emanates. Many Western philosophers have devoted attention to expositions of legal theory, by which they typically mean the rules which should govern the behavior of individuals in relationship to each other and to the state. Analytical jurisprudence seeks answers to the following questions, for example: "What is law?" "What is a state?" "What is a right?" "What is property?" and "What determines a contractual obligation?" From such questions evolved an understanding of the makeup of the legal order. The contribution of Aristotle (384–322 B.C.) includes the *Nicomachean Ethics,* especially Book V, in which he develops and discusses theories of commutative and distributive justice. *The Summa Theologica: Treatise on Law* of Thomas Aquinas (1225–1274) was published as a theological work, but it also made a major effort to organize the science of law as it existed in the thirteenth century. The *Leviathan* (1651), the political philosophy of Thomas Hobbes, contains many discourses on natural law, expressed by Hobbes as "justice, equity, modesty, mercy, and, in sum, doing to others as we would be done to. . . ." The American Founding Fathers assumed the legacy of John Locke. His *Two Treatises of Government* (1759) is acknowledged to be the first modern philosophic defense of government and property based upon the consent of the governed. Locke's arguments provided the theoretical justification for the Declaration of Independence and the United States Constitution. Jeremy Benthem (1748–1832) said that social reforms could best be effected through the legal, not the political, order, and Immanuel Kant substantially added to the force of Benthem's arguments in 1796 with publication of his *Philosophy of Law.* Kant said that law is pure reason and cannot be subject to political manipulation. Kant's thesis is consistent with and antecedent to George Wilhelm Friedrich Hegel's *Philosophy of Right* (1831). Jurisprudence is typically divided into three schools of thought: historical, sociological, and realist. Each school is discussed below.

Friedrich Carl von Savigny (1779–1861) founded the historical school in 1814 with the publication of his *Of the Vocation of Our Age for Legislation and Jurisprudence.* Savigny wrote, "Law grows with the growth, and strengthens with the strength, of the people, and finally dies away as the nation loses its nationality." He maintained that the substance of the law is derived from a subtle national development that eventually concludes in a national legal identity. He acknowledged that law must originate in legislative enactments, but philosophically he eschewed codified law such as Roman law. He argued that since law is construed in direct relationship to the particular social milieu in which it develops, it would be presumptively irrational to assume that what is proper or lawful at one point in time could be equally valid in another. "An age has no need of a code for itself. It would merely compose one for a succeeding and less fortunate age, as we lay up provisions for winter. But an age is seldom disposed to be so provident for posterity." Savigny said the basis of the legal order is the history of a nation's social cognition rather than in the individual's abstract relationship to the state. He therefore emphasized the common spirit of the people, or *Volksgeist.* In founding the historical school, Savigny also contributed substantially to the sociological jurisprudence movement, easily the most pervasive interpretation of jurisprudence in American constitutional law.

Many of the early contributors to sociological jurisprudence were Europeans. Among the most important are the Baron de Montesquieu, who suggested in *The Spirit of the Laws* (1748) that a good law was the result of its conscious adaptation to the spirit and volition of a group of people. A good law must be seen as the product of the interaction between governmental structures and the physical environment of a particular society. "[Laws] should have a relation to the degree of liberty which the constitution will bear, to the religion of the inhabitants, and to their inclinations, riches, numbers, commerce, manners, and customs." Eight years earlier, David Hume had suggested a similar approach to jurisprudence in his *Treatise on Human Nature*. Hume considered law a developing social institution that owed its origins not to individual natures but to accepted social conventions. Other philosophers making important contributions to the early discussion of sociological jurisprudence were Rudolf von Inhering (1818–1892), Max Weber (1864–1920), and Eugen Ehrlich (1862–1922). In 1913 Ehrlich wrote in his *Principles of the Sociology of Law:* "At the present as well as at any other time, the center of gravity of legal development lies not in legislation, nor in juristic science, nor in judicial decision, but in society itself." Sociological jurisprudence came to full flower in the work of Roscoe Pound (1870–1964), for 20 years the Dean of the Harvard University Law School. His most extensive discussion of the subject, *My Philosophy of Law,* was published in 1941. "The legal order," Pound said, "is a regime of social control through politically organized society." The science of law must always be more concerned with an empirical analysis of the law than with law in its abstract form. Rather than being conceived as a theoretical construct, law is more properly conceived as an institution of social control. Sociological jurisprudence became interested in incorporating sociological techniques and research methods in the pursuit of social justice. As a by-product of the industrialism and economic expansion of the late nineteenth and early twentieth centuries, it emphasized law as a partner in social progress. Proponents of the movement rejected abstract law because abstract law recognized no solutions to the problems and challenges inherent in twentieth-century technology. Sociological jurisprudence also rejected the natural law position that an ultimate theory of value can be discovered. There can be no *natural* guide to the resolution of conflict and proscribed behavior, said the movement, and legal rules and precepts must necessarily be only flexible directives rather than rigid restrictions and sanctions envisioning entirely just outcomes. Sociological jurisprudence stressed the social objectives of law, regarding the science of law as merely a means of accomplishing the multivariant purposes of society. Thus the rules of law of a given society are a balancing of competing interests. Each legal decision or opinion is the equalizing of perceived social alternatives. Sociological jurisprudence did demonstrate interest in justice for the individually oppressed person, and it did embrace this principle as a purpose of the law, but more generally it attempted to order conduct in which group action and dynamics were determinative of the public good. This ordering of relations can best be brought about in a society which is homogeneous, static, and cohesive, and one in which there are shared values and traditions. Roscoe Pound issued a challenge to teachers as well as practitioners of the law when he urged lawyers to pursue social rather than legal justice in its narrowest sense. He said that justice may very well be consistent with prevailing societal values and public standards. In summarizing his views Pound wrote in his *Introduction to the Philosophy of Law* (1954):

> For the purpose of understanding the law of today I am content with a picture of satisfying as much of the whole body of human wants as we may with the least sacrifice. I am content to think of law as a social institution to satisfy social wants, so far as such wants may be satisfied or such claims given effect by an ordering of human conduct through politically organized society. For present purposes, I am content to see in legal history the record of a continually wider recognizing and satisfying of human wants or claims or desires through social control and a more embracing and more effective elimination of waste and precluding of friction in human enjoyment of the goods of human experience—in short, a continually more efficacious social engineering.

Some legal writers have argued that sociological jurisprudence is not a philosophy of law at all but is rather an attempt to associate the empiricism of sociological methods with the legal order. This identification has come to be known as the sociology of law. Other authorities say the sociology of law is correctly understood as a general science of society of which considerations of law are a part. Whatever its definition, the sociology of law has received significant attention in modern American legal practice, much of it the result of the etiology of the Brandeis Brief. In 1908, as a practicing attorney, Louis D. Brandeis filed a brief on behalf of the defendant in the case of *Muller v. Oregon* (208 U.S. 412: 1908). Brandeis argued that an Oregon law that set the maximum number of hours per day during which women could work was legal. He looked beyond traditional legal parameters and based his position on supporting sociological data. The data said long working hours were detrimental to the health and morals of working women. Through the employment of such research, Brandeis helped to bring about social reforms that historically had been considered only the purview of legislators. The introduction of sociological evidence thus interjected a normative analysis to aid in the clarification of legal doctrine. The history of Supreme Court interpretations of the due process and equal protection clauses of the Fourteenth Amendment provides a paradigm for the application of the sociological approach to legal reasoning. *Muller* v. *Oregon* is but one example of the Court's application of accepted societal norms prevailing at the time in which the decision was rendered. A more dramatic example is Justice Henry B. Brown's opinion in *Plessy* v. *Ferguson* (164 U.S. 537: 1896). It is fraught with theories of Social Darwinism when it posits racial supremacy, "in this instance the white race," as an absolute social norm. The *Plessy* principle of "separate but equal" established a new standard of racial inequality based on the social science hypotheses of Herbert Spencer and Charles Darwin. Since empirical evidence demonstrated the black race was inferior to the white, it was presumed irrational to grant the black race equal recognition in constitutional law. When Thurgood Marshall, as lawyer for the National Association for the Advancement of Colored People (NAACP), argued the NAACP position in *Brown* v. *Board of Education* (347 U.S. 483: 1954), he also relied on social science literature. Rather than Spencer and Darwin, however, Marshall used Gunnar Myrdal's *An American Dilemma* (1941). Marshall maintained as an empirically verifiable sociological fact that segregated educational institutions had an inherently harmful effect on black children. Noted social psychologist Kenneth Clark testified in the *Brown* case that tests administered by him to black children demonstrated that these children tended to develop a negative awareness of themselves at an early age. Marshall therefore concluded that separate could never be equal. This application of sociological jurisprudence was frequently cited in footnotes explaining the unanimous decision overturning *Plessy*. In *Goesaert* v. *Cleary* (335 U.S. 464: 1948), the Court sustained the constitutionality of a Michigan statute that prohibited the granting of a bartender license to a woman unless she was the wife or daughter of the male owner of the bar. Justice Felix Frankfurter, writing for the majority in a decision consistent with the preponderant social norms of the time, reasoned that Michigan had a legitimate interest in protecting women against "the moral and social problems" that would accompany bartending by women. The state could protect against these problems by "the oversight assumed through ownership of a bar by a barmaid's husband or father . . . [and] minimize the hazards that might confront a barmaid without such protecting oversight." In *Roe* v. *Wade* (410 U.S. 113: 1973), Justice Harry A.

Blackmun devoted an extensive section of his opinion to the positions on abortion held by the American Bar Association (ABA), the American Medical Association (AMA), and the American Public Health Association (APHA). Clearly, the opinions of the AMA and the APHA had more to do with medical evidence than they did with legal standards, but Blackmun chose to emphasize their extralegal authority to lend validity and substance to his legal reasoning.

Legal realism is interested in articulating and demonstrating the marked differences between legal theory and legal practice. Legal realists say the study of law is only an empirical exercise. It is best understood in terms of what is discovered in the courtroom and not necessarily what is discovered in an abstract study of the legal order. Realists are skeptical of those who adopt antiquated or traditional legal theories. Realists such as Kurt Llewellyn and John Dewey are noted for their insistence on the use of logic to guide legal decisions, while other realists such as Glendon Schubert are known for their systematic statistical analyses and mathematical formulae that predict the outcomes of judicial decision making. Jurist and realist Jerome Frank has suggested that the unpredictability of court decisions resides primarily in the elusiveness of the facts of a given case. He argues that the clearest law to follow is that found at the appellate court level since the facts of a particular case have already been established in lower court proceedings. Legal realists maintain that the courts not only find the law but create it as well. In his compendium of lectures, *The Common Law* (1881), the preeminent realist of them all, Oliver Wendell Holmes, Jr., articulated his conception of legal realism as follows:

> The life of the law has not been logic; it has been experience. The felt necessities of the time, the prevalent moral and political theories, intuitions of public policy, avowed or unconscious, even the prejudices which judges share with their fellowmen have had a good deal more to do than the syllogism in determining the rules by which men should be governed. The law embodies the story of a nation's development through many centuries and it cannot be dealt with as if it contained only the axioms and corollaries of a book of mathematics.

Jurisprudence is the science of law. It is an amalgam of philosophic thought, historical analysis, sociological evidence, and legal experience. *See also* COMMON LAW, p. 13; JOHN LOCKE, p. 44; NATURAL LAW AND NATURAL RIGHTS, p. 51.

Significance   The study of jurisprudence allows students of the law to appreciate the fact that ideas about law do not develop in an intellectual or legal vacuum. Rather they evolve from rich sources of thought in other disciplines. Especially in the United States, sociology has helped to shape impressions about law and its impact on those it seeks to serve, protect, and discipline. Jurisprudence enables one better to understand the complex history of the legal ordering of behavior and institutions, and more properly value the heavy responsibility held by those persons society must trust to make the law and render equitable decisions.

John Locke (1632–1704)   British philosopher whose political thought, especially as found in his *Second Treatise of Government* (1690), provided the theoretical base for the American Revolution and constitutionalist movement. John Locke was educated in medicine and philosophy at Oxford. Aside from brief periods of teaching at Oxford, however, he spent most of his working life as an aide to government officials and as a minor official himself. He lived a number of years in Brandenburg, France, and Holland, as well as in his native England. Perhaps the most formative influence on Locke's political thought was Anthony Ashly Cooper, the first Earl of Shaftsbury. Locke was his aide for a number of years. Shaftsbury was a leader of the Whig party, a supporter of religious tolerance for all except Catholics, and a pioneer of British commercial imperialism and colonialism. Locke's *Essay Concerning Human Understanding* (1690) presented a moderate empiricism that inspired the more radical empiricism of Berkeley and Hume. Its representationalist theory of knowledge, which held that we know our ideas of things rather than things themselves, paved the way for Hume's skepticism and Kant's critical philosophy. Locke's most influential political work was his *Two Treatises of Government* (1690), although *A Letter Concerning Toleration*, published in Latin in 1689, was also important. His Preface to the *Treatises* says the work was meant to justify the Glorious Revolution of 1688 that brought William of Orange to the British throne. Scholars now believe, however, that the work was actually written almost a decade earlier and was intended to justify a revolution against the Catholic King James II. The First *Treatise* was simply a refutation of the theory of the divine right of kings. The Second *Treatise* outlined Locke's own political theory. Like Hobbes, Locke believed that human beings start out in a state of nature. But while Hobbes believed that persons in the state of nature were lawless and warlike, Locke believed they are endowed by God with knowledge of the law of nature. He borrowed that concept from Richard Hooker. The main precepts of the law of nature concern the individual's rights to life, liberty, and property. These rights did not prevent Locke from considering slavery legitimate in the case of captives from a just war, however. Locke is preoccupied with defending the right to property, even though he admits this is not an unlimited right. While he defends the right of inheritance, Locke holds that the primary title to property comes from the labor we invest in the property. In order to guarantee that everyone obeys the law of nature, people enter into an "original compact" that inaugurates civil society. Their consent to majority rule limits their personal freedom to some extent, but they thereby gain the protection of written law and the enforcing power of political authority. Locke considered the founding of Rome, Venice, and certain American colonies to have been historical instances of such original compacts. He maintained that the establishment of a particular form of government is a secondary step founded on trust of rulers. It is a more conditional form of consent than is the original compact among the people. Locke insists upon a separation of governmental powers, with the legislature having supreme authority over the executive, which includes the judiciary, and the federative, which supervises relations with other states. The people retain the ultimate right to rebel against a government that has unjustly infringed upon their rights. Locke was a devout Christian, although of a decidedly rationalist bent. In *A Letter Concerning Toleration,* written at the request of Jean le Clerc, a Christian minister in Amsterdam, Locke argues that the "unhappy agreement that we see between the church and state" is the cause of the religious intolerance that injures both civil society and true religion. Religious authorities should restrict their concerns to religious and moral matters and should not try to control political life. Civil authorities should not meddle in religious or moral matters, unless certain religious practices injure the rights of others or disturb the public peace. Locke thus argued that civil toleration should be extended to all religious persuasions— Christian, Jewish, Muslim, and pagan—but with the exception of Roman Catholics and atheists. Roman Catholics were excluded because of their doctrinaire intolerance of other religions and their allegiance to the Pope as their primary earthly sovereign. Atheists were excluded because of their rejection of the religious basis for public morality. *See also* CONSTITUTIONALISM, HISTORICAL DEVELOPMENT OF, p. 16; NATURAL LAW AND NATURAL RIGHTS, p. 51; SOCIAL CONTRACT, p. 61.

Significance   John Locke's philosophy decisively influenced political thinkers in England, France, and the American colonies. Among those most influenced were Voltaire, Montesquieu, the French Encyclopedists, Hamilton, and Jefferson. Locke's *Second Treatise* contained the philosophy underlying Jefferson's Declaration of Independence, especially the Declaration's appeal to self-evident laws of nature, the natural equality of human beings, popular consent as the basis of government, and the right of a people to rebel against an unjust government. Indeed, the final words of the Declaration are an echo of Locke's original compact theory. The *Second Treatise* and *A Letter Concerning Toleration* also bore upon the framing of the Constitution, with its insistence on the separation of church and state, majority rule, the primacy of the legislative branch, and, by way of Montesquieu's refinements, the separation of powers. Locke also influenced American developments in more subtle ways. His tendency to equate the common good with the will of the majority and his emphasis on the rights of private property tended to justify both the neglect of minority rights and the pursuit of economic individualism. The fact that Locke justified revolution not as a path toward an ideal society, as in the French and Russian revolutions, but only as a restoration of the majority's elemental political and economic rights, is reflected in the basically conservative nature of the American Revolution and American political history. John Locke is the single most important figure in the founding of American constitutionalism.

Magna Carta   The "Great Charter" issued by King John at Runnymede on June 15, 1215. Magna Carta became the statutory basis for English liberties while it simultaneously reflected the gradual maturation of secular law in Europe. During the twelfth and thirteenth centuries, there were many instances in France, Germany, Hungary, Italy, and Spain of towns and nobles winning royal charters of liberties because of their developing economic and military strength. William the Conqueror had been powerful enough to resist such charters, but all of his successors to the English throne were forced to grant them to ecclesiastical and baronial lords. The charters were *privilegia,* or laws for particular groups, and were not in any sense laws for the entire realm. King John came to the throne in 1199 inheriting heavy debts from his brother Richard's crusade to the Holy Land and Richard's war with France. John was forced to press his barons for greater and greater financial contributions to the royal treasury. John's position was considerably weakened when he received an interdict and eventual excommunication from Pope Innocent III for his refusal to recognize Stephan Langton's election as Archbishop of Canterbury, an issue on which John eventually relented. Finally in 1215, Langton and William Marshall, the Earl of Pembroke and the most influential of the English barons, convinced the angry secular and ecclesiastical lords to demand a charter of liberties from John rather than fight him in a civil war. They presented John with the *Articles of the Barons,* which served as the basis for Magna Carta. Magna Carta was divided into 63 clauses and covered a large number of issues among which were the rights of the church, of higher nobles, of lesser nobles and freemen, and of towns, tradespeople, and merchants. Rules were laid down for royal officials, especially local ones. Disagreements concerning use of the forests were settled, a clause of Magna Carta that in 1217 was expanded into a separate *Charter of the Forest*. Certain crucial juridical questions were regulated, such as the trial of nobles and freemen by their peers and according to the law of the land; prompt justice; specific locations for trials; and restrictions on writs of *praecipe* as well as writs of inquiry concerning life and limb. One of the most interesting parts of Magna Carta was Clause 61. In that clause the king authorized the establishment of a committee of 25 barons who, in the event of a royal violation of the charter that was not rectified within 40 days, would lead the whole kingdom in confiscating the king's possessions. Despite Magna Carta, however, the barons soon waged war on John. After John's defeat at the Battle of Lewes in 1215, he reissued the charter in its original form. After John's death in 1216, the regent council of the young Henry III issued a revision of the charter in 1217, which served as the basis of Henry's own charter of 1225. It is the Magna Carta of 1225, not the preceding versions, which was included in subsequent English statute rolls and expounded by its classic commentator, Sir Edward Coke. *See also* COMMON LAW, p. 13; CONSTITUTIONALISM, HISTORICAL DEVELOPMENT OF, p. 16; ENGLISH CONSTITUTION, p. 27.

Significance   Magna Carta came to have an importance for constitutionalism that far outweighed its literal and historical meaning. Although its use of "freeman" was broader than any other European document of its time, the rights of freemen still fell within the category of privilege. Yet by the fourteenth century, the English Parliament had universalized a number of Magna Carta's fundamental provisions, so that nine chapters of the 1225 charter still stand in the *English Statute Book*. Some of the language of Magna Carta was incorporated into the constitutions of the early American states and into the federal Constitution of 1787. More influential than the words of Magna Carta, however, was its spirit. It stands as permanent testimony to the human belief in the importance of written law, the limits of absolute monarchy, and the right of rebellion against tyranny. These ideas became fundamental guiding principles in the development of constitutional government in both England and the United States. Yet Magna Carta has not been venerated by everyone. Hobbes and Locke felt that statutory law should be based on natural law rather than on precedent law such as that found in the charter. Petit-Dutaillis (1894) and Edward Jenks

(1904) rejected Magna Carta as a throwback to an earlier feudalism. They said it presented an obstacle to the growth of constitutionalism in England. Current discussions of Magna Carta center on the question of whether a precedent legal system is inherently more or less responsive to social need than a natural law system. Whatever the outcome of the continuing debate, Magna Carta stands unassailed as the most influential statement of early English constitutionalism.

Mayflower Compact   The social covenant signed by the first settlers of Plymouth Plantation in 1620. The Mayflower Compact reads as follows:

> In ye name of God, Amen. We whose names are underwritten, the loyall subjects of our dread soveraigne Lord, King James, by ye Grace of God, of Great Britaine, Franc, & Ireland king, defender of ye faith, &c, haveing undertaken, for ye glorie of God, and advancemente of ye Christian faith, and honour of our king & countrie, a voyage to plant ye first colonie in ye Northerne parts of Virginia, doe by these presents solemnly & mutualy in ye presence of God, and one of another, covenant & combine our selves togeather into a civill body politick, for our better ordering & preservation & furtherance of ye ends aforesaid; and by vertue hereof to enacte, constitute, and frame such just & equall lawes, ordinances, acts, constitutions, & offices, from time to time, as shall be thought most meete & convenient for ye general good of ye Colonie, unto which we promise all due submission and obedience. In witnes whereof we have hereunder subscribed our names at Cap-Codd ye 11 November, in ye year of ye raigne of our soveraigne lord, King James, of England, France, & Ireland ye eighteenth, and of Scotland ye fiftie-fourth. Ano: Dom. 1620.

The main force behind the settlement of Plymouth Plantation, or New Plymouth, were the Separatists, also called Brownists. While the Puritans were content to try to reform the Church of England from within, the Separatists set up independent congregations that embodied their more primitive Christian ideals of doctrine, ritual, and church government. Following the lead of the Reverend Robert Browne, the Separatists insisted that each congregation enter into a covenant providing for the democratic election of ministers and officials and for congregational discipline based on majority rule. Despised by Anglicans and Puritans alike for their "gathered church" doctrine, many Separatists fled to Holland, where their leader there, Henry Ainsworth, gave them the name Pilgrims. William Brewster the Younger formed a Separatist congregation in the Village of Scrooby in Nottinghamshire, with John Robertson as minister and the orphaned William Bradford as one of its members. In 1608, to escape religious persecution, Brewster moved his congregation to Amsterdam and then to Leyden in 1609. Because of the congregation's hardships there, they then decided to move to the New World. After considering agreements with the Virginia Company and the Dutch New Netherlands Company, the Pilgrims finally signed with Thomas Weston's London-based Adventurers to set up a fishing industry in Northern Virginia. Our sole records of the journey are William Bradford and Edward Winslow's *Mourt's Relation* (1622) and Bradford's *Of Plimouth Plantation*, published posthumously in 1856. Having sailed from Holland to England in their own ship, the *Speedwell*, the Pilgrims were joined by the rented *Mayflower*, which contained more Pilgrims and other non-Separatist settlers who had been recruited by the Adventurers Company. After the *Speedwell* proved unseaworthy on two attempted sailings, a reduced contingent of 102 settlers and a crew of 47 finally left Plymouth, England, on September 17, 1620, all aboard the *Mayflower*. Of the settlers embarked, only 40 were Pilgrims. The rest were "strangers," i.e., other freemen, hirelings, and indentured servants. All were lower-middle class in economic status. A few of the strangers, notably Miles Standish and John Alden, had been hired by the Pilgrims in England as "strongmen." When the travelers sighted land at what is now Provincetown, some of the strangers asserted they did not have to abide by the agreements signed in England, since they were landing not in Northern Virginia but in New England. To avert turmoil before landing, therefore, the Pilgrims, probably the Cambridge-educated William Brewster, drafted the Mayflower Compact. Forty-one of the men aboard signed the Compact on November 21, 1620 (Gregorian calendar). The only men who did not sign were one stranger, three hirelings, and two indentured servants. At the same meeting, the Pilgrim John Carver was elected governor with total legislative, executive, and judicial powers. On December 26, the settlers began building their permanent home in the New World, which they named Plymouth. Aided by the English-speaking Indian, Squanto, they made a peace treaty with Massasoit, chief of all the local Indians except the Massachusetts tribe, and began farming, fishing, and trading with the Indians. They set up a strictly communistic economic system, but gradually abandoned it as unworkable beginning in 1623. When Carver died in 1621, Bradford became governor, holding the position until 1656. Because he was weakened by an injury, Bradford asked for the election of an assistant governor. The assistant became seven assistants by 1633, and together the assistant governors formed the Governor's Council, later called the General Court. The governor and his council were elected yearly. By 1623 there was already a limitation on suffrage, and by the mid-1600s, with 232 freemen among the 3,000 inhabitants of

Plymouth Plantation, only those freemen who met stringent property qualifications could vote. In 1626, the Pilgrims bought out their English partners, the Adventurers, but despite their concerted efforts, they never received a royal charter. Between 1636 and 1640, five new towns were founded within Plymouth Plantation—Duxbury, Sandwich, Scituate, Tauton, and Yarmouth. In 1636, the General Court, together with representatives from each of the colony's then-existing towns, Plymouth, Duxbury, and Scituate, adopted the Great Fundamentals, the colony's first constitution. Plymouth's towns used town meetings from the beginning of the settlement, although Sandwich did not establish a formal town government until 1651. The history of Pilgrim Plymouth was closely tied to that of the Puritan Massachusetts Bay Colony. The latter, founded at Salem in 1628, adopted the Pilgrims' organization for its religious congregations, while Plymouth modeled its General Court after that of Massachusetts Bay. In general, however, no love was lost between the two colonies. Plymouth was much more democratic and religiously tolerant than Massachusetts. There were no executions of religious dissenters and no witch convictions in Plymouth. Massachusetts Bay did finally absorb Plymouth Plantation in 1691, when Plymouth was unable to purchase a new charter after the fall of the Stuarts in England. *See also* CONSTITUTIONALISM, HISTORICAL DEVELOPMENT OF, p. 16; FUNDAMENTAL ORDERS OF CONNECTICUT, p. 36; SOCIAL CONTRACT, p. 61.

Significance   The Mayflower Compact was rediscovered in the mid-eighteenth century by historians who idealized it as the foundation of American liberties and the first written constitution. In fact, it was neither. Jefferson did not consult it in drafting the Declaration of Independence, and there is no record of its being mentioned at the Constitutional Convention. Nor was the Mayflower Compact a constitution. The Pilgrim constitution, the Great Fundamentals, was not drafted until 1636. The Compact was rather a social contract, or, in Bradford's words, "a combination made by the Pilgrims before they came ashore, being the first foundation of their government in this place." Although Richard Hooker's theories of social contract and consent of the governed would have been available to the Pilgrims, their more immediate inspiration was Robert Browne's notion of religious covenant. The central ideal of the Mayflower Compact was the consental formation of a civil society to be governed by "just and equal laws," which the covenanters would later enact. Despite their democratic beginning, however, at least for male freemen, the government became a benevolent dictatorship by the governor. The freemen eligible to vote decided only the matters the governor chose to set before them. Nor were the laws completely equal, for it was recommended that punishments vary "according to the nature and quality of the person." Plymouth's compact became a model for several other foundations, however. Roger Williams was expelled from Plymouth for his radical democratic views and founded Providence in 1636 with a similar social contract. Rhode Island became the most democratic and religiously tolerant colony of the original thirteen. The same compact idea underlay the founding of the New England Confederation in 1643. The United Colonies of New England, disrupted by England's creation of the short-lived Dominion of New England, inspired Benjamin Franklin's proposal for an all-colony confederation in 1775. Perhaps the most important legacy of the Mayflower Compact was the institution of the town meeting of Plymouth Plantation's member towns. Thomas Jefferson called the town meeting "the wisest invention ever devised by the wit of man for the perfect exercise of self-government and for its preservation." Given this tradition of active self-government, it was not a coincidence that the first active steps toward American independence were taken near the original home of the Pilgrims, at Lexington and Concord.

Natural Law and Natural Rights   Terms from the vocabulary of moral and political philosophy used to counter positivistic theories of private and public morality. Natural law and natural rights philosophy asserts that the fundamental rules governing human behavior derive from basic characteristics of a human nature common to all. This is true for both our moral obligations (natural law) and for the moral authority to do certain acts (natural rights). Natural law and natural rights are common to all persons of all times and places. As a corollary, if a legislator creates a rule that violates one of the fundamental natural rules, the new rule is immoral and not a valid law. Positivistic moral theories, on the other hand, deny that there is a universal basis for the fundamental rules of human conduct. Instead, positivists say that such rules derive from historical circumstances or simply from arbitrary choice. Thus fundamental rules may vary widely among times and places, groups and individuals. As a corollary, there is no moral basis for distinguishing between morally valid and morally invalid laws. A law is a law. While various natural law and natural rights theories agree on their rejection of positivism, they differ markedly among themselves. The development of these theories can be viewed in four stages: (1) cosmological, (2) juridical, (3) theological-anthropological, and (4) rationalist. In the first three stages, the term *natural rights* is rarely mentioned explicitly. It is implicit in the theories' treatment of justice, i.e., my rights are the correlatives of the obligation of others to be just toward me. In rationalist theory, the term *natural rights* becomes both explicit and dominant.

Socrates, Plato, and Aristotle formulated the key moral concepts that would be incorporated into the classic medieval natural law theories. Given the nature-law split they accepted from their Sophist opponents, however, "natural law" would have seemed a contradiction in terms to them. Natural law in the moral sense was first used by the Greek Stoics of the fourth and third centuries B.C., who in turn greatly influenced Roman thinkers such as Cicero. For the Stoics, the moral life consisted in living harmoniously with the cosmic law of nature established by God or fate.

The next interpretation of natural law and natural rights was formulated by the Roman jurists. Reinterpreting the tripartite division of law introduced by Ulpian, both Isadore of Seville and Gratian distinguished between civil law and natural law. Civil law was proper to each nation, although there was a *jus gentium,* "the law of nations," common to all nations. Natural law was common to human beings wherever they lived, and was superior to civil law, the latter drawing its authority from proper interpretations of the natural law.

The most systematic natural law theory is the theological-anthropological theory developed by Thomas Aquinas. He distinguished three kinds of law: eternal law (God's plan of creation and providence), natural law (the eternal law as embodied in the strivings of human nature and as known by human reason), and human law (human legislation). Aquinas's concept of natural law synthesized juridical theory with Aristotle's doctrine of moral virtue as the habitual and properly integrated exercise of human capacities in pursuit of their natural goals. Aquinas also held that human legislation was authentic law only if it was consonant with the eternal and natural law. Aquinas's theory was weakened by the voluntarism of late medieval scholasticism, but it survived intact in sixteenth-century thinkers such as Richard Hooker. Grotius's seventeenth century version of the *jus gentium,* in which he applied natural law to international relations, was built upon Aquinas's theory.

Concerned that Catholicism had ignored the central role of grace in Christian life, the Reformation held that human nature was so radically perverted by original sin that nature alone could not be the basis of morality. Enlightenment thinkers, especially after Hume's empiricism and skepticism, cast doubt upon our ability to know human nature, even if it were an adequate basis for morality. Thus a new view of natural law began to emerge. This rationalist view rejected the Aristotelian-Thomistic conception of human nature as teleological, and instead portrayed it as a set of physical capacities and needs governed by rationality and freedom. These capacities and needs lacked any particular natural orientation except self-interest. One's moral obligation was simply to live and let live in accordance with self-interest. John Locke reflects the transition from the theological-anthropological stage to the rationalist stage. While he is definitely in the rationalist tradition, he is also influenced by the natural law theory of Richard Hooker. Under rationalist theory, the emphasis of moral philosophy shifted to natural rights. By the nineteenth century, reference to natural law had generally disappeared except in pockets of ecclesiology where Thomism survived. It was a short step from the rationalist doctrine of natural rights to utilitarianism's rejection of the very idea of natural rights. Bentham called the concept "nonsense upon stilts" and led the modern world into a consideration of individual liberties dictated by social utility. Since the Thomistic revival of the late nineteenth century, and especially since the *reductio ad absurdum* of moral positivism under the Nazis, Aquinas's natural law doctrine has received renewed attention. As Protestant-Catholic polemics have receded, interest in natural law theory has been rekindled among Protestant scholars such as Brunner, Althaus, and Wendland. But natural law doctrine is far from the dominant moral philosophy of the 1980s. The most important modern statement of contractarian natural rights theory, John Rawls's *A Theory of Justice*, makes no reference to natural law. *See also* COMMON LAW, p. 13; JURISPRUDENCE, p. 38; JOHN RAWLS, p. 54.

Significance   The development of natural law and natural rights theories was an attempt to clarify how mankind should deal with unjust human laws and behavior, both within and between states. These theories provided the moral rationale for the English Bill of Rights (1689), the American Declaration of Independence (1776), the American Bill of Rights (1789), the French Declaration of the Rights of Man and Citizen (1789), and the United Nations Universal Declaration of Human Rights (1948). They also underlay many acts of civil disobedience in the modern world, not to mention revolutions and such circumscribed discussions of natural law and natural rights as the Nuremberg War Crime Trials. There is universal agreement today that all human beings have certain inalienable rights, whether these rights are grounded in nature or not. The question remains whether and how this belief can be justified. Purely theological arguments aside, the main contemporary justifications for human rights are Kantian, utilitarian, contractarian, and Thomistic. Of these, only the Thomistic view appeals to natural law. The utilitarians have been highly successful in basing individual rights on simple considerations of social usefulness. An adequate theoretical justification of human rights is crucial not only in securing their existence but also in determining their content. Human rights can otherwise degenerate into a distorted version of civil liberties, according to which people have a right to do anything they please, regardless of how what they do affects the common good. Such an extreme view of the content of human rights can eventually provoke a reaction strong enough to threaten the existence of all human rights.

John Rawls (b. 1921)   Contemporary Harvard University moral philosopher who systematically restated the natural rights contractarian theory of justice. John Rawls painstakingly wrote the 600 pages of his definitive *A Theory of Justice* (1971) over a 12-year period. He defends the view that human beings have certain natural rights and that the most secure grounding of both public and private morality is in the idea of social contract. Rawls conceives the ideal social contract more along the lines of Kant than of other contractarians such as Hobbes, Locke, and Rousseau, and he vigorously opposes the utilitarians. The latter deny natural rights by speaking instead of civil liberties meted out according to calculations of social utility. Rawls believes that social justice is more fundamental than individual justice. Most of his book is spent explaining the four stages through which social justice is brought about: (1) the establishment of the principles of social justice in the "original position"; (2) the establishment of constitutional justice in the "constitutional convention"; (3) the establishment of legislative justice in the "legislative stage"; and (4) administrative and judicial application of relevant rules, along with citizen compliance with them in concrete and particular cases. Rawls emphasizes that these four stages and their corresponding principles describe not how people actually do establish and apply the principles of justice but how they ought to do so. Rawls says repeatedly that he wants to achieve a parsimony of assumptions in order to achieve the fullest possible consensus on the principles he derives. He assumes that people are driven only by a desire to maximize their own self-interest, and that they take no interest in the interests of others. To make self-interest work in the cause of fairness, for justice is fairness, Rawls requires the first three stages of choice to be performed behind what he calls a "veil of ignorance." A brief elaboration of Rawls's four stages in the development of social justice follows.

In the first stage, the "original position," people know nothing particular about themselves, whether they are geniuses or idiots, rich or poor, black or white, male or female, American or Russian. Neither do they know anything about their society. Without this ignorance, people who know that fate has given them a greater share of natural and social assets would be tempted to push for a less-than-fair contract, to their own advantage. Rawls says that in such an original position, all self-interested people would choose his "two principles of justice" and the "two priority rules." The two principles of justice are (1) basic liberties such as freedom of conscience and freedom of opportunity must be distributed with absolute equality; and (2) other social goods such as wealth and political power may be distributed unequally only if the inequalities are to the advantage of the least advantaged members of society. The priority rules tell us how to solve conflicts of principle. The first rule says that the first principle of justice is more fundamental than the second principle. The second rule says that the two principles of justice taken together are more important than any other consideration.

In the constitutional convention and the legislative stage the veil of ignorance is partly drawn back so that, while the participants still know nothing about their own individual conditions, they know the relevant facts about their own society. Building on this knowledge and on the principles of justice and priority rules, the participants now establish just political procedures, by which Rawls means a constitution and just laws. The first principle of justice is more important in the constitutional phase; the second principle is more important in the legislative phase. Rawls assumes that the outcome of stages 2 and 3 will be a constitutional democracy with just laws.

In the administrative and judicial application stage, the veil of ignorance is completely removed. Particular cases are judged on the basis of full factual knowledge, the principles of justice and the priority rules, the constitution, and the laws. Good citizens follow the judgments indicated by these combined natural rights forces, and social justice is achieved. *See also* CONSTITUTIONALISM, HISTORICAL DEVELOPMENT OF, p. 16; NATURAL LAW AND NATURAL RIGHTS, p. 51; SOCIAL CONTRACT, p. 61.

Significance   John Rawls is a moral philosopher who enjoys the deep respect of his peers. One measure of the importance of his *A Theory of Justice* is the enormous body of secondary literature it generated almost immediately upon publication in 1971. In its twentieth annual *Nomos* Yearbook, entitled *Constitutionalism* (1979), the American Society for Political and Legal Philosophy included two detailed articles on Rawls. But Rawls has not been without his critics. Robert Nozick's *Anarchy, State, and Utopia* (1974) questions the fairness of the redistributive effects of Rawls's second principle of justice. Other moral philosophers have questioned whether Rawls's hypothetical veil of ignorance can guarantee the moral objectivity he is seeking. Rawls's reliance on rational self-interest as the spring of his moral theory is as questionable for him as it was for earlier contractarians. It is unlikely that moral obligation can ever be reduced to calculations of self-interest. Rawls's initial assumption that human beings are devoid of interest in the interests of others is similar to basing a theory of human physiology on the assumption that humans have no heart. It is an interesting intellectual exercise, but it is contrary to the facts, and it leads to false conclusions about the real human body. Rawls's theory has a noble purpose. Many of his conclusions about the redistribution of social goods and about sacrificing one's life in the cause of justice are worthy of the best traditions in moral philosophy. It is not clear, however, that his assumptions are strong enough to support his conclusions.

Republicanism   The doctrine of government by the people through majority rule or by consent. A republic is a political system based on representation in government by delegates chosen by the people. The principle of representation makes government a reflection of a given culture or society, and limits the power that any individual or group may wield over others. Republicanism forces citizens to work together and compromise, theoretically avoiding extremism by broadening and softening points of view. The doctrine first appeared in the Greek city-states, where the political good was defined in representational and majoritarian terms. It reappeared in medieval constitutional theory in the fourteenth century as the idea of a selected individual acting as an attorney for his fellow citizens. Late medieval political theorists believed that government should act as a balancer and/or mixer of interests for the benefit and satisfaction of the majority. Republicanism flourished in English society with the rise of liberal economic thought and mercantilism in the sixteenth century, with a concomitant mistrust for the king and his ability to govern effectively. Although the living English constitution required that law making be carried out by both the Crown and the Houses of Parliament, the Whig principle of legislative supremacy became so popular that by 1649 Parliament had been established as the supreme law-making body.

There are three theories of representation in the application of republicanism: the mandate theory, the independence theory, and the mandate and independence theories combined. In mandate theory, the representative does only what his or her constituents say they want done. In independence theory, once a representative is chosen the representative is free to do what he or she feels is right. In mandate and independence theory combined, an attempt is made to balance both the constituents' and the representative's interests for reasons of political stability. In mandate theory the representative is a delegate or agent chosen merely to look after the interests of the attentive public. In independence theory it is assumed the representative is typical of those he or she represents, shares their characteristics, but may lead individual interested parties to less parochial opinions. Both mandate and independence theory are concerned about the means by which a representative is chosen, whether it is by election, for example, or by lot, or by a pattern of succession. Republicanism continuously debates the question of what constitutes true and just representation. *See also* ENGLISH CONSTITUTION, p. 27; JOHN LOCKE, p. 44; NATURAL LAW AND NATURAL RIGHTS, p. 51; VIRGINIA PLAN, p. 65.

Significance   Republicanism provides the theoretical basis for the American constitutional system. The writers of the federal Constitution combined the thought of John Locke with their own experience under the English constitution and common law to form the concept of limited government by consent of the governed. The framers had experienced many different types of government in the several colonies. They had suffered under the weak and ineffective government of the Articles of Confederation. They were convinced, therefore, that the best model for government was one in which legislative supremacy, majority rule, popular sovereignty, and representation prevailed. Any federal government should have at least these characteristics, they reasoned, but how much power relative to the states should a central government have? Obviously, to be efficient and effective the central government must have more power than it had under the Articles of Confederation. Yet federal power should be limited to the extent it would not encroach upon local and individual rights. Representation should be maximized, but small groups or factions should be prevented from gaining too much power. The framers were thus attracted to the Virginia Plan, which established a bicameral legislature. The Virginia Plan combined a larger house with greater or more direct representation (smaller groups, specific interests) with a smaller house with less direct representation (larger groups, diversified interests). Small states felt they were disadvantaged because of their small populations. The Connecticut Compromise addressed this concern by establishing equal representation for all states in the Senate, giving the upper house a point of view based on broader and more national interests. The Constitution also guaranteed every state a republican form of government in Article IV, Section 4. The first Supreme Court case concerned with this clause was *Luther* v. *Borden* (7 How. 1: 1849), in which the Court said through

Chief Justice Roger B. Taney that the issue of which of two rival governments in Rhode Island was the proper one should be decided by Congress, not by the Court. The Court held that representation was a political question that should be decided by the people through their representatives. Although the Court has since intervened in the electoral process to ensure the approximate equal value of each citizen's vote, the purpose of the intervention has consistently been to maintain the basic principle of republicanism: government by the people through majority rule.

Separation of Powers   The doctrine and practice of dividing the powers of government among several of its constituent parts in order to prevent the abusive concentration of power in any one part. The separation of powers embodied in the federal Constitution has two dimensions: a *functional* distinction between government and people, and between legislature, executive, and judiciary; and a *territorial* distinction between central and state governments. A related doctrine and practice is that of checks and balances. Sometimes the framers used checks generically for any type of block against absolute power, of which the separation of powers was one example, but more typically they used checks specifically for a device that simultaneously softened and implemented the separation of powers. Checks softened the separation of powers because they allowed, indeed they required, the concurrence of one branch in the work properly assigned to another branch, and they implemented the separation of powers because they specified the controls each part of government had over other parts. In what was hardly an exhaustive list, John Adams counted eight checks and balances in the Constitution: central government vs. states, House vs. Senate, Congress vs. President, Senate vs. President (in treaties and appointments), the people vs. their elected representatives, the Senate vs. the state legislatures (in the original formula for electing United States Senators), and the people vs. the Electoral College.

The territorial separation of powers is discussed in this Dictionary under Federalism (p. 30). This entry concentrates on the functional separation of powers, specifically the division of government into legislative, executive, and judicial branches. The functional separation found in the federal Constitution had both theoretical and practical origins. The first discussion of separation of power theory is found in Greek thought. Plato's distinction between guardians, auxiliaries, and craftsmen in the *Republic* is a division of social functions, however, and not of governmental power. Aristotle's "mean" forms of government, i.e., polity and aristocracy, and his distinction between the deliberative, magistrative, and judicial functions of government (*Politics,* Book IV, Chapters 9–11 and 14–16) were the first true governmental applications of separation theory. In his attempt to analyze the way the Roman Republic combined the power of the consuls, the senate, and the people, Polybius in about 118 B.C. coined the term "mixed" government. His analysis, continued by Cicero in 43 B.C., reappeared in modern form in Sir Thomas Smith's *De Republica Anglorum* (1583) and in James Harrington's *Oceana* (1656). Harrington recommended a division between senate, people, and magistracy. Despite his absolutist practices, Oliver Cromwell three years earlier had written into his *Instrument of Government* a separation of power between the executive (the Lord Protector) and Parliament. John Locke's *Second Treatise of Government* (1690) championed a distinction between the legislative, executive, and federative branches, although he thought the legislature should dominate. Charles de Secondat, better known as the Baron de Montesquieu, is usually credited with having first formulated in his *The Spirit of Laws* (1748) the legislative-executive-judicial separation theory later embodied in the federal Constitution. In fact, however, the Constitution differs from Montesquieu's theory in many essential respects, such as an elected executive, Congress's power to impeach, and the absence of estates. Sir William Blackstone's *Commentaries on the Laws of England* (1765) insisted upon a separation between the executive and the legislative branches. One other author deserves mention, even though his separation theory appeared after the federal Constitution was drafted. In the first part of his *Metaphysics of Morals* (1797), Immanuel Kant elaborated a philosophical justification for Montesquieu's tripartite scheme. More names could be added. In his *Defense of the Constitution* (1786), John Adams claimed to find at least a dozen authors who advocated the doctrine of separation of powers.

Historian Benjamin F. Wright, Jr., has argued that early American governmental experience was at least as important as theory was in shaping the separation of powers in the federal Constitution. The separation between the executive and the legislature had begun with the establishment of the House of Burgesses in Virginia in 1619, especially with its strengthening in 1624. This pattern was substantially copied in all the colonies except Rhode Island and Connecticut, even though the dominance of royal governors hardly made separation an equal division of power. Bicameralism first appeared in Massachusetts in 1644 and eventually spread to all the other colonies except Pennsylvania. Even though its origins are more obscure, a separate judiciary had been established in several colonies by the mid-seventeenth century, and in all the colonies before the Revolution. In the period between 1776 and 1784, all the states except

Rhode Island and Connecticut wrote new constitutions, and all of them except Pennsylvania asserted the importance of separation of powers, especially Virginia, North Carolina, and Georgia. Yet only New York, New Hampshire, and Massachusetts refused to put the executive under the domination of the legislature. This reluctance was because of the hatred the states had for abusive royal governors. All the states except Pennsylvania and Georgia adopted bicameral legislatures. The Articles of Confederation, ratified in 1781, was not influenced by the separation of powers doctrine because of the pervasive distrust of a strong executive and because of the insistence of the individual states upon their autonomy. The few powers allowed to the central government were dominated by the unicameral Congress, with no judicial system and with an executive council so weak it disbanded after its first meeting. It was the inadequacies of government under the Articles that created a consensus in favor of a strong separation of powers in the Constitutional Convention. Benjamin Franklin and Roger Sherman—and, outside the Convention, Thomas Paine—were the sole dissenting voices. Still, the exact shape of the separation of powers in the new government emerged only after extended debate on the convention floor. *See also* CONSTITUTION OF THE UNITED STATES, p. 19; FEDERALISM, p. 30; CARL FRIEDRICH, p. 34.

Significance   Separation of powers is the necessary structural support for the functional division of governmental power that is the foundation of constitutional democracy. It prevents government from obtaining tyrannical power over groups and individuals. The critiques of the federal Constitution's separation of powers doctrine fall into three categories. (1) Totalitarian theorists reject it because they reject any separation of power, favoring instead the concentration of power in an enlightened single authority such as the Philosopher-King, *le Roi-Soleil, il Duce, der Führer,* or the Party. (2) Some proponents of the separation of powers argue that the American version is so extreme as to be inefficient. This group of critics includes many British writers and the American historian J. Allen Smith. (3) Other proponents of the separation of powers argue that the American version is ineffective. They point out that each period of American history has been marked by the unchecked power of one branch or another. In the early years, it was Congress; then came a powerful Supreme Court under John Marshall; in the modern era the nation has a strong presidency, culminating in the imperial presidency of the 1970s and 1980s. Several crucial factors in the recent growth of presidential power were clearly unforeseen by the framers. They include the extra-constitutional role of the president as the head of his party in Congress, the president's ability to appeal directly to the people through the electronic media, and the need of government to deal instantaneously with nuclear attack. Despite the changing fortunes of each functional division of the federal government, the doctrine of separation of powers continues to be the chief structural cornerstone of American constitutionalism.

Social Contract   A theoretical justification for the consensual basis of human society and government. Social contract theory involves two concepts, the governmental contract and the social contract proper, each of which has a history extending back into antiquity. The concept of a governmental contract (*pactum subjectionis*) holds that the relation between a people and its rulers arises from a mutual agreement between both parties. This notion is found in the Old and New Testaments; Roman law; ancient German and Frankish law; feudalism; medieval thought, particularly in Manegold of Lautenbach and Thomas Aquinas; conciliarism, especially in Nicholas of Cusa and Marsilius of Padua; the development of bourgeois economic interests; the Reformation, notably the Huguenots; the Counter-Reformation (Bellarmine, Suarez, and Mariana); modern thinkers (Hobbes, Locke, Hume, Rousseau, Pufendorf, Althusius, Grotius, Kant, and Fichte); and in the constitutional phase of Rawls's *A Theory of Justice* (1971). While the concept of governmental contract was usually invoked as a limitation on governmental authority, including the rights of rebellion and regicide, Hobbes and Spinoza used it also as a justification for absolute monarchy. But most defenders of absolute sovereignty have avoided the dangers of governmental contract theory and instead held theories of the divine right of kings, as in Barclay and Filmer, or papal absolutism.

The concept of a social contract proper (*pactum unionis*) holds that the establishment of any society greater than the family or clan arises from a mutual agreement, historical or hypothetical, among all the individuals of the society. This theory has three main versions, each distinguished by its account of the relationship between the social contract and morality. The first version states that individuals in the state of nature preceding the contract are already subject to a moral natural law. Representatives of this position include Cicero, Richard Hooker, Vitoria, Molina, Locke, and Grotius. The second version states that individuals in the state of nature are not yet under a moral law of any sort. Indeed, the social contract is the foundation of morality, rather than vice versa. Representatives of this position include the Greek Sophists and Epicureans, Hobbes, Spinoza, and Rousseau. Despite his explicit rejection of a social contract, Hume's foundation of both morality and society built upon an informal utilitarian agreement among individuals is not easily distinguished from social contract theory. The third version, held mainly by Kant and those influenced by him, especially Fichte and Rawls, holds that the social contract is preceded by and founded on moral law. But the moral law itself, as seen in the formulation of Kant's categorical imperative, is the result of an ideal original contract with all other human beings. *See also* JOHN LOCKE, p. 44; MAYFLOWER COMPACT, p. 48; NATURAL LAW AND NATURAL RIGHTS, p. 51; JOHN RAWLS, p. 54.

Significance   Social contract theory as a legitimating idea for government enjoys almost universal recognition today, even in those totalitarian regimes where it is violated in practice. The American colonists felt an urgent need for such a legitimating idea. It is seen in the Mayflower Compact of 1620 through the federal Constitution of 1787. Yet the theory of a social contract proper, with the exception of its Kantian and neo-Kantian (Rawlsian) version, has been discarded for several reasons. First, the existence of a state of nature has been discredited by both historians and anthropologists. Second, political thinkers such as Marx and McPherson have exposed the economic individualism that fed the growth of social contract theory. Third, Aristotelians and most twentieth-century Catholic social thinkers have insisted that human sociability and morality are based in human nature itself and are not the creations of arbitrary choice. It is instructive to compare Locke's version of the social contract with Rousseau's. For Locke, individuals who enter into the social contract retain their own wills, even though they are limited by the will of the majority. For Rousseau, individuals abandon their own will to the general will. This difference is reflected in the American and French revolutions respectively, the former concentrating on individual economic freedoms, the latter accelerating into a program for total social reform, often at the expense of individual liberties.

State Constitutions   The fundamental laws of the respective states within the United States of America. State constitutions are not required by the federal Constitution, which provides merely for a "republican form of government" in each state. However, there is a universal tradition of state constitutions antedating the Constitutional Convention and serving as one of its main inspirations. The history of state constitutions can be divided into three phases: colonial charters, revolutionary constitutions, and subsequent developments. Each of the thirteen colonies except New Jersey and Delaware had a charter.

(See Table A-1, p. 465.) Most of these charters were land grants to companies or individuals and included no provisions for self-government by the colonists. Virginia's second charter (1609) required that the London Company's legislation conform with British law and be subject to review by the king in council, a stipulation found in later charters as well. This was not a completely empty requirement because historian E. B. Russell calculated that 5.5 percent of the 8,563 colonial laws were ruled invalid on review. This meant, of course, that company law was limited by a more fundamental law, which laid the foundation for judicial review. It was under the third Virginia charter (1618) that the General Assembly was established, the first instance of representative government in America. The Fundamental Orders drafted by the towns in the Connecticut valley (1639) was the first citizen-drafted constitution in Anglo-American history. William Penn's first version of the Frame of Government for Pennsylvania (1682) contained a closely reasoned statement of the nature of constitutionalism, the first formula for amending a constitution, and the first suggestion of a constitutional convention.

The Revolutionary period of state constitutions began on May 15, 1776, when the Continental Congress began to prepare for independence from Great Britain. New Hampshire and South Carolina had drafted temporary constitutions earlier that year, and Congress now informed them and the other colonies that reconciliation with Great Britain was hopeless and that permanent constitutions were needed. At the same time, Congress began work on the Articles of Confederation, which were approved by Congress in 1777 but not ratified until 1781. The Virginia constitution was completed in June 1776 and served as a model for the others. New Jersey, Delaware, Pennsylvania, Maryland, and North Carolina completed their statements of fundamental law before the end of that year. Georgia and New York (and Vermont, even though it was not yet a state) completed their constitutions in 1777, Massachusetts in 1780, and New Hampshire in 1784. Massachusetts and New Hampshire took longer because their town meetings were determined that the drafting and ratification process would be as democratic as possible. This concern was not so apparent in the other states. Massachusetts is the only state of the original thirteen still operating under its original constitution. The only states that did not draft new constitutions were Connecticut and Rhode Island. They simply revised their colonial charters. Of the Revolutionary era constitutions, only those of New York and Massachusetts provided for an executive who was popularly elected and endowed with broad administrative powers. In all the other states, distrust of kings and royal governors led constitution writers to put the executive and judiciary under the domination of a strong legislature. A number of states, most notably Maryland, set property requirements for voters and officeholders. Few of the state constitutions had well-developed bills of rights, and several had no provisions for amendments.

Subsequent developments in state constitutions are summarized in Table A-2, p. 466. The overwhelming impression one receives from the data is that of constant change. Fourteen states have adopted new constitutions since World War II. Discounting Rhode Island, only 19 states have kept their original constitutions, and even those have been thoroughly revised. By the end of 1979, there had been 4,603 state constitutional amendments. Why this general instability in state constitutions, as compared with the stability of the federal Constitution? One factor is the increasing dominance of the central government, which obviously has limited the powers of the states. Another is faulty governmental structures in state governments that the federal Constitution has been able to avoid. For example, the states eventually decided that total legislative dominance hindered efficient government. They then moved to establish separation of powers among the legislative, executive, and judicial branches. A third factor is that state constitutions have included many laws of a nonfundamental nature. The Louisiana constitution of 1921, for example, contained almost 250,000 words. The current Georgia constitution contains over 600,000 words. The main reasons for such long documents are no doubt that normal legislative processes will adequately regulate certain state and local issues, and the successful struggle of many groups to have their special interests given constitutional protection. A fourth and final reason for instability in state constitutions, dependent in part upon the first three, is that few state constitutions have the sacred aura attached to the federal document. The states use four methods to change their constitutions: (1) legislative proposals (used by all the states); (2) popular initiatives for limited changes (used by 17 states); (3) constitutional commissions (required by statute in 16 states); and (4) constitutional conventions. Constitutional commissions, which study the current constitution and make recommendations for change, were used in 21 states during the 1970s. Constitutional conventions, which adopt proposals for constitutional change, were held in 10 states during the 1970s. In all states but Delaware, the proposals adopted by a constitutional convention must be ratified by the voters. Of all the amendments adopted between 1972 and 1979, most were concerned with taxation and financing (20.2 percent), various state functions (12.1 percent), changes in the legislative branch (11.4 percent), and changes in the judicial branch (11.4 percent). A number of resources for improving state constitutions are available. Beginning with its first edition of the *Model State*

Constitution (1921), the National Municipal League has provided numerous publications and other services. Also helpful in the process of streamlining state constitutions are the Council of State Governments, the United States Advisory Commission on Intergovernmental Relations, and the League of Women Voters. *See also* CONSTITUTIONALISM, HISTORICAL DEVELOPMENT OF, p. 16; CONSTITUTION OF THE UNITED STATES, p. 19; FEDERALISM, p. 30; SEPARATION OF POWERS, p. 58.

Significance   State constitutions have a proud past. They are a clear witness to the deep-rooted American belief in written law. The earliest state constitutions were also the schools in which the framers of the federal Constitution learned their trade. State constitutions guided their citizens through most of the nation's rapid territorial, economic, and population expansion. The present condition of many state constitutions is less shining, however. The modern tendency is to make the state constitution an extended piece of omnibus legislation or a set of guarantees for special interest groups. The state constitution reform movement has attempted to address such problems and foster improvements, maintaining that better state government cannot be worked out by the individual states in isolation. The social, political, and economic problems inherent in contemporary American federalism must be solved before thoroughgoing state constitutional reform can be accomplished.

Virginia Plan   A set of fifteen resolutions or proposals presented to the Constitutional Convention on May 29, 1787, by Edmund Randolph, governor of Virginia. The Virginia Plan, also referred to as the Randolph Plan, although it was written largely by James Madison, proposed the creation of a strong central government. In fact the central government would have virtually unlimited powers, which the Virginia Plan described as "national." The plan said the Articles of Confederation should be "corrected and enlarged" so as to provide for the "common defense, security of liberty, and general welfare" of the nation. The proposal offered by Governor Randolph went far beyond the initial vision of many of the delegates to the convention. They thought the purpose of the meeting was to amend the Articles of Confederation. The Articles had created a federal government with few powers relative to the states. The Virginia Plan provided for a national government with power *over* the states. In the end, much of the plan was included in the Constitution. The Virginia Plan suggested the replacement of the unicameral Continental Congress with a legislature consisting of two houses. It called for the legislature to have the power to legislate "in all cases to which separate states are incompetent, or in which the harmony of the United States may be interrupted by the exercise of individual legislation." The national legislature would also have the power to negate any law passed by the states that it determined to be contrary to the best interests of the union. The proposal included the creation of an executive branch of government to oversee the administration of the laws and a national judiciary of one or more supreme tribunals, along with a system of lower national courts, to interpret the laws. The most controversial part of the Virginia Plan was a proviso that made the voting power of both houses of Congress proportional to "quotas of contribution, or number of free inhabitants, or by the amount of property or population" in each state. Small states rebelled against this idea since they would obviously be disadvantaged in such a system. New Jersey countered with a plan of its own, charging that the Virginia Plan would totally usurp state sovereignty. The debate over proportional versus equal representation was resolved through a compromise approved on July 16 that gave states proportional representation in the House and equal representation in the Senate. The Virginia Plan set the agenda for the entire Constitutional Convention. Its brilliant and innovative propositions captured the imagination of the delegates and forced them either to agree or amend. *See also* CONSTITUTION OF THE UNITED STATES, p. 19; *THE FEDERALIST*, p. 32; SEPARATION OF POWERS, p. 58.

Significance   The Virginia Plan of union provided both foundation and substance for the federal Constitution. It provided the impetus behind the arguments and decisions concerning what type of government the United States was to establish, whether it was to be federal, meaning at this time a confederation of sovereign states, or national. The old Federalists said nationalism would be fatal to liberty. The Nationalists said federalism had proven itself to be incompetent under the Articles of Confederation. The Nationalists finally won the argument, and a central governmental system was established. To make that decision palatable, however, the Senate was converted from a representation of formal property interests to a protection of the interests of the separate states. In summary, the Virginia Plan proposed a bicameral legislature, the power of the legislature to pass laws directly related to individuals, the creation of an executive branch with authority to enforce national laws, and a national judiciary with a Supreme Court. It gave the nation Article IV, Section 3 of the Constitution, which says that the legislature, executive, and judiciary are all bound by the same oath to support the Constitution. It successfully established the Guarantee Clause of Article IV, Section

4, which mandates a republican form of government in every state. The idea of taking a national census from which the allotment for representatives for each state would be derived also came from the Virginia Plan. The success and longevity of the United States Constitution is in no small way indebted to this set of proposals from a remarkable group of men living within a few miles of each other in the Virginia Tidewater. They successfully challenged the Constitutional Convention to share their vision of ordered liberty.

2. The First Amendment

Assembly and Protest, 142

Association, 147

OVERVIEW

The First Amendment states:

> Congress shall make no law respecting an establishment of religion, or prohibiting the free exercise thereof; or abridging the freedom of speech, or of the press; or the right of the people peaceably to assemble, and to petition the Government for redress of grievances.

The several provisions of the First Amendment are designed to protect the sensitive area of personal belief and opinion. The Establishment Clause forbids creation of a state church or direct governmental subsidies to churches. Contention remains, however, about the *extent* to which church and state must be separate. Important establishment criteria, including the often decisive "excessive entanglement" standard, were developed in the church property exemption case, *Walz* v. *Tax Commission of New York City* (397 U.S. 664: 1970). The role of the state in actually advancing religion was explored in *Engel* v. *Vitale* (370 U.S. 421: 1962), in which the Court invalidated a state-sponsored prayer exercise in the public schools. Similarly, the Court struck down an antievolution statute in *Epperson* v. *Arkansas* (393 U.S. 97: 1968). In *Widmar* v. *Vincent* (454 U.S. 263: 1981), the Court prohibited a state university from denying the use of its facilities to a group wanting to use those facilities for religious worship and discussion. Many of the establishment cases considered by the Court have had to do with schools because every state has within its borders both public and parochial schools at the elementary and secondary levels. The Court has been more concerned with the elementary and secondary levels than the college level because it believes the purpose of teaching religion is more encompassing at the lower levels. *Everson* v. *Board of Education* (330 U.S. 1: 1947) upheld state legislation authorizing reimbursement to parents for school transportation, even though some of the parents were sending their children to parochial schools. Similarly, the Court found no violation in off-premises released time religious instruction programs in *Zorach* v. *Clauson* (343 U.S. 306: 1952). Commencing in 1971, the Court considered several important cases involving services or materials made available to nonpublic schools. In *Lemon* v. *Kurtzman* (403 U.S. 602: 1971), the Court struck down a state law

73

authorizing public money to be used for nonpublic school expenses including teacher salaries. In *CPEARL* v. *Nyquist* (413 U.S. 756: 1973), the Court invalidated a New York statute providing repair and maintenance grants, tuition reimbursements, and tax deductions for nonpublic schools. It found problems with the purpose, primary effect, and extent to which governmental and school officials were interacting. The status of various instructional materials was examined in *Wolman* v. *Walter* (433 U.S. 406: 1977). *Tilton* v. *Richardson* (403 U.S. 672: 1971) upheld a federal law allocating building construction grants to church-related colleges and universities.

The Free Exercise Clause of the First Amendment prohibits governmental interference with religious practices. Although the clause absolutely protects religious belief, conduct related to the *pursuit* of belief may be subject to limitation. Generally, a purely secular regulation must be obeyed even by those who find the regulation at odds with their religious belief system. The extent to which the secular regulation concept applies is seen in the compulsory flag salute decision, *West Virginia State Board of Education* v. *Barnette* (319 U.S. 624: 1943), and the license tax decision, *Murdock* v. *Pennsylvania* (319 U.S. 105: 1943). The *Sunday Closing Law Cases* (366 U.S. 421: 1961) permit secular regulation to encroach upon religious practice, but only in the absence of alternate means of achieving secular ends. *Sherbert* v. *Verner* (374 U.S. 398: 1964), *Gillette* v. *United States* (401 U.S. 437: 1971), and *Wisconsin* v. *Yoder* (406 U.S. 205: 1972) provide examples of the way in which the Court has balanced the competing interests of legitimate secular purpose and possible burdens on the free exercise of religion.

The First Amendment prohibits impairment of free speech. The basic principles for free speech cases were established in *Schenck* v. *United States* (249 U.S. 47: 1919), in which the Court held that expression may be regulated where the expression creates a "clear and present danger." *Gitlow* v. *New York* (268 U.S. 652: 1925) modified the *Schenck* standard by permitting restriction of expression if it tended to lead to an injurious result. A sliding scale test for expression was developed in *Dennis* v. *United States* (341 U.S. 494: 1951), where speech that advocated illegal action was examined. Expression through an action substitute or symbolic gesture is protected in *Tinker* v. *Des Moines School District* (393 U.S. 503: 1969). The nature of speech as communication was examined in *Cohen* v. *California* (403 U.S. 15: 1971), in which a state unsuccessfully sought to regulate "offensive" speech. Finally, statutory restrictions imposed on speech may be too broad or vague. *Village of Schaumburg* v. *Citizens for a Better Environment* (444 U.S. 620: 1980) utilizes the overbreadth doctrine to strike down a local ordinance.

The fundamental ingredient of freedom of the press is protection from prior or previous restraint. *Near* v. *Minnesota* (283 U.S. 697: 1931) set out the basic nature of free press protection. The prior restraint doctrine was used to strike down an injunction preventing publication of the Pentagon Papers in *New York Times, Inc.* v. *United States* (403 U.S. 713: 1971). There have been several other key free press policy considerations beyond prior restraint. The extent to which libelous statements are protected was examined in *New York Times, Inc.* v. *Sullivan* (376 U.S. 254: 1964), and plaintiff access to the editorial processes of defendant publications was established in *Herbert* v. *Lando* (441 U.S. 153: 1979). In *Branzburg* v. *Hayes* (408 U.S. 665: 1972), the Court rejected the concept of newsperson's privilege, which would have protected the confidentiality of news sources. The tension between the requirements of fair criminal trials and a free press has prompted numerous Supreme Court decisions. While the press has no special privilege relative to legal processes, *Richmond Newspapers, Inc.* v. *Virginia* (448 U.S. 555: 1980) did hold that press access to trials prevails even over the contrary wishes of a criminal defendant. *Pittsburgh Press Company* v. *Human Relations Commission* (413 U.S. 376: 1973) determined that free press protection does not extend to "commercial speech." The Federal Communication Commission's fairness doctrine was upheld as a proper constraint on the broadcast medium in *Red Lion Broadcasting Company* v. *FCC* (395 U.S. 367: 1969).

The Supreme Court has consistently placed obscenity outside the protection of the First Amendment. Having done so, the central problem becomes fashioning definitional standards that allow protected speech to be distinguished from obscenity. The Court's first major effort to develop such standards came in *Roth* v. *United States* (354 U.S. 476: 1957). After *Roth*, consensus on standards eroded until there was little expression that remained unprotected. *Memoirs* v. *Massachusetts* (383 U.S. 413: 1966) is representative of this development. The Burger Court sought to reestablish clarity in the definition of obscenity in *Miller* v. *California* (413 U.S. 15: 1973). In the wake of *Miller*, many localities attempted to regulate obscenity and adult entertainment. The Court upheld one such attempt through the zoning process in *Young* v. *American Mini Theatres* (427 U.S. 50: 1976). At the same time, one's right privately to possess obscene materials was established in *Stanley* v. *Georgia* (394 U.S. 557: 1969). Besides criminal sanctions, other techniques have been developed to control distribution of obscenity. *Kingsley Books, Inc.* v. *Brown* (354 U.S. 436: 1957) examined the use of injunctions to prevent sales, while *Freedman* v. *Maryland* (380 U.S. 51: 1965) considered film licensure as a means to review content prior to exhibition.

There are occasions in which free expression involves conduct such as assembling, marching, picketing, or demonstrating. It is an area where speech itself is likely to be protected, but where associated conduct may be subject to regulation. The interests of expression must be balanced against the government's interest in maintaining public order. Government may impose restrictions on the time, place, and manner in which expression may occur. In *Adderley* v. *Florida* (385 U.S. 39: 1966), the Court held that jail grounds may be off limits for a demonstration. More recently the Court upheld the right of persons to access a privately owned shopping center to express political views in *PruneYard Shopping Center* v. *Robins* (447 U.S. 74: 1980). Licensure or permit requirements have generally been viewed with suspicion by the Court, as have exparte injunctive proceedings used to restrain assembly before it occurs. In *Carroll* v. *President and Commissioners of Princess Anne* (393 U.S. 175: 1968), the Court struck down an attempt to enjoin a rally of a militant white supremacist organization.

The First Amendment does not explicitly protect the right of association, but it is clearly understood by the Court that group organization is a legitimate means of expression. The freedom to associate is drawn from the several expressed protections of the First Amendment. The character of association as a means of expression is thoroughly developed in *NAACP* v. *Alabama* (357 U.S. 449: 1958), a case involving an attempt by a state to compel disclosure of an organization's membership list. While the Court decided the case on Fourteenth Amendment due process grounds, the principle thrust of the decision was to protect associational freedom. Such a view did not always prevail, however. *Whitney* v. *California* (274 U.S. 357: 1927) reflects a less generous view of association. The Court upheld a state criminal syndicalism statute that permitted guilt by association. More recent decisions have rejected such a position. In *Keyishian* v. *Board of Regents* (385 U.S. 589: 1967), the Court held that mere membership in a particular organization cannot lead to dismissal from public employment. Associational activity as it relates to the electoral process was examined in *Buckley* v. *Valeo* (424 U.S. 1: 1976), a case in which portions of the Federal Election Campaign Act were stricken because of impermissible interference with political campaign expenditures.

The First Amendment entry and an elaboration of the above definitional cases follow.

The First Amendment   Protects personal belief and opinion and action stemming from personal belief and opinion. The First Amendment to the Constitution of the United States was adopted in 1791. It addresses four basic freedoms that its authors deemed imperative to a free society functioning within a democratic government. Those freedoms are (1) freedom of religion, (2) freedom of speech, (3) freedom of the press, and (4) the dual right to assemble peaceably and to petition the government. Freedom of religion is protected by two provisions, one of which prohibits the establishment of religion, while the other ensures the free exercise of religion. By implication a right of association also flows from the First Amendment. Although these rights may or may not be absolute, it has generally been held by the Supreme Court that a balance is required between First Amendment freedoms and the powers of a government to govern effectively. Some eminent jurists have argued that First Amendment rights are indeed absolute, but such jurists have been in the minority. The majority of the Supreme Court throughout the twentieth century has engaged in balancing First Amendment rights with the requirements of public order, and the Court has in fact removed certain conduct from First Amendment protections. The primary issues that have occupied the Court are those requiring line drawing between protected and unprotected activity. Each First Amendment clause will now be taken in turn.

The Establishment Clause was included because the drafters remembered the colonial experience with European state churches. At minimum the clause prohibits government from showing favoritism to a particular church or sect. The Supreme Court, however, has construed the prohibitions more broadly. It has attempted to create standards by which it can distinguish church and state involvements that are forbidden and those that are not. For a policy to withstand the limitations imposed by the clause, a legislative enactment must have a secular purpose, it must have a primary effect that neither advances nor inhibits religion, and it must not excessively entangle church and state authorities. The neutral position to be occupied by the state applies both to spiritual practices such as devotional exercises and to the allocation of public monies for the benefit of religion. The Free Exercise Clause prevents the government from interfering with religious practices. The clause absolutely protects a person's right to believe. The line-drawing problem exists when some kind of conduct is required in addition to belief. As Justice Felix Frankfurter observed in the first flag salute case, conscientious scruples are insufficient to relieve an individual from "obedience to general law not aimed at the promotion or restriction of religious belief." Thus a law that has a legitimate secular purpose may impinge upon the ability of a person to act out religious beliefs. More recently the Court has required that regulations that do interfere with religious practices can only do so in the absence of an alternative to the accomplishment of the legitimate secular objective.

The Court did not have occasion to consider the free speech provision until shortly after World War I. The first important free speech case, *Schenck* v. *United States* (249 U.S. 47: 1919, p. 108) held that the First Amendment would not protect a person who falsely shouted "Fire!" in a crowded theater and thus caused a panic. The authors of the First Amendment, however, were not as concerned with an utterance such as "Fire!" as they were with normal political and social expression. The problems of interpretation for the Court have come largely because the right of expression requires that there be a receiver of speech. There must be communication. Even if the participants in a communication exchange are of limited numbers, there might arise circumstances in which governmental intervention is appropriate. The key is determining *when* that intervention might be justified. The interests of those wishing to express themselves must be weighed against the public interest. That balancing process is complex and has given rise to a typology of expression that distinguishes speech that requires no additional conduct, speech that does require additional conduct, and speech that occurs through symbolism. The Court has fashioned various standards by which it can separate protected from unprotected communication within each of these categories.

The fundamental freedom of the press is also included within the First Amendment. The framers of the Constitution believed that liberty could not be maintained without a free press, which was a check on government. If the press is truly free, it can criticize all branches of the government, public employees, and, particularly, public policy. The doctrine of a free press means the press must be free from government control, printing what it desires without fear of censorship or prior restraint. There are many related issues the framers did not anticipate, however. Since radio and television were unknown in the late eighteenth century, the framers did not anticipate the power of electronic news media. Interference with the rights of those accused of crimes and the fairness of their trials could not be jeopardized in 1791 by prejudicial publicity broadcast over the airwaves. Neither were certain questions of obscenity and commercial speech perceived at the beginning of the American constitutional era. The Supreme Court has had to address each of these issues as they have developed in American history, all the while trying to balance the freedoms mandated in the First Amendment with other individual rights.

The enunciated right of peaceful assembly contains elements of expression found both in the right of free speech and in the right of association. In recent years assembly rights have been associated with the civil-rights movements of the 1960s, with anti-Vietnam demonstrations in the late 1960s and early 1970s, and with other political assemblies. Once again the Court has had to balance peaceful assembly against the protection of other rights, including private property rights and state property rights. Assembly cases usually involve marching, picketing, demonstrating, petition gathering, and similar activities. While free speech may be protected, associated conduct may be subject to regulation by the state. Not only is government interested in protecting property rights, it is also interested in maintaining public order. The essential rule is that government may impose restrictions on the time, place, and the manner in which an expression may occur through assembly. The First Amendment does not expressly protect the right of association. It is drawn from the free speech, peaceful assembly, and right to petition clauses of the First Amendment. While free speech focuses on one's right to express his or her views, the association right focuses on one's right to join a group, and be present at group meetings, but not necessarily to express oneself directly. It is the right to be a member of a group while the group expresses itself without regard to whether an individual member agrees with the group or not. *See also* BILL OF RIGHTS, p. 7; CONSTITUTION OF THE UNITED STATES, p. 19; NATURAL LAW AND NATURAL RIGHTS, p. 51.

Significance　　　The First Amendment was conceived as a constraint on the power of central government. With the exception of the Alien and Sedition Acts of 1798, Congress enacted little legislation that found its way to the Supreme Court on First Amendment challenge until World War I. See, for example, *Schenck* v. *United States* (249 U.S. 47: 1919 p. 108). Soon thereafter the Court was involved in a series of decisions that extended the various components of the First Amendment to the states through the Fourteenth Amendment. For additional discussion of the process of incorporation, see *Hurtado* v. *California* (110 U.S. 516: 1884 p. 206), and *Palko* v. *Connecticut* (302 U.S. 319: 1937 p. 207). Movement toward such an incorporation policy was evident in *Meyer* v. *Nebraska* (262 U.S. 390: 1923), in which the Court struck down a state statute prohibiting the teaching of German to any pre-ninth grade student in either public or private school. In *Meyer*, the Court held that the term "liberty" included, among other things, the right to "acquire useful knowledge" and engage in "common occupations of life," such as teaching. The Court said the Nebraska statute arbitrarily and unreasonably interfered with that liberty to the degree that due process protections of the Fourteenth Amendment had been violated. The free speech protection was formally extended two years later in *Gitlow* v. *New York* (268 U.S. 652: 1925, p. 109) with the Court holding that freedom of speech was "among the fundamental personal rights and 'liberties' protected by the Fourteenth Amendment from impairment by the states." In *Near* v. *Minnesota* (283 U.S. 697: 1931, p. 118), the Court said that it is "no longer open to doubt that the liberty of the press . . . is within the liberty safeguarded by the due process clause of the Fourteenth Amendment from invasion by state action." The right of assembly was incorporated in *DeJonge* v. *Oregon* (299 U.S. 353: 1937). The Court referred to the right of "peaceable assembly" as a right "cognate" and "equally fundamental" to those of free speech and press. It is a right that "cannot be denied without violating those fundamental principles of liberty and justice which lie at the base of all civil and political institutions—principles which the Fourteenth Amendment embodies in the general terms of its due process clause." The free exercise of religion clause was absorbed in *Cantwell* v. *Connecticut* (310 U.S. 296: 1940) with the Court saying the Fourteenth Amendment has "rendered the legislatures of the states as incompetent as Congress to enact such laws." The remaining element of the First Amendment, the Establishment Clause, was made applicable to the states in *Everson* v. *Board of Education* (330 U.S. 1: 1947, p. 89). The Court held that the clause must be extended to the states because it "reflected in the minds of early Americans a vivid mental picture of conditions and practices which they fervently wished to stamp out to preserve liberty for themselves and their posterity." The result of these decisions is that the safeguards residing within the First Amendment stand against unreasonable actions by both national and state governments to circumscribe personal belief and opinion.

ESTABLISHMENT OF RELIGION

Tax Exemptions

***Walz* v. *New York City Tax Commission*, 397 U.S. 664, 90 S.Ct. 1409, 25 L.Ed. 2d 697 (1970)**   Upheld tax exemptions on church-owned property. *Walz* addressed the question of whether tax exemptions for religious property are compatible with the Establishment Clause of the First Amendment. The exemption authorized by state law included "real or personal property used exclusively for religious, educational, or charitable purposes as defined by law and owned by any corporation or association organized or conducted exclusively for one or more such purposes and not operating for profit." Walz, a property owner and taxpayer, contended that the exemption indirectly compelled him financially to support religious organizations owning exempted properties. The Supreme Court upheld the exemption over the dissent of Justice Douglas. In the majority opinion Chief Justice Burger asserted that the First Amendment "will not tolerate either governmentally established religion or governmental interference with religion." As long as those proscribed acts are avoided, "there is room for play in a benevolent neutrality which will permit religious exercise to exist without sponsorship and without interference." Evaluation of policies using the religion clauses rests on "whether particular acts in question are intended to establish or interfere with religious beliefs and practices or have the effect of doing so." The legislative purpose served here is legitimate, Burger said. Historically, common exemptions recognize the "beneficial and stabilizing influences" of the nonprofit groups exempted from taxation. The policy also responds to the "latent danger inherent in the imposition of property taxes." What New York is doing is "simply sparing the exercise of religion from the burden of property taxation levied on private profit institutions." On considering primary effect, the Court introduced the entanglement criterion, which would become a decisive factor in many subsequent establishment cases. The chief justice argued that government involvement with religion existed with or without the exemption. Indeed, "elimination of the exemption would tend to expand the involvement of government by giving rise to tax valuation of church property, tax liens, tax foreclosures, and the direct confrontations and conflicts that follow in the train of those legal processes." While some indirect economic benefits and some involvements result from granting the exemption, they are lesser involvements than collecting the property tax. Finally, the Court rejected any "nexus between tax exemption and establishment of religion." The tax exemption is clearly not "sponsorship since the government does not transfer part of its revenue to churches but simply abstains from demanding that the church support the state." *See also* BILL OF RIGHTS, p. 7; ESTABLISHMENT CLAUSE, p. 80; FIRST AMENDMENT, p. 77.

Significance   *Walz v. Tax Commission of the City of New York* (397 U.S. 664: 1970) provided the Supreme Court a comparatively easy way to handle the establishment issue. Unlike direct aid programs, tax exemption had a long history. The history created a presumption for the practice. While benefits may be conveyed at least indirectly to religion, such tax exemptions were quite distinct from grant programs. The exemptions were also different politically in that they did not generate the divisive debate often associated with direct grant programs. *Walz* was viewed as a strongly accommodationist decision. The specific reference to "benevolent neutrality" was seen as a signal that the state may assume something other than a strictly neutral position regarding religion. At the same time, the new "excessive entanglement" test became a means by which the Burger Court blocked a number of aid programs. See, for example, *Lemon* v. *Kurtzman* (403 U.S. 602: 1971 p. 92). The entanglement test, while not critical to the outcome of *Walz* itself, was to become the principal criterion in many subsequent establishment cases.

Federal Building Grants

Tilton v. *Richardson,* 403 U.S. 672, 91 S.Ct. 2091, 29 L.Ed. 2d 790 (1971)   Allowed use of federal construction monies for projects at church-affiliated institutions of higher education. *Tilton* upheld in a 5–4 decision Title I of the Higher Education Facilities Act of 1963. The act provided construction grants to church-related colleges and universities for buildings and facilities "used exclusively for secular educational purposes." It also prohibited use of funds for any project that may be used for "sectarian instruction, religious worship, or the programs of a divinity school." Applicants for funds must "provide assurances that these restrictions will be respected," and enforcement was to be accomplished by government on-site inspections. The act had a provision through which the government would retain a 20-year interest in the financed facilities, enabling the government to recover at least a portion of the grant if the facility were to be used for other than secular purposes. The Court, through Chief Justice Burger, found the act to have a "legitimate secular objective entirely appropriate for government action" without having the effect of advancing religion. The 20-year limit on governmental interest in preserving the exclusively secular character of building uses was voided, however. The Court found it "cannot be assumed that a substantial structure has no value after that period and hence the unrestricted use of a valuable property is in effect a contribution of some value to a religious body." Key to upholding the act otherwise was the Court's opinion that "excessive entanglement did not characterize the relationship between government and church under the Act." The Court cited three factors that diminished the extent and the potential danger of the entanglement. First, institutions of higher learning are significantly different from elementary and secondary schools. Since "religious indoctrination is not a substantial purpose or activity of these church-related colleges and universities, there is less likelihood than in primary and secondary schools that religion will permeate the area of secular education." Second, the aid provided through the building grants is of a "non-ideological character." The need to monitor buildings would be less than monitoring teachers, for example. Third, entanglement is lessened because the aid comes in the form of a "one-time, single purpose construction grant." There are "no continuing financial relationships or dependencies." The inspections that do occur to monitor use of funds create only minimal contact. These factors also substantially lessen the potential for divisive religious fragmentation in the political arena. Justices Douglas, Black, Marshall, and Brennan dissented. They argued excessive entanglement and the insufficiency of the restrictions cited in the act. The dissenters pointed out that even if the specific buildings funded under the grant were used only for secular purposes, religious institutions were aided by being able to use for religious purposes monies freed by the receipt of the federal grant. *See also* CPEARL V. NYQUIST (413 U.S. 756: 1973), p. 94; FIRST AMENDMENT, p. 77; LEMON V. KURTZMAN (403 U.S. 602: 1971), p. 92; WALZ V. TAX COMMISSION (397 U.S. 664: 1970), p. 80; WOLMAN V. WALTER (433 U.S. 406: 1977), p. 96.

Significance   Tilton v. Richardson (403 U.S. 672: 1971) had substantial impact on First Amendment standards in two ways. First, the entanglement criterion introduced the year before in *Walz* was decisive in *Tilton*. It marked the first application of the standard in a school aid case. Second, Chief Justice Burger developed the distinction between higher education and the elementary-secondary levels of education as a key element in determining the degree to which entanglement existed. Combined with the nature of the bricks and mortar character of the aid, excessive entanglement was not found in *Tilton*. The Court expanded this view in subsequent cases. In *Hunt* v. *McNair* (413 U.S. 734: 1973), for example, the Court upheld a state financing arrangement that involved making proceeds from the sale of revenue bonds available to finance building projects at institutions of higher education, including nonpublic colleges and universities. The monitoring required during the payback period of the program was more extensive than in *Tilton,* but not yet excessive. Similarly, the Court upheld a broad, noncategorical grant program for private colleges, including religiously affiliated institutions, in *Roemer* v. *Board of Public Works of Maryland* (426 U.S. 736: 1976). The Court said the Establishment Clause requires "scrupulous neutrality by the State" but not a "hermetic separation." Although the grants were made annually, the need for close surveillance of purportedly secular activities in *Roemer* was limited enough that it did not constitute excessive entanglement.

School Prayer

***Engel* v. *Vitale,* 370 U.S. 421, 82 S.Ct. 1261, 8 L.Ed. 2d 601 (1962)**   Decided the Establishment Clause prohibited daily recitation of the New York Regents' Prayer. *Engel* generated a great deal of controversy because the spiritual exercise at issue was a prayer composed by a public body, the New York State Board of Regents. The Regents, an agency with broad supervisory authority over the public schools, recommended to school districts that the school day begin with a prayer they specified, although no pupil was to be compelled to join in the recitation of it. The prayer was as follows:

> Almighty God, we acknowledge our dependence on Thee, and we beg Thy blessings upon us, our parents, our teachers and our Country.

The Supreme Court held that by "using its public school system to encourage recitation of the Regents' prayer, the State of New York has adopted a practice wholly inconsistent with the Establishment Clause." The decision was 6–1 with Justice Stewart dissenting and Justices Frankfurter and White not participating. Justice Black wrote for the majority that the Establishment Clause must "at least mean that in this country it is no part of the business of government to compose official prayers for any group of the American people to recite as part of a religious program carried on by government." The exercise "officially establishes the religious beliefs embodied in the Regents' prayer." That the prayer is not overtly denominational or that participation is voluntary cannot save the prayer from a fatal establishment defect, argued Black. The establishment prohibitions go beyond just keeping governmental power and influence from coercing religious minorities to conform to the prevailing officially approved religion. The Establishment Clause rests on the belief that "a union of government and religion tends to destroy government and to degrade religion." The Court said its decision did not indicate a hostility toward religion or prayer. The problem was the state's role in a spiritual exercise. The Court concluded by saying it is "neither sacrilegious nor antireligious to say that each separate government in this country should stay out of the business of writing or sanctioning prayers and leave that purely religious function to the people themselves." Justice Stewart disagreed that the "simple prayer" involved in this case created "an official religion." On the contrary, he maintained that "to deny the wish of these school children to join in reciting this prayer is to deny them the opportunity of sharing in the spiritual heritage of our Nation." *See also* EPPERSON V. ARKANSAS(393 U.S. 97: 1968), p. 86; ESTABLISHMENT CLAUSE, p. 80; EVERSON V. BOARD OF EDUCATION(330 U.S. 1: 1947), p. 89; FIRST AMENDMENT, p. 77; ZORACH V. CLAUSON(343 U.S. 306: 1952), p. 91.

Significance   *Engel* v. *Vitale* (370 U.S. 421: 1962) took a decidedly different direction from previous decisions such as *Everson* v. *Board of Education* (330 U.S. 1: 1947) and *Zorach* v. *Clauson* (343 U.S. 306: 1952). The latter case held, for example, that the Establishment Clause allowed a neutral interaction between church and state. Under such a view, religious practitioners might constitutionally benefit from general secular purpose enactments. *Engel,* however, held that strict separation is required when governmental interaction involves actual spiritual practices. The case prompted a wave of criticism in reaction to invalidating the Regents' prayer. The Court held firm, however, and in the following year struck down other school exercises in *School District of Abington Township* v. *Schempp* (374 U.S. 203: 1963), and in *Murray* v. *Curlett* (374 U.S. 203: 1963). At issue in these cases were legislative enactments that designated recitation of the Lord's Prayer and the reading of Bible passages as spiritual activities to begin each school day. As in *Engel,* the Court found the states' involvement with such practices to be offensive to establishment prohibitions. The Court said in *Abington* that separation was based on a recognition of the teachings of history that powerful sects or groups might bring about a fusion of governmental and ecclesiastical institutions. The other prohibited possibility would be to "convert a dependence of one upon the other to the end that official support of the State or Federal Government would be placed behind the tenets of one or of all orthodoxies." The Court further noted that such establishment limitations do not interfere with free exercise protections. While a state may not use its power to prevent someone from freely exercising, the Free Exercise Clause "has never meant that a majority could use the machinery of the State to practice its beliefs." The reactions to the school prayer and Bible-reading decisions have led to various attempts formally to amend the Constitution to permit voluntary prayer. Given the politically volatile nature of the issue, the Court has generally steered clear of further establishment cases. Instead it has concentrated in recent years on cases related to financial assistance programs. At the conclusion of the 1982 term, the Court upheld the practice of opening legislative sessions with a prayer offered by a state-paid chaplain in *Marsh* v. *Chambers* (77 L.Ed. 2d 1019: 1983). The Court distinguished legislative prayer from school prayer by citing the unique history of the former. The Court noted the practice was first begun with the writing of the Bill of Rights, a clear indication, it said, that the framers of the Constitution did not view legislative prayer as prohibited activity.

Antievolution Law

***Epperson* v. *Arkansas*, 393 U.S. 97, 89 S.Ct. 266, 21 L.Ed. 2d 228 (1968)**   Invalidated a state law that prohibited a teacher in a state-supported school from teaching "the theory or doctrine that mankind ascended or descended from a lower order of animals." Epperson's school district adopted a biology text that contained a chapter on evolution. Epperson was faced with the "literal dilemma" of using the adopted text and simultaneously committing an offense that could subject her to dismissal. She sought a declaratory judgment on the statute and an injunction against her dismissal. The Arkansas Supreme Court sustained the statute, although it avoided responding to the establishment question. The Supreme Court reversed Arkansas in a unanimous decision. The Court said that the First Amendment does not "permit the State to require that teaching and learning must be tailored to the principles or prohibitions of any religious sect or dogma." The Arkansas statute did not satisfy that condition. To the contrary, the Arkansas law "selects from the body of knowledge a particular segment which it proscribes for the sole reason that it is deemed to conflict with a particular religious doctrine." While the study of religion and the Bible "from a literary and historic viewpoint" are compatible with the First Amendment, a state "may not adopt programs or practices in its public schools or colleges which 'aid or oppose' any religion. This prohibition is absolute." The Court included in the prohibition any "preference of a religious doctrine or the prohibition of theory which is deemed antagonistic to a particular dogma." In making an establishment determination, the Court said it must examine the "purpose and primary effect of the enactment." Neither purpose nor primary effect may advance or inhibit religion. In this case, "it is clear that fundamentalist sectarian conviction was and is the law's reason for existence." The motivation for the law was the same as that for the Tennessee "monkey law," to "suppress the teaching of a theory which, it was thought, 'denied' the divine creation of man." The Arkansas statute was not an act of religious neutrality. *See also* BILL OF RIGHTS, p. 7; ESTABLISHMENT CLAUSE, p. 80; FIRST AMENDMENT, p. 77.

Significance   *Epperson* v. *Arkansas* (393 U.S. 97: 1968) took a strict separation position much like that found in *Engel* v. *Vitale* (370 U.S. 421: 1962, p. 84) and *Abington* v. *Schempp* (374 U.S. 203: 1963). The problem in *Epperson,* however, involved embracing a particular religious perspective or doctrine rather than the broader issue of religion versus nonreligion. *Epperson* clearly demands that government should refuse to favor any particular religious doctrine or attempt to disadvantage religious belief that may be distasteful to other religious views. In maintaining its neutral posture, a state may not avoid establishment problems by simply stating a secular purpose or disclaiming religious preference. A Kentucky statute, for example, required the posting of a copy of the ten commandments in every public school classroom in the state. Each posted copy had a small disclaimer saying that "secular application of the ten commandments is clearly seen in its adoption as the fundamental legal code of western civilization and the common law of the United States." A notation was also made that all posted copies were purchased with funds other than public funds. The Supreme Court struck down the statute in *Stone* v. *Graham* (499 U.S. 39: 1980). Calling the declaration of secular purpose "self-serving," the Court found the "preeminent purpose for posting the ten commandments on schoolroom walls is plainly religious in nature." The ten commandments is "undeniably a sacred text" and "no legislative recitation of a supposed secular purpose can blind us to that fact." While the state may integrate the commandments into the school curriculum used in the study of history or comparative religions, the "posting of religious texts on the wall serves no such educational purpose." Thus the enactment failed the secular purpose test, and, despite private funding, the Establishment Clause was violated by the "mere posting of the copies under auspices of the legislature."

Use of Public Facilities

Widmar v. **Vincent, 454 U.S. 263, 102 S.Ct. 269, 70 L.Ed. 2d 440 (1981)**   Reversed a state university's refusal to grant a student religious organization access to university facilities. *Widmar* provided the Supreme Court an opportunity to examine a limitation on religious speech imposed in the name of the Establishment Clause. The limitation came in the form of a state university denying use of its facilities to a group wishing to use those facilities for religious worship and religious discussion. The university made its facilities generally available to registered student organizations and had previously permitted the respondent group to use university facilities. The Supreme Court, with only Justice White dissenting, held that the denial of access was unjustified. The Court found the university had "discriminated against student groups and speakers based on their desire to use a generally open forum to engage in religious worship and discussion." Such a discriminatory and content-based exclusion requires that a state demonstrate a compelling interest for the restriction that is advanced by "narrowly drawn" regulation. The compelling interest claimed by the university was maintenance of "strict separation of church and state." The Court allowed that "the interest of the university in complying with its constitutional obligations may be characterized as compelling." Nonetheless, it may not follow that "an 'equal access' policy would be incompatible with this Court's Establishment Clause cases." While religious groups may benefit from use of the university facilities, "enjoyment of merely 'incidental' benefits does not violate the prohibition against the 'primary advancement' of religion." That the benefits would be incidental was based on the Court's view that "an open forum does not confer any imprimatur of state approval on religious sects or practices." Furthermore, the facilities were available to a "broad class of non-religious as well as religious speakers." The provision of benefits to "so broad a spectrum of groups is an important index of secular effect." Finally, the Court noted that the two religion clauses exist in tension with each other, with Establishment Clause provisions "limited by the Free Exercise Clause and in this case by the Free Speech Clause as well." *See also* BILL OF RIGHTS, p. 7; ESTABLISHMENT CLAUSE, p. 80; FIRST AMENDMENT, p. 77.

Significance   Widmar v. *Vincent* (454 U.S. 263: 1981) resolves the ambiguity between First Amendment expression and First Amendment establishment interests in favor of the former. While a state university must avoid any activity that would have the effect of advancing religion, the Establishment Clause does not provide a compelling enough interest to allow singling religion out for exclusion from access to university facilities. The content-based limitation on expression is particularly suspect. As the Court held in *Carey* v. *Brown* (445 U.S. 914: 1980), a case involving selective regulation of labor picketing, "government may not grant the use of a forum to people whose views it finds acceptable, but deny use to those wishing to express less favored or more controversial views." Content discrimination was the central factor here, too. The Court concluded that "selective exclusions from a public forum may not be based on content alone, and may not be justified by reference to content alone." Nevertheless, a state may be able to justify time, place, and manner restrictions on expression so long as they are not selective. In *Heffron* v. *International Society for Krishna Consciousness, Inc.* (449 U.S. 1109: 1981), the Court upheld a state fair regulation that required the sale, exhibition, or distribution of printed material only from assigned locations. The Court found the regulation reasonable and applicable to all groups, not merely religious organizations.

Bus Transportation

Everson v. *Board of Education of Ewing Township*, 330 U.S. 1, 67 S.Ct. 504, 91 L.Ed. 711 (1947)   Upheld reimbursement of costs of transporting nonpublic school students. *Everson* was the first state school aid case to be argued before the Supreme Court. At issue in *Everson* was a New Jersey statute that authorized local school districts to make "rules and contracts for the transportation of children to and from schools." The Ewing Township Board of Education, acting pursuant to the law, authorized reimbursements to parents covering costs of transporting their children to school using the public transportation system. Some of the reimbursements were made to parents transporting children to local parochial schools. These church schools gave their students, in addition to secular education, regular religious instruction conforming to the religious tenets and modes of worship of the Catholic faith. The Court upheld the reimbursement program in a 5–4 decision. It first explored the nature of the establishment prohibition and concluded, as did Thomas Jefferson, that the clause "intended to erect 'a wall of separation between Church and State.'" But the wall did not require the state to "make it far more difficult" for church schools. The Establishment Clause "requires the state to be neutral in its relations with groups of religious believers and non-believers; it does not require the state to be their adversary." The Court said the reimbursements are not an aid to religion, but rather an attempt to protect the well-being of school children generally. Providing safe transportation is like other "general governmental services" such as police and fire protection, and sewer and water service. Cutting off these kinds of services, services "separable and indisputably marked off from the religious function," would handicap religion unnecessarily. Crucial to the majority's holding was the proposition that institutional religion was not the recipient of aid. Rather, services (reimbursement in this case) were extended directly to students and their parents. The transportation program "does no more than provide a general program to help parents get their children, regardless of their religion, safely and expeditiously to and from accredited schools." This view has become known as the "child benefit" theory, and has been invoked frequently to place certain aid programs outside the coverage of the Establishment Clause. Justices Jackson, Rutledge, Frankfurter, and Burton dissented. Justice Jackson responded to the child benefit theory by saying the "prohibition against establishment of religion cannot be circumvented by a subsidy, bonus, or reimbursement of expense to individuals receiving religious instruction and indoctrination." Justice Rutledge observed that religious content is the reason parents send their children to religious schools. He viewed transportation as an essential component in delivering that religious content. *See also* FIRST AMENDMENT, p. 77; *LEMON V. KURTZMAN* (403 U.S. 602: 1971), p. 92; *TILTON V. RICHARDSON* (403 U.S. 672: 1971), p. 82; *WOLMAN V. WALTER* (433 U.S. 406: 1977), p. 96.

Significance   *Everson v. Board of Education* (330 U.S. 1: 1947) was one of the first full treatments of the Establishment Clause. In addition to placing state enactments within reach of the clause, *Everson* is especially important in that the Court embraced basically an accommodationist position. Despite urging that the wall between church and state be kept "high and impregnable," the Court opted for a neutrality position if the state were not adversarial to religion. The child benefit concept was invented to buttress the Court's view of neutrality by holding that the Establishment Clause does not prevent religious institutions from indirectly benefiting from programs that are themselves neutral with regard to religion. The child benefit approach has been used in more recent school aid cases such as *Board of Education* v. *Allen* (392 U.S. 236: 1968). In *Allen* a New York program to loan textbooks to nonpublic school students was upheld. The Court concluded that the program's purpose was the "furtherance of the educational opportunities available to the young," and that the law "merely makes available to all children the benefits of a general program to lend school books free of charge." The only books available for loan were books found to be suitable for use in public schools and books that were confined to secular substance. With comparable limitations, textbook lending practices have consistently been upheld in such cases as *Meek* v. *Pittinger* (421 U.S. 349: 1975) and *Wolman* v. *Walter* (433 U.S. 406: 1977, p. 96).

Released Time Instruction

***Zorach* v. *Clauson*, 343 U.S. 306, 72 S.Ct. 679, 96 L.Ed. 954 (1952)** Upheld off-campus "released time" for religious education. *Zorach* explored the extent to which the Establishment Clause requires strict separation of church and state with regard to released time religious instruction. The case dispelled some of the criticism generated by the invalidation of a slightly different program in *Illinois ex.rel. McCollum* v. *Board of Education* (333 U.S. 203: 1948) four years earlier. In the New York religious instruction program considered in *Zorach,* students were released from regular classes to receive religious instruction. The religion classes were taught by personnel other than school personnel and were conducted off the school grounds, a point of difference from *McCollum.* Release from school was voluntary and was initiated by a written request from the student's parents. Students not attending religious instruction remained in their regular classrooms. Verification of attendance at religion classes had to be submitted to public school authorities. The Court found the released time approach to be satisfactory in that the program involved "neither religious instruction in public school classrooms nor the expenditure of public funds." The Court did not view the Establishment Clause as requiring "that in every and all respects there shall be a separation of Church and State." To hold otherwise, state and religion "would be aliens to each other—hostile, suspicious, and even unfriendly." Justice Douglas observed in his majority opinion that "We are a religious people whose institutions presume a Supreme

Being." As a result, when government "cooperates with religious activities by adjusting the schedule of public events to sectarian needs, it follows the best of our traditions." While government may not aid or favor religion or any religious sect, there is "no constitutional requirement which makes it necessary for government to be hostile to religion." Justices Black, Jackson, and Frankfurter dissented. Given the presence of the compulsory education law in both *McCollum* and *Zorach,* the dissenters viewed the two situations as equivalent from an establishment perspective. Justice Black observed that the state "makes religious sects the beneficiaries of its power to compel children to attend secular schools." *See also* EVERSON V. BOARD OF EDUCATION (330 U.S. 1: 1947), p. 89; FIRST AMENDMENT, p. 77; WALZ V. TAX COMMISSION (397 U.S. 664: 1970), p. 80.

Significance   Zorach v. Clauson (343 U.S. 306: 1952) softened the separationist position taken in *McCollum.* In doing so, *Zorach* provided a key underpinning for subsequent decisions, especially the decisions of the Burger Court that speak of government taking a position of "benevolent neutrality" toward religion. *McCollum* had found an on-premises released time program to be a governmentally assisted religious activity, and had come closer to the strict separationist language of *Everson* than the *Everson* decision itself. *McCollum,* unlike *Everson,* was an unambiguous decision using the Establishment Clause to invalidate a state enactment. With only one dissent, Justice Reed, *McCollum* held the program to be promotion of religious education through use of tax-supported property and close cooperation between school and religious authorities. *McCollum* advanced the view that the Establishment Clause rested "upon the premise that both religion and government can best work to achieve their lofty aims if each is left free from the other within its respective sphere." The reaction to *McCollum* was fierce since many communities throughout the nation had some form of released time religious instruction program in place. Through emphasis on the off-premises feature of the program in *Zorach,* the Court was able to quiet some of the furor. More important in the long run, however, was the accommodationist language used in *Zorach.* It would be incorporated again and again in subsequent interpretations of the Establishment Clause.

Aid to Nonpublic Schools

Lemon v. Kurtzman, 403 U.S. 602, 91 S.Ct. 2105, 29 L.Ed. 2d 745 (1971)   Prohibited salary supplements for nonpublic school teachers. *Lemon* involved a Pennsylvania statute that authorized reimbursement to nonpublic schools for expenditures "for teachers, textbooks, and instructional materials." The reimbursement was limited to "courses presented in the curricula of the public schools." A school seeking reimbursement needed to identify the separate costs of the eligible "secular educational service." The contested statute specifically prohibited reimbursement for "any course that contains 'any subject matter expressing religious teaching, or the morals or forms of worship of any sect.'" The Supreme Court struck down the statute in a unanimous decision, with Justice Marshall not participating, on the ground that the statute fostered an "excessive entanglement with religion." In assessing the entanglement question, the Court indicated it must "examine the character and purposes of the institutions which are benefited, the nature of aid that the State provides, and the resulting relationship between the government and the religious authority." The main problem was the "ideological character" of teachers. The Court could not "ignore the dangers that a teacher under religious control and discipline poses to the separation of the religious from the purely secular aspects of pre-college education." Although parochial teachers may not intentionally violate First Amendment proscriptions, "a dedicated religious person, teaching in a school affiliated with his or her faith and operated to inculcate its tenets, will inevitably experience great difficulty in remaining religiously neutral." If a state is to make reimbursements available, it must be certain that subsidized teachers do not inculcate religion. The comprehensive and continuing surveillance required to maintain that limit itself becomes an establishment defect since the "prophylactic contacts will involve excessive and enduring entanglement between state and church." Ongoing inspection of school records is a "relationship pregnant with dangers of excessive government direction in church schools." Finally, the Court found entanglement of a different character created by the "divisive political potential of state programs." Continuation of such state assistance will "entail considerable political activity." While political debate is normally a "healthy manifestation of our democratic system . . . political division along religious lines was one of the principal evils against which the First Amendment was intended to protect." *See also* CPEARL V. NYQUIST (413 U.S. 756: 1973), p. 94; FIRST AMENDMENT, p. 77; TILTON V. RICHARDSON (403 U.S. 672: 1971), p. 82; WOLMAN V. WALTER (433 U.S. 406: 1977), p. 96.

Significance   Lemon v. Kurtzman (403 U.S. 602: 1971) clearly reflected the decisive role of the entanglement criterion in establishment cases. The Burger Court's reliance on that criterion has not diminished. The Court again noted the difference between precollege levels of education and higher education as it had defined the distinction in *Tilton*. Religious indoctrination is only an incidental purpose of education at the college level, while educational objectives at the lower levels have a "substantial religious character." *Lemon* emphasizes that the Court sees programs at the elementary and secondary levels as inherently susceptible to entanglement problems. *Lemon* also casts serious doubt on purchase-of-service programs. Monitoring person nel, especially teachers, would be an ongoing obligation that would excessively entangle government and the church school. Transportation and books, on the other hand, have no content to be evaluated or they are subject only to a one-time review. Service items are much more difficult to fit into child benefit coverage than are books and transportation. *Lemon* involved an irresolvable establishment problem. Religion would obviously be advanced in violation of the purpose and effects criteria without the surveillance of teachers. At the same time, the maintenance of a monitoring system produces entanglement defects. Finally, *Lemon* added another dimension to the entanglement test. As nonpublic schools encounter greater financial difficulty, demands to retain or expand aid programs will grow and communities will be divided along religious lines. Such community divisiveness is an end the Establishment Clause must seek to avoid.

Committee for Public Education and Religious Liberty (CPEARL) v. Nyquist, 413 U.S. 756, 93 S.Ct. 2955, 37 L.Ed. 2d 948 (1973) Struck down a statute providing maintenance grants to nonpublic schools and tuition reimbursements and tax deductions for parents of nonpublic school students. *Nyquist* invalidated three financial aid programs for nonpublic elementary and secondary schools established by the New York legislature. One program provided direct money grants to qualified schools in low-income urban areas for maintenance and repair of school facilities and equipment. A second program created a tuition reimbursement plan for parents with annual taxable income of less than $5,000. The third program provided tax deductions to parents failing to qualify for direct reimbursement. The Court found a secular legislative purpose for all three programs, but noted the "propriety of a legislature's purposes may not immunize from further scrutiny a law which either has a primary effect that advantages religion or which fosters excessive entanglement between church and state." The maintenance and repair grants failed the primary effect criterion because there was no restriction on the grant usage. This program advanced religion "in that it subsidized directly the religious activities of sectarian elementary and secondary schools." The Court compared the program upheld in *Tilton* v. *Richardson* (403 U.S. 672: 1971, p. 82), which required restrictions on construction grants for higher education. Certainly public monies could not be distributed to sectarian elementary and secondary schools without similar restrictions. Justice Powell commented, "If the state may not erect buildings in which religious activities are to take place, it may not maintain such buildings or renovate them when they fall into disrepair." The key issue in the reimbursement and tax relief programs was whether use of parents as conduits removed the primary effect and entanglement obstacles. The Court concluded that reimbursement and tax relief were incentives. It was therefore irrelevant "whether or not the actual dollars given eventually find their way into sectarian institutions." The establishment problem is that the program provides incentive or encouragement to send a child to a nonpublic school. The Court resisted engaging in semantic distinctions. "Whether the grant is labeled a reimbursement, a reward or a subsidy, its substantive impact is the same." The Court also refused to accept the argument that reimbursements to low-income parents protected their free exercise options. Noting the tension between the two religion clauses of the First Amendment, the Court found that regardless of the "high social importance of the state's purposes," it may not "justify an eroding of the limitations of the establishment clause now firmly implanted." Finding that the reimbursements and tax relief constituted "encouragement and reward" for sending students to nonpublic schools, a prohibited primary effect, the Court did not need to address the entanglement dimension of the case. It said simply that "assistance of the sort here involved carries grave potential for entanglement in the broader sense of continuing political strife over aid to education." *See also* FIRST AMENDMENT, p. 77; LEMON V. KURTZMAN (403 U.S. 602: 1971), p. 92; TILTON V. RICHARDSON (403 U.S. 672: 1971), p. 82; WALZ V. TAX COMMISSION (397 U.S. 664: 1970), p. 80.

Significance   CPEARL v. *Nyquist* (413 U.S. 756: 1973) reversed a trend. The tone of the Court's opinion in *Walz* v. *Tax Commission* (397 U.S. 664: 1970, p. 80), and the validation of the Higher Education Facilities Act in *Tilton* v. *Richardson* (403 U.S. 672: 1971, p. 82) seemed to suggest the Court was moving toward a pronounced accommodationist position on the Establishment Clause. There was every prospect the Court would view favorably the grant programs allocating public funds for educational activities at sectarian schools. Programs featuring students and parents as the designated targets of aid seemed particularly safe. Despite the ingenious character of the plan in *Nyquist,* the Court said it advanced religion in an impermissible way. A Pennsylvania reimbursement plan closely resembling the New York proposal in *Nyquist* was similarly struck down in *Sloan* v. *Lemon* (413 U.S. 825: 1973). In *Levitt* v. *CPEARL* (413 U.S. 472: 1973), the Court also invalidated state reimbursement to private schools for mandated testing and record-keeping costs. The reimbursement plan made lump sum payments instead of requiring audits to determine "whether a school's actual costs in complying with the mandated service are less than the annual lump sum payment." More crucial was the fact that the testing process was not monitored. "Despite the obviously integral role of testing in the total teaching process, no attempt is made under the statute to assure that internally prepared tests are free of religious instruction." The Court felt it could not ignore the substantial risk that these examinations, prepared by teachers under the authority of religious institutions, would be drafted to inculcate students in the religious precepts of the sponsoring church. More recently, in *Mueller* v. *Allen* (77 L.Ed. 2d 721: 1983), the Court upheld a Minnesota statute that gave parents a state income tax deduction for all educational costs of elementary and secondary level children. Deductions apply to expenses incurred for both public and private schools, even though most benefits will fall to parents of private school students. The Court, in a 5–4 decision, found that Minnesota plan "vitally different" from the plan in *Nyquist.* The Minnesota plan contained several tax deductions and was said to gain secular character from its breadth. It channeled "whatever assistance it may provide to parochial schools through individual parents."

Wolman v. Walter, 433 U.S. 229, 97 S.Ct. 2593, 53 L.Ed. 2d 714 (1977)   Examined a package of six financial aid programs for nonpublic elementary and secondary schools. *Wolman* tested a statute providing aid to private schools in the form of textbooks, standardized testing services, diagnostic and therapeutic services, instructional materials and equipment, and field trip services. All disbursements authorized under the law had equivalent expenditure categories for public schools. The amount of the aid for any category was limited by the amount of per-pupil expenditures for public school students. By varying majorities, the Court upheld four programs and invalidated two. The two invalidated were those providing instructional materials and equipment and field trip services. Only Justices Blackmun and Stewart were in the majority in all six decisions. *Wolman* does not significantly change establishment doctrine as defined by the Burger Court in the numerous school aid cases preceding it, but it does provide a parade example of the way the Court uses the purpose, primary effect, and entanglement criteria in reference to school aid programs. Most of the assistance in question was sufficiently proscribed to satisfy establishment concerns. The textbooks, for example, were lent upon pupil request, and their choices were confined to texts approved for use in public schools. The Court upheld the testing, diagnostic (speech, hearing, and psychological), and therapeutic services because (1) no nonpublic school personnel delivered the services; (2) the services were obtained off public school grounds, i.e., in neutral locations; (3) none of the services advanced ideology; and (4) little need existed to monitor the activities. These components of the aid package passed the purpose, primary effect, and entanglement tests with majorities ranging from 8–1 to 6–3. The instructional materials and field trip services did not fare as well. The Court found that because of the sectarian mission of the nonpublic school, "aid to the educational function of such schools necessarily results in aid to the sectarian school enterprise as a whole." Despite limiting materials to those "incapable of diversion to religious use," these materials "inescapably had the primary effect of providing direct and substantial advancement of the sectarian enterprise." Loaning the materials to the pupil rather than the nonpublic school directly only "exalts form over substance" and cannot alter the judgment that advancement of religion is a primary effect. The field trips were found defective because the nonpublic schools control timing and, within a certain range, the "frequency and destinations" of the trips. The trips are an "integral part of the educational experience, and where the teacher works within and for a sectarian institution, an unacceptable risk of fostering religion is an inevitable by-product." *See also* EVERSON V. BOARD OF EDUCATION (330 U.S. 1: 1947), p. 89; FIRST AMENDMENT, p. 89; LEMON V. KURTZMAN (403 U.S. 602: 1971), p. 92.

Significance   *Wolman* v. *Walter* (433 U.S. 406: 1977) badly splintered the Court. The six component elements in the case produced five different divisions of the justices. The divisions ranged from 6–3 to invalidate the provision of equipment and instructional materials to 8–1 to uphold the provision of special diagnostic services. The pattern of *Wolman* is that services that can be identified as going directly to the nonpublic school student are permitted. Thus, transportation, textbooks, and most off-premise auxiliary services do not violate the Establishment Clause. Other forms of aid relate too closely to the religious purpose of the nonpublic school or run afoul of the entanglement prohibition when monitoring is used to check against impermissible advancement. Failing on one or both of these tests are tuition reimbursements, facility maintenance, instructional materials and equipment, and teacher salary supplements. In 1980, the Court upheld in a 5–4 decision a reimbursement program for mandated testing in *CPEARL* v. *Regan* (444 U.S. 646: 1980). The reimbursement program was similar to one struck down in *Levitt* v. *CPEARL* (413 U.S. 472: 1973), but in *Regan* nonpublic schools had no control over test content and cost-reporting procedures had been tightened. At the conclusion of the majority opinion, Justice White commented on the Court's difficulty in handling the school aid issue. "Our decisions have tended to avoid categorical imperatives and absolutist approaches at either end of the range of possible outcomes. This course sacrifices clarity and predictability for flexibility, but this promises to be the case until the continuing interaction between the courts and the states produces a single, more encompassing construction of the Establishment Clause." Such construction does not appear to be forthcoming in the near future.

FREE EXERCISE OF RELIGION

Compulsory Flag Salute

***West Virginia State Board of Education* v. *Barnette*, 319 U.S. 624, 63 S.Ct. 1178, 87 L.Ed. 1628 (1943)**   Struck down compulsory flag salute requirements for public school students. *Barnette* invalidated a compulsory flag salute, but it did not exempt religion from secular laws. Three years prior to *Barnette,* in *Minersville School District* v. *Gobitis* (310 U.S. 586: 1940), the Court had upheld a flag salute requirement, with only Justice Stone dissenting. Both cases raised the question of whether public school pupils could be compelled, under threat of expulsion and fine, to salute the flag. The Barnette and Gobitis children, members of the Jehovah's Witnesses sect, refused to participate because to do so would have put them in conflict with their religious beliefs. Through Justice Jackson, the six-justice majority in *Barnette* sought to resolve the case on free expression grounds. As an expression issue, the Jehovah's Witnesses behavior could be evaluated by using the "clear and present danger" test, a criterion established in *Schenck* v. *United States* (249 U.S. 47: 1919). Justice Jackson concluded that the children's silence was a form of expression that did not create a clear and present danger. Neither did their refusal to salute the flag "interfere with or deny rights of others to do so." Clear and present danger could justify restriction of expression, but "it would seem that involuntary affirmation could be commanded on even more immediate and urgent grounds than silence." The majority judged that the First Amendment permitted no authority to impose participation in a ceremony "so touching matters of opinion and political attitude." To the contrary, "if there be any fixed star in our constitutional constellation, it is that no official, high or petty, can prescribe what shall be orthodox in politics, nationalism, religion, or other matters of opinion." *See also* BILL OF RIGHTS, p. 7; FIRST AMENDMENT, p. 77; *MURDOCK* V. *PENNSYLVANIA* (319 U.S. 105: 1943), p. 100.

Significance   *West Virginia State Board of Education* v. *Barnette* (319 U.S. 624: 1943) reversed the heavily criticized *Gobitis* decision, but it did so without dismantling the secular regulation rule or encouraging religious preference. The Court opted instead to view free exercise interests as largely contained within expression protections. The compulsory flag salute was offensive because it dealt with matters of belief and opinion, a transgression the First Amendment cannot tolerate regardless of religion. Since the state could not require any child to salute the flag, the Court avoided carving out an exception for Jehovah's Witnesses. The implications of the broader basis for decision can readily be seen by comparing the *Barnette* outcome to the outcome of the earlier flag salute case. *Gobitis* was an example of the secular regulation approach in its purest form. Justice Frankfurter's majority opinion argued that protection of religion does not preclude legislation of a general scope as long as the legislation is not directed against the doctrinal loyalties of particular sects. Even "conscientious scruples" cannot relieve the individual from obedience to general law not aimed at the promotion or restriction of religious beliefs. The secular interest being promoted by flag ceremonies is a preeminent interest. What it seeks is cohesion and national unity, an interest "inferior to none." National unity is the basis of national security. The secular regulation doctrine, decisive in *Gobitis,* emerged from *Murdock* and *Barnette* just three years later as a much less generally applicable justification for state enactments overriding religious expression.

License Tax

***Murdock* v. *Pennsylvania,*319 U.S. 105, 63 S.Ct. 870, 87 L.Ed. 1092 (1943)**   Invalidated a license tax as an impermissible restriction on evangelism. *Murdock* was an exception to the general rule that the free exercise of religion provision of the First Amendment does not exempt an individual from laws that have a valid secular purpose and that do not discriminate against religion or religious believers. *Murdock* involved a municipal license tax that was imposed on all persons selling or canvassing door-to-door. The tax was challenged by Jehovah's Witnesses as an infringement of their ability freely to exercise their religious beliefs. The Supreme Court, in a 5–4 decision, found for the Jehovah's Witnesses. Writing for the majority, Justice Douglas observed that the distribution of religious tracts is "an age old form of missionary evangelism." Such distribution is "as evangelical as the revival meeting," and is a form of religious activity as protected as "worship in the churches and preaching from the pulpit." That monies are obtained through distribution of literature does not transform evangelism into a commercial enterprise. Besides the evangelical character of the Witnesses' solicitation, the Court noted the financial realities of survival and exempted missionary evangelism from taxation on those grounds. While an income tax might be collected from a member of the clergy, it is "quite another thing to exact a tax from him for the privilege of delivering a sermon." If taxes could be collected on religious exercises, the state could make such exercises "so costly as to deprive religion of the resources necessary for its maintenance." Finally, the Court did not find the nondiscriminatory character of the tax sufficient to save it. The tax "does not acquire constitutional validity because it classifies the privileges protected by the First Amendment along with the wares and merchandise of hucksters and peddlers and treats them all alike." Justices Reed, Roberts, Frankfurter, and Jackson dissented, arguing that exemption from the general secular regulation gave religion a preferred status over other forms of expression. *See also* FIRST AMENDMENT, p. 77; *WEST VIRGINIA STATE BOARD OF EDUCATION V.*

BARNETTE(319 U.S. 624: 1943), p. 98; *WISCONSIN V. YODER*(406 U.S. 205: 1971), p. 106.

Significance   *Murdock* v. *Pennsylvania* (319 U.S. 105: 1943) was a departure from earlier free exercise cases. Free exercise holdings had previously established that freedom of religious exercise was not absolute and that religious beliefs would not free an individual from the demands of general secular regulation. The Court upheld compulsory smallpox vaccinations over religious objections in *Jacobson* v. *Massachusetts* (197 U.S. 11: 1905), for example, and it allowed the outlawing of polygamy despite its adverse consequences for Mormons in *Reynolds* v. *United States* (98 U.S. 145: 1878). Just a year prior to *Murdock*, the Court upheld a similar license tax in *Jones* v. *Opelika* (316 U.S. 584: 1942). It said the tax imposed only an incidental burden upon free exercise while allowing a state to "insure orderly living." *Murdock*, however, suggests that injury created by a secular regulation may be too great. In this case, the license tax was imposed on the religious exercise of evangelism, a protected religious practice. Certain regulations, despite their secular purpose and nondiscriminatory administration, simply cannot be applied in some situations. This is especially true when a particular secular regulation has the potential of interfering with the ability of a sect to perpetuate itself. See *Wisconsin* v. *Yoder* (406 U.S. 205: 1971, p. 106). *Murdock* seemed to give religion and religious expression special status, even preferential treatment. Jehovah's Witnesses seemed assured of unregulated solicitations through *Murdock*, but Justice Douglas put the matter in larger perspective when he spoke of First Amendment privileges that "exist apart from state authority." He carefully tied the Witnesses and their form of evangelism into a broad framework of protected expression more fully developed in *West Virginia State Board of Education* v. *Barnette* (319 U.S. 624: 1943, p. 98).

Sunday Closing Laws

***Sunday Closing Law Cases*, 366 U.S. 421 (1961)**   Upheld Sunday restrictions on commercial activity. Four cases challenging state and local prohibitions on Sunday business activities came to the Supreme Court in 1961. Two of the four cases, called the *Sunday Closing Law Cases*, were decided essentially on establishment and equal protection grounds. *McGowan* v. *Maryland* (366 U.S. 421: 1961) and

Two Guys from Harrison–Allentown v. *McGinley* (366 U.S. 582: 1961) were upheld 8–1. In the other two cases, *Gallagher* v. *Crown Kosher Supermarket* (366 U.S. 617: 1961) and *Braunfeld* v. *Brown* (366 U.S. 599: 1961), the petitioners, both orthodox Jews, added free exercise allegations to their establishment and equal protection claims. This tactic weakened their constitutional position, because only Justices Douglas, Brennan, and Stewart found the Sunday closings defective by free exercise standards. The Court said the commercial restrictions in *Gallagher* and *Braunfeld* were legitimate secular regulations, the purpose of which was the designation of a uniform day of rest. The Court held that while the regulation may impose some free exercise burden on the litigants, they were not denied the opportunity for free exercise. They merely had to forgo a day's work. Free exercise only made the practice of their religious beliefs more expensive. The Free Exercise Clause cannot, except in rare circumstances, be used to strike down legislation "which imposes only an indirect burden on the exercise of religion." The Court said the Free Exercise Clause does not require that "legislators enact no law regulating conduct that may in some way result in an economic disadvantage of some religious sects and not to others because of the special practices of the various religions." The Court did offer one important qualification, however. A state may indeed enact a general law the purpose of which is to advance the state's secular goals and which may impose an indirect burden on religious observance. But it may do so only if the state may not "accomplish its purpose by means which do not impose such a burden." Thus the Court fashioned an alternative means factor for evaluating general secular regulations against free exercise challenges. *See also* BILL OF RIGHTS, p. 7; FIRST AMENDMENT, p. 77; *SHERBERT* V. *VERNER* (374 U.S. 398: 1965), p. 103.

Significance   The *Sunday Closing Law Cases* (366 U.S. 421: 1961) modified the secular regulation rule, although the Court rejected free exercise arguments in each of the four cases. It ultimately resolved the issue by weighing the burdens on religious practice flowing from the secular rule. After assessing the competing interests, the Court concluded the burden borne by the sabbatarians was indirect. If the state had required Saturday work, the burden would have been direct and prohibited. What the state did, instead, was deny a person closing a business on Saturday the opportunity to be open on Sunday. The Court's use of the direct-indirect burden approach clearly suggested that at least certain kinds of secular regulations would require exemptions if they survived First Amendment scrutiny at all. The secular regulation rule was altered further by the addition of the alternate means provision. This placed an affirmative obligation on the state to show the lack of alternatives that could accomplish the secular end without imposing a burden on religious exercise. The real impact of these changes became apparent in *Sherbert* v. *Verner* (374 U.S. 398: 1964, p. 103).

Unemployment Compensation

Sherbert v. Verner, 374 U.S. 398, 83 S.Ct. 1790, 10 L.Ed. 2d 965 (1963)   Held that a state may not disqualify a person from unemployment compensation because the person refuses to work on Saturdays for religious reasons. *Sherbert* said the protection of free exercise interests may produce an exemption from secular regulation based on religion. Sherbert was a Seventh-Day Adventist who was discharged from her job because she would not work on Saturday. Saturday is the Sabbath Day for Adventists. Failing to find other employment because of her "conscientious scruples not to take Saturday work," Sherbert filed for unemployment compensation benefits under provisions of South Carolina law. The law required that any claimant is ineligible for benefits if he or she has failed, without good cause, to accept suitable work when offered. Through appropriate administrative proceedings, Sherbert's unwillingness to work on Saturdays was determined to disqualify her from benefits. The Supreme Court held for Sherbert in a 7–2 decision. The burdens imposed on her in this case were too great. She was forced to choose between "following the precepts of her religion and forfeiting benefits," or "abandoning one of the precepts of her religion in order to accept work." Facing such a choice "puts the same kind of burden upon the free exercise of religion as would a fine imposed against appellant for her Saturday worship." The Court failed to find that protection of the unemployment compensation fund from fraudulent claims by unscrupulous claimants feigning religious objections to Saturday work was a sufficiently compelling state interest. Even if the fund were threatened by spurious claims, South Carolina would need to demonstrate that no alternative forms of regulation would combat such abuses. In requiring the religion-based exemption for Sherbert, the Court imposed a requirement of possible differential treatment for those seeking unemployment benefits for refusal to work on Saturdays. The Court suggested, however, that such classification was not the establishment of religion. The decision "reflects nothing more than the governmental obligation of neutrality in the face of religious differences." The holding requires only that "South Carolina may not constitutionally apply the eligibility provisions so as to constrain a worker to abandon his religious convictions." Justices Harlan and White dissented on the ground that the decision required an exemption based upon religion. The decision requires South Carolina to "single out for financial assistance those whose behavior is religiously motivated, even though it denies such assistance to others whose identical behavior (in this case, inability to work on Saturdays) is not religiously motivated." *See also* FIRST AMENDMENT, p. 77; *GILLETTE V. UNITED STATES* (401 U.S. 437: 1971), p. 105; *SUNDAY CLOSING LAW CASES* (366 U.S. 421: 1961), p. 101; *WISCONSIN V. YODER* (406 U.S. 205: 1971), p. 106.

Significance   *Sherbert* v. *Verner* (374 U.S. 398: 1964) was something of a replay of the free exercise issues seen in *Braunfeld* and *Crown Kosher Supermarket*. Sherbert was subjected to economic hardship, like the merchants in the Sunday Closing Cases, but the burden in the Sunday Closing Cases was indirect. In *Sherbert*, the Court found the burden to be impermissibly heavy. Even incidental burdens could be justified only by demonstrating a compelling state interest. The compelling interest criterion is far more demanding than merely showing secular purpose. Coupled with the alternate means requirement carried over from the Sunday Closing Cases, *Sherbert* substantially expanded the protection afforded by the Free Exercise Clause. At the same time, the broadened protection for free exercise produces serious establishment questions. They can be seen clearly in *Thomas* v. *Review Board of the Indiana Employment Security Division* (450 U.S. 707: 1981). Thomas was denied unemployment compensation after voluntarily quitting his job for religious reasons. The Court held the denial of benefits a violation of Thomas's free exercise rights. Only Justice Rehnquist dissented. The Court was even more emphatic than in *Sherbert*, saying, "Where the state conditions receipt of an important benefit upon conduct proscribed by religious faith, or where it denies such a benefit because of conduct mandated by religious belief," a believer is unduly pressured and a burden upon religion exists. While the compulsion may be indirect, the infringement upon free exercise is nonetheless substantial. Justice Rehnquist was wholly dissatisfied with the Court's preferential treatment of Thomas. He noted the Establishment Clause would preclude Indiana from legislating an unemployment compensation law with the exemption stipulated by the Court. He argued that the balance had now tipped too heavily in favor of free exercise protection. *Thomas* "reads the Free Exercise Clause too broadly and it fails to squarely acknowledge that such a reading conflicts with our Establishment Clause cases. As such, the decision simply exacerbates the tension between the two clauses."

Conscientious Objection: Draft

Gillette v. United States, 401 U.S. 437, 91 S.Ct. 828, 28 L.Ed. 2d 168 (1971) Held that religion-based objections to a particular war, as distinct from wars generally, does not entitle a person to exemption from the military draft. *Gillette* examined the specific language of the Selective Service Act, particularly that part of the act that exempted registrants who are "conscientiously opposed to participation in war in any form." Gillette had attempted to limit his objection to participation in the Vietnam War, but the Supreme Court, with only Justice Douglas dissenting, held he was not entitled to such a free exercise exemption. The Court also determined that Congress could provide exemptions to the draft for those having religion-based objections to wars generally without violating establishment prohibitions. While conscription of those with "conscientious scruples" against all wars would violate the free exercise proscription, there are governmental interests of "sufficient kind and weight" to justify drafting people who object to particular wars. The Court determined that the draft laws were not "designed to interfere with any religious ritual or practice, and do not work a penalty against any theological position." In addition, the burdens imposed are incidental when compared to the substantial government interest in creating and administering an equitable exemption policy. The Court also noted the interest of the government in "procuring the manpower necessary for military purposes." These interests permit what Gillette alleged to be an interference with his free exercise rights. The establishment claim was based on the argument that allowing exemption only to those with objection to all wars discriminated against faiths that "distinguish between personal participation in 'just' and 'unjust' wars." The Court held that congressional objectives in requiring objection to all wars were neutral, secular, and did not reflect a religious preference. The Court focused on the need for the exemption to have a neutral basis. Since a virtually "limitless variety of beliefs are subsumable under the rubric 'objection to a particular war,'" the difficulties of operating a fair and uniform conscription system would be substantial. Sorting through the various claims creates a great "potential for state involvement in determining the character of persons' beliefs and affiliations, thus 'entangling government in difficult classifications of what is or is not religious,' or what is or is not conscientious." Acknowledging that some discretion exists under any process that takes individual differences into account, establishment problems would be even greater if conscientious objection of indeterminate scope were involved. *See also* BILL OF RIGHTS, p. 7; FIRST AMENDMENT, p. 77; *SHERBERT* V. *VERNER* (374 U.S. 398: 1964), p. 103.

Significance   *Gillette* v. *United States* (401 U.S. 437: 1971) was unique in singling out a particular war for religion-based conscientious objection to an American draft law. The Selective Service and Training Act of 1940 provided that conscientious objector status did not require affiliation with a religious sect. The claim of exemption required only theistic religious beliefs and training, and not a "merely personal moral code." The Court addressed this language in *United States* v. *Seeger* (380 U.S. 163: 1965), holding a conscientious objector claimant need not declare a belief in a Supreme Being as long as the claimant had beliefs that served in the place of an orthodox belief in God. The term "Supreme Being" was said to mean a broader view of something to which everything else is subordinate. In *Welsh* v. *United States* (398 U.S. 333: 1970), the Court required exemption for a claimant without the basis of his objections resting on religious training or belief as long as the claimant genuinely believed in pacifism. A selective conscientious objector such as Gillette, on the other hand, created problems of implementation so wrought with establishment defects as to outweigh the free exercise interest served by the exemption.

Compulsory Education

***Wisconsin* v. *Yoder,* 406 U.S. 205, 92 S.Ct. 1526, 32 L.Ed. 2d 15 (1972)**   Created a free exercise exemption to a state compulsory school attendance law. *Yoder* did not contest the attendance law as discriminatory against religion, nor was the legitimacy of the state's interest in advancing education challenged per se. The respondents were members of the Old Order Amish and the Conservative Amish Mennonite Church. They had sent their children to public schools through the eighth grade, but they refused to keep their children in public schools until age 16 as required by law. The respondents argued that attendance of Amish children in high school was contrary to their religious beliefs and way of life. It would endanger their salvation, and might threaten the ongoing existence of the sect by exposing Amish children to impermissible worldly influences that would draw them away from their beliefs. The Court, with Justices Powell and Rehnquist not participating, unanimously found for the Amish. It acknowledged the state's paramount responsibility for education, but held that even a fundamental function such as education was not "totally free from the balancing process when it impinges on other fundamental rights and interests." In this instance, the "impact of the compulsory attendance law on respondents' practice of the Amish religion is not only severe, but inescapable." The impact is not confined to "grave interference with important Amish religious tenets," but also the "very real threat of undermining the Amish community and religious practice as it exists today." The effective choice left the Amish was to "abandon belief and be assimilated into society or be forced to migrate to some other and more tolerant region." The Court attempted to confine the holding by emphasizing that the Amish were disputing only one or possibly two years of high school level education. It was training that would be of little value in the agrarian Amish community. Further, the Court noted the noble character of the Amish, specifically mentioning such characteristics as their self-reliance, their peaceful and law-abiding life style, and their unique history. The Amish history and tradition were crucial in connecting their religious beliefs to their unusual way of life, which, in turn, created a unique free exercise injury when the compulsory attendance law was enforced against them. *See also* BILL OF RIGHTS, p. 7; FIRST AMENDMENT, p. 77; SHERBERT V. VERNER (374 U.S. 398: 1964), p. 103.

Significance   *Wisconsin v. Yoder* (406 U.S. 205: 1972) illustrates the extent to which secular regulation has been modified by the Supreme Court. Wisconsin's compulsory education law was clearly a statute of general application with nothing to suggest ill intent with respect to religion or any religious group. The substantial interest a state has in education is unquestioned. Yet when that interest was weighed against the Amish interest in free exercise, the state's interest was said to be subordinate. The main consequences of *Yoder* are seen in the expansion of free exercise protection at the expense of establishment protection. Chief Justice Burger's opinion unmistakably assigns preference to the religious motives of the Amish. At one point, the Chief Justice differentiated between the Amish and Thoreau. If the Amish had "asserted their claims because of their subjective evaluation and rejection of contemporary values accepted by the majority," in a Thoreau-like manner, their claims would not rest on a religious basis. The key establishment problem comes from the Chief Justice's next sentence. "Thoreau's choice was philosophical and personal rather than religious, and such belief does not give rise to the demands of the Religion Clause." *Yoder* thus expands *Sherbert* v. *Verner* (374 U.S. 398: 1964) by requiring a religion-based exemption from an enactment established pursuant to a substantial state interest. As a result, *Yoder* reflects the inevitability of free exercise and establishment conflict when exemptions are created for certain religious groups.

FREE SPEECH

Wartime Speech

Schenck v. *United States*, **249 U.S. 47, 39 S.Ct. 247, 63 L.Ed. 470 (1919)** Established the clear and present danger test for evaluating restrictions of expression. *Schenck* was the first significant free speech case to come before the Supreme Court. At issue were the constraints on speech imposed by the Espionage Act of 1917. The act made it a crime to interfere with recruitment of persons into the armed services. Schenck was convicted of conspiracy to obstruct the draft by printing and distributing materials that urged draft eligible men to resist conscription. The Court unanimously upheld the conviction. Justice Holmes spoke for the Court. He said the right of expression is not absolute. Like other acts, expression is conditional and has boundaries set by the circumstances in which it is done. Even the most "stringent protection of free speech would not protect a man in falsely shouting fire in a theatre and causing a panic." Having established a situational context for evaluating expression, Justice Holmes then described a standard by which the expression could be assessed. The standard was known as clear and present danger. The issue in every case involving expression is "whether the words used are used in such circumstances and are of such a nature as to create a clear and present danger that they will bring about the substantive evil that Congress has a right to prevent." If speech is linked closely enough to illegal action, it is speech that can be restricted. As Justice Holmes put it, "it is a question of proximity and degree." Schenck's expression was intended to have an effect on persons subject to the draft, a point conceded by Schenck. Under certain circumstances such as peacetime, Schenck's expression would not have been sufficiently dangerous to warrant prosecution. But his words were disseminated while the nation was at war. The war context gave quite a different effect to his expression. The clear and present danger test allowed certain speech to be regulated through prosecution as long as the government could show that the expression endangered legitimate governmental functions and societal interests. The test said the danger must be significant and immediate. *See also* DENNIS V. UNITED STATES (341 U.S. 494: 1951), p. 111; FIRST AMENDMENT, p. 77; GITLOW V. NEW YORK (268 U.S. 652: 1925), p. 109.

Significance Schenck v. *United States* (249 U.S. 47: 1919) provided a basic rubric by which expression issues might be examined. Several cases immediately following *Schenck* provided the Court an opportunity to refine further the clear and present danger criterion. In *Frohwerk v. United States* (249 U.S. 204: 1919), a unanimous Court upheld the conviction of an author of several newspaper articles that were highly critical of American involvement in World War I. The Court felt the language of the articles was effectively comparable to Schenck's leaflets. The Court also upheld the conspiracy conviction of Eugene Debs for a speech critical of the war effort in *Debs* v. *United States* (249 U.S. 211: 1919). The speech focused on socialism, "its growth and a prophecy of its success." The Court had no objection to the content of the speech, but made it clear that if the "manifest intent" of a speech encourages those hearing it to obstruct the recruiting service, the "immunity of the general theme may not be enough to protect the speech." In cases involving the Sedition Act of 1918, however, Justices Holmes and Brandeis parted company from the rest of the Court. In *Abrams* v. *United States* (250 U.S. 616: 1919), the Court upheld Abrams's conviction for distribution of materials critical of the government's commitment of forces to Russia in the wake of the Russian revolution. Holmes and Brandeis argued that neither sufficient danger nor proximity had been demonstrated in the case. Only "present danger of immediate evil" warrants limitation of expression, they said, not the "surreptitious publishing of a silly leaflet by an unknown man."

Incitement

Gitlow v. *New York,* 268 U.S. 652, 45 S.Ct. 625, 69 L.Ed. 1138 (1925) Created the "bad tendency" standard for evaluating freedom of expression issues. *Gitlow* modified the clear and present danger test to allow suppression of speech that might tend to produce "substantive evil." *Gitlow* also formally linked the provisions of the

Free Speech Clause of the First Amendment to state enactments through the Due Process Clause of the Fourteenth Amendment. Gitlow, a member of the Left Wing Section of the Socialist party, was convicted under provisions of New York's criminal anarchy statutes for his advocacy of the "overthrow of the government by force, violence, and unlawful means." The criminal advocacy was demonstrated in two published tracts entitled "The Left Wing Manifesto" and "The Revolutionary Age." The Court upheld the New York statute and Gitlow's conviction in a 7–2 decision. It held the statute did not deprive Gitlow of his "liberty of expression," nor did it "penalize the utterance or publication of abstract 'doctrine' or academic discussion having no quality of incitement to any concrete action." Rather, the statute aimed at "language advocating, advising, or teaching the overthrow of organized government by unlawful means." The Court felt the statute was properly focused on advocacy of action directed toward the accomplishment of an illegal purpose, i.e., overthrowing the government. The Court said the police power of the state is appropriately used to "punish those who abuse freedom of expression by utterances inimical to the public welfare." Judgment as to what utterances might be so inimical to the general welfare and "involve such danger of substantive evil" essentially rests with the state's legislative body, and "every presumption is to be indulged in favoring the validity of the statute." Utterances that incite to overthrow the government were found to be "within the range of legislative discretion." As for the point at which the state may intervene, the Court said the "State cannot reasonably be required to measure the danger from every such utterance in the nice balance of a jeweler's scale." A state cannot be said to have acted arbitrarily or unreasonably when it "seeks to extinguish the spark without waiting until it has enkindled the flame or blazed into the conflagration." A state may, in the exercise of its judgment, "suppress the threatened danger in its incipiency." Justices Holmes and Brandeis dissented. Neither felt sufficient danger had been demonstrated. Gitlow's "redundant discourse" simply "had no chance of starting a present conflagration." As in prior speech cases, Holmes invoked the marketplace of ideas argument, asserting that free speech must permit ideas to "compete for acceptance within society." *See also* DENNIS V. UNITED STATES (341 U.S. 494: 1951), p. 111; FIRST AMENDMENT, p. 77; SCHENCK V. UNITED STATES (249 U.S. 47: 1919), p. 108.

Significance   Gitlow v. New York (268 U.S. 652: 1925) had the practical effect of permitting legislatures to restrict expression if it could lead to unlawful ends. The consequences need not be immediate. *Gitlow* permits dousing the spark before it develops into a fire, also referred to as killing the serpent in the egg. *Gitlow* reflected the Court's generally deferential position toward legislative judgments. It explicitly noted the presumption to be indulged in reviewing legislative enactments. In the years following *Gitlow,* however, the Court began to suggest it would be more demanding in cases involving the First Amendment. As opposed to enactments involving economic regulation, for example, legislation touching First Amendment protections would be viewed with suspicion because the Constitution affords First Amendment freedoms a "preferred position." Such a view had its origin in Justice Stone's celebrated footnote in *United States* v. *Carolene Products Company* (304 U.S. 144: 1938). The footnote was frequently cited in the 1940s, especially in labor picketing and free exercise of religion situations. An intermediate position between the preferred position and the *Gitlow* bad tendency doctrine began to evolve after World War II with the balancing test articulated in *United States* v. *Dennis* (341 U.S. 494: 1951).

Subversive Groups

Dennis* v. *United States, 341 U.S. 494, 71 S.Ct. 857, 95 L.Ed. 1137 (1951)   Upheld Sections 2 and 3 of the Alien Registration Act of 1940, the first federal attempt to restrict expression and association since the Alien and Sedition Acts of 1798. *Dennis* examined the constitutionality of the act, particularly the sections that prohibited advocacy of overthrowing the government by force and organizing groups to that end. Dennis was a leader of the Communist party of the United States. The criminal charges brought against him and others were confined to illegal advocacy and conspiracy. The Court upheld the Alien Registration Act, better known as the Smith Act, in a 6–2 decision. Justice Clark did not participate. The Vinson Court had the option of developing a rationale along the lines of *Gitlow* v. *New York* (268 U.S. 652: 1925, p. 109), which permitted the government to declare that advocacy of governmental overthrow is unprotected expression. Or it could utilize the clear and present danger test to determine if sufficient threat existed to warrant restriction in this case. The Court opted for the latter approach, although Chief Justice Vinson reshaped the clear and present danger standard in doing so. Chief Justice Vinson said the severity of the threat involved was heavier than the immediacy or probability of the danger. Regarding immediacy he reasoned, "obviously, the words of the test cannot mean that before the Government may act, it must wait until the putsch is about to be executed, the plans have been laid, and the signal is awaited." Not only is governmental response allowed in such a situation, it is required if the government is "aware that a group aiming at its overthrow is attempting to indoctrinate its members and to commit them to a course whereby they will strike when the leaders feel the circumstances permit." The likelihood of the threat succeeding is not required either. An attempt to overthrow the government by force, even though doomed from the outset, is a "sufficient evil for Congress to prevent it." The Court adopted the sliding scale concept of clear and present danger as articulated by Judge Learned Hand when the Court of Appeals had reviewed the case. Judge Hand's formulation required that courts "ask whether the gravity of the evil, discounted by its improbability, justifies such invasion of free speech as is necessary to avoid the danger." Applying Judge Hand's standard, the Court found the conspiracy to advocate sufficient to bring sanctions against Dennis. Justices Black and Douglas dissented. Justice Black charged the decision "watered down the First Amendment so that it amounts to little more than an admonition to Congress. The Amendment as so construed is not likely to protect any but those safe or orthodox views which rarely need its protection." *See also* GITLOW V. NEW YORK (268 U.S. 652: 1925), p. 109; SCHENCK V. UNITED STATES (249 U.S. 47: 1919), p. 108; WHITNEY V. CALIFORNIA (274 U.S. 357: 1927), p. 149.

Significance   Dennis v. *United States* (341 U.S. 494: 1951) cleared the way for numerous conspiracy convictions under the Smith Act between 1951 and 1957. In *Yates* v. *United States* (354 U.S. 208: 1957), however, the Court severely proscribed Smith Act conspiracy convictions. The Court did not explicitly overrule *Dennis*, but it said the *Dennis* distinction between advocacy of illegal acts and abstract doctrinal advocacy had been ignored by trial courts subsequent to *Dennis*. Whether *Dennis* had really made this distinction is debatable, but the key result of *Yates* was that the government was now required to demonstrate specific illegal acts by party members in order to convict under the Smith Act. Mere membership was insufficient in itself. This clarification weakened the impact of *Dennis*. Four years later, however, the Court upheld the section of the Smith Act making it a crime to be a member of a group advocating forcible overthrow in *Scales* v. *United States* (367 U.S. 203; 1961). In *Scales* the Court did require evidence comparable to that required in

Yates, saying, for example, that in order to gain a conviction under the membership provision, a person's membership had to be both knowing and active, and that the person had to have shown "specific intent to bring about violent overthrow" of the government. The evidentiary requirements established in *Yates* and *Scales* greatly diminished the likelihood of successful prosecutions under the Smith Act.

Symbolic Speech

Tinker v. *Des Moines School District,* **393 U.S. 503, 89 S.Ct. 733, 21 L.Ed. 2d 731 (1969)** Upheld a symbolic gesture as a protected substitute for speech. *Tinker* involved three public school students in Iowa who were suspended from school for wearing black armbands to protest the government's policy in Vietnam. They brought suit to enjoin the school district from enforcing its regulation against the wearing of armbands. The Supreme Court, in a 7–2 decision, said the armbands could be worn. The Court found the "silent, passive expression of opinion, unaccompanied by any disorder or disturbance" to be closely akin to pure speech. While the wearing of the armbands was a symbolic action rather than speech as such, the conduct was a protected right. In this case the state may not prohibit an expression of opinion without evidence the rule is necessary to avoid interference with school discipline or the rights of others. The Court also found the ban defective in that it selectively singled out the symbol representing opposition to the Vietnam War while ignoring other political symbols. Justices Black and Harlan dissented in separate opinions. Both thought school officials must be given the "widest authority in maintaining discipline and good order." Justice Black said a person cannot engage in demonstrations "where he pleases and when he pleases." The armbands in the school setting distracted from the educational process and could, in Justice Black's view, be regulated. Black also lamented the revolutionary era of permissiveness that allowed the public schools to be subjected to the "whims and caprices of the loudest-mouthed." *See also* BILL OF RIGHTS p. 7; COHEN V. CALIFORNIA (403 U.S. 15: 1971), p. 114; FIRST AMENDMENT, p. 77.

Significance *Tinker* v. *Des Moines School District* (393 U.S. 503: 1969) established the standard that symbolic expression may be protected by the Free Speech Clause of the First Amendment. *Tinker* was decided at a time when the United States was undergoing a painful public dialogue about the rights of a minority of its citizens to protest political actions. The nation was reassessing institutional values that had long gone uncontested. The minority reference to "permissiveness" may be understood as reference to a code word of the era for opposition to certain policy choices such as the American involvement in Southeast Asia. The *Tinker* decision had its origins in *Stromberg* v. *California* (283 U.S. 359: 1931), in which the Court struck down a California statute outlawing display of a red flag because it symbolized "opposition to organized government." The Court felt that if such symbolic expression as this could be restricted, more general political debate would be seriously jeopardized. The Court has also had occasion to review similar cases involving symbolic use of the American flag. While it has recognized the government's authority to punish certain improper conduct regarding the flag, the Court has generally permitted the symbolic uses. In *Smith* v. *Goguen* (415 U.S. 566: 1975), for example, the Court reversed a conviction for the "contemptuous" conduct of a person who had sewn a small flag to the seat of his pants. In *United States* v. *O'Brien* (391 U.S. 367: 1968), the Court upheld a conviction for the burning of a draft card in protest of the Vietnam War. The Court said O'Brien's gesture was communicative, but it also found the government's interest in protecting the recruitment of persons for military service prevailed when the competing interests were balanced. In a rather unsupportive statement about symbolic speech, Chief Justice Warren opined that the Court "cannot accept the view that an apparently limitless variety of conduct can be labelled 'speech' whenever the person engaging in the conduct intends thereby to express an idea." More typically, the Court has supported litigants claiming protection for symbolic expression. Yet in *California* v. *LaRue* (409 U.S. 109: 1972) the Court did uphold a liquor control regulation forbidding establishments with liquor licenses from having nude entertainment. The Court did not find performances with sexual overtones protected as symbolic speech.

Offensive Speech

***Cohen* v. *California,* 403 U.S. 15, 91 S.Ct. 1780, 29 L.Ed. 2d 284 (1971)**   Held that offensive expression is entitled to First Amendment protection. Cohen was arrested in the Los Angeles County Courthouse for wearing a jacket upon which were emblazoned the words "Fuck the Draft." At his trial Cohen testified the jacket was his means of stating his intensely held feelings about the draft and American involvement in Vietnam. Cohen was convicted of violating a statute prohibiting "malicious and willful disturbing of the peace" by conduct that is "offensive." The Supreme Court invalidated the statute in a 5–4 decision. The Court ruled that the words were the issue rather than the conduct. It was "speech" that was being prohibited by the state statute. Moreover, the majority held that the California law was vague, the words were not personally directed at anyone, and a state cannot excise epithets as offensive by functioning as a guardian of public morality. Justice Harlan, writing for the majority, said the First Amendment is "designed and intended to remove governmental restraints from the arena of public discussion." A consequence of such freedom "may often appear to be only verbal tumult, discord, and even offensive utterance," but that is the price of the freedom. "We cannot lose sight of the fact that, in what otherwise might seem a trifling and annoying instance of individual distasteful abuse of a privilege, fundamental societal values are truly implicated." Further, the majority was troubled by the "inherently boundless" nature of what California was attempting through the statute. "Surely the State has no right to cleanse public debate to the point where it is grammatically palatable to the most squeamish among us." Finally, Justice Harlan pointed out that language serves a dual communicative function. It conveys not only ideas capable of relatively precise and detailed explication, but it conveys otherwise inexpressible emotions as well. Words are often chosen as much for their emotive as their cognitive force. He concluded, "We cannot sanction the view that the Constitution, while solicitous of the cognitive content of individual speech, has little or no regard for that emotive function which, practically speaking, may often be the more important element of the overall message sought to be communicated." Chief Justice Burger and Justices Blackmun, Black, and White dissented. They said Cohen's "absurd and immature antic" was essentially regulatable conduct. *See also* BILL OF RIGHTS, p. 7; FIRST AMENDMENT, p. 77; *TINKER V. DES MOINES SCHOOL DISTRICT* (393 U.S. 503: 1969), p. 113.

Significance   Cohen v. California (403 U.S. 15: 1971) involved an attempt to punish offensive speech. Such attempts typically take the form of prosecution for breach of the peace. In *Chaplinsky* v. *New Hampshire* (315 U.S. 568: 1942), the Court held that some speech, notably that which is obscene, libelous, and insulting, is not protected by the First Amendment. It is of such slight value that any benefit derived from it is clearly outweighed by the social interest in order and morality. In *Terminello* v. *Chicago* (337 U.S. 1: 1949), the Court reversed the breach of the peace conviction of a highly provocative speaker, holding that a municipal ordinance was inappropriately applied to limit speech that "invites dispute." Two years later, however, the Court upheld the disorderly conduct conviction of a street corner speaker in *Feiner* v. *New York* (340 U.S. 315: 1951). The Court said that when "clear and present danger of riot, disorder, interference with traffic upon the public street, or other immediate threat to public safety, peace, or order appears, the power of the State to prevent or punish is obvious." The dissenters in *Feiner* argued that the speaker ought to have been protected from the hostile crowd and allowed to speak rather than suffering arrest. A somewhat different kind of offensive expression problem was examined in *Federal Communications Commission* v. *Pacifica Foundation* (438 U.S. 726: 1978). Upon receipt of a listener's complaint, the FCC found that a radio station had aired an indecent program. The FCC issued an order to the station threatening subsequent sanction if such broadcasting reoccurred. The Supreme Court upheld the FCC's authority to issue such an order.

Overbreadth Doctrine

***Village of Schaumburg* v. *Citizens for a Better Environment*, 444 U.S. 620, 100 S.Ct. 826, 63 L.Ed. 2d 73 (1980)**   Struck down a local ordinance using the doctrine of overbreadth. In *Village of Schaumburg* the Supreme Court examined a local ordinance that prohibited door-to-door solicitations for contributions by organizations not using at least 75 percent of their receipts for charitable purposes. A charitable purpose excluded such items as salaries, overhead, solicitation costs, and other administrative expenses. An environmental group was denied permission to solicit because it could not demonstrate compliance with the 75 percent requirement. The organization sued claiming First Amendment violations. The Court struck down the ordinance over the single dissent of Justice Rehnquist. The Court's primary objection was the overbreadth of the ordinance. The Court noted that a class of organizations existed to which the 75 percent rule could not constitutionally be applied. These were organizations "whose primary purpose is not to provide money or services to the poor, the needy, or other worthy objects of charity, but to gather and disseminate information about and advocate positions on matters of public concern." The cost of research, advocacy, or public education is typically in excess of 25 percent of funds raised. The Court felt that to lump all organizations failing to meet the 75 percent standard together imposed a direct and substantial limitation on protected activity. While the village interest in preventing fraud may generally be legitimate, the means to accomplish that end must use more precise measures to separate one kind from another. *See also* BILL OF RIGHTS, p. 7; FIRST AMENDMENT, p. 77.

Significance   *Village of Schaumburg* v. *Citizens for a Better Environment* (444 U.S. 620: 1980) is important because it produced a requirement that statutes distinguish sufficiently between lawful and unlawful expression or behavior. In *Coates* v. *Cincinnati* (402 U.S. 611: 1971), the Court struck down a city ordinance that prohibited three or more persons from assembling on public sidewalks and conducting themselves in such a way as to "annoy any police officer or other persons who should happen to pass by." The Court found the ordinance "makes a crime out of what under the Constitution cannot be a crime." It was also impermissibly vague. It conveyed no standard of conduct and "men of common intelligence must necessarily guess at its meaning." Although the overbreadth and vagueness doctrines have often been invoked to invalidate enactments as in *Schaumburg* and *Coates,* some ordinances survive such challenges. In *Grayned* v. *Rockford* (408 U.S. 104: 1972), the Court allowed an antinoise ordinance prohibiting disturbances in the proximity of schools in session. The specific school context separated the restriction from the typically vague and general breach of the peace ordinance. The enactment was seen as a reasonable time, place, and manner restriction. It was narrowly tailored to further Rockford's compelling interest in having undisrupted school sessions and was not an impermissibly broad prophylactic. In *Village of Hoffman Estates* v. *Flipside, Inc.* (456 U.S. 950: 1982), the Court upheld an ordinance requiring a license to sell items designed or marketed for use with illegal cannabis or drugs against claims that the ordinance was both vague and overbroad. The Court ruled that the ordinance merely sought to regulate the commercial marketing of illegal drug paraphernalia and did not reach noncommercial speech. The only potential limit on Flipside's conveying of information was confined to the commercial activity related to illegal drug use. The Court also found the vagueness claim unpersuasive. The "designed for use" provision of the ordinance covered at least some of the items sold at Flipside. The "marketed for use" language provided ample warning to the retailer about licensure and the display practices that could produce violation of the ordinance.

FREE PRESS

Prior Restraint

Near v. *Minnesota*, 283 U.S. 697, 51 S.Ct. 625, 75 L.Ed. 1357 (1931)   Declared that prior restraint of expression is unconstitutional. *Near* was the Supreme Court's first significant censorship decision. The decision established the doctrine of previous or prior restraint, and it emphasized that the core of free press protection is freedom from governmental censorship of published material. The doctrine of prior restraint is built on the proposition that restraint of expression *before* it can occur constitutes a grave threat to free speech. Near published a weekly newspaper that engaged in vicious attacks on various public officials in Minneapolis. He was subsequently enjoined from publication under provisions of a Minnesota statute that authorized the abatement of any "malicious, scandalous and defamatory newspaper, magazine or periodical" as a "public nuisance." The Court found the statute unconstitutional in a 5–4 decision. In doing so the Court first determined that the "liberty of the press and of speech is within the liberty safeguarded by the Due Process Clause of the Fourteenth Amendment from invasion by state action." In an opinion by Chief Justice Hughes, the Court found the statute defective in that it was "not aimed at the redress of individual or private wrongs." Rather, it was aimed at distribution of material "for the protection of the public welfare." While prosecution might legitimately be brought against such publications, the state had insufficient interest to warrant a prior restraint. Chief Justice Hughes argued that the "object of the statute is not punishment, in the ordinary sense, but suppression." The suppression is "accomplished by enjoining publication, and that restraint is the object and effect of the statute." In short, the objectives and means embodied in the statute were the essence of censorship. The Court also pointed out that the statute too seriously limited what might be said about public officials. References to public corruption or malfeasance or neglect of duty create a public scandal by their very nature. Under the statute, they are scandalous and defamatory by definition. The Court said, "the recognition of authority to impose previous restraint upon publication in order to protect the community against the circulation of charges of misconduct, and especially of official misconduct necessarily would carry with it the admission of the authority of the censor against which the constitutional barrier was erected." Disallowing the prior restraint was paramount. While "charges of reprehensible conduct, and in particular official malfeasance, unquestionably create a public scandal, the theory of the constitutional guaranty is that even a more serious public evil would be caused by authority to prevent publication." Justices Van DeVanter, McReynolds, and Sutherland joined in a dissent written by Justice Butler. The dissent argued that the injunction was not a prior restraint in that it could be issued only after a publication had been found to be a nuisance. The dissenters also felt that libel laws were insufficient to suppress such publications. *See also* FIRST AMENDMENT, p. 77; *FREEDMAN V. MARYLAND* (380 U.S. 51: 1965), p. 141; *NEBRASKA PRESS ASSOCIATION V. STUART* (427 U.S. 530: 1976), p. 259; *NEW YORK TIMES V. UNITED STATES* (403 U.S. 713: 1971), p. 119.

Significance   *Near* v. *Minnesota* (283 U.S. 697: 1931) provided the baseline standard in the critical matter of defining prior restraint. *Near* holds such restraint to be heavily suspect, but possibly justifiable in the instance of threats to national security, obscenity, incitements to governmental overthrow or other violence, or interference with private interests. The prior restraint exceptions set forth in *Near* have remained largely undisturbed. Accordingly, the Court struck down a "gag order" intended to safeguard jury selection in a criminal trial in *Nebraska Press Association* v. *Stuart* (427 U.S. 530: 1976, p. 259). It also freed the publication of the Pentagon Papers in *New York Times* v. *United States* (403 U.S. 713: 1971, p. 49). Further, it held that a group wishing to criticize the way a businessman conducted his business may circulate leaflets near the businessman's home and church in *Organization for a Better Austin* v. *Keefe* (402 U.S. 415: 1971). The only restriction upheld came in *Snepp* v. *United States* (445 U.S. 972: 1980), where the Court required an ex–Central Intelligence Agency agent to obtain clearance from the agency prior to publication of any material relating to his former employment with the CIA.

New York Times, Inc v. United States, 403 U.S. 713, 91 S.Ct. 2140, 29 L.Ed. 2d 822 (1971)   Dissolved an injunction against the *New York Times* restraining publication of the Pentagon Papers.

The Pentagon Papers cases examined the question of whether a prior restraint upon publication may be warranted if national security is threatened. The *New York Times* and the *Washington Post* had come into possession of copies of Defense Department documents detailing the history of American involvement in the Vietnam War. After failing to prevent publication by direct request to the newspapers, the Nixon Administration sought injunctions in federal court against the two papers to stop publication of the documents on national security grounds. The Espionage Act of 1917 was cited specifically. An injunction was obtained against the *Times,* but not against the *Post.* The Supreme Court determined that injunctive restraints against either paper were unwarranted in a 6–3 decision. In a brief per curiam opinion, the Court said there is a "heavy presumption" against prior restraint and that the "heavy burden" had not been carried in these cases. Each member of the Court entered an individual opinion. Justices Black and Douglas both rejected prior restraint categorically. Justice Black said that "every moment's continuance of the injunction against these newspapers amounts to a flagrant, indefensible, and continuing violation of the First Amendment." Justice Black recited the history of the Amendment and noted the essential function assigned to the press. The press, he said, "was to serve the governed, not the governors. The Government's power to censor the press was abolished so that the press would remain forever free to censure the Government." Of all the press functions, "paramount among the responsibilities of the free press is the duty to prevent any part of the government from deceiving the people and sending them off to distant lands to die of foreign fevers and foreign shot and shell." Justice Brennan allowed that prior restraint might be possible in the most extreme circumstance, but found no such circumstances present in these cases. The other members of the majority, Justices Stewart, White, and Marshall, focused on the absence of statutory authority for federal courts to issue injunctions such as those sought by the government. It was pointed out that Congress had directly rejected such an option in the debate leading to the passage of the Espionage Act. Justices White and Stewart, however, did indicate concern that national security had been compromised. They suggested that the criminal process could be utilized against the newspapers in this instance. The three dissenters, Chief Justice Burger and Justices Harlan and Blackmun, rejected the majority's First Amendment position, but they were also concerned with the "irresponsibly feverish" and "frenzied" manner in which the cases were handled. Describing the way the cases reached the Court as "frenetic," the Chief Justice said, "the consequence of all this melancholy series of events is that we literally do not know what we are acting upon." *See also* BILL OF RIGHTS, p. 7; FIRST AMENDMENT, p. 77; *NEAR V. MINNESOTA* (283 U.S. 697: 1931), p. 118.

Significance   The *New York Times, Inc.* v. *United States* (403 U.S. 713: 1971) cases represented an important free press challenge. The Supreme Court decision was expected to provide a definitive statement on when prior restraint might constitutionally be imposed, but the decision did not produce such a definitive ruling. The Court's judgment actually hinged on the fairly narrow issue of whether the government had sufficiently demonstrated that immediate and irreparable harm would result from publication of the documents. While the *Times* prevailed, the various opinions did not constitute a strong ruling for freedom of the press. The criminal prosecution of Daniel Ellsberg, who had furnished copies of the documents to the *Times* and the *Post* in the first place, was ultimately dismissed. Thus the Court was precluded from another opportunity to consider the free press issues contained in the Pentagon Papers imbroglio. Similarly, an attempt to prevent publication of an article in *The Progressive* about the manufacture of a hydrogen bomb was resolved prior to the matter reaching the Supreme Court.

Libel

***New York Times, Inc.* v. *Sullivan*, 376 U.S. 254, 84 S.Ct. 710, 11 L.Ed. 2d 686 (1964)**   Held that publications may not be subjected to libel damages for criticism of public officials and their official conduct unless deliberate malice could be shown. *Sullivan* attached stringent conditions to certain kinds of libel actions involving speech attacking public officials. Libel or intentional defamation has not generally been considered a protected expression. A state libel action was brought by a police commissioner in an Alabama court against the *New York Times* for its publication of a paid advertisement that charged police mistreatment of black students protesting racial segregation. It was stipulated that the advertisement contained errors of fact. The trial judge found the statements in the advertisement to be libelous and instructed the jury that injury occurred through publication, and that both compensatory and punitive damages could be presumed. Substantial damages were awarded by the jury, which also found malice on the part of the *Times*. The Supreme Court reversed the judgments in a unanimous decision. The Court's position was that libel law must provide free speech safeguards. To allow unrestricted libel actions "would discourage newspapers from carrying 'editorial advertisements' of this type, and so might shut off an important outlet for the promulgation of information and ideas." Such laws would shackle the First Amendment in its attempt to secure the widest possible dissemination of information from diverse and antagonistic sources. Even the factual errors did not jeopardize the advertisement's protected status. The protection of the advertisement, clearly "an expression of grievance and protest on one of the major public issues of our time," is not contingent on the truth, popularity, or social utility of the ideas and beliefs which are offered. Mistakes or errors of fact are inevitable in free debate and must be protected if freedom of expression is to have the breathing space it needs. Neither does injury to the reputation of a public official itself justify limiting expression. "Criticism of their official conduct does not lose its constitutional protection merely because it is effective criticism and hence diminishes their official reputations." Any rule "compelling the critic of official conduct to guarantee the truth of all his factual assertions—and to do so on pain of libel judgments virtually unlimited in amount—leads to a comparable 'self-censorship.'" Such a rule severely dampens the vigor and limits the variety of public debate. The Court did allow for recovery of damages where it can be proved that statements were made with actual malice, that is, with knowledge that it was false or with reckless disregard of whether it was false or not. In concurring opinions, Justices Black and Goldberg argued for the unconditional insulation of the press from libel suits, at least with regard to public officials. *See also* BILL OF RIGHTS, p. 7; FIRST AMENDMENT, p. 77; *HERBERT V. LANDO* (441 U.S. 153: 1979), p. 123.

Significance   *New York Times, Inc.* v. *Sullivan* (376 U.S. 254: 1964) expanded the Court's experience with seditious libel, a special category of libel that involves defamation of government and its officials. The Alien and Sedition Acts of 1798 would have provided a basic test of seditious libel, but they never reached the Court. The Court has generally included libel in the category of unprotected speech. *Sullivan* provided the Court an opportunity to refine that classification. Libel laws cannot inhibit debate on public issues even if the debate includes strong and unpleasant attacks on the government and its officials. *Sullivan* did hold that public officials could protect themselves through libel actions in situations where false statements were made with reckless disregard of their untruthfulness and with "actual malice." But the *Sullivan* decision approaches an almost unconditional free press position relative to public officials. The Court soon extended *Sullivan* to criminal libel prosecutions in *Garrison* v. *Louisiana* (379 U.S. 64: 1964). In *Garrison,* the Court said that regardless of limitations in other contexts, "where the criticism is of public officials and their conduct of public business, the interest in private reputation is overborne by the larger public interest, secured by the Constitution in the dissemination of the truth." The question of whether groups may be protected from defamatory statements was addressed in *Beauharnais* v. *Illinois* (343 U.S. 250: 1952). The Court upheld an Illinois statute prohibiting derogatory comment about any racial or religious group in a 5–4 decision. The Court said that "we are precluded from saying that speech concededly punishable when directed at individuals cannot be outlawed if directed at groups with whose position and esteem in society the affiliated individual may be inextricably involved." The dissenters in *Beauharnais* vigorously argued that such a law would greatly inhibit public debate. This view eventually prevailed in *Sullivan* and diminished the current applicability of *Beauharnais.*

Editorial Privilege

***Herbert* v. *Lando,* 441 U.S. 153, 99 S.Ct. 1635, 60 L.Ed. 2d 115 (1979)**   Declared that a plaintiff in a libel action is entitled to inquire into the editorial processes of the defendant. Herbert was a retired army officer with extended service in Vietnam. He received widespread media attention when he accused his superior officers of covering up reports of atrocities and other war crimes. Herbert conceded his public figure status, which required him to demonstrate that the defendants had published a damaging falsehood with actual malice. Some three years after Herbert's disclosures, the Columbia Broadcasting System broadcast a report on Herbert and his charges on the television program "60 Minutes." Lando produced and edited the program. He also published an article on Herbert in the *Atlantic Monthly.* Herbert's suit alleged that the "program and article falsely and maliciously portrayed him as a liar and a person who had made war crime charges to explain his relief from command." In attempting to develop proofs for his case, Herbert tried to obtain the testimony of Lando before trial, but Lando refused, claiming the First Amendment protected against "inquiry into the state of mind of those who edit, produce, or publish, and into the editorial process." The Supreme Court found against Lando in a 6–3 decision. The Court held that the First Amendment does not restrict the sources from which a plaintiff can obtain evidence. Indeed, "it is essential to proving liability that plaintiffs focus on the conduct and state of mind of the defendants." If demonstration of liability is potentially possible, "the thoughts and editorial processes of the alleged defamer would be open to examination." Such examination includes being able to inquire directly from the defendants whether they knew or had reason to suspect that their damaging publication was in error. The editorial privilege sought by Lando would constitute substantial interference with the ability of a defamation plaintiff to establish the ingredients of malice. Further, the outer boundaries sought by Lando are difficult to perceive. In response to the concern that opening the editorial process was an intolerable chilling effect, the Court suggested that if the claimed inhibition flows from the fear of liability for publishing knowing or reckless falsehoods, those effects are precisely what the *New York Times* and other cases have held to be consistent with the First Amendment. Spreading false information in and of itself carries no First Amendment credentials. If a plaintiff is able to demonstrate liability from direct evidence "which in turn discourages the publication of erroneous information known to be false or probably false, this is no more than what our cases contemplate." Justices Brennan, Stewart, and Marshall dissented, urging at least a partial privilege for the editorial process. *See also* BILL OF RIGHTS, p. 7; FIRST AMENDMENT, p. 77; *NEW YORK TIMES, INC.* v. *SULLIVAN* (376 U.S. 254: 1964), p. 121.

Significance   Herbert v. Lando (441 U.S. 153: 1979) established that the editorial practices of a defendant publication could be accessed by a plaintiff in an attempt to show malice. *Sullivan* had set in motion the requirement that malice be demonstrated in libel actions brought by public officials. *Lando* carried the implications of such a demonstration to the point of impinging on freedom of the press by rejecting the notion of editorial privilege. Another issue raised in *Sullivan* relates to the matter of public figures. *Sullivan* protected publications from libel suits where critical comment had been made about governmental officials. Soon thereafter, the category of government official was expanded to include public figures, private citizens who are in the midst of public events, or persons who attract wide public attention. In *Rosenbloom* v. *Metromedia, Inc.* (403 U.S. 29: 1971), the Court went so far as to require reckless falsity in all actions, whether the plaintiff was a public official, a public figure, or a private individual. *Gertz* v. *Robert Welsh, Inc.* (418 U.S. 323: 1974) held that an individual did not become a public figure simply because the public was interested in a particular event with which he was associated. Similarly, a federally funded researcher's media response to receipt of a Senator's award for wasting public funds was held insufficient to establish public figure status in *Hutchinson* v. *Proxmire* (443 U.S. 111: 1979).

Newsperson's Privilege

Branzburg v. **Hayes,** 408 U.S. 665, 92 S.Ct. 2646, 33 L.Ed. 2d 626 (1972)   Held that newspersons must disclose sources of information to a grand jury. *Branzburg* rejected the argument of newspersons that they possess a privileged relationship with their sources. After having published reports about drug use and manufacture, Hayes was subpoenaed to appear before a state grand jury and identify those persons he had seen using and making illegal narcotics. Hayes refused to testify and was cited for contempt. Through Justice White, a 5–4 majority of the Supreme Court opined that the First Amendment "does not invalidate every incidental burdening of the press that may result from the enforcement of civil or criminal statutes of general applicability." In balancing the interests of protecting the criminal process and the news gathering function of the press, the former must prevail. The consequential but uncertain burden is not sufficient to treat newspersons differently from other citizens. They must respond to relevant questions put to them in the course of a valid grand jury investigation or criminal trial. The burden in *Branzburg* was not prior restraint, a tax, a penalty on content, or a compulsion to publish. The Court suggested, however, that the impact of its holding would be limited. "Only where news sources themselves are implicated in crime or possess information relevant to the grand jury's task need they or the reporter be concerned about grand jury subpoenas. Nothing before us indicates that a large number or percentage of all confidential news sources fall into either category." Finally, the Court argued that abuse or harassment of the press would be subject to judicial scrutiny and possible intervention. Justice Stewart issued a dissent in which Justices Brennan and Marshall concurred. He said the Court had undermined the historic independence of the press by attempting to annex the journalistic profession as an investigative arm of the government. Justice Stewart argued that freedom of the press requires the ability to gather news which, in turn, is often contingent on a confidential relationship of reporter and source. The dissenters would have required the state to show (1) that probable cause exists to believe a newsperson has relevant information; (2) that the information cannot be obtained from any other source; and (3) that the state has a compelling interest in the information. Justice Douglas also dissented. He said that forcing a reporter before a grand jury has "two retarding effects upon the ear and pen of the press." One is that fear of exposure will cause dissidents to communicate less openly to reporters. The other is that concerns about accountability will cause editors and critics to write with more restrained pens. Douglas suggested more generally that the press has a "preferred position in our constitutional scheme." The position of the press is not designed to enhance profit or set newspeople apart as a favored class. It is intended to "bring fulfill-ment to the public's right to know." *See also* BILL OF RIGHTS, p. 7; FIRST AMENDMENT, p. 77; *RICHMOND NEWSPAPERS, INC. v. VIRGINIA* (448 U.S. 555: 1980), p. 126.

Significance   *Branzburg* v. *Hayes* (408 U.S. 665: 1972) said that even an unconditional freedom to publish would be of limited value if information gathering was unprotected. To protect that function, several states have adopted shield laws designed to protect the confidentiality of sources. No such legislation exists at the federal level, although *Branzburg* did prompt introduction of such proposals. The Burger Court has also rejected other claims of the press regarding its rights in the gathering of information. In *Saxbe* v. *Washington Post, Inc.* (417 U.S. 843: 1974) the Court upheld federal prison regulations that prohibited press interviews with designated or particular inmates. The Court said the Constitution does not impose upon government the "affirmative duty to make available to jour-nalists sources of information not available to members of the public generally." Four years later, in *Houchins* v. *KQED, Inc.* (438 U.S. 1: 1978) the Court upheld a refusal to allow media access to a county jail that had been the site of a prisoner's suicide and other alleged violent incidents, as well as charges of inhumane conditions. The majority saw the case as one involving a "special privilege of access" such as that denied in *Saxbe*. This is "a right which is not essential to guarantee the freedom to communicate or publish."

Trial Access

Richmond Newspapers, Inc. v. Virginia, 448 U.S. 555, 100 S.Ct. 2814, 75 L.Ed. 2d 973 (1980)   Determined that the press has a constitutional right of access to criminal trials. In *Richmond Newspapers* the defendant's counsel requested that a murder trial be closed to the public. The prosecutor expressed no objection, and the trial judge ordered the courtroom cleared. Under Virginia law a trial judge has the discretion to exclude from a trial any person whose "presence would impair the conduct of a fair trial." In a 7–1 decision the Supreme Court held the closure order was a violation of the right of access. The Court said this right of the press was protected under the First Amendment. The majority opinion was written by Chief Justice Burger, with Justice Powell not participating in the decision. Chief Justice Burger began with a lengthy treatment of the history of the open trial. This "unbroken, uncontradicted history, supported by reasons as valid today as in centuries past," forced the Court to conclude "that a presumption of openness inheres in the very nature of a criminal trial under our system of justice." The Court majority said the open trial serves a therapeutic purpose for the community, especially in the instance of shocking crimes. Open trials offer protection against abusive or arbitrary behavior. They allow criminal processes "to satisfy the appearance of justice." While access to trials is not specifically provided in the First Amendment, it is implicit in its guarantees. Without the freedom to attend trials, important aspects of free speech and a free press could be eviscerated. Chief Justice Burger returned to the case at hand in his conclusion. The closure order was defective because the trial judge made no specific finding to support such an order. Alternatives to closure were not explored, there was no recognition of any Constitutional right for the press or the public to attend the proceeding, and there was no indication that problems with witnesses could not have been handled otherwise. In a concurring opinion Justice Brennan said that "open trials play a fundamental role in furthering the efforts of any judicial system to assure the criminal defendant a fair and accurate adjudication of guilt or innocence." The open trial is also the means by which a society becomes aware that it is governed equitably. Justice Rehnquist dissented and recast the issue. For him the issue was "whether any provision in the Constitution may fairly be read to prohibit what the trial judge in the Virginia state court system did in this case." Rehnquist would have permitted the trial judge's order to stand. *See also* BRANZBURG V. HAYES (408 U.S. 665: 1972), p. 125; CHANDLER V. FLORIDA (449 U.S. 560: 1981), p. 262; FIRST AMENDMENT, p. 77; GANNETT COMPANY V. DEPASQUALE (443 U.S. 368: 1979), p. 260; NEBRASKA PRESS ASSOCIATION V. STUART (427 U.S. 530: 1976), p. 259.

Significance   *Richmond Newspapers, Inc.* v. *Virginia* (448 U.S. 555: 1980) clearly distinguished the trial itself from pretrial hearings and elevated the press interest to prevailing weight in the former. In most instances, the Supreme Court has found a criminal defendant to be entitled to insulation from media coverage as a basic requirement of due process in pretrial hearings. Consistent with the objective of minimizing adverse pretrial publicity, the Court allowed closure of pretrial proceedings in *Gannett Company* v. *DePasquale* (443 U.S. 368: 1979). The Court held in *Nebraska Press Association* v. *Stuart* (427 U.S. 530: 1976) that material from a public proceeding or record could not be kept from the public through a court gag order. *Nebraska Press Association* also said the press cannot be restrained from reporting what it observes. A balance of press and criminal defendant interests was struck in *Chandler* v. *Florida* (449 U.S. 560: 1981), in which the Court upheld a policy whereby trials might be broadcast as long as broadcast coverage is not disruptive, intrusive, or prejudicial to the outcome of the trial.

Commercial Press

Pittsburgh Press Company v. ***Human Relations Commission,*** **413 U.S. 376, 93 S.Ct. 2553, 37 L.Ed. 2d 669 (1973)**   Declared that particular kinds of commercial speech may be regulated. The Pittsburgh Press Company was found to be in violation of a Human Relations Commission ordinance because it placed help-wanted advertisements in sex-designated columns. The Commission ordered the newspaper to end the gender-referenced layout of the advertisements. The order was affirmed in Pennsylvania's judicial system. The Supreme Court ruled the order was not prior restraint in a 5–4 decision. The Court first determined the advertisements were commercial speech, not merely because they were advertisements, but because of their commercial content. They were, in fact, "classic examples of commercial speech" because of the proposal of possible employment. They were therefore unlike the political advertisement in *New York Times* v. *Sullivan* (376 U.S. 254: 1964). The Pittsburgh Press Company argued that editorial judgment about where to place an advertisement should control, rather than its commercial content. The Court majority answered that "a newspaper's editorial judgments in connection with an advertisement take on the character of the advertisement and, in those cases, the scope of the newspaper's First Amendment protection may be affected by the content of the advertisement." The kind of editorial judgment involved in this case did not strip commercial advertising of its commercial character. Even more crucial was the fact that the commercial activity involved was illegal employment discrimination. In the Court's view advertisements could be forbidden in this instance just as advertisements "proposing a sale of narcotics or soliciting prostitution" could be forbidden. The justices concluded their opinion by ruling that any First Amendment interest that applies to an ordinary commercial proposal is "altogether absent when the commercial activity itself is illegal and the restriction on advertising is incidental to a valid limitation on economic activity." Dissents were entered by Chief Justice Burger and Justices Douglas, Stewart, and Blackmun. The chief justice wrote that the First Amendment "includes the right of a newspaper to arrange the content of its paper, whether it be news items, editorials, or advertising, as it sees fit." Justice Douglas argued that employment discrimination can be otherwise handled. No ordinance justifies censorship. Justice Stewart felt that, given the Court's holding, there is "no reason why Government cannot force a newspaper publisher to conform in the same way in order to achieve other goals thought socially desirable." If government can "dictate the layout of a newspaper's classified advertising pages today, what is there to prevent it from dictating the layout of the news pages tomorrow?" *See also* BILL OF RIGHTS, p. 7; FIRST AMENDMENT, p. 77; *NEW YORK TIMES, INC.* v. *SULLIVAN* (376 U.S. 254: 1964), p. 121.

Significance   The commercial speech holding in *Pittsburgh Press Company* v. *Human Relations Commission* (413 U.S. 376: 1973) had its origin in *Valentine* v. *Chrestensen* (316 U.S. 52: 1942). The latter decision clearly put commercial speech outside First Amendment coverage. *New York Times* v. *Sullivan* (376 U.S. 254: 1964) substantially narrowed the *Chrestensen* concept of commercial speech, and following *Pittsburgh Press*, the Burger Court narrowed the definition even further. In *Bigelow* v. *Virginia* (421 U.S. 809: 1975), the Court protected the publication of an advertisement by an organization offering services related to legal abortions in another state. The Court held the advertisement "conveyed information of potential interest and value to a diverse audience," not merely a commercial promotion of services. The next year, in *Virginia State Board of Pharmacy* v. *Virginia Citizens Consumers Council, Inc.* (425 U.S. 748: 1976), the Court struck down a statute that made advertising of prescription drugs a form of conduct possibly leading to a suspension of license. The Court argued that even if the advertiser's interest is a purely economic one, such speech is not necessarily disqualified from protection. The consumer and society in general has a "strong interest in the free flow of commercial information." Such a free flow is indispensable in a predominantly free enterprise economy that requires many private economic decisions.

Fairness Doctrine

Red Lion Broadcasting Company v. ***Federal Communications Commission*** **(FCC), 395 U.S. 367, 89 S.Ct. 1794, 23 L.Ed. 2d 371 (1969)**   Upheld a Federal Communications Commission regulation known as the fairness doctrine. Red Lion broadcast a particular program during which the honesty and character of a third party were impugned. The third party demanded free time for a response, but was refused. The FCC then held that Red Lion had failed to satisfy a requirement of equity and equal access. The Supreme Court unanimously upheld the constitutionality of the FCC position. The Court acknowledged that broadcasting is clearly a medium affected by First Amendment interests, but it emphasized some critical differences from the print medium. Among these are the limited number of channels available and the incomparably greater reach of the radio signal. Scarcity of access means Congress "unquestionably has the power to grant and deny licenses," a power vested by Congress in the Federal Communications Commission. The license permits broadcasting, but the licensee "has no constitutional right to be the one who holds the license or to monopolize a radio frequency to the exclusion of his fellow citizens." The Court said the First Amendment does not prevent the government from requiring a license to share a frequency with others and to "conduct himself as a proxy or fiduciary" with obligations to present views that are representative of his community and that would otherwise be barred from the airwaves. Government has an obligation to preserve access for divergent views because of the unique character of the broadcast medium. Justice White said the people retain their interest in free speech by radio and have a collective right to the medium's functioning consistently with the ends and purposes of the First Amendment. It is the "right of the viewers and listeners, not the right of broadcasters, which is paramount." Without regulation through the FCC in the form of such rules as the fairness doctrine, station owners and a few networks would have "unfettered power to make time available only to the highest bidders, to communicate only their own views on public issues, people and candidates, and to permit on the air only those with whom they agreed." The Court concluded that there is no sanctuary in the First Amendment for unlimited private censorship operating in a medium not open to all. *See also* BILL OF RIGHTS, p. 7; FIRST AMENDMENT, p. 77; *HERBERT* v. *LANDO* (441 U.S. 153: 1979), p. 123.

Significance   The thrust of *Red Lion Broadcasting Company* v. *Federal Communications Commission* (395 U.S. 367: 1969) is that a balance must be struck between the First Amendment interests of the broadcast medium and the need to regulate governmentally granted channel monopolies. The fairness doctrine at issue in *Red Lion* had not kept the station from expressing its own views. It had only required that reply time be provided when a station carries a broadcast that attacks an individual personally. The print media may not be required to do the same thing, however. In *Miami Herald Publishing Company* v. *Tornillo* (418 U.S. 241: 1974), the Court overturned a Florida right-to-reply statute that required reply space in a newspaper for any political candidate who was attacked. Such required space was found to be as offensive to the First Amendment as prior restraint. This kind of law authorizes governmental "intrusion into the function of editors in choosing what material goes into a newspaper." Similarly, the Court has also held that the airwaves need not become a common carrier with access guaranteed to any private citizen or group. *Columbia Broadcasting System* v. *Democratic National Committee* (412 U.S. 94: 1973) determined that a broadcaster policy of refusing to sell editorial advertisements was an acceptable practice and not incompatible with the fairness doctrine. The access issue was clouded in 1981 when the Court upheld a right of reasonable access for candidates for federal office in *Columbia Broadcasting System, Inc.* v. *Federal Communications Commission* (449 U.S. 950: 1981).

Obscenity Standards

Roth **v.** *United States,* **354 U.S. 476, 77 S.Ct. 1304, 1 L.Ed. 2d 1498 (1957)**   Established definitional standards for obscenity. *Roth* and its companion case, *Alberts* v. *California,* addressed the issue of whether "obscenity is utterance within the area of protected speech and press." Roth had been convicted of violating the federal obscenity statute by using the mail to distribute "obscene, lewd, lascivious, filthy, or indecent" material. The Supreme Court upheld both convictions. The Court began by holding that the First Amendment was not intended to protect every utterance. As in the case of libel, the Court noted historical evidence that suggested that obscenity also fell outside the scope of protected speech. Obscenity is not included because it is "utterly without redeeming social importance," a judgment reflected in many obscenity statutes in various states and throughout the world. Having thus determined that obscenity is not protected, the Court set about fashioning a definition of obscenity that would permit distinction between protected and unprotected speech. Key to identification of obscenity is its appeal to prurient interests. Treatment of sex per se "is not itself sufficient reason to deny material the constitutional protection of speech and press." The Court sought to establish a standard sufficiently proscribed as not to encroach on material legitimately treating sex. The standard chosen was "whether to the average person, applying contemporary community standards, the dominant theme of the material taken as a whole appeals to prurient interest." Using this standard, the Court concluded that the two statutes under consideration did not offend the First Amendment. Justices Douglas and Black dissented in both cases, saying "any test which turns on what is offensive to the community's standards is too loose, too capricious, too destructive of freedom of expression to be squared with the First Amendment." Justice Harlan concurred in *Alberts* but dissented in *Roth,* saying the "federal interest in dealing with pornography is attenuated," and this ought to be left to the states. *See also* FIRST AMENDMENT, p. 77; *MEMOIRS V. MASSACHUSETTS* (383 U.S. 413: 1966), p. 133; *MILLER V. CALIFORNIA* (413 U.S. 15: 1973), p. 134.

Significance   *Roth* v. *United States* (354 U.S. 476: 1957) clearly established that obscenity is not protected speech and upheld a federal-level attempt to regulate obscenity. The more troublesome issue was differentiating protected speech from unprotected obscenity. The leading definition prior to *Roth* had come from an English case, *Queen* v. *Hicklin* (Law Reports, 3 Queen's Bench 360: 1868). The *Hicklin* test allowed "material to be judged merely by the effect of an isolated excerpt upon particularly susceptible persons." While *Roth* represented progress from the highly restrictive *Hicklin* standard, many questions remained. As the Court struggled with these questions, its definition became less restrictive, and it finally lost all consensus on standards. In *Jacobellis* v. *Ohio* (378 U.S. 184: 1964), for example, the Court essentially held that material need be pornographic in order to be restricted, but no more than two justices could agree on a rationale for the policy. *Memoirs* v. *Massachusetts* (383 U.S. 413: 1966) is also reflective of the Court's inability to construct any consensus on obscenity criteria. The only case producing a more restrictive holding was *Ginzburg* v. *United States* (383 U.S. 463: 1966). The Court upheld Ginzburg's conviction because he commercially exploited the sexual content of the materials he offered for sale. He engaged in pandering. Ginzburg's materials were viewed "against a background of commercial exploitation of erotica solely for the sake of their prurient appeal." In situations where the "purveyor's sole emphasis is on the sexually provocative aspects of his publications, that fact may be decisive in the determination of obscenity." *Ginzburg* modified *Roth* in that materials may pass the initial *Roth* test and yet still be found obscene. While the materials themselves may not be obscene, they can become illicit merchandise through the "sordid business of pandering."

A Book Named "John Cleland's Memoirs of a Woman of Pleasure" v. Attorney General of Massachusetts, 383 U.S. 413, 86 S.Ct. 975, 12 L.Ed. 2d 1 (1966) Reinterpreted the obscenity standards established in *Roth* v. *United States* (354 U.S. 476: 1957). The *Memoirs* case is an example of the obscenity cases that came to the Court in the mid-1960s and muddied, rather than sharpened, the definition of obscenity. In a state proceeding, a book known as *Fanny Hill,* or *John Cleland's Memoirs of a Woman of Pleasure,* was declared obscene. The Supreme Court reversed the finding in a 6–3 decision although the six-justice majority could not agree on an opinion. Chief Justice Warren and Justices Brennan and Fortas based their decision on the state court's misinterpretation and misapplication of the social value criterion of *Roth*. In their view the state erred in determining that a book need not be unqualifiedly worthless before it can be deemed obscene. On the contrary, a book cannot be proscribed unless it is found to be utterly without redeeming social value. "This is so even though the book is found to possess the requisite prurient appeal and to be patently offensive." The three federal criteria, i.e., dominant theme, patent offensiveness, and absence of social value, were to be applied independently. "The social value of the book can neither be weighted against nor canceled by its prurient appeal or patent offensiveness." Justice Douglas concurred in the outcome but said the burden is on the prosecution to prove that a book lacks redeeming social importance. Justice Black took the position that the content of all books is protected by the First Amendment. Justice Stewart would have substituted a hard-core pornography standard to define unprotected content, a level of protection not reached by *Fanny Hill*. In separate dissents, Justices Clark, Harland, and White rejected the elevation of the "utterly without" criterion. In the words of Justice Clark, such a new test damaged *Roth* and "gives the smut artist free rein to carry on his dirty business." Justices Harlan and White argued for greater state prerogatives in handling obscenity. *See also* FIRST AMENDMENT, p. 77; MILLER v. CALIFORNIA (413 U.S. 15: 1973), p. 134; ROTH v. UNITED STATES (354 U.S. 476: 1957), p. 131.

Significance   *Memoirs* v. *Massachusetts* (383 U.S. 413: 1966) was the most permissive of the Warren Court pronouncements on obscenity. It held that the three previously established obscenity criteria—prurient interest, social value, and patent offensiveness—were separate and independent. This was especially important for the social value criterion. If any redeeming social value could be detected, material could not be adjudged obscene despite its appeal to prurient interest and its patently offensive character. Although the Court was badly divided in *Memoirs,* it could be inferred from the case that only hard-core pornography remained as an unprotected class of publication. *Memoirs* also marked the Warren Court's last real effort to grapple with definitional standards for obscenity. In *Redrup* v. *New York* (386 U.S. 767: 1967), the Court declared it would uphold obscenity statutes only to prohibit distribution of obscene materials to juveniles or in cases where such materials were obtrusively thrust upon an unwilling audience. *Redrup* allowed the Court to bypass its stalemate on standards and handle the obscenity matter pragmatically. Earlier the Court had upheld a state prohibition on sales to minors in *Ginsberg* v. *New York* (390 U.S. 629: 1965), and later it upheld federal prosecution of firms sending a second mailing to persons demanding removal of their names from a mailing list in *Rowan* v. *Post Office Department* (397 U.S. 728: 1970).

Miller v. California, 413 U.S. 15, 93 S.Ct. 2607, 37 L.Ed. 2d 419 (1973)   Tightened definitional standards for obscenity. In *Miller* the Burger Court remodeled and reinterpreted Warren Court obscenity holdings. Miller had been convicted of distributing obscene material. His offense was that he had conducted an aggressive book sales campaign by sending unsolicited brochures through the mail. A five-justice majority upheld Miller's conviction and offered a redefinition of the *Roth* (354 U.S. 476: 1957) test. The Court found no fault with *Roth,* but subsequent decisions had "veered sharply away from the *Roth* concept." Thus the need existed to restore its original intent. While many cases had brought about such a need, the major offender was *Fanny Hill,* in which the plurality of the Court produced a "drastically altered test" that required the prosecution to prove a negative. The prosecution had to prove that material was "utterly without redeeming social value—a burden virtually impossible to discharge." See *Memoirs* v. *Massachusetts* (383 U.S. 413: 1966), p. 133. In establishing a revised standard, the Burger Court drew heavily from *Roth*. An obscenity statute must be limited to works that, taken as a whole, appeal to the prurient interest in sex or that portray sexual conduct in a patently offensive way. The material when taken as a whole must lack serious literary, artistic, political, or scientific value. The Court specifically rejected the social value test of *Memoirs*. It also proposed some flexibility in applying its guidelines to specific cases. The nation is "simply too big and too diverse" for a uniform standard of prurient interest or patently offensive sexual conduct. The Court viewed it as unrealistic to base proceedings around an abstract formulation. To require a state to try a case around evidence of a national community standard would be an exercise in futility. The Court asserted that people in different states vary in their tastes and attitudes, and "this diversity is not to be strangled by the absolutism of imposed uniformity." State obscenity trials can therefore base evaluation of materials on the contemporary community standards of the particular state. Justices Brennan, Marshall, and Stewart dissented. They argued that obscenity regulations ought to be confined to the distribution of obscene materials to juveniles and unwilling audiences. In his dissent in *Paris Adult Theatre I* v. *Staton* (413 U.S. 49: 1973), a companion case to *Miller*, Justice Brennan also warned of another expression problem. He said, "The State's interest in regulating morality by suppressing obscenity, while often asserted, remains essentially unfocused and ill-defined." When attempts are made to curtail unprotected speech, protected speech is necessarily involved as well. Thus the effort to serve this speculative interest through regulation of obscene matter "must tread heavily on the rights protected by the First Amendment." Justice Douglas also dissented, offering an absolutist argument for expression in all circumstances. *See also* FIRST AMENDMENT, p. 77; MEMOIRS V. MASSACHUSETTS (383 U.S. 413: 1966), p. 133; ROTH V. UNITED STATES (354 U.S. 476: 1957), p. 131.

Significance   *Miller* v. *California* (413 U.S. 15: 1973) represented the first consensus statement on obscenity standards since *Roth* in 1957. *Miller* is of consequence primarily because the Court's rejection of national community standards prompted highly diverse outcomes relative to obscenity regulations. It also removed the social value criterion as an insurmountable obstacle to prosecution. *Miller* provided examples of the kinds of materials that may be offensive enough to be regulated, but a lack of doctrinal clarity remained. Just a year after *Miller,* the Court unanimously reversed an obscenity conviction in *Jenkins* v. *Georgia* (418 U.S. 153: 1974), overturning a local judgment that the film *Carnal Knowledge* was obscene. The Court cautioned that local juries and their application of community standards are not free from First Amendment boundaries. *Miller* did prompt greater regulation, however, and such regulated activities have generally been supported by the Court. In *New York* v. *Ferber* (458 U.S. 747: 1982), for example, the Court unanimously upheld a statute prohibiting "persons from knowingly promoting a sexual performance by a child under the age of 16." The Court said the states are "entitled to greater leeway in the regulation of pornographic depictions of children." It said that because the state "bears so heavily and pervasively on the welfare of children, the balance of compelling interests is clearly struck, and it is permissible to consider these materials as without First Amendment protection."

Obscenity: Zoning

Young v. *American Mini Theatres, Inc.,* **427 U.S. 50, 96 S.Ct. 2440, 49 L.Ed. 2d 310 (1976)**   Upheld zoning ordinances regulating locations of adult theatres. *Young* approved amendments to Detroit zoning ordinances providing that adult theaters be licensed. They could not be located within 1,000 feet of any two other "regulated uses" or within 500 feet of any residential area. The other "regulated uses" included some ten categories of adult entertainment enterprises. An adult theater was defined as one that presented material characterized by emphasis on "specified sexual activities" or "specified anatomical areas." *Young* was a 5–4 decision against several lines of challenge. First, the Court rejected assertions of vagueness in the ordinance because "any element of vagueness in these ordinances has not affected the respondents." The application of the ordinances to the American Mini Theatres "is plain." As for the licensure requirement, the Court noted that the general zoning laws in Detroit imposed requirements on all motion picture theaters. The Court said, "We have no doubt that the municipality may control the location of theaters as well as the location of other commercial establishments." Establishment of such restrictions in themselves is not prohibited as prior restraint. The "mere fact that the commercial exploitation of material protected by the First Amendment is subject to zoning and other licensing requirements is not sufficient reason for invalidating these ordinances." The Court also considered whether the 1,000-foot restriction constituted an improper content-based classification. The Court said that "even within the area of protected speech, a difference in content may require a different governmental response." Citing the public figure category in libel law and prohibitions on exhibition of obscenity to juveniles and unconsenting adults, the Court held that the First Amendment did not foreclose content distinctions. They "rest squarely on an appraisal of the content of the material otherwise within a constitutionally protected area." Even though the First Amendment does not allow total suppression, the Court held that a state may legitimately use the content of Mini Theatre materials as the basis for placing them in a different classification from other motion pictures. Finally, the Court upheld the regulated use classification on the basis of the city's interest in preserving the character of its neighborhoods. Detroit has a legitimate interest in attempting to preserve the quality of urban life. It is an interest that "must be accorded high respect," and the city must be allowed "a reasonable opportunity to experiment with solutions to an admittedly serious problem." Justices Brennan, Stewart, Marshall, and Blackmun dissented, basing their opinion on the vagueness and content orientation of the ordinance. *See also* BILL OF RIGHTS, p. 7; FIRST AMENDMENT, p. 77; *MILLER* v. *CALIFORNIA* (413 U.S. 15: 1973), p. 134.

Significance   *Young* v. *American Mini Theatres, Inc.* (427 U.S. 50: 1976) represents a new wave of cases raising issues about the local regulation of "adult entertainment." The Court has generally supported local regulation as long as expression is not completely prohibited and as long as a compelling interest can be demonstrated. Meeting these conditions is not always easy, however. In *Erznoznick* v. *Jacksonville* (422 U.S. 205: 1975), the Court struck down an ordinance that prohibited the exhibition of films containing nudity if the screen could be seen from a public street. The Court cited the limited privacy interest or persons on the streets, but it also stressed the overly broad sweep of the ordinance. In *Schad* v. *Borough of Mount Ephraim* (452 U.S. 61: 1981), the Court invalidated a zoning ordinance that banned live entertainment in a borough establishment. Convictions under the ordinance had been secured against an adult bookstore operator for having live nude dancers performing in the establishment. The borough argued that permitting such entertainment would conflict with its plan to create a commercial area catering only to the immediate needs of residents. The Court considered such justification "patently insufficient." The ordinance prohibited a "wide range of expression that has long been held to be within the protection of the First and Fourteenth Amendments."

Private Obscenity

***Stanley* v. *Georgia*, 394 U.S. 557, 89 S.Ct. 1243, 22 L.Ed. 2d 542 (1969)**   Held that a state could not prohibit private possession of obscene materials. Stanley was convicted of possessing obscene films. The films were discovered while federal and state agents searched Stanley's home under authority of a warrant issued in connection with an investigation of Stanley's alleged involvement in bookmaking. The Supreme Court unanimously reversed Stanley's conviction. Justices Stewart, White, and Brennan reversed exclusively on improper search grounds. Stanley's First Amendment claim was based on his "right to read or observe what he pleases—the right to satisfy his intellectual and emotional needs in the privacy of his own home and the right to be free from state inquiry into the contents of his library." Georgia's statute was based on the view that there are "certain types of materials that the individual may not read or even possess." The Court was unpersuaded, saying that "mere categorization of these films as 'obscene' is insufficient justification for such drastic invasion of personal liberties." Although privacy was a key consideration, the Court stressed the First Amendment aspects of *Stanley.* Justifications for regulation of obscenity "do not reach into the privacy of one's own home. If the First Amendment means anything, it means that a State has no business telling a man, sitting alone in his own house, what books he may read or what films he may watch. Our whole constitutional heritage rebels at the thought of giving government the power to control men's minds." The interests of the state are insufficient to protect individuals from obscenity in this fashion. "Whatever the power of the State to control public dissemination of ideas inimical to the public morality, it cannot constitutionally premise legislation on the desirability of controlling a person's private thoughts." Neither may the state justify the prohibition of privately held obscene materials as a means of forestalling antisocial conduct. The state "may no more prohibit mere possession of obscenity on the ground that it may lead to anti-social conduct than it may prohibit possession of chemistry books on the ground they may lead to the manufacture of homemade spirits." The Court also rejected the argument that outlawing possession of obscenity is required to allow enforcement of prohibitions against its distribution. The right to read or observe is dominant and "its restriction may not be justified by the need to ease the administration of otherwise valid criminal laws." *See also* BILL OF RIGHTS, p. 7; FIRST AMENDMENT, p. 77; MILLER V. CALIFORNIA (413 U.S. 15: 1973), p. 134.

Significance   Stanley v. Georgia (394 U.S. 557: 1969) decided that privately held obscene material is a protected right. The Burger Court followed *Stanley,* however, by closing off the means of delivering obscene matter. *United States* v. *Reidel* (402 U.S. 351: 1971) held that obscene material was unprotected expression and could constitutionally be excluded from the mail. On the same day, in *United States* v. *Thirty-Seven Photographs* (402 U.S. 363: 1971), the Court allowed a prohibition on the importation of obscenity from abroad even if it were intended for private use. The following year, in *United States* v. *12 200-ft. Reels of Super 8mm. Film* (413 U.S. 123: 1972), the Court allowed seizure of materials coming into the country from Mexico. The justices declared that the right privately to possess obscene materials did not afford "a correlative right to acquire, sell, or import such material even for private use only." The most noteworthy modification of *Stanley* came in *Paris Adult Theatre I* v. *Staton* (413 U.S. 49: 1973), a companion to *Miller* v. *California* (413 U.S. 15: 1973). *Paris* held that obscene films do not "acquire constitutional immunity from state regulation simply because they are exhibited for consenting adults only." The Court recognized the "legitimate state interests at stake in stemming the tide of commercialized obscenity." It is an interest that includes protecting "the quality of life and the total community environment."

Censorship

***Kingsley Books, Inc.* v. *Brown,* 354 U.S. 436, 77 S.Ct. 1325, 1 L.Ed. 2d 1469 (1957)**   Upheld restrictions on the sale of obscene materials through court order. A section of the New York Code of Criminal Procedure authorized enforcement officials in municipalities to invoke injunctive remedies against the "sale and distribution of written and printed matter found after due trial to be obscene," and to obtain an order for "the seizure, in default of surrender, of the condemned publications." The section entitled the person enjoined to have a trial within one day of the injunction and a decision within two days of the trial. Certain items found in the Kingsley Books establishment were determined obscene, their further distribution enjoined, and their destruction ordered. Kingsley Books did not challenge New

York's authority to prohibit the distribution of obscenity. The appeal focused on the remedial technique, which included the power to enjoin during the course of the litigation. Kingsley Books asserted that such use of the injunctive remedy amounted to an unconstitutional prior restraint. The Supreme Court upheld the injunctive method of the New York code in a 5–4 decision. In approving the approach, the Court compared it to imposing criminal sanctions on booksellers. Rather than requiring the seller "to dread that the offer for sale of a book may without prior warning subject him to criminal prosecution with the hazard of imprisonment," the section of the code at issue "assures him that such consequences cannot follow unless he ignores a court order specifically directed to him for a prompt and carefully circumscribed determination of the issue of obscenity." The Court majority concluded that the code "moves after publication" by enjoining from display or sale "particular booklets theretofore published and adjudged to be obscene." When compared with criminal penalties, the "restraint upon appellants as merchants in obscenity was narrower." The restriction imposed under the code was altogether different from the injunctive restraint found in *Near* v. *Minnesota* (283 U.S. 697: 1931, p. 118). Unlike *Near,* "Section 22-a is concerned solely with obscenity," and it "studiously withholds restraints upon matters not already published and not yet found to be offensive." Chief Justice Warren dissented on the ground that the statute "places the book on trial" with no criteria for "judging the book in context." The matter of use should determine obscenity rather than the quality of the art or literature. Chief Justice Warren concluded by saying the statute "savors too much of book burning." Justices Douglas and Black found the provision for injunction during litigation excessive in that it gave the state "the paralyzing power of a censor." Justice Brennan's dissent cited the absence of a jury as a fatal defect. *See also* FIRST AMENDMENT, p. 77; *FREEDMAN* V. *MARYLAND* (380 U.S. 51: 1965), p. 141; *NEAR* V. *MINNESOTA* (283 U.S. 697: 1931), p. 118.

Significance   *Kingsley Books, Inc.* v. *Brown* (354 U.S. 436: 1957) said that techniques of censoring written materials, especially books, must contain extensive procedural safeguards. In *Smith* v. *California* (361 U.S. 147: 1959), the Court required in addition that a defendant in an obscenity proceding must be shown to have knowledge of the material's contents. Without such knowledge, the bookseller will "restrict the books he sells to those he inspected," and this will constitute a state-imposed "restriction upon the distribution of constitutionally protected as well as obscene literature." Neither can material be prohibited from distribution until it has been subjected to a formal hearing as in *Kingsley.* In *Bantam Books, Inc.* v. *Sullivan* (372 U.S. 58: 1963), the Court struck down a statute that established a commission to convey to booksellers the potential for prosecution if objectionable material was sold. The Court felt these informal sanctions were effective censorship wholly lacking in necessary safeguards.

Film Licensure

Freedman v. *Maryland,* 380 U.S. 51, 85 S.Ct. 734, 13 L.Ed. 2d 649 (1965)   Upheld a film licensure requirement with particular procedural safeguards. *Freedman* explores the fact that most cases challenging obscenity enactments focus on the substantive distinction between protected and unprotected expression. The problem is defining obscenity. *Freedman* targeted the actual technique of censorship. Freedman violated a Maryland statute requiring licensure to exhibit motion pictures. He refused to submit a film to the State Board of Censors prior to showing it. Maryland stipulated that the film would have been licensed had it been submitted. Freedman sought, however, to have movie censorship declared unconstitutional per se. The Court did not go as far as Freedman wanted, but it unanimously reversed his conviction. The Court said a prior restraint mechanism bears a "heavy presumption against its constitutional validity." Specifically, the "administration of a censorship proceeding puts the initial burden on the exhibitor or distributor." The justices went on to outline procedural safeguards "designed to obviate the dangers of the censorship system." First, the "burden of proving that the film is unprotected expression must rest with the censor." Second, while advance submissions may be required, no film may be banned through means "which would lend an effect of finality to the censor's determination." Third, a film cannot be banned unless the process permits judicial determination of the restraint. Fourth, various steps in the process must not take too long. "The exhibitor must be assured that the censor will within a specified brief period, either issue a license or go to court to restrain the showing of the film." Any restraints imposed prior to final judicial determination must be "limited to preservation of the status quo for the shortest fixed period." Finally, the "procedure must also assure a prompt final judicial decision, to minimize the deterrent effect of an interim and possibly erroneous denial of a license." These safeguards are absolute requirements. Without such limitations, "it may prove too burdensome to seek review of the censor's determination." The Court concluded that the Maryland censorship process did not sufficiently incorporate its stipulated safeguards. *See also* BILL OF RIGHTS, p. 7; FIRST AMENDMENT, p. 77; *KINGSLEY BOOKS, INC.* V. *BROWN* (354 U.S. 436: 1957), p. 139.

Significance   *Freedman* v. *Maryland* (380 U.S. 51: 1965) raised serious prior restraint questions. Censorship of films occurred from the time films were first produced, and Supreme Court decisions extended virtually no free press protections for them. As motion pictures evolved, however, their unprotected status changed, and censorship techniques such as those in *Freedman* demanded Court attention. A key case in elevating films to partial coverage by the First Amendment was *Burstyn* v. *Wilson* (343 U.S. 495: 1952). The Court found that it "cannot be doubted that motion pictures are a significant medium for the communication of ideas." Although films may possess a "greater capacity for evil," such potential "does not authorize substantially unbridled censorship." While *Freedman* did not condemn the practice of censorship per se, it established important procedural requirements. Arbitrary interference with exhibitors is not permitted. In *Roaden* v. *Kentucky* (413 U.S. 496: 1973), the Court unanimously determined that a warrantless seizure of a film during its showing by a county sheriff was a prior restraint. Similarly, in *Southeastern Promotions, Ltd.* v. *Conrad* (419 U.S. 892: 1975), the Court held that a city's refusal to rent a city facility for a performance of *Hair* was a prior restraint. The Court said city officials may deny a forum to an obscene production, but such a decision must be made through a properly safeguarded process. In *Heller* v. *New York* (413 U.S. 483: 1973) the Court did uphold the seizure of a film under authority of a warrant from a judge who had viewed it prior to signing the warrant.

ASSEMBLY AND PROTEST

Public Premises

Adderley v. Florida, 385 U.S. 39, 87 S.Ct. 242, 17 L.Ed. 2d 149 (1966)   Held that demonstrators may be barred from assembly on the grounds of a county jail. *Adderley* considered whether certain locations might be put off limits to demonstrations or assemblies.

Adderley and a number of others were convicted of trespass for gathering at a county jail to protest the arrest of several students the day before, as well as local policies of racial segregation at the jail itself. When the demonstrators would not leave the jail grounds when asked, they were warned of possible arrest for trespass. Adderley and others remained on the premises, were arrested, and were subsequently tried and convicted. The Court upheld the convictions in a 5–4 decision. The Court focused on the question of whether the trespass convictions deprived the demonstrators of their freedom of speech. Through Justice Black, the Court majority concluded that "nothing in the Constitution of the United States prevented Florida from even-handed enforcement of its general trespass statute against those refusing to obey the sheriff's order to remove themselves from what amounted to the curtilage of the jailhouse." The fact that the jail was a public building did not automatically entitle the protesters to demonstrate there. The state, no less than a private owner of property, has power to preserve the property under its control for the use to which it is lawfully dedicated. The security purpose to which the jail was dedicated outweighed the expression interests of the protesters. The justices felt that to find for Adderley would be to endorse "the assumption that people who want to propagandize protests or views have a constitutional right to do so whenever and wherever they please." The Court categorically rejected that premise and concluded its opinion by saying the Constitution does not forbid a state to control the use of its own property for its own lawful nondiscriminatory purposes. Justice Douglas dissented, joined by Chief Justice Warren and Justices Brennan and Fortas. Justice Douglas considered the jailhouse "one of the seats of government" and an "obvious center for protest." *See also* FIRST AMENDMENT, p. 77; *PRUNEYARD SHOPPING CENTER* V. *ROBINS* (447 U.S. 74: 1980), p. 144; *TINKER* V. *DES MOINES SCHOOL DISTRICT* (393 U.S. 503: 1969), p. 113.

Significance   *Adderley* v. *Florida* (385 U.S. 39: 1966) illustrated the "speech plus" test. In certain situations speech is defined as conduct beyond oral expression itself. The additional conduct is subject to regulation at a cost to expression. In *Cox* v. *Louisiana* (379 U.S. 536: 1965), the Court upheld a state statute that prohibited picketing near a courthouse. It said a state could legitimately insulate its judicial proceedings from demonstrations. While restrictions were said to be warranted in *Adderley* and *Cox*, breach of the peace convictions of persons demonstrating on the grounds of a state capitol were reversed in *Edwards* v. *South Carolina* (372 U.S. 229: 1963). Similarly, a peaceful sit-in at a public library was protected in *Brown* v. *Louisiana* (383 U.S. 131: 1966). More recently, the Court struck down an ordinance that prohibited picketing in the proximity of school buildings when classes were in session in *Chicago Police Department* v. *Mosley* (408 U.S. 92: 1972). The ordinance was invalidated largely because it excepted labor picketing from the ban. The Court did suggest the city had a legitimate interest in preventing school disruption, however. Time, place, and manner restrictions have generally been recognized by the Court, provided that significant governmental interests can be demonstrated. Trespass on private property was subject to punishment for many years, although civil-rights sit-ins forced a legislative reevaluation of that policy. The Supreme Court successfully avoided dealing with the sit-in issue directly until passage of the Civil Rights Act of 1964. The act prohibited the discriminatory practices in public accommodations that had triggered the sit-in demonstrations in the first place.

Private Property

***PruneYard Shopping Center* v. *Robins,* 447 U.S. 74, 100 S.Ct. 2035, 64 L.Ed. 2d 741 (1980)**   Declared that demonstrators may access privately owned shopping malls to circulate petitions and distribute political pamphlets. *PruneYard* involved a group of high school students who sought to express their opposition to a United Nations Resolution against Zionism. They set up a table near the central courtyard of the shopping center, began distributing pamphlets, and asked patrons of the shopping center to sign a petition. The students were orderly, and no objection to their presence was registered by any shopping center customer. The students were informed by a shopping center security guard that their activity was in violation of a center policy that prohibited all such conduct. The group subsequently filed suit seeking access to the center through a court order. The trial court refused to issue such an order, but the California Supreme Court held that the state constitution entitled the students access to the mall. The United States Supreme Court upheld the California Supreme Court in a unanimous decision. The crucial issue for the Court was whether state-protected rights of expression infringed upon the property rights of PruneYard's owners. Citing the state court opinion, Justice Rehnquist said that "a handful of additional orderly persons soliciting signatures and distributing handbills do not interfere with normal business operations." They "would not markedly dilute defendant's property rights." Three other arguments were developed to support the judgment of the California Supreme Court. First, PruneYard, "by the choice of its owner is not limited to the personal use of the appellants." PruneYard is rather a "business establishment that is open to the public." Any views expressed by center patrons "thus will not likely be identified with those of the owner." Second, the state's insistence that PruneYard's private property be made available was content neutral in that there was "no danger of governmental discrimination for or against a particular message." Finally, PruneYard and its constituent shop owners could easily disclaim any connection to the expression of the demonstrators. They could explain that the "persons are communicating their own messages by virtue of state law." *See also* ADDERLEY V. FLORIDA (385 U.S. 39: 1966), p. 142; BILL OF RIGHTS, p. 7; FIRST AMENDMENT, p. 77.

Significance   *PruneYard Shopping Center* v. *Robins* (447 U.S. 74: 1980) treats the troublesome issue of demonstrator access to private property. The Burger Court position in *PruneYard* represents a compromise between several of its own previous decisions and those of the Warren Court. The Warren Court view is best illustrated in *Amalgamated Food Employees Union* v. *Logan Valley Plaza* (391 U.S. 308: 1968). In *Logan Valley,* the Court upheld the picketing of a business located in a privately owned shopping center, basing the decision directly on the First Amendment. The Burger Court reconsidered *Logan Valley* in *Lloyd Corporation* v. *Tanner* (407 U.S. 551: 1972) and upheld a restriction on handbilling. While the shopping center invites patrons, the Burger Court said, it is not an invitation of unlimited scope. The invitation is to do business with the tenants of the center. There is "no open-ended invitation to the public to use the center for any and all purposes, however incompatible with the interests of both the stores and the shoppers whom they serve." In addition, the restriction did not deprive the persons from distributing their handbills on the public sidewalks surrounding the center. The Burger Court abandoned *Logan Valley* altogether in *Hudgens* v. *National Labor Relations Board* (424 U.S. 507: 1976). In *Hudgens,* union members attempted to picket the retail store of their employer, which was located in a privately owned mall. Citing *Lloyd,* the Court held that the First Amendment "has no part to play in such a case as this." Thus the Burger Court divorced privately owned shopping centers from First Amendment reach. Through the *PruneYard* decision, however, it did allow protection of expression to flow from state constitutional provisions.

Enjoining Assembly

***Carroll* v. *President and Commissioners of Princess Anne*, 393 U.S. 175, 89 S.Ct. 347, 21 L.Ed. 2d 325 (1968)**   Struck down an ex parte injunction prohibiting a rally of a militant white supremacist organization. *Carroll* speaks to the manner by which court restraining orders may be sought to enjoin persons from demonstrating in some way. Such injunctions are frequently, but not always, used in situations where permits or licenses to march or demonstrate have been denied. Carroll, a member of a white supremacist organization known as the National States Rights party, participated in a rally at which aggressively and militantly racist and anti-Semitic speeches were made. At the conclusion of the speeches, it was announced that the rally would be resumed the next night. Local government officials obtained a restraining order in the meantime in an ex parte proceeding. The injunction restrained Carroll and others from holding public meetings for ten days. The Supreme Court struck down the order in a unanimous judgment. The Court's primary objection was to the ex parte procedure. The order was issued "without notice to petitioners and without any effort, however informal, to invite or permit their participation in the proceedings." The Court recognized that ex parte orders may be appropriate in some situations, "but there is no place within the area of basic freedoms guaranteed by the First Amendment for such orders." Absence of an adversary proceeding deprives a trial court of the facts necessary to make a judgment. There is "insufficient assurance of the balanced analysis and careful conclusions which are essential in the area of First Amendment adjudication." The same absence of information makes it more difficult to construct an order in the narrowest and least stifling terms. *See also* ADDERLEY V. FLORIDA (385 U.S. 39: 1966), p. 142; BILL OF RIGHTS, p. 7; FIRST AMENDMENT, p. 77.

Significance   *Carroll* v. *President and Commissioners of Princess Anne* (393 U.S. 175: 1968) established procedural guidelines through which court orders might be obtained against demonstrators. The permit-injunction approach had often been used against civil rights demonstrators. In *Walker* v. *Birmingham* (388 U.S. 307: 1967), the

Court upheld an injunction issued following denial of a parade permit. Walker, Martin Luther King, Jr., and others involved in the proposed parade disobeyed the injunction without seeking appellate review of either the injunction or the permit denial that precipitated the court order. A five-justice majority found the potentially persuasive objections to the Birmingham permit system to be subordinate to the failure of the demonstrators to obey the court order. The dissenters in *Walker* would have voided the injunction on the grounds that the permit system was unconstitutionally discriminatory. Permits are satisfactory as long as they are confined to reasonable time, place, and manner limitations. Permit or license requirements that are not content neutral or that allow too much discretion to permit-granting officials are unacceptable to the Court. A more recent injunction episode involved attempts by the Village of Skokie, Illinois, to prevent an assembly of the National Socialist Party of America, a self-proclaimed Nazi organization. More than half of Skokie's residents are Jewish, and a sizable number are survivors of German concentration camps. Prior to the assembly, an injunction was secured from a state court enjoining the National Socialist Party from a uniformed march, display of swastikas, and distribution of materials that might "promote hatred against persons of the Jewish faith or ancestry." The Illinois Supreme Court refused to stay the injunction. The United States Supreme Court, in *National Socialist Party* v. *Village of Skokie* (432 U.S. 43: 1977), reversed because the denial of the stay at the state level deprived the party of its right to demonstrate for the period until an appellate review could occur. The period was estimated to be a year or more. The Court said that if a "State seeks to impose a restraint of this kind, it must provide strict procedural safeguards including appellate review. Absent such review, the State must instead allow the stay." The party never assembled in Skokie, choosing instead to hold a rally in a Chicago park.

ASSOCIATION

The National Association for the Advancement of Colored People (NAACP) v. Alabama, 357 U.S. 449, 78 S.Ct. 1163, 2 L.Ed. 2d 1488 (1958) Examined the nature of constitutional protection for the freedom of association. *NAACP* involved an attempt by the state of Alabama to compel disclosure of the NAACP membership list as a means of inhibiting the operation of the organization. Alabama sought to enjoin NAACP activities within the state because the association had failed to comply with a statutory requirement that all out-of-state corporations file certain information. Among the documents the NAACP was ordered to produce was a list of all names and addresses of members and agents in Alabama. The association refused to disclose such a list and was cited for contempt and fined. The Supreme Court reversed the contempt judgment unanimously. The Court's opinion provided the foundation of the concept of the constitutional right of association. In its opinion the Court first had to resolve the matter of standing. Alabama argued that the NAACP could not "assert constitutional rights pertaining to the member," but the Court found the association's "nexus with them is sufficient to permit that it act as their representative." The Court determined in fact that the NAACP is the "appropriate party to assert these rights, because it and its members are in every practical sense identical." The Court then moved on to the infringement of protected freedoms threatened by the compulsory disclosure. It recognized that "effective advocacy of both public and private points of view, particularly controversial ones, is undeniably enhanced by group association." The compelled disclosure was viewed as affecting "adversely the ability of the petitioner and its members to pursue their collective effort to foster beliefs which they admittedly have a right to advocate." The Court saw disclosure as having adverse consequences in two ways. First, the NAACP itself would likely suffer diminished financial support and fewer membership applications. Second, disclosure of the identity of members might prompt "economic reprisal, loss of employment, threat of physical coercion, and other manifestations of public hostility." The Court found that Alabama had not shown a "controlling justification for the deterrent effect on the free enjoyment of the right to associate which disclosure of membership lists is likely to have." *See also* FIRST AMENDMENT, p. 77; KEYISHIAN V. BOARD OF REGENTS (385 U.S. 589: 1967), p. 151; WHITNEY V. CALIFORNIA (274 U.S. 357: 1927), p. 149.

Significance   The *National Association for the Advancement of Colored People* v. *Alabama* (375 U.S. 449: 1958) marked the beginning of a new era for associational rights. In a similar judgment, *Shelton* v. *Tucker* (364 U.S. 479: 1960), the Court struck down a state statute requiring every public school teacher to disclose annually every organization supported by his or her membership or contribution. The Court determined that even a legitimate inquiry into a teacher's fitness and competence "cannot be pursued by means that broadly stifle fundamental personal liberties when the end can be more narrowly achieved." Associational ties have also been an issue with respect to admission to the bar. In *Baird* v. *State Bar* (401 U.S. 1: 1971), the Court held that applicants to the bar may not be compelled to disclose organizational memberships. "Views and beliefs are immune from bar association inquisitions designed to lay a foundation for barring an applicant from the practice of law." In *Law Students Civil Rights Research Council, Inc.* v. *Wadmond* (401 U.S. 154: 1971), however, the Court upheld bar admission inquiries into character and fitness, including questions probing membership in associations advocating unlawful overthrow of the government. While not directly involving the disclosure issue, the NAACP was able to affirm another dimension of associational freedom in *NAACP* v. *Button* (371 U.S. 415: 1963). *Button* upheld the NAACP's strategy of representing membership interests through litigation. Many states had enacted antisolicitation laws prohibiting the "stirring up" of lawsuits. In the case of the NAACP, the Court recognized such activity as a means for achieving lawful objectives and a form of political expression. Indeed, "for such a group, association for litigation may be the most effective form of political association." Litigation seeking vindication of constitutional rights is a different matter from avaricious use of the legal process purely for personal gain.

Whitney v. California, 274 U.S. 357, 47 S.Ct. 641, 7 L.Ed. 1095 (1927)   Upheld a state criminal syndicalism statute making it a crime to belong to an organization advocating use of unlawful force to achieve its political objectives. *Whitney* was one of the first cases in which the Supreme Court examined the conviction of a political radical. The right of association is not explicitly provided in the First Amendment, yet there is a recognized relationship between group association and the freedom of expression and assembly protected by the First Amendment. *Whitney* tested the limits of the relationship. Whitney was convicted of violating California's Criminal Syndicalism Act, which prohibited organizing and being a member of a group advocating unlawful force as a political weapon. She had participated in a convention of the Communist Labor Party of California that had passed resolutions advocating various revolutionary acts. Whitney asserted she had not supported the resolutions nor had she wished the party to urge violation of California's laws. She was convicted because she had remained at the convention and had not disassociated herself from the party after the resolutions were adopted. The Supreme Court upheld her conviction in a unanimous decision. The

Court's opinion by Justice Sanford argued guilt by association. The Court refused to reexamine the jury's fact determination that Whitney had not sufficiently detached herself from the party. The Court simply noted that remaining in attendance until the close of the convention and maintaining membership "manifested her acquiescence." The justices said that California's approach did not restrain free speech or assembly. The "essence of the offense denounced by the Act is the combining with others in an association for the accomplishment of the desired ends through the advocacy and use of criminal and unlawful methods." Because such united and joint action constituted an even greater threat to public peace and security, a state may reasonably exercise its police power to prevent groups from "menacing the peace and welfare of the State." Justice Brandeis wrote a concurring opinion joined in by Justice Holmes. Justice Brandeis urged use of the clear and present danger test in cases such as this. If insufficient danger flowed from the discussion, resolutions such as those of the Communist Labor Party may be protected. Justice Brandeis offered that "the wide difference between advocacy and incitement, between preparation and attempt, between assembling and conspiracy must be borne in mind. In order to support a finding of clear and present danger, it must be shown either that immediate serious violence was to be expected or was advocated or that past conduct furnished reason to believe that such advocacy was contemplated." *See also* DENNIS V. UNITED STATES (341 U.S. 494: 1951), p. 111; KEYISHIAN V. BOARD OF REGENTS (385 U.S. 589: 1967), p. 151; NAACP V. ALABAMA (357 U.S. 449: 1958), p. 147.

Significance   Whitney v. *California* (274 U.S. 357: 1927) seemed to provide license for convicting political radicals because of their association alone, but the Court began to disengage from *Whitney* almost immediately. In *Fiske* v. *Kansas* (274 U.S. 380: 1927), the Court reversed a criminal syndicalism conviction of a labor organizer because of insufficient evidence in linking his organization to illegal activity. In *DeJonge* v. *Oregon* (299 U.S. 353: 1937) and *Herndon* v. *Lowry* (301 U.S. 242: 1937), the Court reversed convictions of admitted members of the Communist Party because as individuals neither defendant had violated a criminal law. While an organization may have criminal objectives, simply attending a peaceful meeting called by such an organization cannot transfer criminal liability. The formal end to *Whitney* came in *Brandenburg* v. *Ohio* (395 U.S. 444: 1969), in which the Court unanimously struck down a state syndicalism statute. The defendant in this case was the leader of a Ku

Klux Klan group who had spoken at a Klan rally. The Court said "the mere abstract teaching of the moral propriety or even moral necessity for a resort to force and violence is not the same as preparing a group for violent action and steeling it for such action." Accordingly, a statute that fails to draw this distinction impermissibly intrudes on First Amendment freedoms. *Whitney* was decided at a time when large segments of the American people were preoccupied with a "Red scare." It was also prior to the time that the utility of group association was widely appreciated. The impact of *Whitney* in the 1980s is negligible, but it establishes a useful historical perspective on the right of association.

Keyishian v. *Board of Regents*, **385 U.S. 589, 87 S.Ct. 675, 17 L.Ed. 2d 629 (1967)**   Required that more than "mere membership" in organizations be demonstrated before the imposition of restrictions on associational rights. *Keyishian* examined New York statutory provisions known collectively as the Feinberg Law, which authorized the Board of Regents to monitor organizational memberships of state employees. The board was required to generate a list of subversive organizations. Membership in any one of them was prima facie evidence of disqualification from public employment, including appointments to academic positions. While the person being terminated could have a hearing, the hearing could not address the matter of the subversive classification of the organization. Keyishian and several other faculty members in the state university system were dismissed because of their membership in the Communist Party. The Court struck down the Feinberg Law in a 5–4 decision. The majority rejected the premise that "public employment, including academic employment, may be conditioned upon the surrender of constitutional rights which could not be abridged by direct government action." The Court found "mere membership" to be an insufficient basis for exclusion. "Legislation which sanctions membership unaccompanied by specific intent to further the unlawful goals of the organization or which is not active membership violates constitutional limitations." The Court also said the statutes "sweep overbroadly in association which may not be proscribed." The regulations "seek to bar employment both for association which legitimately may be proscribed and for association which may not be sanctioned." The flaw of overbroad sweep was as fatal as the flaw of vagueness. The dissenters, Justices Clark, Harlan, Stewart, and White, reacted strongly by saying the Court majority "has by its broadside swept away one of our most precious rights, namely the right of self-preservation." *See* *also* DENNIS V. UNITED STATES (341 U.S. 494: 1951), p. 111; NAACP V. ALABAMA (357 U.S. 449: 1958), p. 147; WHITNEY V. CALIFORNIA (274 U.S. 357: 1927), p. 149.

Significance   *Keyishian* v. *Board of Regents* (385 U.S. 589: 1967) overturned *Adler* v. *Board of Education* (342 U.S. 485: 1952), decided fifteen years earlier. *Adler* had found the Feinberg Law constitutional, deciding that teachers "have no right to work for the State in the school system on their own terms." The state may inquire into the fitness and suitability of a person for public service and past conduct may well relate to present fitness. In addition, one's associates, past and present, may properly be considered in determining fitness and loyalty. "From time immemorial, one's reputation has been determined in part by the company he keeps." Shortly after *Keyishian,* in *United States* v. *Robel* (389 U.S. 258: 1967), the Court voided a McCarron Act provision that prohibited any member of a Communist action organization from working in a defense facility. As in *Keyishian,* the Court found the statute "casts its net across a broad range of associational activities, indiscriminately trapping membership which can be constitutionally punished and membership which cannot be so proscribed." In a decision predating *Keyishian* and *Robel* by a year, but using similar rationale, the Court struck down a loyalty oath provision that imposed penalties upon anyone taking the oath who might later become a member of a subversive organization. The case was *Elfbrandt* v. *Russell* (384 U.S. 11: 1966). The Burger Court did uphold a loyalty oath in *Cole* v. *Richardson* (405 U.S. 676: 1972), which required public employees to uphold and defend the federal and state constitutions and to oppose the overthrow of federal or state governments by illegal means. *Cole* found the oath sufficient in that it did not impose specific action obligations on persons taking it. It required only a general commitment to abide by constitutional processes.

Electoral Process

Buckley v. Valeo, 424 U.S. 1, 96 S.Ct. 612, 46 L.Ed. 2d 659 (1976)   Examined the constitutionality of the Federal Election Campaign Act of 1974. *Buckley* considered the act against various First Amendment challenges, including the possibility that regulation of the electoral process impinges upon individual and group expression. The Federal Election Campaign Act was passed in the wake of Watergate. It sought to protect the electoral process by (1) limiting political campaign contributions, (2) establishing ceilings on several categories of campaign expenditures, (3) requiring extensive and regular disclosure of campaign contributors and expenditures, (4) providing public financing for presidential campaigns, and (5) creating the Federal Election Commission to administer the act. Suit was filed by a diverse collection of individuals and groups that included United States Senator James Buckley, the Eugene McCarthy presidential campaign, the Libertarian Party, the American Conservative Union, and the New York Civil Liberties Union. By differing majorities, the Court upheld those portions of the act that provided for campaign contribution limits, disclosure, public financing, and the election commission. The section imposing limits on expenditures was invalidated. In a per curiam opinion, the Court said the act's contribution and expenditure ceiling "reduces the quantity of expression because virtually every means of communicating ideas in today's society requires the expenditure of money." The Court distinguished, however, between limits on contributions and limits on those things for which the contributions might be spent. While the latter represents substantial restraint on the quantity and diversity of political speech, limits on contributions involve "little direct restraint." The contributor's freedom to discuss candidates and issues is not infringed in any way. Even though contributions may underwrite some costs of conveying a campaign's views, the contributions must be transformed into political expression by persons other than the contributor. The Court acknowledged a legitimate governmental interest in protecting the "integrity of our system of representative democracy" from quid pro quo arrangements that might arise from financial contributions. Expenditure limits, on the other hand, severely burden one's ability to speak one's mind and engage in vigorous advocacy. Neither is the First Amendment to be used to equalize political influence. "The concept that government may restrict the speech of some elements of our society in order to enhance the relative voice of others is wholly foreign to the First Amendment." By striking the expenditure limits, the Court allowed unlimited use of personal wealth or expenditures made on behalf of campaigns separate from the actual campaign organization of a candidate. On the matter of disclosure, the Court agreed that the requirement might deter some contributions but viewed it as a "least restrictive means of curbing the evils of campaign ignorance and corruption." The Court also upheld the act's public financing provisions by rejecting a claim that a differential funding formula for major and minor parties was unconstitutional. *See also* FIRST AMENDMENT, p. 77; *NAACP v. ALABAMA* (357 U.S. 449: 1958), p. 147; *WHITNEY v. CALIFORNIA* (274 U.S. 357: 1927), p. 149.

Significance   *Buckley* v. *Valeo* (424 U.S. 1: 1976) generated important followup questions regarding regulation of the electoral process. In *First National Bank of Boston* v. *Bellotti* (435 U.S. 765: 1978), the Court struck down a state statute prohibiting the use of corporate funds for the purpose of influencing a referendum question. Without a showing that the corporation's advocacy "threatened imminently to undermine democratic processes," the state has no interest sufficient to limit a corporation's expression of views on a public issue. In *Consolidated Edison Company* v. *Public Service Commission of New York* (447 U.S. 530: 1980), the Court overturned a state commission order prohibiting utilities from enclosing inserts discussing public policy issues in billing envelopes. The Court said the order was aimed at the pro–nuclear energy content of the insert and was not justifiable as a time, place, or manner restriction on speech. Finally, in *Citizens Against Rent Control/Coalition for Fair Housing* v. *City of Berkeley* (450 U.S. 908: 1981), the Court struck down a municipal ordinance limiting contributions to organizations formed to support or oppose ballot issues. With only Justice White dissenting, the Court drew heavily on *Buckley* and concluded that the ordinance went too far in restraining individual and associational rights of expression.

3. The Fourth Amendment

OVERVIEW

The Fourth Amendment states:

> The right of the people to be secure in their persons, houses, papers, and effects, against unreasonable searches and seizures, shall not be violated, and no Warrants shall issue, but upon probable cause, supported by Oath or affirmation, and particularly describing the place to be searched, and the persons or things to be seized.

The Fourth Amendment requires that invasions of privacy occur only under authority of a warrant. A warrant is to be issued by a neutral party based upon probable cause and must particularly describe what is to be searched for or seized. Probable cause is given its basic definition in *Draper* v. *United States* (385 U.S. 307: 1959), while neutral party and particularity are discussed in *Coolidge* v. *New Hampshire* (403 U.S. 443: 1971) and *Ybarra* v. *Illinois* (444 U.S. 85: 1979), respectively.

Contemporary application of the Fourth Amendment involves other warrant issues as well. *United States* v. *Harris* (403 U.S. 573: 1971) weighs the use of information from informants to establish probable cause. *Steagald* v. *United States* (451 U.S. 204: 1981) distinguishes the interests protected by arrest and search warrants and considers whether an arrest warrant for one individual can cover the search of another individual's home. *Zurcher* v. *Stanford Daily* (436 U.S. 547: 1978) decides whether a state is prevented from issuing a search warrant simply because the possessor of the place to be searched is not suspected of criminal conduct. *Katz* v. *United States* (389 U.S. 347: 1967) and *Dalia* v. *United States* (441 U.S. 238: 1979) examine the authorization requirements for electronic surveillance and covert entry to implement an approved surveillance. *Mapp* v. *Ohio* (367 U.S. 643: 1961) and *Stone* v. *Powell* (428 U.S. 465: 1976) discuss the exclusionary rule, a rule of evidence that disallows use of evidence secured by means of an unreasonable search.

Failure to secure a warrant does not necessarily make a search unreasonable. Several warrant exceptions have evolved. *Chimel* v. *California* (395 U.S. 752: 1969) and *United States* v. *Edwards* (415 U.S.

800: 1974) explore unwarranted searches conducted incident to valid arrests. The "exigent circumstance" exception is developed in *Michigan* v. *Tyler* (436 U.S. 499: 1978), and the "plain view" exception is described in *Washington* v. *Chrisman* (455 U.S. 1: 1982). Searches of automobiles have generally been viewed as exigent situations, with several aspects of these searches examined in *Chambers* v. *Maroney* (399 U.S. 42: 1970), *United States* v. *Robinson* (414 U.S. 218: 1973), *South Dakota* v. *Opperman* (428 U.S. 364: 1978), and *Robbins* v. *California* (453 U.S. 420: 1981). The cases of *Terry* v. *Ohio* (392 U.S. 1: 1968) and *Brown* v. *Texas* (443 U.S. 47: 1979) provided the Court an opportunity to consider the "stop and frisk" search technique. The matter of consent search is treated in *Schneckloth* v. *Bustamonte* (412 U.S. 218: 1973) and *United States* v. *Matlock* (415 U.S. 164: 1974). In the former case the suspect himself gave consent; in the latter permission was obtained from someone other than the suspect under investigation.

The Fourth Amendment entry and an elaboration of the above definitional cases follow.

The Fourth Amendment   Safeguards American citizens from unreasonable searches and seizures. The Fourth Amendment was included in the Bill of Rights as the direct result of the British imposition in the American colonies of writs of assistance. These general warrants allowed for arbitrary searches and seizures of persons and property. They proliferated in the years immediately preceding the American Revolution when they were issued to seize contraband smuggled into the colonies in violation of acts of parliament imposing duties and tariffs on imports. In *Lopez* v. *United States* (373 U.S. 427: 1963), Justice William J. Brennan said, "The evil of the general warrant is often regarded as the single immediate cause of the American Revolution." As early as 1761 James Otis, a prominent Boston lawyer and merchant, was railing against the use of writs of assistance. John Adams considered such condemnations the foundation of the Revolution. Of Otis's denunciations Adams wrote, "Then and there was the first scene of the first act of opposition to the arbitrary claims of Great Britain. Then and there the child Independence was born." When the child was more mature, it insisted on specific language to ensure that probable cause existed to issue a warrant. It said that name, place, and things sought must be identified. Further, the warrant must issue from a neutral magistrate who would be a disinterested third party between the individual citizen and the law enforcement officer seeking the warrant. Yet the Fourth Amendment only extended to the federal government in early American history. After passage of the Fourteenth Amendment in 1868, coverage of the Fourth Amendment could be extended to the states through the Fourteenth Amendment's Due Process Clause. The modern nationalization of the Fourth Amendment was dramatically interpreted by the Supreme Court in such cases as *Mapp* v. *Ohio* (367 U.S. 643: 1961), *Ker* v. *California* (374 U.S. 23: 1963), *Aguilar* v. *Texas* (378 U.S. 108: 1964), and *Chimel* v. *California* (395 U.S. 752: 1969). The wind changed, however, with Richard M. Nixon's "law and order mandate" in 1968, and with his appointment of Warren E. Burger as Chief Justice of the United States. With more conservative appointments such as this, decisions of the Court have gradually moved from limiting the scope of permissible searches and seizures to limiting the scope of the rights of criminal defendants, including the parameters of permissibility. In 1973, for example, the Burger Court upheld full searches of individuals lawfully arrested for traffic violations without the existence of evidence of probable cause (*United States* v. *Robinson*, 414 U.S. 218; *Gustafson* v. *Florida*, 414 U.S. 260). Thus specific abuses under the Fourth Amendment are reinterpreted over time. *See also*

BILL OF RIGHTS, p. 7; *CHIMEL V. CALIFORNIA* (395 U.S. 752: 1969), p. 175; *MAPP V. OHIO* (367 U.S. 643: 1961), p. 172.

Significance   The Fourth Amendment established an absolute right against threat of unreasonable intrusion by agents and officials of the newly formed American government. The clamor for the Fourth Amendment, as well as the other nine amendments in the Bill of Rights, came out of the state constitutional ratifying conventions. The delegates to the Maryland convention said, for example, that the adoption of the Fourth Amendment was necessary because "a free people" must be provided a constitutional check effective to "safeguard our citizens" against the issuance of general warrants. In making their arguments, many of the states relied heavily on the language of Sir William Blackstone's *Commentaries on the Laws of England,* Volume IV, in which general warrants were declared to be illegal. Elements of Blackstone's language found their way into both the Constitution and the Bill of Rights. The English constitution did forbid the issuance of general writs. In 1766 Parliament expressly declared all general warrants for search and seizure illegal, but abuses of both common and statutory law were prevalent in Great Britain and in the American colonies in the late eighteenth century. Just prior to the American Revolution, members of Parliament were in fact debating the abuses of the general warrant process. Among the discussants were Sir Edward Coke, Sir Matthew Hale, and especially Lord Camden, who found the general warrant wholly outside the spirit of the English constitution. Lord Camden was quoted by a justice of the United States Supreme Court as late as 1886, when Joseph P. Bradley wrote in *Boyd* v. *United States* (116 U.S. 616) that Camden's exposition expressed "the true doctrine on the subject of searches and seizures." It furnished "the true criteria of the reasonable and unreasonable character of such searches." The true doctrine and the true criteria are settled in American jurisprudence as the sanctity of a citizen's home and person. Hopefully the fundamental values safeguarded by the framers' prohibition against unreasonable searches seizures will far outlast changing historical circumstances.

Probable Cause

Draper v. United States, 385 U.S. 307, 70 S.Ct. 329, 3 L.Ed.2d 327 (1959)   Examined criteria for establishing probable cause.

Draper was arrested in Chicago by a federal agent who neither knew Draper nor had seen him commit any criminal offense. The experienced agent had been told by a "previously reliable" informant that Draper was engaged in narcotics distribution and that Draper would be arriving in Chicago by train. The arrest of Draper occurred at the railroad station, where the officer recognized Draper from the physical description provided by the informant. A search conducted incident to the arrest yielded heroin. Draper was subsequently convicted on narcotics charges, and the heroin was admitted into evidence. With only Justice Douglas dissenting, the Supreme Court upheld the search. The critical question for the Court was whether the arresting officer had probable cause to make the arrest. In dealing with probable cause, the Court emphasized that the evidence needed to satisfy the standard is quite different from that needed to prove guilt. The Court said, "We deal with probabilities. These are not technical; they are the factual and practical considerations of everyday life on which reasonable and prudent men, not legal technicians, act." The arresting officer had found the informant accurate and reliable in the past, and the arresting officer "would have been derelict in his duties" had he not pursued the information. As a standard of probable cause, the Court suggested it exists where reasonably trustworthy information known to authorities is sufficient "to warrant a man of reasonable caution in the belief that an offense has been or is being committed." Thus the arresting officer had probable cause, his arrest of Draper was valid, and the search of Draper incident to the arrest could produce admissible evidence. *See also* FOURTH AMENDMENT, p. 159; PROBABLE CAUSE, p. 446; *TERRY* V. *OHIO* (392 U.S. 1: 1968), p. 188; *UNITED STATES* V. *HARRIS* (403 U.S. 573: 1971), p. 165.

Significance   Arrest and search incident to an arrest, without a warrant, depend upon whether the arresting officer has probable cause. Even where the arresting officer is acting on hearsay information, he or she is entitled to consider such information in determining whether the officer has probable cause within the meaning of the Fourth Amendment. *Draper* v. *United States* (385 U.S. 307: 1959) provides the perspective that while an arrest or search is a governmental intrusion, and while a warrant can authorize the intrusion, a warrantless arrest and search are legally permitted if probable cause exists. Probable cause is defined as the level of evidence or knowledge required to convince a neutral third party, typically a judge or magistrate, to issue a warrant. The test applied is essentially the same test an officer must use in searching without a warrant. *Draper* establishes that probable cause relates to reasonable inferences rather than technical judgments drawn from rigid legal requirements. It is clear that probable cause does not require support conclusive of guilt. It deals with probabilities. The probabilities must be sufficiently high in the judgment of the magistrate to focus closely enough on a person or a place to justify an authorized invasion of privacy. The probable cause standard can be met by providing evidence such as direct observation of criminal acts by a law enforcement officer or indirect observation by citizens or informants, physical evidence, or accounts of crimes by witnesses. The *Draper* test requires a nonneutral police officer to exercise the same judgment as a neutral judge. When an officer makes a warrantless search the question is, Did the officer have probable cause to make an arrest and a search pursuant to that arrest?

Neutral Magistrate

Coolidge v. *New Hampshire,* **403 U.S. 443, 91 S.Ct. 2022, 29 L.Ed.2d 564 (1971)**   Considered who shall make the determination of probable cause. During an investigation of Coolidge, some evidence was obtained from his home without a search warrant. After his arrest, following warrantless seizure of guns and other evidence, a warrant to search Coolidge's automobile was obtained by the state. The arrest and search warrants, however, had been issued by the state attorney general acting as a justice of the peace, a practice permitted under state law. Prior to issuing the warrants, the attorney general had supervised the police investigation of the case, and he subsequently served as chief prosecutor at Coolidge's trial. An incidental issue was that during the investigation, Coolidge's automobile, parked in his driveway, was towed to the police station, where it was searched three times over the course of more than a year. Several search exemption questions stemmed from this fact. The Supreme Court concluded that the warrants issued by the attorney general were irreparably flawed. The majority said the Fourth Amendment offers protection by requiring that inferences made from evidence "are drawn by neutral and detached magistrates instead of being judged by the officer engaged in the often competitive enterprise of ferreting out crime." The Court felt that "there could hardly be a more appropriate setting than this for a *per se* rule of disqualification" because "prosecutors and police simply cannot be asked to maintain the requisite neutrality with regard to their own investigations." Since the attorney general could not be regarded as the "neutral and detached magistrate required by the Constitution, the search stands on no firmer ground than if there had been no warrant at all." New Hampshire subsequently tried to establish that the search fit one of the several warrant requirement exceptions, specifically, (1) as incident to the arrest, (2) the auto search exigency, and (3) the plain view doctrine. The Court rejected each of the claims. *See also* FOURTH AMENDMENT, p. 159; NEUTRAL MAGISTRATE, p. 435; WARRANT p. 460.

Significance The decisive holding in *Coolidge* v. *New Hampshire* (403 U.S. 443: 1971) was that the search warrant issued by the attorney general was invalid inasmuch as he was not a "neutral and detached magistrate." The appropriate authorizing party must have no direct interest in the search. Officials within the judicial branch are typically viewed as the neutral party most appropriately vested with the power to issue warrants. The basic constitutional rule is that searches conducted outside the judicial process, without prior approval by a judge or magistrate, are per se unreasonable under the Fourth Amendment. In *Johnson* v. *United States* (333 U.S. 10: 1948), the Court said the Fourth Amendment would become a "nullity" and would leave privacy to "police discretion" if judgments relative to the sufficiency of cause to conduct a search were left to other than "neutral and detached" magistrates. The required neutrality can also disappear if the magistrate issuing the warrant stands to gain financially. In *Connally* v. *Georgia* (429 U.S. 245: 1977), the Court found a Georgia statute allowing warrants to be issued by unsalaried justices of the peace who collected a fee only when a warrant was issued to be in violation of the neutrality requirement. A judge may compromise neutrality by participating in the execution of the warrant as well. In *Lo-Ji Sales, Inc.* v. *New York* (442 U.S. 319: 1979), a judge issued an open-ended warrant for seizure of allegedly obscene materials. He accompanied the police in the execution of the warrant and listed on the warrant additional seized items that he determined to be obscene. The Court unanimously condemned the practice because the judge "undertook to telescope the processes of the application for warrants, the issuance of the warrant, and its execution," and because it was "difficult to discern when he was acting as a 'neutral and detached' judicial officer and when he was one with the police and prosecutors in the executive seizure." The clear effect of *Coolidge* is that judicial officers typically possess the requisite neutrality to issue warrants, but a warrant issued by a nonneutral official makes the search essentially warrantless.

Warrant Particularity

Ybarra v. Illinois, 444 U.S. 85, 100 S.Ct. 338, 62 L.Ed.2d 238 (1979)   Defined the degree of particularity that must be described in search warrants. Ybarra was a customer at a tavern that underwent a warrant-authorized search. The warrant specified the tavern and the bartender as the subjects of the search. In executing their duties, officers performed a "cursory weapons search" on all the tavern patrons under provisions of Illinois law. The officer patting down Ybarra "felt a cigarette pack with objects in it," but did not remove the packet from Ybarra's pocket. The officer eventually returned to Ybarra, removed the packet, and found heroin. Ybarra's motion to suppress this evidence was denied, and he was convicted of possession of a controlled substance. The Supreme Court reversed the conviction in a 6–3 decision. Illinois attempted to justify the search on two bases. First, Illinois contended the initial weapons search was reasonable and the follow-up search was sufficient as an outgrowth of a reasonable frisk. The majority rejected this argument, saying, "the State is unable to articulate any specific fact that would have justified a police officer at the scene in even suspecting that Ybarra was armed and dangerous." Illinois's second argument was to justify the search as included in the warrant issued for the search of the bar and bartender. That argument was rejected as well. The Court said, "a person's mere propinquity to others independently suspected of criminal activity does not, without more, give rise to probable cause to search that person." It is necessary to focus on an individual in order to effect a search. The Court concluded that "a search or seizure of a person must be supported by probable cause particularized with respect to that person." The expectations of privacy require the protection of particularity, and this "requirement cannot be undercut or avoided by simply pointing to the fact that coincidentally there exists probable cause to search or seize another or to search the premises where the person may happen to be." The dissenters in *Ybarra,* Chief Justice Burger and Justices Blackmun and Rehnquist, argued that the search was reasonable as incident to the execution of the warrant. They would also have upheld the search on stop and frisk grounds. *See also* FOURTH AMENDMENT, p. 159; NEUTRAL MAGISTRATE, p. 435; PROBABLE CAUSE, p. 446; *TERRY* V. *OHIO,* p. 188.

Significance   *Ybarra* v. *Illinois* (444 U.S. 85: 1979) invalidated an Illinois statute that authorized officers in the execution of a valid search warrant to search any person encountered on the warrant-covered premises. The problem with the statute was its failure to meet the Fourth Amendment's "particularity" requirement for warrants. The particularity provision in the Amendment reflected intense feelings held by the authors of the Constitution against invasions of privacy committed under authority of the "general warrant" common in eighteenth-century England. The general warrant was a broad license under which virtually unrestricted searches could occur. Warrants obtained in compliance with the Fourth Amendment must make some reference to the person who is to be searched. That reference may be other than an actual name as long as it allows a reasonably reliable identification of the person to be searched. In the absence of any warrant reference, an officer must have a reasonable suspicion that a person encountered in a search is armed and dangerous. Such suspicion would permit a frisk as described in *Terry* v. *Ohio* (392 U.S. 1: 1968). In the *Ybarra* case no reasonable inference of danger was said to exist. The Court did note that the warrant "did not allege that the bar was frequented by persons illegally purchasing drugs." This reference suggests that had it been established at the time the warrant was obtained that patrons were often engaged in related criminal conduct in the tavern, this fact may have had a bearing on determining the sufficiency of the search of Ybarra, even though it occurred incidental to the execution of a warrant search of the tavern itself. Nonetheless, the clear message of *Ybarra* is the necessity for particularity in warrants.

Informants and Probable Cause

***United States* v. *Harris*, 403 U.S. 573, 91 S.Ct. 2075, 29 L.Ed.2d 723 (1971)**   Weighed the adequacy of a search conducted with a warrant issued on the basis of information provided by an unnamed informant. The informant, deemed to be a "prudent person" by the investigator seeking the warrant, was left unnamed because the person "fears for their [sic] life and property should their [sic] name be revealed." The Supreme Court held, in a 5–4 decision, that the warrant was properly issued. The partial concurrences among the majority made the decision even closer than 5–4, however. The Court suggested that Fourth Amendment issues such as this are governed by "practical and not abstract" considerations and that affidavits for warrants "must be tested and interpreted by magistrates and courts in a common sense and realistic fashion." Given this approach, the Court found the affidavits supporting the warrant request sufficient because (1) "they contained substantial basis for crediting the hearsay"; (2) the informant had personally observed the reported conduct; and (3) the affidavits cited "prior events within the affiant's own knowledge." The Court also said that a police officer's knowledge of a suspect's reputation could be utilized in evaluating information obtained from an informant. To disallow such knowledge would be to "ignore a 'practical consideration of everyday life' upon which an officer (or a magistrate) may properly rely in assessing the reliability of an informant's tip." Justice Harlan, joined by Justices Douglas, Brennan, and Marshall, dissented. His main contention related to the credibility of the informant. The informant in this case "had not been shown to possess any of the common attributes of credibility." The informant's name had not been disclosed to the magistrate, and his disclosures had not been corroborated. In short, Justice Harlan argued, this is "precisely the sort of informant whose tip should not be the sole basis for the issuance of a warrant." *See also* DRAPER V. UNITED STATES (385 U.S. 307: 1959), p. 160; FOURTH AMENDMENT, p. 159; PROBABLE CAUSE, p. 446.

Significance   United States v. Harris (403 U.S. 573: 1971) said that hearsay may be used when seeking a warrant provided some conditions are satisfied. *Aguilar* v. *Texas* (378 U.S. 108: 1964) established two key criteria. First, information must be provided that speaks to the reliability and trustworthiness of the informant. This is a special problem when the informant is unnamed or anonymous. Second, the substance of the informant's information must be supported by other evidence. In *Spinelli* v. *United States* (393 U.S. 410: 1969), the Court reversed a conviction because insufficient support had been provided for a tip from an anonymous informant. Clearly, therefore, the identity of an informant *is* a factor in assessing credibility. If the identity of an informant is either withheld or unknown, *Spinelli* requires additional support to compensate. *Spinelli* also demanded that the basis upon which the informant concluded that criminal conduct had occurred be fully developed. *Harris,* however, relaxed the warrant standards. It directly modified *Spinelli* by holding that information about the reputation of the person to be searched could be used to support the warrant request. Further, *Harris* held that previous receipt of reliable information was not requisite to demonstrating an informant's reliability. *Harris* reinterpreted both *Aguilar* and *Spinelli* by assigning more weight to a suspect's reputation and by deferring to the experience and knowledge of police officers in assessing the credibility of information from informants. A modification of standards regarding information tips occurred in *Illinois* v. *Gates* (454 U.S. 1140: 1983) as the Court abandoned the "two-pronged test" of *Aguilar* and *Spinelli*. The Court substituted the "totality of circumstances" approach in determining probable cause for search warrants. The *Aguilar* and *Spinelli* elements of informant veracity, reliability, and basis of knowledge remain as considerations for magistrates issuing warrants, but the totality approach is said to be more flexible in *Gates* and "will better achieve the accommodation of public and private interests that the Fourth Amendment requires than does the approach that has developed from *Aguilar* and *Spinelli*." While the impact of this adjustment will have to be measured over time, *Gates* seems to constitute a major policy shift.

Third-Party Searches

***Zurcher* v. *Stanford Daily*, 436 U.S. 547, 98 S.Ct. 1970, 56 L.Ed.2d 525 (1978)**   Discussed whether a state is prevented from issuing a search warrant simply because the possessor of the place to be searched is not suspected of criminal conduct. A demonstration occurred on the hospital premises of Stanford University. During the demonstration a number of persons, including police officers sent to contain the demonstration, were injured. The *Stanford Daily,* a student newspaper, published several articles and photographs of the incident. It was thought the *Daily* had photographs that could lead to the identification of the demonstrators who had assaulted the officers. A warrant was issued, and the police searched the *Daily* offices. The *Daily* sought a declaratory judgment against those connected with the warrant authorizing the search. In a 5–3 decision (Justice Brennan not participating), the Supreme Court upheld the warrant. The majority, through Justice White, offered several controlling observations in support of its decision. First, probable cause relates to evidence sought. When the state can show probable cause in regard to evidence that may be found by a search, a warrant is issued and an invasion of privacy is justified. Second, warrants may be issued to search any property. "Nothing on the face of the Amendment suggests that a third-party search warrant should not normally issue." Third, the majority rejected the argument that only the property of those suspected of an offense may be subject to a search. Justice White said it is "untenable to conclude that property may not be searched unless its occupant is reasonably suspected of crime and is subject to arrest." Finally, the majority felt that the press interests were handled within the warrant process. The "preconditions for a warrant . . . should afford sufficient protection against the harms that are assertedly threatened by warrants for searching newspaper offices." The three dissenters, Justices Stewart, Stevens, and Marshall, argued that the newspaper should not be subjected to a warrant search. They would have issued a subpoena that would allow the "newspaper itself an opportunity to locate whatever material might be requested and produce it." *See also* FOURTH AMENDMENT, p. 159; PROBABLE CAUSE, p. 446.

Significance   *Zurcher* v. *Stanford Daily* (436 U.S. 547: 1978) held that no special protection of privacy interests flows from the First Amendment. Further, the conditions necessary for the issuance of a search warrant provide adequate safeguards to First Amendment rights, i.e., if applied with exactitude the conditions of issuance of such a warrant do not endanger the press's ability to gather, analyze, and disseminate news. *Zurcher* permits warrant searches of places neither owned nor occupied by persons actually suspected of criminal conduct. The sole protection is the process through which warrants are obtained. That process requires demonstration that there is a reasonable expectation that evidence relating to a criminal investigation is located in the place searched. Relevant evidence can often be found with third parties. Evidence for investigations of white-collar crime might be located in bank, medical, and insurance records, for example. As computer-dependent record keeping develops, probabilities increase dramatically that potentially valuable evidence is stored in anonymous third-party locations. The Court was asked in *Zurcher* to preclude such searches, but the Court found the safeguards afforded by the warrant process to be adequate. Another policy option rejected by the Burger Court in *Zurcher* was the subpoena approach to obtaining evidence from third parties. Since subpoenas do not require a showing of probable cause, they possess the liability of possible indiscriminate use. At the same time, the subpoena technique does allow the third party to control the search and maintain the privacy of other materials on the premises. Justice Stewart, in dissent, joined by Justice Marshall, was very concerned that freedom of the press was endangered by this discussion. Not only would the newsroom be "disrupted" by a lengthy search, but the possibility of disclosure of information received from confidential sources would tend to prevent the press from fulfilling "its constitutionally designated function of informing the public." Justice Stevens filed a separate dissent, creating the 5–3 split.

Electronic Surveillance

***Katz* v. *United States,* 389 U.S. 347, 88 S.Ct. 507, 19 L.Ed.2d 576 (1967)** Established the Fourth Amendment protections afforded in the area of electronic surveillance. Katz was convicted on federal gambling charges. The key evidence against him was recordings of telephone conversations obtained by the FBI through a microphone installed in a public telephone booth. With only Justice Black dissenting, the Supreme Court held that the incriminating recordings could not be used against Katz. The decision said the protection of the Fourth Amendment "protects people, not places." The phonebooth itself is not a protected area as such. Rather, as Katz entered the phonebooth, he brought with him an expectation of privacy. What Katz "seeks to preserve as private, even in an area accessible to the public, may be constitutionally protected." Even if he could be seen from outside, he deserved protection from the "uninvited ear," and he should be able to "assume that the words he utters into the mouthpiece will not be broadcast to the world." Thus, expectations of privacy are critical to application of the Fourth Amendment. The Court qualified its decision, however, by adding that the protections of the Fourth Amendment are not absolute. Electronic surveillance is not foreclosed altogether. The government's surveillance of Katz was flawed because it failed to secure prior authorization. Even though the government had probable cause to believe Katz was using the phone for criminal purposes, and despite the limited scope and duration of the surveillance, the Court insisted on advance authorization. If probable cause, appropriate limitations on scope and duration, and prior review are present, invasions of privacy through electronic surveillance techniques are permissible. *See also* DALIA v. UNITED STATES(441 U.S. 238: 1979), p. 170; ELECTRONIC SURVEILLANCE, p. 406; FOURTH AMENDMENT, p. 159.

Significance Technology has allowed invasions of privacy in ways unimagined at the time the Fourth Amendment was written. *Katz* v. *United States* (389 U.S. 347: 1967) established that wiretaps and electronic surveillance are searches of a kind covered by the Fourth

Amendment. The decision brought to an end a long-standing policy to the contrary. The first critical decision on wiretapping came in *Olmstead* v. *United States* (277 U.S. 438: 1928). Olmstead and a number of others were convicted on conspiracy to violate the Prohibition Act. The convictions were gained largely through evidence obtained by tapping telephone lines. The Court held that the Fourth Amendment only protected an individual from the seizure of tangible things, and the conversations were not tangible. Further, the amendment only protected against physical entry onto Olmstead's property. The conversations presented in evidence were obtained without trespass. While not going so far as to declare that wiretaps and electronic surveillance violated the Fourth Amendment, *Katz* and *Berger* v. *New York* (338 U.S. 41: 1967) reversed *Olmstead* and tightly proscribed this kind of evidence gathering. Such surveillance could only be undertaken with prior judicial authorization, and such approval was contingent on a demonstration of probable cause. Further, *Katz* and *Berger* applied relatively stringent standards relative to the scope and duration of authorized surveillance. These standards were subsequently embodied in the Omnibus Crime Control Act of 1968.

Dalia v. United States, 441 U.S. 238, 99 S.Ct. 1682, 60 L.Ed.2d 177 (1979)   Examined whether covert entry is permissible in implementing an approved surveillance. Dalia tried to have certain evidence suppressed on the ground that the surveillance equipment used to intercept various conversations was illegally installed. The *Dalia* decision said among other things that covert entry to install surveillance equipment must be explicitly and separately authorized by the judicial authority approving the surveillance request. A 5–4 majority of partial concurrences held that the covert entry in *Dalia* did not violate the Fourth Amendment, however. The Court rejected the argument that the Fourth Amendment proscribes all covert entries, noting that it is "well established that law officers may constitutionally break and enter to execute a search warrant where such entry is the only means by which the warrant effectively may be executed." Second, the majority rejected the argument that Title III of the Omnibus Crime Control and Safe Streets Act of 1968 itself limited use of covert entry. Need for the surveillance must be demonstrated in accordance with the statute's requirements, but "nowhere in Title III is there any indication that the authority of courts . . . is to be limited to approving those methods of interception that do not require covert entry for installation of intercepting equipment." Finally, the majority rejected the assertion that even if Title III allows covert entry, explicit authorization is required prior to implementation. The Court said such explicit authorization would "promote empty formalism." The Fourth Amendment does not "require that a Title III surveillance order include a specific authorization to enter covertly the premises described in the order." Justices Brennan, Marshall, Stewart, and Stevens dissented. They distinguished surveillance requiring covert or illegal entry from nontrespassory surveillance. The former should not be viewed "as a mere mode of warrant execution." The dissenters would have required specific judicial approval. They felt the Crime Control Act, given its detail elsewhere, would have expressly authorized covert entry had it intended to do so. The majority's decision "converts silence into thunder." *See also* ELECTRONIC SURVEILLANCE, p. 406; FOURTH AMENDMENT, p. 159; *KATZ V. UNITED STATES* (389 U.S. 347: 1967), p. 169.

Significance   The Omnibus Crime Control and Safe Streets Act of 1968 moved wiretape and electronic surveillance into a different era. *Dalia v. United States* (441 U.S. 238: 1979) is one of a series of Burger Court decisions providing interpretation of the act, which basically prohibited communication interception except under particular conditions. The exceptions are structured around controls such as prior judicial approval and the other limitations required in *Katz* v. *United States* (389 U.S. 347: 1967). In addition, the statute permitted emergency surveillance without judicial authorization for up to 48 hours in cases involving national security. The Burger Court, however, unanimously found surveillance of domestic political activists under the emergency provisions to be deficient in *United States* v. *United States District Court* (407 U.S. 297: 1972). The Burger Court has otherwise upheld provisions of the act and has demonstrated a very literal approach to construction of the act's provisions. For example, in *United States* v. *Giordano* (416 U.S. 505: 1974), the Court had occasion to examine the procedures by which applications for approved interceptions are made. The act requires that applications be signed by the attorney general or a specially designated assistant attorney general, but in this case the applications were signed by an executive assistant. The Court reversed Giordano's conviction because of the process deviation. At the same time, *Dalia* reflects the Court's unwillingness to demand more than the statute explicitly requires. The case suggests that the key element in providing protections from abuse in this sensitive area is the prior judicial authorization for the surveillance. Once the surveillance is approved, the means of executing the surveillance are beyond judicial supervision. According to *Dalia,* any limitations on implementation must come through legislative initiative.

Exclusionary Rule

Mapp v. *Ohio*, 367 U.S. 643, 81 S.Ct. 1684, 6 L.Ed.2d 1081 (1961)   Considered whether products of unreasonable searches or seizures must be excluded from state criminal proceedings. The police who conducted a warrantless search of Mapp's residence were looking for evidence of a bombing and for materials associated with gambling. Instead they found "obscene" materials. The materials were confiscated, and Mapp was subsequently convicted for their possession. The Supreme Court, in a 6–3 decision, held that a state was required to exclude illegally obtained evidence. In applying the exclusionary rule to the states, the majority argued that the right of privacy was of sufficient priority to warrant the most effective methods of implementation. The means of protecting privacy other than the exclusionary rule were found to be "worthless and futile." The Court felt compelled to "close the only courtroom door remaining open to evidence secured by official lawlessness in flagrant abuse of that basic right." The Court had refused to extend the rule to state proceedings in earlier cases, but in *Mapp* the majority determined that the Fourth Amendment remains "an empty promise" unless secured through the exclusionary rule. Justices Harlan, Frankfurter, and Whittaker dissented and focused on three areas of concern. First, they were unsatisfied that *Mapp* was the proper case through which to reconsider prior decisions on the exclusionary rule because *Mapp* was brought and argued primarily on obscenity grounds. Second, the dissenters asserted that prior cases had sufficiently addressed general due process dimensions of privacy. Third, they concluded that states ought to be free to adopt or reject the exclusionary rule at their discretion. The key concern was state power versus federal power. The proper position of the Supreme Court should be to "forbear from fettering the States with an adamant rule which may embarrass them in coping with their own peculiar problems in criminal law enforcement." *See also* EXCLUSIONARY RULE, p. 409; FOURTH AMENDMENT, p. 159; *STONE* V. *POWELL* (428 U.S. 465: 1976), p. 173.

Significance   *Mapp* v. *Ohio* (367 U.S. 643: 1961) extended the exclusionary rule to state criminal proceedings. The exclusionary rule is aimed at deterring police misconduct in the conduct of searches and in preserving the integrity of trial courts by insulating them from tainted evidence. The exclusionary rule is a highly controversial device for serving these objectives because its utilization has crime control costs. Further, imposition of the rule by the United States Supreme Court preempts a policy decision previously retained by the states. Clearly *Mapp* was a decision that had fundamental policy impact. The decision had evolved over many years. Initially, admissibility of search evidence was governed by common law. In *Weeks* v. *United States* (232 U.S. 383: 1914), the Supreme Court adopted the rule in federal cases, at least for evidence illegally obtained by federal agents. The Court chose not to extend the rule to the states, however. As late as 1949 the Court held that the rule was not required at the state level despite the linkage of the provisions of the Fourth Amendment to the states via the Fourteenth Amendment. See *Wolf* v. *Colorado* (338 U.S. 25: 1949). Though the *Wolf* decision was maintained through the next decade, the Court showed signs of altering its course. In *Elkins* v. *United States* (364 U.S. 206: 1960), the Court ended the "silver platter" practice. *Elkins* closed a loophole left from *Weeks* that allowed evidence illegally seized by state authorities to be handed on a "silver platter" to federal authorities for use in federal proceedings. Extension of the exclusionary rule to all state proceedings in *Mapp* was therefore a major policy adjustment. It was an attempt by the Warren Court to create serious disincentives to search misconduct and to locate the monitoring function for search practices with state trial judges.

Stone v. Powell, 428 U.S. 465, 96 S.Ct. 3037, 49 L.Ed.2d 1067

(1976) The consolidation of two cases drawing together elements of the exclusionary rule, federalism, and *habeas corpus* review. In a state proceeding, Powell was convicted of murder. In that trial Powell had sought to have the weapon in his possession at the time of his arrest excluded from evidence. The arrest was for vagrancy. The trial judge rejected his claim, as did a state appellate court. Powell then sought *habeas corpus* review in a federal district court. Relief was denied by the district court, but Powell prevailed before the United States Court of Appeals. The Supreme Court, however, reversed the Court of Appeals in a 6–3 decision. The key question for the majority was the extent to which federal *habeas corpus* review ought to be available to state prisoners who had adverse decisions on search issues in state criminal proceedings. The majority focused on *habeas* jurisdiction under the applicable statute and on whether the utility of the exclusionary rule outweighed the "costs of extending it to collateral review of Fourth Amendment claims." The majority concluded that "where the State has provided an opportunity for full and fair litigation of a Fourth Amendment claim, a state prisoner may not be granted habeas corpus relief on the ground that evidence obtained in an unconstitutional search or seizure was introduced at his trial." The majority expressed its dissatisfaction with the exclusionary rule. Justice Powell, making reference to the usual reliability of physical evidence suppressed by the exclusionary rule, spoke of how the rule can "deflect the truthfinding process" and how it "often frees the guilty." In his concurring opinion, Chief Justice Burger referred to the exclusionary rule as a "Draconian, discredited device." Rather than reconsider the rule itself, the majority chose to limit opportunities for federal court review. Justices Brennan, Marshall, and White dissented from the restriction of the "availability of a federal forum for vindicating those federally guaranteed rights." *See also* EXCLUSIONARY RULE, p. 409; FEDERALISM, p. 30; FOURTH AMENDMENT, p. 159; *HABEAS CORPUS*, p. 419; *MAPP V. OHIO* (367 U.S. 643: 1961), p. 172.

Significance   *Stone* v. *Powell* (428 U.S. 465: 1976) reflected the controversial character of the exclusionary rule, as well as the growing disaffection with it. Disaffection has been manifest in two ways. First, when given situations in which the rule might have been extended, the Burger Court has consistently refused to do so. In *United States* v. *Calandra* (414 U.S. 338: 1974), the Court held that the rule did not apply to grand jury proceedings. It said the rule had "never been interpreted to proscribe the use of illegally seized evidence in all proceedings," and that "extension of the exclusionary rule would seriously impede the grand jury." Second, the Burger Court has been receptive to modification of the rule. While the Court has chosen to retain it, decisions such as *Powell* have narrowed the impact of such cases as *Mapp* v. *Ohio* (367 U.S. 643: 1961). *Powell* gave the Court the opportunity to limit federal *habeas corpus* jurisdiction as a method by which state prisoners could receive collateral review on search issues. The case diminishes the possibility of federal judges' intervening in state cases featuring search issues where those issues have had a "full and fair" review within the state courts. *Powell* thus conveys greater conclusiveness to state determinations about the applicability of the exclusionary rule. An alternative to the exclusionary rule is to bring civil action against offending officers. In *Bivens* v. *Six Unknown Named Agents of the Federal Bureau of Narcotics* (403 U.S. 388: 1971), the Court ruled that allegations of Fourth Amendment violations by federal officers acting "under color of federal law" are actionable under 28 U.S.C. Section 1331(a).

Warrantless Search

Chimel* v. *California, 395 U.S. 752, 89 S.Ct. 2034, 23 L.Ed.2d 685 (1969) Examined limitations on warrantless searches when conducted incident to a legal arrest. Chimel was arrested at his home. The police proceeded to conduct a warrantless search of Chimel's home, including the garage and attic. Certain items were found and admitted into evidence at his trial over his objection. The Supreme Court reversed his conviction in a 7–2 decision. The majority, through Justice Stewart, said that officers have two primary interests when making an arrest. The first is to "remove any weapons that [the arrestee] might seek to use in order to resist or effect his escape." Second, the Court allowed that it is "entirely reasonable for the arresting officer to search for and seize any evidence on the arrestee's person in order to prevent its concealment or destruction." The question in *Chimel* is the extent to which an actual search may be conducted toward either or both these ends. *Chimel* concludes that the area to be searched incident to an arrest is narrowly confined. The Court defined this area as one "within his [the arrestee's] immediate control." That is an area "from within which he might gain possession of a weapon or destructible evidence." Such an area clearly did not extend to an entire residence. The Court argued that there is "no comparable justification . . . for routinely searching through all the desk drawers or other closed or concealed areas in that room itself." The latter kind of search may only proceed under authority of a search warrant. *Chimel* thus significantly closed the scope of a permissible search stemming from a valid arrest. Justices Black and White dissented on the ground that despite the failure actually to obtain the warrant, probable cause could have been shown. By requiring the warrant, the dissenters felt that evidence would be needlessly jeopardized. Further, Black and White argued that the arrest "supplies an exigent circumstance justifying police action." That exigent circumstance allows recovery of evidence of a crime, and that evidence would have been jeopardized by delaying the search in order to obtain a warrant. *See also* FOURTH AMENDMENT, p. 159; *UNITED STATES V. EDWARDS* (415 U.S. 800: 1974), p. 176; WARRANT PARTICULARITY, p. 460.

Significance   Like many cases before it, *Chimel* v. *California* (395 U.S. 752: 1969) recognized the warrant exception that applies when searches are conducted while making a lawful arrest. Such searches are justified as a means of protecting the safety of arresting officers and others as well as preventing the destruction of evidence. *Chimel* addressed the *extensiveness* of a search attending an arrest. In cases prior to Chimel, the Court had held that full premises searches could occur. See *Harris* v. *United States* (331 U.S. 145: 1947) and *United States* v. *Rabinowitz* (339 U.S. 56: 1950). *Chimel,* however, imposed more stringent limits on the area that could reasonably be searched. While prior cases had given consideration to the "control" an arrestee might have over weapons or evidence on the premises, *Chimel* both restricted and supplanted such precedents as *Harris* and *Rabinowitz* by inserting the qualifier "immediate" on the term control. Thus *Chimel* permitted warrantless searches incident to lawful arrests, but greatly limited their scope. Officers may only search that area from which an arrestee might be able to access a weapon or evidence. If a fuller search of the premises is desired, *Chimel* requires a warrant.

United States v. Edwards, 415 U.S. 800, 94 S.Ct. 1234, 39 L.Ed.2d 771 (1974)   Examined the question of how long after a person is taken into custody a search can take place incident to the arrest. Edwards was arrested around 11 P.M. for attempting to break into a post office. From paint chips found at the scene, investigators had reason to believe Edwards's clothing contained material evidence of the crime. Edwards's clothing was taken from him without warrant the following morning, some ten hours after his arrest. The clothing did yield paint chips similar to those on the window sill of the post office, and over Edwards's objection, the clothing was admitted in evidence at his trial. Edwards appealed his conviction on the ground that the search had not been incident to his arrest. The Supreme Court disagreed with Edwards in a 5–4 decision. The majority, through Justice White, emphasized that seizure of Edwards's clothing would have been permitted at the time Edwards was taken into custody. The delay in this instance occurred because it "was late at night; no substitute clothing was then available for Edwards to wear, and it would certainly have been unreasonable for the police to have stripped respondent of his clothing and left him exposed in his cell throughout the night." Delay until the next morning was a "normal incident" to the custodial arrest, and "reasonable delay" in effecting the seizure "does not change the fact that Edwards was no more imposed upon than he could have been at the time and place of the arrest or immediately upon arrival at the place of detention." The dissenters, Justices Douglas, Stewart, Brennan, and Marshall, felt the delay invalidated the search. Justice Stewart remarked that "the mere fact of an arrest does not allow the police to engage in warrantless searches of unlimited geographic or temporal scope." The dissenting justices believed the search must be "substantially contemporaneous with the arrest." *See also* CHIMEL V. CALIFORNIA (395 U.S. 752: 1969), p. 175; FOURTH AMENDMENT, p. 159; MICHIGAN V. TYLER (436 U.S. 499: 1978), p. 178.

Significance   *United States* v. *Edwards* (415 U.S. 800: 1974) examined whether the warrant exception permitting a search incident to a lawful arrest allows that incidental search to occur the next day. Clearly the search must occur within the same general time frame as the arrest. If too much time elapses, or the arrestee is fully secured, the necessity for the warrant exception diminishes. The *Edwards* decision provides some flexibility. *Edwards* does not require that searches incident to arrest must occur immediately following the arrest. The greater the delay, however, the greater the burden on demonstrating continuing necessity. In *Edwards,* the incidental search was not conducted on a location, but upon clothing. The majority agreed that the actual arrest and the subsequent processing of Edwards had concluded, but the delayed seizure of the clothing could be justified. Certainly an immediate confiscation of Edwards's clothing would have been permitted as incidental to his arrest. That seizure would have occurred but for the late night arrest and the unavailability of substitute clothing. The presence of those two factors provided the basis for tolerating the delay. At the same time, Edwards's place of residence could not have been subjected to a warrantless search on the following day. *Edwards* permits flexibility as long as necessity and reasonableness for the delay can be shown. Distinct from a search conducted incident to an arrest is an inventory search of an arrested person and any container or article in his possession. In *Illinois* v. *Lafayette* (77 L. Ed.2d 65: 1983) the Court upheld the search of an arrestee's shoulder bag, saying, "justification for such searches does not rest on probable cause." A warrant is not required in this case because "every consideration of orderly police administration benefiting both police and the public points toward the appropriateness of the examination of the shoulder bag prior to [the defendant's] incarceration." The Court concluded that "even if less intrusive means existed of protecting some particular types of property, it would be unreasonable to expect police officers to make fine and subtle distinctions in deciding which containers or items may be searched."

Michigan v. Tyler, 436 U.S. 499, 98 S.Ct. 1942, 56 L.Ed. 2d 486 (1978)   A consideration of the concept of exigent circumstance as an exception to the search warrant requirement. A fire began about midnight in a store co-owned by Tyler. Before the fire was fully extinguished, the fire chief made a cursory inspection of the fire scene. Among the things noted at the time were containers of flammable liquid. The police were immediately informed, and a fuller investigation commenced. After leaving the scene for several hours, both police and fire officials returned to the unsecured location around 8 A.M., more systematically examined the scene, and seized evidence. In the days that followed, additional visits to the scene were made, and additional evidence, largely in the form of photographs, was obtained. None of the inspections, either those taking place during the fire itself or those occurring up to 30 days after the fire, was conducted with a warrant or with Tyler's consent. The Supreme Court, with Justice Brennan not participating, unanimously ruled that the searches occurring during and immediately after the fire had satisfied the conditions of the exigent circumstance exception. Those occurring more than nine hours after the fire did not satisfy the exigent circumstance conditions. The majority rejected the argument that no privacy interests remained, that badly burned premises have been abandoned, and that searches by officials other than police are not encompassed by the Fourth Amendment. Warrants are generally required, and an official must show more than "the bare fact that a fire has occurred." Even though there is a "vital social objective in ascertaining the cause of the fire, the magistrate can perform the important function of preventing harassment by keeping that invasion to a minimum." However, this search was subject to the exigent circumstance exception. The Court said, "A burning building clearly presents an exigency of sufficient proportions to render a warrantless entry 'reasonable.'" The authorities were properly on the premises, and could thus seize evidence in plain view. Justice Stewart argued that "it would defy reason to suppose that a fireman must secure a warrant or consent before entering a burning structure to put out the blaze. And once in the building for this purpose, firefighters may seize evidence of arson that is in plain view." Justices Marshall and White would have restricted the warrantless search up to the point the fire was extinguished. They would have required a warrant for the return inspection the morning after the fire. Justice Rehnquist considered the search of a "routine, regulatory" nature and would have placed it outside the conventional Fourth Amendment coverage. *See also* FOURTH AMENDMENT,

p. 159; WARRANTLESS SEARCH, p. 461; *UNITED STATES* v. *EDWARDS* (415 U.S. 800: 1974), p. 176.

Significance   Warrantless searches are permitted if exigent or emergency circumstances can be demonstrated. *Michigan* v. *Tyler* (436 U.S. 499: 1978) examined the exigent circumstance exception associated with entry onto burning property. The exigent circumstance exception is based upon the recognition that prior authorization through a warrant may simply be impossible under the conditions. To expect an officer to interrupt the "hot pursuit" of a suspect to obtain a warrant to continue the chase onto private property is generally regarded as unreasonable. Key to proceeding without a warrant is demonstrating a compelling emergency. In *Tyler*, the Court found the presence of fire fighters on the burning private property to be justified. Once legally on the property, the officers could reasonably investigate the origin of the fire. The investigation was permitted because it could be related not only to the preservation of potential evidence of crime, but also because it was necessary to reduce the likelihood of the fire's recurring. Thus the fire was viewed as an emergency sufficient to allow the fire officials to be on the premises legally. The legal presence also allowed warrantless investigation for a reasonable time following the onset of the fire. The searches that occurred on days following the fire were not seen as contemporaneous with the exigency that permitted the initial legal entry onto the property. Once property can be secured, the exigency ends and no necessity for proceeding without a warrant remains. See also *Mincey* v. *Arizona* (437 U.S. 385: 1978).

Steagald v. *United States*, 451 U.S. 204, 101 S.Ct. 1642, 68 L.Ed.2d 38 (1981)

Held that an arrest warrant for one individual cannot cover the search of the home of another individual. Federal agents, possessing an arrest warrant for Ricky Lyons, went to the home of Gary Steagald in search of Lyons. Though the officers failed to find Lyons, they did find evidence leading to the arrest of Steagald. The search of Steagald's home that produced the evidence was conducted without a search warrant. The Court disallowed the search in a 7–2 decision. The majority distinguished between arrest and search warrants and concluded that the arrest warrant for Lyons had no bearing on "petitioner's privacy interest in being free from an unreasonable invasion and search of his home." Given that no exigent circumstances could be shown, Steagald was entitled to judicial determination of probable cause through the warrant process. To hold otherwise "would create a significant potential for abuse." Police, using only an arrest warrant for a particular person, "could search all the homes of that individual's friends and acquaintances." An arrest warrant might thus "serve as the pretext for entering a home in which police have a suspicion, but not probable cause to believe that illegal activity is taking place." The Court pointed out that "an arrest warrant alone will suffice to enter a suspect's own residence to effect his arrest." The Court acknowledged that the exigent circumstance doctrine would apply to most situations. In this instance, however, the Court felt that law enforcement authorities would not have been seriously impeded in their efforts by the warrant requirement, thus the exigent circumstance doctrine did not apply. The two dissenting members of the Court, Justices White and Rehnquist, argued that the burden on law enforcement was heightened by the warrant requirement and that the privacy interests of Steagald were sufficiently protected by the arrest warrant. *See also* DRAPER V. UNITED STATES (385 U.S. 307: 1959), p. 160; FOURTH AMENDMENT, p. 159; PROBABLE CAUSE, p. 446.

Significance   Steagald v. United States (451 U.S. 204: 1981) determined that an arrest warrant issued against one individual does not adequately protect the privacy interests of any unnamed person. A valid arrest warrant is a limited authorization entitling officers to search the premises on which the named person is located at the time of arrest. The Court distinguished the interests protected by arrest and search warrants. The former protect an individual from unreasonable seizure. The latter "safeguards an individual's interest in the privacy of his home and possessions." The officers in this case attempted to use the arrest warrant for more than the seizure of suspect Lyons. Probable cause standards were satisfied relative to the arrest of Lyons, but police suspicions that Lyons might be found at Steagald's residence, or that Steagald himself might be in possession of contraband, were "never subjected to the detached scrutiny of a judicial officer." That left Steagald's privacy interests protected only by "the agent's personal determination of probable cause." Without exigent circumstances "such judicially untested determinations are not reliable enough to justify entry into a person's home." Prior to *Steagald* the Court determined in *Payton* v. *New York* (445 U.S. 573: 1980) that, in the absence of exigent circumstances, officers may not enter a person's residence without a warrant to make "routine felony arrests." Both *Steagald* and *Payton* reflect the Court's view that privacy interests must be protected through the warrant process, and the bypassing of that process can only occur in the presence of exigent circumstances.

Washington v. Chrisman, 455 U.S. 1, 102 S.Ct. 812, 70 L.Ed.2d 778 (1982) Involved a plain view seizure of evidence located in a residence some distance from the place of a legitimate arrest. Chrisman was stopped by a campus police officer for illegally possessing liquor. The officer asked Chrisman for identification. Chrisman had no identification on him and requested that he be permitted to return to his dormitory room to obtain it. The officer agreed and accompanied him to the residence hall. The officer stood at the open door of Chrisman's room and watched him look for identification. While waiting, the officer noticed what he believed to be marijuana lying "in plain view" on a desk in the room. The officer entered the room, confirmed that the substance was marijuana, and advised Chrisman and his roommate of their rights. The students consented to a broader search of the room, which yielded more marijuana and LSD. The students subsequently sought to have the evidence suppressed on the ground that the officer was not entitled to enter the room and either examine or seize the marijuana and LSD without a warrant. In a 6–3 decision, the Supreme Court upheld the search. The plain view doctrine was critical for the majority. The doctrine "permits a law enforcement officer to seize what clearly is incriminating evidence or contraband when it is discovered in a place where the officer has a right to be." The majority concluded that the officer had properly accompanied Chrisman to his room, and that remaining at the doorway was irrelevant to sustaining the warrantless search. The officer had "an unimpeded view of and access to the area's contents and its occupants." The officer's "right to custodial control did not evaporate with his choice to hesitate briefly in the doorway." He had a "right to act as soon as he observed the seeds and the pipe. This is a classic instance of incriminating evidence found in plain view when a police officer, for unrelated but entirely legitimate reasons, obtains lawful access to an individual's area of privacy." Justices Brennan, Marshall, and White dissented, saying the plain view doctrine "does not authorize an officer to enter a dwelling without a warrant to seize contraband merely because the contraband is visible from outside the dwelling." For them, the failure of the officer to enter the room with Chrisman was a fatal defect. Further, the exigency of custody pursuant to arrest did not justify, in the officer's mind, entry into the room. *See also* COOLIDGE V. NEW HAMPSHIRE (403 U.S. 443: 1971), p. 162; FOURTH AMENDMENT, p. 159; WARRANTLESS SEARCH, p. 461.

Significance *Washington* v. *Chrisman* (455 U.S. 1: 1982) rested upon the plain view exception to the warrant requirement. Chrisman drew heavily upon *Harris* v. *United States* (390 U.S. 234: 1968) and *Coolidge*

v. *New Hampshire* (403 U.S. 443: 1971). *Harris* involved discovery of evidence while securing an impounded car as defined in department regulations. *Harris* held that evidence may be seized that is "in the plain view of an officer who has the right to be in a position to have that view." Controlling for *Harris* was the recognition that the officer had legally opened the door to Harris's car before finding the seized evidence. The *Harris* decision did not permit warrantless entry of a residence, however, simply because an officer notes contraband through a window. *Coolidge* sharpened *Harris* by saying that "plain view alone is never enough to justify the warrantless seizure of evidence." The exigent circumstance alone can provide the basis for the warrantless seizure of evidence in plain view. *Coolidge* also established that plain view discoveries "must be inadvertent." Anticipated discovery cannot be included within plain view and must be handled through a warrant. *Chrisman* reiterates that legal entry by an officer must occur prior to the plain view discovery and seizure. Standing in the doorway of the students' room was a legal crossing of the "constitutionally protected threshold;" thus the seizure of the evidence noticed in plain view was permissible.

Automobile Searches

Chambers v. Maroney, 399 U.S. 42, 90 S.Ct. 1975, 26 L.Ed.2d 419 (1970)   Considered the distinction between residences and automobiles in applying Fourth Amendment protections. Following an armed robbery a description of the robbers and their car was broadcast. Police stopped a car meeting the description and arrested the occupants. The car was taken to the police station and subsequently searched without a warrant. The search produced both weapons used and property taken in the robbery. Following his conviction Chambers sought *habeas corpus* relief on the ground of unconstitutional search. The Supreme Court unanimously rejected Chambers's claim, with Justice Blackmun not participating. The majority cited prior cases that recognized "a necessary difference between a search of a store, dwelling house or other structure . . . and a search of a ship, motor boat, wagon or automobile." The Court said that "the circumstances that furnish probable cause to search a particular auto for particular articles are most often unforeseeable; moreover, the opportunity to search is fleeting, since a car is readily movable." Given this situation an "immediate search is constitutionally permissible." The Court could have chosen to require immobilization of the car until a warrant could be obtained, but it rejected this course as only a "lesser" intrusion. In the Court's view there was no difference between "seizing and holding a car before presenting the probable cause issue to a magistrate and . . . carrying out an immediate search without a warrant." As long as probable cause exists, either course is permitted. Since Chambers's car was properly under the control of the police, there was "little to choose in terms of practical consequences between an immediate search without a warrant and the car's immobilization until a warrant is obtained." *See also* FOURTH AMENDMENT, p. 159; *HABEAS CORPUS*, p. 419; *ROBBINS* V. *CALIFORNIA* (453 U.S. 420: 1981), p. 186; *SOUTH DAKOTA* V. *OPPERMAN* (428 U.S. 364: 1978), p. 185; *UNITED STATES* V. *ROBINSON* (414 U.S. 218: 1973), p. 183.

Significance   *Chambers* v. *Maroney* (399 U.S. 42: 1970) provided a contemporary reiteration of the "moving vehicle" exception to the warrant requirement first introduced in 1925 in *Carroll* v. *United States* (267 U.S. 132). The moving vehicle doctrine allows a warrantless vehicle search because the mobility of vehicles creates a particular exigency, i.e., the possibility that the vehicle could be moved out of the jurisdiction. The same standards of probable cause exist, however, as would apply if a warrant could be feasibly sought. The searching officer must be able to support a belief that the vehicle contains seizable materials. *Carroll* thus created a key distinction between vehicles and places of residence. Mobility of the former creates a generally applicable warrant exception. *Chambers* expanded upon *Carroll* by allowing the mobility exigency to pertain if the vehicle was first taken to the police station. *Chambers* rejected the need to obtain a warrant once the vehicle had been secured, which broadens the scope of the exception. It is also clear from *Chambers* that the rationale that applies to automobiles extends to other movable conveyances such as trucks, ships, planes, and mobile homes.

United States v. Robinson, 414 U.S. 218, 94 S.Ct. 467, 38 L.Ed.2d 427 (1973)   Discussed whether a traffic violation may trigger an arrest that then provides the basis for a full search. Robinson was stopped by a police officer who had reason to believe Robinson was driving with a revoked license. Probable cause was satisfied in that the same officer had stopped Robinson only four days earlier and had found Robinson's license to have been revoked. The officer put Robinson under a full-custody arrest and conducted a thorough search. The search yielded a packet containing heroin capsules, and Robinson sought to have the evidence suppressed. The

Supreme Court upheld the search in a 6–3 decision. The question faced by the Court was that though Robinson had been legally arrested, was the full search justified since it could not yield any evidence pertaining to the traffic offense? The majority argued that a custodial arrest allowed a full search and that such a situation was not bound by the limits placed on investigative searches under stop and frisk guidelines. The Court asserted that "standards traditionally governing a search incident to lawful arrest are not . . . commuted to the stricter *Terry* standards by the absence of probable fruits or further evidence of the particular crime for which the arrest is made." Further, custodial arrests subject officers to "extended exposure" to danger, more so than the "fleeting contact" of stop and frisks; thus a fuller search than a cursory weapons frisk can be justified. The majority concluded that if the arrest is lawful, authority to search is established, and the full search is "not only an exception to the warrant requirement of the Fourth Amendment, but is also a 'reasonable' search under that Amendment." The dissenters, Justices Douglas, Brennan, and Marshall, disagreed with the majority on two crucial points. First, they felt it was necessary to require establishment of probable cause relative to the seized evidence after the arrest. Without having to justify searches on a case-by-case basis, the full arrest might simply be "a pretext for searching the arrestee." Second, the dissenters rejected the argument that a search of personal effects was appropriate even if it could be justified that Robinson was required to empty his pockets. The minority could not agree that "simply because some interference with an individual's privacy and freedom of movement has lawfully taken place, further intrusions should automatically be allowed despite the absence of a warrant that the Fourth Amendment would otherwise require." *See also* CHAMBERS v. MARONEY (399 U.S. 42: 1970), p. 182; CHIMEL v. CALIFORNIA (395 U.S. 752: 1969), p. 175; FOURTH AMENDMENT, p. 159; PROBABLE CAUSE, p. 446; STOP AND FRISK, p. 455; TERRY v. OHIO (392 U.S. 1: 1968), p. 188.

Significance   *United States* v. *Robinson* (414 U.S. 218: 1973) held that a traffic violation may provide the basis for a lawful custodial arrest. The custodial arrest, in turn, permits a full warrantless search of the person and the area within the arrestee's "immediate control" incident to that lawful arrest. The primary impact of *Robinson* is found in the breadth of the warrant exception permitted. *Robinson* allowed a full search, not a search confined to discovery of weapons. The Court explicitly distinguished the situation from *Terry* v. *Ohio* (392 U.S. 1: 1968), and the stricter stop and frisk guidelines. The *Robinson* search was not connected to finding evidence related to the offense for which Robinson was under arrest. The search in *Robinson* also differed from such incident-to-arrest searches as in *Chimel* v. *California* (395 U.S. 752: 1969) in that no arrest warrant authorized Robinson's detention. The Court took *Robinson* one step further in *Gustafson* v. *Florida* (414 U.S. 260: 1973), decided the same day as *Robinson*. *Gustafson* permitted a search incident to a custodial arrest from a traffic violation even though state law and department regulations permitted the officer merely to issue a traffic citation. *Robinson* and *Gustafson* are among the more permissive decisions relative to Fourth Amendment limits upon unreasonable search conduct. *Robinson* is limited, however, to the "traffic stop" for a full custodial arrest, and is not authority for a stop to issue a ticket or to warn a driver. In *Robinson,* the officer had probable cause to believe the driver was driving on a revoked license, a serious offense in all states' traffic codes.

South Dakota v. Opperman, 428 U.S. 364, 96 S.Ct. 3092, 49 L.Ed.2d 1000 (1978)   Involved a warrantless inventory search of an impounded automobile. Opperman's car was impounded for numerous parking violations. A police officer noted some personal property in the car, and, following established inventory practices, inventoried the contents of Opperman's car. During the inventory marijuana was discovered in the unlocked glove compartment. Opperman was subsequently prosecuted for possession of marijuana. He sought to have the evidence suppressed, but his motion was denied, and he was convicted. The Supreme Court affirmed the conviction 5–4. In addition to the mobility dimension involved with automobiles, the majority stressed that there is a diminished "expectation of privacy with respect to one's automobile" as distinct from "one's home or office." The primary function of automobiles is transportation, and a car "seldom serves as one's residence or as the repository of personal effects." In the course of its "community caretaking functions," police often take automobiles into custody. Impounded cars are routinely secured and inventoried in order to protect the owner's property, minimize claims against the police over lost or stolen property, and to protect police from potential danger. The majority found these "caretaking procedures" to be an established practice within state law. The search was not unreasonable because the inventory was "prompted by the presence in plain view of a number of valuables inside the car." *Opperman* never suggested that this "standard procedure, essentially like that followed throughout the country, was a pretext concealing an investigatory police motive." A dissent authored by Justice Marshall was joined by Justices Brennan, Stewart, and White. It emphasized there was "no reason to believe that the glove compartment of the impounded car contained any particular property of any substantial value." In addition the minority deferred to Opperman's locking of the car as adequate protection of his property. The police could show no further need for protection. Finally, the police made no attempt to secure Opperman's consent. In short the dissenters objected to the result of the holding, which "elevates the conservation of property interests—indeed mere possibilities of property interests—above the privacy and security interest protected by the Fourth Amendment." *See also* CHAMBERS V. MARONEY (399 U.S. 42: 1970), p. 182; FOURTH AMENDMENT, p. 159; WARRANTLESS SEARCH, p. 461; ROBBINS V. CALIFORNIA (453 U.S. 420: 1981), p. 186.

Significance   South Dakota v. Opperman (428 U.S. 364: 1978) broadened permissible seizures under the plain view doctrine by approving the warrantless entry into an impounded car for purposes of conducting a standard inventory. While the Court limited the *Opperman* holding to the facts of that case, two points stand out in the opinion. First, authorities were allowed to seize criminal evidence from a car that was entered with neither a warrant nor with probable cause to believe that evidence of a crime was located in it. The rationale was the "diminished expectation of privacy" attached to a car and the various needs served by conducting the inventory. Second, the Court suggested that such inventories ought not to be evaluated in probable cause terms. In a footnote the Court observed that the "probable cause approach is unhelpful when analysis centers upon the reasonableness of routine administrative caretaking functions." The majority maintained that *Opperman* represented "standard practice" for the police, and there existed no suggestion of any investigatory motive. Had there been such a motive, the investigation would have been a "subterfuge for criminal investigation" and would not have been permitted.

Robbins v. California, 453 U.S. 420, 101 S.Ct. 2841, 69 L.Ed.2d 744 (1981)   Considered the opening of wrapped packages discovered during an automobile search. A station wagon was stopped by officers because it was being driven erratically. The officers smelled marijuana smoke and proceeded to pat down the driver. A vial of liquid was discovered that precipitated a search of the passenger compartment of the car. Marijuana and associated paraphernalia were discovered. After putting the driver in the police car, officers opened the station wagon tailgate and found a recessed luggage compartment containing two packages wrapped in an opaque plastic. The officers unwrapped the packages and found marijuana bricks. Robbins's motion to suppress the evidence was denied at his trial, and he was convicted of various drug offenses. Six Supreme Court justices voted to reverse the conviction. Although unable to agree on an opinion, five members of the Court agreed that the warrantless opening of the packages violated the Fourth Amendment. The opaque wrapping insulated the packages from warrantless search because they "manifested an expectation that the contents would remain free from public examination." The majority opined that the Fourth Amendment protects "people and their effects." These effects may be located in suitcases, briefcases, or opaque plastic bags. The Court acknowledged exceptions to this position. The plain view exception will apply where "contents can be inferred from their outward appearance," but the container in question "must so clearly announce its contents, whether by its distinctive configuration, its transparency, or otherwise, that its contents are obvious to an observer." The majority concluded that the opaque container (packages) in this case could not be opened without a warrant even though the search of the automobile had been lawful. Justice Stewart wrote the opinion for the majority. It was concurred in by Justices Brennan, White, and Marshall. Justice Powell concurred in a separate opinion. Chief Justice Burger also concurred in the judgment but wrote no opinion. The remaining three justices, Blackmun, Rehnquist, and Stevens, each wrote separate dissenting opinions. The opinion of the Court is an opinion of only four justices, therefore, although two others concurred. *See also* CHAMBERS v. MARONEY (399 U.S. 42: 1970), p. 182; FOURTH AMENDMENT, p. 159; SOUTH DAKOTA v. OPPERMAN (428 U.S. 364: 1978), p. 185; UNITED STATES v. ROBINSON (414 U.S. 218: 1973), p. 183.

Significance   *Robbins* v. *California* (453 U.S. 420: 1981), reversing the lower courts, held that a closed container found in a lawfully searched car is constitutionally protected to the same extent as are closed containers or closed pieces of luggage found anywhere else. There exists no distinction between containers or suitcases and property worn or carried about the person. Such a distinction would have no basis in the language or meaning of the Fourth Amendment, which protects people and their effects whether the effects are personal or impersonal. The majority also found that there were no objective criteria by which such a distinction could be made. Unless a closed container found in an automobile is such that its contents may be said to be in plain view, those contents are fully protected by the

Fourth Amendment. In the trial the evidence was not sufficient to justify an exception to the rule on the ground that the contents of the packages in question could be inferred from their outward appearance. In *United States* v. *Chadwick* (433 U.S. 1: 1977) the Court refused to permit the warrantless search of a locked footlocker taken from the trunk of an automobile. The locked container conveyed a privacy expectation for the contents that required warrant protection, especially since authorities had gained control of the footlocker itself. In *Arkansas* v. *Sanders* (442 U.S. 753: 1979) the Court similarly rejected the automobile exception as the basis for a warrantless search of everything found within a car during a legal warrantless search. *Robbins* refines *Chadwick* and *Sanders* by extending the expectation of privacy concept to any closed container, although allowing plain view seizures for those containers that obviously contain contraband. A sealed container may be lawfully opened for inspection at borders and places of entry into the United States. The Court held in *Illinois* v. *Andreas* (77 L.Ed.2d 1003: 1983) that if contraband is discovered during such an inspection, the container may be resealed, delivered, and reopened without a search warrant at the time the receiver takes delivery.

Stop and Frisk

***Terry* v. *Ohio*, 392 U.S. 1, 88 S.Ct. 1868, 20 L.Ed.2d 889 (1968)**   Examined the practice of stop and frisk and established basic guidelines for a limited warrantless search conducted on persons behaving in a suspicious manner. A police officer of 39 years' service observed two men, later joined by a third, acting "suspiciously." Specifically, the officer felt the men were "casing" a particular store. The officer approached the men, identified himself as a police officer, and requested identification. Upon receiving an unsatisfactory response to his request, the officer frisked the men. Terry was found to have a gun in his possession, and was subsequently charged and convicted for carrying a concealed weapon. The Supreme Court upheld the validity of the stop and frisk practice, with only Justice Douglas dissenting. It was admitted in *Terry* that the officer did not have "probable cause" to search Terry. Indeed, this is why *Terry* is important in recent Fourth Amendment cases: The majority distinguished between a frisk and a full search. The Court concluded that the officer was entitled to conduct a cursory search for weapons. Such a search is "protective," and while it constitutes an "intrusion upon the sanctity of the person," it is briefer and more limited than a full search. The frisk was justified by the need to discover weapons that may be used to harm the officer or others. Thus, where the officer "observes unusual conduct which leads him reasonably to conclude in light of his experience that criminal activity may be afoot," where he identifies himself as a police officer, and where "nothing in the initial stages of the encounter serves to dispel his reasonable fear for his own or others' safety," he is entitled to conduct a cursory search. Justice Douglas argued that probable cause had not been satisfied with respect to the weapons charge, i.e., the officer had no basis to believe Terry was carrying a weapon; thus the search was invalid. *See also* BROWN V. TEXAS (443 U.S. 47: 1979), p. 190; FOURTH AMENDMENT, p. 159; STOP AND FRISK, p. 455.

Significance Terry v. *Ohio* (392 U.S. 1: 1968) provided law enforcement authorities with the capability of executing preventive actions. Not only did *Terry* allow police to stop a person in situations deemed to be "suspicious," but *Terry* authorized a limited weapons pat-down. Controlling in *Terry* was observed behavior that would justify or give cause for making the stop. Given cause to stop, the officer was entitled to conduct at least a cursory search. *Terry* does not allow a full search unless the cursory search yields a weapon that leads to an actual custodial arrest. In *Sibron* v. *New York* (392 U.S. 40: 1968), a case decided with *Terry*, the Court disallowed a stop and frisk that netted a package of narcotics because the searching officer could not demonstrate cause for the stop. There was no reason to infer that Sibron was armed at the time of the stop or presented a danger to the officer. The Court felt the search of Sibron was a search for evidence, not for weapons. The Court noted this same absence of focused suspicion in the tavern frisk case, *Ybarra* v. *Illinois* (444 U.S. 85: 1979). The Burger Court expanded upon *Terry* in *Adams* v. *Williams* (407 U.S. 143: 1972), when it permitted a frisk based upon an informant tip as opposed to an officer's own observations. In *Pennsylvania* v. *Mimms* (434 U.S. 106: 1977) the Court held that an officer could order a lawfully detained driver out of his automobile. Once out, the *Terry* standard must still be met. The Court concluded that considerations of an officer's safety justified having a driver leave a car, and if cause exists to proceed with a frisk, a pat-down is permissible. *Terry* and the cases that build upon it authorize substantial latitude for a cursory weapons search if observed or reported behavior can focus sufficient suspicion. Two recent cases further define the scope of *Terry*. In *United States* v. *Place* (77 L.Ed.2d 110: 1983) the Court held that suspicious luggage may be seized at an airport and subjected to a sniff test by a narcotics detection dog. In this case the permissible limits of a *Terry* stop were exceeded, however, when the luggage was kept for 90 minutes, the suspect was not informed of where the luggage would be taken, and detention officers failed to specify how the luggage might be returned. *Terry* was also extended in *Michigan* v. *Long* (77 L.Ed.2d 1201: 1983), when the Court allowed a protective search of the passenger compartment of a stopped car. The majority ruled that "*Terry* need not be read as restricting the preventative search to the person of the detained suspect." Search of the passenger compartment of a car is permissible as long as the police "possess an articulable and objectively reasonable belief that the suspect is potentially dangerous." Contraband discovered in the course of such a protective search is admissible evidence.

Brown v. Texas, 443 U.S. 47, 99 S.Ct. 2637, 61 L.Ed.2d 357 (1979)

Examined a Texas "stop and identify" statute that made it a crime to refuse to report one's name and address when requested by a police officer. Brown was arrested and convicted of violating the statute after being stopped by a police officer who had observed Brown and another person "walking in opposite directions" in an area of "high incidence of drug traffic." The Supreme Court unanimously set aside the conviction. The Court's brief opinion began with a reiteration of the basic expectations of a proper search. A search or seizure "must be based on specific, objective facts." To detain a person for questioning, an officer must "have reasonable suspicion, based on objective facts, that the individual is involved in criminal activity." The officer stopping Brown could not sufficiently demonstrate "a reasonable suspicion" that Brown was involved in criminal conduct. Nothing in Brown's behavior "was different from the activities of other pedestrians in that neighborhood." Neither the fact the neighborhood was "frequented by drug users" nor the "understandable desire to assert a police presence" was seen as sufficient to "negate Fourth Amendment guarantees." Chief Justice Burger concluded the opinion by saying, "In the absence of any basis for suspecting appellant of misconduct, the balance between the public interest and appellant's right to personal security and privacy tilts in favor of freedom from police interference." *See also* FOURTH AMENDMENT, p. 159; STOP AND FRISK, p. 455; TERRY V. OHIO (392 U.S. 1: 1968), p. 188.

Significance   *Brown* v. *Texas* (443 U.S. 47: 1979) is representative of several Burger Court decisions that underscored the reasonable suspicion criterion for stop and frisks. The Warren Court found sufficient cause existed for a stop in *Terry* v. *Ohio* (392 U.S. 1: 1968).

But several more recent cases, including *Brown,* provided examples of insufficient cause. In *United States* v. *Brignoni-Ponce* (442 U.S. 873: 1975), the Court held that vehicle stops to search for illegal aliens were impermissible unless specific cause could be shown. Random stops of vehicles simply on the basis of observed substantial trafficking in aliens was inadequate. More recently the Court held that police could not randomly stop automobiles to check license and registration without some focused suspicion of a violation. To stop a driver an officer must have cause comparable to the cause required to stop a person on foot. At the same time the Court upheld a search under a stop and identify ordinance later held to be unconstitutional. In *Michigan* v. *DeFillipo* (443 U.S. 31: 1979), a person was arrested after providing "unresponsive and evasive answers" to inquiries posed by a police officer under an ordinance that allowed police to stop and question any individual whose behavior "warrants investigation." Drugs were discovered in the search performed following arrest for the ordinance violation. A six-justice majority determined the arrest was made in good faith and that the products of the search could be used, even though the ordinance itself was later found defective. A vagueness criterion has also been applied to this type of ordinance. In *Kolender* v. *Lawson* (75 L.Ed.2d 903: 1983) the Court struck down a California law requiring persons who "loiter or wander on the streets" to provide "credible and reliable" identification, and to "account for their presence" when requested. The majority ruled that the statute was vague and that it vested virtually complete discretion in police officers to determine if the enactment requirements had been satisfied. While stop and frisk remains a valuable law enforcement practice, *Brown* firmly established that reasonable suspicion must exist for such a stop to occur.

Consent Searches

***Schneckloth* v. *Bustamonte*, 412 U.S. 218, 93 S.Ct. 2041, 36 L.Ed.2d 854 (1973)**   Explored what is involved in determining the voluntariness of consenting to a search. A police officer stopped an automobile occupied by six persons including Bustamonte. After requesting identification and establishing that the car was owned by the brother of one of the occupants, the officer asked if he could search the interior of the car. The owner's brother agreed. When the officer asked whether the trunk opened, the owner's brother took the car keys and opened the trunk. Several stolen checks were found in

the trunk and were subsequently entered into evidence at Bustamonte's trial. The Supreme Court upheld the use of the evidence.
The key to the case was a determination of whether consent had been
voluntarily given. A six-justice majority said "two competing
concerns must be accommodated in determining the meaning of
a 'voluntary' consent—the legitimate need for such searches
and the equally important requirement of assuring the absence
of coercion." Such problems cannot be "resolved by any infallible touchstone." The Court stressed the "totality of circumstances"
in making judgments in these kinds of cases and concluded that
consent had been voluntarily given in *Bustamonte*. The majority rejected the argument that consent must be evaluated in the same way
as a waiver of rights pertaining to a fair trial. The majority opted
not to require that individuals know of their right to refuse consent
in order to establish a voluntary consent. The dissenters, Justices
Douglas, Brennan, and Marshall, argued that before consent could
be obtained, a person must be informed of his or her right to refuse consent. *See also* FOURTH AMENDMENT, p. 159; EXIGENT CIRCUM-
STANCE, p. 410; *UNITED STATES V. MATLOCK* (415 U.S. 164: 1974),
p. 193.

Significance   In *Schneckloth* v. *Bustamonte* (412 U.S. 218: 1973), the
Court refused to require that persons be informed that they need not
consent to searches. *Schneckloth* effectively distinguishes between
search and self-incrimination situations, holding that an individual
need be apprised of legal options only in the instance of self-
incrimination. While the *Schneckloth* decision still requires that the
prosecution bear the burden of proof in showing that a consent was
voluntarily obtained, *Schneckloth* excludes knowledge of the right to
withhold consent as an absolute element of showing voluntary consent. A number of states use the more demanding standard that all
persons must be informed that they may opt not to consent to a
search. Presuming a consent has been voluntarily obtained, there
remains the question of how much the consent allows authorities to
search. Consent may be limited to specific places to be searched or
specific items to be searched for. If it cannot be shown that an
unlimited search has been voluntarily consented to by a suspect, the
search ought to be carefully limited. Consent may also be withdrawn,
and searches continued after consent is revoked must be otherwise
defensible. Even a suspect's consent may be insufficient to uphold a
search. The Court held in *Florida* v. *Royer* (75 L.Ed.2d 229: 1983) that
if a suspect is detained beyond the permissible bounds of an investigative stop, his consent to a search of his suitcases becomes "tainted by
the illegal detention." Finally, the voluntariness standard says the

person consenting to a search must actually possess the capacity to consent. See *United States* v. *Matlock* (415 U.S. 164: 1974).

United States v. Matlock, 415 U.S. 164, 94 S.Ct. 988, 39 L.Ed. 242 (1974)   Considered whether a third party may consent to a search. Matlock was convicted of bank robbery. Part of the evidence used against him was stolen money found during a warrantless search in a bedroom Matlock shared with someone else. Consent for the search yielding the stolen money was obtained from the other person, not Matlock. The Supreme Court upheld the search in a 6–3 decision. The majority stressed the decisive element in determining the adequacy of a third-party consent was joint occupancy or control. The Court found such joint control present in this case because (1) Matlock had often represented the other person as his wife; (2) the consenting person "harbored no hostility" toward Matlock; and (3) the person had admitted cohabitation out of wedlock with Matlock, a criminal offense in the state of the search. The majority concluded she was in a position to give valid consent to the search. The dissent was similar to that in *Schneckloth* v. *Bustamonte* (412 U.S. 218: 1973). Justices Douglas, Brennan, and Marshall argued that consent cannot be obtained unless the consenting party is informed of the right to refuse consent. Their central thrust was that a waiver of the right to privacy cannot be effectively made if "he is totally ignorant of the fact that, in the absence of his consent, such invasions of privacy would be constitutionally prohibited." Justice Douglas also pointed out that no exigent circumstance prevailed here; thus authorities had every opportunity to secure a warrant prior to the conduct of the search. *See also* EXIGENT CIRCUMSTANCE, p. 410; FOURTH AMENDMENT, p. 159; *SCHNECKLOTH* V. *BUSTAMONTE* (412 U.S. 218: 1973), p. 191.

Significance   *United States* v. *Matlock* (415 U.S. 164: 1974) provided guidance in the matter of third-party consent searches. If the suspect does not offer consent, the question becomes whether anyone may legally consent to a search of the suspect's premises. In *Matlock,* the Court targeted the "common authority" criterion. If a third party shares common authority over a place or items within a place, that person may properly consent to the search. Generally, common authority would cover consent by a spouse or persons otherwise living together such as in *Matlock.* Consent in these situations, however, may be limited if there are places or items within the shared premises that are "exclusively used" by the nonconsenting other party. Parents may generally consent to searches of rooms occupied by minor children within the parents' premises. Minors, on the other hand, typically may not provide consent to search shared premises. The ability to consent is independent from possessing title to the premises to be searched. Accordingly, a landlord may not legally consent to the search of a leased room or rooms, nor may the employee or agent of any landlord consent to a search on behalf of a tenant. This applies even to short-term renters in hotels or motels. *Matlock* permits third-party consent searches if the third party has common authority over the premises to be searched. The common authority criterion prevails over all others in determining the legality of a third-party consent search.

4. The Fifth Amendment

OVERVIEW

The Fifth Amendment states:

> No person shall be held to answer for a capital, or otherwise infamous crime, unless on a presentment or indictment of a Grand Jury, except in cases arising in the land or naval forces, or in the Militia, when in actual service in time of War or public danger; nor shall any person be subject for the same offence to be twice put in jeopardy of life or limb; nor shall be compelled in any criminal case to be a witness against himself, nor be deprived of life, liberty, or property, without due process of law; nor shall private property be taken for public use, without just compensation.

The Fifth Amendment provides protection for the individual at both ends of the criminal process. It requires a charge by means of a grand jury indictment, and when the process is concluded, it prohibits a person from being "twice put in jeopardy" for the same offense. The protections of the Fifth Amendment were not applied to the states until well into the twentieth century, however. Chief Justice John Marshall said in *Barron* v. *Baltimore* (7 Peters 243: 1833) that the Bill of Rights applied only in federal cases. While *Barron* has never been formally overturned, ratification of the Fourteenth Amendment created new possibilities for applying all or part of the Bill of Rights to the states. An example of the Supreme Court's refusal to apply criminal procedure protections to the states is *Hurtado* v. *California* (110 U.S. 516: 1884), in which California was not required to indict on presentment of a grand jury. In *Palko* v. *Connecticut* (302 U.S. 319: 1937), the Court rejected the view that the Fourteenth Amendment made safeguards of the Bill of Rights against double jeopardy effective against the states. But the *Palko* decision established a doctrine of "selective incorporation" that by 1983 had left only the Grand Jury Clause of the Fifth Amendment and the Excessive Fines and Bail Clause of the Eighth Amendment outside the corpus of incorporated criminal procedures.

197

The evolution of Fifth Amendment standards includes a number of benchmark cases. *Costello* v. *United States* (350 U.S. 359: 1953) allowed relative informality in grand jury inquiries and established wide operating room for them. *United States* v. *Washington* (431 U.S. 181: 1977) examined the extent to which a grand jury witness must be warned of the possible consequences of his or her testimony. Each of these cases conveys that charging is very different from guilt adjudication. The enduring double jeopardy issues have been when jeopardy "attaches" and when it constitutes "sameness." *Breed* v. *Jones* (421 U.S. 519: 1975) found that jeopardy begins when fact finding on the charge begins. *Waller* v. *Florida* (397 U.S. 387: 1970) found that sameness is constituted when multiple sovereignties, in this case a state and a municipality, simultaneously prosecute for the same offense. *Price* v. *Georgia* (398 U.S. 323: 1970) and *Bullington* v. *Missouri* (451 U.S. 430: 1981) considered retrial situations in which the concept of "implicit acquittal" applies. *Ashe* v. *Swenson* (397 U.S. 436: 1970) incorporated the doctrine of "collateral estoppel" into double jeopardy protection.

The Fifth Amendment also protects persons from having to provide testimony against themselves. The landmark *Miranda* v. *Arizona* (384 U.S. 436: 1966) decision required that any person being interrogated be apprised of his or her right to say nothing. Statements made without such prior warning are inadmissible, although *Harris* v. *New York* (401 U.S. 222: 1971) allowed use of such statements to impeach the defendant's own testimony at trial. *Michigan* v. *Tucker* (417 U.S. 433: 1974), *Brewer* v. *Williams* (430 U.S. 387: 1977), and *North Carolina* v. *Butler* (441 U.S. 369: 1979) examined waiver of the *Miranda* protections and the status of statements made following partial *Miranda* warnings. *Carter* v. *Kentucky* (450 U.S. 288: 1981) dealt with inferences that can be drawn from a defendant's failure to testify and jury instructions relative to that silence. *Estelle* v. *Smith* (451 U.S. 454: 1981) considered whether testimony from a psychiatrist who had conducted a court-ordered competency examination may be used at the sentencing stage of a proceeding.

Self-incrimination questions have also arisen relative to evidence other than testimony that may be derived from a defendant. *Schmerber* v. *California* (384 U.S. 757: 1966), *Neil* v. *Biggers* (409 U.S. 188: 1972) and *Manson* v. *Braithwaite* (432 U.S. 98: 1977) took into account identification techniques and defendant-derived evidence such as lineups, showups, photographic identification, and blood samples in relation to the privilege against self-incrimination. *Kastigar* v. *United States* (406 U.S. 441: 1972) looked at immunity as an approach to satisfying the self-incrimination protection.

The Fifth Amendment entry and an elaboration of the above definitional cases follow.

The Fifth Amendment   Provides protections for persons in the criminal process, particularly that no one shall be deprived of life, liberty, or property without due process of law. The Fifth Amendment was an American adaptation of elements of the English common law tradition. In contrast to the language of the Fourth Amendment, whose etiology was based on specific colonial experiences with the British use of the general warrant, the language of the Fifth Amendment was based on what Blackstone referred to as "universal maxims." The Fifth Amendment contains five separate clauses: (1) "No person shall be held to answer for a capital, or otherwise infamous crime, unless on a presentment or indictment of a Grand Jury, except in cases arising in the land or naval forces, or in the Militia, when in actual service in time of War or public danger." The language is James Madison's. He had before him Article VIII of the Constitution of North Carolina (1776), which said, "No freedman shall be put to answer any criminal charge but by indictment, presentment, or impeachment." Madison also had a resolution from the Massachusetts ratifying convention of 1788 saying it was necessary to obtain an indictment by grand jury before trial of any crime. The states were often working from Sir William Blackstone's *Commentaries on the Laws of England,* Volume IV, in which he wrote, "Whenever any capital offence is charged, the same law requires that the accusation be warranted by the oath of 12 men before the party shall be put to answer it." Blackstone thus summarized an English common law tradition dating from the time of William the Conqueror's petit jury in the eleventh century. The tradition was reiterated over the generations as the rule that no case could be prosecuted until a duly sworn grand jury had attested that grounds existed for such prosecution. In modern America the federal grand jury is composed of not less than 16 nor more than 23 members, although the states in some cases use a one-person grand jury, usually a trial judge. The Supreme Court held that the Grand Jury Clause of the Fifth Amendment does not extend to the states under its construction of the Due Process Clause of the Fourteenth Amendment. Hence indictment by grand jury is held absolute only in federal criminal proceedings. The Exception Clause regarding land or naval forces and the militia attempts to avoid potential conflicts between civilian and military tribunals. The armed forces have their own system of justice in place, although the Supreme Court has ruled in a number of cases that certain criminal procedure rights extend also to military personnel. In general, however, the federal courts have confined their rulings on military personnel to the question of whether the defendant and the crime were in fact subject to the Uniform Code of Military Justice at the time of the alleged offense.

(2) ". . . nor shall any person be subject for the same offence to be twice put in jeopardy of life or limb." Blackstone said it was "a universal maxim of the common law of England that no man is to be brought into jeopardy of his life more than once for the same offence." This principle of "non bis in idem" was based initially on a holding in twelfth-century English courts that if a person were tried for violation of an ecclesiastical canon, he could not then be tried for the same infraction in the civil courts. The Archbishop of Canterbury, Thomas Becket, declared in reaction to an edict of Henry II that to do otherwise would violate "the standards of common law." In 1641, barely 20 years after the Plymouth Settlement, the Massachusetts Body of Liberties provided that "no man shall be sentenced by Civil Justice for one and the same crime, offence, or trespass." John Locke added in his draft of the North Carolina Fundamental Constitutions of 1669 that "no cause shall be twice tried in any one court, upon any reason or pretense whatsoever." In modern American criminal proceedings, jeopardy attaches when a defendant is formally charged with an offense and the trial has commenced before a competent court. The word "commence" applies in a jury trial to the time the jury is impaneled and sworn. In a court trial it applies to the time the first witness is sworn. The protection against double jeopardy was extended to state actions by the due process clause of the Fourteenth Amendment in *Benton* v. *Maryland* (395 U.S. 784: 1969).

(3) ". . . nor shall be compelled in any criminal case to be a witness against himself." The origins of this clause were in the practices of the English Star Chamber Court, where persons even suspected of some offense were interrogated before any formal accusation had been made. The questions were leading and were intended to elicit a confession. It was not uncommon to gain confessions in Star Chamber with the help of threats or torture. As late as the seventeenth century it was common practice in England for a defendant to be questioned at trial only by the prosecutor or the judge. Thus the English system of justice at the time was redolent with forced confessions. The early American knowledge of and determination to reform this system was reflected in the Virginia Bill of Rights. It stated flatly that no one can be "compelled to give evidence against himself." A number of state constitutional ratifying conventions later insisted that the Virginia model be followed. By 1886 Justice Joseph P. Bradley could affirm what had become the American tradition in *Boyd* v. *United States* (116 U.S. 630): "Any compulsory discovery made by extorting the oath is contrary to the principles of free government." Ten years later the tradition was summarized by Justice Henry B. Brown in *Brown* v. *Walker* (161 U.S. 591: 1896):

The change [from abject coercion to more humane influences] in the English criminal procedure in that particular seems to be founded upon no statute and no judicial opinion, but upon a general and silent acquiescence of the court in a popular demand. But, however adopted, it has become firmly imbedded in English, as well as in American jurisprudence. So deeply did the inequities of the ancient system impress themselves upon the minds of the American colonists that the states, with one accord, made a denial of the right to question an accused person a part of their fundamental law, so that a maxim, which in England was a mere rule of evidence, became clothed in this country with the impregnability of a constitutional enactment.

Malloy v. *Hogan* (378 U.S. 1: 1964) mandated applicability of the self-incrimination clause to the states under the Fourteenth Amendment.

(4) ". . . nor be deprived of life, liberty, or property, without due process of law." The words "due process of law" came from Article XIII of the Constitution of New York. The drafter of the Bill of Rights, James Madison, was greatly influenced in his word choice by fellow *Federalist* author Alexander Hamilton. Hamilton argued persuasively that insertion of the phrase "due process" would remove any doubt it was "the process and proceedings of the courts of justice" being addressed. Thus the *courts* would interpret the legitimate rights of citizens, not legislative bodies, which could presumably enact legislation to "disfranchise or deprive" citizens of *any* right. Because of the clause's general thrust and applicability, the Supreme Court historically has been reluctant to give it precise definition. The Court prefers to rely on "the gradual process of judicial inclusion and exclusion," as in *Davidson* v. *New Orleans* (96 U.S. 97: 1878). Justices have attempted consistently to distinguish, however, between substantive due process and procedural due process, a practice especially evident in interpretations of the Due Process Clause of the Fourteenth Amendment. *Black*'s *Law Dictionary* distinguishes substantive and procedural due process in the following way:

Substantive due process. Such may be broadly defined as the constitutional guarantee that no person shall be arbitrarily deprived of his life, liberty or property; the essence of substantive due process is protection from arbitrary and unreasonable action. *Babineaux* v. *Judiciary Commission*, La., 341 So.2d 396,400.

Procedural due process. Those safeguards to one's liberty and property mandated by the 14th Amend., U.S. Const., such as the right to counsel appointed for one who is indigent, the right to a copy of a transcript, the right of confrontation; all of which are specifically provided for in the 6th Amendment and made applicable to the states' procedure by the 14th Amendment.

Central meaning of procedural due process is that parties whose rights are to be affected are entitled to be heard and, in order that they may enjoy that right, they must be notified. *Parham* v. *Cortese,* 407 U.S. 67, 92 S.Ct. 1983, 1994, 32 L.Ed.2d 556. REASONABLE NOTICE AND OPPORTUNITY TO BE HEARD AND PRESENT ANY CLAIM OR DEFENSE ARE EMBODIED IN THE TERM "PROCEDURAL DUE PROCESS." *In re Nelson,* 78 N.M. 739, 437 P. 2d 1008.

Substantive due process requires that the Supreme Court be convinced that not only the procedure for enforcing the law but *the law itself* is fair, reasonable, and just. Thus the Court has struck down laws regulating hours of labor and forbidding employers to discharge workers for union membership and activity, as in *West Coast Hotel* v. *Parrish* (300 U.S. 379: 1937). The perils of such power under substantive due process review were articulated by Justice Lewis F. Powell, Jr. in *Moore* v. *East Cleveland* (431 U.S. 494: 1977):

> . . . substantive due process has at times been a treacherous field for this Court. There are risks when the judicial branch gives enhanced protection to certain substantive liberties without the guidance of the more specific provisions of the Bill of Rights. As the history of the Lochner era demonstrates, there is reason for concern lest the only limits to such judicial intervention become the predilections of those who happen at the time to be members of this Court. That history counsels caution and restraint. But it does not counsel abandonment.

(5) ". . . nor shall private property be taken for public use, without just compensation." The founding fathers considered property rights to be absolute and inherent. Again, this holding is based in English common law dating from the Magna Carta. The citizen's power of eminent domain is described in *Black's Law Dictionary* as "the highest and most exact idea of property remaining in the government, or in the aggregate body of the people in their sovereign capacity." The precise parameters for the legitimate taking of private property for public use remain elusive. The Supreme Court has followed a case-by-case approach to definition of them. In *Penn Central* v. *City of New York* (438 U.S. 104: 1978), the Court said it recognized the guarantee contemplated by the Eminent Domain Clause of the Fifth Amendment. It was

> designed to bar Government from forcing some people alone to bear public burdens which, in all fairness and justice, should be borne by the public as a whole. This Court quite simply has been unable to develop any set formula for determining when justice and fairness require that economic injuries caused by public action be compensated by the government, rather than remain disproportionately concentrated on a few persons.

Although there is no set formula for compensating economic injuries under the Fifth Amendment, the Court showed in *United States* v. *Sioux Nation of Indians* (448 U.S. 371: 1980) that it does indeed arrive at compensation figures. The Court said the Sioux were entitled to $17 million because the federal government had exceeded its powers in taking the Black Hills from the Sioux in 1877. Thus the Court felt the Black Hills were worth $17 million in 1877. The Sioux said the justices were better lawyers than they were economists. *See also* BILL OF RIGHTS, p. 7; COMMON LAW, p. 13; JOHN LOCKE, p. 44; MAGNA CARTA, p. 46.

Significance   The Fifth Amendment has been the basis of more Supreme Court decisions than any other article of the Bill of Rights or of the Constitution itself. The broad and dramatic interpretations of the Due Process Clause after passage of the Fourteenth Amendment in 1868 makes it the lynchpin of American constitutional law. The Fifth Amendment's provision proscribing self-incrimination has become one of the foremost privileges incurring to citizens of the United States. "Pleading the Fifth" has found its way into the American vernacular, with Justice Arthur J. Goldberg stating the significance of the popular notice in *Murphy* v. *Waterfront Commission* (378 U.S. 52: 1964):

> The privilege against self-incrimination reflects many of our fundamental values and most noble aspirations: our unwillingness to subject those suspected of crime to the cruel trilemma of self-accusation, perjury, or contempt; our preference for an accusatorial rather than an inquisitorial system of criminal justice; our fear that self-incriminating statements will be elicited by inhumane treatment and abuses; our sense of fair play which dictates 'a fair state-individual balance by requiring the government to leave the individual alone until good cause is shown for disturbing him and by requiring the government in its contest with the individual to shoulder the entire load.' 8 Wigmore, *Evidence*, 717; our respect for the inviolability of human personality and of the right of each individual 'to a private enclave where he may lead a private life,' *United States* v. *Grunewald*, 233 F.2d 556; our distrust of self-deprecatory statements; and our realization that the privilege, while sometimes 'a shelter to the guilty,' is often 'a protection to the innocent.' *Quinn* v. *United States*, 349 U.S. 155, 162.

The fact that the Supreme Court can review on both substantive and procedural due process grounds under the Fifth and Fourteenth Amendments gives the Supreme Court unparalleled power in modern democratic governments. Although due process, in Daniel

Webster's words, fundamentally may only provide that a court "hear before it condemns," it has in American practice been elaborated to provide a series of checkpoints for the courts to assure the preservation of a distinctly American tradition, that it is better for the guilty to go free than for one innocent person to be deprived of life, liberty, or property.

Incorporation

Hurtado v. California, 110 U.S. 516, 4 S.Ct. 111, 28 L.Ed. 232 (1884) Considered whether a state criminal procedure appeal should incorporate or nationalize the Bill of Rights to create equivalent federal and state procedural standards. Throughout most of the nineteenth century, appeals of state criminal cases did not come before the United States Supreme Court. The policy was based on the view that procedural protections in the Bill of Rights for those accused of criminal conduct did not apply to the states. In *Barron* v. *Baltimore* (7 Peters 243: 1833) Chief Justice John Marshall declared that the limits on governmental power expressed in the Bill of Rights applied only to "the government created by the instrument," i.e., the federal government, and not to "the distinct governments," i.e., the states. Since Chief Justice Marshall was not disposed to generous interpretations of state power, the power he was willing to give the states in *Barron* remained the controlling precedent until passage of the Fourteenth Amendment in 1868. The Fourteenth Amendment reopened consideration of the relationship of the Bill of Rights and the states, for clearly the proscriptions of the Amendment were directed at the states. The first important constitutional skirmish in this regard came in the *Slaughterhouse Cases* (16 Wallace 36: 1873). Using the doctrine of dual citizenship, the Supreme Court said the Fourteenth Amendment absolutely did not nationalize the Bill of Rights. But *Slaughterhouse* did not involve criminal procedures. *Hurtado* did. Hurtado had been convicted of murder. He claimed denial of due process because he had been charged through a process known as information rather than through indictment by a grand jury. Hurtado argued that the Due Process Clause of the Fourteenth Amendment embraced the Grand Jury Clause of the Fifth Amendment and extended the Grand Jury Clause to the states. With only Justice John Marshall Harlan dissenting, the Supreme Court rejected Hurtado's claim. Writing for the Court, Justice Stanley Matthews said that if it had been the intention of the authors of the Fourteenth

Amendment to require grand juries at the state level, they would have included "explicit declarations to that effect." Further, reference to due process in the Fifth Amendment is entirely separate from reference to the grand jury in the same amendment. Since due process means the same thing in both the Fifth and the Fourteenth Amendments, neither amendment ties the grand jury to due process. Finally, Justice Matthews argued that historically grand jury indictment was not an essential component of due process. The grand jury indictment was "merely a preliminary proceeding." In his dissent Justice Harlan asserted that the Fourteenth Amendment totally incorporated and absorbed the Bill of Rights. He viewed everything in the Bill of Rights as so closely linked to the "principles of liberty and justice lying at the root of our civil and political institutions" that no state can depart from them without violating due process. *See also* BILL OF RIGHTS, p. 7; FIFTH AMENDMENT, p. 201; *PALKO* V. *CONNECTICUT* (302 U.S. 319: 1937), p. 207.

Significance   *Hurtado* v. *California* (110 U.S. 516: 1884) established that states are not required to indict on presentment of a grand jury. That opinion still prevails after a hundred years. Other aspects of the incorporation question regarding criminal procedures have evolved differently, however. Not much change was seen in *Maxwell* v. *Dow* (176 U.S. 581: 1900), in which the Court held that a state criminal conviction using a jury of eight persons neither deprived the defendant of due process nor diminished the privileges of federal citizenship. But in *Twining* v. *New Jersey* (211 U.S. 78: 1908), although the Court refused to apply the self-incrimination protection to the states, it did consider the possibility that certain national citizenship rights might be protected from state violations. It said "fundamental" rights might qualify. The definitive break in the incorporation logjam came in *Gitlow* v. *New York* (268 U.S. 652: 1925), in which the Court held that the free speech protection of the First Amendment applied to the states. With *Gitlow* the direction and rate of evolutionary change regarding the incorporation doctrine was irreversibly changed, and it became inevitable that state criminal procedures would be affected.

Palko v. Connecticut, 302 U.S. 319, 58 S.Ct. 149, 82 L.Ed. 288 (1937)   Described "selective incorporation" as a device for determining when Bill of Rights protections should be applied to the states. *Palko* came to the Supreme Court as a double jeopardy case. Under provisions of state law, the prosecution successfully appealed a trial in which Palko had been convicted of second-degree murder and sentenced to life imprisonment. At the retrial Palko was convicted of first-degree murder and sentenced to death. Palko said he had been "twice put in jeopardy," a violation of the Fifth Amendment. He maintained the double jeopardy prohibition reached Connecticut through the Due Process Clause of the Fourteenth Amendment. The Court disagreed with Palko and upheld his retrial in a 7–2 decision. Writing for the majority, Justice Benjamin N. Cardozo accepted the task of distinguishing between those Bill of Rights guarantees such as freedom of speech and freedom of the press, which had already been extended to the states by 1937, and protections such as double jeopardy, which the Court said in *Palko* did not apply. The "rationalizing principle" of Justice Cardozo was based on the judgment of whether a particular right is "of the very essence of a scheme of ordered liberty." Certain processes such as a jury trial or grand jury indictment "may have value and importance," but to abolish or bypass them would not violate "a principle of justice so rooted in the tradition and conscience of our people as to be ranked as fundamental." The rights the states must protect are of a "different plane of social and moral values." The absorption process must consider "the belief that neither liberty nor justice would exist if they were sacrificed." In determining on which side of the incorporation line a challenged practice falls, Justice Cardozo said the Court must ask if the defendant has been subjected to a "hardship so acute and shocking that our polity would not endure it." In the instance of double jeopardy, the Court said the answer must surely be no. Connecticut was not "attempting to wear the accused out" through endless trials, but only to have a trial "free from the corrosion of substantial legal error." No fundamental principle had been violated. Palko was executed. *See also* BILL OF RIGHTS, p. 7; FIFTH AMENDMENT, p. 201; *HURTADO V. CALIFORNIA* (110 U.S. 516: 1884), p. 206.

Significance   *Palko v. California* (302 U.S. 319: 1937) rejected the view that the Fourteenth Amendment made provisions of the Bill of Rights effective against the states. The Supreme Court later overturned *Palko* on the double jeopardy holding when it extended protection against double jeopardy to the states in *Benton* v. *Maryland* (395 U.S. 784: 1969). But the idea of selective incorporation remains as a legacy of the Cardozo reasoning in *Palko*. Ten years after *Palko* the Court used the selective approach against the total incorporation approach when it refused to apply the privilege against self-incrimination to the states in *Adamson* v. *California* (332 U.S. 46: 1947). Justice Black's dissent in *Adamson* is regarded as the classic total incorporation statement. When the search and seizure provision of the Fourth Amendment was incorporated in *Wolf* v. *Colorado* (338 U.S. 25: 1949), it was applied within the "ordered liberty" approach of *Palko*. The Warren Court made extensive changes in criminal justice policy by drawing the incorporation line of *Palko* to include most of the rights of the accused in the Bill of Rights. The Warren Court's reliance on *Palko* is illustrated in *Malloy* v. *Hogan* (378 U.S. 1: 1964) and *Duncan* v. *Louisiana* (391 U.S. 145: 1968), which incorporated self-incrimination and jury trials, respectively. Only the Grand Jury Clause of the Fifth Amendment and the Excessive Fines and Bail Clause of the Eighth Amendment currently stand outside the corpus of incorporated criminal procedures.

Grand Jury

Costello v. United States, 350 U.S. 359, 76 S.Ct. 406, 100 L.Ed. 397 (1953) Examined whether grand juries must utilize the same procedural and evidentiary rules as are required for jury trials. Costello, an organized crime figure, was indicted by a grand jury for tax evasion. He claimed that the grand jury indictments had been based on hearsay evidence and should be dismissed. Costello was subsequently convicted. A unanimous Court upheld the conviction based on the challenged indictments. The Court held that no constitutional provision "prescribes the kind of evidence upon which grand juries must act." The work of grand juries was intended not to be "hampered by rigid procedural or evidentiary rules." Citing the history out of which the English grand jury system evolved, the Court noted that grand jurors could "act on their own knowledge and were free to make their presentments or indictments on such information as they deemed satisfactory." The Court noted the excessive delays that would be produced by challenges to indictments on grounds of evidence inadequacy. It would mean that a defendant could "insist on a kind of preliminary trial to determine competency and adequacy of the evidence before the grand jury." Such is not required by the Fifth Amendment. The Court concluded its opinion by reiterating that a preliminary trial "would run counter to the whole history of the grand jury institution, in which laymen conduct their inquiries unfettered by technical rules." See also BRANZBURG V. HAYES (408 U.S. 665: 1972), p. 125; FIFTH AMENDMENT, p. 201; GRAND

JURY, p. 418; *UNITED STATES V. WASHINGTON* (431 U.S. 181: 1977), p. 210.

Significance   *Costello* v. *United States* (350 U.S. 359: 1953) graphically demonstrated the broad operating latitude the Supreme Court has typically extended to grand juries. *Costello* reflects the categorical distinction between the charging process and processes designed to adjudicate guilt. Without question the grand jury can operate more informally. Procedural and evidentiary rules were referred to as possible "impediments" to the charging role of grand juries. Although decided in 1953, the position of *Costello* remains virtually unaltered, and the consequences of the case are apparent in at least three ways. First, *Costello* underscored the investigative function of grand juries and the Court's view that grand juries must be exposed to the widest range of information in performing the accusatorial function. All other interests are generally subordinate to this end. Second, because of the primacy of the investigatory role, *Costello* enhances the influence of the prosecutor in guiding the operations of a grand jury. The greater the level of informality allowed in grand jury proceedings, the greater the discretion that can be utilized by the prosecutor in selecting witnesses and other evidence for grand jury consideration. Third, *Costello*'s emphasis on informality raises certain questions regarding protection of witnesses' rights, specifically the right against self-incrimination and the right of assistance of counsel. Other problems have been noted related to the use of immunity and the threat of the contempt power. The latter can be seen in *Branzburg* v. *Hayes* (408 U.S. 665: 1972), where a reporter was compelled to disclose information to a grand jury or be subjected to penalties for contempt.

United States v. Washington, 431 U.S. 181, 97 S.Ct. 1814, 52 L.Ed.2d 238 (1977)   Considered the question of whether a grand jury witness must be specifically warned that he may be indicted by that grand jury. Further, must he be explicitly informed that if he is indicted, his testimony may be used against him at his trial? Washington was not warned of either possibility, but the Supreme Court held 7–2 that his grand jury statements were admissible at his trial. The majority concluded that the Fifth Amendment does not "preclude a witness from testifying voluntarily in matters which may incriminate him." Unless compulsion can be shown, the Fifth Amendment does not automatically apply because testimony has an incriminating effect. Once Washington had been warned generally that he could remain silent and that statements he made could be used against him, that advice "eliminated any possible compulsion to self-incrimination which may otherwise exist." The Court went on to say, "Even in the presumed psychologically coercive atmosphere of police custodial interrogation, *Miranda* does not require that any additional warnings be given simply because the suspect is a potential defendant." The majority sought to discount Washington's challenge with other distinctions as well. First, the Court felt he had been warned adequately to allow him to know his status as a potential defendant. Given all that transpired, "by the time he testified respondent knew better than anyone else" his status. Second, the majority was not convinced that any additional warnings would have aided Washington. Chief Justice Burger offered that "potential defendant warnings add nothing of value to protection of Fifth Amendment rights." Justices Brennan and Marshall dissented, arguing that persons who are "targeted" as potential defendants ought to receive greater protection from the Fifth Amendment and that continued interrogation of such witnesses ought to continue only after a voluntary and intelligent waiver of the Fifth Amendment is made by the witness. *See also* COSTELLO V. UNITED STATES (350 U.S. 359: 1953), p. 209; FIFTH AMENDMENT, p. 201; GRAND JURY, p. 418.

Significance   *United States* v. *Washington* (431 U.S. 181: 1977) was one of several cases decided by the Burger Court involving grand jury practices. In *United States* v. *Mandujano* (425 U.S. 564: 1976), a person was indicted by a grand jury for making false statements to the grand jury. The defendant attempted to have the grand jury testimony suppressed on the ground that he had not received complete *Miranda* warnings prior to his appearance. A unanimous Court concluded that the testimony need not be suppressed. The Court stressed two themes in *Mandujano*. First, the *Miranda* decision "did not perceive judicial inquiries and custodial interrogation as equivalents." The grand jury setting is so "wholly different from custodial police interrogation" that to apply *Miranda* to grand juries is an "extravagant expansion never remotely contemplated by the Court in Miranda." Second, the Court deferred to the broadest view of the grand jury's investigative function. The Court spoke of witnesses being "legally bound to give testimony" and having an "absolute duty to answer all questions." While the privilege against self-incrimination can be asserted, the Court clearly did not wish to interfere with the grand jury's capacity to conduct a complete inquiry. In *United States* v. *Calandra* (414 U.S.

338: 1974), the Court refused to extend the exclusionary rule to grand jury proceedings. Once again the Court spoke of the need to maintain broad investigative powers for grand juries. Extending the exclusionary rule would "seriously impede" grand jury inquiries and "unduly interfere with the effective and expeditious discharge of the grand jury's duties." The policy preferences reflected in *Washington* prevailed because the grand jury function is clearly distinct from guilt adjudication at the trial stage. Since the grand jury is designed to investigate and accuse, the Court decided it can best perform that function by using the widest range of evidence available. That evidence may properly come before a grand jury through procedures substantially less formal and protective than those found at the trial stage.

Double Jeopardy

***Waller* v. *Florida*, 397 U.S. 387, 90 S.Ct. 1184, 25 L.Ed.2d 435 (1970)**   Examined the question of whether a state and a municipality are separate sovereign entities, each able to prosecute criminal offenses based on the same act. Waller was convicted for destruction of city property, an ordinance violation. The state later tried him for theft of the property. The damage to the property had occurred while it was being illegally taken. Waller was convicted of grand larceny in the second proceeding, and he appealed on double jeopardy grounds. The Supreme Court vacated the second conviction in a unanimous decision. The Court rejected the notion that separate sovereignty between a state and a municipality is analogous to the relationship between the states and the federal government. The Court argued that political subdivisions of states have never been "considered as sovereign entities." Instead, they have been viewed as "subordinate governmental instrumentalities created by the State to assist in carrying out state governmental functions." While the Constitution permits dual prosecution of an individual for federal and state offenses stemming from the same act, Waller could not be so prosecuted by a municipal and a state government. As applied in that context, the Court said the "dual sovereignty theory is an anachronism, and the second trial constituted double jeopardy." *See also* ASHE v. SWENSON (397 U.S. 436: 1970), p. 213; BREED v. JONES (421 U.S. 519: 1975), p. 216; BULLINGTON v. MISSOURI (451 U.S. 430: 1981), p. 217; DOUBLE JEOPARDY, p. 403; FIFTH AMENDMENT, p. 201; PRICE v. GEORGIA (398 U.S. 323: 1970), p. 215.

Significance   *Waller* v. *Florida* (397 U.S. 387: 1970) said the existence of multiple instrumentalities of government below the federal level in the United States creates the potential for successive prosecutions in conflict with double jeopardy protections. The counterpart issue of successive federal-state prosecutions was first treated in *United States* v. *Lanza* (260 U.S. 377: 1922). *Lanza* held that successive federal-state prosecutions were permissible on dual sovereignty grounds. The two sovereignties derive "power from different sources" and are "capable of dealing with the same subject-matter within the same territory." When each level defines certain behaviors as crimes and undertakes prosecution of violators, each "is exercising its own sovereignty, not that of the other." Federal and state authorities have coordinated their activities in recent years, and, as a general practice, the federal government does not commence prosecutions in cases where state prosecutions have been initiated. For the same reasons of dual sovereignty, the double jeopardy prohibition does not preclude simultaneous prosecutions in two or more states if the criminal act occurred in more than one state. Because sovereignty flows from the source of authority, the dual sovereignty concept cannot apply in the *Waller* instance because local units are creations of state power. Conclusion of a criminal proceeding in a municipal jurisdiction or a state court constitutionally precludes a subsequent prosecution for the same criminal act in the other.

Ashe v. *Swenson*, 397 U.S. 436, 90 S.Ct. 1189, 25 L.Ed. 2d 469 (1970)

Considered whether the principle of collateral estoppel is contained within the double jeopardy protection in state criminal proceedings. Collateral estoppel is a legal principle that prohibits relitigation of an issue once a valid judgment has been made on that issue. Six persons were robbed while they were playing poker. Ashe was charged with armed robbery of each of the six players, i.e., six separate offenses. He was also charged with theft of the getaway car. Ashe was tried for robbing one of the victims and was acquitted. The jury found the evidence "insufficient" to convict. Several weeks later Ashe was tried for the robbery of another of the victims and was convicted. With only Chief Justice Burger dissenting, the Supreme Court reversed Ashe's conviction. Five justices concurred in three different opinions. The majority felt the only issue in dispute in the first trial was the identification of Ashe as one of several robbers. The jury had resolved that question in the negative. Substituting one victim for another "had no bearing whatever upon the issue of whether the petitioner was one of the robbers." The majority found the fact issue of the two trials to be identical and suggested the "situation is constitutionally no different" than had the state attempted to reprosecute Ashe for the robbery of the first victim. The two offenses were the same. Chief Justice Burger's dissent focused on two points. First, Burger felt that collateral estoppel had been extended too far. If the double jeopardy protection is intended to prohibit harassment of an accused through repeated prosecution, use of collateral estoppel was "truly a case of expanding a sound basic principle beyond the bounds—or needs—of its rationale and legitimate objectives." Second, Burger disagreed that the fact question in the second case was the same as the first. Using the same evidence test, Burger concluded that the evidence required to convict was at least partially different in the second case. *See also* BREED V. JONES (421 U.S. 519: 1975), p. 216; BULLINGTON V. MISSOURI (451 U.S. 430: 1981), p. 217; COLLATERAL ESTOPPEL, p. 396; DOUBLE JEOPARDY, p. 403; FIFTH AMENDMENT, p. 201; PRICE V. GEORGIA (398 U.S. 323: 1970), p. 215; WALLER V. FLORIDA (397 U.S. 387: 1970), p. 212.

Significance   Ashe v. Swenson (397 U.S. 436: 1970) addressed the most troublesome double jeopardy question, that of "sameness." The double jeopardy protection prevents a second prosecution only if charges are brought for the same offense. Thus determination of sameness is fundamental. With a large number of acts defined as crimes, it is likely that multiple prosecutions can arise out of overlapping offenses and single transactions. Prior to *Ashe*, one of two criteria was typically used in handling this problem. The first related to evidence required to convict on particular charges. If the "same evidence" was required for both, the offenses were deemed the same for purposes of double jeopardy. If, however, at least one element of each offense could not be proved with common evidence, the offenses were said to be different. The "same evidence" approach created limits to the protection afforded against reprosecution because of the overlapping character of contemporary criminal codes. The same evidence criterion does, however, preclude prosecution for included offenses, offenses that are generally less serious than a connected greater offense but are so tightly related that one cannot convict on the greater charge without convicting on the lesser charge as well. In *Brown v. Ohio* (432 U.S. 161: 1977), for example, the Court held that prosecution for auto theft, a greater offense, following conviction for joyriding, a lesser included offense arising out of theft of the car, was prohibited based on the same evidence test. *Brown* also said the "same evidence" was the test to be applied in determining sameness. In some instances the "same transaction" test is substituted for determining sameness of offense. This test measures offenses by actions. Though multiple charges arising out of a single incident may be brought in consolidated proceedings, the transaction test prevents multiple prosecutions for criminal conduct occurring in a single episode. The primary defect of the transaction test is that the definition of transaction remains vague. What are the actual parameters of a single transaction? Application of the collateral estoppel principle in *Ashe* provides some clarification of the sameness problem. *Ashe* forbids reprosecution in cases where a person has been acquitted on the basis of an ultimate fact issue present in the second case. Since the fact issue has been resolved in the defendant's favor previously, a second prosecution cannot constitutionally occur.

Price v. *Georgia,* 398 U.S. 323, 90 S.Ct. 1757, 26 L.Ed.2d 300 (1970)

Involved the concept of "implicit acquittal" by which it can be said that if a jury chooses to convict an individual on a lesser included charge, the jury acquitted the individual on the greater charge. Price was convicted of manslaughter although the state had charged Price with murder. Price appealed his conviction on jury instruction grounds and had his conviction set aside by a Georgia appellate court. Price was then retried with the indictment again charging him with murder. The jury again convicted Price of manslaughter, and Price appealed on double jeopardy grounds, claiming impermissible jeopardy on the murder charge in the second trial. The Supreme Court agreed with Price in a unanimous decision. Justice Blackmun did not participate. Chief Justice Burger wrote for the majority that "the first verdict, limited as it was to the lesser included offense, required that the retrial be limited to that lesser offense." The Chief Justice emphasized that the double jeopardy protection "flows inescapably" from a concern about "risk of conviction," and Price was "twice put in jeopardy." Price's jeopardy on the murder charge "ended when the first jury 'was given a full opportunity to return a verdict' on that charge and instead reached a verdict on a lesser charge." Burger concluded the opinion by suggesting that there was no effective difference between direct or explicit acquittal and one "implied by a conviction on a lesser included offense when the jury was given a full opportunity to return a verdict on the greater charge." *See also* ASHE v. SWENSON (397 U.S. 436: 1970), p. 213; BREED v. JONES (421 U.S. 519: 1975), p. 217; BULLINGTON v. MISSOURI (451 U.S. 430: 1981), p. 217; DOUBLE JEOPARDY, p. 403; FIFTH AMENDMENT, p. 201; WALLER v. FLORIDA (397 U.S. 387: 1970), p. 212.

Significance   *Price* v. *Georgia* (398 U.S. 323: 1970) raises and settles the question of implicit acquittal, but it also addresses the more general question of the extent to which the double jeopardy protection applies to a case where a defendant successfully appeals a conviction. Reprosecution is typically permitted. The Court advanced a waiver rationale in *Green* v. *United States* (355 U.S. 184: 1957), saying that an appealing defendant is waiving double jeopardy protection by requesting that the conviction be reversed. Although the waiver argument is not wholly persuasive, and while some cases subsequent to *Green* have seemed to temper the waiver approach, defendants remain vulnerable to the reinstitution of charges following a successful appeal. The exception to the retrial rule applies to those cases where the successful appeal has determined that the conviction was based on legally deficient evidence. See *Burks* v. *United States* (437 U.S. 1: 1978). The "implicit acquittal" principle of *Price* applies at this point. It limits the charge on reprosecution to no greater than the equivalent of the original conviction. Thus, if a jury opted to convict to a lesser included level at the initial trial, the retrial is limited to a charge no more serious than that lesser included offense. *Price* sets the limitation on the scope of reprosecution following a successful appeal.

Breed v. **Jones, 421 U.S. 519, 95 S.Ct. 1779, 44 L.Ed.2d 346 (1975)**   Decided when jeopardy actually begins or attaches. The case involved a 17-year-old boy who was adjudicated in a juvenile court proceeding but was later transferred to adult court for prosecution because he was "unfit for treatment as a juvenile." Jones appealed his adult court conviction claiming he had been "in jeopardy" in his juvenile proceeding and that initiation of charges against him in the adult court was foreclosed by the double jeopardy prohibition. The Supreme Court agreed with Jones in a unanimous decision. The Court's holding rested primarily on its perception of jeopardy. The Court said it was "simply too late in the day" to think that a juvenile is "not put in jeopardy at a proceeding whose object is to determine whether he has committed acts that violate criminal law," a proceeding "whose potential consequences include both the stigma inherent in such a determination and the deprivation of liberty for many years." So, despite attempts to make juvenile proceedings different from trials of adults, the juvenile process resembles the adult process closely enough to create jeopardy. The Court also rejected the contention that the prosecution of Jones as an adult was merely a continuation of the prosecution begun at the juvenile level. While the Court agreed the case "had not yet reached its conclusion" in the juvenile proceeding in that no sentence had been assigned, it determined the failure to sentence Jones had not in any way limited Jones's risk or jeopardy. Putting Jones "at risk" was viewed as the decisive aspect of jeopardy. The juvenile court, "as the trier of facts, began to hear evidence," and at that point Jones's jeopardy began. If the juvenile authorities wished to preserve flexibility in terms of treatment or sentence options, those matters should have been considered prior to initiating proceedings in the juvenile court. If a defendant cannot be suitably treated as a delinquent, the Court urged that transfer occur "prior to adjudicatory hearings." *See also* ASHE V. SWENSON (397 U.S. 436: 1970), p. 213; BULLINGTON V. MISSOURI (451 U.S. 430: 1981), p. 217; DOUBLE JEOPARDY, p. 403; FIFTH AMENDMENT, p. 201; PRICE V. GEORGIA (398 U.S. 323: 1970), p. 215; WALLER V. FLORIDA (397 U.S. 387: 1970), p. 212.

Significance   *Breed* v. *Jones* (421 U.S. 519: 1975) decided the issue of when jeopardy begins. This is a critical determination in that a person must be in jeopardy once before he or she can be protected against a second jeopardy. In the *Jones* case, jeopardy began when the juvenile authorities began to hear evidence in the adjudication of Jones. A person is "at risk" for double jeopardy purposes when the proceeding begins. More specifically, the risk begins at the time a jury is chosen or when a court begins to take evidence. A judgment on that evidence by a jury or a court need not occur. Immunity from future prosecution on the original charges does not extend to cases where the defendant initiated a cessation of trial proceedings. Nor does it extend to those cases where the defendant successfully appeals following a conviction and has the conviction vacated on grounds other than evidence insufficiency. A case that does not reach the evidence stage, stopping at some preliminary point, affords no protection from further prosecution on the same charges. Neither dismissal of charges at a preliminary hearing nor dismissal of an indictment before a trial actually commences, precludes those same charges from being brought again.

Bullington v. Missouri, 451 U.S. 430, 101 S.Ct. 1852, 68 L.Ed.2d 270 (1981)   Raised the question of whether the double jeopardy protection applies to the sentencing process. Bullington had been sentenced to life imprisonment by a jury in the second stage of a bifurcated process in which the determination of guilt was separate from the sentence. Bullington was subsequently granted a new trial on certain procedural grounds. The prosecutor indicated the death penalty would be sought at the second trial. Bullington claimed that double jeopardy barred the death penalty following his conviction at the second trial. A five-member majority of the Supreme Court agreed with him. Through Justice Blackmun, the majority acknowledged that the Court had resisted attempts to extend the double jeopardy clause to sentencing in the past, but the majority found the bifurcated death penalty process sufficiently different from other sentencing situations to act in this case. Given the process used, the majority concluded that sentencing was analogous to the guilt adjudication stage of other cases. The process gives sentencing the "hallmarks of the trial on guilt or innocence." Thus, if a jury acquits a defendant on a more extreme penalty option, it forecloses that sentence from being utilized in a retrial. The Court found the "implicit acquittal" principle applicable here just as if Bullington's jury had chosen to convict of a lesser included offense. Chief Justice Burger and Justices Powell, White, and Rehnquist dissented. They disagreed that the sentence process was analogous to the trial stage even in a bifurcated proceeding. They argued there was an inherent difference in the nature of the issues requiring response. The dissenters further stated that there are statutory boundaries to sentencing choices that have no guilt stage counterparts. They concluded that Missouri ought to be able to pursue imposition of the statutorily authorized penalty at the second trial just as it had at the first. *See also* ASHE V. SWENSON (397 U.S. 436: 1970), p. 213; BREED V. JONES (421 U.S. 519: 1975), p. 216; DOUBLE JEOPARDY, p. 403; FIFTH AMENDMENT, p. 201; PRICE V. GEORGIA (398 U.S. 323: 1970), p. 215; WALLER V. FLORIDA (397 U.S. 387: 1970), p. 212.

Significance   Bullington v. Missouri (451 U.S. 430: 1981) focused on the question of whether a person may receive a more severe sentence on retrial even if the charge is not more serious. *Price v. Georgia* (398 U.S. 323: 1970) confirmed that a person cannot be retried for a more serious charge following a successful appeal. In *North Carolina v. Pearce* (395 U.S. 711: 1969), the Court held that the double jeopardy protection did not prohibit a more severe sentence as such. As a safeguard against vindictive sentence increases, however, *Pearce* required that the more severe sentence be based on new information not available at the initial sentencing. *Bullington* went beyond *Pearce* in extending the double jeopardy coverage and the "implicit acquittal" principle where juries make sentencing judgments in a two-stage process. Despite *Bullington* the Court has limited the extent to which the double jeopardy protection impinges on sentencing. In *United States v. DiFrancesco* (449 U.S. 819: 1980), the Court held that provisions of the Organized Crime Control Act of 1970 allowing for the government to appeal sentences imposed under the "dangerous special offender" section of the statute do not offend the double jeopardy protection. A five-justice majority found that even though a successful appeal might cause a lenient sentence to be replaced by a more severe one, the policy did not violate the double jeopardy prohibition against either multiple trials or multiple punishments.

Self-Incrimination

Miranda v. *Arizona*, 384 U.S. 436, 86 S.Ct. 1602, 16 L.Ed.2d 694 (1966)   Examined custodial interrogation practices. The *Miranda* decision was based on the relationship between the Fifth Amendment's privilege against self-incrimination and the Sixth Amendment's right to counsel in the pretrial period. The groundwork for *Miranda* began two years earlier in *Escobedo* v. *Illinois* (1964). In a controversial 5–4 decision, the Court overturned the conviction of Escobedo, holding that when a police investigation begins to focus on a particular individual, and when interrogation turns from mere information gathering to eliciting a confession, the American legal system requires that the individual must be allowed to consult with legal counsel. *Miranda* and three companion cases allowed the Warren Court to develop this theme further and broaden its application. The Court was particularly concerned with the interrogation environment, believing it to be a closed process and inherently coercive. Chief Justice Warren said, "Even without employing brutality . . . the very fact of custodial interrogation exacts a heavy toll on individual liberty and trades on the weaknesses of individuals." He added, "It is obvious that such an interrogation environment is created for no other purpose than to subjugate the individual to the will of the examiner. This atmosphere carries its own badge of intimidation." The majority specified four warnings that must be administered at the time of arrest, prior to beginning interrogation. The "Miranda Rules" require that an arrested person (1) be told of his or her right to remain silent, (2) be told that anything he or she says can be used against the accused in court, (3) be told that he or she has a right to consult with an attorney prior to questioning and that failure to request counsel does not constitute waiver of the right, and (4) be told that counsel will be provided to the accused in the event that he or she cannot afford counsel. *Miranda* v. *Arizona* (384 U.S. 436: 1966) held that statements made by the accused without these warnings are inadmissible in a trial. *See also* BREWER V. WILLIAMS (430 U.S. 387: 1977), p. 223; ESTELLE V. SMITH (451 U.S. 454: 1981), p. 227; HARRIS V. NEW YORK (401 U.S. 222: 1971), p. 220; MICHIGAN V. TUCKER (417 U.S. 433: 1974), p. 222; NORTH CAROLINA V. BUTLER (441 U.S. 369: 1979), p. 225; SELF-INCRIMINATION CLAUSE, p. 448.

Significance   *Miranda* v. *Arizona* (384 U.S. 436: 1966) instituted extensive changes in constitutional policy involving rights of the accused. No single decision of the Warren Court has had more impact except, perhaps, *Mapp* v. *Ohio* (367 U.S. 643: 1961). The Warren Court clearly assigned high priority to confronting inappropriate police practices. It recognized the utility of defense counsel as a means of discouraging misconduct. Basically it tried to give meaning to constitutional protections and to prevent them from becoming empty formalisms. Protection against self-incrimination, for example, could be achieved by extending the right to counsel to critical pretrial stages, hence the linkage of the two provisions in *Miranda*. The decision intensified criticism of the Warren Court's approach to defining rights of the accused. The Court's detractors felt that *Miranda* made confessions virtually impossible to secure, thus hand-cuffing law enforcement authorities. Many felt the Court had pre-empted legislative prerogatives in setting law enforcement standards. The negative feeling toward *Miranda* was manifested in the Omnibus Crime Control Act of 1968. Provisions of this legislation softened some of the *Miranda* requirements, at least at the federal level. Federal judges, for example, were given greater latitude in determining the voluntariness of incriminating statements. It was left to the Burger Court to determine the status of *Miranda* for state trials. Several Burger Court decisions have closed the scope of its provisions. In *Harris* v. *New York* (401 U.S. 222: 1971), for example, the Court held that a statement judged inadmissible because of *Miranda* defects could be used to impeach a defendant should he or she take the witness stand. The Burger Court has rejected opportunities to overrule *Miranda*, however, and seems to be embarked on a case-by-case examination of *Miranda* standards.

Harris v. New York, 401 U.S. 222, 91 S.Ct. 643, 28 L.Ed.2d 1 (1971)   Considered whether statements made by a defendant in violation of *Miranda* could be used to impeach that defendant's own testimony at his trial. *Miranda* established that criminal defendants must be informed of their right against self-incrimination and their right to assistance of counsel. While Harris was testifying at his own trial, he was asked during cross-examination whether he had made any statements immediately following his arrest. When he claimed he could not recall making any statements, the statements he in fact made were introduced into evidence for the purpose of impeaching Harris's credibility. The jury instruction attempted to differentiate between use of statements for impeachment purposes and their use as evidence of guilt. The jury was instructed it could not do the latter. Harris was subsequently convicted. The Supreme Court rejected his appeal in a 5–4 decision. The majority said that *Miranda* is not an absolute prohibition against the use of statements taken without proper warnings. *Miranda* bars the prosecution from "making its case with statements" taken in violation of *Miranda*. But "it does not follow from *Miranda* that evidence inadmissible against an accused in the prosecution's case in chief is barred for all purposes." Use of such evidence, however, must satisfy conditions of trustworthiness. Crucial to the outcome in *Harris* is the use of statements made in an adversary process, specifically impeachment of a witness through cross-examination. The "impeachment process here undoubtedly provided valuable aid to the jury in assessing petitioner's credibility." The majority felt that information was of more value than guarding against the "speculative possibility" that police misconduct would be encouraged. The majority emphasized the need to maintain the integrity of the trial itself. A defendant can testify in his own defense, but does not have "the right to commit perjury." Once the defendant takes the witness stand, the prosecution can "utilize the traditional truth-testing devices of the adversary process." Chief Justice Burger concluded the opinion by saying, "The shield provided by *Miranda* cannot be perverted into a license to use perjury by way of a defense, free from the risk of confrontation with prior inconsistent utterances." The dissenters, Justices Douglas, Black, Brennan, and Marshall, argued that statements that are tainted should not be used under any circumstance. They felt the decision would "seriously undermine" the maintenance of constitutional protections against police misconduct. *See also* BREWER V. WILLIAMS (430 U.S. 387: 1977), p. 223; FIFTH AMENDMENT, p. 201; MICHIGAN V. TUCKER (417 U.S. 433: 1974), p. 222; MIRANDA V. ARIZONA (384 U.S. 436: 1966), p. 219; NORTH CAROLINA V. BUTLER (441 U.S. 369: 1979), p. 225; SELFINCRIMINATION CLAUSE, p. 448; STONE V. POWELL (428 U.S. 465: 1976), p. 173.

Significance   *Harris v. New York* (401 U.S. 222: 1971) seriously qualified *Miranda*. The Court allowed *Miranda*-defective statements and confessions to be utilized to impeach a defendant, as opposed to being used in making the case in chief. *Harris* reflects the Burger Court's reluctance fully to embrace the *Miranda* holding, as well as its

Court's reluctance fully to embrace the *Miranda* holding, as well as its general unwillingness to disturb the dynamics of the adversary process. The basic thrust of *Harris* is that a jury ought to be given every opportunity to assess a defendant and the defense being advanced. The underlying theme of *Harris* was reiterated in *Oregon* v. *Hass* (420 U.S. 714: 1975) by a 6–2 margin. The *Harris-Hass* rule does not apply, however, where statements are obtained involuntarily. In *Mincey* v. *Arizona* (437 U.S. 385: 1978), the Court ruled that interrogation of a defendant hospitalized in critical condition produced involuntary and untrustworthy responses. They could not be used even for impeachment purposes. The Court has also held that post-warning silence cannot be used to impeach a defendant. In *Doyle* v. *Ohio* (426 U.S. 610: 1976), two defendants offered exculpatory explanations at their trial, explanations not previously shared with police or prosecutors. They were cross-examined as to why they had withheld their stories until the trial. A six-justice majority concluded that "silence in the wake of these [*Miranda*] warnings may be nothing more than the arrestee's exercise of these *Miranda* rights." On the other hand, silence occurring previous to receiving *Miranda* warnings may be used for impeachment purposes on the grounds that the silence was not "induced by the assurances contained in the *Miranda* warnings."

Michigan v. Tucker, 417 U.S. 433, 94 S.Ct. 2357, 41 L.Ed.2d 182 (1974)   Raised questions about the administration of *Miranda* rules. Tucker was questioned before *Miranda,* but the trial occurred after *Miranda* had been published. Tucker was advised that statements he made could be used against him, but was not thoroughly advised about his right to access an attorney. In particular he was not told that counsel could be furnished him, despite his indigent status. There is no way of knowing whether the defendant understood his right to an attorney. What is clear is that he was not *told* he could have a lawyer without cost. During the ensuing interrogation, Tucker named an alibi witness. The actual statements of this witness turned out to discredit Tucker's alibi, and Tucker was convicted. Thus, without assistance of counsel, Tucker provided the decisive evidence against himself through his own alibi witness. With only Justice Douglas dissenting, the Court upheld Tucker's conviction. The Court said *Miranda* indeed precluded admission at trial of the statements made by Tucker during his interrogation. But this did not cover the naming of a third party, which was done voluntarily. The protection from self-incrimination is aimed at certain kinds of practices, none of which were involved in the naming of the alibi witness. The Court did find that *Miranda* was "disregarded" to the extent that the full warnings were not executed. In retrospect *Miranda* clearly applied, but the disregard was "inadvertent." More important, so long as "the police conduct did not abridge respondent's constitutional privilege against self-incrimination, but departed only from the prophylactic standards set by this Court in *Miranda*," testimony from the witness named by the defendant need not be excluded. The Court felt that use of the exclusionary rule in cases where police actions were "pursued in complete good faith" served no purpose relative to deterring police misconduct. The Court emphasized the flexible character of *Miranda*. Failure to give full *Miranda* warnings "does not entitle the suspect to insist that statements made by him be excluded in every conceivable context." *Miranda* protections must be evaluated from a broader perspective. Justice Rehnquist remarked, "Just as the law does not require that a defendant receive a perfect trial, just a fair one, it cannot realistically require that police investigating serious crimes make no errors whatsoever." Furthermore, the information provided by the witness was reliable and subject to the "testing process" of an adversary trial. There was "no reason to believe that Henderson's [the witness'] testimony is untrustworthy simply because respondent [Tucker] was not advised of his right to appointed counsel." *See also* BREWER v. WILLIAMS (430 U.S. 387: 1977), p. 223; FIFTH ADMENDMENT, p. 201; HARRIS v. NEW YORK (401 U.S. 222: 1971), p. 220; MIRANDA v. ARIZONA (384 U.S. 436: 1966), p. 219; NORTH CAROLINA v. BUTLER (441 U.S. 369: 1979), p. 225; SELF-INCRIMINATION CLAUSE, p. 448.

Significance   Michigan v. *Tucker* (417 U.S. 433: 1974) decided that incomplete administration of *Miranda* did not necessarily invalidate use of statements secured subsequent to the incomplete warnings. Whether the derived evidence could be used would depend on the reliability of the evidence itself. Generally, evidence derived from statements or confessions that are improperly obtained cannot be used. The derived evidence is contaminated by the tainted confession. *Tucker* reiterated the Burger Court's strong predisposition for exposing the trial process to the fullest range of reliable evidence, even if the evidence was derived from a flawed and inadmissible confession. Since Tucker disclosed the witness voluntarily and the witness's subsequent testimony was viewed as trustworthy, failure fully to advise Tucker of his *Miranda* protections was a subordinate interest.

Brewer v. Williams, 430 U.S. 387, 97 S.Ct. 1232, 51 L.Ed.2d 424 (1977)   Involved incriminating statements made by a defendant in the absence of his attorney. Williams was arrested, arraigned, and jailed in Davenport, Iowa, for abducting and murdering a young child in the city of Des Moines. Williams consulted with attorneys in both cities and was advised to make no statements to the police. As Williams was being transported from Davenport to Des Moines, he indicated unwillingness to be interrogated until his attorney was present but said he would make a full statement at that time. Nonetheless, one of the officers, aware that Williams was a former mental patient and deeply religious, sought to elicit statements from Williams relative to the location of the child's body. The officer suggested to Williams that the child's parents were entitled to a "Christian burial" for their child. Williams eventually made a number of incriminating statements and directed the police to the location of the child's body. Williams was subsequently tried and convicted. Evidence relating to statements made during his transportation to Des Moines were admitted at his trial over his objections. The Supreme Court held 5–4 that the evidence was inadmissible and the conviction void. The decision hinged on whether Williams had knowingly and intelligently waived his right to counsel. There was no dispute that the police officer had deliberately attempted to elicit information from Williams and that the "Christian burial speech" was "tantamount to interrogation." The majority concluded that the right to counsel had not been waived. It said that waiver required "not merely comprehension but relinquishment." That the defendant had relied heavily on advice of counsel throughout, that he had consulted with attorneys at both ends of his trip, and that he had specifically mentioned making a statement *after* completing the trip and consulting with his attorney, all were evidence of his unwillingness to waive his right to counsel. The officer elicited incriminating statements "despite Williams' express and implicit assertions of his right to counsel." Regardless of the "senseless and brutal" character of the offense, what had occurred was "so clear a violation" of Williams's constitutional protection that it "cannot be condoned." The dissenters were outraged. Chief Justice Burger called the result "intolerable." The dissenters held that Williams had not been compelled or coerced. Further, they noted that Williams's guilt was beyond doubt, and that to apply "the draconian judicial doctrine" called the exclusionary rule to cases such as *Williams* was highly inappropriate. *See also* EXCLUSIONARY RULE, p. 409; FIFTH ADMENDMENT, p. 201; *HARRIS* V. *NEW YORK* (401 U.S. 222: 1971), p. 220; *MICHIGAN* V. *TUCKER* (417 U.S. 433: 1974), p. 222; *MIRANDA* V. *ARIZONA* (384 U.S. 436: 1966), p. 219; *NORTH CAROLINA* V. *BUTLER* (441 U.S. 369: 1979), p. 225; SELF-INCRIMINATION CLAUSE p. 448.

Significance   Brewer v. Williams (430 U.S. 387: 1977) highlights the relationship between assistance of counsel and the protection from self-incrimination. The Court established in *Miranda* that preservation of the privilege against self-incrimination is best accomplished by providing an accused with access to defense counsel. *Brewer* conveys that the Court is reluctant to allow waiver of counsel in interrogation situations. *Brewer* also raised questions about what constitutes interrogation. The Court found the "Christian burial speech" to be "tantamount to interrogation," intentionally designed to elicit incriminating statements. But *Brewer* does not fully define what constitutes an interrogation. The Court generally holds that *Miranda* safeguards apply when interactions occur that the police know may reasonably be expected to elicit an incriminating response. Thus warnings must be given whenever an officer, through any action verbal or otherwise, is likely to prompt an incriminating response. See *Rhode Island* v. *Innis* (446 U.S. 291: 1980). The Court has held firm on the counsel waiver issue. It will not accept a voluntary confession from a defendant after he or she has requested defense counsel and the counsel is not present for the confession. In *Oregon* v. *Bradshaw* (000 U.S. 000: 1983) the Court did rule, however, that a prisoner's question, "Well, what is going to happen to me now?" constituted initiation of further conversation that could yield admissible statements against him.

North Carolina v. Butler, 441 U.S. 369, 99 S.Ct. 1755, 60 L.Ed.2d 286 (1979)   Considered whether the waiver of a constitutional right need be explicit. Butler was arrested and informed of his *Miranda* rights. He was given an "Advice of Rights" form, which he read and said he understood. He refused, however, to sign the waiver provision at the bottom of the form, although he indicated he was "willing to talk." Butler subsequently tried to have statements made during the ensuing conversation suppressed. The case revolved around a determination of whether Butler had actually waived his rights. The Supreme Court decided that Butler's statements could be admitted. The majority in an opinion written by Justice Stewart, joined by Chief Justice Burger and Justices White, Blackmun, and Rehnquist, held that while explicit waiver is usually strong proof of the validity of a waiver, it is not "inevitably either necessary or sufficient to establish the waiver." The Court said further, "the question is not one of form, but rather whether the defendant in fact knowingly and voluntarily waived the rights delineated in *Miranda*." The burden of demonstrating the adequacy of a waiver rests with the prosecution, and the prosecution's "burden is great." However, "in at least some cases waiver can be clearly inferred from the actions and words of the person interrogated." Waivers must be evaluated in terms of the facts and circumstances of each case. The Court's judgment was that Butler made a knowing and voluntary waiver even though it was not explicit. The majority clearly rejected the establishment of an "inflexible *per se* rule" requiring explicit waiver. The dissenters, Justices Brennan, Marshall, and Stevens, argued that an affirmative or explicit waiver is required to satisfy *Miranda*. Justice Powell did not participate in the case. The dissenting justices claimed that *Miranda* recognized that custodial interrogation is "inherently coercive," and that ambiguity must be "interpreted against the interrogator." They would have required a "simple prophylactic rule requiring the police to obtain express waiver." *See also* BREWER V. WILLIAMS (430 U.S. 387: 1977), p. 223; FIFTH AMENDMENT, p. 201; HARRIS V. NEW YORK (401 U.S. 222: 1971), p. 220; MICHIGAN V. TUCKER (417 U.S. 433: 1974), p. 222; MIRANDA V. ARIZONA (384 U.S. 436: 1966), p. 219; SELF-INCRIMINATION CLAUSE, p. 448.

Significance   North Carolina v. Butler (441 U.S. 369: 1979) specifies what must be done by a defendant to waive the associated rights of assistance of counsel and protection from self-incrimination. The *Miranda* protections may be waived, but the waiver must be voluntary, knowing, and intelligent. It may not be the product of coercion, trick, threat, persuasion, or inducement. While the waiver need not be written or explicit, it cannot be presumed from silence under any circumstances. The burden rests with the prosecution to demonstrate that a waiver was freely, knowingly, and intelligently made. Determinations of the adequacy of a waiver are to be based on the "totality of the circumstances" of a particular case and may include such matters as the background and overall conduct of the defendant. *Butler* provides some latitude by not requiring a firm rule relative to explicit waiver. At the same time it clarifies and maintains the general protections afforded by *Miranda*. The latter was intended to draw a clear and bright line obviating the need for a case-by-case determination of voluntariness. *Butler* brings the Court full circle. The dissent recognizes that *Butler* implicitly, if not explicitly, overruled part of *Miranda*'s clear holding.

Carter v. Kentucky, 450 U.S. 288, 101 S.Ct. 1112, 67 L.Ed.2d 241 (1981)   Involved a defendant who chose not to testify in his own defense. Carter requested a specific jury instruction indicating he was not obligated to testify and that his failure to testify should not prejudice him in any way. The trial judge refused the request, and Carter was convicted. The Supreme Court reversed the conviction with only Justice Rehnquist dissenting. The majority found that the Fifth Amendment does more than simply preclude adverse comment on the defendant's silence. The "defendant must pay no court-imposed price for the exercise of his constitutional privilege not to testify." And that penalty "may be just as severe when there is no adverse comment" and the jury "is left to roam at large with only its untutored instincts to guide it." A defendant is entitled to request special mention of his choice not to testify so as to "remove from the jury's deliberations any influence of unspoken adverse inferences." The Court noted the impact of the jury instruction and concluded that a trial judge "has an affirmative constitutional obligation to use that tool when a defendant seeks its employment." While those instructions may not prevent jurors from speculating about a defendant's silence, the "unique power of the jury instruction . . . [can] reduce that speculation to a minimum." Justice Rehnquist argued in dissent that the instruction requested by Carter was a matter to be determined at the state level rather than by construction of the Fifth Amendment. Rehnquist felt Carter was not constitutionally entitled to such special instruction. *See also* FIFTH AMENDMENT, p. 201; MIRANDA V. ARIZONA (384 U.S. 436: 1966), p. 219; SELF-INCRIMINATION CLAUSE, p. 448.

Significance   Carter v. Kentucky (450 U.S. 288: 1981) is a milestone in the evolution of self-incrimination standards. An important related case is *Twining* v. *New Jersey* (211 U.S. 78: 1908), in which the Court refused to examine a New Jersey law permitting a jury instruction that an unfavorable inference could be drawn from the defendant's unwillingness to take the stand in his or her own defense. The Court held in *Twining* that the Fifth Amendment privilege against self-incrimination did not extend to the states, thus no specific practice allegedly abridging it could be considered. Essentially the same position was taken 40 years later in *Adamson* v. *California* (332 U.S. 46: 1947), where prosecutorial comment on a defendant's failure to testify was permitted. When the Supreme Court overturned *Twining* and *Adamson* relative to state applicability of the self-incrimination protection in *Malloy* v. *Hogan* (378 U.S. 1: 1964), the comment practice was a primary target. It was declared unconstitutional a year later in *Griffin* v. *California* (380 U.S. 609: 1965). *Carter* extends the "no comment" rule one last step.

Estelle v. Smith, 451 U.S. 454, 101 S.Ct. 1866, 67 L.Ed. 2d 359 (1981)   Decided whether testimony by a psychiatrist who conducted a competency examination of a defendant prior to the defendant's trial can be offered at the penalty phase of the trial. A competency examination does not immediately suggest self-incrimination issues, but they emerge in *Estelle*. Prior to Smith's murder trial, the prosecution made clear its intention to seek the death penalty. The Court ordered a competency examination. Smith was found competent, and was tried and convicted. A separate sentencing hearing is required for the death penalty in Texas. It must be found, among other things, that the defendant is likely to commit more violent crime if given the opportunity. It was to this question that the psychiatrist's testimony was directed, and Smith was sentenced to death. The Supreme Court reversed the sentence in a unanimous decision. The opinion by Chief Justice Burger made several statements about the right against self-incrimination. First, it applies to the sentencing stage just as it does to the guilt adjudication stage of a trial. Its availability "does not turn on the type of proceeding, but on the nature of the statement or admission and the exposure which it invites." Second, that the statements made by Smith were "uttered in the context of a psychiatric examination does not remove them from the reach of the Fifth Amendment." That they were nontestimonial in nature was irrelevant. Third, Smith should have been warned of his right to remain silent and that statements made to the psychiatrist could be used at a capital sentencing proceeding. The Court found Smith to be in the same position as a person subjected to a custodial interrogation by police. The psychiatrist may have been "neutral" in some respects, but when he went beyond simply reporting results of the examination and testified for the prosecution at the penalty stage, "his role changed and became essentially like that of an agent of the State recounting unwarned statements made in a post-arrest custodial setting." In sum the Court reiterated that the protection against self-incrimination is as "broad as the mischief against which it seeks to guard." The Court also found a defect on right to counsel grounds, concluding that the right had attached to Smith prior to the examination and counsel should have been present at what proved to be a "critical stage of the aggregate proceedings against respondent." *See also* FIFTH AMENDMENT, p. 201; *MIRANDA* V. *ARIZONA* (384 U.S. 436: 1966), p. 219; SELF-INCRIMINATION CLAUSE, p. 448.

Significance   *Estelle* v. *Smith* (451 U.S. 454: 1981) was a strong statement by the Burger Court of its commitment to the interests protected by *Miranda* v. *Arizona* (384 U.S. 436: 1966). *Smith* also reflects the wide scope to which self-incrimination coverage has evolved. *Smith* refers to "exposure" in regard to the protection provided by the privilege against self-incrimination. This exposure is distinct from and more inclusive than protection based upon the type of legal proceeding taking place. Thus self-incrimination coverage attaches also to juveniles as well as sentencing and competency examinations. By making it clear that exposure can exist in contexts other than traditional legal proceedings, the *Smith* decision broadens the scope of the privilege. Recognition that statements need not be in the form of actual testimony is particularly significant in terms of the expanded scope of the privilege. *Smith* is one of the Burger Court's strongest pronouncements regarding self-incrimination.

Blood Samples

***Schmerber* v. *California*, 384 U.S. 757, 86 S.Ct. 1826, 16 L.Ed.2d 908 (1966)**   Explored whether the privilege against self-incrimination extends to defendant-derived evidence of a non-communicated nature. The privilege clearly covers communicated testimony. *Schmerber* involved a driving-while-intoxicated conviction in which critical evidence against the defendant came in the form of blood test results. The blood sample upon which the tests were performed was taken over Schmerber's objection. Schmerber challenged the conviction on search, self-incrimination, assistance of counsel, and general due process grounds. A five-justice majority rejected all of his contentions. The majority held that taking the blood sample "constituted compulsion for the purposes of the privilege." The critical question in *Schmerber* was whether the blood sample actually constituted making Schmerber "a witness against himself." The Court concluded that the scope of the self-incrimination protection did not extend far enough to reach Schmerber. The privilege applied only against compelling evidence against the accused "from his own mouth." The evidence must be testimonial, i.e., the words or communications of the accused. The majority likened the blood sample to fingerprints and other means of identification. It said that making the suspect provide "real or physical evidence does not violate it" (the privilege against self-incrimination). The Court opined that in Schmerber's case, "not even a shadow of testimonial compulsion upon or enforced communication by the accused was involved either in extraction or in chemical analysis." Schmerber's "testimonial capacities were in no way implicated." In the majority's view Schmerber, "except as a donor, was irrelevant to the results of the test." Dissents were written by Chief Justice Warren and Justices Douglas, Fortas, and Black. The dissents ranged across the issues raised by Schmerber, but Justice Black's argument was representative of the minority's concerns about self-incrimination. He said, "To reach the conclusion that compelling a person to give his blood to help the State convict him is not equivalent to compelling him to be a witness against himself strikes me as quite an extraordinary feat." The dissenters rejected the majority's distinction between verbal testimony and physical evidence. See also FIFTH AMENDMENT, p. 201; *MANSON V. BRAITHWAITE* (432 U.S. 98: 1977), p. 232; *NEIL V. BIGGERS* (409 U.S. 188: 1972), p. 230.

Significance   *Schmerber* v. *California* (384 U.S. 757: 1966) is the definitive ruling on blood samples and self-incrimination. *Schmerber* held simply that blood samples, because they are not "testimonial" in character, are not covered by the privilege against self-incrimination. As long as the sample is not taken in a manner which "shocks the conscience," analysis conducted on the sample is admissible evidence. The Court has also permitted states to admit into evidence a person's refusal to submit to a blood-alcohol test. In *South Dakota* v. *Neville* (74 L.Ed.2d 748: 1983) the Court held that since the offer of taking the test is "clearly legitimate, the action becomes no less legitimate when the State offers a second option of refusing the test, with attendant penalties for making that choice." Use of test results based on breath, urine, skin, and other samples obtained from a suspect's body are also covered under the *Schmerber* decision. Extending *Schmerber*, the Court has held that samples of a person's handwriting or voice may be used for identification purposes. In *Gilbert* v. *California* (388 U.S. 263: 1967), the Court said that while one's voice and handwriting are a means of communication, a sample of handwriting or a voice exemplar, independent of the content of what is written or said, is an "identifying physical characteristic" that is outside the protection of the privilege against compelled self-incrimination. Warren Court decisions such as *Schmerber* and *Gilbert* clearly distinguish protected testimonial incrimination from unprotected nontestimonial evidence. The Burger Court has maintained the distinction. The only constraints on nontestimonial evidence stem from the Fourth Amendment and the guidelines flowing from it governing seizure of evidence.

Identification Procedures

Neil v. Biggers, 409 U.S. 188, 93 S.Ct. 375, 34 L.Ed.2d 401 (1972)   Examined the confrontation process and clarified some of the criteria for admitting identifications as evidence in a trial. Direct confrontation by a witness is frequently used to identify persons suspected of criminal acts. Biggers was convicted of rape. The single most significant piece of evidence against him was the testimony of the rape victim. She had identified Biggers as two police officers walked him past her. This confrontation, or showup, occurred seven months after the crime. A lineup for identification purposes was not used because the police could not assemble a sufficient number of other persons resembling the accused. The Supreme Court ruled that the showup was adequate and upheld Biggers's conviction in a 5–3 decision, Justice Marshall not participating. The majority ruled that a defendant must demonstrate that the identification process was "so unnecessarily suggestive and conducive to irreparable mistaken identification" as to deny due process. That determination is to be made through examination of the "totality of the circumstances." The primary evil to be prevented is "a very substantial likelihood of irreparable misidentification." A confrontation may be suggestive, but not so suggestive as to make misidentification likely. The identification of Biggers was suggestive because he was the only person placed before the victim, but it was not too suggestive because other factors supported the reliability of the victim's identification. The Court noted several criteria that must be used in evaluating the reliability of the identification. The factors include (1) the opportunity of the witness to "view the criminal at the time of the crime"; (2) the witness's "degree of attention"; (3) how accurate the witness's "prior description" of the suspect has been; and (4) the "level of certainty demonstrated by the witness" at the confrontation. On the basis of these factors, the Court concluded that even though the showup has been suggestive, the witness's identification had been reliable enough. Justices Brennan, Douglas, and Stewart dissented on the ground that the identification procedure in the case was too suggestive. *See also* FIFTH AMENDMENT, p. 201; *MANSON* V. *BRAITHWAITE* (432 U.S. 98: 1977), p. 232; *SCHMERBER* V. *CALIFORNIA* (384 U.S. 757: 1966), p. 229.

Significance   *Neil* v. *Biggers* (409 U.S. 188: 1972) provides generally applicable standards by which the reliability of identifications can be assessed. The Supreme Court has never held that requiring a person to be viewed by a witness violates due process rights. It has, however, circumscribed confrontational identification processes in such cases as *Neil*. The *Neil* criteria are not always decisive because the confrontation technique is excessively suggestive in itself. For example, a lineup that contains only one person dressed in the manner described by a witness, only one person approximating the physical description provided by the witness, only one person who appears in a second lineup who had appeared in an earlier lineup, are confrontations that make "identifications virtually inevitable." See *Foster* v. *California* (394 U.S. 400: 1969). Such a confrontation is categorically prohibited. If the confrontation is not too suggestive, the reliability of the identification is evaluated further using the *Neil* criteria. The Court has also determined that post-indictment confrontations are a sufficiently critical stage in the criminal process that a suspect is entitled to assistance of counsel at that point.

Manson v. Braithwaite, 432 U.S. 98, 97 S.Ct. 2243, 53 L.Ed.2d 140 (1977)   Involved a photographic identification challenged as being both suggestive and unnecessary. An undercover police officer purchased heroin from a person in a lighted apartment hallway. The transaction took several minutes, during which time the officer was in close physical proximity to the seller. After the transaction, the officer described the seller to another officer. Based on the physical description, the second officer concluded the seller was Braithwaite and gave a single photograph of Braithwaite to the first officer. The first officer examined the photograph and identified Braithwaite as the seller. The photograph and the officer's identification were received as evidence at Braithwaite's trial. Braithwaite was convicted. With only Justices Brennan and Marshall dissenting, but with Justice Stevens filing a separate concurring opinion, the Supreme Court upheld Braithwaite's conviction. The crucial question for the Court was whether the reliability of the identification outweighs the procedural problems with it. The procedures used in this case were both suggestive and unnecessary. Only one photograph had been supplied to the undercover officer, and there had been no emergency or exigent circumstance present. Therefore the Burger Court had two basic policy options. The first was to adopt a firm rule precluding the use of evidence stemming from suggestive or unnecessary identification procedures with no consideration of the reliability of the identification. The other was to evaluate the reliability of each identification based on the "totality of circumstances." The majority chose the latter course. The Court concluded that while an absolute prohibition might best deter police misconduct, such a rule "goes too far since its application automatically and peremptorily, and without consideration of alleviating factors, keeps evidence from the jury that is reliable and relevant." The Court said, "reliability is the lynchpin in determining the admissibility of identification testimony." Since the officer had sufficient time to observe the seller, was attentive, could accurately describe him, was certain of the identification, and had made the identification soon after the heroin sale, his testimony identifying Braithwaite was reliable. *See also* EXCLU-SIONARY RULE, p. 409; FIFTH AMENDMENT, p. 201; *NEIL* V. *BIGGERS* (409. U.S. 188: 1972), p. 230.

Significance   Manson v. *Braithwaite* (432 U.S. 98: 1977) decided that the Supreme Court would not adopt a per se rule of exclusion for needlessly suggestive and unnecessary photographic identification. Given the Burger Court's disenchantment with the exclusionary rule generally, it was hardly unexpected that the Court chose not to impose the rule in *Manson*. What the Burger Court chose instead was to base admissibility of identifications on their reliability. It called reliability the "lynchpin" of such testimony. The reliability focus brings into play the criteria discussed in *Neil* v. *Biggers* (409 U.S. 188: 1972) for evaluating confrontation identifications. In addition *Manson* holds that the suggestiveness of photographic identifications may be tempered by an inability to gather photographs of other persons. The Court said that an exigency may exist that requires a witness to examine only one photograph of a suspect, although the Court conceded that no such exigency existed in *Manson*. Typically witnesses examine spreads of many photographs, as when "mug-books" are used, and identifications that may occur in this way are usually not suggestive. The *Manson* holding provides greater latitude in photographic identification techniques in that it allows identifications determined to be reliable to carry decisive weight against allegations of suggestive or unnecessary procedures.

Immunity

Kastigar v. United States, 406 U.S. 441, 92 S.Ct. 1653, 32 L.Ed.2d 212 (1972)   Examined the extent of immunity from prosecution. Kastigar was subpoenaed to testify before a federal grand jury. He was granted "derivative use" immunity, which prohibits direct use of the compelled testimony or any information derived from that testimony. Kastigar argued that the derivative use immunity granted him was not coextensive with his jeopardy and refused to testify. He was then found to be in civil contempt and jailed. In a 5–2 decision, with Justices Brennan and Rehnquist not participating, the Supreme Court upheld the contempt. Kastigar argued that only complete or transactional immunity would satisfy the protections of the Fifth Amendment. Transactional immunity prohibits prosecution for any transaction about which the person was compelled to testify. The Court disagreed. It found derivative use immunity to be "coextensive with the scope of the privilege against self-incrimination." The immunity "need not be broader" than the protection "afforded by the privilege." In the majority's view, "the privilege has never been construed to mean that one who invokes it cannot subsequently be prosecuted." If a subsequent prosecution does occur, the prosecution has the "affirmative duty to prove that the evidence it proposes to use is derived from a legitimate source wholly independent of the compelled testimony." The majority felt this protection was "substantial" and "commensurate with that resulting from invoking the privilege itself." Justices Douglas and Brennan dissented in favor of requiring full transactional immunity. *See also* FIFTH AMENDMENT, p. 201; IMMUNITY, p. 422; SELF-INCRIMINATION CLAUSE, p. 448.

Significance   *Kastigar* v. *United States* (406 U.S. 441: 1972) focused on the critical immunity issue of coextensiveness. The immunity granted a witness in exchange for testimony must cover or be coextensive with the vulnerability created by compelling the witness to testify. Prior to 1970, witnesses who were compelled to testify were granted transactional immunity, which is total immunity. It insulates a witness from prosecution for *any transaction* about which the witness is required to testify regardless of how serious a crime is involved or how tangential the crime is to the primary issue under investigation. In 1970 Congress passed the Organized Crime Control Act, which authorized a more limited immunity. This immunity is confined to using the testimony itself or information derived from the testimony. It is called "derivative use," "use," or "testimonial" immunity. The key feature of such immunity is that a witness may be prosecuted subsequent to testifying as long as the evidence used against him or her can be shown to be independent of the compelled testimony. The real significance of Kastigar is that it established a less rigorous definition of coextensiveness than had existed before. It approved limited immunity as sufficiently meeting the protections afforded by the privilege against self-incrimination. While the testimony itself cannot be used directly or indirectly, compelled testimony may prompt investigation because authorities are aware of a witness's guilt. Immunity policy requires consideration of the balance between self-incrimination interests and the interest of public security served by gaining information about criminal activities. *Kastigar* shifts the balance point in favor of public security interests.

5. The Sixth Amendment

OVERVIEW

The Sixth Amendment states:

> In all criminal prosecutions, the accused shall enjoy the right to a speedy and public trial, by an impartial jury of the State and district wherein the crime shall have been committed, which district shall have been previously ascertained by law, and to be informed of the nature and cause of the accusation; to be confronted with the witnesses against him; to have compulsory process for obtaining witnesses in his favor, and to have the Assistance of Counsel for his defense.

The provisions of the Sixth Amendment are aimed at providing a criminal defendant with a fair trial. The trial must occur without unnecessary delay. *Barker* v. *Wingo* (407 U.S. 514: 1972) defined criteria by which speedy trial claims are evaluated. A defendant is also entitled to confront witnesses against him. *Pointer* v. *Texas* (380 U.S. 400: 1965) held the Confrontation Clause applicable to the states and required that the defense have an opportunity to cross-examine witnesses. *Chambers* v. *Mississippi* (410 U.S. 284: 1973) explored the relationship between the Confrontation Clause and the heresay rule of evidence. *Washington* v. *Texas* (388 U.S. 14: 1967) established that a state cannot statutorily deny a defendant access to a witness and that a criminal defendant can compel witnesses to appear for the defense.

The Sixth Amendment entitles a criminal defendant to trial by an impartial jury. What constitutes impartiality is a continuing issue before the Supreme Court. These standards prevail: (1) Juries must be selected in a manner that does not systematically discriminate against any population group. Yet *Swain* v. *Alabama* (380 U.S. 202: 1965) held that particular juries need not proportionately reflect a community's population. (2) Potential racial prejudice may be probed during the *voir dire* examination of prospective jurors. Yet *Ristaino* v. *Ross* (424 U.S. 589: 1976) mandates such inquiries only in cases where such prejudice is a strong likelihood. (3) Jurors who would never impose the death penalty in capital cases can be excluded from service, but the Supreme Court said in *Witherspoon* v. *Illinois* (391 U.S. 510: 1968) that jurors with only serious reservations about the death penalty cannot be excluded. (4) A 12-person jury is not constitutionally required by *Williams* v. *Florida* (399 U.S. 78: 1970). (5) A unanimous jury in state criminal trials is not constitutionally required by *Apodaca* v. *Oregon* (406 U.S. 404: 1972).

A criminal trial must be relatively insulated from media coverage in order to protect the due process interests of a defendant. Such excessive media coverage as occurred in *Sheppard* v. *Maxwell* (384 U.S. 333: 1966) requires strong judicial action. Yet a trial judge may not issue a restraining order on the media, as in *Nebraska Press Association* v. *Stuart* (427 U.S. 539: 1976), because it is an unconstitutional prior restraint. The prior restraint rule does not extend to a pretrial suppression hearing, where the media were denied access in *Gannett Company* v. *DePasquale* (443 U.S. 368: 1979). The closed proceeding did not apply to the trial itself in *Gannett,* however, a position emphasized in *Chandler* v. *Florida* (449 U.S. 560: 1981). In *Chandler* the Supreme Court held that electronic media coverage of a trial is permissible as long as such coverage is neither disruptive nor prejudicial.

The Sixth Amendment provides that the accused "have the Assistance of Counsel for his defence." A defendant may not be prevented from availing himself or herself of counsel. The key questions evolving from this clause are whether counsel is actually required in criminal cases as a condition of due process, and whether provisions of the clause bind state criminal proceedings. *Powell* v. *Alabama* (287 U.S. 45: 1932), *Gideon* v. *Wainwright* (372 U.S. 335: 1963), and *Argersinger* v. *Hamlin* (407 U.S. 25: 1972) required counsel in state capital, felony, and misdemeanor trials, respectively. *United States* v. *Wade* (388 U.S. 218: 1967) is representative of cases extending counsel to critical stages of the criminal process other than the trial itself. *Faretta* v. *California* (422 U.S. 806: 1975) summarized the Court's holding on the issue of self-representation.

Pleading guilty to a criminal charge effectively waives the Sixth Amendment protections inherent in the trial process. Pleading guilty also constitutes ultimate self-incrimination in relation to the purposes of the Fifth Amendment. The Supreme Court has consistently upheld the constitutionality of plea bargaining as a part of the guilty plea as long as the latter is made knowingly and voluntarily. *Boykin* v. *Alabama* (395 U.S. 238: 1969) and *Brady* v. *United States* (397 U.S. 742: 1970) examined characteristics of an acceptable plea and criteria for evaluating what constitutes a "knowing and voluntary" plea. *Santobello* v. *New York* (404 U.S. 257: 1971) required that all promises made to a defendant as an inducement to plead guilty must be fulfilled. In *Bordenkircher* v. *Hayes* (434 U.S. 357: 1978), the Court allowed use of threats of more serious charges as a legitimate bargaining approach by prosecutors. The Court required only that the threatened charges be legally sufficient.

Until 1967 juvenile proceedings were viewed as nonadversarial, civil in character, and generally unlike adult criminal prosecutions. *In re Gault* (378 U.S. 1: 1967) dramatically altered those presuppositions in favor of applying formal Fifth and Sixth Amendment standards to juvenile proceedings. *In re Winship* (397 U.S. 358: 1970) took *Gault* a step further by replacing the civil standard of proof of guilt with the more rigorous standard of "beyond a reasonable doubt." Although most procedural safeguards are now equivalent in adult and juvenile proceedings, the Court has not removed all distinctions. In *McKeiver* v. *Pennsylvania* (403 U.S. 441: 1971) it said trial by jury is not constitutionally required in juvenile cases.

The Sixth Amendment entry and an elaboration of the above definitional cases follow.

The Sixth Amendment   Mandates a fair trial for criminal defendants. Like the Fifth Amendment, the Sixth is based in traditions of English common law. Abuses of laws intended to safeguard the rights of criminal defendants were common in colonial America. Most of the constitutions of the first thirteen states contained language designed to correct them. The Virginia Bill of Rights, written by George Mason, put the concern this way in Article VIII:

> In all capital or criminal prosecutions, a man hath a right to demand the cause and nature of his accusation, to be confronted with the accusers and witnesses, to call for evidence in his favour, and to a speedy trial by an impartial jury of twelve men of his vicinage, without whose unanimous consent he cannot be found guilty; nor can he be compelled to give evidence against himself.

The state constitutional ratifying conventions, with North Carolina taking the lead, insisted that the principle of trial by jury is one of the most fundamental rights accruing to the citizens of a democracy. It was not enough that the protection also appears in Article III, Section 2, of the Constitution:

> The Trial of all cases, except in Cases of Impeachment, shall be by Jury; and such Trial shall be held in the state where the said Crimes shall have been committed. . . .

The immediate cause of such deep concern was the British practice in colonial America of sending defendants to England for trial. Colonists believed to be guilty of violating the trade laws or stamp acts, for example, were tried by the British Admiralty Court in England without benefit of a jury. On October 21, 1774, the Continental Congress declared unequivocally that "the seizing of or attempting to seize any person in America in order to transport such person beyond the sea for trial of offences committed within the body of a county in America, being against the law, will justify, and ought to meet with, resistance and reprisal." In that part of the Declaration of Independence containing the litany of "repeated injuries and usurpations" suffered by the colonies, the following complaints appear: ". . . For depriving us in many cases of the benefits of Trial by Jury; for transporting us beyond seas to be tried for pretended offences. . . ." It was a sore subject. The colonists also insisted that provisions of Magna Carta be remembered on the subject of speedy trials. A person accused of a crime must not be kept in prison an unreasonable period of time *before* trial of the facts. It is essential to the guarantee that persons unjustly accused will not be incarcerated for a crime not committed.

> That this right [to a speedy trial] was considered fundamental at this early period in our history is evidenced by its guarantee in the

constitutions of several of the states of the new nation as well as by its
prominent position in the Sixth Amendment. . . . The history of
the right to a speedy trial and its reception in this country clearly
establish that it is one of the most basic rights preserved by our
Constitution. (*Klopfer* v. *North Carolina*, (386 U.S. 213: 1967)

Klopfer applied Sixth Amendment rights to the states. The found-
ers were equally concerned that the Bill of Rights embody the
English common law tradition holding that one accused of a criminal act should have available the bill of indictment containing the
charges against him. The assumption implicit in this clause of the
Sixth Amendment is that if a defendant is aware of the precise
charges levied against him or her, an appropriate defense can be
mounted. The Supreme Court has opined that the Constitution is not
specific on the process by which a defendant is to be informed, but
there is no doubt of the right of the accused to demand such
information. Again, modern doctrine reflects old belief. The Virginia
ratifying convention stated simply, "A man hath a right to demand
the cause and nature of his accusation."

A clause of the Sixth Amendment that did not originate in the
English common law tradition was the guarantee of compulsory
process. Until 1787 it was well settled in the conduct of English trials
that persons accused of felonies or treason were not allowed to
introduce witnesses in their own behalf. After 1787 this general law
was abolished in England, but there were restrictions on the number
and kinds of witnesses who could be summoned. Not only did the
constitutional ratifying conventions have this immediate precedent
before them in 1789, they also had the American tradition that "all
criminals shall have the same privileges of Witnesses as their Prosecutors." Such a provision was in the charters of both Pennsylvania and
Delaware as early as 1701. The idea found its way into other colonial
statements of legal principle as well, so that the first Congress of the
United States was prepared to guarantee compulsory process in the
Federal Crimes Act of 1790. This statute (18 U.S.C., Section 563)
remains in force. It says in part,

> Every person who is indicted of treason or other capital crime . . .
> shall be allowed, in his defense, to make any proof that he can
> produce by lawful witnesses, and shall have the like process of
> the court to compel his witnesses to appear at his trial, as is
> usually granted to compel witnesses to appear on behalf of the
> prosecution.

In *Rosen* v. *United States* (245 U.S. 467: 1918), the Supreme Court
declared that defendants should be allowed to summon in their
behalf all witnesses competent to testify with knowledge to the facts of

the case. *Washington* v. *Texas* (388 U.S. 14: 1967) brought the Compulsory Process Clause under the Due Process Clause of the Fourteenth Amendment and applied it to state actions. The right of compulsory process is now an unchallenged part of American criminal procedure, as is the right of access to counsel.

Prior to 1836, defendants in the English court system were allowed access to counsel only in cases where the charge was treason. Even then the access was limited to arguing points of law with the permission of the judge. Blackstone said, "It is a settled rule at common law that no counsel shall be allowed a prisoner upon his trial, upon the general issue in any capital crime, unless some point of law shall arise to be debated." Blackstone then condemned the practice as inhumane to the treatment of English prisoners and defendants. As in the case of compulsory process, the American tradition was different, however. The charters of Pennsylvania and Delaware also established a legal right to counsel, although it was limited to the right to retain counsel at one's own expense. This right was codified both in the Judiciary Act of 1789 and the Federal Crime Act of 1790. Thus if a defendant could afford to retain counsel, his right to counsel was guaranteed. Several twentieth-century Supreme Court decisions dramatically reinterpreted this tradition. In *Powell* v. *Alabama* (287 U.S. 45: 1932) the Court determined that states were required to furnish counsel as an extension of the due process guarantee of the Fourteenth Amendment. In *Johnson* v. *Zerbst* (304 U.S. 458: 1938) the Court required that counsel be given to all indigents in federal cases unless the defendant could, in the opinion of the presiding judge, competently and intelligently waive that right. In *Gideon* v. *Wainwright* (372 U.S. 335: 1963) the Court said:

> The right of one charged with a crime to counsel may not be deemed fundamental and essential to fair trials in some countries, but it is in ours. From the very beginning, our state and national constitutions and laws have laid great emphasis on procedural and substantive safeguards designed to assure fair trials before impartial tribunals in which every defendant stands equal before the law. This noble ideal cannot be realized if the poor man charged with crime has to face accusers without a lawyer to assist him.

Three years later the Court said in *Miranda* v. *Arizona* (384 U.S. 436: 1966) that as soon as an accused person is in custody and police interrogation has begun, he or she must be informed of the right to counsel in order to be afforded all the protections of due process. Thus the evolution of the Sixth Amendment phrase "have the Assistance of Counsel for his defence" has made legal representation an absolute constitutional guarantee. *See also* BILL OF RIGHTS, p. 7; COMMON LAW, p. 13; MAGNA CARTA, p. 46.

Significance   The Sixth Amendment provides rights that differentiate the American system of jurisprudence from many others in the modern world. Yet the set of requirements mandating a fair trial represent one of the more interesting misunderstandings in the history of criminal procedure. It has been commonly agreed that Magna Carta contained the linguistic structure for trial by jury. Evidence now suggests, however, that the concept of trial by jury was contemplated neither in form nor function at Runnymede. This part of Sixth Amendment guarantees emerged full-blown in the Plymouth Colony in 1623, where it was required that all criminal facts to be adjudicated should be tried by a jury of twelve "honest men to be impanelled by authority, in form of a jury upon their oaths." The Plymouth tradition that these twelve persons should unanimously agree on a verdict survives in federal criminal procedures to this day, although the Supreme Court has ruled that in state actions a unanimous-decision jury is not always necessary to convict a defendant. Another early American tradition surviving intact is the principle that a trial for any criminal offense shall take place in the district in which the alleged offense took place. Such a holding became the impetus for state and local court systems. Later interpretations of it have allowed for changes of venue depending on circumstances determined appropriate by the presiding judge. Similarly, later interpretations of what constitutes a fair trial and a proper jury have evolved according to the due process and equal protection standards of the Fourteenth Amendment. It is now Supreme Court doctrine that impartiality in the composition of a jury must reflect the sociological makeup of the trial district's population. By the same token the idea of witness confrontation has evolved from the right of those accused of treason to confront witnesses against them under England's Treason Act of 1696 to modern rules of procedure that take strongly into account a trial's reliance on evidence and testimony brought by witnesses. The Supreme Court stated what continues to be the status of this clause of the Sixth Amendment in *Kirby* v. *United States* (174 U.S. 47: 1899):

> A fact which can be primarily established only by witnesses cannot be proved against the accused except by witnesses who confront him at the trial, upon whom he can look while being tried, whom he is entitled to cross-examine, and whose testimony he may impeach in every mode authorized by the established rules governing the trial or conduct of criminal cases.

The Sixth Amendment's guarantee of the right to counsel assures that all other provisions of the amendment are monitored by persons with legal knowledge. The right to counsel has been extended to every corner and aspect of the criminal procedures process: to the states, to the poor, and to persons immediately after being put in custody. In no other modern government have so many safeguards been assigned to the rights of persons accused of crimes.

Speedy Trial

Barker v. ***Wingo,*** **407 U.S. 514, 92 S.Ct. 2182, 33 L.Ed.2d 101 (1972)** Established criteria by which claims of denial of speedy trial may be evaluated. *Klopfer* v. *North Carolina* (386 U.S. 213: 1967) had already decided that the speedy trial provisions of the Sixth Amendment applied to the states. Defendant Barker was charged with murder and had a trial date set. Between the original trial date, October 21, 1958, and October 1963, Barker's trial was continued 17 times. Barker did not object to the first 11 continuances because he was on pretrial release through most of the period. When eventually tried, Barker was convicted and sentenced to life. The Supreme Court unanimously upheld Barker's conviction. Before fashioning a speedy trial test in the case, Justice Powell considered the unique character of the speedy trial protection. He called it "generically different" from other constitutional protections because there is a "societal interest in providing a speedy trial which exists separate from, and at times in opposition to, the interests of the accused." The speedy trial concept is also "amorphous" and "vague," more so than other rights of the accused. Writing for the Court, Justice Powell rejected specific timetables and the "on demand" approach as inflexible. Instead he devised a "balancing test" for evaluating speedy trial claims. The test contained four elements and "compels courts to approach speedy trial cases on an *ad hoc* basis." The four factors identified are (1) length of delay; (2) reasons offered by the government (prosecution) to justify the delay; (3) the defendant's assertion of his or her right to a speedy trial; and (4) prejudice to the defendant in terms of pretrial incarceration, anxiety, and impairment of the defense itself. Applying these criteria to Barker, the Court concluded that despite the lengthy delay, Barker's defense was not prejudiced. He was on release throughout most of the period, and he failed seriously to assert the right to a speedy trial. *See also* FIFTH AMENDMENT, p. 201; SIXTH AMENDMENT, p. 241; SPEEDY TRIAL, p. 452.

Significance Barker v. *Wingo* (407 U.S. 514: 1972) provides a uniquely two-edged protection in relation to a speedy trial. The defendant must be protected from lengthy pretrial detention and diminution of the capacity to offer a defense, but the prosecutor's case must be similarly protected from erosion by delay. *Barker* established several criteria for assessing when a speedy trial has not occurred. In fashioning the four criteria listed above, the Court rejected both the fixed-time and "demand-waiver" approaches. Instead the Court opted for a balance test, which is compatible with the Burger Court's general preference for examining the "totality of the circumstances." Three other cases speak to the matter of when the speedy trial protection begins, i.e., when the clock starts to run. *United States* v. *Marion* (404 U.S. 307: 1971) examined a three-year delay between a criminal act and the filing of charges. The Court concluded that the speedy trial guarantee does not apply "until the putative defendant in some way becomes an 'accused.'" *United States* v. *Lovasco* (431 U.S. 783: 1977) also considered pre-indictment delay. In *Lovasco* the prosecution had a chargeable case within a month of the crime but did not seek indictment for an additional 17 months. The delay was attributed to an inability to finish the investigation of the case against Lovasco as well as several others. Compounding the situation was the fact that the defendant lost the testimony of two witnesses who died during the 18-month delay. Nonetheless the Court found for the prosecution and refused to find an investigative delay prior to indictment a fatal defect. The Court refused to require prosecutors to charge as soon as evidence might be minimally sufficient. The Court did recognize that "reckless" pre-indictment delay or delay aimed at gaining an advantage did constitute a denial of due process. Finally, in *United States* v. *MacDonald* (456 U.S. 1: 1982) a murder case that drew national attention, the Court found that the time between dismissed charges brought within the military system of justice and the subsequent filing of civilian charges is not subject to speedy trial protection. Thus the burden of demonstrating violation of the speedy trial protection clearly rests with the defense, and cases such as *Marion, Lovasco,* and *MacDonald* reflect the Court's preference for limiting the stages or time periods to which the speedy trial protection applies. In the meantime Congress has legislated a speedy trial time period for federal courts. An accused must be brought to trial within 70 days of his or her first court appearance to answer criminal charges. That time period can be tolled for various reasons, usually consistent with defense requests. Some states have also enacted speedy trial legislation, frequently allowing six months from the time of arraignment. The balancing test of *Barker* still applies, however, especially to the states. On balance, for example, six months may or may not violate the *Barker* criteria.

Confrontation

***Pointer* v. *Texas*, 380 U.S. 400, 85 S.Ct. 1065, 13 L.Ed.2d 923 (1965)** Considered the applicability to the states of the Confrontation Clause of the Sixth Amendment, which requires that the accused "be confronted with the witnesses against him." Pointer was tried for robbery. His chief accuser provided a detailed account of the crime at a preliminary hearing, an occasion at which Pointer was unrepresented by defense counsel. At the trial the prosecution used transcripts of the testimony of the witness from the preliminary hearing because the witness had moved to another state. Pointer was convicted. A unanimous Supreme Court reversed the conviction, saying the right to cross-examine a witness was a central aspect of confrontation. Inclusion of the confrontation protection in the Sixth Amendment reflected the framers' belief that "confrontation was a fundamental right essential to a fair trial." As for the practice in Texas of allowing use of a transcript, the Court said the confrontation protection would have been satisfied had the statements been made at a "full-fledged hearing" where Pointer had been represented by counsel with "a complete and adequate opportunity to cross-examine." Absent that condition, what occurred was an unconstitutional denial of the Sixth Amendment right of confrontation. *See also* CHAMBERS V. MISSISSIPPI (410 U.S. 284: 1973), p. 248; CONFRONTATION CLAUSE, p. 397; SIXTH AMENDMENT, p. 241.

Significance *Pointer* v. *Texas* (380 U.S. 400: 1965) applied the confrontation right to state trial proceedings for the first time. The Supreme Court held specifically that the right to confront and cross-examine witnesses is a fundamental right essential to a fair trial and is obligatory on state courts by virtue of the Fourteenth Amendment. *Pointer* is one of a series of cases in which the Warren Court extended to defendants in state courts rights of accused persons long protected in federal courts. The right to confront historically has meant that witness and defendant must be present in the courtroom for the various stages of the judicial process. Though that expectation generally holds, it is not inflexible. A defendant may waive the right to presence and choose not to attend any or all of the proceedings. A defendant's courtroom behavior may also become sufficiently disruptive to justify his or her removal from the courtroom as a requisite to continuing, as in *Illinois* v. *Allen* (397 U.S. 337: 1970). The capability to cross-examine, however, remains the heart of the confrontation protection. Soon after *Pointer,* the Court reinforced its decision in *Bruton* v. *United States* (391 U.S. 123: 1968). Bruton was tried in a federal court. A postal inspector gave testimony that described an oral confession by Bruton's codefendant. The confession implicated both the codefendant and Bruton. The trial judge instructed the jury that the confession was inadmissable hearsay and must be disregarded in deciding Bruton's guilt. The Supreme Court held the instruction was insufficient protection. The use of the codefendant's confession "added substantial, perhaps even critical, weight to the Government's case in a form not subject to cross-examination, since Evans [the codefendant] did not take the stand." While conceding that some situations might be remedied by jury instructions, the remedy did not apply here. The introduction of the confession "posed a substantial threat" to Bruton's capability to confront. "In the context of a joint trial we cannot accept limiting instructions as an adequate substitute for the petitioner's constitutional right of cross-examination. The effect is the same as if there had been no instruction at all."

Chambers v. **Mississippi, 410 U.S. 284, 93 S.Ct. 1038, 35 L.Ed.2d 297 (1973)**   Considered the effect of state rules of evidence on the exercise of the right of cross-examination. Defendant Chambers was charged with murder. He called a particular witness in order to introduce the witness's written confession to the crime. The witness repudiated his confession, at which point Chambers sought to cross-examine him as an adverse witness. The request was denied, as were other efforts to use the witness, because of hearsay limitations and a state rule that a party may not impeach his or her own witness. With only Justice Rehnquist dissenting, the Supreme Court reversed Chambers's conviction. Justice Powell's opinion for the majority emphasized the "realities of the criminal process." Defendants must be able fully to explore testimony from all witnesses including their own because "in modern criminal trials defendants are rarely able to select their witnesses; they must take them where they find them." Impeaching his own witness may be crucial to a defendant's ability to put on a defense. In addition, such rules of evidence as the hearsay rule must allow exceptions and not "be applied mechanistically to defeat the ends of justice." Exception must occur where "constitutional rights directly affecting the ascertainment of guilt are implicated." Thus Chambers was deprived of his constitutional right of confrontation. *See also* CONFRONTATION CLAUSE, p. 397; *POINTER* V. *TEXAS* (380 U.S. 400: 1965), p. 247; SIXTH AMENDMENT, p. 241.

Significance   *Chambers* v. *Mississippi* (410 U.S. 284: 1973) clearly reflects the view that a trial is a productive fact-finding process only if reliable evidence can be fully considered. The Confrontation Clause is designed to ensure evidence reliability by providing for cross-examination and requiring a witness to testify under oath. Further, the testimony of witnesses in open court can be assessed in terms of the witness's behavior or manner. The Confrontation Clause entitles a defendant to examine and perhaps challenge the full range of evidence against him in an attempt to develop the best factual defense. As seen in *Chambers,* the Burger Court has been generally unreceptive to attempts to limit the examination/cross-examination process. *Chambers* is another Fourteenth Amendment extension of a federally protected right to the states. The Court held that the due process right found in the Fourteenth Amendment included the Sixth Amendment right to confront and cross-examine witnesses. In *Davis* v. *Alaska* (415 U.S. 308: 1974), the Court applied the *Chambers* decision to a case where a defendant had been denied the opportunity to disclose and develop during cross-examination the juvenile record of a crucial prosecution witness. While disclosure of the witness's status as a juvenile delinquent would conflict with the state's policy of preserving confidentiality of juvenile proceedings, a seven-member majority decided that disclosure of the witness's status was necessary to impeach the credibility of the witness. There are practical limits, however. In *Ohio* v. *Roberts* (448 U.S. 56: 1980), the Court returned to a variation of the *Pointer* fact situation. A witness after testifying at a preliminary hearing did not appear at the trial despite several subpoenas. A state statute permitted use of preliminary hearing testimony of a witness who could not be produced at the trial. The defendant objected to the use of the transcript despite the fact that the witness had originally been called by the defense, since her preliminary hearing testimony had not been entirely favorable to his defense. The Supreme Court concluded that a sufficiently good-faith effort had been made to locate the witness and that the prior testimony bore "sufficient indicia of reliability" to be used under these circumstances.

Compulsory Process

Washington v. Texas, 388 U.S. 14, 87 S.Ct. 1920, 18 L.Ed.2d 1019 (1967)   Examined whether the compulsory process provision of the Sixth Amendment, which gives the accused the right to obtain witnesses in his or her favor, applies to the states through the Fourteenth Amendment, and whether a state may prohibit "principals, accomplices, or accessories" in the same crime from being witnesses for each other. Defendant Washington, charged with murder, wished to use Charles Fuller as a defense witness. Fuller was a coparticipant with Washington in the alleged crime. Washington was denied use of Fuller as a witness by Texas statute. Fuller could testify for the prosecution under Texas law, however. The Supreme Court unanimously reversed Washington's conviction. The Court held that the right of compulsory process for the defense "stands on no lesser footing than other Sixth Amendment rights" previously held applicable to the states. The Court considered it fundamental because it is the "right to present a defense." Thus the Court subordinated the trial court's interest in deterring perjury to the defendant's right to present a defense. The Court was unconvinced that codefendants would perjure themselves on behalf of codefendants anyway. If a witness is convicted and awaiting sentence, or simply awaiting trial, "common sense would suggest that he often has a greater interest in lying in favor of the prosecution rather than against it." The Court concluded that to think that "criminals will lie to save their fellows but not to obtain favors from the prosecution for themselves is indeed to clothe the criminal class with more nobility than one might expect to find in the public at large." *See also* BLACKSTONE'S *COMMENTARIES*, p. 11; COMPULSORY PROCESS, p. 397; SIXTH AMENDMENT, p. 241.

Significance   *Washington v. Texas* (388 U.S. 14: 1967) extended to state actions through the Fourteenth Amendment the expectation that a defendant in a criminal case can present, through his or her own witnesses and evidence, an alternate version of the facts. The ability to subpoena witnesses can be of paramount importance to a defense against criminal charges. In *Washington,* the Court opined, the state of Texas arbitrarily denied a defendant the right to have the material testimony of a witness, thus denying him the right to compulsory process. The compulsory process provision of the Sixth Amendment has not frequently been before the Supreme Court. The Burger Court has rendered two decisions in this regard, both of which found for the defendant in appeals focusing on violation of the compulsory process protection. *Webb* v. *Texas* (409 U.S. 95: 1972) involved judicial intimidation of a defense witness. The witness, serving a sentence on a prior criminal conviction, was admonished by the trial judge about the "dangers of perjury," how a perjury conviction would mean substantial supplement of the sentence being served, and how perjury would impair chances of parole. The witness decided not to testify, and Webb argued that his only witness had been coerced into not testifying by the trial judge. The Supreme Court agreed. It cited the judge's "threatening" remarks as effectively driving the witness from the stand and denying Webb due process. In *Cool* v. *United States* (409 U.S. 100: 1972), the Court again ruled for the defendant because the defense was impaired by an improper jury instruction. Defendant Cool relied on the testimony of a codefendant. The witness, while admitting his own guilt, testified that Cool had nothing to do with the crime. The trial judge gave the jury "a lengthy 'accomplice instruction' to be used in evaluating Vogles' [the codefendant's] testimony." The judge suggested that the testimony was "open to suspicion" and that unless the jury believed the testimony "beyond a reasonable doubt," it should be discarded. The Supreme Court concluded "the clear implication of the instruction was that the jury should disregard Vogles' testimony. . . ." An instruction of that kind "places an improper burden on the defense." Thus *Washington, Webb,* and *Cool* establish a firm expectation that the defense will be able to present a full and undeterred case.

Jury Selection

Swain v. *Alabama*, **380 U.S. 202, 85 S.Ct. 824, 13 L.Ed.2d 759 (1965)** Examined the effects of racial exclusion on the Sixth Amendment's requirement that the accused be tried by an impartial jury. A black defendant was convicted of rape by an all-white jury. On appeal it was asserted the jury impaneling process was discriminatory in the selection of venire panels, in the selection of jurors from venire panels, and in the use of the strike system, a form of peremptory challenge. The facts seemed to support Swain's contentions. Jury-eligible blacks constituted 26 percent of the population of Talladega County, Alabama, but only 10–15 percent of the grand and petit jury panels had been black for at least a decade. While blacks served on a high proportion of grand juries, including the grand jury that indicted Swain, no black had served on a petit jury in the county since 1950. Eight blacks were on the venire in Swain's case, but two were exempt, and the remaining six were struck by the prosecutor. The Court, in an opinion authored by Justice White, found for Alabama in a 6–3 decision. The majority stressed that Alabama had not "totally excluded" blacks from the panels, and while the selection process was "somewhat haphazard," it concluded that "an imperfect system is not equivalent to purposeful discrimination." The lack of systematic or process-wide discrimination was decisive in the mind of the Court. The majority also concluded that the peremptory challenge was not directly subject to the trial court's control. Thus use of the strike in a particular case is not a denial of equal protection. The critical doctrine emerging from *Swain* is that a defendant "is not constitutionally entitled to demand a proportionate number of his race on the jury which tries him nor on the venire or jury roll from which petit jurors were drawn." Neither the jury roll nor the venire "need be a perfect mirror of the community or accurately reflect the proportionate strength of every identifiable group." Justices Goldberg, Douglas, and Warren dissented. They held that a *prima facie* case of discrimination had been made. *See also* RISTAINO V. ROSS (424 U.S. 589: 1976), p. 254; SIXTH AMENDMENT, p. 241; WITHERSPOON V. ILLINOIS (391 U.S. 510: 1968), p. 253.

Significance   *Swain* v. *Alabama* (380 U.S. 202: 1965) modified the doctrine established in *Norris* v. *Alabama* (294 U.S. 587: 1935). The *Norris* case, an appeal growing out of the notorious Scottsboro trial, prohibited systematic exclusion of persons from jury service on the basis of race. *Norris* allowed discriminatory practice to be inferred from statistics demonstrating inequity of access. *Swain* came before the Supreme Court because more subtle methods of discrimination had since been designed to minimize the involvement of blacks and others in jury service. The Court's decision in *Swain* did not abandon the basic thrust of *Norris* in terms of systematic exclusion, but it made the burden of proving discriminatory practice much more difficult. Though less compelling facts than were present in *Swain* have prevailed in more recent cases in establishing a *prima facie* case of discrimination, there remains no specific expectation that general population ratios will be reflected in specific juries. See *Castaneda* v. *Partida* (430 U.S. 482: 1977). Cases such as *Taylor* v. *Louisiana* (419 U.S. 522: 1975) and *Duren* v. *Missouri* (439 U.S. 357: 1979) have rejected certain state selection methods on the grounds that they systematically exclude women from jury service. But the Court has continued generally to defer to the states in the establishment and administration of techniques designed to draw juries that are a representative cross-section of the community.

Witherspoon v. Illinois, 391 U.S. 510, 88 S.Ct. 1770, 20 L.Ed.2d 776 (1968) Explored the Sixth Amendment requirement that the jury in a criminal case be both impartial and representative of the community, and determined whether a state law could exclude from jury service in a capital case any person who possessed "conscientious scruples against capital punishment" or had "opposition to the same." Utilizing an Illinois statute, the prosecution eliminated nearly half of the prospective jurors by challenging *all* who expressed qualms about the death penalty. Most of the challenge process was accomplished without ascertaining whether the scruples of prospective jurors would compel them to vote against capital punishment. Defendant Witherspoon claimed that a jury that excluded persons with reservations about capital punishment was no longer impartial or representative. The Supreme Court agreed, and voided the death sentence recommended by Witherspoon's "death qualified" jury. While not holding that Witherspoon's jury was more likely to convict given its composition, the Court did find the jury to be "woefully short" of impartiality on the sentence issue. The majority said it would be appropriate to exclude those prospective jurors who could never impose the death sentence, but not those who only had reservations. When Illinois excluded those with qualms against capital punishment, it "crossed the line of neutrality." It produced a jury "uncommonly willing to condemn a man to die." Justices Black, Harlan, and White dissented. They felt that jury neutrality would be seriously breached by requiring those with reservations to serve on a jury. To the three dissenters, *Witherspoon* was a case of "plain bias." Their concern was that the Court majority had imposed a requirement that "those biased on one of the critical issues in the trial should be represented on a jury." *See also* RISTAINO V. ROSS (424 U.S. 589: 1976), p. 254; SIXTH AMENDMENT, p. 241; SWAIN V. ALABAMA (380 U.S. 202: 1965), p. 251.

Significance Witherspoon v. *Illinois* (391 U.S. 510: 1968) found that a jury cannot be selected that is uncommonly willing to condemn a person to death. Yet the Court refused to announce a per se constitutional rule requiring the reversal of every jury selected in the Illinois fashion. The Court said simply that in this case the jury "fell woefully short of that impartiality to which petitioner was entitled under the Sixth and Fourteenth Amendments." Writing for the majority, Justice Stewart found it "clear" that imposing the death penalty by a "hanging jury" would deprive the defendant of his life without due process of law. *Witherspoon* is one of several important Burger Court decisions about jury size and the unanimity principle. In *Davis* v. *Georgia* (429 U.S. 122: 1976), the Court voided the death sentence of a state prisoner whose sentence had been imposed by a jury from which one prospective juror had been excluded because of general reservations about the death penalty. In *Adams* v. *Texas* (448 U.S. 38: 1980), the Court considered whether a state could exclude from a jury those unable to swear under oath that the extant possibility of the death penalty would not affect their deliberations. With only Justice Rehnquist dissenting, the Court decided that *Witherspoon* required reversal of the oath process. While still allowing exclusion of those who cannot be impartial, the majority was not satisfied that irrevocable opposition could be inferred from failure to swear to the impossibility of imposing the death penalty. *Davis* and *Adams* clearly convey the Burger Court's intention to extend the selection expectations established in *Witherspoon*.

Ristaino v. Ross, 424 U.S. 589, 96 S.Ct. 1017, 47 L.Ed.2d 258 (1976)   Considered the question of whether a defendant is constitutionally entitled to ask questions specifically directed toward racial prejudice during the *voir dire* examination of prospective jurors. The trial judge denied the defendant's motion to pose the question, and a black defendant was subsequently convicted in a state court of violent crimes against a white victim. The Supreme Court concurred in the trial judge's decision in a 6–2 vote. Justice Stevens did not participate. Justice Powell reasoned for the majority that the Constitution "does not always entitle a defendant to have questions posed during *voir dire* specifically directed to matters that conceivably might prejudice veniremen against him." Though circumstances might warrant specific questions about racial prejudice, these were matters to be handled through the exercise of "sound discretion" by the trial court, a function "particularly within the province of the trial judge." The mere fact that the victim and the defendant were of different races was not in itself something that was "likely to distort the trial." Therefore the defendant was not entitled to *voir dire* questions pursuing race prejudice. Justices Brennan and Marshall dissented. *See also* SIXTH AMENDMENT, p. 241; SWAIN V. ALABAMA (380 U.S. 202: 1965), p. 251; WITHERSPOON V. ILLINOIS (391 U.S. 510: 1968), p. 253.

Significance   *Ristaino* v. *Ross* (424 U.S. 589: 1976) is representative of the Burger Court's view of what kinds of questions a defendant is entitled to pursue during a *voir dire* examination. The *voir dire* process refers to a series of questions posed to prospective jurors to determine their impartiality. A prospective juror found to be partial on the basis of his or her responses is excused from service on a given jury "for cause." The supervision of *voir dire* rests with the trial judge. *Ristaino* decided that a trial judge's discretion has been properly exercised when a defendant is denied the opportunity to probe the racial prejudice of prospective jurors simply because the defendant and victim of the crime are of different races. *Ristaino* underscored the requirement that a defendant must demonstrate unusual circumstances such as the presence of a racial issue as an actual component of a particular case. A similar holding involving national origin was made in *Rosales-Lopez* v. *United States* (451 U.S. 182: 1981), in which a Mexican defendant, at trial for illegally bringing Mexican aliens into the country, wished to ask potential jurors about possible prejudice toward Mexicans. In *Ham* v. *South Carolina* (409 U.S. 524: 1973) the Court concluded that questions relating to racial prejudice *were* appropriate given the defendant's visibility in the civil-rights movement in the locality of his trial. *Ristaino, Ham,* and *Rosales-Lopez* place the monitoring of the jury selection process, specifically the conduct of the *voir dire* examination, exclusively in the hands of the trial judge.

Jury Size

Williams v. **Florida, 399 U.S. 78, 90 S.Ct. 1893, 26 L.Ed.2d 446 (1970)**   Considered whether a jury of less than 12 persons satisfied the constitutional requirement of *Duncan* v. *Louisiana* (391 U.S. 145: 1968) that no state could deny trial by jury in a criminal case. The Court found that Florida's trial of Williams with a jury of 6 persons met the requirement. Justice White concentrated on three principles in the majority opinion. First, while the jury is deeply rooted in our legal history, he said he found nothing from historical evidence to suggest the framers intended that exactly 12 persons should always serve on a jury, or that the number 12 was an "indispensable component" of the Sixth Amendment. Second, juries should be large enough to promote group deliberation, free from "outside attempts at intimidation." The Court found nothing to lead it to believe that this goal was "in any meaningful sense less likely to be achieved when the jury numbers six than when it numbers twelve."

Third, juries must "provide a fair possibility for obtaining a representative cross section of the community." The Court found the difference between 12 and 6 to be "negligible" in this regard. As long as selection processes prevent arbitrary or discriminatory exclusions, the Court felt "the concern that the cross-section will be significantly diminished if the jury is decreased in size from 12 to six seems an unrealistic one." Justice Marshall dissented, arguing that the Fourteenth Amendment required a 12-member jury in cases where a defendant such as Williams could be sent to prison for the remainder of his life upon conviction. Justice Blackmun did not participate in the decision. *See also* APODACA V. OREGON (406 U.S. 404: 1972), p. 256; JURY, p. 431; SIXTH AMENDMENT, p. 241.

Significance　　*Williams* v. *Florida* (300 U.S. 78: 1970) represented an unexpected departure from English common law tradition. The tradition clearly acknowledged a jury of 12 persons. When *Duncan* v. *Louisiana* (391 U.S. 145: 1968) established the fundamental character of the jury trial at the state level, it presumed state juries would have 12 jurors, as do federal juries. The rationale offered by the Court in *Williams* has been subjected to serious criticism, particularly as it relates to the deliberative and representational aspects of 12- versus 6-person juries. The Court did establish subsequently that 6 was the constitutionally acceptable *minimum*. In *Ballew* v. *Georgia* (435 U.S. 223: 1978) the Court considered a conviction by a 5-member jury in a state obscenity case. A unanimous Court, including all five members who had voted in the *Williams* majority eight years earlier, found a 5-member jury to be constitutionally defective. The Court's opinion used as its rationale the reasons offered by critics of the *Williams* decision. The Court found that "effective group deliberation" and the ability adequately to represent a cross-section of the community was seriously threatened by a 5-member jury. Critics say the difference between 6 and 5 appears to be entirely arbitrary. The *Williams* decision provided the states with considerable latitude in utilizing juries in criminal cases.

Jury Unanimity

Apodaca v. *Oregon,* **406 U.S. 404, 92 S.Ct. 1628, 32 L.Ed.2d 184 (1972)**　　Addressed the question of conviction by less than a unanimous jury. Apodaca was convicted by the 9–3 vote of an Oregon jury. The Supreme Court upheld the conviction. The majority "perceived no difference" between the unanimous and nonunanimous jury. Both fulfilled the "interest of the defendant in having the judgment of his peers interposed between himself and the officers of the State." In response to the argument that nonunanimity detracted from the reasonable doubt standard, the majority replied that the standard of reasonable doubt "did not crystallize in this country until after the Constitution was adopted." Thus it was not directly required by the Sixth Amendment. The petitioner also argued that nonunanimity diminished the representativeness of a jury and allowed convictions "to occur without the acquiescense of minority elements within the community." The Court majority rejected this argument by saying it is not necessary that every "distinct voice in the community" be represented on every jury. The majority also rejected the notion that minority viewpoints would not be adequately represented even where convictions were obtained. They "found no proof for the notion that a majority will disregard its instructions and cast its vote for guilt or innocence based on prejudice rather than the evidence." Justices Blackmun and Powell concurred separately. Justice Blackmun admitted "great difficulty" with the prospect of a 7–5 conviction. A 9–3 conviction was, however, "a substantial" enough majority for Blackmun. Justice Powell would retain the unanimity requirement at the federal level to honor the Sixth Amendment but allow the states to deviate from unanimity. Justices Brennan, Marshall, Douglas, and Stewart dissented, citing "diminution of verdict reliability" because juries not needing unanimity need not deliberate as fully, and possibly not deliberate at all. Justice Marshall, in a separate dissent, focused on the "beyond reasonable doubt" standard, feeling the doubts of the three impeached the verdict of the nine. See also JURY, p. 431; SIXTH AMENDMENT, p. 241; WILLIAMS V. FLORIDA (399 U.S. 78: 1970), p. 255.

Significance   Apodaca v. Oregon (406 U.S. 404: 1972) highlights the issue of confidence in jury decisions. Has the reasonable doubt standard been eroded and the likelihood of successful prosecutions increased with the *Apodaca* standard? Some would answer yes to both parts of the question. Like the 12-person jury, the unanimity standard had been viewed as an integral part of the criminal process. It still is in the federal courts. Taken together with *Williams* v. *Florida* (399 U.S. 78: 1970), *Apodaca* leaves the jury trial a less effective right of the accused than had been the case prior in state proceedings. The Court has established that conviction in a state criminal case coming on a 5–1 vote is unsatisfactory. In *Burch* v. *Louisiana* (441 U.S. 130: 1979) the unanimous opinion of the Court was that when a constitutional minimum of six jurors sits on a criminal case, nothing less than unanimity will suffice. *Apodaca* establishes that nonunanimous convictions on votes that may be split as much as 9–3 are adequate, however. The sufficiency of margins less than 9–3 for 12-person juries, and split decisions from juries numbering more than 6 but less than 12, remain to be defined. *Apodaca* and *Williams* opened doors relative to jury decision and size long thought locked shut. Many states have accepted the Court's invitation to alter their policies accordingly.

Pretrial Publicity

***Sheppard* v. *Maxwell*, 384 U.S. 33, 86 S.Ct. 1507, 16 L.Ed.2d 600 (1966)**   Considered whether pervasive pretrial publicity, most of which was highly adverse to the defendant, deprived him of the fair trial mandated by the Sixth Amendment. Every stage of the *Sheppard* case was subjected to intensive media coverage, from inquest through indictment to the trial itself. The general substance of the coverage given Sheppard was hostile. Jurors were subjected to continuous publicity. Sheppard was eventually convicted of the murder of his wife, but the Supreme Court reversed the conviction with only Justice Black dissenting. The Court focused its discussion on the failures of the trial judge adequately to provide Sheppard with the "judicial serenity and calm to which he was entitled." Specifically, the trial judge should have (1) used stricter rules governing media use of the courtroom, (2) better insulated the witnesses from media representation, (3) limited the flow of information to the media from principals in the case, and (4) admonished the media to monitor the accuracy of their reports. The Court found the failure properly to insulate the jury the most glaring error in the trial. Several jurors admitted hearing media broadcasts about the case while serving. The Court said Sheppard's fair trial turned into an avoidable "carnival," and Sheppard was deprived of the fair trial to which he was entitled. *See also* CHANDLER V. FLORIDA (449 U.S. 560: 1981), p. 262; GANNETT COMPANY V. DEPASQUALE (443 U.S. 368: 1979), p. 260; NEBRASKA PRESS ASSOCATION V. STUART (427 U.S. 539: 1976), p. 259.

Significance   *Sheppard* v. *Maxwell* (384 U.S. 333: 1966) focused on the tension existing between a defendant's right to a fair trial and the First Amendment right of a free press. The press has always had the potential negatively to impact on the fairness of criminal proceedings, but technical developments in the broadcast media have increased that potential dramatically. Virtually an entire community can be reached with information that may have a prejudicial effect on a particular case. The *Sheppard* case portrays these prejudicial effects at their worst. The result was that the Court did not require Sheppard to identify any *actual* prejudice to him. Since the totality of the circumstances raised the *possibility* of prejudice, that was sufficient to grant him relief. Even with the excesses that occurred in *Sheppard*, the Court resisted restricting the press. Instead the Court focused on the trial judge as the key figure in ensuring a fair trial. It talked about the option of delaying a trial until publicity had subsided or of changing the venue of a case. It emphasized how the *voir dire* examination could have been used to determine whether prejudicial publicity existed. It suggested sequestering or isolating juries in particularly visible cases. The caution of the Court in addressing press behavior prompted initiatives elsewhere. The industry itself, through meetings with representatives of trial courts, began to fashion principles of conduct for criminal case coverage. Much of the press now voluntarily complies. A subsequent decision, *Murphy* v. *Florida* (421 U.S. 794: 1975), provided more clarity on the question of when reported information becomes prejudicial. The Court said in *Murphy* that prospective jurors need not be "totally ignorant" of a case. They need only be able to "reach a verdict based on the evidence presented in the court." Press treatment of a case, especially one governed by self-imposed limits, does not necessarily mean that the publicity is either prejudicial or adverse. The *Sheppard* case, however, clearly demonstrated the need for certain safeguards to ensure a fair trial for criminal defendants.

Nebraska Press Association v. Stuart, 427 U.S. 530, 96 S.Ct. 2791, 49 L.Ed.2d 683 (1976) Examined the propriety of a "gag order" on the media as a way of preventing prejudicial pretrial publicity in violation of the fair trial requirement of the Sixth Amendment. *Sheppard* v. *Maxwell* (384 U.S. 33: 1966) placed the responsibility for maintaining a fair trial environment with the trial judge. In this case Judge Stuart restrained the media from "publishing or broadcasting accounts of confessions or admissions made by the accused or facts 'strongly implicative' of the accused" until such time as a jury was impaneled. The crime itself was the murder of six persons. Compliance with the order, as modified by the Nebraska Supreme Court, was achieved. The Supreme Court reviewed the case even though the order had expired by the time the case was argued. The Court unanimously rejected the gag order, noting also that the trial judge "acted responsibly, out of a legitimate concern, in an effort to protect the defendant's right to a fair trial." Nonetheless the Court viewed the restraining order as excessive. It suggested that truly extraordinary prejudicial publicity must be present in order to consider an action as severe as restraint. Given that the gag is a denial of free speech, the Court said it must review carefully whether the record justifies such an "extraordinary remedy." Included in such an examination are certain factors: (1) the "nature and extent" of the coverage, (2) alternative measures and their likely impact on mitigating publicity, and (3) the effectiveness of the gag order in preventing damaging and prejudicial publicity. The Court concluded that the record was not sufficient on the last two factors in this instance. Although the Court did not rule out the possibility that a restraining order might be sustained under certain circumstances, Judge Stuart's order was found to be excessive and a denial of the Nebraska Press Association's First Amendment rights. See also CHANDLER V. FLORIDA (449 U.S. 560: 1981), p. 262; GANNETT COMPANY V. DEPASQUALE (443 U.S. 368: 1979), p. 260; SHEPPARD V. MAXWELL (384 U.S. 333: 1966), p. 258.

Significance   Nebraska Press Association v. Stuart (427 U.S. 539: 1976) dealt with whether the press should be precluded from publishing what it already knows. This is a different problem from Sheppard v. Maxwell (384 U.S. 333: 1966), which focused on remedies after prejudicial pretrial publicity had already occurred. Stuart looked at the gag order as a means of stemming pretrial publicity before the fact. The prior-restraint considerations of Stuart had been suspect for 25 years before the case was decided. While Stuart stopped short of invalidating the gag rule altogether, the clear thrust of the decision was to impose conditions virtually impossible to satisfy. The case then becomes a kind of intermediate point between a policy course stressing after-the-fact remedies and an approach that would close judicial proceedings to the public and the press. It is apparent from Stuart that prohibiting the press from reporting what they observe directly in open court is the least favored approach.

Pretrial Proceedings

Gannett Company v. DePasquale, 443 U.S. 368, 99 S.Ct. 2898, 61 L.Ed.2d 608 (1979)   Posed the question of whether the media could be denied access to a pretrial suppression hearing. If the press is allowed to observe a judicial proceeding, it generally will be allowed to report what it observed. Since both the defense and prosecution agreed to close the proceeding at issue in *Gannett,* the case really asked whether the public has an independent right to an open pretrial judicial hearing. In a 5–4 decision, the Court upheld the closed hearing. The majority reasoned that pretrial suppression hearings, as distinct from trials, pose "special risks of unfairness." The objective of such hearings is to screen out unreliable or illegally obtained evidence. Pretrial publicity about such evidence could "influence public opinion" and "inform potential jurors of inculpatory information wholly inadmissible at the actual trial." As for the public's independent right to access, the Court stressed two points. First, public interest in the application of the Sixth Amendment does not create "a constitutional right on the part of the public." The public interest is protected by the participants in the adversary process. Thus the public has no claim that could displace the defendant's desire to close the proceeding. Second, the common law tradition recognizes the difference between a pretrial proceeding and the trial itself. "Pre-trial proceedings, precisely because of [a] concern for a fair trial, were never characterized by the degree of openness as were actual trials." Justices Blackmun, Brennan, Marshall, and White dissented. They concentrated on the benefits of open processes and what they considered to be unconstitutional limitations on the press. Justice Blackmun said that casting fair trial rights in terms of the accused is "not sufficient to permit the inference that the accused may compel a private proceeding simply by waiving that right." In addition, open proceedings are educative, allow police and prosecutorial performances to be scrutinized, and protect both the public and the defendant from partiality. The appearance of justice is important. "Secret hearings—though they are scrupulously fair in reality—are suspect by nature." *See also* CHANDLER V. FLORIDA (449 U.S. 560: 1981), p. 262; NEBRASKA PRESS ASSOCIATION V. STUART (427 U.S. 539: 1976), p. 259; SHEPPARD V. MAXWELL (384 U.S. 333: 1966), p. 258.

Significance   *Gannett Company* v. *DePasquale* (443 U.S. 368: 1979) sidesteps the censorship question raised in *Nebraska Press Association* v. *Stuart* (427 U.S. 539: 1976). The press was not prohibited from publishing information it already possessed in the *Gannett* case. Rather than consider infringement of the First Amendment rights of a free press, *Gannett* focused on whether a defendant's interest in closing a pretrial hearing supersedes the public's interest in an open proceeding. The decision clearly raised the prospect of all judicial proceedings, even trials, being closed at the initiative of the defense. The Court refused to take that step in *Richmond Newspapers, Inc.* v.

Commonwealth of Virginia (448 U.S. 555: 1980). In *Richmond* the Court would not permit closure of trial to the public and media despite the defendant's request that this be done. With only Justice Rehnquist dissenting, the Court held that trials could not "summarily close courtroom doors" without interfering with First Amendment protections. Thus the potential for closure begun in *Gannett* was checked in *Richmond*. Remaining from *Gannett*, however, and reinforced by *Richmond*, is a great deference to trial judge discretion in dealing with closure. *Richmond* makes clear that closing trials is extreme, but if some overriding and demonstrable defendant interest can be shown, they may indeed be closed to the public and the press.

Media Coverage of Trials

Chandler v. *Florida*, 449 U.S. 560, 101 S.Ct. 802, 66 L.Ed.2d 740 (1981)   Examined implementation of media coverage provisions in a trial where the defendant objected to such coverage as a violation of the Sixth Amendment's requirement of a fair and impartial trial. The Florida Supreme Court, as part of the Florida Code of Judicial Conduct, constructed a canon that permitted electronic media and still photographic coverage of trial and appellate proceedings. The canon conveyed authority over all media coverage to the presiding trial judge. The Supreme Court decided in *Chandler* that, absent a specific showing of prejudice, the Florida program was constitutional. Chief Justice Burger wrote for a unanimous Court, with Justice Stevens not participating. He said that an absolute ban on broadcast coverage could not be justified because of potential risk. The Court preferred the Florida approach because it provided safeguards for certain problem cases. The Florida guidelines "place on trial judges positive obligations to be on guard to protect the fundamental right of the accused to a fair trial." The "mere presence" of the broadcast media does not "inherently" adversely affect the process. The burden is on the defendant to show that his case was influenced by the coverage. The Florida process allows review on appeal of allegations of compromised proceedings because of media coverage. Chandler could demonstrate no specific adverse impacts "on the trial participants sufficient to constitute a denial of due process." *See also* GANNETT COMPANY V. DEPASQUALE (443 U.S. 368: 1979), p. 260; NEBRASKA PRESS ASSOCIATION V. STUART (427 U.S. 539: 1976), p. 259; SHEPPARD V. MAXWELL (384 U.S. 333: 1966), p. 258.

Significance   *Chandler* v. *Florida* (449 U.S. 560: 1981) reflects the Supreme Court's deference to the discretion of trial judges in managing problems relating to media coverage of criminal trials. Just as in *Gannett Company* v. *DePasquale* (443 U.S. 368: 1979) and *Richmond Newspapers, Inc.* v. *Commonwealth of Virginia* (448 U.S. 555: 1980), the Court left critical assessments of possible adverse effects of coverage to the presiding judge. This approach squares with the Burger Court's preference for letting the "totality of circumstances" provide the basis for resolving questions of law. *Chandler* also represents a swing away from *Gannett,* a swing begun in *Richmond Newspapers.* Courtroom coverage by electronic media has the potential to be most problematic in terms of fair trial standards. Yet in *Chandler* the Court refused to find such coverage inherently violative of due process as the Warren Court had in *Estes* v. *Texas* (381 U.S. 532: 1965). *Chandler* placed the burden of proof with the defendant by requiring the accused to demonstrate prejudice. *Gannett* had allowed an accused simply to request closure. Absent a demonstration of adverse effect, a defendant cannot simply terminate coverage or achieve closure by request alone. The experiment in Florida warrants ongoing attention to determine whether benefits or any liabilities emerge as a result of more extensive media coverage. The Federal Judicial Conference prohibits the use of photography or reading devices in federal courts.

Assistance of Counsel

Powell v. Alabama, 287 U.S. 45, 53 S.Ct. 55, 77 L.Ed. 158 (1932)   Raised the constitutional issue of whether the assistance-of-counsel provisions of the Sixth Amendment required appointment of counsel in a state capital case. *Powell* is a case arising out of the infamous "Scottsboro" trial, in which seven black defendants were convicted of rape of two white women in Alabama in 1931. Powell and his codefendants were on trial for their lives in a wholly hostile environment. They were indigent, and they were illiterate. Trial counsel was not named for the defendants until the morning of the trial. All seven defendants were found guilty. The Supreme Court reversed the convictions in a 7–2 decision. In doing so the Court determined that the Due Process Clause of the Fourteenth Amendment encompassed assistance of counsel because counsel was "fundamental" to due process. Through this process the counsel provisions of the federal Constitution are extended to state criminal proceedings, at least in capital cases. The trial judge in the Scottsboro case failed to give reasonable time and opportunity to secure counsel for the preparation of a defense. Given the extreme circumstances of the case, this "failure of the trial court to make an effective appointment of counsel constituted denial of due process within the meaning of the Fourteenth Amendment." In a capital case where the defendant is unable to employ counsel and is "incapable adequately of making his own defense because of ignorance, feeblemindedness, illiteracy or the like," a trial judge, whether requested to or not, must assign counsel for him as a necessary requisite of due process. The assignment obligation can only be fulfilled if counsel is assigned in time to allow the "giving of effective aid in the preparation and trial of the case." A criminal defendant requires "the guiding hand of counsel at every step in the proceeding against him." Although the Court did not indicate the stage of the proceedings where counsel might be required, clearly it was required at the trial stage at the latest in a state criminal proceedings. *See also* ARGERSINGER V. HAMLIN (407 U.S. 25: 1972), p. 266; GIDEON V. WAINWRIGHT (372 U.S. 335: 1963), p. 264; UNITED STATES V. WADE (388 U.S. 218: 1967), p. 267.

Significance   *Powell* v. *Alabama* (387 U.S. 45: 1932) was a limited decision in that it involved only capital cases at the state level and was bound by an unusual fact situation. Nonetheless, *Powell* had substantial impact on policy regarding assistance of counsel in two ways. First, it tied the Sixth Amendment Counsel Clause to the states through the Due Process Clause of the Fourteenth Amendment for the first time, albeit only for capital cases at the trial stage. Second, *Powell* changed the direction of the evolution of Court policy on assistance of counsel. For some time prior to *Powell,* many argued that the Sixth Amendment merely allowed a defendant to have counsel. *Powell* became the basis for establishing assistance of counsel as a requirement of fairness. It was only a matter of time until the Court examined the requirement of providing counsel in noncapital felonies. In *Johnson* v. *Zerbst* (304 U.S. 458: 1938), the Court ruled that in all federal felonies counsel must be provided to indigent defendants. Although limited to federal cases, *Zerbst* extended *Powell* beyond capital cases and established that without a knowing and voluntary waiver, counsel must be appointed for federal criminal trials. *Zerbst* also took *Powell* to the threshold of application of a parallel counsel policy at the state level, accomplished in *Gideon* v. *Wainwright* (372 U.S. 335: 1963).

Gideon v. Wainwright, 372 U.S. 335, 83 S.Ct. 792, 9 L.Ed.2d 799 (1963)   Considered whether states must provide counsel in all felony cases under the Sixth Amendment provision that the accused shall "have the Assistance of Counsel for his defense." *Powell v. Alabama* (287 U.S. 45: 1932) had established that states had an obligation to provide counsel to indigent criminal defendants in *capital* cases. Gideon was charged with a property felony in Florida. He was unable to secure his own defense counsel and requested appointment of counsel for his trial. The request was denied, and Gideon was convicted and sentenced to five years imprisonment. The Supreme Court reversed his conviction in a unanimous and landmark decision. Had Gideon been prosecuted for a federal offense, he would have had counsel appointed under provisions of *Johnson* v. *Zerbst* (304 U.S. 458: 1938). But the governing precedent in state cases was *Betts* v. *Brady* (316 U.S. 455: 1942), which required "special circumstances" in order to necessitate appointment of counsel. *Gideon* gave the Court an opportunity to reconsider *Betts*. The Court concluded that *Betts* was wrong and that denial of counsel to indigent, noncapital, felony defendants violated the basic concept of due process. The fundamental right to a fair trial "could not be realized if the poor man charged with a crime has to face his accuser without a lawyer to assist him." The Court said that *Betts* "had departed from the sound wisdom upon which the Court's holding in *Powell* v. *Alabama* rested," that *Betts* was "an anachronism when handed down," and "should now be overruled." *See also* ARGERSINGER V. HAMLIN(407 U.S. 25: 1972), p. 266; FARETTA V. CALIFORNIA (422 U.S. 806: 1975), p. 269; POWELL V. ALABAMA (287 U.S. 45: 1932), p. 263; UNITED STATES V. WADE (388 U.S. 218: 1967), p. 267.

Significance   *Gideon* v. *Wainwright* (372 U.S. 335, 1963) confirmed a position on counsel in state felony trials that had been evolving since the day *Betts* v. *Brady* (316 U.S. 455: 1942) was decided. The evolution took two forms. First, *Betts* provided that trial courts find "special circumstances" before appointing counsel. Initially these special circumstances included capital cases, physical or mental handicap, or a very young defendant. Over time the Court broadened the concept of special circumstances and made denial of counsel in many cases impossible. Between the late 1940s and the *Gideon* decision, no state conviction was affirmed by the Supreme Court over claims of denial of counsel. The Court was clearly moving toward the position it enunciated in *Gideon*. Second, many states on their own initiative adopted a policy of requiring counsel in all felony cases. By the time *Gideon* was decided, almost half of them had already embraced the *Gideon* position, at least for the trial stage of criminal proceedings. The attorneys general of 22 states submitted an *amicus curiae* brief to the Supreme Court on behalf of Gideon. Unlike some of the other Warren Court decisions dealing with rights of the accused, the *Gideon* holding was generally well received. It ended the uncertainties stemming from the special circumstances rule and established that all felony cases require counsel at the trial stage. With *Gideon* in place, the Court could move on two other critical questions: (1) Does the counsel requirement extend to misdemeanor-level criminal cases? (2) Are there other stages in the criminal process comparable to the trial stage that also require assistance of counsel? Thus *Gideon* reshaped policy on assistance of counsel, but it also refocused other inquiry in a way that eventually produced related landmark decisions such as *Miranda* v. *Arizona* (384 U.S. 436: 1966). Gideon's lawyer on appeal was Abe Fortas, himself appointed a Supreme Court Justice in 1965. A popular book on the development of the case, *Gideon's Trumpet* by Anthony Lewis (New York: Vintage Books, 1964), was widely read and highly regarded in the late 1960s. The book was described by one reviewer as "how one lonely man, a poor prisoner, took his case to the Supreme Court—and changed the law of the United States."

Argersinger v. *Hamlin,* 407 U.S. 25, 92 S.Ct. 2006, 32 L.Ed.2d 530 (1972)   Extended to misdemeanors the *Gideon* doctrine that defendants in felony cases must be provided with a lawyer if they are indigent. *Gideon* v. *Wainwright* (372 U.S. 335: 1963) required that all indigent felony defendants be provided counsel at state expense. Argersinger was convicted of an offense punishable by up to six months imprisonment. He was indigent and unrepresented by counsel. In a unanimous decision the Supreme Court found his trial and conviction to be constitutionally defective. The opinion of the Court stressed these points: (1) The Court found nothing historically to indicate Sixth Amendment rights should be retractable in cases involving petty offenses. (2) The nature of the legal issues of a case should be the criterion for assessing necessity of counsel. Cases where lesser terms of imprisonment result may not be any less complex than cases where lengthy sentences may occur. (3) Given the assembly-line character of misdemeanor proceedings, assistance of counsel may be especially important. The basic holding of *Argersinger* is that absent a "knowing and intelligent waiver," no defendant may receive jail or prison time unless the defendant was represented by counsel at his or her trial. Several members of the Court wrote concurring opinions addressing the decision's implementation problems, but the basic holding was unanimous and included all four appointees of President Nixon. *See also* GIDEON V. WAINWRIGHT (372 U.S. 335: 1963), p. 264; POWELL V. ALABAMA (287 U.S. 45: 1932), p. 263; UNITED STATES V. WADE (388 U.S. 218: 1967), p. 267.

Significance   *Argersinger* v. *Hamlin* (407 U.S. 25: 1972) reveals stress stemming from implementation and operational considerations. On the one hand, the Court wished to extend *Gideon* and did so with fairly strong language. On the other hand, the Court was faced with implementation of policy where the court system is most congested and where pressures for "assembly-line justice" are most acute. *Argersinger* was a compromise. It required counsel in misdemeanor cases, recognizing that the legal needs of defendants in these cases may be equal to or greater than defendants in felony cases. It also provided trial judges with the choice of not appointing counsel at all, although in refusing to do so the trial judge might forfeit imprisonment as a sentence option. Despite the problems in implementing it, *Argersinger* has fundamentally altered the process of justice in misdemeanor courts, often called "city courts," "municipal courts," or "Justice of the Peace courts." It has also produced important legislation at the state and local level. Many cities, for example, now appoint or contract with counsel to provide legal assistance to persons who desire to try misdemeanor charges. Some states have decriminalized most traffic offenses in order to avoid the consequences of *Argersinger*. *Argersinger* was refined in *Scott* v. *Illinois* (440 U.S. 367: 1979), where the Supreme Court held that a state court does not have to appoint counsel where imprisonment is authorized for a particular offense but is not actually imposed. *Argersinger* and *Scott* together require greater caution by state and local governments in criminal proceedings. Many local judges are loath to imprison for misdemeanor convictions where counsel is not present, unless the defendant was made aware of his or her right to counsel before tendering a guilty plea. The *Scott* emphasis on actual incarceration was reinforced in *Lassiter* v. *Department of Social Services* (452 U.S. 18: 1981), where the Court held that counsel need not be provided to an indigent parent at a hearing that could terminate her status as a parent. The Court said an indigent litigant was entitled to counsel only when the litigant is threatened with the deprivation of physical liberty.

Critical Stages for Assistance of Counsel

United States v. Wade, 388 U.S. 218, 87 S.Ct. 1926, 18 L.Ed.2d 1149 (1967)   Considered whether counsel must be present at a post-indictment lineup session. Once the Supreme Court determined in *Gideon* v. *Wainwright* (372 U.S. 335: 1963) that assistance of counsel was a fundamental ingredient of due process at the trial stage of any felony prosecution, it followed that assistance of counsel at other stages in the criminal process would have to be evaluated. *Wade* represents a number of cases that define the stages critical enough to require assistance of counsel. The Court vacated Wade's conviction and ordered a new trial, saying the post-indictment process was "peculiarly riddled with innumerable dangers and variable factors which might seriously, even crucially, derogate from a fair trial." Denial of counsel at this stage was seen as critical. There exists "grave potential for prejudice, intentional or not, in the pre-trial lineup." The presence of counsel "can often avert prejudice and assure a meaningful confrontation at trial." The Court's conclusion was that there was "little doubt" that the lineup was a "critical stage," a stage at which Wade was entitled to aid of counsel. *See also* ARGERSINGER V. HAMLIN (407 U.S. 25: 1972), p. 266; GIDEON V. WAINWRIGHT (372 U.S. 335: 1963), p. 264; POWELL V. ALABAMA (287 U.S. 45: 1932), p. 263.

Significance   United States v. Wade (388 U.S. 218: 1967) settled the question of whether earlier or later stages of criminal proceedings other than trial similarly required assistance of counsel. The Warren Court approached the issue by defining the concept of "critical stages." A critical stage is where advice of counsel may be essential to protecting a defendant's rights and where the outcome of the criminal process as a whole is substantially affected. Within five years of *Gideon*, pretrial steps or proceedings such as custodial interrogation prior to charging, post-charge investigations, and preliminary hearings and identifications such as the lineup in *Wade* were found to be critical stages requiring assistance of counsel. These rulings came in *Miranda* v. *Arizona* (384 U.S. 436: 1966); *Massiah* v. *United States* (377 U.S. 201: 1964); and *White* v. *Maryland* (373 U.S. 59: 1963), respectively. Even before *Gideon*, counsel provisions had been extended to arraignments in *Hamilton* v. *Alabama* (368 U.S. 52: 1961). Expansion of the concept of critical stage also occurred with respect to post-trial proceedings. In *Douglas* v. *California* (372 U.S. 353: 1963) the Court held that counsel was required for those appeals that are a matter of right. To the present point in the development of critical stage doctrine, counsel is not required for second or discretionary appeals. See *Ross* v. *Moffitt* (417 U.S. 600: 1974). Counsel is required for juvenile proceedings, however, as in *In re Gault* (378 U.S. 1: 1967), and at the sentencing stage of adult criminal proceedings. In *Mempa* v. *Rhay* (389 U.S. 128: 1967) the Court said that an individual is entitled to counsel in a proceeding where probation is revoked and a sentence is to be imposed. These cases demonstrate the exceptionally high priority assigned by the Supreme Court to making legal counsel available to all persons at most stages of the criminal charge process. They reflect the Court's recognition that other constitutional protections are best preserved through assistance of counsel.

Self-Representation

***Faretta* v. *California,* 422 U.S. 806, 95 S.Ct. 2525, 45 L.Ed.2d 562 (1975)** Considered whether a state criminal defendant's defense of himself met the Sixth Amendment requirement of assistance of counsel. By the mid-1970s it was clearly established that a person being tried on a criminal charge in either a state or federal court must be afforded the right of assistance of counsel. A six-justice Supreme Court majority held that Faretta could constitutionally assist and defend himself. The majority, through Justice Stewart, recognized that self-representation may be an unwise course for a criminal defendant, but the Court said it is "one thing to hold that every defendant, rich or poor, has the right to the assistance of counsel, and quite another to say that a State may compel a defendant to accept a lawyer he does not want." Free choice was crucial to the majority decision. The choice of a defense belongs to the defendant, including the question of counsel. Although the defendant's choice may be "ultimately to his own detriment, his choice must be honored." A trial judge must make the defendant "aware of the dangers and disadvantages of self-representation" so that the record can reflect that the defendant made a choice with "eyes open." The criterion by which the determination is to be made is not technical. It makes no difference "how well or poorly Faretta had mastered the intricacies of the hearsay rule and the California code provisions." The decision rested with his "knowing exercise of the right to defend himself." In the case appealed the majority concluded that Faretta had been denied a constitutional right to "conduct his own defense." Chief Justice Burger and Justices Blackmun and Rehnquist dissented. Burger could find no Sixth Amendment right to represent oneself. The "spirit and logic" of the amendment required that the accused receive "the fullest possible defense." He did not agree with the freedom-of-choice argument of the majority, and opined that the trial court retains discretion to reject a waiver of counsel. The chief justice was concerned that greater congestion of the courts would follow *Faretta,* and that the quality of justice would suffer. Blackmun also found the

Sixth Amendment to stop short of conveying a right of self-representation. He felt the decision would cause "procedural confusion without advancing any significant strategic interest of the defendant." *See also* GIDEON V. WAINWRIGHT (372 U.S. 335: 1963), p. 264; POWELL V. ALABAMA (287 U.S. 45: 1932), p. 263; SIXTH AMENDMENT, p. 241.

Significance   *Faretta v. California* established the rule that a defendant has a right to carry on his or her own defense without violating the assistance-of-counsel requirement of the Sixth Amendment. The case runs absolutely counter to many recent Supreme Court decisions that found "the guiding hand of counsel" indispensable to due process. *Faretta* not only recognizes the option of self-representation but accords it the status of a protected right on par with assistance of counsel. *Faretta* holds in addition that a defendant need not demonstrate even minimal levels of legal skill to exercise the right of self-representation. Like any other constitutional provision, the right to counsel may be waived voluntarily. *Faretta* clearly leaves a number of substantive questions to future consideration. One relates to effectiveness of counsel. *Faretta* would seem to foreclose a defendant's making appeal on the grounds of ineffective counsel after exercising the right to self-representation. The question of effectiveness of counsel has long been troublesome for the courts, with no precise standards in place for cases where it has been at issue. The most generally recognized criterion is the "mockery of justice" standard, but this standard requires extraordinary ineffectiveness. Representative of cases where the Court has rejected claims of ineffective assistance is *Jones* v. *Barnes* (103 S.Ct. 3308: 1983), in which the Court held that counsel assigned to handle an appeal for a convicted defendant need not raise every issue suggested by the defendant. For courts to "second-guess reasonable professional judgments and impose on appointed counsel a duty to raise every 'colorable' claim suggested by a client would disserve the goal of vigorous and effective advocacy." As more specific and perhaps more stringent standards evolve by which the performance of attorneys in criminal cases may be assessed, the Court will likely have to reexamine its holding in *Faretta*.

Plea Bargaining

***Boykin* v. *Alabama*, 395 U.S. 238, 89 S.Ct. 1709, 23 L.Ed.2d 274 (1969)**   Addressed some of the conditions that must be present for a guilty plea to be acceptable. An overwhelming majority of American criminal defendants plead guilty rather than face a trial. Defendant Boykin pled guilty to five counts of robbery and was sentenced to death by a jury. The record showed that the trial judge asked no questions of the defendant at the time of the plea, that the defendant did not address the court in any way, and that the defendant did not testify at his sentencing proceeding. He was represented by counsel throughout. A six-member majority of the Supreme Court found the plea insufficient. The Court focused on the trial judge's error of accepting the plea without an "affirmative showing that it was intelligent and voluntary." The majority held that a plea is "more than a confession, it is a conviction." Waiver of such rights as trial by jury, confronting one's accusers, and the protection from self-incrimination simply cannot be taken from a silent record. Justice Fortas did not participate in the case. Justices Black and Harlan dissented primarily on the grounds that the record was only silent as opposed to showing that the plea was neither voluntary nor unknowing. They also emphasized that Boykin had not targeted this problem in his appeal. Rather he argued the death penalty issue. The dissenters were concerned that the states should not be required to adhere to the same requirements as the federal courts in taking pleas. *See also* BORDENKIRCHER V. HAYES (434 U.S. 357: 1978), p. 275; BRADY V. UNITED STATES (397 U.S. 742: 1970), p. 272; SANTOBELLO V. NEW YORK (404 U.S. 257: 1971), p. 273.

Significance   *Boykin* v. *Alabama* (395 U.S. 238: 1969) established that the plea of guilty constitutes more than a confession. It stands as a conviction equivalent to a jury finding. It involves the waiver of several protections such as self-incrimination, trial by jury, confrontation of accusers, and forfeiture of the presumption of innocence. *Boykin* established minimum Sixth Amendment standards and federal-state uniformity regarding guilty pleas. Because of *Boykin*, no federal or state judge can accept a plea of guilty without questioning the defendant as to whether the charge is understood by him, whether the potential sentence that may result from pleading guilty to the charge is understood by him, and whether promises or threats have been made. The defendant must be made aware that many constitutional protections are being waived. The basis of *Boykin* was to ensure that the plea of guilty was the defendant's knowing and voluntary choice. Although *Boykin* does not require it, some jurisdictions place a summary of the case against a defendant in the record. In the absence of satisfactory responses to any of the judge's inquiries, a trial judge has the discretion of refusing to accept a guilty plea and having the case scheduled for trial. Today in federal courts a mandatory rule (Rule 11, Federal Rules of Criminal Procedure) stipulates the steps to be taken by the judge in considering a plea of guilty. The steps must comply with *Boykin*. Most state courts have similar code or rule requirements. Thus the plea process takes considerably more time than before *Boykin*, but the *Boykin*-type appeal rarely occurs anymore. It is widely thought that the *Boykin* process results in considerably higher judicial standards being imposed at the trial level.

Brady v. United States, 397 U.S. 742, 90 S.Ct. 1463, 25 L.Ed.2d 747 (1970)   Examined the effect of a potential death sentence on the voluntariness of a plea. Are pleas acceptable if they are taken against the possibility of the imposition of the death penalty should a defendant be convicted on the same charge by a jury? Brady had been charged with kidnapping and demanded a jury trial. He changed his mind when a codefendant pled guilty to a comparable charge and became available to testify against him. The Supreme Court upheld Brady's plea. Justice White wrote the opinion of the Court. He opined that knowledge and voluntariness are the two critical ingredients of an acceptable plea. Present those two elements, motivation to avoid a possible death sentence was not a defect per se. After examining the "totality of the circumstances," the Court felt there was no evidence to suggest that Brady would have undergone a trial "but for" the capital punishment potential or that he "was so gripped by fear of the death penalty" that he could not make a rational decision. Brady was assisted by counsel throughout. Justices Brennan, Marshall, and Douglas concurred in the result of the case, but were concerned that under the Court's narrow definition of involuntariness, a defendant could make a rational or knowing, but still an involuntary, plea. *See also* BORDEN-KIRCHER V. HAYES (434 U.S. 357: 1978), p. 275; BOYKIN V. ALABAMA (395 U.S. 238: 1969), p. 270; SANTOBELLO V. NEW YORK (404 U.S. 257: 1971), p. 273.

Significance   *Brady* v. *United States* (397 U.S. 742: 1970) decided that the voluntariness of a plea should be determined case by case based on the totality of the circumstances present when the plea is offered. Fearing the imposition of a death penalty does not, per se, destroy the voluntary element necessary before a plea may be accepted. In *United States* v. *Jackson* (390 U.S. 570: 1968) the Supreme Court held the death penalty provisions of the Federal Kidnapping Act (the Lindbergh Law) unconstitutional on the grounds that they tended to "discourage defendants from insisting on their innocence and demanding trial by jury." The *Brady* plea had been taken almost ten years before *Jackson* and could have been handled by a determination that *Jackson* would not apply retroactively. The Burger Court, however, chose to modify *Jackson* by substituting the "totality of circumstances" standard. *Brady* had the effect of making challenges of pleas on the grounds of involuntariness much more difficult than under the Warren Court rule in *Jackson*. The *Brady* decision also dealt with the status of guilty pleas more generally. The Burger Court chose to comment positively on plea bargaining. The Court said it would not find a plea deficient when "motivated by the defendant's desire to accept the certainty or probability of a lesser penalty rather than face a wider range of possibilities" through a jury trial. Justice White itemized the benefits that accrue to both defendant and the state through the process of plea bargaining. He suggested it was this "mutuality of advantage" that explained the great frequency of dispositions of criminal cases by means of the plea. While particular pleas may be suspect, the Burger Court clearly endorsed the practice of plea bargaining in *Brady*.

Santobello v. *New York,* 404 U.S. 257, 29 S.Ct. 495, 30 L.Ed.2d 427 (1971)

Considered the issue of what happens when the state fails to honor a commitment made during plea-bargaining discussions. Santobello was indicted for two felonies and agreed to enter a guilty plea in exchange for no sentence recommendation by the prosecuting attorney. At the sentencing hearing, delayed twice at defendant's initiative, a new prosecuting attorney appeared. Apparently ignorant of his colleague's promise, the new prosecutor recommended the maximum sentence, which Santobello received. The trial judge said, however, he was not influenced by the prosecutor's recommendation. The Court concluded that Santobello's sentence must be vacated, although a minority of the Court (Justices Marshall, Brennan, and Stewart) argued that the defendant should be allowed to withdraw his guilty plea entirely. On the basic sentence question, the Court said the condition of no sentence recommendation was an integral part of the bargain made with the prosecutor. The Court did not forgive the failure of one prosecutor to communicate the elements of the negotiation to his successor. The prosecutor's office has "the burden of 'letting the left hand know what the right hand is doing' or has done." The Court said further, "the breach of agreement was inadvertent," but that "does not lessen its impact." *Santobello* represented to the Court "another example of an unfortunate lapse in orderly prosecutorial procedures," presumably a product of excessively high caseloads. But while workload "may well explain these episodes, it does not excuse them." The plea process "must be attended by safeguards to insure the defendant what is reasonably due in the circumstances." The position of the Court was that where pleas "rest in any significant degree on a promise or agreement of the prosecutor, such promise must be fulfilled." *See also* BOYKIN V. ALABAMA (395 U.S. 238: 1969), p. 270; BRADY V. UNITED STATES (397 U.S. 742: 1970), p. 272; BORDENKIRCHER V. HAYES (434 U.S. 357: 1978), p. 275.

Significance   Santobello v. *New York* (404 U.S. 257: 1971) illustrates the problems attendant to a congested court system where over 90 percent of criminal cases are disposed of by means of the plea. The system requires nontrial dispositions in order to keep pace with case volume. Most cases are passed from one assistant prosecutor to another within a prosecutor's office as the next stage of the process is reached. The left hand does not always know what the right hand has done. Plea bargaining has long been a suspect practice anyway. The National Advisory Commission on Criminal Justice Standards and Goals strongly urged the abolition of plea bargaining in the early 1970s. *Santobello* addresses several important issues related to the Advisory Commission's recommendations. First, the Court established the basic expectation that where promises are instrumental in achieving a plea, the integrity of the bargaining process must be maintained and the promises honored. *Santobello* defines a performance standard for prosecutors. Second, *Santobello* permits a defendant in a criminal case to enforce a plea agreement against the government. Although *Santobello* involved only a prosecutorial recommendation, it raised the specter of a prosecutor offering to dismiss other counts against a defendant, and not prosecuting for similar offenses within a given time. The lower courts have frequently invoked *Santobello* when a defendant alleges and proves a plea agreement has been violated. It is not uncommon for courts to dismiss criminal proceedings when prosecutorial authorities have reneged on a plea. This kind of specific enforcement may be the most important aspect of *Santobello*. Third, *Santobello* gave the Court an opportunity to speak generally to the status of plea bargaining. The Court gave the practice a strong endorsement. It referred to plea bargaining as an "essential component of the administration of justice. Properly administered, it is to be encouraged." The Court itemized several reasons why plea bargaining should be regarded not only as essential, but as "highly desirable." The advantages included finality, pretrial confinement, conservation of scarce resources, and enhancement of rehabilitative prospects. Taken with the positive language found in *Brady* v. *United States* (397 U.S. 742: 1970), the *Santobello* language and decision can be viewed as foreclosing the possibility that the Court will call for the abolition of plea bargaining in the near future.

Bordenkircher v. Hayes, 434 U.S. 357, 98 S.Ct. 663, 54 L.Ed.2d 604 (1978)   Weighed the question of how far a prosecutor should go in putting a criminal defendant under pressure to plead guilty. After defendant Hayes refused to plead to a particular felony indictment, the prosecutor carried out his threat to have the defendant reindicted under Kentucky's habitual offender statute. The statute allowed the possibility of a mandatory life sentence. Threat of this action was conveyed by the prosecutor during the course of plea negotiations. A jury subsequently convicted Hayes of the original charge and made an additional finding that he was eligible for a life term under the recidivist statute. Hayes appealed, claiming violation of due process. The Supreme Court decided against Hayes 5–4. The majority's decision took two lines of argument. First, the Court acknowledged the breadth of prosecutorial discretion in the charging process. The majority found little difference between charging initially and offering to drop the recidivist part of the subsequent charge. Second, the Court said the plea-bargaining process should be afforded substantial operating margin. The bargaining process should entertain the whole range of options available to the defendant. In this case, Hayes was informed of what the prosecutor would do if he did not plead guilty, and since he was properly chargeable under the recidivist statute, the prosecutor had not acted improperly. The Court concluded that the prosecutor "openly presented the defendant with the unpleasant alternatives of foregoing trial or facing charges on which he was plainly subject to prosecution." This was not viewed as a deprivation of due process. And, "in the 'give and take' of plea bargaining, there is no such element of punishment or retaliation so long as the accused is free to accept or reject the prosecutor's offer." The four dissenters—Justices Brennan, Marshall, Blackmun, and Powell—viewed the prosecutorial conduct as creating "a strong inference of vindictiveness." While expressing general deference to prosecutorial discretion, the minority thought the prosecutor had intended to discourage and penalize Hayes for pursuing his constitutional rights to a trial. Justice Powell concluded by saying, "Implementation of a strategy calculated solely to deter the exercise of constitutional rights is not a constitutionally permissible exercise of discretion." *See also* BOYKIN V. ALABAMA (397 U.S. 238: 1969),

p. 270; BRADY V. UNITED STATES (397 U.S. 742: 1970), p. 272; SANTOBELLO V. NEW YORK (404 U.S. 257: 1971), p. 273.

Significance   Bordenkircher v. Hayes (434 U.S. 357: 1978) extended substantial latitude to the prosecutor in plea-bargaining situations. The Court majority was unwilling to view the prosecutor's conveyed incentives to plead guilty as either punitive or malicious threats. Thus *Bordenkircher* defined the plea-bargaining setting itself as one permitting broad prosecutorial discretion. The narrow holding in the case should cause it to be viewed with caution, however. One of the majority justices, Justice Potter Stewart, has since left the Court, and the dissent was strong. Nevertheless *Bordenkircher* clarified for a while the opinion of the Court in *Blackledge v. Perry* (417 U.S. 21: 1974), and it freed the plea-bargaining process from the limitations of *Blackledge*. Perry was convicted of a misdemeanor. He pursued his statutory right to a retrial and was subsequently charged with a felony for the same conduct that was originally charged as a misdemeanor. The Court disallowed the substitute charge on the grounds that the recharging was motivated by vindictiveness. An actual retaliatory motive need not be shown. The Court's perception of vindictiveness sufficient to "deter a defendant's exercise of the right to appeal" was the crucial factor in *Blackledge*. Some observers felt the thrust of *Blackledge* might carry over to the plea process itself. *Bordenkircher* resolved the doubt otherwise and enhanced the leverage a prosecutor may bring to bear in plea-bargaining negotiations.

Juvenile Justice: Legal Protections for Juveniles

In Re Gault, **378 U.S. 1, 87 S.Ct. 1428, 18 L.Ed.2d 257 (1967)**   Examined the extent to which juvenile proceedings must provide constitutional protections similar to those afforded adult criminal defendants. Gerald Gault, age 15, was found to have made a lewd telephone call and was committed to the state industrial school as a delinquent. He faced the possibility of having to remain there until he was 21 years of age. For an adult the maximum punishment for such an offense would have been a $50 fine or confinement for not more than 60 days. Gault's parents appealed the outcome, claiming (1) they had been given inadequate notice of the charges; (2) the complainant had not testified; (3) they had not been offered counsel; (4) Gerald had not been warned that any statements he made could be used against him; (5) no records had been made of the hearing; and (6) Arizona law permitted no appeal in a juvenile proceeding. With only Justice Stewart dissenting, the Supreme Court found for Gault. The majority, through Justice Fortas, recognized that juvenile and adult proceedings had been intentionally different up to that point in history. Fortas declared, however, that the proceedings could not remain dissimilar with regard to basic constitutional protections. He suggested that the essential difference between Gault's case and adult criminal cases is that safeguards available to adults were discarded for the juvenile. Although some benefits derive from handling juveniles differently, i.e., more informally, there must be procedural protections. "Under our Constitution, the condition of being a boy does not justify a kangaroo court." The holding in *Gault* required that delinquency proceedings that may lead to detention must provide juveniles with access to counsel, with appointed counsel in instances of indigency, adequate notification of charges with a right to confront witnesses, and with the privilege against self-incrimination. In his dissent Justice Stewart dwelt on traditional juvenile-adult procedural differences, urging that juvenile proceedings not become full-blown adversary proceedings. *See also* IN RE WINSHIP (397 U.S. 358: 1970), p. 278; MCKEIVER V. PENNSYLVANIA (403 U.S. 441: 1971), p. 279; SIXTH AMENDMENT, p. 241.

Significance   In re Gault (378 U.S. 1: 1967) challenged the long-standing view that juvenile proceedings are categorically different from adult criminal proceedings. A juvenile "conviction," for example, was not supposed to be viewed as a conviction by future employers and adult courts. Judges, however, usually had access to juvenile "convictions" when the former juvenile found himself later before an adult court. For many years prior to *Gault*, juvenile courts were seen as places where the state acted as *parens patriae* (benevolent parent) rather than as an adversary. Juvenile proceedings came to be regarded as civil in character and substantially more informal than adult criminal trials. They were viewed as being free from due process expectations in any strict sense. The characteristic of informality had been the strength of juvenile courts and the main source of problems as well. The *parens patriae* assumption sometimes produced insensitivity to legal procedures, and it was such insensitivity that the Court attacked in *Gault*. The case was but one of a series of decisions by the Warren Court extending due process rights to categories of persons not previously enjoying them. *Gault* was actually the second Warren Court decision addressing due process in juvenile courts. The first case, *Kent* v. *United States* (383 U.S. 541: 1966), preceded *Gault* by a year. *Kent* involved the waiver of jurisdiction by a juvenile court to allow transfer of a juvenile's case to adult court. The Court imposed several specific procedural requirements on the waiver process, including a hearing, representation by counsel, and access to all records and reports on the juvenile germane to the waiver. While *Kent* was limited to relatively few cases, it clearly conveyed the Court's interest in juvenile rights and procedural fairness in juvenile courts. The effects of *Gault* are substantial. The procedural requirements of juvenile courts have now been formalized to the extent that many current proceedings bear little resemblance to juvenile court activities of 25 years ago. While certain differences yet remain between juvenile and adult processes, the adjudicatory hearing in juvenile court contains most of the ingredients of the trial of an adult defendant.

Juvenile Justice: Reasonable Doubt

In Re Winship, **397 U.S. 358, 90 S.Ct. 1068, 25 L.Ed.2d 368 (1970)**   Examined the question of whether the reasonable doubt standard is required in juvenile proceedings. Using the preponderance of evidence standard as provided by state statute, Winship was found to have stolen money. A six-justice Supreme Court majority determined that proving guilt beyond a reasonable doubt was an essential element of due process in proving the case, however. The reasonable doubt standard should be required at the adjudicatory stage of any juvenile proceeding in which the juvenile is charged with an act constituting a crime if committed by an adult. Justice Brennan argued for the majority that a criminal defendant would be at "severe disadvantage" if guilt could be determined on the strength "of the same evidence as would suffice in a civil case." The reasonable doubt standard emphasizes the "necessity of reaching a subjective state of certitude of the facts" at issue. As for the need to extend the standard to juvenile proceedings, Brennan said that "civil labels and good intentions do not themselves obviate the need for criminal due process standards in juvenile courts." These more rigorous evidentiary standards would not interfere with confidentiality, informality, flexibility, and the speed with which juvenile proceedings occur. They would not compel "States to abandon or displace any of the substantive benefits of the juvenile justice process." Justices Black, Burger, and Stewart dissented. Justice Black expressed concern that the Court was supplementing constitutional provisions. In a literalist dissent, he maintained there was no expressed language in the Bill of Rights regarding standards of evidence as distinct from counsel and self-incrimination. The dissent of Burger and Stewart took issue with the notion that a juvenile proceeding was a "criminal prosecution." They said the *Winship* decision further eroded the differences between juvenile and criminal courts. Burger and Stewart also registered unhappiness with "strait-jacketing" states with due process requirements in juvenile matters. They said the juvenile justice process needed fewer rather than more "trappings of legal procedures and judicial formalism," concluding that the juvenile system must have "breathing room and flexibility" to survive. Juvenile courts could not withstand "repeated assaults" from the Supreme Court. *See also* IN RE GAULT (378 U.S. 1: 1967), p. 276; MCKEIVER V. PENNSYLVANIA (403 U.S. 441: 1971), p. 279; SIXTH AMENDMENT, p. 241.

Significance   In re Winship (397 U.S. 358: 1970) gave the Supreme Court an opportunity to use the Due Process Clause of the Fourteenth Amendment as a means to establish fairness standards beyond those expressly contained in the Bill of Rights. *Winship* profoundly affected juvenile as well as adult criminal proceedings. Prior to *Winship* the reasonable doubt standard was only presumed to apply to adults. *Winship* specifically joined the reasonable doubt standard and the concept of due process for juveniles as well. *Winship,* following soon after *In re Gault* (378 U.S. 1: 1967), seemed to remove juvenile processes from the status of civil proceedings and place them alongside adult criminal trials. That it did not completely do so can be seen in such cases as *McKeiver* v. *Pennsylvania* (403 U.S. 441: 1971). A distinct new direction was apparent from *Gault* and *Winship,* however. Juvenile authorities must deal with the legal requirements essential to the fair operation of courts. They must be more aware of juvenile conduct that has an adult counterpart, rather than merely of "status" offenses such as truancy, which are improper conduct only for those of the status of juvenile. The informality that marked juvenile processes before *Gault* is clearly a thing of the past in *Winship.*

Juvenile Justice: Jury Trial

McKeiver **v. *Pennsylvania*, 403 U.S. 441, 91 S.Ct. 1976, 29 L.Ed.2d 677 (1971)**   Examined whether juveniles are entitled to jury trials in the adjudicative stage of state delinquency proceedings. *In re Gault* (378 U.S. 1: 1967) and *In re Winship* (397 U.S. 358: 1970) brought a number of process changes to the juvenile justice system. In a 6–3 decision, the Supreme Court held that these process changes in the direction of due process expectations for juvenile proceedings did not mean that all rights assured to an accused adult would automatically extend to juveniles. Jury trials would be one of the excepted rights. Through Justice Blackmun, the majority referred to the traditional differences between adult and juvenile processes. Despite *Gault* and other cases incorporating certain constitutional protections for juveniles, the Court maintained a selective approach. It was clearly trying to "strike a judicious balance" between "procedural orderliness" and the more informal approach of juvenile courts. The majority did not wish to remake juvenile proceedings into a "fully adversarial process" by making access to a jury a required element of the juvenile process. This policy might diminish the "idealistic prospect of an intimate, informal protective proceeding." Further, the majority felt that use of a jury would not improve the fact-finding function of juvenile courts. Rather it might "provide an attrition of the juvenile court's assumed ability to function in a unique manner." Use of the jury would also bring into juvenile courts the "traditional delays, the formality, and the clamor of the adversary system and, possibly, the public trial." The majority said that if such formality is "superimposed" on the juvenile court, there is "little need for its separate existence." The dissenters, Justices Douglas, Black, and Marshall, took issue with the majority's willingness to subordinate a constitutional protection such as the jury trial to the special objectives of the juvenile process. They felt that "where a state uses its juvenile court proceedings to prosecute a juvenile for a criminal act and to order 'confinement' until the child reaches 21 . . . then he is entitled to the same procedural protection as an adult." *See also* IN RE GAULT (378 U.S. 1: 1967), p. 276; IN RE WINSHIP (397 U.S. 358: 1970), p. 278; SIXTH AMENDMENT, p. 241.

Significance   *McKeiver* v. *Pennsylvania* (403 U.S. 441: 1971) allowed the Burger Court to establish that the changes in juvenile rights brought by *Gault* and *Winship* would not remove all distinctions between adult and juvenile proceedings. *McKeiver* preserved the thrust of the rationale that created separate juvenile courts in the late nineteenth century. The Burger Court was not unsympathetic to the basic tightening and formalizing of procedural requirements in juvenile processes, however. It would later extend juvenile rights to cases involving double jeopardy protection. At the same time, *McKeiver* said that juvenile proceedings were not quite a fully adversarial process needing all the constitutional guarantees of adult proceedings. *McKeiver* also decided that considerations of due process did not compel states to provide juveniles with the right to a jury trial. The Court did suggest that state legislatures may opt for jury trials or that state appellate courts may require them through construction of state constitutions. Thus juvenile processes were not to be regarded as full-blown criminal proceedings, although states were free to structure juvenile proceedings more tightly if they wished. *McKeiver* halted the steamroller approach to providing all the due process rights of adults to juveniles.

6. The Eighth Amendment

OVERVIEW

The Eighth Amendment states:

> Excessive bail shall not be required, nor excessive fines imposed, nor cruel and unusual punishments inflicted.

The first clause of the Eighth Amendment provides protection from the imposition of disproportionate or inordinately high bail or fines for criminal offenses. Bail accomplishes pretrial release of a defendant by defining the conditions of the release and by specifying sanctions for "bail skipping" while the defendant is on release. Thus an attempt is made to assure the defendant's appearance at subsequent proceedings. Pretrial release allows a person charged with a crime to retain his or her freedom while awaiting trial. It is a key component of the doctrine that a person is presumed innocent until proven guilty. The Supreme Court has ruled that bail is excessive when it is set higher than an amount that can reasonably be expected to "assure the presence of the accused at trial" (*Stack* v. *Boyle,* 342 U.S. 1: 1951). In its opinion in *Duncan* v. *Louisiana* (391 U.S. 145: 1968), the Supreme Court noted that Louisiana's rejection of sufficient property pledged as bail for a petitioner's release worked against the petitioner and was maintained "in bad faith and for purposes of harassment." The few Court decisions involving the excessive bail issue have typically focused on a defendant's inability to pay and on the imposition of a jail term resulting from indigence. While sitting as a Circuit Judge, Justice William O. Douglas stated in *Bandy* v. *United States* (81 S.Ct. 197: 1960), "It would be unconstitutional to fix excessive bail to assure that a defendant will not gain his freedom. Yet in the case of an indigent defendant, the fixing of bail in even a modest amount may have the practical effect of denying him release."

Congress and state legislatures have attempted to define the parameters of the Excessive Bail Clause of the Eighth Amendment. In 1966, for example, Congress passed the Bail Reform Act, which itemizes criteria to be considered in making pretrial release judgments. Most state legislatures followed the 1966 act with reforms of their own, but for certain serious offenses and/or for defendants with previous and extensive criminal records, many state courts deny bail altogether. Some legal experts feel this practice is not incompatible with the excessive bail prohibition. Most jurisdictions also allow defendant release without posting money per se. Release on recognizance may be available to defendants who have demonstrable and sufficient ties to a community, such as the presence of a family or a job or other factors that contribute to the likelihood that the defendant will appear at subsequent court proceedings of his or her own volition.

The Supreme Court has established the following standards for its interpretation of the second clause of the Eighth Amendment, the cruel and unusual punishments section: (1) Punishment cannot involve torture or be inordinately cruel. (2) Punishment cannot be disproportionate or excessive relative to the offense (*Coker* v. *Georgia,* 433 U.S. 584: 1977; *Hutto* v. *Davis,* 437 U.S. 678: 1968). (3) Punishment can be imposed only for bona fide criminal offenses (*Robinson* v. *California,* 370 U.S. 660: 1962). In *Trop* v. *Dulles* (356 U.S. 86: 1958) the Court said the Cruel and Unusual Punishments Clause draws its meanings from "evolving standards of decency that mark the progress of a maturing society." Thus the interpretation of what constitutes cruel and unusual punishment is a fluid concept in which the status of a particular punishment such as the death penalty may change as society's values evolve and/or mature.

The Court initially considered the question of excessive and disproportionate punishment in a noncapital context in the case of *Robinson* v. *California* (370 U.S. 660: 1962), where the Court held that California's imposition of criminal penalties could not stand merely because competent authority had determined that a defendant was addicted to narcotics. The Court considered it cruel and unusual punishment to impose criminal penalties on someone whose only "offense" was addiction to narcotics. *Robinson* was especially important because it extended the clause to state actions. In *Rummel* v. *Estelle* (445 U.S. 263: 1980) the Court considered the constitutionality of the imposition of mandatory life sentences for repeat offenders.

The dominant cruel and unusual punishment theme in recent years has been the clause's application to the death penalty. The constitutionality of such a penalty, including procedures by which it may be imposed and actual methods of execution, have all been examined by the Supreme Court. The Court held the death penalty to be defective in *Furman* v. *Georgia* (408 U.S. 238: 1972) because those with the authority to impose such a sentence could exercise complete discretion over the terms of capital punishment. Imposition of the death penalty constituted cruel and unusual punishment because its application was arbitrary, discriminatory, and capricious. In *Gregg* v. *Georgia* (428 U.S. 153: 1976) the Court declared that capital punishment was not unconstitutional per se and could be used where sufficient "structure" was provided for its imposition. The decision in *Woodson* v. *North Carolina* (428 U.S. 280: 1976) invalidated the holding that made the death penalty mandatory for particular and specified offenses. In *Coker* v. *Georgia* (433 U.S. 584: 1977) the Court considered the substantive rather than the procedural aspects of the death penalty and ruled that the death penalty was excessive, cruel, and unusual when imposed as punishment for the offense of rape.

Two cases decided in 1983 significantly affect the death penalty discussion. *Barefoot* v. *Texas* (77 L.Ed.2d 1090: 1983) gave the Court an opportunity to specify guidelines for the increasing number of death-sentenced petitioners entering the appellate stages of the federal *habeas corpus* process. *Barclay* v. *Florida* (77 L.Ed.2d 1134: 1983) gave notice to sentencers that they cannot depart from statutory guidelines in determining the aggravating circumstances necessary for imposing the death penalty.

The significance of the Cruel and Unusual Punishments Clause is illustrated by the Supreme Court's extending its interpretation of the clause to allow for review of all noncapital sentence policies and penal objectives established by state legislatures, including the adequacy of prison facilities and confinement conditions. The Court found, for example, that the practice of double-celling prisoners in a maximum-security state prison did not violate the cruel and unusual punishment clause. It has opined on numerous occasions that it is an ongoing function of the Court to scrutinize claims of violations of prisoners' rights through the Cruel and Unusual Punishments Clause, and thus preside over the evolving standards of the Eighth Amendment (*Rhodes* v. *Chapman*, 452 U.S. 337: 1981).

The Eighth Amendment entry and an elaboration of several of the above definitional cases follow.

The Eighth Amendment   Protects the principle that one is presumed innocent until proven guilty and proscribes cruel and unusual punishments. The Eighth Amendment is divided into two clauses, the first saying, "excessive bail shall not be required, nor excessive fines imposed," the second adding, "nor cruel and unusual punishments inflicted." Like other provisions of the Bill of Rights, the Eighth Amendment originated in English common law. Centuries of English statutory law contributed to the tradition that individual liberties would be offended if an accused person were not afforded the opportunity to be "admitted to bail." The accused must be presumed innocent until trial of the facts and evidentiary proceedings prove otherwise. In 1679, for example, the Habeas Corpus Act required "persons imprisoned for bailable offenses to be set free on bail, so that the King's subjects could no longer be detained in prison in such cases where by law they are bailable." Section 20 of Magna Carta had earlier stipulated that no excessive fines should be imposed upon subjects of the Crown. A major defect of English statutory law, however, was that for centuries no limit was set on the amount of bail a judge could demand. The resulting abuses in the bail system were not eliminated until passage of the English Bill of Rights after the Revolution of 1688. Like the language of excessive bail and fines, the language of the Eighth Amendment clause proscribing cruel and unusual punishments also comes from the reign of William and Mary. In 1689 the English Parliament was forced to adopt a Bill of Rights as the result of widespread abuses of individual liberties during the reign of the Stuarts. The Bill of Rights was directly the result of the cruel punishments imposed during the days of the infamous Court of Star Chamber. A major difference between the English and the American bills of rights was that the former had only legislative standing, while the latter had constitutional weight and status. The American authors of the Eighth Amendment also chose to substitute for the words "ought to" in the English Bill of Rights the imperative words "shall not" in the American Bill of Rights. The change made the amendment enforceable by the courts, not subject to future legislative caveats. The Virginia, North Carolina, and New York ratifying conventions urged the inclusion of the Eighth Amendment in the Bill of Rights, knowing implicitly of the violations of the safeguards purported to be contained in the English Bill of Rights through their study of Blackstone's *Commentaries.* Blackstone characterized the violations as "barbarous punishments." Punishments in the colonies during the years prior to the Revolutionary War were quite severe. *See also* BILL OF RIGHTS, p. 7; COMMON LAW, p. 13;

CONSTITUTIONALISM; HISTORICAL DEVELOPMENT OF, p. 16; MAGNA CARTA, p. 46.

Significance   The Eighth Amendment assures that the amount of bail imposed on a criminal defendant is commensurate with the alleged offense. Presumption of guilt is not fixed before trial of the facts. The bail clause was codified in the Judiciary Act of 1789 and further elaborated in the Bail Reform Act of 1966. In *Stack* v. *Boyle* (342 U.S. 1: 1951), Chief Justice Fred M. Vinson, writing for the Supreme Court majority, made the following statement concerning the established American tradition of bail admittance and imposition:

> From the passage of the Judiciary Act of 1789 to the present Rules of Criminal Procedure, federal law has unequivocally provided that a person arrested for a noncapital offense *shall* be admitted to bail. This traditional right to freedom before conviction permits the unhampered preparation of a defense, and serves to prevent the infliction of punishment prior to conviction. . . . Unless this right to bail before trial is preserved, the presumption of innocence, secured only after centuries of struggle, would lose its meaning.

The second clause of the Eighth Amendment illustrates the dynamic and evolutionary processes at work in American constitutional law. In *Weems* v. *United States* (217 U.S. 349: 1910), the Supreme Court established that the Cruel and Unusual Punishments Clause of the amendment was to be interpreted in light of the social values of the time. Subsequent Courts have reiterated the *Weems* standard that the Eighth Amendment "is not fastened to the absolute but may acquire meaning as public opinion becomes enlightened by humane justice."

Noncapital Cruel and Unusual Punishment

Robinson v. *California,* 370 U.S. 660, 82 S.Ct. 1417, 8 L.Ed.2d 758 (1962)   Invalidated a California statute that made addiction to narcotics a crime. The question before the Warren Court in this case was whether the Eighth Amendment prohibition against cruel and unusual punishment precluded a state from making narcotics addiction a crime. Lawrence Robinson had been convicted in the Los Angeles Municipal Court of addiction to narcotics, a misdemeanor, and sentenced to 90 days in jail. Robinson was not under the influence of drugs at the time of his arrest, and the only evidence against him was the testimony of the arresting officer who observed scars and needle marks on Robinson's arms. The California courts upheld the conviction, and Robinson appealed to the United States Supreme

Court. In a 6–2 decision, with Justice Frankfurter not participating, the Supreme Court struck down the California statute as one that contemplated punishment of an individual based solely on the presence of a particular condition or status, rather than punishment for an overt criminal act. The majority opinion, written by Justice Potter Stewart, said that a statute suggesting that a chronic condition is an "offense" may render a person "continuously guilty of the offense." As the Court viewed it, the statute subjected an individual to potential prosecution "at any time prior to [that individual's] reform." Further, the statute's focus on this "status of addiction" reached in scope to a person who might never have used or possessed narcotics, nor have been engaged in any other "antisocial behaviors" in the state of California. The criminal offense approach to the problem of narcotics addiction could not stand because addiction was not unlike other illnesses, such as venereal disease and mental illness. The Court reasoned that legislation making the contracting of an illness a criminal offense would "doubtless be universally thought to be an infliction of cruel and unusual punishment." The majority concluded that the 90-day jail sentence imposed on Robinson was not a problem in an abstract sense, but the particular penalty had to be considered in the context of the particular offense. Justice Stewart wrote, "Even one day in prison would be cruel and unusual punishment for the 'crime' of having a common cold." The Court's emphasis, therefore, was not focused on the *method* of punishment so much as the *nature* of the "crime" for which the punishment was considered. The dissenters, Justices Clark and White, were critical of the Court's unwillingness to defer to California's initiative in responding to drug addiction. Justice Clark thought the statute created something akin to "civil commitment," and would have permitted California to require some treatment for those "who have lost the power of self-control." In his concurring majority opinion Justice Douglas responded by observing that "the addict is a sick person [who] may, of course, be confined for treatment or for the protection of society. Cruel and unusual punishment results not from confinement, but from convicting the addict of a crime." *See also* COKER v. GEORGIA (433 U.S. 584: 1977), p. 298; EIGHTH AMENDMENT, p. 289; RUMMEL v. ESTELLE (445 U.S. 552: 1980), p. 292.

Significance   *Robinson* v. *California* (370 U.S. 660: 1962) clarified the relationship of the cruel and unusual punishment prohibition to the states through the Due Process Clause of the Fourteenth Amendment. It also established that the prohibitions envisioned in the Cruel and Unusual Punishments Clause contain limitations on the kinds of behavior and conditions that can properly be considered criminal.

The decision in *Robinson* integrated the concepts of criminal intent and overt criminal acts into the Cruel and Unusual Punishments Clause. Criminal punishment therefore requires criminal behavior. The broader immediate effect was to place in jeopardy all laws that focus on a particular condition or status. Vagrancy ordinances became suspect, for example, and many states decriminalized certain kinds of behavior in which the victim of the crime and the person charged with the crime were the same person. Other states reduced from felonies to misdemeanors certain types of antisocial behavior. Still other states opened treatment facilities for alcoholics and drug abusers, while simultaneously abolishing the previously construed criminal nature of the condition. *Robinson* also raised questions about the constitutionality of punishments that were the products of a nonpunishable condition or status. In *Powell* v. *Texas* (392 U.S. 514: 1968), for example, the Court considered whether a chronic alcoholic could be convicted of public intoxication. In this case the Court did not extend *Robinson* to include symptomatic behavior in a 5–4 decision. The Court distinguished *Powell* from *Robinson,* saying that Powell was not being punished for his alcoholism, but for being drunk in public.

Excessive Imprisonment

Rummel v. *Estelle,* **445 U.S. 552, 100 S.Ct. 1133, 63 L.Ed.2d 382 (1980)**   Assessed mandatory life sentences for repeat offenders. Rummel was sentenced to life imprisonment under a Texas recidivist law that provided that a third felony conviction mandated such a penalty. Rummel's three felony convictions came over a ten-year period and were for property offenses totaling $239.11. Rummel's appeal argued that the penalty was so disproportionate that it constituted cruel and unusual punishment. A five-member Supreme Court majority rejected Rummel's appeal. Justice William H. Rehnquist focused on three points for the majority. First, he argued that outside the issue of capital punishment, the disproportionality argument should seldom apply. Second, he suggested that Rummel's likelihood of parole must be considered. Parole is "an established variation on imprisonment," and a "proper assessment of Texas' treatment of Rummel could hardly ignore the possibility that he will not actually be imprisoned for the rest of his life." Finally, Justice Rehnquist said that Texas ought to have latitude in dealing with repeat offenders. The Eighth Amendment does not require Texas "to treat him in the same manner as it might treat him were this

his first 'petty property offense.'" The duration of imprisonment is a matter "largely within the discretion of the punishing jurisdiction." Justices Powell, Brennan, Marshall, and Stevens dissented. They did not see the disproportionality criterion as reserved for capital offenses. They also maintained that the possibility of parole was extraneous to the assessment of the punishment itself. After comparing Texas's statute with recidivist statutes in other states, the dissenters concluded the Texas statute was excessive and disproportionate in Rummel's case. *See also* COKER V. GEORGIA (433 U.S. 584: 1977), p. 298; EIGHTH AMENDMENT, p. 289; ROBINSON V. CALIFORNIA (370 U.S. 660: 1962), p. 290.

Significance   *Rummel* v. *Estelle* (445 U.S. 552: 1980) considered the possible disproportion of prison sentences apart from the problem of excess in capital punishment. The Supreme Court decided that the criteria used to assess Georgia's choice of penalty for rape in *Coker* v. *Georgia* (433 U.S. 584: 1977) were not directly applicable in *Rummel*. The Court said great deference ought to be extended to legislative judgments where prison sentences are involved. While Texas had the most extreme habitual offender statute in the country, it differed in degree rather than in kind from other states. Short of differences in kind, the Eighth Amendment should not be used to invalidate judgments that are "peculiarly" matters for the legislature. Two years later, in *Hutto* v. *Davis* (454 U.S. 370: 1982), the Court upheld the imposition of two consecutive 20-year prison terms and two $10,000 fines for the crime of possession and distribution of nine ounces of marijuana. Building on *Rummel* the Court said there was no way to "make any constitutional distinction between a term of years and a shorter or longer term of years." While expressing some concern about the severity of the sentence received by prisoner Davis, the Court refrained from finding for him. To have done so would be "invariably a subjective decision," and courts should be "reluctant to review legislatively mandated terms of imprisonment." *Rummel* and *Davis* seemed to suggest that Eighth Amendment challenges of prison sentences would not be successful. Comity, notions of substituting federal judicial opinion for that of state legislatures, and a strict constructionist view of the Constitution help explain the Court's decisions in *Rummel* and *Davis*. But in *Solem* v. *Helm* (77 L.Ed.2d 637: 1983), the Court invalidated a life sentence without the possibility of parole under South Dakota's recidivist statute. It found the sentence disproportionate. Justice Blackmun joined the four dissenting justices from *Rummel* to form a new 5–4 majority that essentially embraced the arguments rejected in *Rummel*. Rather than overturn

Rummel, however, the Court found *Helm* "clearly distinguishable." The Court noted the less serious and passive character of Helm's crime, which was issuing a "no account" check in the amount of $100, and the relatively minor nature of his six previous offenses. Key to distinguishing *Rummel* was the impossibility of Helm's parole. While Rummel could have reasonably expected to become eligible for early parole, Helm stood little chance of having his sentence commuted. Chief Justice Burger said for the dissenters in *Helm* that *Rummel* clearly governed and that the decision in *Helm* "blithely discards any concept of stare decisis, trespasses gravely on the authority of the States, and distorts the concept of proportionality of punishment by tearing it from its moorings in capital cases."

Death Penalty

***Furman* v. *Georgia,* 408 U.S. 238, 92 S.Ct. 2726, 33 L.Ed.2d 346 (1972)**   Considered the constitutionality of capital punishment in the context of the Eighth Amendment. In *Furman* the Supreme Court examined the means by which state prisoners were sentenced to death in an effort to determine if the exercise of discretion by the sentencing authority constituted cruel and unusual punishment. The Court invalidated statutes that allowed for unguided sentencer discretion in a 5–4 decision. Following a brief *per curiam* opinion, each member of the majority issued his own concurring opinion. *Furman* produced a total of 133 pages in opinions, including dissents by Chief Justice Burger, and Justices Blackmun, Powell, and Rehnquist. Justice Potter Stewart, whose opinion is most often cited in *Furman* discussions, emphasized the arbitrariness of unstructured discretion. He found the lack of definition in the statutes to be particularly problematic, because it left an inordinate amount of discretion in the hands of the sentencer. The resulting subjective judgments created cruel and unusual punishment. Justice Stewart found the death penalty in such cases to be cruel "in the same way that being struck by lightning is cruel." The recipients of the death penalty become a "capriciously-selected, random handful." A "freakishly imposed" penalty is cruel and unusual. In his concurring opinion Justice Byron R. White cited the infrequency of the imposition of capital punishment as a factor in its diminished impact as a deterrent. He found the death penalty to be cruel by virtue of its occasional application. Justice William O. Douglas suggested the death penalty was not only capriciously imposed but was also imposed in a racially discriminatory manner. Justices William J. Brennan and

Thurgood Marshall said capital punishment was a cruel and unusual punishment per se. It was unconstitutional on its face and not defensible under any circumstances. The dissenting opinions differed from those of the majority on three main points. First, the dissenters criticized the perceived judicial activism of the majority. According to Justice Rehnquist, the majority's decision had to be viewed as "an act of will" and not as a proper statement of law. Second, the dissenters maintained that capital punishment did not offend contemporary standards of humaneness. Third, the minority held that competent juries were capable of rendering reasonable decisions even in the absence of specific statutory guidance. The minority pointed to the infrequency of the imposition of the death penalty as a reflection of the proper exercise of "sensitivity and caution" by judges and juries. Discretion was an asset rather than a liability. *See also* COKER v. GEORGIA (433 U.S. 584: 1977), p. 298; EIGHTH AMENDMENT, p. 289; GREGG v. GEORGIA (428 U.S. 153: 1976), p. 295; WOODSON v. NORTH CAROLINA (428 U.S. 280: 1976), p. 297.

Significance   *Furman* v. *Georgia* (408 U.S. 238: 1972) established standards by which sentencers could or could not impose the death penalty. It also reversed the holding that a multistage or bifurcated conviction and sentencing process was not required of the states (*McGautha* v. *California,* 402 U.S. 183: 1971). *Furman* reflected the Court majority's desire to examine the effects of flawed sentencing processes in terms of the Cruel and Unusual Punishments Clause of the Eighth Amendment. The Court believed unguided sentencer discretion to be the principal defect of many state statutes, and *Furman* signaled the states to make revisions accordingly. The Court suggested two approaches for addressing the discretion issue. One was the provision of guidance to sentencers by a more careful definition of those offenses for which the death penalty might be imposed. The other was to remove sentencer discretion by imposing a mandatory death sentence as the automatic result of conviction for certain crimes. By 1976, 35 state legislatures had taken one or the other of these options in a thoroughgoing revision of *Furman*-flawed capital punishment statutes.

Gregg v. Georgia, 428 U.S. 153, 96 S.Ct. 2909, L.Ed. 859 (1976)   Examined whether the death penalty was a cruel and unusual punishment per se. Many state legislatures responded to *Furman* v. *Georgia* (408 U.S. 238: 1972) by revising their capital punishment statutes to structure sentencer discretion. In three cases, *Gregg* v. *Georgia* (428 U.S. 153: 1976), *Proffitt* v. *Florida* (428 U.S. 242: 1976), and *Jurek* v. *Texas* (428 U.S. 262: 1976), the Supreme Court upheld statutes as revised by Georgia, Florida, and Texas. The Court said the death penalty included in the revised statutes "does not invariably violate the Constitution." Justice Potter Stewart, writing for the majority of seven, said that the Court may not "require the legislature to select the least severe penalty possible so long as the penalty selected is not cruelly inhumane or disproportionate." He found society willing to endorse the death penalty, since 35 state legislatures had provided for the death penalty after *Furman*. Thus contemporary standards were not offended. Justice Stewart said retribution was a sufficient legislative objective to support the statutes. He viewed capital punishment as an "expression of society's moral outrage at particularly offensive conduct." The Court also considered whether death was an excessive penalty in itself, deciding in Justice Stewart's words that when life has been taken, death is not invariably "disproportionate." It is "an extreme sanction, suitable to the most extreme crimes." As for the statutory flaws alleged in *Furman,* Justice Stewart concluded that the state statute revisions adequately remedied the defects. Arbitrariness was eliminated through several procedural revisions; all the statutes contained bifurcated trial-sentence processes; the guilt discrimination stage was separated from the sentencing stage; and the statutes required appellate review and structured sentencer discretion through definition of aggravating and mitigating circumstances. A sentencer could not consider imposing death in the absence of aggravating circumstances. In summary, the Court's opinion was that sentencer discretion had been adequately structured in the state statutes. Justices Marshall and Brennan dissented. Both suggested that capital punishment was constitutionally offensive under any circumstances. Justice Marshall argued that a punishment may be excessive, and therefore cruel and unusual, even though there may be public support of it. He found the majority's ideas about retribution as the basis for punishment to be the "most disturbing" aspect of the *Gregg* decision. *See also* COKER V. GEORGIA (433 U.S. 584: 1977), p. 298; EIGHTH AMENDMENT, p. 289; FURMAN V. GEORGIA (408 U.S. 238: 1972), p. 294; WOODSON V. NORTH CAROLINA (428 U.S. 280: 1976), p. 297.

Significance   *Gregg* v. *Georgia* (428 U.S. 153: 1976) clarified several central issues regarding capital punishment. First, the Court held that death is a constitutionally permissible penalty for murder, given certain conditions. Second, *Gregg* acknowledged that retribution can serve as a sufficient basis for legislative decisions regarding penal policy. And third, *Gregg* determined that structuring sentencer discretion through the definition of aggravating and mitigating circumstances adequately remedied the problems cited in *Furman* v. *Georgia* (408 U.S. 238: 1972). *Gregg* focused on the special character of the death penalty. It is unique in "severity and finality" from every other punishment. While the death penalty may not be cruel and unusual punishment as such, its utilization requires the application of extensive substantive and procedural safeguards. *Gregg* reveals the Court's preference for leaving implementation of capital punishment to the guided discretion of judges and juries. The position taken by the Court in *Gregg, Proffitt,* and *Jurek* established the foundation for current judicial policy regarding the death penalty.

Woodson v. North Carolina, 428 U.S. 280, 96 S.Ct. 2978, 49 L.Ed.2d 944 (1976)   Examined the adequacy of the mandatory death sentence. Several states responded to *Furman* v. *Georgia* (408 U.S. 238: 1972) with revisions in their capital punishment statutes making the death penalty mandatory for certain offenses. A five-justice Supreme Court majority held that the mandatory approach was "unduly harsh and unworkably rigid." The five said allowing some discretion in sentencing was more compatible with evolving standards of societal decency, a frequently mentioned criterion in cruel and unusual punishment cases. The fact that juries possessing discretion infrequently impose capital punishment suggests that capital punishment is viewed as "inappropriate" in a large number of cases. A second defect cited by the majority was that mandatory sentences did not remedy *Furman* flaws. The mandatory approach "papers over" the problem of jury discretion. There are no standards by which to determine "which murderer shall live and which shall die." Neither does the mandatory approach allow a review of arbitrary death sentences. The third flaw in the mandatory approach was said to be its undifferentiating character. The statutes did not allow for the consideration of factors particular to the crime and the defendant. They precluded consideration of "compassion or mitigating factors." The statutes treated all convicted persons "as members of a faceless, undifferentiated mass to be subjected to the blind infliction of the penalty of death." The four dissenters, through Justice Rehnquist, were troubled by the majority's process focus. Justice Rehnquist felt the Court should confine itself to a simple determination of whether a punishment is cruel. The Court had already concluded in *Gregg* v. *Georgia* (428 U.S. 153: 1976) that capital punishment was not a cruel and unusual punishment per se. To invalidate the statute on procedural grounds was therefore inappropriate. *See also* COKER V. GEORGIA (433 U.S. 584: 1977), p. 298; EIGHTH AMENDMENT, p. 289; FURMAN V. GEORGIA (408 U.S. 238: 1972), p. 294; GREGG V. GEORGIA (428 U.S. 153: 1976), p. 295.

Significance   Woodson v. *North Carolina* (428 U.S. 280: 1976) gave the Court an opportunity to choose between two alternative approaches to capital punishment. *Woodson* clearly reflected the Court's preference for retaining some discretion with sentencers in capital cases. To implement capital punishment reasonably, the sentencer must evaluate the specific details of a particular case against criteria defined by state legislatures. The mandatory approach precludes consideration of the factors that may make a case unique. That is its fatal flaw. The Court has since underscored the inadequacy of the mandatory approach. In striking down a Louisiana statute that called for capital punishment for the deliberate killing of a fire fighter or police officer, the Court said, "It is incorrect to suppose that no mitigating circumstances can exist when the victim is a police officer." (See *Harry Roberts* v. *Louisiana,* 431 U.S. 633: 1977.) Neither can the scope of sentencer considerations be improperly restricted. In *Lockett* v. *Ohio* (438 U.S. 586: 1978) the Court held that limiting a sentencer to a narrow range of possible mitigating circumstances was unsatisfactory. In *Eddings* v. *Oklahoma* (455 U.S. 104: 1982) the Court remanded the case of a 16-year-old boy sentenced to death by a trial judge who determined that, as a matter of state law, he could not consider as a mitigating circumstance the youth's "unhappy upbringing and emotional disturbance." Thus *Woodson* struck a middle ground between complete sentencer discretion and the complete mandating of the sentence of death. Is the mandating of sentences other than death not equally offensive to the Eighth Amendment? That question was left to other cases for resolution.

Coker v. Georgia, 433 U.S. 584, 97 S.Ct. 2861, 53 L.Ed. 982 (1977)   Established that the death penalty could not constitutionally be imposed as a sentence for the rape of an adult woman. *Gregg* v. *Georgia* (428 U.S. 153: 1976) did not address the question of whether murder was a necessary requisite to the imposition of capital punishment. In *Coker* a seven-justice majority developed two lines of argument against the death penalty for rape. Writing for the Court, Justice Byron R. White said, first, that society did not endorse capital punishment for rape. This was reflected in the refusal of 32 of the 35 states making post-*Furman* adjustments to their capital punishment statutes to include rape of an adult woman as a capital crime. Even in Georgia juries did not typically impose the death penalty in rape cases, suggesting that juries found the penalty disproportionate when it was available. Justice White argued in the second place that the death penalty was an excessive punishment for rape. Because the death penalty is unique in its "severity and revocability," it is excessive for a defendant "who does not take human life." The crime of rape "does not compare with murder." Dissents were offered by Chief Justice Burger and Justice Rehnquist, who contended the death penalty for rape was not excessive. They believed that states ought to be afforded extensive latitude and opportunity to deal with this particular crime. The Chief Justice concluded that it is not "constitutionally impermissible" for states to make the "solemn judgment" to utilize the death penalty to combat the complete violation of a woman's dignity and personhood. *See also* EIGHTH AMENDMENT, p. 289; FURMAN V. GEORGIA (408 U.S. 238: 1972), p. 294; GREGG V. GEORGIA (428 U.S. 153: 1976), p. 295; RUMMEL V. ESTELLE (445 U.S. 263: 1980), p. 292; WOODSON V. NORTH CAROLINA (428 U.S. 280: 1976), p. 297.

Significance   Coker v. Georgia (433 U.S. 584: 1977) produced a substantive limitation on the imposition of the death penalty. *Furman* v. *Georgia* (408 U.S. 238: 1972), *Gregg* v. *Georgia* (428 U.S. 153: 1976), and *Woodson* v. *North Carolina* (428 U.S. 280: 1976) had focused primarily upon procedural aspects of capital punishment, such as sentencer discretion and two-stage proceedings. They established that punishments that are excessive or disproportionate relative to the offense are cruel and unusual. *Coker* added that death is a disproportionate punishment for the offense of rape of an adult woman, and the case clearly implied that capital punishment is excessive for any offense other than murder. In *Coker* the Court attempted to establish a set of criteria by which excess could be evaluated. It suggested that public attitudes toward a particular offense were germane. These attitudes are reflected in legislative judgments about criminal penalties. Excess can therefore be judged in sentences that substantially depart from penalties thought to be appropriate in the majority of states. The Court found that Georgia was the only state in the union to have authorized the death penalty for rape. Since 35 states had occasion to review their statutes following *Furman,* the Court concluded that Georgia's choice of punishment was at too great a variance from the norm. In addition the Court found that Georgia juries rejected the death penalty in over 90 percent of rape case convictions, which the Court considered another indication of the excess of the law. Using the disproportionality rationale, the Court extended *Coker* to persons who aid and abet felony murder in *Enmund* v. *Florida* (458 U.S. 782: 1982). The Court ruled that the Eighth Amendment precludes imposing the death penalty on a person who aids and abets a felony in which murder is committed by others, but who "neither took life, attempted to take life, nor intended to take life" himself. A discussion of disproportion and excess in a noncapital context can be found in *Rummel* v. *Estelle* (445 U.S. 263: 1980).

Barefoot v. Texas, 77 L.Ed.2d 1090 (1983)   Reviewed the process through which death penalty appeals are handled and established guidelines for lower courts in handling them. Barefoot was convicted of murder and appealed directly to the Texas appellate courts. Barefoot focused his appeal on the practice in Texas of using psychiatric testimony during sentencing to speak to the aggravating factor of future danger to society. The psychiatric testimony practice is described in *Estelle* v. *Smith* (451 U.S. 454: 1981). When the United States Supreme Court refused to accept Barefoot's case, he began *habeas corpus* proceedings first in the state courts of Texas and then in Federal District Court. The Federal District Court denied a writ of *habeas corpus,* but it did issue a certificate of probable cause, which enabled Barefoot to go to the Court of Appeals. There he sought a stay of execution. After taking arguments on both the merits of the *habeas corpus* appeal and the petition for a stay of execution, the Court of Appeals denied the stay. Barefoot then asserted he was entitled to a separate response on the merits of his *habeas corpus* appeal. The Supreme Court upheld the Court of Appeals in a 6–3 decision. Justice Byron R. White wrote for the Court. He said the primary avenue for review of criminal cases is direct appeal and that process was fully utilized by Barefoot. While federal *habeas corpus* review is important, it is "secondary and limited." Federal courts "are not forums in which to relitigate state trials." Neither is the *habeas* process one through which a defendant is "entitled to delay an execution indefinitely." Justice White then examined Barefoot's specific claim. Barefoot was indeed entitled to a decision on the merits given the fact his case was not frivolous and it had received a certificate of probable cause. Although the Court of Appeals did not formally affirm the District Court denial of *habeas,* there was "no question that the Court of Appeals ruled on the merits of the appeal." To affirm formally would have been advisable, but it would be "unwarranted exaltation of form over substance" to remand the case. Simply because the Court of Appeals "moved swiftly to decide the stay does not mean its treatment of the merits was cursory or inadequate."

Noting the increasing number of death-sentenced petitioners entering the appellate stages of the federal *habeas* process, Justice White took this opportunity to present guidelines for the process. The Court did not want others to infer that what occurred in *Barefoot* should be "accepted as the norm or as the preferred procedure." The Court's guidelines first required district court judges to be very selective in issuing certificates of probable cause. Needed for certification is a "substantial showing" that a federal right has been denied. Asserting the severity of the death penalty "does not in itself suffice to warrant the automatic issuing of a certificate." Second, the certificate entitles the petitioner to a decision on the merits. A stay must be issued in situations where it is needed "to prevent the case from becoming moot by the petitioner's execution." Third, courts of appeals "may adopt expedited procedures" for handling *habeas* appeals. Assuming proper notice, "arguments on the merits may be heard at the same time as the motion for the stay is considered." They may be treated in a single opinion. Finally, the Court warned that stays are not automatic simply because petitions for certiorari are filed. The Court also affirmed the lower-court judgment regarding the use of psychiatric testimony. Justice White said that to disallow such evidence treating a defendant's future behavior is "somewhat like asking us to disinvent the wheel." The adversary process was seen as an adequate safeguard against the unreliability of such testimony. Justices Marshall, Blackmun, and Brennan objected to the expedited process allowed by *Barefoot*. Justice Marshall thought the decision "perverse." It permitted "special truncated procedures" for *habeas* appeals raising substantial questions, whereas defendants with lesser sentences must follow ordinary appellate procedures. Justice Marshall could not imagine a class of cases for which "summary procedures would be less appropriate than capital cases." He expressed the hope that few circuit judges would adopt them. The three dissenters also vigorously objected to the use of psychiatric testimony for sentencing in capital cases. *See also* CERTIORARI, p. 390; EIGHTH AMENDMENT, p. 289; *HABEAS CORPUS,* p. 419.

Significance   *Barefoot* v. *Texas* (77 L.Ed.2d 1090: 1983) reaffirmed that capital punishment is not inherently a cruel and unusual punishment in violation of the Eighth Amendment. It means death penalty appeals will move through the courts more quickly. It probably means the number of *habeas corpus* appeals moving past the district court level will decrease, with some of the appeals currently making their way to the Supreme Court being eliminated. The other effects of this 1983 decision are not yet clear.

Barclay v. Florida, 77 L.Ed.2d 1134 (1983)   Addresses the issue of aggravating factors that must be present for the death penalty to be imposed. The clear command in *Gregg* v. *Georgia* (428 U.S. 153: 1976) was that sentencers must be guided when considering the death penalty. Contemporary capital punishment statutes therefore contain lists of both aggravating and mitigating circumstances that must be evaluated when making the sentence judgment. Mitigating circumstances are considered in *Woodson* v. *North Carolina* (428 U.S. 280: 1976). Barclay was convicted of first-degree murder, a crime apparently racially inspired. The trial judge set aside the jury recommendation of life imprisonment and ordered the death penalty. The judge made his own determination that several statutory aggravating circumstances were present. He also defined the defendant's extensive criminal record as an aggravating circumstance. The judge discussed what he believed to be the racial motive for the crime and "compared it with his own experience in the army in World War II, when he saw Nazi concentration camps and their victims." Barclay contended his death sentence was invalid because the judge considered his criminal record as an aggravating circumstance in the absence of statutory authorization and because the judge improperly mentioned "racial hatred" and "his own experiences" in the sentencing opinion. The Supreme Court agreed with Barclay regarding the judge's use of Barclay's criminal record but affirmed the death sentence nonetheless in a 6–3 decision. Through Justice William H. Rehnquist, the Court was emphatic that sentencers are not permitted to redefine sentencing guidelines or add factors to the statutory list of aggravating circumstances. While the Eighth Amendment does not preclude use of other evidence, Florida law prohibited consideration of nonstatutory factors in this case. The more crucial question was whether the inappropriate consideration of Barclay's prior criminal record contaminated the findings of statutory aggravating circumstances and disturbed the overall balance of aggravating and mitigating factors. The Court ruled that the other findings were independent of and undisturbed by the reference to Barclay's criminal record. The Court allowed the trial judge to take account of the racial motive of the crime. Barclay's professed desire to "start a race war" was relevant to several statutory aggravating factors, and the judge's discussion of it was "neither irrational nor arbitrary." Comparison to Nazi concentration camps was seen as an appropriate way of weighing this "heinous, atrocious and cruel" aggravating circumstance. The purpose of statutory standards is to remove arbitrariness, but they do not make sentencing determinations "mechanical and rigid." Justice Rehnquist said it is "fitting for the moral, factual, and legal judgment to play a meaningful role in sentencing." The statutory standards themselves must be reasonable, and they must provide genuine guidance for identifying those offenders for whom capital punishment is appropriate. *See also* GREGG V. GEORGIA (428 U.S. 158: 1976), p. 295; EIGHTH AMENDMENT, p. 289; WOODSON V. NORTH CAROLINA (428 U.S. 280: 1976), p. 297.

Significance   *Barclay v. Florida* (77 L.Ed.2d 1134: 1983) gave notice to sentencers that they cannot depart from statutory guidelines in determining aggravating circumstances for imposing the death penalty. This is not to say the Supreme Court will ignore statutory language it deems vague and ambiguous. It struck down such language in *Godfrey v. Georgia* (446 U.S. 420: 1980). In *Zant v. Stephens* (103 S.Ct. 2733: 1983) the Court underscored the jury's independence in determining aggravating circumstances where statutes are clear. In *Zant* a jury had found three statutory aggravating factors and imposed the death penalty. One of the factors was later found defective for reason of vagueness, but the Court held the remaining two factors properly fulfilled the requirements for such a penalty. In *California v. Ramos* (74 L.Ed.2d 19: 1983) the Court permitted an instruction that told the jury at the penalty stage of a trial that sentence of life imprisonment without the possibility of parole could be commuted to a sentence that included potential parole. This information, known as the Briggs Instruction, was viewed by the Court as providing data that focused the jury's attention on "probable future dangerousness," a service that helped the jury "individualize" its deliberation. Justices Brennan, Marshall, Blackmun, and Stevens thought the instruction prompted the death sentence. Justice Marshall said it was misleading in that it invited speculation and guesswork. The Briggs Instruction injected into the capital sentencing process "a factor that has no relation to the nature of the offense or the character of the offender."

7. Equal Protection and Privacy

OVERVIEW

This chapter is devoted to an examination of equal protection under the law, permitted and prohibited classifications, and the matter of privacy. In order to address these issues it is necessary to begin with the Fourteenth Amendment.

The Fourteenth Amendment states:

SECTION 1. All persons born or naturalized in the United States, and subject to the jurisdiction thereof, are citizens of the United States and of the State wherein they reside. No State shall make or enforce any law which shall abridge the privileges or immunities of citizens of the United States; nor shall any State deprive any person of life, liberty, or property, without due process of law; nor deny to any person within its jurisdiction the equal protection of the laws.

SECTION 2. Representatives shall be apportioned among the several States according to their respective numbers, counting the whole number of persons in each State, excluding Indians not taxed. But when the right to vote at any election for the choice of electors for President and Vice-President of the United States, Representatives in Congress, the Executive and Judicial officers of a State, or the members of the Legislature thereof, is denied to any of the male inhabitants of such State, being twenty-one years of age, and citizens of the United States, or in any way abridged, except for participation in rebellion, or other crime, the basis of representation therein shall be reduced in the proportion which the number of such male citizens shall bear to the whole number of male citizens twenty-one years of age in such State.

SECTION 3. No person shall be a Senator or Representative in Congress, or elector of President and Vice-President, or hold any office, civil or military, under the United States, or under any State, who, having previously taken an oath, as a member of Congress, or as an officer of the United States, or as a member of any State legislature, or as an executive or judicial officer of any State, to support the Constitution of the United States, shall have engaged in insurrection or rebellion against the same, or given aid or comfort to the enemies thereof. But Congress may by a vote of two-thirds of each House, remove such disability.

SECTION 4. The validity of the public debt of the United States, authorized by law, including debts incurred for payment of pensions and bounties for services in suppressing insurrection or rebellion, shall not be questioned. But neither the United States nor any State shall assume or pay any debt or obligation incurred in aid of insurrection or rebellion against the United States, or any claim for the loss or emancipation of any slave; but all such debts, obligations and claims shall be held illegal and void.

SECTION 5. The Congress shall have power to enforce, by appropriate legislation, the provisions of this article.

The Fourteenth Amendment is familiar to most American citizens because of its due process of law language. Such language has been utilized by the Supreme Court frequently in extending protection afforded under the first ten amendments to the states, particularly in criminal procedure cases. Although it is clear the Fourteenth Amendment was drafted with the slavery issue and the Civil War in mind, it was not utilized to any great extent by the Supreme Court for 50 years after its ratification in 1868. When it was used, it was generally in an economic context in relationship to corporations claiming due process for business purposes.

Section 1 of the Fourteenth Amendment has the familiar phrase "nor shall any State deny to any person within its jurisdiction the equal protection of the laws." Equal protection is impossible to define precisely, but the phrase was intended to guarantee newly freed slaves equality of treatment and the enjoyment of basic civil and political rights. Like the Due Process Clause, however, considerable time passed before the Supreme Court began to interpret and apply the Equal Protection Clause against abridgement of civil and political rights.

The cases that follow are divided into three sections. The first section addresses the issue of racial discrimination, long a problem in American society. The persistence of the problem has required the courts to utilize the Due Process, Equal Protection, and Privileges and Immunities Clauses of the Fourteenth Amendment, the voting provisions of the Fifteenth Amendment, the Due Process Clause of the Fifth Amendment, the Interstate Commerce Clause, civil rights statutes passed by Congress under the Necessary and Proper Clause, and the enforcement clauses of the Thirteenth, Fourteenth, and Fifteenth Amendments in an orchestrated effort to redress the effects of prejudice in American society.

The language of the Fourteenth Amendment was largely directed toward the Supreme Court's decision in *Dred Scott* v. *Sandford* (60 U.S. 393: 1857). The Court ruled in that case that black people, their slave status notwithstanding, were not citizens within the meaning of the Constitution. Even after ratification of the Fourteenth Amendment, the Court moved slowly to read full black citizenship into American jurisprudence. Indeed, in the *Civil Rights Cases* (109 U.S. 3: 1883), the Court held that only discrimination that involved "state action" fell within the Court's constitutional purview. Neither could it address private discrimination. Even when state action was obviously involved, the Supreme Court insulated a large part of discrimination in the states by creating the separate but equal doctrine of *Plessy* v. *Ferguson* (163 U.S. 537: 1896).

It took 82 years for the Supreme Court to modify its initial response to the intent of the drafters of the Fourteenth Amendment. It did so in *Sweatt* v. *Painter* (339 U.S. 629: 1950), which struck down a state law requiring separation of the races at state law schools. *Sweatt* was but a breath away from the landmark *Brown* v. *Board of Education* (*Brown I,* 374 U.S. 483: 1954; and *Brown II,* 349 U.S. 294: 1955), decisions that halted constitutional tolerance of segregation in public education. A series of clarification cases followed, including *Swann* v. *Charlotte-Mecklenburg Board of Education* (402 U.S. 1: 1971) and *Milliken* v. *Bradley* (418 U.S. 717: 1974).

The state action concept necessary for the Court to intervene was broadened over the years, but *Washington* v. *Davis* (426 U.S. 229: 1976) and *Village of Arlington Heights* v. *Metropolitan Housing Development Corporation* (429 U.S. 252: 1977) modified that concept by holding that prohibited state action turns on discriminatory *intent* rather than discriminatory *impact.* The Court simultaneously upheld several state initiatives aimed at curbing racial inequalities. It determined that race could be a permissible consideration in university admission procedures in the case of *Regents of the University of California* v. *Bakke* (438 U.S. 265: 1978). The Court also addressed nonschool issues involving minority contractor set-asides in federal construction grants in *Fullilove* v. *Klutznick* (448 U.S. 448: 1980). It recently permitted the Internal Revenue Service to withdraw tax exempt status from a racially discriminatory private school in *Bob Jones University* v. *United States* (76 L.Ed.2d 157: 1983). Although not addressed in this chapter, the Equal Protection and Due Process Clauses are closely related in jury selection. *Swain* v. *Alabama* (380 U.S. 202: 1965, p. 251) discusses the Court's expectations on this issue.

The second section of equal protection cases covers an extension of coverage to classifications other than those based on race. Such an expansion of scope has been called the new equal protection. It was the Warren Court that began to entertain the possibility that the Equal Protection Clause might apply to other classifications, but expanding the scope of the clause meant that legitimate and illegitimate classifications had to be distinguished. An invalid classification impinges on fundamental rights, such as the right to vote. The reapportionment decisions of *Baker* v. *Carr* (369 U.S. 186: 1962) and *Reynolds* v. *Sims* (377 U.S. 533: 1964) are illustrative of such an invalid classification. *Mobile* v. *Bolden* (446 U.S. 55: 1980) examined the racial impacts of redistricting. *South Carolina* v. *Katzenbach* (383 U.S. 301: 1966) is included despite its Fifteenth Amendment foundation because it upheld the congressional initiative taken in the Voting Rights

Act of 1965. *Shapiro* v. *Thompson* (394 U.S. 618: 1969) struck down a residency requirement for public assistance because it interfered with the fundamental right to unencumbered movement from state to state. If a fundamental right is involved, the Court imposes more stringent standards of review on the classification. Also deserving strict scrutiny are classifications said to be "suspect." Alienage was found to be such a classification in *Graham* v. *Richardson* (403 U.S. 365: 1971). The Court struck down a state law disadvantaging illegitimate children in *Weber* v. *Aetna Casualty & Surety Company* (406 U.S. 164: 1972), although the standard of review for illegitimacy was not set at the more stringent level. Age classifications such as the mandatory retirement decision of *Massachusetts Board of Retirement* v. *Murgia* (427 U.S. 307: 1976) have generally been found to have a rational basis that frees them from the more demanding standard. In *San Antonio Independent School District* v. *Rodriguez* (411 U.S. 1: 1973), the Court did not find that indigency-based classifications require the more stringent review, although indigency has long been considered a threat to due process requirements in a criminal justice context. Most troublesome for the Court has been the extent to which the Equal Protection Clause applies to gender-based classifications. It struck down differential housing and medical benefits in military service in *Frontiero* v. *Richardson* (411 U.S. 677: 1973) with only a single dissent, but a majority of the Court could not agree that gender was a suspect classification. By 1981 the Court was ready to permit Congress to authorize a male-only draft registration in *Rostker* v. *Goldberg* (453 U.S. 57: 1981). In *County of Washington* v. *Gunther* (450 U.S. 907: 1981), the Court ruled that Title VII of the Civil Rights Act of 1964 can provide the basis for job-related sex discrimination suits beyond the equal pay for equal work issue. Earlier, in *Kahn* v. *Shevin* (416 U.S. 351: 1979), the Court upheld a benevolent classification that favored women by providing a property tax exemption for widows, but not widowers. The case of *Vlandis* v. *Kline* (412 U.S. 441: 1973) altered the focus of equal protection issues by introducing the concept of irrebuttable presumptions. This approach raised the question of whether a classification makes a presumptive judgment and then precludes an affected person from addressing the classificatory judgment.

There is a final section of cases involving privacy rights. While privacy is not strictly an equal protection issue, the Equal Protection Clause is one of several clauses used by the Court in responding to privacy issues. The concept of privacy is not explicitly addressed anywhere in the Constitution. The idea that certain aspects of life are simply beyond governmental intrusion evolved over time. In *Griswold* v. *Connecticut* (381 U.S. 479: 1965), the Supreme Court established privacy as a constitutional *value*. The Court fashioned the right of privacy from several specific protections in the Bill of Rights and the Fourteenth Amendment.

Invasion of privacy was the basis of the Court's decision in *Roe* v. *Wade* (410 U.S. 113: 1973), which struck down the prohibition of abortion. *Wade* entitled a woman to an abortion by saying it was a private right free from governmental obstacles. *City of Akron* v. *Akron Center for Reproductive Health, Inc.* (76 L.Ed.2d 687: 1983) struck down a city ordinance containing restrictions on *access* to abortion. Included in the ordinance was a mandatory 24-hour waiting period, a parental consent requirement for unmarried minors, a detailed informed consent provision compelling specific statements from a patient's physician, and a requirement that abortions after the first trimester be performed in a hospital. While the Court has protected the right to abortion on privacy grounds, cases such as *Harris* v. *McRae* (448 U.S. 297: 1980) have determined that government need not pay for abortions. The scope of the right of privacy outside the abortion context remains unclear. Considerations of privacy led the Court to invalidate a housing ordinance limiting occupancy to single families in *Moore* v. *East Cleveland* (431 U.S. 494: 1977) because the Court said the enactment interfered too greatly with family life.

The essential definitional cases involving equal protection and privacy follow. The reader is urged to pay particular attention to the cases cited in the *Significance* section of each entry for further reference.

The Equal Protection Clause   Provision contained in the Fourteenth Amendment which prohibits unreasonable classifications. The Equal Protection Clause is one of the changes made in the Constitution after the Civil War. The Thirteenth Amendment outlawed slavery, the Fifteenth Amendment prohibited interference with the right to vote, but the Fourteenth Amendment provided the broadest adjustment to the Constitution. Section 1 contained the phrase "nor shall any State deny to any person within its jurisdiction the equal protection of the laws." At the time the Equal Protection Clause was aimed at guaranteeing former slaves equal treatment under the law and certain basic civil rights. The Supreme Court made an effort to confine the language of the clause to blacks in the *Slaughterhouse Cases* (16 Wall. 36: 1873). *Slaughterhouse* held that the clause was to be used when state laws "discriminated with gross injustice and hardship" against "newly emancipated negroes." The Court said federal authority could be used only where racial discrimination occurred by action of a state because the coverage of the clause was aimed only at "that race and that emergency." After confining the clause to racial classifications, the Court set out in following years to define the nature of the protections afforded to blacks under the clause. The early decisions were less than generous. In 1883, the Court struck down the Civil Rights Act of 1875, ruling that the Equal Protection Clause applied only to state action. The holding in the *Civil Rights Cases* (103 U.S. 3: 1883, p. 321) was consistent with the Court's position in *Slaughterhouse*. It placed private acts of discrimination outside the reach of the Equal Protection Clause and the courts. The Court categorically rejected the argument that the clause authorized Congress to "create a code of municipal law for the regulation of private rights." The Fourteenth Amendment authorized only corrective rather than general legislation that "may be necessary and proper for counteracting such laws as the States may adopt." Regulation of private discrimination, if it were to occur at all, was left to state discretion and initiative. Soon thereafter a comprehensive network of state segregation statutes or Jim Crow laws was enacted. The Court found the segregative approach to be constitutional in *Plessy* v. *Ferguson* (163 U.S. 537: 1896, p. 322), using the separate but equal doctrine. The Court said Jim Crow statutes only made a legal distinction between races and had "no tendency to destroy the legal equality of the two races." No constitutional provision could go further and "abolish distinctions based upon color, or to enforce social, as distinguished from political, equality, or a commingling of the two races upon terms unsatisfactory to either." Little attention was paid to the equivalent-treatment-under-separate-circumstances idea until certain professional education cases came to the Court in the 1950s. Then the equality aspect of the separate but equal doctrine was carefully examined. Separate but equal was struck down in the landmark decision of *Brown* v. *Board of Education I* (347 U.S. 483: 1954, p. 326). The Court found that racial segregation imposed by law materially interfered with equal educational opportunity. Subsequently the Court used the Equal Protection Clause to require that affirmative steps be taken to desegregate where constitutional violations could be shown. The authority of the federal courts to mandate relief in such situations was extensively applied. The Supreme Court went on to hold that race can be a permissible consideration in university admission procedures and in establishing policies extending preferential treatment to those subjected to past discrimination. The state action requirement still provides some insulation for private discrimination, however, even though the Court has become more receptive to claims that private discriminators are acting closely enough to state authority to be reached. While softening the line of demarcation between private and state acts, the Court has kept purely private discrimination outside the scope of the Equal Protection Clause and has modified the nature of state action criteria by holding that prohibited behavior turns on discriminatory *intent* rather than discriminatory *impact*. Nonetheless, the Court has allowed the Internal Revenue Service to withdraw tax exempt status from a private university engaged in racially discriminatory practices in *Bob Jones University* v. *United States*, 76 L.Ed.2d 157: 1983, p. 341. *See also* CLASSIFICATION, p. 394; REVERSE DISCRIMINATION, p. 447; SEPARATE BUT EQUAL, p. 449; STATE ACTION, p. 454.

Significance   The Equal Protection Clause had a limited impact on public policy for many years. It was reserved exclusively for racial discrimination and was not always aggressively applied even in that context. The Due Process Clause of the Fourteenth Amendment proved to be of far greater policy significance than the Equal Protection Clause as a means of examining the reasonableness of state legislation. The character of equal protection began to change in the post–New Deal period, however, as the Court became more extensively involved with civil liberties questions. The Warren Court in particular began to consider application of the Equal Protection Clause to classifications in addition to race. The expanding scope of the clause is sometimes called the new equal protection. Because most legislation engages in some form of classification, the clause became an attractive vehicle for challenges. The Equal Protection Clause does not preclude the use of classifications. It merely requires that a classification be reasonable. The main problem of the new equal protection is that of distinguishing reasonable and permissible classifications from arbitrary and impermissible ones. Legislatures are generally afforded wide discretion in making classifications. Legislative classifications are typically evaluated by the rationality test, which is a standard reflecting the Court's understanding that the drawing of lines that create distinctions is peculiarly a legislative task as well as an unavoidable one. Classifications are presumed to be valid under this approach and need not achieve perfection. If the legislative objective is legitimate, a classification may be used as long as it rationally relates to its objective. This doctrine places the burden of proof on the party claiming the legislation has no rational or reasonable basis. Under certain circumstances, a classification may be subjected to the strict scrutiny standard, a closer examination requiring a state to show more than reasonableness for a classificatory scheme. The state must demonstrate a serious need or a compelling interest that can only be addressed by use of the challenged classification. Thus the burden of proof shifts to the state in cases in which strict or close scrutiny is used. The strict scrutiny standard applies when the classification impinges on a fundamental right, understood as a right expressly protected, such as freedom of speech, religious exercise, or the right to vote. Or a fundamental right may be a right fashioned by implication, such as the right to cross state lines or the right to have an abortion. In *Shapiro* v. *Thompson* (394 U.S. 618: 1969, p. 349), the Court struck down a residency requirement for public assistance benefits because the classification inhibited movement of persons from state to state. The Court said a classification that touches on the fundamental right of interstate movement is "patently unconstitutional." Similarly, interference with the fundamental right of an impaired and undiluted vote prompted the Court to develop the one person–one vote principle in legislative apportionment cases. The close scrutiny standard also applies if the classification is "suspect." A suspect class is one that is saddled with such disabilities, or is the recipient of such purposeful unequal treatment over time, or is a class that occupies such a politically powerless position, as to require extraordinary protection within the political process. Classifications based on race and alienage are considered to be inherently suspect. The racially conscious affirmative action policies upheld by the Court have demonstrated a compelling interest served by the classification. If a classification is to be used in such situations, it must also be precisely drawn or carefully tailored, and it must employ the least drastic means possible to achieve its particular legislative objectives. The Court has striken a number of gender-based classifications, but to date has not found gender to be a suspect class. Some members of the Court have suggested that gender receive heightened, although not strict, scrutiny. Neither are such classifications as age, illegitimacy, or wealth considered to be suspect, although the Court has required that indigent criminal defendants be entitled to appointed counsel and free transcripts for appeals. The new equal protection has dramatically altered the scope of the Equal Protection Clause, and it is likely that new ground will continue to be broken in this policy area.

Right of Privacy   A protection drawn from several constitutional provisions placing certain aspects of life beyond the reach of governmental intrusion. The right of privacy was first acknowledged by the Supreme Court in *Griswold* v. *Connecticut* (381 U.S. 479: 1965, p. 369). The view that the Constitution afforded such protection had existed for some time, however. As early as 1928, in the wiretapping case of *Olmstead* v. *United States* (277 U.S. 438: 1928), Justice Brandeis offered a classic dissent, stating the Fourth and Fifth Amendments conferred the "right to be let alone." Justice Brandeis regarded this as "the most comprehensive of rights and the right most valued by civilized men." While Justice Brandeis found the Fourth and Fifth Amendments to be a sufficient source for the right of privacy, the rest of the Court had more difficulty finding a constitutional mandate for the protection of privacy. Several additional possibilities have been suggested by individual justices in subsequent cases. The First Amendment has been cited, for example, as providing some insulation for privacy interests. In *Stanley* v. *Georgia* (394 U.S. 557: 1969, p. 138), a case involving privately possessed obscene materials, Justice Marshall said regulation of obscenity cannot "reach into the privacy of one's own home." He added that "if the First Amendment means anything, it means that a state has no business telling a man, sitting alone in his own house, what books he may read or what films he may watch." In another obscenity case, *Paris Adult Theatre I* v. *Staton* (413 U.S. 49: 1973), Justice Brennan also looked to the First Amendment as a protection for "sexually oriented materials" for consenting adults. The First Amendment has also been used to protect the anonymity of a voluntary association. In *NAACP* v. *Alabama* (357 U.S. 449: 1958, p. 147), Justice Harlan cited the "vital relationship between freedom to associate and privacy in one's associations."

Justice Harlan argued in *Griswold* that the Due Process Clause of the Fourteenth Amendment also offered protection against invasions of privacy. In his view, the Connecticut prohibition on the distribution of contraceptives violated basic values "implicit in the concept of ordered liberty," thus contravening the protection of the Due Process Clause. Justice Harlan said that while other constitutional provisions might be relevant in this instance, the Due Process Clause was sufficient in itself. It stands "on its own bottom" when a right as fundamental as privacy is concerned. The Due Process Clause must not, in Justice Harlan's opinion, be limited to merely procedural safeguards. Rather, the clause is a "rational continuum which includes a freedom from all substantial arbitrary impositions and purposeless restraints." The Connecticut birth control enactment failed due process muster because its substantive focus was an "intolerable and unjustifiable invasion of privacy in the conduct of the most intimate concerns of an individual's personal life." *Roe* v. *Wade* (410 U.S. 113: 1973, p. 371), the landmark abortion decision, also grounded its privacy holding on due process considerations. Justice Brennan has seen privacy secured by the Equal Protection Clause of the Fourteenth Amendment in certain situations. *Eisenstadt* v. *Baird* (405 U.S. 438: 1972) involved a state prohibition on the sale of contraceptives to unmarried persons. The Court struck down the statute. *Griswold* had already established that such regulation could not be applied to married persons because the right of privacy inhered in the marital relationship. *Eisenstadt* was based on the view that married couples were "two individuals with a separate intellectual and emotional make-up." Given that, if the "right of privacy means anything," it must mean that the "individual, married or single, is to be free from unwarranted governmental intrusion into matters so fundamentally affecting a person as the decision whether to bear or beget a child."

Finally, the Ninth Amendment has been mentioned as supporting a constitutional right to privacy. This amendment states that "the enumeration in the Constitution of certain rights shall not be construed to deny or disparage others retained by the people." In his concurrence in *Griswold,* Justice Goldberg argued for the recognition of privacy as a constitutionally protected right by saying the Ninth Amendment "lends strong support" to the proposition that the liberty protected by the Fifth and Fourteenth Amendments "is not restricted to rights specifically mentioned in the first eight amendments."

The Court's approach in the pivotal *Griswold* decision drew indirectly from most of those arguments for privacy. Justice Douglas, author of the Court's opinion in *Griswold,* saw the issue as lying within a zone of privacy created by several fundamental constitutional guarantees. Justice Douglas developed his right of privacy doctrine through the concept of penumbra. According to *Black's Law Dictionary*, a penumbra is an "implied power" that is "engrafted" on another. To Justice Douglas, specific Bill of Rights guarantees have penumbras formed by "emanations from those guarantees that help give them life and substance." Justice Douglas made reference to the right of association contained in the penumbra of the First Amendment as an illustration. When one draws together the right of association from the First Amendment, the quartering of soldiers prohibition from the Third Amendment, the unreasonable search and seizure protections from the Fourth Amendment, the self-incrimination privilege from the Fifth Amendment, and the retention language of the Ninth Amendment, a constitutional right of privacy emerges. *See also* GRISWOLD V. CONNECTICUT (381 U.S. 479: 1965), p. 369; ROE V. WADE (410 U.S. 113: 1973), p. 371; SUBSTANTIVE DUE PROCESS, p. 456.

Significance   The right of privacy emanates from an aggregation of various Bill of Rights protections. *Griswold* v. *Connecticut* (381 U.S. 479: 1965, p. 369) provided the Supreme Court an opportunity to develop both the concept and the approach. *Griswold* sought to keep the Court from appearing to engage in the second-guessing of legislative policy choices. Justice Douglas declared that the Court does not sit as a super-legislature trying to determine the wisdom, need, and propriety of laws that touch economic problems, business affairs, or social conditions. He intentionally declined use of the Due Process Clause of the Fourteenth Amendment as a source of privacy protection in an attempt to avoid comparisons with the substantive due process predispositions of the Court in the early twentieth century. Nonetheless, the Connecticut statute was stricken because it operated "directly on an intimate relation of husband and wife and their physician's role in one aspect of their relationship." Justice Douglas's efforts notwithstanding, the Court's holding in *Griswold* raised the possibility that the new right of privacy could be used indiscriminately to strike down legislative enactments. In his *Griswold* dissent, Justice Black argued that the only limit of the Court's use of a natural law due process philosophy in reviewing legislation would be the Court's own restraint. Justice Black was concerned that the elevation of privacy to the status of a constitutional right was the creation of a means whereby the Court could substitute its views of appropriate social policy for the views of legislative bodies. There was a general concern that *Griswold* reflected the view that persons were entitled to freedom from regulation in a broad sense. These concerns touched on matters of fundamental proportion and consequence. Since *Griswold,* the Court has both enlarged and confined the right of privacy doctrine. Cases such as *Eisenstadt* and *Wade* broadened the concept of privacy, taking it from interpersonal relationships to the level of individual choice. At the same time, however, the Court rejected the view that the right of privacy is unlimited or absolute in character. In *Wade,* the Court held that assertions of the right of privacy must be weighed against state regulatory interests. Accordingly a number of decisions since *Wade* have rejected claims of privacy infringement. Given their relatively recent origin, the evolution of right of privacy standards is still in a definitional phase.

RACIAL DISCRIMINATION

Citizenship

Dred Scott **v.** *Sandford,* **60 U.S. (19 How.) 393, 15 L.Ed. 691 (1857)**   Held that blacks, their slave status notwithstanding, were not citizens of the United States. *Dred Scott* v. *Sandford* was one of the Supreme Court's first major rulings on civil liberties. It explored the nature of citizenship, the institution of slavery, and it was a factor in precipitating the Civil War. It also prompted the policies embodied in the Fourteenth Amendment. Dred Scott was a black slave from Missouri who had been taken by his master to the free state of Illinois and then to the Louisiana Territory, an area designated "free" under terms of the Missouri Compromise of 1820. Scott ultimately returned to the slave state of Missouri, where he brought suit claiming his residency in free areas had altered his status as a slave. The Missouri Supreme Court held that Missouri law governed despite Scott's residence elsewhere. Scott then pressed his suit in federal court. The case could have been resolved by a court holding that Scott's status was a matter of Missouri law, but the Supreme Court chose to address the substance of the case, largely because two justices wanted to make it an occasion to examine slavery critically. The remainder of the Court decided against Scott in a 7–2 decision, with each member of the Court entering a separate opinion. In what is viewed as the Court's prevailing sentiment, chief justice Taney opined that Scott was not entitled to sue because he was not a citizen. He was not a citizen because he was black and a slave. The chief justice contended that at the time the Constitution was written, blacks were regarded as "beings of an inferior order and altogether unfit to associate with the white race, either in social or political relations." Blacks were property. Chief Justice Taney invoked the concept of dual citizenship to foreclose Scott's claims. Federal citizenship is conferred only through federal action, he said, and no matter how extensive the privileges and immunities conferred elsewhere, they neither carried over to Missouri nor could they affect Scott's ineligibility for federal citizenship. The chief justice said no state can "introduce a new member into its political community created by the Constitution of the United States. It cannot make him a member of this community by making him a member of its own." Neither can a state "introduce any person, or description of persons, who were not intended to be embraced in this new political family, which the Constitution brought into existence, but here intended to be excluded from it." Scott's noncitizen status also flowed from his still being a slave. Chief Justice Taney asserted that Scott had never achieved free status under provisions of the Missouri Compromise because that enactment was unconstitutional. In the Court's view, Congress did not have the authority to designate certain territories as free. To do so would deprive slaveholders of their due process property rights. The two dissenters, Justices Curtis and McLean, split from the majority on every issue in the case. Justice Curtis in particular disputed Chief Justice Taney's proposition that blacks were not citizens at the time the Constitution was ratified. He noted that there were several states where those "descended from African slaves were not only citizens of those States, but such of them had the franchise of electors, on equal terms with other citizens." To Justice Curtis, "it would be strange if we were to find in that instrument anything which deprived of their citizenship any part of the people of the United States who were among those by whom it was established." *See also* CIVIL RIGHTS CASES (109 U.S. 3: 1883), p. 321; EQUAL PROTECTION CLAUSE, p. 313; FOURTEENTH AMENDMENT, p. 412.

Significance   The citizenship questions of *Dred Scott* v. *Sandford* (60 U.S. 393: 1857) were rendered moot by adoption of the Fourteenth Amendment in 1868. Indeed, the first sentence of Section 1 reversed *Dred Scott*. Although the Fourteenth Amendment was very narrowly interpreted initially, as in the *Slaughterhouse Cases* (16 Wall. 36: 1873), its provisions have since become the foundation for civil liberties and civil-rights protections in modern America. *Dred Scott* provided the political impetus for a tragic Civil War fought over the extent to which federal authority could be brought to bear on the issue of slavery.

Eventually it paved the way for public policy adjustments that gave the descendents of Dred Scott equal protection of the laws.

State Action

***Civil Rights Cases,* 109 U.S. 3, 3 S.Ct. 18, 27 L.Ed. 835 (1883)** Limited the applicability of the Equal Protection Clause to situations where the state is an actual party to the discriminatory conduct. The *Civil Rights Cases* were an aggregation of suits that challenged the constitutionality of the Civil Rights Act of 1875, passed on the authority conferred by the Fourteenth Amendment. The cases specifically challenged the power of Congress to regulate private acts of racial discrimination. The Civil Rights Act provided that all persons "shall be entitled to the full and equal enjoyment of the accommodations, advantages, facilities and privileges of inns, public conveyances and theaters." In addition to its prohibitions of private discriminatory behavior in public accommodations, the act also assumed federal control over situations where state and local governments failed to protect citizens from discrimination by other private citizens. Over the vigorous dissent of Justice Harlan, the Court struck down the act. Justice Bradley's opinion for the Court stressed that the Fourteenth Amendment did not extend to Congress an unlimited source of legislative power. The amendment was intended to "provide modes of relief against State legislation, or State action." The Fourteenth Amendment did not "invest Congress with power to legislate upon subjects which are within the domain of State legislation" or "authorize Congress to create a code of municipal law for the regulation of private rights." The Fourteenth Amendment authorized Congress to enact corrective rather than general legislation that "may be necessary and proper for counteracting such laws as the States may adopt or enforce, and which, by the amendment, they are prohibited from making or enforcing." The Civil Rights Act of 1875 was defective in that it was not corrective, it referred to no State violation, and it impermissibly reached into the domain of local jurisprudence and laid down rules for the conduct of individuals. Justice Bradley expressed the fear that if Congress had authority to pass such legislation it would be difficult "to see where it is to stop." Nor did Justice Bradley think the Thirteenth Amendment authorized such legislation. He indicated that "mere discrimination on account of race or color was not regarded as a badge or slavery." Justice Harlan felt that the Thirteenth Amendment was a sufficient power source, saying that "such discrimination practiced by corporations and individuals in the exercise of their public or quasi-public functions is a badge of servitude the imposition of which Congress may prevent under its power." Critical for Justice Harlan was the "public convenience" or accommodation nature of the enterprises covered by the Civil Rights Act. *See also* EQUAL PROTECTION CLAUSE, p. 313; FOURTEENTH AMENDMENT, p. 412; *PLESSY V. FERGUSON* (163 U.S. 537: 1896), p. 322; *WASHINGTON V. DAVIS* (426 U.S. 229: 1976), p. 333.

Significance   The state action requirement established by the *Civil Rights Cases* (109 U.S. 3: 1883) remains in force, but discrimination in privately owned public accommodations is now regulated. The Court eventually became receptive to assertions that a close relationship exists between state authority and discriminating activity. In *Burton* v. *Wilmington Parking Authority* (365 U.S. 715: 1961), the Court found that the state had become a party to discrimination by a restaurant that leased space in a municipal parking facility. The state had not required equal access to all patrons. Granting a liquor license to a racially exclusive private club, however, was held not to alter the club's private character in *Moose Lodge #107* v. *Irvis* (407 U.S. 163: 1972). Congress was also able to bypass the state action requirement by regulating access to public accommodations through the Commerce Clause in the Civil Rights Act of 1964. The Court upheld the public accommodations title of the statute, provisions of which looked very much like those of the Civil Rights Act of 1875. In *United States* v. *Guest* (383 U.S. 745: 1966), the Court upheld a federal indictment of private individuals for the violation of a murder victim's civil rights. While the Court found state action present, six members of the Court said Congress has the power to reach wholly private acts that violate Fourteenth Amendment protections. The Burger Court has yet to take the indicated final step and abandon the state action requirement altogether.

Separate but Equal

***Plessy* v. *Ferguson*, 163 U.S. 537, 16 S.Ct. 1138, 41 L.Ed. 256 (1896)**   Established the doctrine of separate but equal. *Plessy* v. *Ferguson* addressed the question of state-mandated segregation. In the *Civil Rights Cases* (109 U.S. 3: 1883, p. 321), the Supreme Court limited the coverage of the Equal Protection Clause to situations where the state was a party to acts of discrimination. A number of

Southern states simultaneously established comprehensive segregation through legislative enactments that required separate accommodations for each race. Louisiana enacted a statute that compelled all railroads operating within the state "to provide equal but separate accommodations for the white and colored races." Plessy, a black passenger on a railway car, was subjected to criminal penalties for his refusal to leave the white section. Plessy appealed his conviction on Thirteenth and Fourteenth Amendment grounds, but the Court rejected the appeal in an 8–1 decision. Justice Brown began the Court's opinion by dispatching the Thirteenth Amendment contentions. A statute that implies merely a legal distinction between races "has no tendency to destroy the legal equality of the two races or reestablish a state of involuntary servitude." The Fourteenth Amendment claims were more difficult. The Fourteenth Amendment in Justice Brown's view was intended to provide both races with equality before the law, but it was also *limited* to legal equality. The Amendment was not designed "to abolish distinctions based upon color, or to enforce social, as distinguished from political, equality, or a commingling of the two races upon terms unsatisfactory to either." Statutory segregation does not necessarily imply the inferiority of either race to the other, and it is a policy option within the competency of the state legislatures in the exercise of their police power. Legislatures must have discretion to act with reference to "established usages, customs, and traditions of the people" as they reasonably attempt to promote the people's comfort and preserve public peace and good order. The Court majority categorically rejected the proposition that "social prejudices may be overcome by legislation, and that equal rights cannot be secured to the negro except by an enforced commingling of the two races." Such equality could only occur as the result of natural affinities, because the Constitution cannot put social inequality "upon the same plane." With such reasoning the Court established the separate but equal doctrine. The sole dissent in the case was entered by Justice Harlan, who argued that no superior, dominant, ruling class of citizens existed under the Constitution. The Constitution simply did not permit caste because it is color-blind and cannot tolerate classes among citizens. To segregate on the basis of race is "a badge of servitude wholly inconsistent with the civil freedom and the equality before the law established by the Constitution. It cannot be justified on any legal ground." Neither was Justice Harlan impressed by the statute's requirement that equivalent facilities be provided. He said the "thin disguise of equal accommodations for passengers in railroad coaches will not mislead anyone, nor atone for the wrong done this day." *See also* BROWN V. BOARD OF EDUCATION I (347 U.S. 483: 1954), p. 326; EQUAL PROTECTION CLAUSE, p. 313; FOURTEENTH AMENDMENT, p. 412; SWEATT V. PAINTER (339 U.S. 629: 1950), p. 324.

Significance   The words of Justice Harlan's dissent in *Plessy* v. *Ferguson* (163 U.S. 537: 1896) were prophetic. For several decades the Court used the separate but equal doctrine without paying serious attention to whether facilities were actually equivalent. The only successful challenges to segregation in public carriers prior to 1954 typically involved interstate travelers who allowed, or forced, the Court to base its holding on the impermissible burdens segregation imposed on the free flow of interstate commerce. See, for example, *Morgan* v. *Virginia* (328 U.S. 373: 1946). Following the Court's renunciation of the separate but equal doctrine in *Brown I* (347 U.S. 483: 1954, p. 326), it added to the public education focus of *Brown* state-mandated segregation in transportation, public accommodations, and municipal facilities. Nonetheless, the separate but equal doctrine served as the rationale for constitutional segregation for the better part of six decades.

Graduate Education

Sweatt v. *Painter,* 339 U.S. 629, 70 S.Ct. 848, 94 L.Ed. 1114 (1950)   Held that intangible factors may be considered in determining whether professional educational programs are comparable under the separate but equal doctrine. *Sweatt* v. *Painter* involved a comparison of the educational facilities at two state law schools in Texas. The equivalence of segregated facilities had not been seriously examined by the Court for several decades following *Plessy* v. *Ferguson* (163 U.S. 537: 1896, p. 322). Educational inequalities then became the setting in which the deficiencies of the separate but equal doctrine were examined. Challenges were first directed at the advanced degree level. Sweatt was precluded from admission to the University of Texas Law School by statute because he was black. Sweatt's state court suit was postponed to give Texas time to establish a separate law school for blacks. Sweatt persisted in his effort to enter the white law school, however, even after a black law school was opened. The Supreme Court unanimously reversed the finding of the state court that the facilities were equivalent. It ordered that Sweatt be admitted to the white law school. Sweatt had argued that the Court should reverse separate but equal as a constitutional doctrine, but the Court chose to focus on the narrower issue of the institutional equivalence of the two law schools. Chief Justice Vinson authored the Court's opinion, beginning with obvious and easily measured items such as the size of the faculties, the breadth of course offerings, the capacity of the libraries, and opportunities for specialization. On the basis of these factors, the Court concluded there was not "substantial equality in the educational opportunities offered white and Negro law students by the State." More important to the Court, however, were the differences between the two schools "in qualities which are incapable of objective measurement." Chief Justice Vinson included among the intangibles such items as faculty reputation, the position and influence of alumni, and tradition and prestige. The black law school was also deficient because it provided law studies in an academic vacuum. Pointing out that a black lawyer would be practicing in a real world with many white lawyers, witnesses, jurors, judges, and other officials, the Chief Justice said a black law school simply could not qualify as a proving ground for legal learning and practice because of its isolation. The opinion concluded by saying, "it is difficult to believe that one who had a free choice between these law schools would consider the question close." *See also* BROWN V. BOARD OF EDUCATION I (347 U.S. 483: 1954), p. 326; EQUAL PROTECTION CLAUSE, p. 313; FOURTEENTH AMENDMENT, p. 412; *PLESSY V. FERGUSON* (163 U.S. 537: 1896), p. 322.

Significance   *Sweatt v. Painter* (339 U.S. 629: 1950) was actually the last of a series of decisions involving segregation in higher education. The first of these cases, *Missouri ex. rel. Gaines v. Canada* (305 U.S. 337: 1938), was decided 12 years before *Sweatt*. Gaines had been denied admission to the University of Missouri Law School. Unlike Texas, Missouri had no alternative law school to offer Gaines. The all-white school proposed instead to underwrite Gaines's costs at a law school in an adjacent state. Gaines rejected the offer and continued his effort to gain entry to the University of Missouri. The Court ruled that Gaines was entitled to admission. It reaffirmed the basis of that decision in *Sipuel v. Board of Regents of the University of Oklahoma* (332 U.S. 631: 1948). In another decision rendered on the same day as *Sweatt*, *McLaurin v. Oklahoma State Regents* (339 U.S. 637: 1950), the Court said a black graduate student could not be segregated within a state university. Although the decisions involving graduate education had been focused narrowly, it was clear from cases such as *Sweatt* and *McLaurin* that the stage was being set for a full-scale reexamination of the separate but equal doctrine. Less than two years later, the Court agreed to examine segregation in elementary and secondary level public education.

School Segregation

Brown* v. *Board of Education I, 347 U.S. 483, 74 S.Ct. 686, 98 L.Ed. 873 (1954)   Overruled the separate but equal doctrine and held racial segregation in public schools to be unconstitutional. *Brown* v. *Board of Education I* was a Kansas case but had companion cases from Delaware, Virginia, South Carolina, and the District of Columbia. Each was premised on different facts and different local conditions, but all raised the common legal question of the constitutionality of racial segregation in public schools. After taking arguments in December 1952, the Court postponed a decision and ordered reargument of the issues in December 1953. During the intervening year, Earl Warren succeeded Fred M. Vinson as chief justice. The decision that came the following May was unanimous, and the opinion was written by the new chief justice. He began by considering whether those persons who proposed the Fourteenth Amendment intended it to apply to school segregation. He found the Amendment's history to be illusive and the evidence generally inconclusive. Neither was the separate but equal doctrine helpful, because, unlike *Sweatt* v. *Painter* (339 U.S. 629: 150, p. 251), black and white schools appeared substantially equal when tangible factors were used to evaluate them. Chief Justice Warren declared that resolution of the issue must come from an examination of "the effect of segregation itself on public education." This could not be done by turning the clock back to 1868, when the Fourteenth Amendment was adopted, or even to 1896, when *Plessy* v. *Ferguson* was decided. Rather, the Court was obliged to consider public education in the light of its full development and its present place in American life. The chief justice spoke of the importance of education, calling it the basis of good citizenship. He said it was instrumental in awakening a child to cultural values. It was the key to success in life. In fact education was "perhaps the most important function of state and local government." Given the fundamental character of education, therefore, opportunity to acquire it must be made available to all on equal terms. The controlling question was whether segregation deprived minority children of equal educational opportunity. The Court concluded that it did. The basis of the Court's judgment was extensive psychological evidence that showed that segregation negatively affected the educational development of minority students. "To separate them from others of similar age and qualifications solely because of their race generates a feeling of inferiority as to their status in the community that may affect their hearts and minds in a way unlikely ever to be undone." The doctrine of separate but equal has no place in public education, the Court said. Separate educational facilities are inherently unequal. *See also* BROWN V. BOARD OF EDUCATION II (349 U.S. 294: 1955), p. 327; EQUAL PROTECTION CLAUSE, p. 313; MILLIKEN V. BRADLEY(418 U.S. 716: 1974), p. 331; SWANN V. CHARLOTTE-MECKLENBURG BOARD OF EDUCATION(402 U.S. 1: 1971), p. 329.

Significance   *Brown* v. *Board of Education I* (347 U.S. 483: 1954) held that the Equal Protection Clause of the Fourteenth Amendment prohibits the segregation of public schools anywhere in the United States. In *Bolling* v. *Sharpe* (347 U.S. 497: 1954), the companion to *Brown* from the District of Columbia, the Court substituted the Due Process Clause of the Fifth Amendment because the Equal Protection Clause could not be used to limit federal actions. The Court held that the concepts of equal protection and due process, both stemming from the American ideal of fairness, are not mutually exclusive. While the justices did not suggest that the two concepts are always interchangeable, they recognized that "discrimination may be so unjustifiable as to be violative of due process." Since segregation in the District's schools was not reasonably related to any proper governmental objective, black students "are burdened in a fashion which constitutes an arbitrary deprivation of their liberty in violation of the Due Process Clause." Having found constitutional violations in all of the five cases involving official or de jure segregation, the Court then separated the remedy questions and docketed them for later argument. *Brown* v. *Board of Education II* (349 U.S. 294: 1955) addressed enforcement of the decision in *Brown I*. The broad implications of the decision were apparent immediately, however. Although *Brown I* had focused on segregation in public education, it had the effect of establishing a constitutional prohibition on race as a classification. Soon thereafter, the Court extended the *Brown* holding to other areas, such as transportation and municipal facilities. Yet the question of whether segregation that existed unofficially or de facto was subject to the same relief as segregation that existed officially or de jure remained unanswered for several years following *Brown I*.

Desegregation Order

Brown v. Board of Education II,349 U.S. 294, 75 S.Ct. 753, 99 L.Ed. 1083 (1955)   Established guidelines by which public school desegregation could begin. *Brown* v. *Board of Education II* was devoted to implementation of the desegregation of public schools as mandated by the Court's decision in *Brown* v. *Board of Education I* (347 U.S. 483: 1954, p. 326). The Supreme Court chose to remand all five original cases back to the lower federal courts from which they had come because "full implementation may require solution of varied local school problems." The Court saw the primary responsibility for elucidating, assessing, and solving these problems resting with local school authorities. The role of the courts was defined as considering "whether the action of school authorities constitutes good faith implementation of the governing constitutional principles." Lower federal courts were to be guided by equitable principles in fashioning specific decrees. Recourse to equity law allowed courts practical flexibility in shaping their remedies and the facility for adjusting and reconciling public and private needs. While supervising courts could take into account the public interest in eliminating obstacles in making an orderly transition to school systems operated in accordance with constitutional principles set forth in *Brown I*, the Court warned that in doing so, "the vitality of these constitutional principles cannot be allowed to yield simply because of disagreement with them." The Court specified a timetable. Local authorities were expected to make a "prompt and reasonable start toward full compliance." Additional time might be available presuming that school districts could establish "that such time is necessary in the public interest and is consistent with good faith compliance at the earliest practicable date." The Court said that constitutional violations must be relieved "with all deliberate speed." *See also* BROWN V. BOARD OF EDUCATION I (347 U.S. 483: 1954), EQUAL PROTECTION CLAUSE, p. 313; *MILLIKEN* V. *BRADLEY* (418 U.S. 717: 1974), p. 331; *SWANN* V. *CHARLOTTE-MECKLENBURG BOARD OF EDUCATION* (402 U.S. 1: 1971), p. 329.

Significance   Reaction to *Brown* v. *Board of Education II* (349 U.S. 294: 1955) was intense and varied. There was widespread support and applause for the end of separate but equal in public education. The temperate character of the order in *Brown II* diffused potential opposition from a large middle group. Nonetheless, substantial resistance developed. In some places the reactions were violent. The situation in Little Rock, Arkansas, is illustrative. The state legislature passed a state constitutional amendment registering opposition to the desegregation decisions and enacted legislation "relieving school children from compulsory attendance at racially mixed schools." Since school was to begin in the fall of 1957 under a desegregation plan designed by the Little Rock School Board, the Governor of Arkansas, Orval Faubus, sent units of the Arkansas National Guard to

Central High School in Little Rock and placed it "off limits" to black students. Crowds gathered and violence was threatened. The school board sought postponement of *Brown* implementation because of "extreme public hostility." In *Cooper* v. *Aaron* (358 U.S. 1: 1958), the Court unanimously found the situation "directly traceable" to provocative actions by state officials and rejected the request to postpone. The Court firmly indicated that "constitutional rights of respondents are not to be sacrificed or yielded to the violence and disorder which have followed upon the actions of the Governor and Legislature." Another form of resistance in segregated areas was to close the public schools altogether. One such attempt was made in Prince Edward County, Virginia, a school district involved in one of the original suits decided in *Brown I*. Under a freedom of choice provision of state law, local authorities closed the public schools. Education was made available to white students through private schools financed by means of a complex mixture of state monies and local tuition grants. In *Griffin* v. *County School Board of Prince Edward County* (377 U.S. 218: 1964), the Court upheld a lower-court injunction against this technique. The Court said it had "no doubt of the power of the court to give this relief to enforce the discontinuance of the county's racially discriminatory practices." The most common form of resistance, however, was simply to delay any change from the dual school system. The Court in *Green* v. *County School Board of New Kent County* (391 U.S. 430: 1968) termed "intolerable" local plans that "at this late date fail to provide meaningful assurance of prompt and effective disestablishment of a dual school system." The following year, in *Alexander* v. *Holmes County Board of Education* (396 U.S. 19: 1969), the Court ended the all deliberate speed proviso of *Brown II* and ordered operation of only unitary school systems "at once." The latter two cases clearly established an affirmative obligation for local authorities to desegregate public schools with no further delay.

Intradistrict Busing

Swann v. ***Charlotte-Mecklenburg Board of Education*, 402 U.S. 1, 91 S.Ct. 1267, 28 L.Ed.2d 554 (1971)**   Upheld a lower-court desegregation order that included intradistrict busing. *Swann* v. *Charlotte-Mecklenburg County Board of Education* examined at length the scope and character of remedies to be used by federal judges in eliminating public school segregation under the Equal Protection Clause of the Fourteenth Amendment. *Swann* was the first case in which the Supreme Court said that busing was a reasonable approach to achievement of racially integrated public schools. In 1965, the Charlotte-Mecklenburg school district was required to devise a desegregation plan. The plan, approved by a federal court, had a substantial number of black students still attending schools identifiable as "black." Various Supreme Court decisions had spoken of the obligation to eliminate all vestiges of a dual school system, and so more extensive desegregation was sought. Finding the Charlotte-Mecklenburg plan inadequate, another district court had a plan of its own prepared by a court-appointed desegregation expert. The new plan involved extensive transportation of elementary level students and was adopted by the district court as part of its desegregation order. The school board appealed, arguing the remedy was excessive. The Supreme Court unanimously rejected the school board's argument and upheld the lower court's entire remedy, including busing. The opinion of the Court was written by Chief Justice Burger. He said the controlling objective was the elimination of all vestiges of state-imposed segregation. Judicial authority may be invoked, he said, if local school authorities fail in their affirmative obligation to do so. The scope of judicial authority to remedy past wrongs is broad, for breadth and flexibility are inherent in equitable remedies. Such power is not unlimited, however. It may be exercised "only on the basis of a constitutional violation." Remedial authority does not put judges automatically in the shoes of school authorities whose powers are plenary. Judicial authority enters only when local authority defaults. The Court believed the district court had appropriately taken corrective action in the case. It then proceeded to review the student assignment element of the remedy order. It found the use of racial population ratios a "useful starting point in shaping a remedy" rather than an inflexible requirement. As for alteration of attendance zones, the Court felt "administratively awkward, inconvenient and even bizarre" arrangements may be required to eliminate dual school systems. Neighborhood schools can be maintained only where there is no constitutional violation. If attendance zones are to be altered, student transportation becomes essential. The Court concluded that local school boards may properly be required to "employ bus transportation as one tool of school desegregation." *See also* BROWN V. BOARD OF EDUCATION I (347 U.S. 483: 1954), p. 326; BROWN V. BOARD OF EDUCATION II (349 U.S. 294: 1955), p. 327; EQUAL PROTECTION CLAUSE, p. 313; MILLIKEN V. BRADLEY (418 U.S. 717: 1974), p. 331.

Significance   The Supreme Court upheld an extensive busing order in *Swann* v. *Charlotte-Mecklenburg Board of Education* (402 U.S. 1:

1971). The Court made it clear, however, that busing was not an absolute ingredient of desegregation orders and that mathematical ratios were only to be used to dismantle segregated districts and not to achieve racial balance. It also said in *Swann* that district courts would retain power to deal with future problems, but year-by-year adjustments of racial composition were not required. The question of *re*segregation was addressed in *Pasadena City Board of Education* v. *Spangler* (427 U.S. 424: 1976). The Court held that once a district has been desegregated, school authorities need not readjust pupil assignments to reflect population shifts. Unless it could be shown that official actions had caused resegregative shifts in population, continued court involvement would constitute pursuit of racial balance rather than creation of a unitary school system. *Swann* expressly prohibited the former. Although the Court did not categorically endorse busing, it did strike down a statute prohibiting assignment of students on account of race and involuntary busing to that end in *North Carolina State Board of Education* v. *Swann* (402 U.S. 43: 1971), a companion to the Charlotte-Mecklenburg case.

Interdistrict Busing

***Milliken* v. *Bradley I*, 418 U.S. 717, 94 S.Ct. 3112, 41 L.Ed.2d 1069 (1974)** Invalidated a busing order involving the Detroit school system and 53 suburban school districts. *Milliken* v. *Bradley* addressed the critical question of whether desegregation orders could cross district lines and combine urban districts and outlying suburban districts. Such questions had remained unanswered following the Court's endorsement of busing in *Swann* v. *Charlotte-Mecklenburg Board of Education* (402 U.S. 1: 1971, p. 329). Response to the question would determine the extent to which school districts outside the South could be desegregated. Suit was brought by Bradley and others charging that the Detroit school system had been racially segregated by action of local as well as state school authorities. The district court did find violations and considered several desegregation plans. It rejected one plan involving only the City of Detroit because so few white students were available for reassignment that the plan would only "accentuate the racial identifiability of the district as a black school system." Instead, the court chose a plan that involved busing students between the Detroit district and 53 suburban districts. The Supreme Court overturned the multidistrict remedy in a 5–4 decision. Chief Justice Burger offered that such a consolidation would "give rise to an array of other problems in financing and operating this new school system." The new super school district would require that the federal court become a de facto legislative authority to resolve many complex questions, and the school superintendent for the entire area. The chief justice thought few judges could act effectively in these capacities. The Court found a more fundamental flaw, however, in the district court's order. The scope of the order exceeded the scope of the violation demonstrated. The chief justice ruled that before a consolidation or cross-district order could occur, it must be shown that a "constitutional violation within one district produces a significant segregative effect in another district." The Court concluded that without an interdistrict violation, and interdistrict effect, there is no constitutional wrong calling for an interdistrict remedy. To hold otherwise would allow a "wholly impermissible remedy based on a standard not hinted at in *Brown I* or *Brown II.*" Justices Douglas, Brennan, White, and Marshall dissented. Justice White criticized the majority for fashioning out of "whole cloth an arbitrary rule that remedies for constitutional violations occurring in a single Michigan school district must stop at the school district line." Referring to the Court's decision as a "great step backward," Justice Marshall felt the decision was a "reflection of a perceived public mood that we have gone far enough in enforcing the Constitution's guarantee of equal justice." He feared the decision would encourage metropolitan areas to be divided into two cities, one white and one black. *See also* BROWN V. BOARD OF EDUCATION I (347 U.S. 483: 1954), p. 326; BROWN V. BOARD OF EDUCATION II (349 U.S. 294: 1955), p. 327; EQUAL PROTECTION CLAUSE, p. 313; SWANN V. CHARLOTTE-MECKLENBURG BOARD OF EDUCATION (402 U.S. 1: 1971), p. 329.

Significance   Milliken v. Bradley I, (418 U.S. 717: 1974) was decided by the Court in 1974, but it returned three years later as *Milliken* v. *Bradley II* (433 U.S. 267: 1977). The second case involved a decree that not only assigned pupils throughout the Detroit school district, but also required a number of additional educational activities such as remedial reading, intensified student testing and counseling, and extensive in-service teacher training. The Court unanimously upheld the lower-court order, saying that despite the compensatory character of the remedy, it "does not change the fact that it is part of a plan that operates prospectively to bring about the delayed benefits of a unitary school system." The troublesome question of the status of de facto segregation has continued to escape direct response. In *Keyes* v. *School District No. 1* (413 U.S. 189: 1973), the Court held that actions undertaken in support of de facto segregated schools constituted de jure segregation. In two recent cases from Ohio, *Columbus Board of Education* v. *Penick* (443 U.S. 449: 1979) and *Dayton Board of Education* v. *Brinkman* (443 U.S. 526: 1979), the Court upheld systemwide busing as a remedy because both systems were officially segregated at the time *Brown I* was decided. Given the encompassing interpretation the Court put on the concept of de jure segregation in these cases, the need to determine the constitutionality of de facto segregation has diminished significantly.

Job Discrimination: Intent

Washington v. *Davis,* 426 U.S. 229, 96 S.Ct. 2040, 48 L.Ed.2d 597 (1976)   Required demonstration of intent in order to prove employment discrimination. *Washington* v. *Davis* considered the question of whether statutory standards prohibiting racial discrimination in employment under Title VII of the Civil Rights Act of 1964 are the same as the constitutional standards for adjudicating claims of invidious racial discrimination. The Court held that the latter required not only a showing of impact, but intent as well. *Washington* v. *Davis* involved a written personnel test that was administered to all prospective federal employees including those who, like Davis, sought positions on the Washington, D.C., police force. The test, called Test 21, was ostensibly used to measure verbal aptitude. Four times as many black applicants failed the test as whites. Davis claimed that the test was not reasonably related to one's performance as a police officer and that it discriminated against black applicants. In a 7–2 decision, the Supreme Court upheld use of the test. The Court's opinion was written by Justice White, who took exception to the understanding of the Court of Appeals that litigants proceeding under Title VII "need not concern themselves with the employer's possibly discriminatory purpose but instead focus solely on the racially differential impact." Justice White declared that this "is not the constitutional rule." The Court has "never held that the constitutional standard is identical to the standards applicable under Title VII, and declines to do so today." A law "neutral on its face and serving ends otherwise within the power of government to pursue" is not invalid because it may affect a greater proportion of one race than another. While disproportionate impact is not irrelevant, it is not the sole touchstone of impermissible discrimination. Justice White termed "untenable" the proposition that the Constitution could keep government from seeking modestly to upgrade the communicative abilities of its employees. The Court was unconvinced the test was a purposeful device to discriminate. Such evidence as the affirmative effort of the police department to recruit black officers, the changing racial composition of the recruit classes and the force in general, and the relationship of the test to the training program addressed the issue of intent. In this case the evidence "negated any inference that the Department discriminated on the basis of race." The Court concluded that to apply the Title VII approach to constitutional adjudication involves a more probing judicial review of "seemingly reasonable acts of administrators than is appropriate under the Constitution." The Court also observed that if all legislation designed to serve neutral ends is invalidated because in practice it benefits or burdens one race more than another, the results would be extremely far-reaching. Justices Brennan and Marshall dissented, arguing that once discriminatory impact is demonstrated, the employer must prove how the challenged practice has a demonstrable relationship to successful performance of the job for which it was used. *See also* CIVIL RIGHTS CASES (109 U.S. 3: 1883), p. 313; EQUAL PROTECTION CLAUSE, p. 321; *VILLAGE OF ARLINGTON HEIGHTS V. METROPOLITAN HOUSING DEVELOPMENT CORPORATION* (429 U.S. 252: 1977), p. 335.

Significance   *Washington* v. *Davis* (426 U.S. 229: 1976) held that discriminatory intent must be shown to establish a constitutional violation. *Davis* distinguished situations in which constitutional provisions such as equal protection are involved from those based upon federal civil-rights statutes. While certain practices may be found in violation of federal law, such as Title VII, those practices may not be constitutional violations. The disproportionate impact standard set forth in *Griggs* v. *Duke Power Company* (401 U.S. 424: 1971) still applied to situations arising under Title VII. In *Griggs* the Court refused to permit an employer to use a high school diploma and scores on an intelligence test as a qualifying condition for employment. Unanimously the Court held that once a plaintiff shows unequal or disproportionate impact, the employer must demonstrate a relationship between the challenged practice and job performance. The intent element surfaced more recently in a Title VI suit brought by black and Hispanic police officers laid off when financial problems beset New York City. Title VI bars racial or ethnic discrimination by recipients of federal monies. In a fragmented decision, the Court held in *Guardians Association* v. *Civil Service Commission of the City of New York* (103 S.Ct. 3221: 1983) that without a showing of discriminatory intent, compensatory relief such as back pay and retroactive seniority was not available through Title VI.

Housing Discrimination: Intent

Village of Arlington Heights v. *Metropolitan Housing Development Corporation,* 429 U.S. 252, 97 S.Ct. 555, 50 L.Ed.2d 450 (1977)   Held that intent must be shown to establish an equal protection violation in a local government zoning decision affecting housing. In *Village of Arlington Heights* v. *Metropolitan Housing Development Corporation,* the Supreme Court upheld a local zoning ordinance against charges of racial discrimination. In doing so, the Court reaffirmed the holding in *Washington* v. *Davis* (426 U.S. 229: 1976, p. 333), which required proof of discriminatory intent. The Court went on to provide assistance in identifying the factors that might allow determination of discriminatory purpose. The Metropolitan Housing Development Corporation (MHDC) wished to build racially integrated low- and middle-income housing in the Village of Arlington Heights. MHDC contracted to purchase a site, but the sale was contingent on having the tract rezoned from single-family to multiple-family dwelling status. The Village refused to rezone, claiming the particular area had always been zoned for single-family use, and that the multiple-family classification had historically been reserved for locations adjacent to commercial areas. The zoning decision was challenged as racially discriminatory. In a 5–3 decision, Justice Stevens not participating, the Court reversed a Court of Appeals decision, rendered prior to *Davis,* holding the zoning decision to be in violation of the Equal Protection Clause. At the same time the Court unanimously agreed to remand the case for consideration of statutory claims under the Fair Housing Act. Justice Powell spoke for the majority and reiterated the *Davis* rule that proof of racially discriminatory intent or purpose is necessary to find an equal protection violation. Justice Powell said that courts should generally defer to legislative and administrative judgments that balance numerous competing considerations. He stated, however, that race "is not just another competing consideration." When a discriminatory purpose is shown to be a motivating factor in a policy, judicial deference is no longer justified. Determining whether a discriminatory purpose exists demands sensitive inquiry. Justice Powell offered several suggestions. Certainly the "impact of the official action" is an "important starting point." Without a clear pattern, unexplainable on grounds other than race, other evidence must be considered. Historical background may be a useful source if it reveals a series of official actions taken for invidious purposes. Sequences of events leading to the challenged decision may be relevant. So, too, would be departures from normal procedural sequence or if factors usually considered important strongly favor a decision contrary to the one reached. Finally, courts might defer to legislative or administrative history, especially where there are contemporary statements by members of the decision-making body, minutes of its meetings, or reports. Although the decision impacted heavily on minorities in Arlington Heights, the Court did not find proof of discriminatory purpose as it examined the record using these criteria. *See also* CIVIL RIGHTS CASES (109 U.S. 3: 1883), p. 321; EQUAL PROTECTION CLAUSE, p. 313; *WASH-INGTON* V. *DAVIS* (426 U.S. 229: 1976), p. 333.

Significance   *Village of Arlington Heights* v. *Metropolitan Housing Development Corporation* (429 U.S. 252: 1977) refused to find a local zoning decision in violation of the Equal Protection Clause without a showing of discriminatory intent. *Arlington Heights* follows a long line of significant Fourteenth Amendment cases involving discrimination in housing. In *Buchanan* v. *Warley* (245 U.S. 60: 1971), the Court struck down several segregative housing ordinances. Three decades later, in *Shelley* v. *Kraemer* (334 U.S. 1: 1948), it ruled that private restrictive convenants could not be enforced in state courts. Such covenants were agreements among private property owners not to sell or rent to various specified minorities, usually blacks. *Shelley* assumed that court enforcement made the state a party to the discrimination. On the same state action grounds, the Court ruled in *Reitman* v. *Mulkey* (387 U.S. 369: 1967) that a state could not repeal open-occupancy statutes by referendum without encouraging discriminatory conduct. Federal proscription of private discrimination in conveying property through a century-old civil-rights statute was upheld in *Jones* v. *Alfred H. Mayer Company* (392 U.S. 409: 1968). In *James* v. *Valtierra* (402 U.S. 137: 1971), the Court permitted a state constitutional provision requiring referendum approval of all low-income housing projects. As in *Arlington Heights,* the Court refused to hold that use of the referendum technique presumed discriminatory or prejudicial purpose. Where discrimination is a motive, courts are able to construct broad remedies. In *Hills* v. *Gautreaux* (425 U.S. 284: 1976), the Court approved a plan that made public housing available in suburban areas because violations to which the Department of Housing and Urban Development had been a party were found to exist both in Chicago and in adjoining areas. *Arlington Heights* is a pivotal case in that it took the Court in a new direction. After years of expanding the concept of state action, *Arlington Heights* decreased the need to show discriminatory purpose in equal protection cases.

Reverse Discrimination

***Regents of the University of California* v. *Bakke,*438 U.S. 265, 98 S.Ct. 2733, 57 L.Ed.2d 750 (1978)**   Rejected use of quotas in university admission procedures, but permitted use of race as a factor in recruiting heterogeneous student bodies. *Regents of the University of California* v. *Bakke* represented the Supreme Court's first discussion of the merits of affirmative action. The troublesome question posed by affirmative action programs is whether preference may be extended to a particular racial or ethnic group in order to correct historical inequalities. Can certain intentional preferences constitutionally be permitted because of their compensatory character? The medical school at the University of California at Davis admitted 100 students annually. To assure minority representation within the student body, 16 places were reserved for minority applicants. Bakke, a white applicant, was twice denied admission although his credentials were better than some of the minority applicants admitted under the affirmative action policy. Bakke brought suit arguing that the racially sensitive quota system at Davis violated Title VI of the Civil Rights Act of 1964. The act prohibited discrimination in programs receiving federal funding. The Court resolved the case by finding for both sides. In a 5–4 split, the Court ruled that the Davis quota system was impermissible and ordered that Bakke be admitted. At the same time, the Court also held in a 5–4 vote that a state university may take race into account in allowing for a diverse student body. Each issue split the Court into two blocs of four members each, with Justice Powell providing the decisive vote on each judgment. Justice Powell joined Chief Justice Burger and Justices Rehnquist, Stewart, and Stevens on the quota component, but aligned himself with Justices Brennan, Marshall, White, and Blackmun on the issue of limited affirmative action efforts. Justice Powell's opinion rejected the quota approach and the injustice of racial classifications generally. The Fourteenth Amendment confers protection to individuals, he said. The "guarantee of equal protection cannot mean one thing when applied to one individual and something else when applied to a person of another color." Justice Powell rejected the view that race was not a suspect classification when applied to the white majority because the purpose of such classification was benign. Individuals within that class "are likely to find little comfort in the notion that the deprivation they are asked to endure is merely the price of membership in the dominant majority and that its imposition is inspired by the supposedly benign purpose of aiding others." Noting that the white majority itself was composed of various minority groups, Justice Powell feared that courts would forever be asked to assess the degree of discrimination each has suffered and the redress each was due. By "hitching the meaning of the Equal Protection Clause to these transitory considerations, we would be holding, as a constitutional principle, that judicial scrutiny of classifications touching on racial and ethnic background may vary with the ebb and flow of political forces." Justice Powell did, however, recognize attainment of a diverse student body as a constitutionally permissible goal for an institution of higher education. Indeed, he said the nation's future depends upon leaders trained through wide exposure, which comes through a diverse student body. He referred to the Harvard admissions program, which assigns a plus to particular racial or ethnic backgrounds, but still treats each applicant as an individual in the admissions process. In striking the Davis quota system, the Court said it need not reach the broader constitutional question of race as a factor in admissions decisions. It was enough to say Title VI required Bakke's admission and the striking of Davis's reserved seat policy. A majority of the Court saw the Davis program as educationally sound and sufficiently important to justify the use of race-conscious admissions programs. The Davis approach did not "stigmatize any discrete group or individual," and thus was adequate as a means of remedying the effects of past societal discrimination. *See also* EQUAL PROTECTION CLAUSE, p. 313; *FULLILOVE V. KLUTZNICK* (448 U.S. 448: 1980), p. 339; *WASHINGTON V. DAVIS* (426 U.S. 229: 1976), p. 333.

Significance   *Regents of the University of California v. Bakke* (438 U.S. 265: 1978) was a compromise holding. While the Court rejected quotas as such, it still allowed universities to manipulate admissions to produce heterogeneous student bodies. The Court had an opportunity to deal with the reverse discrimination issue four years earlier in *DeFunis v. Odegaard* (416 U.S. 312: 1974). DeFunis argued that he had been denied admission to the University of Washington Law School because of a preferential admissions policy very much like that used at Davis. DeFunis, however, had been admitted to the law school under court order and was actually close to graduation at the time the case was presented to the Supreme Court. Five members of the Court decided the case was moot and avoided speaking to the equal protection question. Following *Bakke,* a more positive affirmative action decision came from the Court in *United Steelworkers of America* v. *Weber* (443 U.S. 193: 1979). The Court upheld a private and voluntary employee training program against a challenge of Title VII of the Civil Rights Act of 1964. The program gave selection preference to black employees for training, although not to the total exclusion of white employees.

Minority Preferences

Fullilove **v.** *Klutznick,* **448 U.S. 448, 100 S.Ct. 2758, 65 L.Ed.2d 202 (1980)**   Allowed a portion of federal construction grant funds to be reserved or "set aside" for businesses owned and operated by racial minorities. *Fullilove* v. *Klutznick* examined the central affirmative action issue of whether the use of quotas is permissible under the Fourteenth Amendment. The Public Works Employment Act of 1977 contained a minority business enterprise (MBE) section that required at least 10 percent of federal monies designated for local public works projects to be set aside for businesses owned by minorities. Implementation of the policy was designed to come through grant recipients who were expected to seek out MBEs and provide whatever assistance or advice might be necessary to negotiate bonding, bidding, or any other historically troublesome process. The policy was challenged by a number of nonminority contractors, but was upheld by the Supreme Court in a 6–3 decision. Chief Justice Burger said the MBE section must be considered against the background of ongoing efforts directed toward deliverance of the century-old promise of equality of economic opportunity. The chief justice noted that a program using racial or ethnic criteria, even in a remedial context, calls for close examination, "yet we are bound to approach our task with appropriate deference." The Court's analysis involved two steps, the constitutionality of Congress's objectives and the permissibility of the means chosen to pursue the objectives. The Court ruled that Congress had ample evidence to conclude that minority businesses had impaired access to public contracting opportunities, that their impaired access had an effect on interstate commerce, and that the pattern of disadvantage and discrimination was a problem that was national in scope. Thus Congress had the authority to act. The Court then turned to the means used. Racial or ethnic criteria may be used in a remedial fashion as long as the program is narrowly tailored to achieve the corrective purpose. The Court rejected the view that in developing remedies Congress must act in a wholly color-blind fashion. No organ of government has a more comprehensive remedial power than Congress. Where Congress can prohibit certain conduct, "it may, as here, authorize and induce state action to avoid such conduct." The Court recognized that some nonminority contractors who may not themselves have acted in a discriminatory manner may lose some contracts. Such a result, outside the legislative purpose, is an unfortunate but incidental consequence. As Congress attempts to effectuate a limited and properly tailored remedy to cure the effects of prior discrimination, such a sharing of the burden by innocent parties is not impermissible. Justices Stewart, Rehnquist, and Stevens disagreed. They argued that "government may never act to the detriment of a person solely because of that person's race." Racial discrimination is invidious by definition, and that rule cannot be any different when the persons injured by a racially biased law are not members of a racial minority. As for the corrective character of the legislation, Justice Stewart remarked that Congress is not a court of equity and has "neither the dispassionate objectivity nor the flexibility that are needed to mold a race-conscious remedy around the single objective of eliminating the effects of past or present discrimination." *See also* BOARD OF REGENTS V. BAKKE (438 U.S. 265: 1978), p. 337; EQUAL PROTECTION CLAUSE, p. 313; REVERSE DISCRIMINATION, p. 447; WASHINGTON V. DAVIS (426 U.S. 229: 1976), p. 333.

Significance Fullilove v. Klutznick (448 U.S. 448: 1980) upheld the use of set-asides or reserved funds for minority business enterprises as a method of remedying past discrimination in the construction industry. A year before *Fullilove,* the Court had approved a preferential employment training plan in *United Steelworkers of America* v. *Weber* (443 U.S. 193: 1979). The plan, a component of a collective bargaining agreement, sought to reduce racial imbalances in a corporation's skilled or craft work force. The plan gave preference to unskilled black employees over white employees, even white employees with greater seniority, in admission to training programs that taught the skills needed to become a craft worker. In a 5–2 decision, the Court held that Title VII of the Civil Rights Act of 1964 did not categorically preclude private and voluntary affirmative action plans. To prohibit such plans would produce a result inconsistent with the intent of the Civil Rights Act. It would be ironic if Title VII, "triggered by a nation's concern over centuries of racial injustice," was interpreted as the "legislative prohibition of all voluntary, private, race-conscious efforts to abolish traditional patterns of racial segregation and hierarchy." *Fullilove* and *Weber* together adopt the proposition that equal protection allows compensatory policies for groups that have demonstrably been disadvantaged in the past.

Tax Exempt Status

***Bob Jones University* v. *United States,* 76 L.Ed.2d 157 (1983)**
Ruled that the federal government may revoke or deny tax exemptions to private educational institutions practicing racial discrimination. The heart of the dispute in *Bob Jones University* v. *United States* was an Internal Revenue Service (IRS) interpretation of two sections in the Internal Revenue Code. Section 501 (c)(3) allowed tax exemptions for institutions "organized and operated exclusively for religious, charitable, or educational purposes," while Section 170 granted charitable deductions for contributors to such entities. The IRS determined in 1970 that the provisions could not apply to private schools engaged in racial discrimination. It issued a revenue ruling that such schools were no longer charitable institutions. Bob Jones University admitted black students but denied admission to applicants who were "known to advocate" interracial marriage or dating or were married to a person of a different race. The University said its discriminatory policies were justified because they were required by religious beliefs. The Supreme Court upheld the IRS determination to withdraw exempted status from Bob Jones in an 8–1 ruling. The University argued that as long as it remained either a religious or an educational institution, it need not also be charitable to qualify for the exemption. The Court responded through Chief Justice Burger by saying that Section 501 (c)(3) must be interpreted against the background of congressional intent. The Court found "unmistakable evidence" that "entitlement to tax exemption depends on meeting certain common law standards of charity—namely, that an institution seeking tax exempt status must serve a public purpose and not be contrary to established public policy." The exempted institution "must demonstrably serve and be in harmony with the public interest," because all taxpayers are affected by exemptions or deductions granted by the government. Other taxpayers in effect become indirect or vicarious donors. The institution, therefore, cannot have objectives "so at odds with the common community conscience as to undermine any public benefit that might otherwise be conferred." As

a result, racially discriminatory schools cannot be viewed as providing a benefit within the context of charitable or within congressional intent underlying Sections 170 and 501 (c)(3). The Court's focus then turned to the authority of the IRS to make its ruling. Bob Jones argued that only Congress itself could alter the scope of the two sections. The Court disagreed. The chief justice noted that Congress refused to reverse the ruling despite numerous opportunities. Chief Justice Burger called the congressional nonaction significant and thought it hardly conceivable that Congress was not abundantly aware of what was going on. Similarly, public policy at the time of the ruling was unmistakably clear on the issue of racial discrimination. It would be "anomalous for the Executive, Legislative, and Judicial Branches to reach conclusions that add up to a firm public policy on racial discrimination, and at the same time have the IRS blissfully ignore what all three branches of the Federal Government had declared." Finally, the Court dismissed the argument that the discrimination was based on sincerely held religious beliefs. The chief justice wrote that religious liberty may be limited if the state is pursuing an overriding governmental interest. The interest in eliminating racial discrimination was seen as a fundamentally overriding interest that "substantially outweighs whatever burden denial of tax benefits places on petitioners' exercise of their religious beliefs." Justice Rehnquist dissented. While agreeing that national policy is opposed to racial discrimination and that Congress has the power to further that policy by denying tax exemptions, Justice Rehnquist felt that Congress had yet actually to do so. "Whatever the reasons for the failure, this Court should not legislate for Congress." *See also* EQUAL PROTECTION CLAUSE, p. 313; FIRST AMENDMENT, p. 77; FREE EXERCISE CLAUSE, p. 413.

Significance   The decision in *Bob Jones University* v. *United States* (76 L.Ed.2d 157: 1983) permits denial of tax exempt status to private educational institutions practicing racial discrimination even if such behavior is grounded in religious doctrine. The holding clearly subordinates the burden imposed on a religious institution through the loss of an exemption to the interest of eliminating racial discrimination. Previous to the *Bob Jones* case, the Court had ruled in *Norwood* v. *Harrison* (413 U.S. 455: 1973) that state-purchased textbooks could not be loaned to private schools practicing racial discrimination. In *Runyon* v. *McCrary* (427 U.S. 160: 1976), the Court held that private schools could be prohibited from racially exclusive admissions practices. The *Bob Jones* case is of greater significance in that it establishes the priority of combating racial discrimination over religious beliefs and recognizes the broad governmental authority vested in administrative agencies to pursue that policy.

THE NEW EQUAL PROTECTION

Reapportionment

Baker v. Carr, 369 U.S. 186, 82 S.Ct. 691, 7 L.Ed.2d 663 (1962)   Held that legislative apportionment was a matter properly before federal courts. *Baker* v. *Carr* abandoned the position that apportionment was a political question not subject to resolution by the judicial branch. By the middle of the twentieth century, gross malapportionment existed for most state legislative districts as well as for Congress. Years of inattention to shifting populations had produced highly inequitable representation. Baker and others brought suit in Federal District Court in Tennessee, claiming that despite significant growth and shifts in the population of Tennessee, legislative districts were still apportioned on the basis of a 1901 statute. The Court through Justice Brennan said the federal courts possessed jurisdiction in the case because the equal protection claim was not "so attenuated and unsubstantial as to be absolutely devoid of merit." Precedent would seem to have foreclosed the Court from adjudicating *Baker* by virtue of the political question doctrine in *Colegrove* v. *Green* (328 U.S. 549: 1946). The *Colegrove* decision held that the enjoining of an election because of malapportionment was beyond the Court's competence. Apportionment was of a "peculiarly political nature and therefore not meet for judicial determination." Thus the Court viewed the matter in separation of power terms. For the judiciary to involve itself would "cut very deep into the very being of Congress. Courts ought not to enter this political thicket." Justice Brennan traced the history of the doctrine and concluded that its application revealed a definite pattern. "Prominent on the surface of any case held to involve a political question is found a textually demonstrable constitutional commitment of the issue to a coordinate political department." Guaranty Clause claims and the conduct of foreign affairs were especially reflective of this category. A second category of political question issues involved cases where there was a lack of judicially discoverable and manageable standards for resolving such cases, or where it was impossible to decide without an initial policy determination clearly outside judicial discretion. Justice Brennan said the apportionment question fit neither of those categories. It was rather an equal protection problem containing claims of arbitrary and capricious action by the State of Tennessee. Justices Frankfurter and

Harlan dissented. Justice Frankfurter, who had written the Court's opinion in *Colegrove*, felt the *Baker* case was controlled by the political question doctrine and that the decision was a "massive repudiation of the experience of our whole past in asserting destructively novel judicial power." The Court must, in Justice Frankfurter's view, maintain "complete detachment, in fact and in appearance, from political entanglements and by abstention from injecting itself into the clash of political forces in political settlements." Justice Harlan remarked that those who consider the Court's authority as based on wise exercise of self-restraint and discipline in constitutional adjudication "will view the decision with deep concern." *See also* EQUAL PROTECTION CLAUSE, p. 313; LEGISLATIVE APPORTIONMENT, p. 384; *MOBILE* V. *BOLDEN* (446 U.S. 55: 1980), p. 346; *REYNOLDS* V. *SIMS* (377 U.S. 533: 1964), p. 344; *SOUTH CAROLINA* V. *KATZENBACH* (383 U.S. 301: 1966), p. 348.

Significance   Baker v. Carr (369 U.S. 186: 1962) allowed the matter of reapportionment to be brought to federal courts. *Baker* did not attempt to develop particular standards regarding reapportionment, but left in its wake a great deal of activity directed toward relieving malapportionment. The Court's first indication of a standard that could guide redistricting came in *Gray v. Sanders* (373 U.S. 368: 1963). The voting practice at issue was the unit system, a technique by which statewide officials were nominated in Georgia. While the Court distinguished this process from legislative districting, it held that the Equal Protection Clause required persons to have an equal vote. Specific reference to "one man, one vote" was made in *Gray*. The following year the Court applied the one man–one vote standard to apportionment of congressional districts in *Wesberry* v. *Sanders* (376 U.S. 1: 1964).

Reynolds v. Sims, 377 U.S. 533, 84 S.Ct. 1362, 12 L.Ed.2d 506 (1964)   Established requirements for the apportionment of bicameral state legislatures. *Reynolds v. Sims*, accompanied by several companion cases from other states, held that the one man–one vote principle applied to both houses of state legislatures. *Reynolds* involved a challenge of the apportionment of Alabama House and Senate districts, a districting system allegedly based on the 1900 census. A six-justice majority struck down both the existing districts as well as a proposal based on the federal concept, a plan that apportioned only one house on the basis of population. The Court's opinion was written by Chief Justice Warren, who saw the central question as whether there are any constitutionally cognizable principles that would justify departures from the basic standard of equality among voters in the apportionment of seats in state legislatures. The gravity of the issue was reflected in the observation that "the right of suffrage can be denied by a debasement or dilution of the weight of a citizen's vote just as effectively as by wholly prohibiting the free exercise of the franchise." Chief Justice Warren declared that legislators represent people, not trees or acres. Legislators are elected by voters, not farms or cities or economic interests. People must have an unimpairable capacity to elect representatives, and the weight of a citizen's vote cannot be made to depend on where he lives. Population is of necessity the starting point for the consideration of, and the controlling criterion for judgment in, legislative apportionment controversies. The constitutional demands of equal protection require that a legislative vote is not diluted when compared with other citizens living elsewhere in the state. Equal protection also demands that both chambers of state legislatures be apportioned on the basis of population. The Court rejected the federal analogy approach calling it "inappropriate and irrelevant." Proposing such plans is often "little more than an after-the-fact rationalization offered in defense of maladjusted state apportionment arrangements." The Court found that electing both houses on the basis of population was compatible with the concept of bicameralism. It said the composition and complexion of the two houses would differ substantially. Thus population-based representation, "as nearly of equal population as is practicable," became the rule, with only small deviations allowable for flexibility or to prevent gerrymandering. Justices Harlan, Stewart, and Clark dissented. They called the decision "profoundly ill-advised and constitutionally impermissible." All three felt that a state ought to be able to choose any electoral legislative structure it thinks is best suited to the interests, temper, and customs of its people. The dissenters rejected the idea that equal protection requirements could only be met by "uncritical, simplistic, and heavy-handed application of sixth-grade arithmetic." *See also* BAKER v. CARR (369 U.S. 186: 1962), p. 343; APPORTIONMENT, p. 384; MOBILE v. BOLDEN (446 U.S. 55: 1980), p. 346; SOUTH CAROLINA v. KATZENBACH (394 U.S. 301: 1966), p. 348.

Significance   Reynolds v. Sims (377 U.S. 533: 1964) established stringent population guidelines for the apportionment of districts in state legislatures. The extent to which the Warren Court would tolerate deviation from the one man–one vote standard was reflected in *Lucas* v. *Forty-Fourth General Assembly* (377 U.S. 713: 1964), one of the companions to *Reynolds.* In *Lucas,* the Court rejected a plan with a 3.6 to 1 variance in one house and a 1.7 to 1 variance in the other house on equal protection grounds. The ruling was made despite approval of the plan in a statewide referendum. The Burger Court permitted deviations of slightly more than 16 percent in *Mahan* v. *Howell* (410 U.S. 315: 1973). The variance was permitted because it was done "to advance the rational state policy of respecting the boundaries of political subdivisions" and did not otherwise exceed constitutional limitations. Following *Reynolds,* the Court was asked to consider whether the one man–one vote rule applied to local units of government. In *Avery* v. *Midland County* (390 U.S. 474: 1968), the Court held that when local governments elect representatives from single-member districts, good faith attempts must be undertaken to make those districts equal in population. The considerations given to equal protection in apportioning legislative districts have been defined as carrying over to other electoral situations. In *Kramer* v. *Union Free School District* (395 U.S. 621: 1969), the Court held that a state could not restrict participation in school district elections to district property owners and parents of children in the school system. Despite the original controversy and the contention that representation might effectively be calculated on a basis other than population, the democratic premise underpinning *Reynolds* has been generally accepted.

Reapportionment and Race

Mobile v. **Bolden,** **446 U.S. 55, 100 S.Ct. 1490, 64 L.Ed. 2d 47 (1980)**   Upheld a municipal at-large election process against claims that such a system diluted minority group voting influence. *Mobile* v. *Bolden* considered whether malapportionment of legislative districts violated the Equal Protection Clause of the Fourteenth Amendment because it debased the value of an individual's vote. A Federal District Court found a constitutional violation in the election process in Mobile, Alabama, and ordered that a single-member district structure replace the current at-large system. The Supreme Court found the at-large plan to be constitutionally adequate and reversed the District Court in a 6–3 decision. Critics of the at-large or multi-member district approach argue that some elements of the electorate are unrepresented. The Court noted that criticism of the at-large election is rooted in its winner-take-all aspect and its tendency to submerge minorities. The specific question posed in *Bolden* was whether the at-large scheme had been established for the purpose of reducing the impact of black voters. No finding was made by the trial court that black voters had been deprived of the privilege of voting or hampered in the registration process. The Court had previously found in such cases as *White* v. *Regester* (412 U.S. 755: 1973) that the multi-member election system was not unconstitutional per se. Constitutional violations occur in apportionment systems only "if their purpose were invidiously to minimize or cancel out the voting potential of racial or ethnic minorities." To demonstrate such a violation, a plaintiff must prove that the disputed plan was conceived or operated as a purposeful device to further racial discrimination. A showing that a particular group has not elected representatives in proportion to its members is not sufficient. The Court said that while black candidates in Mobile have been defeated, that fact alone does not work a constitutional deprivation. The Court also rejected the relevance of discrimination by the city in the context of municipal employment and the dispensing of public services. Evidence of possible discrimination by city officials in other contexts is "tenuous and circumstantial evidence of the constitutional invalidity of the electoral system under which they attained their offices." The Burger Court concluded that past cases show "the Court has sternly set its face against the claim, however phrased, that the Constitution somehow guarantees proportional representation." Justices Brennan, Marshall, and White dissented. They argued that a sufficient discriminatory impact had been shown. Justice Marshall said the Court's decision meant that "in the absence of proof of discrimination by the State, the right to vote provides the politically powerless with nothing more than the right to cast meaningless ballots." *See also* BAKER V. CARR (369 U.S. 186: 1962), p. 343; APPORTIONMENT, p. 384; REYNOLDS V. SIMS (377 U.S. 533: 1964), p. 344.

Significance   Mobile v. Bolden (446 U.S. 55: 1980) held that discriminatory intent must be demonstrated before an electoral system can be found constitutionally defective. But what if the intent is benevolent? What if an apportionment plan is designed to make more likely the electoral success of minorities? The Court upheld such a plan in *United Jewish Organizations of Williamsburgh, Inc.* v. *Carey* (430 U.S. 144: 1977), where district lines in New York were redrawn to enhance the possibility of electing racial minorities to the state legislature. The plan split a group of Hasidic Jews, formerly concentrated in a single state Assembly and Senate district, into two districts. Suit was brought claiming voter reassignment had been based on race. The Court upheld the redistricting plan, finding that other voters in the county involved were not denied an opportunity to participate in the political process. The Court also held that considerations of race could be made in an attempt to comply with provisions of the Voting Rights Act of 1965, as in *South Carolina* v. *Katzenbach* (383 U.S. 301: 1966, p. 348). As long as considerations of race were directed toward the achievement of racial equality, they were permissible. Plans that actually disenfranchise are clearly unconstitutional, however. In *Gomillion* v. *Lightfoot* (364 U.S. 339: 1960), the Court held that a plan that restructured the boundaries of a city so that most black residents were placed outside the city limits was in violation of both the Fourteenth and Fifteenth Amendments.

Voting Rights Act of 1965

South Carolina v. ***Katzenbach,*** **383 U.S. 301, 86 S.Ct. 803, 15 L.Ed.2d 769 (1966)**   Upheld the Voting Rights Act of 1965. *South Carolina* v. *Katzenbach* explored how the Fifteenth Amendment protects the right to vote and provides Congress with authority to enact appropriate legislation to further that objective. The Voting Rights Act of 1965 abolished devices, such as the literacy test and accumulated poll taxes, by which citizens had been disqualified from voting. The act also provided for extensive federal supervision of elections and required that any new conditions of voter eligibility be reviewed by the attorney general before implementation. Provisions of the act were triggered if less than 50 percent of citizens of voting age were registered to vote or where fewer than 50 percent of the voting age population had participated in the 1964 presidential election. Chief Justice Warren wrote the opinion of the Court. He noted that the purpose of the act was "to banish the blight of racial discrimination in voting, which has infected the electoral process in parts of our country for nearly a century." The Court accorded great deference to an act dedicated to such a purpose even if Congress had exercised power in an inventive manner. Referring to the stringent remedies and their implementation without prior adjudication, the Court said that litigation was inadequate when discrimination was widespread and persistent. Following nearly a hundred years of systematic resistance to the Fifteenth Amendment, Congress might well decide to shift the advantage of time and inertia from the perpetrators of the evil to its victims. The targeted nature of the act's coverage was a reasonable legislative option. Congress determined that voting discrimination "presently occurs in certain sections of the country. In acceptable legislative fashion, Congress chose to limit its attention to the geographic areas where immediate action seemed necessary." In sum, the Court viewed the act as an array of potent weapons marshalled to combat the evil of voting discrimination. They were weapons that constitute "a valid means for carrying out the commands of the Fifteenth Amendment." *See also* BAKER V. CARR (369 U.S. 186: 1962), p. 343; FIFTEENTH AMENDMENT, p. 412; MOBILE V. BOLDEN (446 U.S. 55: 1980), p. 346; REYNOLDS V. SIMS (377 U.S. 533: 1964), p. 344.

Significance   In upholding the Voting Rights Act of 1965, *South Carolina* v. *Katzenbach* (383 U.S. 301: 1966) targeted voting practices involving non–English-speaking voters for the first time. The act had provisions intended for the large Spanish-speaking Puerto Rican population in New York. They were upheld on equal protection grounds in *Katzenbach* v. *Morgan* (384 U.S. 641: 1966). The act had a five-year limitation but was extended in 1970, 1975, and 1982. The 1970 extension banned the use of literacy tests. The same extension also set the minimum voting age at 18 throughout the country. The Court held in *Oregon* v. *Mitchell* (400 U.S. 112: 1970), however, that Congress could only establish age qualifications for federal elections. States retained control over state and local elections. Ratification of the Twenty-sixth Amendment in 1971 superseded the Court's decision in *Oregon* v. *Mitchell.* Primary elections also have attained constitutional status. After several decisions to the contrary, the Court held in *United States* v. *Classic* (313 U.S. 299: 1941) that the federal government could regulate primaries because of their integral role in the overall election process. In *Smith* v. *Allwright* (321 U.S. 649: 1944), the Court found that political parties conducting racially exclusive primaries were acting as an agent of the state and thus were in violation of the Fifteenth Amendment. The Court also outlawed the poll tax for state elections in *Harper* v. *Virginia State Board of Elections* (383 U.S. 663: 1966), holding that such a tax discriminated in an invidious fashion.

Residency Requirements

***Shapiro* v. *Thompson,* 394 U.S. 618, 89 S.Ct. 1322, 22 L.Ed.2d 600 (1969)**   Held that residency requirements for welfare eligibility impermissibly restricted the right to move freely from state to state. *Shapiro* v. *Thompson* was a pivotal case in the development of expanded equal protection coverage under the Fourteenth Amendment. Once the Court decided the Equal Protection Clause might apply to classifications other than racial ones, the Court was forced to examine the scope of the protection afforded and the standards by which classifications might be assessed. It determined the legislative classifications that interfered with "fundamental rights" were "suspect" and demanded "close scrutiny" by the courts. *Shapiro* involved a woman trying to obtain support under the Aid to Families with Dependent Children (AFDC) public assistance program. She was denied assistance because she could not satisfy the state's one-year residency requirement. The Court found the residency requirement invalid in a 6–3 decision. The Court said the effect of the waiting period requirement was to create two classes of needy resident families indistinguishable from each other except that one is composed of residents who have resided in the state a year or more, and the other is composed of residents who have resided less than a year. The purpose of the requirement was to deter migration of needy persons into the state, and thus preserve the fiscal integrity of state public assistance programs. But the Court said inhibiting migration is constitutionally impermissible. It is a long-recognized right of citizens "to be free to travel throughout the length and breadth of our land uninhibited by statutes, rules, or regulations which unreasonably burden or restrain this movement." The right of interstate travel was held to be a fundamental right, and a classification that would "chill" the assertion of such a right is "patently unconstitutional." Classifications such as this that touch on the fundamental right of interstate movement must be assessed by the stricter standard of whether they promote a compelling state interest, and the arguments submitted by the state were not compelling. Chief Justice Warren and Justices Harlan and Black dissented, with Justice Harlan saying the branch of the compelling interest doctrine associated with fundamental rights, as distinct from the branch dealing with suspect classes, is "unfortunate, unnecessary, and unwise when extended beyond racial classifications." *See also* EQUAL PROTECTION CLAUSE, p. 313; FOURTEENTH AMENDMENT, p. 412; RIGHT TO TRAVEL, p. 459.

Significance   *Shapiro* v. *Thompson* (394 U.S. 618: 1969) led to the elimination of many residency requirements where provision of public services is involved, and it reduced voting registration residency requirements to a short duration. Some residency requirements have survived, however, as in the case of state university tuition, e.g., *Vlandis* v. *Kline* (412 U.S. 441: 1973), and divorces, e.g., *Sosna* v. *Iowa* (419 U.S. 393: 1975). *Shapiro* was the first of a series of cases involving access to public assistance as a matter of right. *Shapiro* did not directly address the question of whether welfare was to be protected as a fundamental right. Soon after *Shapiro*, the Court again refused to address that problem in *Dandridge* v. *Williams* (397 U.S. 471: 1970). It upheld a ceiling on monthly aid to be received by any one family. The ceiling policy was challenged as overbroad, but the Court said the concept of overreaching "has no place in cases which establish social and economic regulations." While some aid payment disparities may be produced, the imperfection of classifications does not necessarily produce equal protection violations as long as there is a reasonable basis for the regulation. In *Jefferson* v. *Hackney* (406 U.S. 535: 1972), the Court allowed Texas to reduce aid payment limits to AFDC recipients as well as those receiving Old Age Assistance, Aid to the Blind, and Aid for Permanently and Totally Disabled Persons. The recipients of AFDC were overwhelmingly black and Hispanic, while the other categories of recipients were largely white. The Court held that the aid levels of the various programs need not be comparable. In *Graham* v. *Richardson* (403 U.S. 265: 1971, p. 351), the Court did invalidate a state law imposing limitations on access to welfare benefits on the basis of alienage. It also ruled in *Goldberg* v. *Kelly* (397 U.S. 254: 1970) that welfare recipients are entitled to formal hearings before welfare benefits can be terminated. While the Court has established some limits on the use of residency requirements and protected access to public assistance benefits, none of its cases has established residency as a suspect classification. Neither has welfare been established as a fundamental right, although the United States recognized the special position of various forms of welfare by signing the Universal Declaration of Human Rights in 1948.

Alienage

Graham v. Richardson, 403 U.S. 365, 91 S.Ct. 1848, 29 L.Ed.2d 534 (1971) Prohibited state classifications based on alienage. *Graham* v. *Richardson* held that classifications based on alienage were "suspect" and subject to a review more stringent than the rational basis test. Richardson was a lawfully admitted resident alien who had become permanently and totally disabled. She applied for public assistance benefits under provisions of the Social Security Act that offer financial assistance to persons with disabilities she had. She met all requirements for benefits except for a 15-year residency requirement for aliens. The Supreme Court ruled the requirement to be unconstitutional on Fourteenth Amendment grounds in a unanimous decision. Justice Blackmun's opinion for the Court said that states generally have been accorded broad discretion to classify, especially in the areas of "economics and social welfare." Yet "classifications based on alienage, like those based on nationality or race, are inherently suspect and subject to close judicial scrutiny." Aliens are a prime example of a discrete and insular minority for whom such heightened judicial solicitude is appropriate. The Arizona requirement was defective because it created two classes of needy persons, indistinguishable except with respect to whether they are or are not citizens of the United States. Arizona sought to justify its classification on the basis of "a special public interest in favoring its own citizens over aliens in the distribution of limited resources such as welfare benefits." The Court disagreed that such a special interest existed even though Arizona had "a valid interest in preserving the fiscal integrity of its programs." But a state cannot accomplish even valid purposes by invidious distinctions, and "the saving of welfare costs cannot justify an otherwise invidious classification." The fiscal integrity rationale was found no more compelling in *Graham* than in *Shapiro* v. *Thompson* (394 U.S. 618: 1969, p. 349). Unlike *Shapiro*, however, the justification is "particularly inappropriate where the discriminated class consists of aliens." Aliens, like citizens, pay taxes and may be called into the armed forces. Unlike the short-term residents involved in *Shapiro*, aliens may live within a state for many years, work in the state, and contribute to the economic growth of the state. Thus no special public interest approach can apply to distribution of tax benefits to which aliens have contributed on an equal basis with residents of the state. Finally, the Court held that the federal government has overriding and superior authority in this field. Federal power is preemptive of state regulation, and Congress "has not seen fit to impose any burden or restriction on aliens who become indigent after their entry into the United States." *See also* EQUAL PROTECTION CLAUSE, p. 313; FOURTEENTH AMENDMENT, p. 412; *SHAPIRO* v. *THOMPSON* (394 U.S. 618: 1969), p. 349.

Significance   *Graham* v. *Richardson* (403 U.S. 365: 1971) found alienage to be a suspect classification when used by states as the basis for denial of welfare benefits. In *Sugarman* v. *Dougall* (413 U.S. 634: 1973), the Court used the *Graham* rationale to strike down a state civil service statute precluding aliens from competing for state civil service jobs. Alienage does not retain suspect status in all contexts, however. In *Matthews* v. *Diaz* (426 U.S. 67: 1976), the Court unanimously upheld a Social Security Act provision denying medicare supplemental medical insurance to aliens unless they had been admitted for permanent residence and had resided in the United States for at least five years. The Court deferred to the federal government's comprehensive authority regarding immigration and citizenship and evaluated the classification using the less stringent rationality test. Alienage classifications are also subject to the rational standard test rather than the compelling state interest test associated with strict scrutiny when vital governmental functions are involved. In *Foley* v. *Connelie* (435 U.S. 291: 1978), the Court upheld a New York regulation limiting state police appointments to citizens. Suggesting that it would be inappropriate to require every statutory exclusion of aliens to clear the high hurdle of strict scrutiny, the Court held that the police function is a basic function of government and the right to govern may be reserved to citizens. In *Ambach* v. *Norwich* (441 U.S. 68: 1979), the Court upheld a statute preventing a noncitizen from becoming certified to teach in the public schools. Again using the rational basis test, the Court held that a state could restrict the performance of those functions that go to the heart of representative government to persons who have become part of the process of self-government. The same approach was used in upholding a California law requiring "peace officers," including deputy probation officers, to be citizens. (See *Cabell* v. *Chavez-Salido*, 454 U.S. 432: 1982.) It is clear the Supreme Court subjects to strict scrutiny any restriction on aliens that affects their economic interests, but it uses a s stringent standard when the restriction involves political activity.

Illegitimacy

***Weber* v. *Aetna Casualty and Surety Company,* 406 U.S. 164, 92 S.Ct. 1400, 31 L.Ed.2d 768 (1972)**   Struck down a state classification based on legitimacy as a violation of the Equal Protection Clause of the Fourteenth Amendment. *Weber* v. *Aetna Casualty and Surety Company* examined the classification of illegitimacy and held that a state handling claims for worker's compensation benefits may not disadvantage the unacknowledged illegitimate child of a deceased worker. Henry Stokes had died from employment-related injuries. At the time of his death, Stokes was living with four legitimate minor children, one unacknowledged minor, and Willie Mae Weber, the mother of the unacknowledged minor. Stokes's wife had been committed to a mental institution prior to his death. After Stokes's death, a second illegitimate child of Stokes and Weber was born. The Louisiana worker's compensation law places unacknowledged illegitimate children in a class of "other dependents," a class of lower status than that of "children." The "other dependents" class may recover worker's compensation benefits only if the higher class of survivors does not exhaust the maximum benefits. The four legitimate offspring of Stokes were awarded the statutory maximum, leaving nothing to the two unacknowledged illegitimate children. In an 8–1 decision, the Supreme Court said this statutory scheme violated the Equal Protection Clause of the Fourteenth Amendment. Justice Powell's opinion declared the statute to be unacceptable even though it was limited to unacknowledged illegitimate children and did not prohibit recovery altogether. The less favorable position into which the unacknowledged illegitimate child was placed was said to be fatal because "such a child may suffer as much from the loss of a parent as a child born within wedlock or any illegitimate later acknowledged." Louisiana law precluded acknowledgement of the illegitimate child even if the father had wished to do so. Justice Powell observed that "the burdens of illegitimacy, already weighty, become doubly so when neither parent nor child can legally lighten them." He suggested the Court's inquiry into such cases turned on two questions: What legitimate state interest does the classification promote? and, What fundamental personal rights might the classification endanger? The Court did not take issue with Louisiana's interest in protecting legitimate family relationships, but it did not feel the challenged statute promoted that interest. "Persons will not shun illicit relations because their offspring may not one day reap the benefits of workmen's compensation." While illegitimacy has been socially condemned through the ages, Justice Powell thought that visiting this condemnation on the head of an infant is illogical and unjust. Penalizing the illegitimate child is simply an ineffectual way of deterring the parent. Justice Rehnquist felt the Court was engaged in a highly subjective review of what constituted legitimate state interests and how those interests might be advanced in relation to fundamental personal rights. He would have deferred to Louisiana's distinction between legitimate and unacknowledged illegitimate children. *See also* FOURTEENTH AMENDMENT, p. 412; RIGHT OF PRIVACY, p. 316.

Significance   *Weber* v. *Aetna Casualty and Surety Company* (406 U.S. 164: 1972) said that a state could not deny equal benefit recovery opportunities to unacknowledged illegitimate children. But the

Supreme Court has never been able to determine conclusively the exact character of illegitimacy as a classification or the level of scrutiny it deserves. The Court has scrutinized the problem more closely than the rationality test would require, but it has never found illegitimacy to be a suspect class deserving the strictest scrutiny. Examples of the Court's criss-crossing path in dealing with this classification follow. In *Levy* v. *Louisiana* (391 U.S. 68: 1968), the Court struck down a law that denied unacknowledged illegitimate children opportunity to recover wrongful death damages for their mothers. The statute was viewed as sufficiently arbitrary that impermissible discrimination could be found by use of standards less demanding than strict scrutiny. In *Labine* v. *Vincent* (401 U.S. 532: 1972), however, the Court upheld a state succession law that denied illegitimate children inheritance rights equal to those of legitimate children. The Court said a state had the power to protect and strengthen family life as well as to regulate the disposition of property. *Weber* was next in sequence and resembled more closely the approach taken in *Levy*. *Matthews* v. *Lucas* (427 U.S. 495: 1976) then held that a requirement demanding proof of dependency by illegitimate children seeking social security death benefits was a rational means of protecting against survivor benefits being paid to children who were not dependent. The Court noted in *Lucas* that statutory classifications based on illegitimacy fall into "a realm of less than strict scrutiny." Claiming that such less-than-strict scrutiny was not "toothless," the Court a year later struck down an Illinois statute that precluded illegitimate children from inheriting property from their fathers in *Trimble* v. *Gordon* (430 U.S. 762: 1977). Using a rationale closely resembling that of *Weber,* the Court found the classification too remote from a legitimate state purpose to pass review. Finally, in *Pickett* v. *Brown* (103 S.Ct. 2199: 1983), the Court disallowed a statute barring paternity suits brought on behalf of illegitimate children more than two years after their birth. The Court unanimously concluded that the state infringed upon the illegitimate's opportunity to secure support and that the two-year period did not sufficiently advance the state's interest in preventing litigation of stale and possibly fraudulent claims.

Age

Massachusetts Board of Retirement v. Murgia, 427 U.S. 307, 96 S.Ct. 2562, 49 L.Ed.2d 520 (1976)   Upheld a mandatory retirement age of fifty for uniformed police officers against Fourteenth Amendment challenge. *Massachusetts Board of Retirement* v. *Murgia* illustrates the rationality test for invalidating classifications. In reviewing challenged classification schemes, the Supreme Court has used different evaluative criteria or standards, the least stringent of which is the rationality test. It would invalidate classifications only if they are arbitrary and have no demonstrable justification. The rationality test is typically used in reviewing age-based classifications. In *Murgia,* a provision of state law required that uniformed state police officers retire at age fifty. Key to the Court's holding in the case was the criterion used to assess the mandatory retirement policy. Murgia argued that the age classification was a "suspect class" and entitled to a "strict scrutiny" review, a more stringent review than that associated with the rationality test. The Court disagreed and held that Murgia did not belong to a suspect class. His claim could be reviewed using the rationality test. In a 7–1 decision, Justice Stevens not participating, the Court upheld the mandatory retirement law and determined that the strict scrutiny approach should be used only when the classification impermissibly interferes with the exercise of a fundamental right or operates to the particular disadvantage of a suspect class. In the Court's view the Massachusetts policy involved neither situation. It proceeded using the rational basis standard, a relatively relaxed criterion reflecting the Court's awareness that the drawing of lines creating distinctions is peculiarly and unavoidably a legislative task. The legislature's actions are presumed to be valid under this approach, and "perfection in making the necessary classification is neither possible nor necessary." In this instance, the legislature sought "to protect the public by assuring the physical preparedness of its uniformed police." Given the fact that physical ability generally declines with age, the Court found the mandatory retirement policy rationally related to the state's objective. It concluded by saying the choice of policy by Massachusetts may not be the best means and that a more just and humane system could possibly be devised, but under the rational basis test the enactment did not deny equal protection. Justice Marshall dissented from the use of the less demanding test because of its failure sufficiently to safeguard equal protection interests. He would have preferred a flexible standard that would have examined more carefully the means chosen by Massachusetts. To Justice Marshall, the means chosen "forced retirement of officers at age fifty and is therefore so overinclusive that it must fall." *See also* EQUAL PROTECTION CLAUSE, p. 313; FOURTEENTH AMENDMENT, p. 412; CLASSIFICATION, p. 394.

Significance Massachusetts Board of Retirement v. Murgia (427 U.S. 307: 1976) said a mandatory retirement policy for uniformed police officers was rational. Soon after *Murgia,* the Court upheld a mandatory retirement policy for Foreign Service officers in *Vance* v. *Bradley* (440 U.S. 93: 1979). Again the Court found a retirement policy rationally related to the legislative goal of assuring the professional capacity of persons holding critical public service positions. In this case, Foreign Service officers have to undergo special rigors associated with overseas duty. Justice Marshall dissented and reiterated his call for a more demanding standard in reviewing such legislation. In *Equal Employment Opportunity Commission* v. *Wyoming* (75 L.Ed.2d 18: 1983), the Court ruled that state and local governments are not immune from provisions of the Age Discrimination in Employment Act. This act prohibits employer discrimination against any employee or potential employee because of age. The Court made it clear, however, that the judgment did not compel a state to abandon policies that can demonstrate age as a bona fide occupational qualification. Central to the decisions in both *Murgia* and *Bradley* was the holding that compulsory retirement would better ensure good job performance by limiting the age of employees. Both cases sought to maximize the physical capabilities of persons performing certain lay functions. The question of physical qualifications for professional training programs was addressed in *Southeastern Community College* v. *Davis* (440 U.S. 979: 1979). Davis sought admission to a registered nursing program at a state community college despite a hearing disability. She was denied admission. She filed suit under the Rehabilitation Act of 1973, which prohibits discrimination against "an otherwise qualified handicapped person, solely by reason of his handicap." The Court unanimously held that an educational institution may impose reasonable physical qualifications for admission to a clinical training program. The Court did not require the college to make program adjustments to accommodate handicapped persons.

Wealth

San Antonio Independent School District v. Rodriguez, 411 U.S. 1, 93 S.Ct. 1278, 36 L.Ed.2d 16 (1973) Approved a state system for financing public education using locally levied property taxes. *San Antonio Independent School District* v. *Rodriguez* raised two provocative questions. First, Is access to public education one of the fundamental rights a state can limit only by showing a compelling interest? Second, Does indigency constitute a suspect class under evolving equal protection standards under the Fourteenth Amendment? The San Antonio case involved a challenge of the funding mechanisms for public education in Texas. A portion of the educational costs was provided by state appropriations, with local districts supplementing these revenues by locally levied property taxes. Suit was brought asserting that this funding approach created inequities among school districts because some were disadvantaged by low or limited property tax bases. It was argued that the differences in property tax yields produced impermissible disparities in per pupil expenditures. In a 5–4 decision, the Court rejected the argument that wealth discrimination had occurred or that a fundamental right had been violated. The Court distinguished *Rodriguez* from prior cases involving indigency. Indigents are unable to pay for a particular benefit so that "an absolute deprivation of a meaningful opportunity to enjoy that benefit occurs." Even in the poorest of school districts, however, children were receiving some kind of public education. This led the Court to conclude that the Texas system "does not operate to the particular disadvantage of any suspect class." Even showing wealth discrimination would not have provided "an adequate basis for invoking strict scrutiny." Neither is education a fundamental right. While noting historical dedication to public education in the United States, the Court said the importance of a service performed by the state does not determine whether it must be regarded as fundamental for purposes of examination under the Equal Protection Clause. The Court also thought the Texas system was implemented in an effort to extend public education and improve its quality. That differentiated it from other situations in which the Court had applied strict scrutiny. Furthermore, for the Court to void the educational financing system in Texas would require it to intrude in an area in which it had traditionally deferred to state legislatures. The Court said it was impossible to devise a scheme of taxation free of all discriminatory impacts. Although the Texas system "provides less freedom of choice with respect to expenditures from some districts than for others, the existence of some inequality in the manner in which the state's rationale is achieved is not alone a sufficient basis for striking down the entire system." Insofar as wealth was concerned, the Equal Protection Clause "does not require absolute equality or precisely equal advantages." Justices Brennan, Marshall, Douglas, and White dissented. They criticized the majority's "rigidified approach to equal protection analysis." The minority would have deemed education a fundamental right and found the Texas financing system invidiously discriminatory. *See also* EQUAL PROTECTION CLAUSE, p. 313; FOURTEENTH AMENDMENT, p. 412; CLASSIFICATION, p. 394.

Significance   *San Antonio Independent School District* v. *Rodriguez* (411 U.S. 1: 1973) upheld a school financing system that produced disparities in local tax yields against claims that such inequities constituted impermissible economic discrimination. Similarly, in *James* v. *Valtierra* (402 U.S. 137: 1971), the Court had upheld a state constitutional requirement that all low-income housing projects be approved by local referendum. It said a procedure that disadvantages a particular group does not always deny equal protection. Wealth classification has been invalidated when it interferes with a fundamental right. In *Harper* v. *Virginia State Board of Education* (383 U.S. 663: 1966), the Court declared a state poll tax unconstitutional because it discriminated against the poor. The Court said the qualification to vote should have no relation to wealth. The impacts of indigency have also been extensively recognized with respect to ensuring the fundamental rights of those accused of crimes. The vulnerability of indigents in this context is seen in *Tate* v. *Short* (401 U.S. 391: 1971), where the Court held that an indigent person could not be jailed as a substitute for payment of penal fines.

Gender

Frontiero v. Richardson, 411 U.S. 677, 93 S.Ct. 1764, 36 L.Ed.2d 583 (1973)   Voided statutes treating servicemen and servicewomen differently in the allocation of housing allowances and medical benefits. *Frontiero* v. *Richardson* illustrates the extent of the Court's disagreement about classification by gender and whether it ought to be scrutinized. The Burger Court first utilized the Equal Protection Clause to invalidate a gender-based classification in the early 1970s. While the Court has continued to hold that sex discrimination is forbidden by the Equal Protection Clause of the Fourteenth Amendment, it has failed to develop any consensus on the matter. *Frontiero* involved a female air force lieutenant who sought higher housing and medical allowances by having her husband declared a dependent. Such benefits were automatically granted with respect to the wife of a male member of the uniformed services. Frontiero argued that the policy was discriminatory in two ways. From a procedural standpoint, only female members were required to demonstrate spouse dependency. As a matter of substance, a male member receives benefits even if he provides less than half of his wife's support. A similarly situated female does not receive such benefits. With only Justice Rehnquist dissenting, the Court invalidated the statutory provisions. The eight-justice majority was fragmented, however, on the standard by which gender classification ought to be evaluated. Justices Brennan, Douglas, White, and Marshall viewed sex classifications, like those of race, alienage, and national origin, as inherently suspect and therefore subject to close judicial scrutiny. Justice Brennan noted a long history of sex discrimination, rationalized by an attitude of romantic paternalism that, "in practical effect, put women not on a pedestal, but in a cage." Sex is an "immutable characteristic determined solely by the accident of birth." To impose special disabilities on women because of their sex runs counter to the concept that legal burdens should bear some relationship to individual responsibility. What gives sex classification its suspect status, argued Justice Brennan, is that the "sex characteristic frequently bears no relation to ability to perform or contribute to society." The result is that women are often invidiously relegated to inferior legal status without regard to actual capabilities. A policy achieving nothing more than administrative convenience through different treatment by gender is "the very kind of legislative choice forbidden by the Equal Protection Clause." Chief Justice Burger and Justices Powell, Stewart, and Blackmun also found the statute unconstitutionally discriminatory, but refused to go so far as to label gender an inherently suspect class. They resolved the case using the less stringent rational basis test. Justice Powell said an expansion to suspect status had far-reaching implications, but it was also preemptive and premature given current consideration of the Equal Rights Amendment. *See also* COUNTY OF WASHINGTON V. GUNTHER (450 U.S. 907: 1981), p. 363; EQUAL PROTECTION CLAUSE, p. 313; KAHN V. SHEVIN (416 U.S. 351: 1973), p. 365; ROSTKER V. GOLDBERG (453 U.S. 57: 1981), p. 361; CLASSIFICATION, p. 394.

Significance   Frontiero v. Richardson (411 U.S. 677: 1973) prohibited differential treatment of servicemen and servicewomen. Until the 1970s, the Court found no constitutional defect in sex-based classifications. In *Goesaert* v. *Cleary* (335 U.S. 464: 1948), the Court upheld a law denying a bartenders' license to all women except the wives or daughters of bar owners, saying that states were not precluded from drawing "a sharp line between the sexes." *Reed* v. *Reed* (404 U.S. 71: 1971), however, struck down an Idaho law giving preference to males over females in administering estates. Using the rationality test, the Court unanimously concluded that the Equal Protection Clause does not permit states to place persons into different classes on the basis of criteria wholly unrelated to the objective of the statute. In *Stanton* v. *Stanton* (421 U.S. 7: 1975) the Court carried the holdings of *Reed* and *Frontiero* to a Utah statute that set the age of majority at 21 for males and 18 for females. The case involved a divorce decree ordering child support payments for a son through age 21 and a daughter only through age 18. While again refusing to find sex an inherently suspect class, the Court held that the statute contained nothing rational relative to the provision of child support. Notwithstanding the "old notions" used to justify the decree, the Court said the classification "does not survive an equal protection attack." No test could be used, "compelling state interest, rationality, or anything in between." In *Craig* v. *Boren* (429 U.S. 190: 1976), the Court struck down an Oklahoma statute that permitted females to buy 3.2 percent beer at age 18 while prohibiting males to do so until age 21. The Court said gender classifications must serve important governmental objectives and be substantially related to reaching those objectives, and the Oklahoma statute did not survive those criteria.

Rostker v. Goldberg, 453 U.S. 57, 101 S.Ct. 2646, 69 L.Ed.2d 478 (1981) Ruled that Congress constitutionally could exclude women from registering for a possible military draft without violating the due process limitations of the Fifth Amendment. *Rostker* v. *Goldberg* involved the Military Selective Service Act and the power it gave the president to require "every male citizen" and male resident aliens of appropriate age to register for potential conscription. Suit was brought by Goldberg and a number of others subject to the registration order by President Carter, claiming the gender classification violated the Due Process Clause of the Fifth Amendment. The Court disagreed in a 6–3 decision. Justice Rehnquist delivered the opinion of the Court. He said that congressional judgments warrant particular deference when the issue involves raising and regulating the armed forces. Congressional authority is at its apogee in this policy area. Against that background, the Court turned to the issue of gender-based registration. Unlike previous sex discrimination cases, this one involved an enactment in which the legislative body "did not act unthinkingly or reflexively." The decision to exempt women from registration was not the accidental by-product of a traditional way of thinking about women. On the contrary, the policy was considered at great length, and Congress clearly expressed its purpose and intent. The Court upheld the classification primarily because males and females are not similarly situated with respect to combat duty. Women are statutorily restricted from such duty. By viewing the draft of combat troops in time of national emergency and registration for that draft as part of the same function, the Court found basis for distinguishing the situations of males and females. Justice Rehnquist said the Constitution "requires that Congress treat similarly situated persons similarly, not that it engage in gestures of superficial equality." Congress was entitled to focus on the question of military need rather than equity. Justices White, Brennan, and Marshall dissented. Justice White pointed out that a draft could recruit personnel for both combat and noncombat needs. In his view women should not have been excluded for that reason alone. Justice Marshall rejected the categorical exclusion of women and called for heightened scrutiny of gender-based classifications. Justice Marshall was unpersuaded that the combat restrictions on women were relevant to the registration process, nor did he think the classification advanced any legitimate purpose. Registration of women "in no way obstructs the government interest in preparing for a draft of combat troops." *See also* COUNTY OF WASHINGTON V. GUNTHER (450 U.S. 907: 1981), p. 363; EQUAL PROTECTION CLAUSE, p. 313; FRONTIERO V. RICHARDSON (411 U.S. 677: 1973), p. 359.

Significance   Rostker v. Goldberg (453 U.S. 57: 1981) held that Congress had a rational basis for male-only draft registration. Despite its greater receptivity to claims of sex discrimination, the Burger Court has not found gender classification to be inherently suspect. In *Personnel Administrator* v. *Feeney* (442 U.S. 256: 1979), the Court upheld a state policy extending preferential status to military veterans for state employment. It found no discriminatory intent in the advantage given veterans over nonveterans, a class composed of both men and women, despite the policy's adverse impact on women. See *Washington* v. *Davis* (426 U.S. 229: 1976), p. 333. In *Parham* v. *Hughes* (441 U.S. 347: 1979), the Court upheld a Georgia statute that permitted fathers of legitimate or legitimated children to sue for the wrongful death of the child. The Court found the policy to be a rational means for dealing with the matter of proving paternity. The Court also held that the policy did not reflect any overbroad generalizations about men as a class. Finally, in *Michael M.* v. *Sonoma County Superior Court* (450 U.S. 464: 1981), the Court upheld a statutory rape law prohibiting sexual intercourse with a female under 18 years of age. The Court ruled that statutes cannot make overbroad generalizations based on sex that are entirely unrelated to any differences between men and women. The statute was permissible because it addressed a substantial inequity between men and women based on "the harmful and inescapably identifiable consequences of teenage pregnancy." Further, the risk of pregnancy "constitutes a substantial deterrence to young females." The statute creating criminal sanctions for males "serves roughly to equalize the deterrent on the sexes."

Gender: Employment

County of Washington v. *Gunther,* **450 U.S. 907, 101 S.Ct. 2242, 68 L.Ed.2d 751 (1981)** Held that Title VII of the Civil Rights Act of 1964 covered more than equal pay for equal work claims. *County of Washington* v. *Gunther* allowed the Court to clarify the relationship between two federal enactments treating sex-based wage discrimination. Title VII of the Civil Rights Act of 1964 barred employment discrimination. The Equal Pay Act of 1963 prohibited wage differentials based on sex for persons performing equivalent work. Title VII contained a reference to the Equal Pay Act through a provision of the Bennett amendment, which exempted from the Equal Pay Act differences in wage stemming from seniority, merit, or work quantity. The question in *Gunther* was whether the Bennett amendment made Title VII and the Equal Pay Act coextensive relative to wage discrimination, or whether Title VII provided broader protection than situations in which unequal pay for equal work was involved. Gunther, a female guard at a county jail, brought suit under Title VII claiming wage disparity between male and female guards for substantially similar, but not identical, work. In a 5–4 decision, the Court ruled that the Bennett amendment permitted Title VII litigation to go beyond equal pay for equal work claims. Justice Brennan's opinion stressed that the objective of the Bennett amendment was to make the two statutes compatible by specifying some affirmative defenses that would apply in situations where pay disparities existed for equal work. To confine Title VII to the equal work standard of the Equal Pay Act would mean that a woman who is discriminatorily underpaid could obtain no relief, no matter how egregious the discrimination might be, unless her employer also employed a man in an equal job in the same establishment at a higher rate of pay. The majority rejected the view that Congress had intended the Bennett amendment "to insulate such blatantly discriminatory practices from judicial redress under Title VII." Rather, Title

VII was used by Congress "to strike at the entire spectrum of disparate treatment of men and women resulting from sex stereotypes." Chief Justice Burger and Justices Stewart and Powell joined in a vigorous dissent written by Justice Rehnquist. The dissenters felt the intent of Congress in Title VII was that claims of gender-based wage discrimination were contingent on a showing of equal work. The minority was highly critical of the majority's judicial activism. Justice Rehnquist said the Court's decision was based on the majority's "unshakable belief that any other result would be unsound public policy." He charged that "the Court is obviously more interested in the consequences of its decision than in discerning the intention of Congress," and that "the Court relies wholly on what it believes Congress should have enacted." The decision was "simply a case where the Court superimposed on Title VII a gloss of its own choosing." *See also* CIVIL RIGHTS ACT OF 1964, p. 393; EQUAL PROTECTION CLAUSE, p. 313; *FRONTIERO V. RICHARDSON* (411 U.S. 677: 1973), p. 359; *ROSTKER V. GOLDBERG* (453 U.S. 57: 1981), p. 361.

Significance   *County of Washington* v. *Gunther* (450 U.S. 907: 1981) held that Title VII challenges of sex-based wage discrimination are not limited to claims of unequal pay for equal work. While the Court explicitly said that its decision did not embrace the comparable work concept, *Gunther* did mean that women bringing wage discrimination suits need only show that gender was used in a discriminatory fashion in setting a rate of pay. *Gunther* also reflects a broadening view of the Burger Court about what constitutes sex discrimination. In *Geduldig* v. *Aiello* (417 U.S. 484: 1974), the Court had allowed a state disability insurance program to exempt coverage of wage losses from normal pregnancies. Rather than finding a classification by sex, the Court held that the two classes were divided on the basis of pregnancy, and the nonpregnant class consisted of both men and women. Three subsequent cases, however, have found the Court moving away from the *Geduldig* position. In *Newport News Shipbuilding and Dry Dock Company* v. *EEOC* (77 L.Ed.2d 89: 1983), the Court struck down a health plan that did not provide the same pregnancy coverage for wives of male employees as it provided for female employees. In *Los Angeles Department of Water and Power* v. *Manhart* (435 U.S. 702: 1978), the Court held that requiring female employees to make higher contributions to retirement programs than men violated Title VII, despite the statistical probability that a woman would collect more retirement benefits because of greater longevity. The counterpart to *Manhart* came in *Arizona Governing Committee for Tax Deferred Annuity and Deferred Compensation Plans* v. *Norris* (77 L.Ed.2d 1236: 1983), in which the Court invalidated an employer-sponsored retirement plan that provided smaller benefits to women by using sex-based actuarial tables reflecting greater longevity for women. The Court said the classification of employees on the basis of sex was no more permissible at the pay-out stage of a retirement plan than at the pay-in stage.

Gender: Benevolent

Kahn v. Shevin, 416 U.S. 351, 94 S.Ct. 1734, 40 L.Ed.2d 189 (1973)   Upheld a state statute that provided a property tax exemption to widows, but not widowers. *Kahn* v. *Shevin* explored the fact that not all gender-based classifications convey disabilities to women. A number of enactments use gender as a benevolent classification, and *Kahn* allowed such a preferential policy. A Florida statute provided widows with an annual $500 exemption on property taxes. No similar benefit existed for widowers. The Supreme Court found the classification permissible in a 6–3 decision. Justice Douglas wrote the brief opinion of the Court. He noted that "the financial difficulties confronting the lone woman in Florida or in any other State exceed those facing the man." Whether the cause was overt discrimination or "the socialization process of a male dominated culture," a woman finds the job market inhospitable. Justice Douglas referred to data showing income disparities between males and females. This disparity was likely to be exacerbated for the widow. Unlike the male, the widow will be thrust into "a job market with which she is unfamiliar, and in which, because of her former economic dependency, she will have fewer skills to offer." The tax exemption was designed to further the policy of "cushioning the financial impact of spousal loss upon the sex for whom that loss imposes a disproportionately heavy burden." The Court differentiated this situation from that of *Frontiero* v. *Richardson* (411 U.S. 677: 1973), where benefits were granted on a gender basis solely for administrative convenience. The differentiation that favored females over males in granting the tax exemption in *Kahn* was a reasonable rather than an arbitrary distinction. States are to be permitted large leeway in making such classifications. Justices Brennan, White, and Marshall dissented. They argued that gender-based classifications are suspect and require more justification than the state offered. The dissenters also felt the statute was "plainly overinclusive," and that the state should have been required to prove that its interests could not have been served by a more precisely tailored statute or by use of feasible and less drastic means. For the dissenters, Florida could have advanced the interest of ameliorating the effect of past economic discrimination against women without categorically excluding males or including widows of substantial economic means. *See also* BENEVOLENT CLASSIFICATION, p. 388; *COUNTY OF WASHINGTON* V. *GUNTHER* (450 U.S. 907: 1981), p. 363; EQUAL PROTECTION CLAUSE, p. 313; *FRONTIERO* V. *RICHARDSON* (411 U.S. 677: 1973), p. 359; *ROSTKER* V. *GOLDBERG* (453 U.S. 57: 1981), p. 361.

Significance	Kahn v. *Shevin* (416 U.S. 351: 1973) upheld benevolent classifications. In *Califano* v. *Webster* (430 U.S. 313: 1977), the Court allowed a provision of the Social Security Act that permitted a woman to exclude more low-earning years than a male could exclude in calculating an average wage for use in the benefit formula. The objective of the provision was "the permissible one of redressing our society's longstanding disparate treatment of women." The Court also upheld a gender-based differential requiring mandatory discharge of naval officers who failed to be promoted within a specified period of time in *Schlesinger* v. *Ballard* (419 U.S. 498: 1975). Women were permitted four more years to gain promotion because women officers were not "similarly situated" to men. They had fewer opportunities to gain the needed professional service required for promotion. Nevertheless, the Court has found some benevolent gender classifications actually to be punitive and therefore invalid. In *Weinberger* v. *Wiesenfeld* (420 U.S. 636: 1975), for example, the Court found that social security survivor benefits for widows with minor children discriminated against women in that their compulsory social security contributions produced less protection for their survivors than the comparable contributions of men. Using the same reasoning, the Court set aside dependency requirements in the Federal Old-Age, Survivors, and Disability Insurance Benefits Program in *Califano* v. *Goldfarb* (430 U.S. 199: 1977). From the perspective of the two wage earners, the act "plainly disadvantages women contributors as compared with similarly situated men." Finally, in *Orr* v. *Orr* (440 U.S. 268: 1979), the Court voided an Alabama statute authorizing alimony payments to women but not to men. Justice Brennan suggested that benevolent gender classification carries "the inherent risk of reinforcing stereotypes about the proper place of women." Even compensatory objectives must be carefully tailored. Here the state's purpose could be as well served by a gender-neutral classification as by one that classifies by gender. The latter carries with it the baggage of sexual stereotypes.

Irrebuttable Presumptions

Vlandis v. *Kline,* 412 U.S. 441, 93 S.Ct. 2230, 37 L.Ed.2d 63 (1973)   Invalidated a classification based on residency because it constituted an irrebuttable presumption. *Vlandis* v. *Kline* examines whether equal protection issues may be assessed by using a framework in which a classification is presumed to exist, while those affected by the classification are prohibited from disputing their status. In *Vlandis,* the Court struck down an irrebuttable presumption. Connecticut required nonresident state university students to pay higher tuition and higher fees than state residents. If the legal address of a married student was outside the state at the time of application for admission to the university, such a person would forever remain a nonresident student. Similarly, if an unmarried person had a legal address outside Connecticut at any time during the year prior to seeking university admission, that person would permanently and irrebuttably retain nonresident status. At issue in the case was not the residency classification per se, but rather the "conclusive and unchangeable presumption" attached to it. Kline and others claimed that she had a constitutional right to controvert that presumption of nonresidence by presenting evidence that she was a bona fide resident. Connecticut sought to justify the presumption through its interest in equalizing the cost of public higher education between state residents and nonresidents. The Court ruled that rather than ensuring that only its bona fide residents receive their full subsidy, the Connecticut presumption also ensured that some bona fide residents, like Kline, do *not* receive their full subsidy. They can never do so while they remain students. The Court also refused to allow Connecticut to turn its classification into a policy that "favors with the lower rate only its established residents, whose past tax contributions to the State have been higher," because the statutory provisions are "so arbitrary as to constitute a denial of due process of law." Finally, the Court rejected Connecticut's justification of administrative convenience and certainty. Such an interest "cannot save the conclusive presumption from invalidity where there are other reasonable and practicable means of establishing the pertinent facts on which the State's objective is premised." Thus *Vlandis* held that irrebuttable presumptions are prohibited when the presumption is not necessarily or universally true, and when there are reasonable alternative means of making the crucial determination. Chief Justice Burger and Justices Rehnquist and Douglas dissented, taking issue with application of the language of strict scrutiny to a Due Process Clause issue. The dissenters also felt Connecticut was free to pursue a policy that favored established state residents. *See also* EQUAL PROTECTION CLAUSE, p. 313; IRREBUTTABLE PRESUMPTION, p. 427; *MASSACHUSETTS BOARD OF RETIREMENT V. MURGIA* (427 U.S. 307: 1976), p. 355.

Significance   *Vlandis* v. *Kline* (412 U.S. 441: 1973) struck down a state residency requirement because it was based on a conclusive or irrebuttable presumption. A provision of the Food Stamp Act was likewise invalidated in *United States Department of Agriculture* v. *Murry* (413 U.S. 508: 1974). The act withheld food stamp eligibility from households with an 18-year-old "who is claimed as a dependent child for Federal tax purposes by a taxpayer who is not a member of an eligible household." The Court ruled that the provision created a conclusive presumption that such a household is not in need, and that the presumption was not a rational measure of need. In *Cleveland Board of Education* v. *LaFleur* (414 U.S. 632: 1974), the Court struck down a requirement that pregnant teachers take an unpaid leave at least five months prior to their child's expected date of birth and not return to work until the semester following the child's attaining an age of three months. The Court noted the failure of the regulation to make individual determinations of a teacher's capacity to continue teaching. The rule served no legitimate purpose, and it unnecessarily penalized the female teacher for asserting her right to bear children. An irrebuttable presumption is not categorically prohibited, however. In *Weinberger* v. *Salfi* (422 U.S. 749: 1975), the Court upheld a duration-of-relationship requirement for survivor benefits under social security. By law, benefits are denied to wives and stepchildren in cases where the marriage occurred less than nine months prior to the death of the wage earner. The Court ruled that Congress could reasonably conclude that a broad prophylactic rule could protect against the possibility of persons entering marriage simply to claim benefits upon the anticipated early death of the wage earner. The restriction also obviated the necessity for large numbers of individual determinations. Further, it protected large numbers of claimants who satisfy the rule from the uncertainties and delays of administrative inquiry into the circumstances of their marriages. In *Massachusetts Board of Retirement* v. *Murgia* (427 U.S. 307: 1976, p. 000), the Court upheld a mandatory retirement age against arguments that individual fitness determinations were a more reasonable approach.

RIGHT OF PRIVACY

Basic Characteristics

Griswold v. *Connecticut*, 381 U.S. 479, 85 S.Ct. 1678, 14 L.Ed.2d 510 (1965)   Struck down state birth control regulation as an impermissible invasion of privacy. *Griswold* v. *Connecticut* addressed the fact that the Constitution contains no expressed right of privacy. *Griswold* fashioned such a right out of various provisions of the Bill of Rights. The Court was presented with the occasion to consider the privacy issue through review of a Connecticut statute that made it a crime to use birth control devices or provide counsel on their use. Griswold was arrested and convicted for violation of the statute. The Supreme Court voided the statute in a 7–2 decision, although members of the majority differed in their views about the source of the privacy protection. The opinion of the Court was offered by Justice Douglas. He disclaimed that the Court should act as a "super-legislature" making determinations about the "wisdom, need, and propriety of laws that touch economic problems, business affairs, or social conditions." At the same time, however, the Connecticut statute "operates directly on an intimate relation of husband and wife and their physician's role in one aspect of that relation." The Court could intervene because "various guarantees create zones of privacy." These zones are formed by emanations from "penumbras" of specific Bill of Rights guarantees. Justice Douglas developed the freedom of association as an example. In such cases as *NAACP* v. *Alabama* (357 U.S. 449: 1958, p. 147), the Court protected the privacy of association as a right peripheral to the First Amendment. The protection of association came from a First Amendment penumbra under which privacy is protected from governmental intrusion. The emanations that cast the penumbras draw from Bill of Rights guarantees and give them life and substance. The several guarantees involved here include the First Amendment, the privacy of the home that comes from the Third and Fourth Amendments, and the self-incrimination provision of the Fifth Amendment, and the Ninth Amendment. Justices Harlan and White used the Due Process Clause of the Fourteenth Amendment to find that "the enactment violates basic values implicit in the concept of ordered liberty." Justices Black and Stewart dissented. Justice Black noted the absence of a specific constitutional provision and accused the Court of engaging in wholly inappropriate substantive second-guessing. He said the Court does not possess the power "to measure constitutionality by our belief that legislation is arbitrary, capricious or unreasonable, or accomplishes no justifiable purpose, or is offensive to our own notions of civilized standards of conduct." Justice Black compared the Court's approach to that of the substantive due process cases of an earlier era and felt it "no less dangerous when used to enforce this Court's views about personal rights than those about economic rights." *See also* MOORE V. EAST CLEVELAND (431 U.S. 494: 1977), p. 376; RIGHT OF PRIVACY, p. 316; *ROE* V. *WADE*(410 U.S. 113: 1973), p. 371.

Significance　　*Griswold* v. *Connecticut* (381 U.S. 479: 1965) defined privacy as a constitutionally protected right. The key question remaining after *Griswold* was the scope of the protection and where the boundaries and criteria for application of the right were located. Initially the Court enlarged upon the privacy protection defined in Griswold, particularly as it affected procreation. In *Eisenstadt* v. *Baird* (415 U.S. 438: 1972), the Court struck down a Massachusetts statute limiting distribution of contraceptives to married persons. Justice Brennan argued that "if the right of privacy means anything, it is the right of the individual, married or single, to be free from unwarranted governmental intrusion into matters so fundamentally affecting a person as the decision whether to bear or beget a child." *Eisenstadt* became the cornerstone of the highly controversial abortion decision of *Roe* v. *Wade* (410 U.S. 113: 1973, p. 371). In a related case, the Court invalidated a New York law prohibiting contraceptive sales to minors in *Carey* v. *Population Services International* (431 U.S. 678: 1977). Boundaries began to appear in the mid-1970s as the Court talked of privacy rights as attaching to such matters as marriage, procreation, and the family. Outside those contexts, claims of invasion of privacy have fared badly. In *Kelley* v. *Johnson* (425 U.S. 238: 1976), for example, the Court upheld regulations on the hairstyles, mustaches, and beards of police officers. In *Paul* v. *Davis* (424 U.S. 693: 1976), the Court refused to find a privacy violation in the case of a person who had been described in a police flyer as a shoplifter, even though he had never been formally charged with the offense. Finally, in *Whalen* v. *Roe* (429 U.S. 589: 1977), the Court unanimously upheld a New York law requiring that computer lists be maintained to identify persons receiving certain categories of prescription drugs. Thus privacy is a conditional right that is most subject to limitation when asserted outside a broadly defined family context.

Abortion

Roe v. *Wade,* 410 U.S. 113, 93 S.Ct. 705, 35 L.Ed.2d 147 (1973)   Held that criminal abortion statutes impermissibly encroach upon a person's right of privacy as guaranteed by the Due Process Clause of the Fourteenth Amendment and other provisions of the Constitution. *Roe* v. *Wade* was by far the most controversial outgrowth of the privacy protection doctrine. *Wade* involved a Texas statute that made it a crime to perform an abortion except when preserving the mother's life. It was typical of many nineteenth-century criminal abortion laws. In a 7–2 decision, the Court struck down the prohibition. Justice Blackmun's opinion began with an historical survey of laws proscribing abortion. This led him to a three-pronged rationale for the prohibition. The objectives of such statutes were to (1) discourage illicit sexual conduct, (2) protect pregnant women from the hazardous abortion procedure, and (3) protect prenatal life. Only the final justification, protection of prenatal life, offered any possibility of being a sufficiently important interest for the state. It was, however, a very limited interest because the language and meaning of the Fourteenth Amendment applies "only postnatally." The term "person" as used in the Amendment "does not include the unborn." Furthermore, the privacy protection is broad enough to encompass a woman's decision whether or not to terminate her pregnancy. It might appear, therefore, that the woman's choice was to be absolutely insulated from regulation. That is not quite so, for there comes a time in every pregnancy when the state's interests "become sufficiently compelling to sustain regulation of the factors that govern the abortion decision." Justice Blackmun established a timetable for these interests based upon the three trimesters of a pregnancy. During the first trimester, a state has no interest whatsoever. Throughout the second trimester, the state could regulate the conditions under which abortions occur. The pregnant woman, in consultation with her physician, was still free to determine, without regulation by the state, whether or not to terminate the pregnancy. The state's interest in protecting potential life begins with the final trimester when the fetus becomes viable or has the capability of meaningful life outside the mother's womb. This approach allowed Justice Blackmun to suggest that the Court need not resolve the difficult question of when life begins. When doctors, philosophers, and theologians "are unable to arrive at any consensus, the judiciary is not in a position to speculate as to the answer." Justices White and Rehnquist dissented, charging the majority with excessive exercise of judicial power. Neither saw any consideration of privacy that could justify striking down the Texas statute. *See also* CITY OF AKRON v. AKRON CENTER FOR REPRODUCTIVE HEALTH, INC. (76 L.Ed.2d 687: 1983), p. 372; GRISWOLD v. CONNECTICUT (381 U.S. 479: 1965), p. 369; HARRIS v. MCRAE (448 U.S. 297: 1980), p. 374; RIGHT OF PRIVACY, p. 316.

Significance   Roe v. Wade (410 U.S. 113: 1973) established a woman's right to have an abortion. *Doe* v. *Bolton* (410 U.S. 179: 1973) was a companion case to *Wade* in which a Georgia law was also invalidated. The Georgia enactment was less than five years old at the time of review and was thought to be representative of reform or enlightened abortion legislation. The Court found the statute overly restrictive in several ways and thus caused an impermissible encroachment on protected privacy. First, the statute required that all abortions take place in certified hospitals, even during the first trimester. Second, a committee of hospital staff persons was required to approve the procedure. Third, the judgment of the woman's physician needed confirmation by at least two other physicians. The statute was also flawed because of a residency requirement. However, the Court has sustained legislation requiring notification of parents prior to a minor's having an abortion. In *H.L.* v. *Matheson* (450 U.S. 398: 1981), the Court limited the use of public funds for abortion, and in *Harris* v. *McRae* (448 U.S. 297: 1980), the Court attempted to keep the right to abortion as established in *Wade* free from obstacles. In *Colautti* v. *Franklin* (439 U.S. 379: 1979), the Court held a Pennsylvania viability statute unconstitutional because it subjected physicians to possible criminal prosecution if certain specified techniques were not used when a fetus "is" or "may be" viable. The Court felt the requirement was too vague. It subjected physicians to threat in the absence of intent. The statute was also seen as having a "chilling effect" on the willingness of physicians to perform abortions.

Abortion Regulation

City of Akron v. Akron Center for Reproductive Health, Inc., **76 L.Ed.2d 687 (1983)**   Invalidated several restrictive regulations on abortion. *City of Akron v. Akron Center for Reproductive Health,*

Inc. strongly reaffirmed the Supreme Court's position that the constitution guarantees the right to an abortion free from governmental restrictions. The restrictions examined came in a city ordinance thought to be a model for abortion regulation. The ordinance contained five key elements. (1) All abortions performed after the first trimester must occur in a hospital. (2) Unmarried minors under 15 must have parental consent or a court order to obtain an abortion. (3) Attending physicians must convey specific statements about the fetus as a "human life," about fetus viability, and about the physical and emotional complications that may result from an abortion, all in order to ensure that the patient's consent is informed. (4) Abortions could not be performed within 24 hours of the signing of a consent form. (5) "Humane and sanitary" disposal of "fetal remains" must accomplished. The Court held the restrictions to be unconstitutional in a 6–3 decision. The opinion was written by Justice Powell, who emphasized the fundamental role of precedent in a society governed by the rule of law. He explicitly reaffirmed *Roe* v. *Wade* (410 U.S. 113: 1973, p. 371) and then turned to the challenged components of the Akron ordinance. The second-trimester hospitalization requirement imposed a significant obstacle by creating additional costs and the possibility of having to travel to find available facilities. New abortion techniques developed since *Roe* v. *Wade* made it possible to perform abortions safely on an outpatient basis. The consent requirement was deficient in that Akron "may not make a blanket determination that all minors under the age of 15 are too immature to make this decision." The informed consent provision was excessive because "much of the information required is designed not to inform the woman's consent but rather to persuade her to withhold it altogether." The Court also found this section to be an intrusion upon the discretion of the pregnant woman's physician. The 24-hour waiting period failed to demonstrate furtherance of any legitimate state interest. The fetus disposal issue was set aside as impermissibly vague as a definition of conduct for which physicians could be prosecuted. A dissent was entered by Justice O'Connor, joined by Justices White and Rehnquist. Justice O'Connor rejected the trimester reasoning of *Roe* as "a completely unworkable method of accommodating the conflicting personal rights and compelling state interests that are involved." She said an analytical framework that varies according to the stages of pregnancy precludes sound constitutional theory or the need to apply neutral principles. Standards are continually in flux because they are linked to ever-changing medical technology. This relationship puts the *Roe* framework on a collision course with itself because technology will inevitably move forward the point at which a state may regulate while simultaneously moving backward the point of viabiously moving lity at which the state may proscribe abortions. None of the regulations enacted by Akron were burdensome in Justice O'Connor's view. They were rather the expression of legitimate state interest in protecting potential human life, an interest that exists throughout the pregnancy. *See also* HARRIS v. MCRAE (444 U.S. 297: 1980), p. 374; RIGHT OF PRIVACY, p. 316; ROE v. WADE (410 U.S. 113: 1973), p. 371.

Significance   As in *City of Akron* v. *Akron Center for Reproductive Health, Inc.* (76 L.Ed.2d 687: 1983), most enactments imposing restrictions on abortions have been invalidated. In *Planned Parenthood of Central Missouri* v. *Danforth* (428 U.S. 52: 1976), the Court rejected spousal consent, or parental consent in the case of an unmarried minor, for all abortions. It said a state cannot delegate a veto power the state itself is absolutely and totally prohibited from exercising. The Court reiterated its position on consent requirements in *Bellotti* v. *Baird II* (443 U.S. 622: 1979) by rejecting a parental consent requirement because it provided no process by which the minor's own capacity to make the decision could be examined. Several abortion regulations have received the Court's approval, however. In *H.L.* v. *Matheson* (450 U.S. 398: 1981), the Court upheld a parental *notification* provision if the patient was a minor, although parental *consent* for the abortion was not required. Regulations in the two companion cases to *Akron* were also upheld. In *Planned Parenthood Association of Kansas City* v. *Ashcroft* (76 L.Ed.2d 733: 1983), statutory provisions involving parental consent, mandatory pathological examination of all abortion tissue, and attendance of a second physician for abortions after 12 weeks, were upheld. The Missouri consent section was approved because, unlike *Akron*, it contained a process by which a minor could be determined mature enough to make the decision, thus bypassing parental or judicial consent. In *Simopoulos* v. *Virginia* (76 L.Ed.2d 755: 1983), a hospital requirement for second-trimester abortions was upheld because licensure was available for outpatient clinics.

Medicaid Abortion Funding

***Harris* v. *McRae*, 448 U.S. 297, 100 S.Ct. 2671, 75 L.Ed.2d 784 (1980)**   Held that federal medicaid funds could not be used to cover abortion costs. *Harris* v. *McRae* examined the constitutionality of congressional restrictions on medicaid reimbursements for costs of abortions. The restrictions, known as the Hyde Amendment, limited federal funds for abortions to those cases where the mother's life was jeopardized by a full-term pregnancy or for rape or incest victims, provided "such rape or incest has been reported promptly to a law enforcement agency or public health service." The Supreme Court upheld the Hyde Amendment against equal protection and due process challenges in a 5–4 decision. The Court concluded that the right to have an abortion as established in *Roe* v. *Wade* (410 U.S. 113: 1973, p. 371) carried with it no entitlement to federal funding to cover an abortion's costs. The funding limitation imposed no restriction on access to abortions, and while indigency may make it more difficult, perhaps impossible, for some women actually to have abortions, the enactment did not create or affect the indigency. The Hyde Amendment merely reflected a value choice favoring childbirth over abortion. It placed no governmental obstacle in the path of a woman who chooses to terminate her pregnancy. By means of unequal subsidization of abortion and other medical services it encourages alternative activity. The Hyde Amendment leaves an indigent women with at least the same range of choice in deciding whether to obtain a medically necessary abortion as she could have had if Congress had chosen to subsidize no health care costs at all. The freedom to be protected from governmental interference in such personal decisions as abortion does not also confer an entitlement to such funds as may be necessary to realize all the advantages of that freedom. Finally, the majority concluded that the Hyde Amendment was rationally related to a legitimate governmental objective. The incentives that make childbirth a more attractive alternative bear a direct relationship to the legitimate congressional interest in protecting potential life. That abortion was singled out for more extensive restriction than other medical services was viewed as rational in that abortion is inherently different from other medical procedures. No other procedure involves the purposeful termination of potential life. Justices Brennan, Marshall, Blackmun, and Stevens dissented. Justice Brennan referred to the Hyde Amendment as "a transparent attempt by the Legislative Branch to impose the political majority's judgment of the morally acceptable and socially desirable preference on a sensitive and intimate decision that the Constitution entrusts to the individual." The amendment "both by design and in effect serves to coerce indigent pregnant women to have children that they would otherwise elect not to have." Justice Brennan also detected factors beyond the woman's indigency as interfering with her free choice of an abortion. He argued that the "fundamental flaw in the Court's due process analysis is its failure to acknowledge that the discriminatory distribution of benefits of governmental largesse can discourage the exercise of fundamental liberties as effectively as can an outright denial of those rights through criminal and regulatory sanctions." *See also* GRISWOLD V. CONNECTICUT (381 U.S. 479: 1965), p. 369; RIGHT OF PRIVACY, p. 316; *ROE* V. *WADE*(410 U.S. 113: 1973), p. 371.

Significance   *Harris* v. *McRae* (448 U.S. 297: 1980) was not the Court's first experience with restrictions on public monies for covering the costs of abortions. It was the most extensive, however, in that it included therapeutic abortions. In *Maher* v. *Roe* (432 U.S. 464: 1977), the Court upheld a Connecticut restriction on funding for elective or nontherapeutic abortions while subsidizing childbirth. *Maher* was the foundation of *McRae*. The Court decided two other cases on the same day as *Maher*, both of which upheld limitations on funding for abortions. In *Beal* v. *Doe* (432 U.S. 438: 1977), it held that the federal medicaid program did not require a participating state to bear costs of nontherapeutic abortions. The extent to which the Court was irreconcilably split on these cases can be seen in the harsh dissent offered by the usually mild-mannered Justice Blackmun. In *Beal* he remarked that "there is another world out there, the existence of which the Court, I suspect, either chooses to ignore or fears to recognize." He felt the Court's decision was punitive and tragic for the indigent. Implicit is the condescension that she may go elsewhere for her abortion. "I find such condescension disingenuous and alarming, almost reminiscent of 'let them eat cake.'" The other companion to *Maher, Poelker* v. *Doe* (42 U.S. 519: 1977), allowed a municipality to provide subsidized hospital services for childbirth while excluding services for nontherapeutic abortions.

Definition of Family

Moore **v. *City of East Cleveland,* 431 U.S. 494, 97 S.Ct. 1932, 52 L.Ed.2d 531 (1977)**   Ruled that a municipality through a zoning ordinance did not have authority to restrict occupancy of a private home to persons defined as family. *Moore* v. *City of East Cleveland* involved an ordinance that limited occupancy of a dwelling unit to members of a "single family." The zone of privacy issue involved in the case had provided the basis for numerous challenges of legislation since *Griswold* v. *Connecticut* (381 U.S. 479: 1965, p. 369). Most successful applications of the invasion of privacy approach have been in situations where matters of family were involved in some way. In the East Cleveland ordinance, "family" was defined very narrowly to include essentially parents and children. Moore lived in her home with her son and two grandsons. She was found in violation of the ordinance because the grandsons were cousins rather than brothers. Although the Court could not agree on common language, a five-justice majority found the ordinance unconstitutional. The opinion of the Court was written by Justice Powell, who characterized the ordinance as "slicing deeply into the family itself." He said such an enactment compels the Court to act aggressively. "When a city undertakes such an intrusive regulation of the family, the usual judicial deference to the legislature is inappropriate." That posture was demanded because the Court had long recognized that freedom of personal choice in matters of marriage and family life is one of the liberties protected by the Due Process Clause of the Fourteenth Amendment. Justice Powell acknowledged that the family is not beyond regulation, but governmental interests in doing so must be very carefully examined, as well as the means chosen to advance those interests. The interests asserted by East Cleveland were served only marginally by the ordinance. Justice Powell noted the risk involved when "the judicial branch gives enhanced protection to certain substantive liberties without the guidance of more specific provisions of the Bill of Rights." Although history counsels caution and restraint as a general rule, it does not counsel abandonment. Nor does it require what the city urges, i.e., cutting off any protection of family rights at the first convenient boundary, the boundary of the nuclear family. Justice Brennan concurred and said the zoning power "is not a license for local communities to enact senseless and arbitrary restrictions which cut deeply into private areas of protected family." He also charged that the ordinance was the imposition of "white suburbia's preference in patterns of family living," a preference reflecting "cultural myopia" and insensitivity to the concept of the extended family. Justices Stewart, White, and Rehnquist disagreed that the ordinance interfered with an aspect of family life deserving constitutional protection. The three did not feel that Moore's claim was sufficient for heightened protection under the Due Process Clause. Chief Justice Burger also dissented, but based his disagreement on the ground that Moore had not fully exhausted the administrative remedies available to her. *See also* FOURTEENTH AMENDMENT, p. 412; GRISWOLD V. CONNECTICUT (381 U.S. 479: 1965), p. 369; RIGHT OF PRIVACY, p. 316.

Significance   Moore v. *City of East Cleveland* (431 U.S. 494: 1977) set aside an ordinance that attempted to restrict occupancy of a home to persons within the ordinance definition of family. Prior to *Moore*, the Court had upheld a zoning ordinance in *Belle Terre* v. *Boraas* (416 U.S.

1: 1974) that limited land use to single-family dwellings. The ordinance defined family more broadly than the enactment in *Moore*, and the Court deferred to the permissible legislative objectives of regulating population density and preventing congestion and noise. In *Zablocki* v. *Redhail* (434 U.S. 374: 1978), the Court found that the right of privacy precluded interference with a person's desire to marry. A state statute required any person under an order to pay child support to obtain authorization to marry. Permission was contingent on showing that support obligations were current and that the children involved "would not likely thereafter become public charges." Redhail was denied a marriage license because he had failed to make support payments for a previously fathered child. The Court held the statute unconstitutional because it barred certain classes from ever marrying. They were "coerced into foregoing the right to marry." The right of privacy is limited to traditional marital relationships in *Doe* v. *Commonwealth Attorney for the City of Richmond* (425 U.S. 901: 1976). The Court summarily affirmed a three judge district court dismissal of a privacy challenge to the use of a state sodomy statute against homosexuals. The lower court found that homosexuality was "obviously no portion of marriage, house, or family life," and that a state may impose criminal sanctions on conduct "even when committed in the home, in the promotion of morality and decency."

8. *Legal Words and Phrases*

Abstention   A policy designed to reduce conflict between federal and state courts. Abstention allows a federal court to withhold exercise of its jurisdiction on a federal constitutional issue until a state court has rendered a judgment on such state law as may have a bearing on the federal question.

Significance   The doctrine of abstention maintains that a federal court should not assume jurisdiction in a case until the uncertainties of state law are addressed by the appropriate state courts. Abstention by the federal court may prevent or minimize conflict by limiting federal court interference in matters that pertain primarily to state law. Abstention also permits a federal court to relinquish its jurisdiction if the federal court determines that the central issue in a case has been appropriately resolved at the state level. A particular form of abstention is known as comity. Comity is a courtesy by which one court extends deference to another in the exercise of authority. Comity is offered out of respect and good will rather than obligation. Like abstention, it is aimed at preventing friction between courts, both of which may have legitimate jurisdictional claims in a case.

Adversary Proceeding   A legal contest that involves a real contest between two opposing parties. In an adversary proceeding, formal notice is served on the party against whom an action has been filed to allow that party an opportunity to respond. An adversary proceeding is different from an ex parte proceeding, where only one party appears. An adversary proceeding also differs from a summary proceeding, where no significant fact dispute exists and where the court may hasten and simplify the resolution of an issue. *See also* ADVISORY OPINION, p. 381; CASE OR CONTROVERSY, p. 389.

Significance   An adversary proceeding forces a plaintiff and defendant in a legal action to contest each other with evidence gathered in support of their respective cases. The system is generally regarded as the most effective means of the evaluation of evidence. The adversary system also features a diffusion of power among its principal participants, such as judge, prosecutor, jury, and defense counsel. Each actor helps to produce a check and balance effect, thus safeguarding against arbitrary or abusive judgments.

Advisory Opinion   A response by a judge or court to a legal question posed outside a bona fide case or controversy. An advisory opinion is a reply to an abstract or hypothetical question. It has no binding effect unless it is legally accepted by the requesting body. *See also* CASE OR CONTROVERSY, p. 389; DECLARATORY JUDGMENT, p. 401.

Significance   An advisory opinion may not be rendered by a federal court because of the constitutional provision limiting jurisdiction of federal courts to an actual case or controversy. The limitation is designed to preserve separation of powers and keep the judiciary from certain political entanglements that might adversely affect the judicial branch. Several states allow the rendering of an advisory opinion in order to clarify state legislation without the necessity of burdensome litigation.

Aggravating Circumstances   Elements that increase the severity of a criminal act. Aggravating circumstances go beyond the legal aspect of a particular crime. The presence of such a circumstance is required to distinguish guilty persons who may be sentenced to death. To be sentenced to death for murder in most states, at least one aggravating circumstance must be shown beyond a reasonable doubt. This is done to isolate the most grievous offenses. An aggravating circumstance may be (1) a substantial history of serious assaultive criminal convictions; (2) a capital offense committed during the course of another capital offense; or (3) a crime especially heinous or a crime involving torture or "wantonly vile" acts. *See also* BARCLAY V. FLORIDA (77 L.Ed.. 2d 1134: 1983), p. 302; CRUEL AND UNUSUAL PUNISHMENT, p. 401; GREGG V. GEORGIA (428 U.S. 238: 1976), p. 295; WOODSON V. NORTH CAROLINA (428 U.S. 280: 1976), p. 297.

Significance   An enumeration of aggravating circumstances provides structure and guidance to sentencers in death penalty cases. Such an enumeration is required by the Supreme Court in *Furman v. Georgia* (408 U.S. 238: 1972). Distinct from an aggravating circumstance is a *mitigating* circumstance. The latter is a factor that diminishes or reduces a convicted person's culpability. The presence of at least one mitigating circumstance may preclude imposition of capital punishment. Typical mitigating circumstances are youth, no prior criminal history, and emotional disturbance or duress.

Amicus Curiae   A person or organization submitting a brief to a court expressing views on a legal question before the court. An amicus curiae, literally meaning "friend of the court," is not an actual party to an action. He, she, or it is an interested third party who attempts to provide the court with information or arguments that may not have been offered by the actual parties. *See also* BRIEF, p. 389.

Significance Amicus curiae participation is a common court-related interest group activity. It typically occurs in cases with substantial public interest ramifications. As the Supreme Court considered whether a woman has a constitutional right to an abortion in *Roe* v. *Wade* (410 U.S. 113: 1973), amicus briefs were submitted by 36 pro-abortion and 11 anti-abortion organizations. Some of the groups filed jointly. Amicus arguments tend to focus on the broader implications of a particular case. Submission of an amicus brief is not a matter of right, however. With the exception of amicus participation by an agency of the federal government, an amicus brief may be filed only with the consent of both parties in an action, on motion to the court, or by invitation of the court.

Appeal A request to an appellate or superior court to review a final judgment made in an inferior or lower court. Appellate jurisdiction is the power placed in appeals courts to conduct such a review. It empowers the superior court to set aside or modify the lower-court decision. An appeals court has several options in reviewing a lower-court decision. It may affirm, which means the lower-court result is correct and must stand. It may reverse or vacate, which means it sets aside the lower-court ruling. Vacated judgments are often remanded to the lower court for further consideration. If an appellate decision overrules a precedent, it supersedes the earlier decision and the authority of the decision as precedent. A party seeking appeal is typically referred to as the *appellant* or *petitioner,* while the party against whom an action has been filed is the *appellee* or *respondent.* Appellate jurisdiction is distinguished from original jurisdiction. In the former, some other court or agency must render a judgment in a case before an appeal can be sought. *See also* CERTIORARI, p. 390; EQUITY JURISDICTION, p. 407; JUDICIAL REVIEW, p. 429; ORIGINAL JURISDICTION, p. 430.

Significance Appeals courts are generally structured on two levels. One is an intermediate court that handles cases initially, and the other is a superior or supreme court. Appellate jurisdiction is conveyed through constitutional or statutory mandate. Federal appellate jurisdiction is granted by Article III of the Constitution, which says that the Supreme Court possesses such jurisdiction "both as to law and fact, with such exceptions and under such regulations as the Congress shall make." Appeals may be undertaken as a matter of right where the appellate court, typically an intermediate appeals court, must review a case. Other appeals occur at the discretion of the appeals court. The writ of certiorari is a discretionary route of access to the appellate jurisdiction of the United States Supreme Court. Review as a matter of right is subject to some discretion by the Supreme Court, as in the writ of appeal. The party seeking the appeal has a right to review, but the Court may reject the appeal for want of a substantial federal question.

Apportionment   The allocation of the number of representatives a political unit may send to a legislative body. Apportionment is based upon population, and it is a requirement of equal protection that legislatures have districts of substantially equal populations. Prior to 1962 the Supreme Court had considered legislative apportionment a political question, a matter not subject to resolution by the judicial branch. In *Baker* v. *Carr* (369 U.S. 186: 1962), however, the Court held apportionment to be a justiciable issue. *See also* BAKER V. CARR (369 U.S. 186: 1962), p. 343; JUSTICIABILITY, p. 432; POLITICAL QUESTION, p. 442; *REYNOLDS* V. *SIMS* (377 U.S. 533: 1964), p. 344.

Significance   Apportionment evolved to the one man–one vote rule, although *Baker* itself did not establish that standard. *Baker* created a relatively stringent expectation of population equivalence for single-member legislative districts. The one man–one vote standard now applies to all levels of government, including local units.

Arraignment   A pretrial proceeding at which an accused person is formally charged. During an arraignment, the accused is given a copy of the information or indictment against him or her, and is asked to respond to the charges. The options available at the arraignment are to plead guilty, not guilty, or nolo contendere. Nolo contendere expresses a wish not to contend the charges. The accused may also stand mute, which is entered as a plea of not guilty. *See also* BAIL, p. 387; GRAND JURY, p. 418.

Significance   Arraignment is one of several steps in the criminal justice process. It is designed to safeguard an accused against arbitrary or vindictive actions by the state. An arraignment must occur within a short period of time following an arrest. The constitutional protections to which the accused is entitled are reiterated at the arraignment, and his or her bail status may also be reviewed. In some jurisdictions a brief proceeding called an arraignment occurs prior to formal charging. This first appearance or presentment allows the rights of the accused to be reviewed and the pretrial release question to be addressed. A formal hearing to charge must still occur in jurisdictions that define arraignment in this way.

Assembly, Right to A fundamental right provided by the First Amendment. The right of assembly provides that the people are entitled "peaceably to assemble, and to petition the government for redress of grievances." It includes the right to protest governmental policies as well as to advocate particular, even distasteful, views. The right to assemble generally involves "speech plus." This is expression with an associated action component such as a demonstration or a march. While the people have a right peaceably to assemble, the government also has a legitimate function to maintain order. The two interests may collide. The right of assembly does not provide absolute protection. In the words of Justice Black, the right of assembly does not include expression whenever and however and wherever one pleases. The government can impose regulations on the time, place, and manner of assembly, provided that substantial interests, such as preventing threats to public order, can be shown. Thus certain locations such as jail grounds may be constitutionally placed off limits as a place of demonstration. Similarly, the right to assemble does not protect such actions as inciting breaches of the peace, the obstruction of traffic, or seizure of a local public library. Time, place, and manner regulations must be evenhandedly applied and must be wholly unrelated to the content of the expression involved. *See also ADDERLEY V. FLORIDA* (385 U.S. 39: 1966), p. 142; *CARROLL V. PRESIDENT AND COMMISSIONERS OF PRINCESS ANNE* (393 U.S. 175: 1968), p. 146; FREE SPEECH CLAUSE, p. 416; *PRUNEYARD SHOPPING CENTER V. ROBINS* (447 U.S. 74: 1980), p. 144; SPEECH PLUS, p. 451.

Significance The right to assemble is fundamental for people in a democratic society. As in matters involving free expression, restrictions on the right to assemble are suspect. They must be content-neutral. As long as demonstrators do not interfere with normal business operations, they may access such private property as a shopping center. *PruneYard Shopping Center v. Robins* (447 U.S. 74: 1980) placed the protection for assembly such as this under applicable state constitutional provisions. Assembly that requires prior governmental approval or permit is also suspect, although content-neutral permit systems are likely to be constitutionally acceptable if they are confined to reasonable time, place, and manner restrictions.

Association, Right of   The legal right of a group of people acting together to advance a mutual interest or achieve a common objective. The right of association is not expressly protected by the First Amendment. It is derived from safeguards for expression and assembly contained in the First Amendment. The utility of association as a means of achieving political and social goals was acknowledged by the Supreme Court in *NAACP* v. *Alabama* (357 U.S. 449: 1958). The Court said, "Effective advocacy of both public and private points of view, particularly controversial ones, is undeniably enhanced by group association." Given the fundamental role of associational activity, government bears an obligation to ensure that interference with such activity does not occur. The Court struck down a state membership disclosure requirement in *NAACP* v. *Alabama* because the regulation adversely affected the ability of the NAACP and its members "to pursue their collective effort to foster beliefs which they admittedly have a right to advocate." Associational activity was also protected in *Baird* v. *State Bar* (401 U.S. 1: 1971), in which the Court held that applicants for admission to the bar may not be compelled to disclose organizational memberships. *See also* FREE SPEECH CLAUSE, p. 416; KEYISHIAN V. BOARD OF REGENTS (385 U.S. 589: 1967), p. 151; LOYALTY OATH, p. 433; NAACP V. ALABAMA (357 U.S. 449: 1958), p. 147; OVERBREADTH DOCTRINE, p. 440; WHITNEY V. CALIFORNIA (274 U.S. 357: 1927), p. 149.

Significance   The right of association may have positive effects in a democracy, but regulation may still be imposed. The most troublesome association cases have involved statutory attempts to proscribe subversive organizations and prohibit criminal syndicalism. Syndicalism refers to the takeover of the means of industrial production by workers. Criminal syndicalism involves the advocacy of, or participation in, unlawful acts to achieve political change. Many states had criminal syndicalism statutes that were upheld initially because association itself was seen as concerted action threatening public security. (See *Whitney* v. *California*, 274 U.S. 357: 1927.) The Warren Court rejected this approach because such laws were directed at "mere abstract teaching" or advocacy that is not necessarily related to unlawful acts. Decisions such as *Keyishian* v. *Board of Regents* (385 U.S. 589: 1967) found "mere membership" in a subversive organization to be insufficient grounds for exclusion from public employment. The Court said laws that sanction membership unaccompanied by specific intent to further the unlawful goals of the organization violate constitutional limitations. The right of association is most often protected from regulation by means of the overbreadth doctrine, which cautions that restrictive statutes tend to trap association members indiscriminately. Associational protection has also been applied to organizational involvement in the electoral process.

Bad Tendency Test   A standard used by the Supreme Court to evaluate the reasonableness of restrictions on speech and press. The bad tendency test permits restriction of expression if the expression tends to involve a danger of "substantive evil" or if it could lead to unlawful ends. In *Gitlow* v. *New York* (268 U.S. 652: 1925), the Court said a state may reasonably "extinguish the spark without waiting until it has enkindled the flame or blazed into the conflagration." It may also "suppress the threatened danger in its incipience." *See also* CLEAR AND PRESENT DANGER TEST, p. 395; FREE SPEECH CLAUSE, p. 416.

Significance   The bad tendency test is one of the standards developed by the Supreme Court for reviewing restrictions imposed on free speech and press. It is the least favorable standard the Court has utilized to judge expression. It presumes the constitutionality of restrictive enactments. The approach has sometimes been referred to as killing the serpent in the egg.

Bail   Monetary security used to ensure the future appearance of an accused at proceedings to adjudicate criminal charges. In exchange for posting bail, an accused is released from custody pending completion of the adjudicatory process. If the accused appears at all required proceedings, whatever security has been posted is returned, regardless of the outcome of the case. Bail is forfeited by failure to appear. While pretrial release may be denied for certain serious offenses, the Eighth Amendment prohibits excessive bail. Excess has been held to mean the imposition of pretrial release conditions beyond what is necessary to ensure subsequent appearances. *See also* EIGHTH AMENDMENT, p. 289.

Significance   Bail is closely related to the assumption of the American legal system that accused persons are innocent until they are proven guilty. Pretrial release is one way of acting out this assumption. If an accused person is to be released before trial, such release may be accomplished in one of several ways. He or she may post an amount of money set by a judicial officer. In some jurisdictions a partial payment or a deposit is sufficient. Property may be used in lieu of money. In the event the accused cannot raise the full amount of bail, or does not possess property that might serve as collateral, a bail bondsman may be used. For a nonreturnable fee, a bail bondsman guarantees to the court that the bail levied against the accused will be covered if the accused fails to appear. An alternative approach to pretrial release involves release on personal recognizance. Instead of posting money or property, an accused may be released because there are sufficient family- or work-related factors to minimize the likelihood of flight. Release on recognizance is limited to persons charged with less serious offenses. Releasing an accused before trial is consistent with the presumption of innocence and the view that bail is simply and exclusively a guarantee of a later appearance rather than the imposition of punishment. Some jurisdictions use bail as a method of detaining defendants thought to be dangerous and likely to commit additional crimes.

Balancing Test   An approach to judicial decision making in which free speech interests are weighed against other societal interests to determine if restraint of speech is warranted. The balancing test presumes that constitutionally protected rights are not absolute. It assesses the extent to which governmental authority may be exercised to protect society from substantial damage. *See also* BAD TENDENCY TEST, p. 387; CLEAR AND PRESENT DANGER TEST, p. 395; FREE SPEECH CLAUSE, p. 416.

Significance   The balancing test may use particular values that load the scale, notably the clear and present danger test and the bad tendency test. Otherwise, balancing may be employed on a case-by-case basis with standards that may or may not utilize abstract value systems. The balancing test is often used in reviewing Equal Protection Clause cases and First Amendment issues.

Benevolent Classification   A preferential classification of persons conveying favorable treatment to them. A benevolent classification establishes an advantage for a particular group. Other classifications may convey disabilities to a designated group in terms of regulation, for example. *See also* CLASSIFICATION, p. 394; *KAHN* V. *SHEVIN* (416 U.S. 351: 1973), p. 365; REVERSE DISCRIMINATION, p. 447.

Significance   A benevolent classification can only pass equal protection scrutiny if the legislative objective is not unnecessarily discriminatory. The objective is usually to implement an ameliorative policy designed to remedy past inequities as a form of affirmative action. An example of a benevolent classification is a Florida property tax exemption for widows but not for widowers. The exemption was intended to soften the financial impact of the death of a husband because such a loss imposes a disproportionately heavy burden on women.

Brief   A written document presented to a court in support of a party's position on a legal question. A brief contains a statement of the facts, applicable law, and arguments drawn from the facts and the law urging a judgment compatible with the interests of the party submitting the brief. In a law school context, a brief is a short outline of a case studied by the student and prepared for recitation and review. *See also* AMICUS CURIAE, p. 382.

Significance   A brief is the medium through which legal arguments are placed before courts. Briefs are generally submitted by the parties themselves, although third-party briefs from amicus curiae may also be submitted. If a brief is compelling enough, it may secure the court's judgment and opinion.

Case or Controversy   A properly asserted legal claim made in a manner appropriate for judicial response. A case or controversy may be decided by federal courts under Article III of the Constitution. For a case to constitute a bona fide controversy sufficient to satisfy Article III requirements, it must possess several elements. (1) It must involve parties who are truly contending or adverse. (2) There must exist a recognizable legal interest arising out of a legitimate fact situation. (3) The issue must be capable of judicial enforcement by judgment. The case must be justiciable. A person bringing a claim or petitioning a court is known as a *party* or a *litigant*. The initiating party to a legal action is also called a *plaintiff* or a *petitioner*. The party against whom such action may be brought is a *defendant* or a *respondent*. Cases are named for the parties involved. The designation *et al.* is used after the first-named party in a suit where there are several plaintiffs or defendants. Cases designated *in re* are proceedings that are not wholly adversarial, such as a juvenile case *in re*, or "in the matter of," John Doe. The abbreviations *ex rel* may be made when a legal action is initiated by the state at the instigation of a party with a private interest in the result. *See also* ADVISORY OPINION, p. 381; JUSTICIABILITY, p. 432; STANDING, p. 452.

Significance   A case or controversy is a justiciable case. In *Aetna Life Insurance Company* v. *Haworth* (300 U.S. 227: 1937), the Supreme Court described a justiciable case as one in which the controversy is "definite and concrete, touching the legal relations of parties having adverse legal interests." Such a controversy must also be "real and substantial, admitting of specific relief through a decree of a conclusive character." A true case or controversy is opposite from a hypothetical or abstract question upon which a court might render an advisory opinion.

Certiorari   A writ or order to a court whose decision is being challenged to send up the records of the case so a higher court can review a lower-court decision. *Certiorari* means "to be informed" and is granted to the losing party by the Supreme Court if four justices agree the writ should be issued. Until 1891 the Court was formally obliged to take all appeals that came through the federal court system or that concerned a federal question and were appealed from the highest state courts. In 1890 the Court had to deal with some 1,816 cases, a near physical impossibility for the justices. The problem of an overcrowded docket was then addressed by the Everts Act of 1891, by which Congress created three-judge circuit courts of appeals as intermediaries between the federal district courts and the Supreme Court. The act restricted the means of appeal to the Supreme Court by introducing discretionary certiorari power. Through certiorari the Court could decline to hear certain cases if a given number of justices felt they were not sufficiently important. Denial of a certiorari petition means the decision of the Circuit Court is upheld. Despite the Everts Act, the Court's workload continued to expand, however. It was occasioned by major increases in population, a more extensive governmental administrative apparatus, and the widespread use of the writ of error, by which cases came to the Court by assertion of legal error committed by a court below. The Judiciary Act of 1925 largely did away with the writ of error and gave the Court even wider discretion in broad classes of cases by reaffirming the writ of certiorari. In the years following the Judiciary Act of 1925, the proportion of certiorari petitions granted by the Court never exceeded 22 percent. Certiorari is one of four ways by which cases come before the Supreme Court. The others are appeal, the extraordinary writ, and certification. Certification is a process through which a lower court requests a higher court to resolve certain issues in a case while the case is still pending in the lower court. *See also* APPEAL, p. 383.

Significance   The certiorari power is the Supreme Court's principal means of keeping abreast of its work. It can also be an effective administrative tool in the hands of a skillful chief justice. When Charles Evans Hughes became chief justice in 1930, for example, he read and summarized all certiorari petitions coming to the Court. He weeded out some as easily disposable and put them on a separate list before the Saturday conference of the justices. In conference Chief Justice Hughes attempted to average only about three and one-half minutes for discussion of each certiorari petition. Since his preparation far exceeded that of the other justices, his views on whether to grant certiorari petitions were seldom challenged. Thus a chief justice, as chief administrative officer of the Court, can restrict access to the Court by his manipulation of certiorari petitions. He can also direct the Court's attention to policy areas he thinks are important, as when Chief Justice Hughes expanded the Court's scrutiny of *in forma pauperis* petitions to the point where *habeas corpus* arguments by prisoners became an important part of the Court's docket. *In forma pauperis* means "in the manner of a pauper" and refers to permission extended to an indigent to proceed with a legal action without having to pay court fees and other costs associated with litigation. The scope of the Supreme Court's certiorari jurisdiction is much broader than that afforded by any other means of access to the Court, including the writ of appeal. The writ of certiorari extends to any civil or criminal case in the federal courts of appeal regardless of the parties, the status of the case, or the amount in controversy. Any state court decision that involves the construction and application of the federal Constitution, treaties, or laws, or the determination of a federal title, right, privilege, or immunity falls within the Court's certiorari jurisdiction. Certiorari allows the Supreme Court to enter the policy-making process virtually at any point it chooses.

Child Benefit   An approach to establishment of religion questions which allows indirect aid to religious institutions by focusing upon individual recipients of aid rather than a church or denomination. Child benefit theory has permitted transportation and textbooks to be provided to students of nonpublic schools, although the Establishment Clause prohibits government from aiding institutional religion. The theory says it is the individual student who receives the assistance and not a religious body. In *Everson v. Board of Education* (330 U.S. 1: 1947), the Supreme Court held that provision of certain "general governmental services," such as police and fire protection, sewer and water services, and transportation, are the kinds of services "indisputably marked off from the religious function." The Court said religion would be unnecessarily handicapped if such services were not permitted. *See also* ESTABLISHMENT CLAUSE, p. 408; *EVERSON V. BOARD OF EDUCATION* (330 U.S. 1: 1947), p. 89.

Significance   Child benefit reasoning has been effectively used to place certain governmental programs outside the coverage of the Establishment Clause. The theory reflects a position on church-state relations that has been termed "benevolent neutrality" or "accommodationist."

Chilling Effect   The consequence of a policy or practice that discourages the exercise of a legal right. A chilling effect comes when persons perceive the possibility of sanctions or reprisals if their rights are exercised. A convicted person may not be sentenced more heavily after retrial, for example, because he or she successfully appealed the initial conviction. The possibility of a heavier sentence would have a chilling effect because it would penalize persons pursuing their constitutional right to appeal. It would also inhibit persons in prison from filing appeals. *See also* FREE SPEECH CLAUSE, p. 416; OVERBREADTH DOCTRINE, p. 440; PRIOR RESTRAINT, p. 444.

Significance   Chilling effect problems are often encountered in relation to First Amendment rights. In *Pittsburgh Press Company v. Commission on Human Relations* (413 U.S. 376: 1973, p. 000), the Supreme Court said a special problem of prior restraint on expression is that it induces excessive caution by speakers who wish to steer clear of restricted areas. A self-imposed regulation of expression occurs. Laws that are vague and create uncertainties about what can be said chill free expression.

Citizenship   One's status as a person who is entitled to all the rights and privileges guaranteed and protected by the Constitution of the United States. Citizenship is conferred by Congress. Since the Civil Rights Act of 1866, all persons born or naturalized in the United

States are citizens of the United States. The Fourteenth Amendment reiterated that language in Section 1. The term "dual citizenship" refers to a person's status as a citizen of the United States and the state in which he or she resides, or to the holding of citizenship in two countries. *See also* PRIVILEGES AND IMMUNITIES CLAUSES, p. 445.

Significance   Citizenship is elaborated in two privileges and immunities clauses of the United States Constitution. The Constitution requires, for example, that citizens of a particular state have parity with citizens of all other states. The *Slaughterhouse Cases* (16 Wallace 36: 1873) emphasized the distinct character of federal and state citizenship. *Slaughterhouse* held that privileges and immunities conferred by state citizenship were outside federal reach through the Fourteenth Amendment. Such an interpretation took a very narrow view of the substance of federal citizenship. It covered only such things as interstate travel and voting. While subsequent decisions have extended the meaning of citizenship in the Fourteenth Amendment, *Slaughterhouse* is still controlling in that it precludes use of privileges and immunities language in protecting citizens by federal authority.

Civil Rights Act of 1964   A federal law designed to eliminate racial discrimination. The Civil Rights Act of 1964 was the most comprehensive legislation of its kind since Reconstruction. The act contained several key policy thrusts, the most significant being Title II, dealing with public accommodations. The provisions of the title are very similar to those of the Civil Rights Act of 1875, which was struck down in the *Civil Rights Cases* (109 U.S. 3: 1883, p. 321). Title II prohibited discrimination in hotels, motels, restaurants, theaters, and other public halls and arenas.

Significance   The Civil Rights Act of 1964 was tied to the regulatory power stemming from federal authority to protect interstate commerce and all that affects it. The stricken 1875 statute had been based upon legislative power presumed to flow from the Fourteenth Amendment. The use of the commerce power in 1964 was upheld in *Heart of Atlanta Motel* v. *United States* (379 U.S. 241: 1964). Title III enabled the Justice Department to undertake suits to desegregate noneducational public facilities. Title IV was aimed at school segregation. It authorized greater federal involvement in achieving desegregation of local school districts. Title V broadened the power of the Civil Rights Commission to include all situations where equal protection had been denied. Title VI authorized the withholding of federal funds from any state or local program that discriminated in education or anywhere else. The threatened loss of federal revenue for school districts failing to desegregate became an effective means for encouraging compliance. Title VII prohibited employment discrimination. It established the Equal Employment Opportunity Commission to enforce the title. Federal court litigation has increased dramatically since passage of the Civil Rights Act of 1964. The civil-rights focus has since turned to issues of employment discrimination based on race, gender, and age. The act settled the issue of equality in public accommodations to the extent that litigation in that subject area has virtually stopped.

Class Action A suit brought by several persons on behalf of a larger group whose members have the same legal interest. A class action is indicated when a group is so large that individual suits are impractical. Group suits have been used frequently in recent years and are often the means by which civil-rights, consumer, and environmental questions are litigated. A class action is sometimes called a representative action. It can be brought in both federal and state courts. It must be certified by a trial court at the outset, and all class members must be made aware of the suit and given an opportunity to exclude themselves. Certification involves a determination that the asserted class actually exists and that those persons bringing the action are members of the class.

Significance A class action provides economy and efficiency in the adjudication of an issue. It significantly reduces the possibility of conflicting judgments resulting from numerous individual suits. Several limitations apply to a class action. In *Zahn* v. *International Paper Co.* (414 U.S. 291: 1973), the Supreme Court held that to use federal diversity jurisdiction for class actions, each member of the class must have suffered an injury amounting to at least $10,000 in value. The Court also said in *Eisen* v. *Carlisle* & *Jacqueline* (417 U.S. 156: 1974) that the initiators of a class action must notify, at their own expense, all members of the class. The impact of these decisions has been to reduce the number of large consumer and environmental suits. The more numerous smaller class actions have not been adversely affected.

Classification A division of the population into two or more groups for purposes of allocating a benefit or imposing a restriction. In order to be a permissible classification, a legislative enactment must not be arbitrary or impose such disabilities as to be in violation of the Due Process or Equal Protection Clauses. *See also* BENEVOLENT CLASSI-FICATION, p. 388; EQUAL PROTECTION CLAUSE, p. 313; REVERSE DIS-CRIMINATION, p. 447.

Significance   A classification is typically evaluated by the Supreme Court through the rational basis test, a deferential and relaxed standard. Classifications are presumed valid. If a legislative enactment pursues a legitimate objective, the classification is permitted if it rationally relates to the objective. The Supreme Court may, however, place legislative classifications under closer examination or "strict scrutiny." Close or strict scrutiny transfers the burden of proof to the state and demands more than a showing of reasonableness. A compelling state interest must be demonstrated in these instances and a critical need established. The state must also show that its compelling interest cannot be served through other than classificatory means. The strict scrutiny standard applies when the classification affects a fundamental right such as the right to vote, to speak freely, and to travel freely between and among the states. Classifications are also subjected to strict scrutiny if they touch a "suspect" class. Such a class is one that has been so damaged by long-term and purposeful discrimination that extraordinary protection is required. Classifications based on race and alienage are inherently suspect.

Clear and Present Danger Test   A standard used to determine if a particular expression is protected by the First Amendment. The clear and present danger test was first articulated in *Schenck* v. *United States* (249 U.S. 47: 1919), a case involving an Espionage Act prosecution for obstruction of military recruitment. The Supreme Court upheld Schenck's conviction, saying that expression is a conditional freedom that must be evaluated in a situational context. Each situation must be reviewed to determine whether expression occurs in such a way and is of "such nature as to create a clear and present danger that it will bring about the substantive evil which legislatures are empowered to prevent." If speech is linked closely enough to illegal acts, it may be restricted. The Court said it was a matter of proximity and degree. *See also* BAD TENDENCY TEST, p. 387; FREE SPEECH CLAUSE, p. 416; *SCHENCK* V. *UNITED STATES* (249 U.S. 47: 1919), p. 108; SLIDING SCALE TEST, p. 450.

Significance   The clear and present danger test presumes that free speech is not an absolute right. The test is designed to justify interference with speech only when the government can show that the speech creates a danger both substantial and immediate. In this respect clear and present danger is a more demanding test for restrictive enactments than the bad tendency test.

Collateral Estoppel　　A legal principle that prohibits relitigation of an issue once a final fact judgment has been made. Collateral estoppel is based on the doctrine of *res judicata*, which means "a matter already decided." *See also* ASHE V. SWENSON (397 U.S. 436: 1970), p. 213; DOUBLE JEOPARDY, p. 403.

Significance　　Collateral estoppel was first developed in civil litigation. The Fifth Amendment protection from double jeopardy was held to include the right to argue or claim collateral estoppel in criminal cases in *Ashe* v. *Swenson* (397 U.S. 436: 1970, p. 213). *Ashe* prohibited reprosecution in cases where an acquittal in a prior case was based on a fact issue introduced in the second case. Since the fact issue had been resolved in the defendant's favor initially, it could not be relitigated in another criminal prosecution. The *Ashe* decision clarified the same offense criterion traditionally used in double jeopardy cases. The collateral estoppel doctrine prevents prosecution of different offenses if previously resolved fact questions would be reconsidered in a later case.

Community Standards　　A criterion used in the evaluation of obscenity. The community standards test was first introduced in *Roth* v. *United States* (356 U.S. 476: 1957). The Warren Court said in *Roth* that "community" should refer to national standards. National norms were perceived as being less restrictive and more permissive than local standards. Defining standards in national terms also made criteria for adjudicating obscenity issues more uniform. It places the Supreme Court at the center of the process of determining what constitutes obscenity. *See also* MEMOIRS V. MASSACHUSETTS (383 U.S. 413: 1966), p. 133; MILLER V. CALIFORNIA (383 U.S. 15: 1973), p. 134; OBSCENITY, p. 437; ROTH V. UNITED STATES (354 U.S. 476: 1957), p. 131.

Significance　　Community standards criteria have been a major source of disagreement in the Supreme Court's treatment of obscenity. The Burger Court abandoned the Warren Court approach in *Miller* v. *California* (413 U.S. 15: 1973), saying that to require obscenity prosecutions to use national standards was "an exercise in futility." The Court said the nation is simply too big and diverse to expect that fixed and uniform standards can be formulated. Rather the standards should be drawn from each local community and applied in concert with "limiting instructions on the law." The Court rejected as neither realistic nor constitutionally sound a requirement that would have "the people of Maine or Mississippi accept the standards of Las Vegas or New York City." Defining community standards in local terms created the prospect of a more restrictive and diverse approach to the regulation of obscenity.

Compulsory Process   The Sixth Amendment right of a person to have witnesses in his or her favor. Compulsory process protects the defendant's right to present a defense that includes witnesses who may not want to appear voluntarily. A defendant may subpoena a party and compel his or her presence. A subpoena is the command of a court requiring a person to appear at a legal proceeding and offer testimony on a particular matter. A *subpoena duces tecum* is a process by which physical items such as papers or records are produced at such a proceeding. *See also* WASHINGTON V. TEXAS (388 U.S. 14: 1967), p. 250.

Significance   Compulsory process was extended to the states in *Washington* v. *Texas* (388 U.S. 14: 1967, p. 250), in which the Supreme Court determined that the right was fundamental. The compulsory process provision of the Sixth Amendment has been interpreted more broadly than the right to subpoena witnesses. It has been held to prevent a state from denying access to certain categories of witnesses, such as coparticipants in an alleged crime. Similarly, it prevents a state from creating situations in which a witness for the defense is diminished in value by a judicial action or jury instruction. The compulsory process protection establishes a substantial expectation that the defense will be able to present a full and unimpaired alternative version of the facts.

Confrontation Clause   The Sixth Amendment entitlement that an accused person must be confronted with the witnesses against him or her. The Confrontation Clause is often thought to be synonymous with the right to cross-examine accusers or adverse witnesses, but cross-examination is only one element of the clause's broader objective of fully exposing reliable evidence to the fact-finding process. The Confrontation Clause requires that witnesses be brought to open court and placed under oath and thereby under threat of perjury. Their testimony as well as their manner and presence is assessed there. *See also* CHAMBERS V. MISSISSIPPI (410 U.S. 284: 1973), p. 248; POINTER V. TEXAS (380 U.S. 400: 1965), p. 247; SIXTH AMENDMENT, p. 241.

Significance   The Confrontation Clause entitles an accused person to challenge the evidence against him or her in an attempt to present the best factual defense possible. An accused person is therefore given the opportunity to be present at all proceedings against him or her, and a relatively unrestricted examination/cross-examination process can be utilized. The Supreme Court found the right of confrontation to be a fundamental right and has applied it to the states through the Fourteenth Amendment in *Pointer* v. *Texas* (380 U.S. 400: 1965).

Consent Search   A person's right to waive Fourth Amendment protections and consent to a search. Consent search involves the critical question of whether consent has been voluntarily given. The Supreme Court has determined that the voluntariness issue cannot be resolved by any infallible touchstone, but can only be resolved by looking at the totality of circumstances. In doing so, two competing concerns must be accommodated. One is the legitimate need for searches. The other is the need to assure the absence of coercion in gaining consent. *See also* SCHNECKLOTH V. BUSTAMONTE (412 U.S. 218: 1973), p. 191; THIRD-PARTY SEARCH, p. 457; UNITED STATES V. MATLOCK (415 U.S. 164: 1974), p. 193.

Significance   Consenting to a search means waiving a constitutional protection. The Supreme Court has established that the burden of proving the voluntariness of such consent rests with the prosecution and cannot be inferred from silence. The Court has not gone so far as to require that persons be informed that they may withhold consent, although a number of states have done so. Assuming consent is voluntary, a person may limit his or her consent to particular places to be searched and specific items to be searched for. Once granted, consent may be withdrawn. Even uncoerced consent cannot purge taint stemming from an impermissible action occurring prior to consent. If a person is illegally detained, for example, any subsequent search is flawed.

Contempt   Any act that obstructs the administration of justice by a court or that brings disrespect on a court or its authority. Contempt may be *direct* in that it occurs in the presence of the court and constitutes a direct affront to the court's authority. While some due process protections apply to contempt, it is generally a summary order through which penalties of fine or imprisonment may be directly imposed by the court. Contempt may be *indirect* in that the behavior that demonstrates contempt may occur outside the court-room. It is necessary to distinguish between criminal and civil contempt. Criminal contempt is an act of obstruction or disrespect typically occurring in the courtroom. A party who acts in an abusive manner in court is in criminal contempt. He or she may receive a fine and/or imprisonment for up to six months summarily imposed. Civil contempt results from failure to comply with the order of a court. Civil contempt is designed to coerce compliance with an order to protect the interests of the party on whose behalf the order to judgment was issued. Civil contempt ends when the desired conduct or compliance occurs. A legislative contempt power also exists. It may be used if a disturbance is created within a legislative chamber or if persons subpoenaed to appear before legislative committees fail to testify. Congressional contempt is not summarily imposed, however. It is handled through the standard criminal process with trial occur-ring in a federal district court if an indictment has been secured from a grand jury.

Significance   The contempt power provides courts with leverage to maintain courtroom decorum appropriate for judicial proceedings. Contempt enables a court to punish disruptive or disrespectful conduct, and it serves as a deterrent to such conduct. The contempt power also permits courts to compel compliance with a court order, backstopping the authority of all such orders.

Counsel, Assistance of   A protection of the Sixth Amendment that entitles any accused person to have "assistance of counsel for his defense." The assistance of counsel provision in its early construction was confined to preventing the government from keeping an accused from securing his or her own counsel. There was no expectation that counsel was required or would be provided in the instance of defendant indigency. The Supreme Court has gradually expanded the coverage of the counsel language, however, to require the appointment of defense counsel in all federal and state felony cases, and finally in all misdemeanor cases involving confinement to jail as a possible sentence. Juvenile delinquency proceedings also require the appointment of counsel. *See also ARGERSINGER* v. *HAMLIN* (407 U.S. 25: 1972), p. 266; CRITICAL STAGE, p. 400; *GIDEON* v. *WAINWRIGHT*

(372 U.S. 335: 1963), p. 264; POWELL V. ALABAMA (287 U.S. 45: 1932), p. 263; UNITED STATES V. WADE (388 U.S. 218: 1967), p. 267.

Significance   The assistance of counsel doctrine has developed around two points. First, the aid provided by counsel is invaluable in criminal cases, and due process requires "the guiding hand of counsel" for an accused charged with a criminal offense. Justice Black remarked in *Gideon* v. *Wainwright* (372 U.S. 335: 1963) that lawyers are necessities, not luxuries. Second, a defendant should not be denied assistance of counsel because of his or her indigency. Any person who is charged with a criminal offense and who is not able to afford counsel cannot have a fair trial unless counsel is provided. The right to counsel has also been extended to various critical stages of the criminal process both before and after trial. A critical stage is defined as any step in the criminal process where the advice of counsel may be essential to protecting the rights of an accused person, or where the defendant's overall fate is substantially affected. Currently recognized as critical stages are custodial interrogations, preliminary hearings, arraignments, post-indictment lineups, sentencing and probation revocation hearings, and appeals. Assistance of counsel is also a part of the civil trial process. While such assistance is not constitutionally mandated for civil trials, federal appellate courts have held that less strict adherence to evidentiary rules and less formal discovery compliance ought to be applied by trial courts when one of the parties is unrepresented by counsel. In the case of an unrepresented prisoner plaintiff in civil-rights actions, counsel is often appointed by the trial judge to ensure fairness.

Critical Stage   The point in a criminal proceeding at which an accused person is entitled to assistance of counsel. Critical stage assistance is essential to protecting the rights of an accused person and may substantially affect the criminal process as a whole. *See also* COUNSEL, ASSISTANCE OF, p. 399; GIDEON V. WAINWRIGHT (372 U.S. 335: 1963), p. 264; UNITED STATES V. WADE (388 U.S. 218: 1967), p. 267.

Significance   Critical stage was defined only in terms of the trial itself until 1963. Assistance of counsel was not needed elsewhere in the criminal process. Once trial assistance was mandated for all felony prosecutions in *Gideon* v. *Wainwright* (372 U.S. 335: 1963), however, it was inevitable that other stages in the criminal process would be examined as well. Soon after *Gideon,* such stages as custodial interrogations, post-indictment investigations, preliminary hearings, and post-indictment identifications were found to be critical. Even prior to *Gideon,* counsel requirements had been extended to arraignments. The critical stages of post-trial proceedings have been defined as sentencing, probation revocations, and appeals. The large number of recognized critical stages reflects the high priority assigned to assistance of counsel by the Supreme Court. An accused must have access to legal counsel throughout the criminal process to satisfy due process requirements.

Cruel and Unusual Punishment   A criminal penalty prohibited by the Eighth Amendment. Cruel and unusual punishment standards have been drawn from evolving standards of decency. The status of a particular punishment may change as society's values change. Currently the Supreme Court has said that punishments that involve torture or cruelty are prohibited, as are punishments that are degrading. *See also* EIGHTH AMENDMENT, p. 289; MANDATORY SENTENCE, p. 434.

Significance   The cruel and unusual punishment doctrine holds that punishments must "comport with human dignity." They cannot be imposed upon a status or condition, and they must be proportionate to the offense. The death penalty, a punishment unique in terms of its severity and irrevocability, does not invariably offend the cruel and unusual punishment prohibition. Procedural flaws may make the imposition of the death penalty impermissible, however. It may not be imposed without a two-stage or bifurcated trial and sentencing process. The sentencer must be provided with sufficient guidance for making a determination of death. He or she must specify aggravating circumstances in assessing the gravity of a particular offense, and the sentencer must consider any and all mitigating circumstances. The mandatory sentence of death is not permitted because it does not allow for mitigating circumstances.

Declaratory Judgment   A form of relief invoked when a plaintiff seeks a declaration of his or her rights. A declaratory judgment does not involve monetary damages but is an assessment of a party's rights prior to an injury occurring. It differs from a conventional action in that no specific order is issued by the court. It differs from an advisory opinion in that parties have a bona fide controversy in a declaratory judgment proceeding, although actual injury has not yet occurred. The federal courts are empowered to render declaratory judgments by the Federal Declaratory Judgment Act of 1934. In a declaratory judgment proceeding there must be a real controversy, but the plaintiff is uncertain of his or her rights and seeks adjudication of them. As in injunctive relief, a declaratory judgment request is a petition for a court to exercise its powers of equity. No jury is permitted. The judge is asked to declare what the law is regarding the controversy. *See also* ADVISORY OPINION, p. 381.

Significance   Declaratory judgment actions are a comparatively recent development in American jurisprudence because the traditional concept was that courts could only act when a plaintiff was entitled to a coercive remedy. A plaintiff may find it necessary, however, to determine if he or she is bound by contractual language that the plaintiff believes to be void or unenforceable for some reason. If the plaintiff should fail to comply, he or she is risking suit for breach of contract and consequential damages. The declaratory judgment procedure is helpful to all parties because it circumvents the necessity of a possible breach and the lengthy litigation that such action invites. Contract and patient disputes frequently form the basis of declaratory judgments. Courts are reluctant to issue them on broad public policy issues.

De Jure   A Latin term meaning "by right." A de jure action flows directly from an official pronouncement. It is used in contrast to de facto as a legal qualifier. *De facto* means "in fact," and is a condition that has status as a function of its existence or through established practice.

Significance   The terms *de jure* and *de facto* may be used in a variety of contexts to modify or qualify a condition. They have often been used in describing conditions of racial segregation. De jure segregation is intended and specifically sanctioned by law. Such legally sanctioned segregation was struck down by the Supreme Court in *Brown* v. *Board of Education I* (347 U.S. 483: 1954, p. 326). De facto segregation occurs without formal assistance of government. In its de facto form, segregation has social and economic causes outside the established constitutional system.

Diversity Jurisdiction   A civil case with a plaintiff and a defendant from different states. Diversity jurisdiction deals with the problem of diversity of citizenship. The description of federal court jurisdiction in Article III of the Constitution provides that "federal judicial power shall extend to cases between citizens of different states" or between citizens and aliens. Since the Constitution did not establish inferior federal courts, and since only Congress is permitted to confer such jurisdiction, diversity jurisdiction lies wholly within the control of Congress. Diversity jurisdiction was first conferred upon lower federal courts in the Judiciary Act of 1789, but a $50 controversy had to exist before the federal courts could enforce their jurisdiction. The amount in controversy was raised to $10,000 in 1958. *See also* CASE OR CONTROVERSY, p. 389; ORIGINAL JURISDICTION, p. 440.

Significance   Diversity jurisdiction is periodically debated in Congress among those who would abolish it altogether, those who would reduce it dramatically, and those who would retain it as it is. Proponents of abolition point to the cost to federal taxpayers, the intervention of federal courts in state law matters, and the redundancy and uncertainty that exists when a dual system of courts addresses the same issues. Opponents of change argue the possibility of home party bias against nonresidents, the value of two-system interaction, and the multiplicity of civil actions that the federal courts, for procedural reasons, are better equipped to handle. Diversity jurisdiction exists where there is a diversity of citizenship or where there is an interstate aspect to a legal action. Suits below the dollar threshold and that involve no substantial federal issue are conveyed to state courts. Diversity jurisdiction was established for the federal courts originally because state courts might be biased against litigants from out-of-state. The political interests of the federalists were well served by having federal court jurisdiction touch on state and local matters. Diversity of citizenship cases constitute a large portion, about 30 percent, of the current civil caseload in federal courts. The potential for substantial conflict between federal and state law litigated in federal courts under diversity jurisdiction was minimized by the Supreme Court's decision in *Erie Railroad* v. *Tompkins* (304 U.S. 64: 1938). The Court held that state statutory or common law is always to be applied in diversity cases.

Double Jeopardy   A Fifth Amendment provision that no person shall be "subject for the same offense to be twice put in jeopardy of life or limb." Double jeopardy precludes the state from repeatedly subjecting a citizen to the ordeal of prosecution for a given offense with the possibility of eventual conviction on the charge. The ban on double jeopardy was extended to the states by the Warren Court in *Benton* v. *Maryland* (395 U.S. 784: 1969). The Double Jeopardy Clause was seen by the Court as representing "a fundamental ideal in our constitutional heritage." The clause does not prevent both federal and state levels of government from prosecuting persons for the same criminal act on the basis of dual sovereignty, however. Bank robbery, for example, is both a federal and a state crime if the bank has federal insurance coverage. Successive prosecutions at the state and local levels are precluded because local units of government are subordinate instrumentalities of the state. Dual sovereignty does not exist within a state. In a jury trial jeopardy commences when the jury is sworn. In a nonjury trial jeopardy commences when the first witness is sworn. Cases dismissed prior to the commencement of double jeopardy in either proceeding may be reinstated. The Double Jeopardy Clause does not apply to cases where a defendant successfully appeals following a conviction and has the conviction set aside on grounds other than insufficiency of evidence. Reprosecution in such situations is limited to a charge no greater than the equivalent of the original conviction that prompted the appeal. A sentence may be more severe following successful reprosecution without violating the Double Jeopardy Clause if multiple punishments have been imposed. *See also* ASHE V. SWENSON (397 U.S. 436: 1970), p. 213; BREED V. JONES (421 U.S. 519: 1975), p. 216; BULLINGTON V. MISSOURI (451 U.S. 430: 1981), p. 217; COLLATERAL ESTOPPEL, p. 396; FIFTH AMENDMENT, p. 201; IMPLICIT ACQUITTAL, p. 423; PRICE V. GEORGIA (398 U.S. 323: 1970), p. 215; WALLER V. FLORIDA (397 U.S. 387: 1970), p. 212.

Significance   A double jeopardy determination is frequently made difficult by what constitutes sameness. Sameness is usually resolved by precluding prosecutions for two offenses where the same evidence is required to prove guilt. A "same transaction test," which views offenses in terms of similar actions by the defendant, may also be used. Neither approach clearly delineates sameness, however. The doctrine of collateral estoppel is held to be part of the double jeopardy protection and provides some assistance in solving the sameness problem. It forbids reprosecution in cases where an accused has been acquitted on the basis of an ultimate fact issue relitigated in the second trial. Another double jeopardy problem is created by the declaration of a mistrial after jeopardy has attached. If the defendant makes the mistrial motion, ordinarily there is no double jeopardy issue. But if the prosecution makes the motion, or if the judge grants a mistrial without a motion, an ambiguous situation is created. In the latter two situations, jeopardy may be double on a reprosecution unless the mistrial was manifestly necessitated.

Due Process Clauses   Constitutional provisions designed to ensure that laws will be reasonable both in substance and in means of implementation. Due process language is contained in two clauses of the Constitution of the United States. The Fifth Amendment prohibits deprivation of "life, liberty, or property, without due process of law." It sets a limit on arbitrary and unreasonable actions by the federal government. The Fourteenth Amendment contains parallel language aimed at the states. Due process requires that actions of government occur through ordered and regularized processes. It subjects those processes to constitutional and statutory limits in the protection of individual rights. There are two kinds of due process. The first is *procedural due process,* which focuses on the methods or procedures by which governmental policies are executed. It guarantees fairness in the processes by which government imposes regulations or sanctions. Procedural due process requires that a person be formally notified of any proceeding in which he or she is a party, and that he or she be afforded an opportunity for an impartial hearing. Additional procedural rights have been enumerated in the Bill of Rights. Through the process of incorporation, most Bill of Rights protections have been applied to the states through the Due Process Clause of the Fourteenth Amendment. *Substantive due process* represents the second kind of due process. It involves the reasonableness of policy content. Policies may deny substantive due process when they do not rationally relate to legitimate legislative objectives or when they are impermissibly vague. *See also* FIFTH AMENDMENT, p. 77; FOURTEENTH AMENDMENT, p. 412; INCORPORATION, p. 425; PROCEDURAL DUE PROCESS, p. 446; SUBSTANTIVE DUE PROCESS, p. 456.

Significance   Due process is an evolving concept that undergoes continuing adjustment and refinement. The two due process clauses provide the Supreme Court an ongoing opportunity to consider and define the legal contours of fairness. The heart of the matter is reasonableness. If the substance of a government policy, or the procedures used to implement it, are adjudged to be arbitrary and unreasonable, the Court can nullify the policy or practice under the due process clauses.

Editorial Privilege   The extent to which publishers may be insulated from the need to disclose information about editorial judgments. Editorial privilege is a form of benefit. A benefit is a privilege possessed by a person or a class of persons providing an advantage over other persons or classes. In some instances a privilege exempts one from some obligation because his or her office or function would be impaired. If the editorial process is confidential, for example, a plaintiff in a libel action may not be able to inquire of a publisher about the source of information used by the publisher. Neither could the plaintiff inquire about the information-gathering process itself or the bases upon which journalistic judgments were made, including a publisher's state of mind. In *Herbert* v. *Lando* (441 U.S. 153: 1979), the Supreme Court rejected the position that editorial privilege prevents access to the editorial process by a plaintiff seeking to demonstrate malice in a libel action. *See also* HERBERT V. LANDO (441 U.S. 153: 1979), p. 123; LIBEL, p. 433; NEWSPERSON'S PRIVILEGE, p. 436; *NEW YORK TIMES* V. *SULLIVAN,* p. 121.

Significance   Editorial privilege tends to protect publishers from successful libel actions. The privilege safeguards the freedom of the press by allowing wide latitude in the making of editorial judgments. *Lando* shows that editorial privilege is limited, however.

Electronic Surveillance   The observing or monitoring of a person by electronic means. Electronic surveillance includes telephone wiretaps and a wide variety of mechanisms that permit eavesdropping. Electronic surveillance was not considered to fall under the purview of the Fourth Amendment until recently, because neither physical entry onto private property had occurred, nor had seizure of tangible items taken place. In the late 1960s the Supreme Court reinterpreted the Fourth Amendment to create a protection for personal privacy, and this reinterpretation extended Fourth Amendment coverage to electronic surveillance. Congress subsequently enacted the Omnibus Crime Control Act of 1968, incorporating certain proscriptions on surveillance fashioned by the Court from its review of Fourth Amendment requirements. The act mandates use of an application procedure to obtain prior approval for electronic surveillance. The process closely resembles that used in obtaining a warrant. An unapproved emergency surveillance may occur for up to 48 hours provided a threat to national security is involved. *See also* DALIA V. UNITED STATES (441 U.S. 238: 1979), p. 170; KATZ V. UNITED STATES (389 U.S. 347: 1967), p. 169; WARRANT, p. 460.

Significance   Electronic surveillance constitutes a substantial threat to personal privacy. Modern technology is advanced enough that many sophisticated forms of intrusion yield thorough results. While the Supreme Court has not forbidden such surveillance altogether, its use is extensively regulated. The various means of executing an authorized surveillance need not be separately approved by judicial officers.

En Banc   A decision or proceeding made or heard by the entire membership of a court. En banc distinguishes cases having full participation from the more typical use of only a fraction of a court's membership to hear a particular case. En banc is sometimes used in reference to state and federal intermediate appellate courts, which generally assign only three members of the larger panel to hear appeals.

Significance   The United States Supreme Court and a state's highest appellate tribunal always sit en banc. An en banc court in United States Court of Appeals cases is usually ordered only in highly controversial cases or in cases where one or more of the court's panels have disagreed on a major point of law.

Equity Jurisdiction   The power of a court to grant relief or remedy to a party seeking court assistance outside principles of the common law. Equity jurisdiction permits judgments based on perceptions of fairness that supplement common law doctrines. *Relief* is assistance extended by a court to an injured or aggrieved party justified by these considerations. A *remedy* is the specific means, such as an injunction, by which a court intervenes to protect a legal right or interest through its equity jurisdiction. In *Brown* v. *Board of Education II* (349 U.S. 294: 1955), for example, the Supreme Court mandated that lower federal courts issue relief decrees shaped by equitable principles. The Court characterized equity as having a practical flexibility in its approach to constructing remedies. The lower courts were to reconcile public and private needs with decrees framed by perceptions of fairness and justice. A *show cause* proceeding is a process in equity jurisdiction with the rules of equity applying. A show cause order may be issued by a court to require a party to appear and explain why an action should not take place. Anyone opposed to the action has an opportunity to express his or her position and produce evidence in support of his or her interest. If the affected party does not appear or present acceptable reasons, the proposed show cause action will take place. The burden of proof is on the party required to show cause. *See also* APPEAL, p. 383; COMMON LAW, p. 13; INJUNCTION, p. 427.

Significance   Equity jurisdiction in the United States is placed in the same courts that possess jurisdiction over statutory and common law. In Great Britain courts of equity are structurally separate from courts having jurisdiction over legal matters. Considerations of equity in American courts protect against injustices occurring through proper but too rigid application of common law principles or where gaps exist in the common law.

Establishment Clause   The portion of the First Amendment that forbids Congress from enacting any law respecting an establishment of religion. The Establishment Clause in its most narrow construction would hold that no official or state church can be established in the United States and that no particular religion can be preferred by government action. A still more rigorous construction would have an absolute separation of church and state. The Supreme Court has generally steered a course near, but not quite reaching, the latter position. *Everson* v. *Board of Education* (330 U.S. 1: 1947) provided definitions on the subject as well as a linkage of the establishment prohibition to the states. *Everson* said the Establishment Clause erected a wall of separation between church and state that precluded government from aiding all religions or preferring one religion over another. Neither could government aid religion in preference to nonreligion, nor participate in the affairs of any religious organization. A closely related position is defined as the concept of governmental neutrality toward religion. The neutrality position does not prohibit all interaction of church and state. It only forbids governmental policies that aid or handicap religion. Yet another interpretation of the Establishment Clause accommodates certain governmental associations to religion. This position allows what Chief Justice Burger has termed "benevolent neutrality" in *Walz* v. *Tax Commission of New York City* (397 U.S. 664: 1970). Benevolent neutrality presumes that government need not act as an adversary of religion to avoid establishment prohibitions. *See also* CHILD BENEFIT, p. 391; *CPEARL V. NYQUIST* (413 U.S. 756: 1973), p. 94; *ENGEL V. VITALE* (370 U.S. 421: 1962), p. 84; *EVERSON V. BOARD OF EDUCATION* (330 U.S. 1: 1947), p. 89; *WALZ V. TAX COMMISSION OF NEW YORK CITY* (397 U.S. 664: 1970), p. 80.

Significance   The Establishment Clause has been interpreted in recent years to mean that government should not be prevented from providing benefits to people simply because they' have religious beliefs. Government's provision of such services as fire protection should not constitute an establishment of religion in this view. The

Supreme Court has also developed a construct known as "child benefit" for establishment challenges of various educational aid programs. Under the child benefit doctrine, textbooks distributed to nonpublic school students benefit individual students rather than institutional religion. Contemporary establishment cases are generally evaluated using three criteria. First, government policy must have a secular legislative purpose. The prayer and Bible-reading programs struck down by the Court in the early 1960s were seen as having spiritual rather than secular purposes. Second, no enactment can have as its principal or primary effect the advancement or inhibition of religion. Third, no statute may foster an excessive entanglement of government and religion. The entanglement criterion was crucial in several school aid cases because the Court felt government would be placed in a continuous monitoring relationship with religious institutions. Church and state would be brought into an impermissible pattern of regular and close interaction. The Court saw heated debate over various aid programs creating such ongoing divisiveness in American communities that undesirable entanglement was the inevitable result.

Exclusionary Rule   A court-fashioned rule of evidence that in criminal trials prohibits the use of items gained from an unconstitutional search or seizure. The exclusionary rule was designed to give effect to the Fourth Amendment prohibition against unreasonable searches and seizures. The rule is highly controversial and is not explicitly required by the Fourth Amendment. Until 1914, common law provided that evidence obtained in violation of the Fourth Amendment could still be used in a criminal trial. *Weeks* v. *United States* (232 U.S. 383: 1914) broke from that tradition and established the exclusionary rule in federal cases. The Supreme Court said that, without the rule, the Fourth Amendment is of no value and "might as well be stricken from the Constitution." The Court refrained, however, from taking a parallel step for state criminal trials. In *Wolf* v. *Colorado* (338 U.S. 25: 1949), the Court chose to leave the states free to choose whether the rule would operate in their courts. In 1949 the Court did not see the rule as essential enough that it must be extended to the states. *Mapp* v. *Ohio* (367 U.S. 643: 1967, p. 172) overruled *Wolf* and established the rule comprehensively. Since *Mapp*, the Court has had occasion to consider the exclusionary rule quite often. While the Court has chosen to retain the rule, dissatisfaction with it is apparent. Two patterns are revealed in the Court's recent handling of the problem. First, the rule will not be extended beyond the trial setting. The Burger Court rejected extension of it to grand

jury proceedings in *United States* v. *Calandra* (414 U.S. 338: 1974). The
Court allowed illegally obtained evidence to be used in a civil tax
proceeding in *United States* v. *Janis* (429 U.S. 874: 1976). Second, the
Court is willing to limit the coverage of the rule. It allowed otherwise
inadmissible evidence to be used in impeaching a defendant's trial
testimony in *Oregon* v. *Hass* (420 U.S. 714: 1975), and it limited *habeas
corpus* access to the federal courts in state search cases in *Stone* v. *Powell*
(428 U.S. 465: 1976, p. 173).

Significance   The exclusionary rule is justified in many ways. It is
seen by some as an indispensable doctrine for making operational the
personal protections guaranteed by the Fourth Amendment. The
rule creates disincentives for police misconduct in the search context
by making the products of such searches inadmissible. Others argue
that the exclusionary rule protects the integrity of the courts by
keeping the judicial process free of illegally seized evidence. Criticisms of the rule are numerous and substantial, however. Many
regard it as excessive because it goes beyond Fourth Amendment
provisions. The costs of the rule are seen as too high because it
often results in criminal conduct going unpunished. Further, it
tends to defeat the best test of evidence, which is its reliability.
The rule frequently allows suppression of reliable evidence because
the means of obtaining it were flawed. In sum, critics of the exclusionary rule argue that instead of sanctioning police officers the
rule rewards criminal defendants. The rule is clearly threatened as
political pressures mount to modify it. The exclusionary rule survives because its detractors have not been able to find an adequate
alternative.

Exigent Circumstance   An exception to the warrant requirement because the special demands of a situation make normal
warrant expectations impractical or impossible. Exigent circumstance searches include searches of automobiles, for example. The
exigency or emergency is created by the unforeseen need to search
and the fleeting opportunity to accomplish the search because of the
vehicle's mobility. A stop and frisk encounter is also an exigent
circumstance. In *Michigan* v. *Tyler* (436 U.S. 499: 1978, p. 178), the
Supreme Court also permitted a warrantless search of a fire scene
under the exigent circumstance exception. The Court held that a
burning building "clearly presents an exigency of sufficient proportions" to permit a reasonable warrantless entry. It would defy reason
to require a warrant or consent to be secured before entering a

burning building. Once on the premises to fight the fire, police and fire officials are entitled to gather visible evidence. A hot pursuit chase may also create sufficient exigency to allow a warrant exception. The exigent circumstance doctrine takes cognizance of the impossibility of completing the warrant process in certain situations where making a search or an arrest may be demanded. *See also* HOT PURSUIT, p. 421; MICHIGAN V. TYLER (436 U.S. 499: 1978), p. 178; WARRANTLESS SEARCH, p. 460.

Significance   The exigent circumstance doctrine is an exception to the warrant requirement for searches and arrests. It is necessitated by situational demands that make the normal processes impossible. The exception reflects the opinion that Fourth Amendment protections are not absolute, yet it places the burden of justifying an exigent circumstance on law enforcement officers.

Fairness Doctrine   A Federal Communications Commission policy that requires the holder of a broadcast license to afford a reasonable amount of air time to issues of public significance and to replies by persons of differing viewpoints from those expressed by the station. The fairness doctrine, also known as the equal time provision, is enforced by the Federal Communications Commission through its licensure authority. *See also* FREE PRESS CLAUSE, p. 415; *RED LION BROADCASTING COMPANY, INC.* v. *FCC* (395 U.S. 367: 1969), p. 130.

Significance   The fairness doctrine has been upheld by the Supreme Court against First Amendment challenge in *Red Lion Broadcasting Company, Inc.* v. *FCC* (395 U.S. 367: 1969). The Court distinguished the broadcast medium from the print medium, saying the fairness doctrine was necessary for broadcasting because of the scarcity of access to the airwaves and because licensees could otherwise monopolize the medium.

Federal Question   The jurisdiction to hear cases involving issues related to the United States Constitution, federal laws, or treaties. A federal question is one involving judicial powers conferred in Article III of the Constitution.

Significance   A federal question must be shown by parties wishing to access the federal courts. Their case or controversy must be within the power of the federal courts to adjudicate. An exception can occur when citizens of two different states are adversaries in a legal action. The Supreme Court frequently refuses to review cases because it believes a substantial federal question is not present.

Fifteenth Amendment   A post–Civil War amendment added to the Constitution in 1870. The Fifteenth Amendment provides that "the right of the citizens of the United States to vote shall not be denied or abridged by the United States or by any State on account of race, color, or previous condition of servitude." A second section of the Amendment empowered Congress to pass appropriate enforcement legislation. The Fifteenth Amendment did not extend the right to vote per se, but prohibited racial discrimination in voting. *See also* FOURTEENTH AMENDMENT, p. 313; *SOUTH CAROLINA* V. *KATZENBACH* (383 U.S. 301: 1966), p. 348; THIRTEENTH AMENDMENT, p. 458.

Significance   The Fifteenth Amendment left control over voting to the states, which placed qualifications for voting within the purview of state legislatures. Early decisions of the Supreme Court acknowledge that federal power could be exercised if citizens were denied the opportunity to vote in state elections on racial grounds. It was not until the Second World War, however, that the Supreme Court used the Fifteenth Amendment to reach the more sophisticated discriminatory techniques used in several states, such as the white primary and qualifying tests. Congressional initiatives based on the Fifteenth Amendment did not appear until the Voting Rights Act of 1965. The Voting Rights Act abolished such devices as the literacy test and poll tax, by which people had been disqualified from voting since Reconstruction. The act also provided for extensive federal supervision of elections and required that any new voter eligibility criterion be reviewed by the attorney general prior to its implementation. The Supreme Court unanimously upheld the Voting Rights Act in *South Carolina* v. *Katzenbach* (383 U.S. 301: 1966), saying an aggressive and inventive legislative approach was appropriate given nearly a century of systematic resistance to the Fifteenth Amendment. The Court's ruling in *Katzenbach* clearly established broad federal power over voting practices in the United States.

Fourteenth Amendment   A post–Civil War amendment added to the Constitution in 1868. The Fourteenth Amendment was designed to expand the Thirteenth Amendment as the basis for federal civil-rights authority. The amendment was also aimed at forcing southern compliance with newly established political rights for blacks.

The provisions of Section 1 constitute the heart of the amendment. It begins by declaring that "all persons born or naturalized in the United States, and subject to the jurisdiction thereof, are citizens of the United States and the State wherein they reside." This language reversed the citizenship holding in *Dred Scott* v. *Sandford* (19 Howard 393: 1857). The privileges and immunities provision then follows. This provision was intended to combat the effects of the Black Codes and allow federal authority to be used to protect and advance the civil rights of black citizens. The *Slaughterhouse Cases* decision (16 Wallace 36: 1873) neutralized this thrust through use of the dual citizenship concept. Dual citizenship allowed the Supreme Court to ascribe civil and political rights of major consequence to the states. Section 1 also says that no state shall deprive any person of life, liberty, or property without due process of law. The Due Process Clause ultimately allowed the Court to apply most Bill of Rights guarantees to the states in a process known as incorporation. The clause also enabled the Court to engage in a substantive review of state policies, particularly those regulating private property rights. Section 1 concludes by saying that no state shall deny to any person within its jurisdiction the equal protection of laws. The function of this provision was to prohibit unjustified classifications that might discriminate unreasonably. Section 5 empowers Congress "to enforce by appropriate legislation, the provisions of this article." Early attempts to do so were unsuccessful because the Court held that congressional power might only be used in a remedial fashion in cases where the state was itself an active participant in impermissible discrimination. The state action requirement survives, although the scope of federal legislative power conferred by the Fourteenth Amendment has been expanded considerably. *See also* CLASSIFICATION, p. 394; DUE PROCESS CLAUSES, p. 405; EQUAL PROTECTION CLAUSE, p. 313; INCORPORATION, p. 425; PRIVILEGES AND IMMUNITIES CLAUSES, p. 445; STATE ACTION, p. 454.

Significance   The Fourteenth Amendment brought a federal presence to the protection of civil rights, but early interpretations of the amendment preserved a dominant role for the states in this policy area. Only recently has the amendment produced major changes, primarily through expanded construction of the Due Process and Equal Protection Clauses. The Fourteenth Amendment has become the cornerstone of civil-rights policy and the principal means by which Bill of Rights guarantees have been extended to the states.

Free Exercise Clause   The clause of the First Amendment that restricts Congress from passing any law prohibiting the free exercise of religion. The Free Exercise Clause restrains government from compelling worship or belief and from making any right or privilege contingent on religious belief. Since *Cantwell* v. *Connecticut* (310 U.S. 296: 1940), the Free Exercise Clause has applied to the states through the Fourteenth Amendment. The clause presents problems of differentiation stemming from actions that flow out of beliefs. While belief is an absolute right, associated conduct may be regulated under certain circumstances. Most government enactments are of wide scope and are not aimed at any particular religious group. *See also* ESTABLISHMENT CLAUSE, p. 408; FIRST AMENDMENT, p. 77; *GILLETTE V. UNITED STATES* (401 U.S. 437: 1971), p. 105; *SHERBERT V. VERNER* (374 U.S. 398: 1964), p. 103; *SUNDAY CLOSING LAW CASES* (366 U.S. 421: 1961), p. 101; *WEST VIRGINIA STATE BOARD OF EDUCATION V. BARNETTE* (319 U.S. 624: 1943), p. 98; *WISCONSIN V. YODER* (406 U.S. 205: 1972), p. 106.

Significance   Free Exercise Clause cases typically involve conflicts between laws serving a wide and secular purpose on the one hand, and the religious interests of individuals on the other. Religion may not be used to exempt a person from compliance with secular law designed to safeguard the public's safety or health. The Supreme Court said in *Reynolds* v. *United States* (98 U.S. 145: 1878), the Mormon polygamy case, that "to permit professed doctrines of religious beliefs to prevail over the law of the land would permit every citizen to become a law unto himself." A classic illustration of the secular regulation approach to free exercise interpretation is seen in the first compulsory flag salute case, *Minersville School District* v. *Gobitis* (310 U.S. 586: 1940). Through Justice Frankfurter, the Court held that religious protections do not preclude legislation of a general secular nature as long as the legislation does not take direct aim at a sect. Justice Frankfurter said that even conscientious scruples cannot relieve an individual from obedience to general law. Modification of the secular regulation criterion came in the *Sunday Closing Law Cases* (366 U.S. 421: 1961), when the Warren Court attempted to provide further protection for religious exercise. The Court said that enactments must use the least restrictive means possible when pursuing secular objectives. A state must show that it could not have achieved a secular objective through an alternative method imposing less of a burden on religious exercise. The full impact of this modification is seen in *Sherbert* v. *Verner* (374 U.S. 398: 1964), where the Court held against a state unemployment compensation benefit system because it failed to demonstrate that no alternative forms of regulation could protect the system from fraudulent claims. Although less antithetical to religious exercise than the unmodified secular purpose test standing alone, the new approach raised the prospect of favoring religious preference. Such a course is laden with Establishment Clause difficulties because greater protection afforded religious practice means greater advantage for religion. This is an outcome precluded by the establishment prohibition.

Free Press Clause   A clause of the First Amendment prohibiting Congress from enacting any law abridging the freedom of the press. The Free Press Clause restrains both the federal government and the state from imposing prior restraint on the print media. A prior or previous restraint is a restriction on publication before it takes place or before published material can be circulated. Such restraint typically occurs through licensure or censorship procedures. The First Amendment prohibits prior restraint because restriction of expression before it can occur constitutes a threat both to free speech and to free press. Exceptions to the prohibition may be justified if publication threatens national security, incites overthrow of the government, is obscene, or interferes with the private rights of other persons. The basic dimensions of prior restraint were established in *Near v. Minnesota* (283 U.S. 697: 1931) and in *New York Times, Inc. v. United States* (403 U.S. 317: 1971), the Pentagon Papers case. *See also* FREE SPEECH CLAUSE, p. 416; LIBEL, p. 433; *NEAR V. MINNESOTA* (283 U.S. 697: 1931), p. 118; *NEW YORK TIMES, INC. V. SULLIVAN*(376 U.S. 354: 1965), p. 121; *NEW YORK TIMES, INC. V. UNITED STATES*(403 U.S. 713: 1971), p. 119; OBSCENITY, p. 437; *PITTSBURGH PRESS COMPANY V. COMMISSION ON HUMAN RELATIONS* (413 U.S. 376: 1973), p. 128; PRIOR RESTRAINT, p. 444; *RED LION BROADCASTING COMPANY V. FEDERAL COMMUNICATIONS COMMISSION* (395 U.S. 367: 1969), p. 130.

Significance   The Free Press Clause protects the information-gathering function of the press, although an absolute right of access and confidentiality of sources does not exist. Freedom of the press occasionally collides with the fair trial interests of criminal defendants. Some limitations may therefore be imposed on the press to minimize prejudicial pretrial publicity. The press cannot be barred from criminal trials, however, and it cannot be restrained from reporting what is observed there except in extraordinary circumstances. The broadcast media are permitted to cover criminal proceedings provided they do so with no adverse consequences to the accused. Several forms of published expression remain unprotected by the Free Press Clause. Obscenity, for example, has consistently been held to be subject to government regulation. Another area outside Free Press Clause protection is libel, which is printed material falsely and maliciously defaming a person. Despite its unprotected character, libel has been narrowly defined by the Supreme Court, especially where public officials are concerned. Debate on controversial public issues cannot be inhibited by threats of libel actions. Finally, the Court has held that commercial speech is not fully protected. Commercial speech is advertising intended to promote the sale of a product or a service. The broadcast medium is affected by a First Amendment interest, but is subject to government licensure regulation anyway because of the difficulty of access to the airwaves.

Free Speech Clause   A clause of the First Amendment that provides comprehensive protection for expression. The Free Speech Clause is absolute in prohibiting Congress from making any law that abridges the freedom of speech. Free Speech Clause coverage has been extended to the states through the Due Process Clause of the Fourteenth Amendment. In the case of *Schenck* v. *United States* (249 U.S. 47: 1919), the Supreme Court held that the First Amendment did not convey unlimited protection for expression, however, despite the absolutist language of the clause. Once the Court found that expression could be regulated, it became necessary to establish boundaries for when it could be regulated. Several categories of expression and several tests for evaluating expression have evolved. *See also* ASSEMBLY, RIGHT TO, p. 385; ASSOCIATION, RIGHT OF, p. 386; BAD TENDENCY TEST, p. 387; BALANCING TEST, p. 388; CLEAR AND PRESENT DANGER TEST, p. 395; PURE SPEECH, p. 447; SPEECH PLUS, p. 451; SYMBOLIC SPEECH, p. 457.

Significance   The Free Speech Clause protects pure speech more than any other form of expression. Pure speech is communication that has no additional action element. In order for pure speech to be restricted, it must create a clear and present danger. If the expression advocates unlawful acts, for example, and involves a substantial and immediate danger of a kind the government is empowered to prevent, the expression loses its protection. Advocacy of abstractions is not seen as having a sufficiently close connection to action. This kind of expression is permitted virtually unrestricted use. A less rigorous standard than clear and present danger is the bad tendency test, which allows regulation if there is a chance that substantive evil will occur. Another way of evaluating expression is through use of a balancing test. This standard weighs the expression interest against societal interests in an effort to determine if restriction of speech is warranted in a particular case. A form of balancing is a sliding scale formulation in which the gravity of the threat is weighed against the likelihood of the threat's coming to pass. Once speech has gone beyond its pure form to require action, the conduct becomes a possible object of regulation even though the expression itself may be protected. This is called "speech plus," which may take such forms as picketing or demonstrating. Such situations draw not only on the Free Speech Clause but on the First Amendment right to assemble as well. These kinds of expression may be subject to time, place, and manner restrictions provided the restrictions are evenhandedly applied and are content-neutral. Symbolic expression, i.e., gestures that are substituted for words, is recognized as having the same character of expression. Symbolic expression may be regulated only if the surrogate action is itself unlawful or subject to regulation.

Fundamental Right   Protection extended to a right expressly stated or implied in the Constitution. A fundamental right occupies a preferred position in American jurisprudence. It receives demanding review by the courts. If classificatory legislation affects a fundamental right, for example, the legislation is subject to the standards of strict scrutiny. The state must demonstrate that a compelling need is served by any enactment impinging on a fundamental right. *See also* PRE-FERRED POSITION DOCTRINE, p. 444; RIGHT, p. 448.

Significance   A fundamental right may be expressly provided in the Constitution, or it may have evolved to a preferred status. Fundamental rights include the right to interstate travel, participation in the political process, opportunity to adjudicate legal issues, privacy, personal autonomy, and abortion. Such services as public welfare assistance and public medical care have not been viewed by the Supreme Court as fundamental rights. Residence requirements used as a condition of receiving welfare assistance or medical care have been struck down as impermissible restrictions on the fundamental right of unhindered interstate movement.

Gag Order   An order by a court directed to media representatives prohibiting the reporting of a court proceeding. A gag order is an injunction intended to minimize publicity that might prejudice a criminal trial. Except in extreme circumstances, the Supreme Court has limited the use of such an order as a violation of freedom of the press. A gag order is also an order from a court preventing a disruptive litigant from further interference with a court proceeding. The order might go so far as to bind and literally gag an unruly litigant, as in *Illinois* v. *Allen* (397 U.S. 337: 1970). A gag order may be issued against the lawyers and litigants in a case prohibiting them from discussing certain aspects of the case. Sometimes a gag order results in sealing portions of a file or the transcripts of certain testimony in a trial in order to protect infants, mentally ill persons, or a patent or trade secret. *See also* INJUNCTION, p. 427; *NEBRASKA PRESS ASSOCIATION* V. *STUART* (427 U.S. 539: 1976), p. 259.

Significance   A gag order is used to prevent prejudicial pretrial publicity. It is an extreme measure and constitutes a substantive encroachment on freedom of the press. Other alternatives such as change of venue or delay in the commencement of a criminal prosecution are more accepted means of protecting the fair trial rights of an accused person.

Grand Jury   An investigative body that makes accusations rather than determines guilt. The grand jury evaluates information generated on its own or brought to it by a prosecutor. If it determines that probable cause exists, it returns an indictment against an accused person. The indictment signifies that the grand jury feels a trial on specific charges is warranted. In English law the grand jury had the function of protecting persons from being tried arbitrarily. An American grand jury typically ranges from 12 to 23 persons with selection occurring under guidelines that require neutral and nondiscriminatory processes. See *Alexander* v. *Louisiana* (405 U.S. 625: 1972). Grand juries operate in secret as a protection of persons it may not indict. Witnesses appear before grand juries under subpoena. Failure to provide information desired by a grand jury may result in a witness being cited for contempt, as in *Branzburg* v. *Hayes* (408 U.S. 665: 1972, p. 125). Upon hearing all testimony relating to a particular person, the grand jury determines by a simple majority vote whether to indict. While grand juries may function through their own initiative, they are usually guided and sometimes dominated by a prosecutor. The latter determines which witnesses will appear and which evidence will be developed. The prosecutor has virtually complete discretion in grand jury proceedings through control of relevant information. Grand juries usually indict persons whom prosecutors want to be indicted. A person need not appear before a grand jury to be indicted. Witnesses who do appear usually are not permitted counsel at the proceeding itself, although out-of-room consultation during the proceeding is often permitted. A witness must be advised of his or her rights against self-incrimination, but this warning may be quite general. See *United States* v. *Washington* (431 U.S. 181: 1977 p. 210). The Fifth Amendment requires grand juries in the American federal system. The requirement has never been extended to the states, however. In *Hurtado* v. *California* (110 U.S. 516: 1884, p. 206), the Supreme Court held that California's use of the information process, instead of the grand jury, did not deny due process. *Hurtado* gave the states the opportunity to determine their own preferential procedure for bringing criminal charges. Thirty-two states have elected to use the grand jury, at least for some portion of their criminal proceedings. Only eight states use it for all cases. Decisions subsequent to *Hurtado* have enhanced the investigative power of grand juries. An alternative accusatorial process to grand jury indictment is the information. This procedure allows a prosecutor to submit charges against a person supported by sufficient evidence in the view of a trial court of appropriate jurisdiction. *See also* COSTELLO V. UNITED STATES (350 U.S. 359: 1953), p. 209; FIFTH AMENDMENT, p. 201; UNITED STATES V. WASHINGTON (431 U.S. 181: 1977), p. 210.

Significance   The grand jury function is completely different from the guilt adjudication function. Grand jury proceedings have therefore been freed from the rigorous procedural and evidentiary standards used at trials. See *Costello* v. *United States* (350 U.S. 359: 1953, p. 209). The relaxation of procedural constraints was intended to maximize the opportunity for a grand jury to consider as much evidence as possible before making its decision to charge. Flexibility designed to enhance the investigative power of grand juries has some costs, however. Procedural protections of witnesses are less extensive than at the trial stage, and a heightened potential for misconduct exists relative to contempt and immunity practices. The state of Michigan permits a one-person grand jury. This person is always a trial judge, and he or she functions in the same manner as a grand jury composed of laypersons.

Habeas Corpus   A Latin term meaning "you have the body." *Habeas corpus* was a procedure in English law designed to prevent governmental misconduct, especially the improper detention of prisoners. Its primary purpose was to force jailers to bring a detained person before a judge who would examine the adequacy of the detention. If the judge found the person improperly in custody, he could order the prisoner's release through a writ of *habeas corpus*. A *writ* is an order from a court requiring the recipient of the order to do what the order commands. In American law the preliminary hearing functions as a point of examination into the propriety of pretrial detention as well as the charges brought against an accused person.

Article I, Section 9, of the United States Constitution provides that the "privilege of the Writ of Habeas Corpus shall not be suspended, unless when in Cases of Rebellion or Invasion the Public Safety may require it." President Lincoln attempted to suspend the writ early in the Civil War, but it was determined in *Ex parte Merryman* (17 Fed. Cas. No. 9487: 1861) that suspension was entirely a congressional prerogative. Congress subsequently authorized President Lincoln to suspend the writ of *habeas corpus* at his discretion. This action was challenged and was eventually decided by the Supreme Court in *Ex parte Milligan* (4 Wallace 2: 1866). A unanimous Court said the president could not suspend *habeas corpus* under any circumstances. A five-member majority held that Congress did not have the power either. There has been no subsequent attempt to suspend *habeas corpus* in the United States.

Significance   *Habeas corpus* today involves federal court review of state criminal convictions. After the Fourteenth Amendment was ratified, Congress enlarged *habeas corpus* to include persons already convicted and in custody in the states. These prisoners could apply for a writ of *habeas corpus* if they believed a violation of the Constitution or federal statutes had occurred in their cases. The allegations of violations were limited to jurisdictional issues at the time, but this apparently insignificant change began a transformation of the traditional concept of *habeas corpus*. It eventually turned *habeas corpus* into a virtual substitute for the conventional appeals process. Several Supreme Court decisions have expanded the *habeas corpus* remedy. *Frank* v. *Mangum* (237 U.S. 309: 1915) held that *habeas corpus* review existed when states failed to provide an effective means for convicted prisoners to pursue alleged violations of their federal constitutional rights. *Brown* v. *Allen* (344 U.S. 443: 1953) said that federal courts could reexamine a prisoner's constitutional allegations even if the state had provided corrective processes. The defendant had only to exhaust the processes. In *Fay* v. *Noia* (372 U.S. 391: 1963), the Court determined that even if all state processes are not utilized, a defendant can access the federal courts through a *habeas corpus* application. The number of state prisoners seeking *habeas corpus* relief in the early 1940s was slightly over one hundred annually. By the early 1970s there were over eight thousand applications per year. The Burger Court has been critical of this trend. It frequently expresses disapproval of *habeas corpus* being taken "far beyond its historical bounds and in disregard of the writ's central purpose." See *Schneckloth* v. *Bustamonte* (412 U.S. 218: 1973). In its most significant response to the issue to date, the Burger Court held in *Stone* v. *Powell* (428 U.S. 465: 1972, p. 173) that the *habeas corpus* remedy is not available to state prisoners, at least those pursuing Fourth Amendment search violations, when the defendant had been afforded a full and fair opportunity to press the allegations in a state court. While *habeas corpus* still provides substantial access for state prisoners, the scope of the remedy has been reduced in the last decade.

Hearsay   A statement by a witness repeating the words of another person rather than testifying on the basis of direct knowledge. Hearsay evidence brings statements made out of court into a legal proceeding. Hearsay is generally prohibited because the party whose out-of-court statement is offered cannot be subjected to tests of credibility through cross-examination. *See also* CONFRONTATION CLAUSE, p. 397.

Significance   The hearsay rule is designed to ensure that testimony coming before a court is reliable. Assertions that occur in open court and survive direct confrontation by the opposing party are regarded as credible, and the hearsay rule protects this method of screening evidence. There are exceptions to the hearsay rule, but before a court allows hearsay it must be convinced of both the reliability of hearsay testimony and the compelling need to use it.

Hot Pursuit   An exception to the rule that a law enforcement officer has authority to make arrests only within his or her jurisdiction. The hot pursuit doctrine allows an officer to arrest a fleeing suspect who has gone beyond the officer's assigned area of authority. *See also* EXIGENT CIRCUMSTANCE, p. 410; WARRANT, p. 460; WARRANTLESS SEARCH, p. 460.

Significance   Hot pursuit is established both in common law and by statute. Attempts to go after a suspect after an unreasonable interruption, however, are not permitted under the hot pursuit rule. Hot pursuit also permits a warrant exception to allow police officers to chase a fleeing suspect onto private premises. Such a chase constitutes an exigent circumstance that relieves an officer of normal warrant requirements, at least prior to making a search or arrest.

Identification Procedures   Methods used to assist a witness in recognizing and identifying an accused person. Identification procedures usually involve direct confrontation in a lineup or a showup. Identification may also be made from photographs. Such procedures are permissible as long as they are not unnecessarily suggestive and conducive to mistaken identification. *See also* CRITICAL STAGE, p. 400; *MANSON V. BRAITHWAITE* (432 U.S. 98: 1977), p. 232; *NEIL V. BIGGERS* (409 U.S. 188: 1972), p. 230; SELF-INCRIMINATION CLAUSE, p. 448.

Significance   Identification procedures are admissible in criminal cases under a totality of circumstances doctrine, with the reliability of the identification being the key consideration. Reliability rests upon the opportunity of the witness to observe the criminal at the time of the offense, the attentiveness of the witness at that time, the accuracy of the witness's description of the suspect, and the witness's level of certainty at the time of confrontation with the suspect. Without sufficient reliability, identification testimony may not be used. Recent Supreme Court decisions have declared postindictment lineups to be a critical stage in the criminal process requiring assistance of counsel for the defendant.

Immunity   Part of the privilege against self-incrimination. Immunity prevents a person from involuntarily becoming a witness against himself or herself. The government can compel a person to disclose incriminating evidence, but when a witness is granted immunity, he or she cannot be prosecuted based upon the compelled testimony. *See also* KASTIGAR V. UNITED STATES (406 U.S. 441: 1972), p. 233; SELF-INCRIMINATION CLAUSE, p. 448.

Significance   Immunity was first considered by the Supreme Court in the late nineteenth century. In *Counselman* v. *Hitchcock* (142 U.S. 547: 1892), the Court held that the federal immunity statute was defective in that it left a witness vulnerable to prosecution based on evidence derived from compelled testimony. Four years later, in *Brown* v. *Walker* (161 U.S. 591: 1896), the Court was asked to determine whether immunity could shield a witness beyond the prevention of actual prosecution. The Court decided that disgrace or impairment of reputation, which were possible consequences of involuntary testimony, were outside the coverage of the self-incrimination privilege. They need not be addressed when granting immunity. The matter of personal disgrace arose again in the mid-twentieth century during the investigations conducted into political subversion and national security. In *Ullman* v. *United States* (350 U.S. 422: 1956), the Court upheld provisions of the Immunity Act of 1954, which authorized immunity for testimony in national security cases. *Ullman* and *Brown* both held that self-incrimination only protects from danger of prosecution, not the danger of disgrace and the costs stemming from it. Immunity is typically used to obtain evidence from one person leading to the conviction of another. It allows information to develop that is not readily available through other investigative techniques. Given the frequent use of immunity, a critical question revolves around how extensive it must be. It must extend to direct use of the testimony itself, known as *use immunity*, but it frequently includes more. *Counselman* held that a witness must be protected from prosecution based on evidence derived from compelled testimony, known as *derived use immunity*. Even derived use immunity is limited, however. It does not prevent prosecution of a witness for a crime about which he or she may have involuntarily testified as long as the evidence used in the prosecution was developed wholly apart from the witness's testimony. *Transactional immunity* is the most inclusive form of immunity. It prevents prosecution for any matter or transaction about which the witness testifies. In *Kastigar v. United States* (406 U.S. 441: 1972, p. 233), the Court determined that derivative use immunity satisfied the prohibition against self-incrimination and that transactional immunity "affords the witness considerably broader protection than does the Fifth Amendment privilege." Derived use immunity is coextensive with the protection to which a person is entitled under the Fifth Amendment. *Kastigar* did require, however, that if a witness is subsequently charged, the prosecution must bear the burden of demonstrating that the evidence is independent of the witness's compelled testimony. Grants of immunity also apply across jurisdictions. When the Supreme Court made the self-incrimination protection applicable to the states in *Malloy* v. *Hogan* (378 U.S. 1: 1964), it also looked at federal-state reciprocity on grants of immunity. In *Murphy* v. *Waterfront Commission of New York* (378 U.S. 52: 1964), it ruled that a witness granted immunity to testify at a state or federal proceeding could not be prosecuted at the other level based on the compelled testimony.

Implicit Acquittal   Prohibits charging a criminal defendant with a more serious offense on retrial than the charge upon which he or she was convicted at the first trial. Implicit acquittal acknowledges that a criminal defendant remains in continuing jeopardy if the defendant has obtained a reversal of a criminal conviction. The prohibition on double jeopardy does not preclude a retrial on the original charge if an acquittal has not been effected. Implicit acquittal applies to the level of charge for the retrial. If the initial judgment was to a lesser included offense, retrial must be limited to that lesser included offense. Double jeopardy absolutely bars reprosecution following an acquittal on a charge, but if a jury chooses to convict a defendant for a lesser included offense, the jury has implicitly acquitted on the more serious charge. The Supreme Court said in *Price* v. *Georgia* (398 U.S. 323: 1970, p. 215) that a defendant's "jeopardy on the greater charge had ended when the first jury was given a full opportunity to return a verdict on that charge and instead reached a verdict on the lesser charge." *See also* BULLINGTON v. MISSOURI (451 U.S. 430: 1981), p. 217; DOUBLE JEOPARDY, p. 403; PRICE v. GEORGIA (398 U.S. 323: 1970), p. 215.

Significance   Implicit acquittal addresses a complex double jeopardy question. The double jeopardy prohibition clearly bars reprosecution on a charge already found inadequate by a jury. The implicit acquittal doctrine precludes a reprosecution at a level more serious than the original conviction on the ground that a jury consciously rejected conviction at that level, thus implicitly acquitting the accused of that charge. The Supreme Court has applied the implicit acquittal doctrine to the sentencing process in cases where sentence is determined through a proceeding that resembles a trial on guilt or innocence. A two-stage sentencing procedure is used in capital punishment situations for that reason.

Implied Power   Authority not expressly conveyed in the Constitution or in statutes but inferred as stemming from expressly authorized grants of power. Implied power necessarily flows from expressed power and provides the means for the achievement of expressed power.

Significance   Implied power was first treated by the Supreme Court in *McCulloch* v. *Maryland* (4 Wheaton 316: 1819). At issue was the authority of Congress to establish a national bank, clearly not one of the enumerated powers of Article I of the Constitution. Chief Justice Marshall nonetheless upheld creation of the bank on implied power grounds. The Court decided that the Necessary and Proper Clause of Article I, Section 8, gave Congress wide discretion in the selection of methods by which it could carry out its policy judgments. Chief Justice Marshall said that if the objective sought by Congress is itself permissible, any means plainly adopted to that end were also permitted unless specifically prohibited by the Constitution. *McCulloch* thus established broad implied power as an aspect of legislative power.

Inherent power is distinguished from implied power in that inherent power is authority beyond that expressly conferred or reasonably inferred. Implied power must be drawn from expressly granted power by reasonable inference.

In Camera　　Means "in chambers" but refers to any kind of proceeding in which a judge conducts court business in private. In camera proceedings are held in a judge's chambers or any other location closed off to spectators.

Significance　　In camera refers to the private review of written materials by a judge. The materials may be in the possession of one party who does not want to disclose them to an opposing party. The judge reviews the materials to determine if they are legally admissible. If they are, the materials are then disclosed to the other side.

Incorporation　　The extent to which the federal Bill of Rights acts as a limitation on state governments. Incorporation was originally defined in *Barron* v. *Baltimore* (7 Peters 243: 1833). Through Chief Justice Marshall, the Supreme Court held that the Bill of Rights constrained only "the government created by the instrument," the federal government, and not the "distinct governments," the states. *Barron* was controlling until ratification of the Fourteenth Amendment in 1868. The Fourteenth Amendment reopened the question of incorporation because it clearly directed its proscriptions to the states. Several schools of thought developed about how to resolve the matter. The most sweeping recommendation was to apply all Bill of Rights provisions to the states through the Due Process Clause of the Fourteenth Amendment. The clause prohibits a state from denying liberty without due process. Those advocating total incorporation viewed the term *liberty* as an all-inclusive shorthand for each of the rights enumerated in the Bill of Rights. The approach was vigorously advocated by the first Justice John Marshall Harlan and by Justice Hugo L. Black, but it has never prevailed. A second opinion rejected any structural linkage of due process to the Bill of Rights and held simply that the Due Process Clause requires states to provide fundamental fairness. Due process is assessed under this standard by criteria of immutable principles of justice, or, as suggested by Justice Benjamin N. Cardozo in *Palko* v. *Connecticut* (302 U.S. 319: 1937), elements implicit in the concept of ordered liberty. Application of such standards would occur on a case-by-case basis. The third opinion is a hybrid of the first two and is known as *selective incorporation*. The selective approach resembles the fundamental fairness position in that it does not view as identical those rights contained in the Bill of Rights and those rights fundamental to fairness. Unlike the fundamental fairness approach, however, the selective view holds that rights expressly contained in the Bill of Rights, if adjudged fundamental, are incorporated through the Fourteenth Amendment and are applicable at the state level regardless of the circumstances of a particular case. If the self-incrimination provision of the Sixth Amendment were determined to be fundamental, for example, it would apply in full to any state case bringing whatever substantive standards it preferred into federal courts. The selective approach created an honor roll of Bill of Rights provisions, some viewed as fundamental and wholly incorporated and a few others as less important and not worthy of incorporation. *See also* BILL OF RIGHTS, p. 7; FEDERALISM, p. 30; *HURTADO V. CALIFORNIA* (110 U.S. 516: 1884), p. 206; *PALKO V. CONNECTICUT* (302 U.S. 319: 1937), p. 207.

Significance   Incorporation focuses on the degree to which Bill of Rights guarantees apply to the states. The question assumed important status soon after ratification of the Fourteenth Amendment and remained unresolved for many years. The Supreme Court finally settled on the selective incorporation approach, which allowed the Warren Court to apply most Bill of Rights safeguards to the states. The Warren Court added many provisions to the list developed under the preceding fundamental fairness doctrine. The only Bill of Rights provisions that have not been incorporated are the grand jury requirement of the Fifth Amendment and the Excessive Bail and Fine Clause of the Eighth Amendment.

Informant   A person who provides information to authorities about criminal violations. Informant data are used to further an investigation and may be offered to support an attempt to establish probable cause in the warrant process. Since the information obtained from an informant is typically represented by another person through an affidavit, it is hearsay information. Hearsay may be used if the informant is reliable, the information is credible, and some corroborative evidence exists to support the substance of the informant's data. Additional supportive evidence may be required when the informant is unnamed or anonymous. *See also* HEARSAY, p. 421;

PROBABLE CAUSE, p. 446; *UNITED STATES* v. *HARRIS* (403 U.S. 573: 1971), p. 165; WARRANT, p. 460.

Significance   An informant generally provides information for such considerations as money or favored treatment in reference to his or her own criminal conduct. In *Illinois* v. *Gates* (454 U.S. 1140: 1983), the Burger Court moved to a totality of circumstances approach in determining probable cause when informants are used. The Court wanted to create more flexibility for warrant-issuing magistrates. The use of informants is a common law enforcement technique, and the *Gates* decision reinforces that tradition.

Injunction   An order prohibiting a party from acting in a particular way or requiring a specific action by a party. An injunction allows a court to minimize injury to a person or group until the matter can otherwise be resolved, or an injunction may prevent injury altogether. An injunction was used in the Pentagon Papers cases to keep the *New York Times* and the *Washington Post* from publishing sensitive Defense Department documents. See *New York Times* v. *United States* (403 U.S. 713: 1971, p. 119). Failure to comply with an injunction is a contempt of court. Once issued, an injunction may be annulled or quashed. *See also* EQUITY JURISDICTION, p. 407.

Significance   An injunction may be temporary or permanent. Temporary injunctions, known as interlocutory injunctions, are used to preserve a situation until the issue is resolved through normal processes of litigation. A permanent injunction may be issued upon completion of full legal proceedings. School segregation cases, such as *Brown* v. *Board of Education I* (347 U.S. 483: 1954, p. 236), characteristically were cases in which injunctions were sought. An injunction is an example of a court exercising its equity jurisdiction as opposed to its legal jurisdiction.

Irrebuttable Presumption   A judgment about an issue of fact that is presumed final and unchangeable. An irrebuttable presumption is often used in equal protection litigation. In such cases, the Supreme Court considers whether a classification presumes correctly that a condition is true and whether it justifiably denies anyone affected by the classification presumptive relief. *See also*

MASSACHUSETTS BOARD OF RETIREMENT V. MURGIA (427 U.S. 307: 1976), p. 355; *VLANDIS V. KLINE* (412 U.S. 441: 1973), p. 367.

Significance   An irrebuttable presumption is not always illegal, but the Court has generally struck down those presumptions where the presumed fact is not universally true or where there exist reasonable alternative means of making the critical determination. In *Massachusetts Board of Retirement* v. *Murgia* (427 U.S. 307: 1976, p. 355), however, the Court upheld a presumptive mandatory retirement age for uniformed police officers against arguments that individual fitness determinations were a more reasonable approach.

Irreparable Injury   A wrong or damage that has no sufficient remedy. An irreparable injury is the kind of injury for which monetary compensation is not adequate, or it is an injury that cannot be corrected or repaired. The possibility of an irreparable injury is one of the conditions precedent to granting an injunction. Plaintiffs often aver to the court that the type of injury they have suffered, or will suffer if the court does not intervene, is, or will be, irreparable. *See also* EQUITY JURISDICTION, p. 407; INJUNCTION, p. 427.

Significance   Irreparable injury must be demonstrated before many courts will grant injunctive relief. A potential irreparable injury might be media disclosure of military secrets or an unauthorized disposal of chemical waste into the environment. A case can be made in either instance to enjoin such activity because recovery from the harm caused might be impossible.

Judicial Activism   An approach to appellate decision making associated with activist behavior by members of the United States Supreme Court. Judicial activism sees the appellate courts as playing an affirmative policy role. Judicial activists are inclined to find constitutional violations, and they sometimes invalidate legislative and executive policy initiatives. *See also* JUDICIAL SELF-RESTRAINT, p. 429; JUSTICIABILITY, p. 432; PREFERRED POSITION DOCTRINE, p. 444.

Significance   Judicial activism is sometimes described as legislation by justices to achieve policy outcomes compatible with their own social priorities. A judicial activist will find more issues appropriate for judicial response than will an apostle of judicial self-restraint. An example of judicial activism is the Warren Court's judgment that legislative apportionment was a justiciable issue in *Baker* v. *Carr* (369 U.S. 186: 1962), and the Court's subsequent formulation of the one person–one vote districting standard. Critics of this form of activism felt the Court had encroached on legislative prerogatives. Activism need not coincide with a liberal policy orientation. Classic examples of judicial activism can be found in the 1930s as the Court struck down numerous pieces of New Deal legislation in the interest of preserving laissez-faire economic doctrine. The judicial activist sees the Court as appropriately and legitimately asserting itself in the policy-making process even if its policy objectives differ from those of the legislative and executive branches. Justices William O. Douglas and William J. Brennan and Chief Justice Earl Warren are generally considered to be the leading proponents of judicial activism.

Judicial Review   The power of a court to examine the actions of the legislative and executive branches and declare them unconstitutional. Judicial review may also find a statute or action compatible with the federal or state constitution. The power of judicial review was discussed extensively at the Constitutional Convention of 1787, but it was not included in the Constitution as an expressly delegated judicial function. The Supreme Court first asserted the power in the case of *Marbury* v. *Madison* (1 Cranch 37: 1803) under the leadership of Chief Justice John Marshall. *See also* JUDICIAL ACTIVISM, p. 428; JUDICIAL SELF-RESTRAINT, p. 429.

Significance   Judicial review was established in *Marbury* when the Supreme Court determined that a section of the Judiciary Act of 1789 unconstitutionally expanded the original jurisdiction of the Court. The Court asserted that it must, under such circumstances, be able to void enactments that conflict with the Constitution. Chief Justice Marshall considered judicial review to be "the very essence of judicial duty." The arguments for judicial review became so firmly rooted in American jurisprudence that the doctrine became one of the principal means by which courts participate in the shaping of public policy.

Judicial Self-Restraint   A philosophy and style of judicial decision making that minimizes the extent to which judges apply their personal views to the legal judgments they render. Judicial self-restraint is particularly useful in analyzing the behavior of the United States Supreme Court. The term describes a self-imposed limitation seen by the judges who practice it as the decision-making approach most compatible with democratic principles. It is opposite from judicial activism. *See also* JUDICIAL ACTIVISM, p. 428; JUSTICIABIL-ITY, p. 432.

Significance   Judicial self-restraint holds that courts should defer to the policy judgments made by the elected branches of government. Judges who adhere to the philosophy of restraint impose a more restrictive definition of justiciability and adhere more strictly to judicial precedent. Self-restraint does not necessarily coincide with a conservative policy orientation. Exercise of self-restraint by deferring to a legislative enactment mandating establishment of a minimum wage or an aggressive Equal Employment Opportunity Commission program, for example, might yield a liberal policy result. Judicial self-restraint is a perception of the judicial role that limits the exercise of judicial power and views the legislative and executive branches as the appropriate sources of major policy initiatives. Among the leading advocates of judicial self-restraint in the history of the Supreme Court are Justices Felix Frankfurter and the second Justice John Marshall Harlan.

Jurisdiction   The power of a court to act, including its authority to hear and to decide cases. Jurisdiction defines the boundaries within which a particular court may exercise judicial power. Judicial power is specifically conveyed through the definition of jurisdiction. The jurisdiction of federal courts is described in Article III of the Constitution in the case of the Supreme Court, and in acts of Congress in the case of the lower federal courts. A limitation on jurisdiction is that it may extend only to those issues that Article III specifies as lying within the judicial power of the United States. Federal judicial power may extend to classes of cases defined in terms of substance and party as well as to cases in law and equity stemming directly from the federal Constitution, federal statutes, treaties, or those cases falling into the admiralty and maritime category. Federal judicial power also extends to cases involving specified parties. Regardless of the substance of the case, federal jurisdiction includes actions (1) where the federal government itself is a party; (2) between two or more states; (3) between a state and a citizen of another state; (4) between citizens of different states; (5) between a state and an alien; (6) between a citizen of a state and an alien; and (7) where foreign ambassadors are involved. State constitutions and statutes usually define the jurisdiction of state courts. They often do so in terms of the amount of money sued for in civil actions and the maximum punishment allowed in criminal actions. Jurisdiction also refers to the location of the parties and the court. A court located in a particular county may be the only court that has jurisdiction in a lawsuit involving two residents of that county, or it may be the only court that has jurisdiction to hear a criminal case when the crime has occurred within that county. The concept of location of jurisdiction is technically a question of venue, however, and not one of jurisdiction. If the power of a court is questioned on the basis of location, it is usually because the court lacks the proper venue. If an issue is properly before a court, a *judgment* may be rendered. A judgment is the final ruling of a court on a matter properly before it. The judgment of a court may also be called its decision or decree. Judgment on occasion also refers to the reasoning underlying a decision, but more typically the rationale of a decision is called the *opinion.* One such judgment may be to dismiss, which is to dispose of a case with no further consideration of it. A court may also issue a stay, which suspends some action or proceeding until a further event transpires. *See also* APPEAL, p. 383; DIVERSITY JURISDICTION, p. 402; EQUITY JURISDICTION, p. 407; ORIGINAL JURISDICTION, p. 440.

Significance Jurisdiction conveys authority to courts to act in particular cases. Federal court jurisdiction is defined in provisions of the Constitution and federal statutes. Jurisdiction routes particular kinds of issues or parties to the appropriate judicial forum. While the authority of courts may overlap to some degree, the lines of differentiation are usually quite clear. The independence of federal and state court jurisdictions was designed to maintain the respective sovereignty of the two levels of government.

Jury A specific number of citizens called to render a judgment on various issues of fact in a legal proceeding. A jury in its most common form is the grand jury and the petit or ordinary trial jury. The grand jury hears evidence and determines whether a person must stand trial on a criminal charge. A petit jury makes an actual determination of guilt in a criminal or civil trial. Article IV of the Constitution mandates jury trials in criminal cases. The right is repeated in the Sixth Amendment, which entitles the accused to "a public trial, by an impartial jury." The Seventh Amendment preserves the right of jury trial in civil cases where the amount in controversy exceeds $20. In 1968, the Supreme Court extended the jury trial provision in criminal cases to the states because it said trial by jury is "fundamental to the

American scheme of justice." Selection of jurors must conform to constitutional and statutory guidelines. Juries must be selected in ways that do not systematically exclude any segment of the population, although no particular jury needs to reflect proportionately a community's population. The venire or jury pool from which a particular jury is to be drawn is created by random selection from a master list of registered voters within a political jurisdiction. Once the venire has been established, a *voir dire* examination is conducted to determine if the potential jurors are impartial. Jurors whose responses to questions during *voir dire* are not acceptable are excused for cause. Following *voir dire,* counsel for either party may exclude jurors through a strike or peremptory challenge. Juries are typically composed of 12 persons, but states are permitted to use juries of as few as 6 persons in criminal or civil cases. Federal civil juries may be smaller than 12 people, but in criminal proceedings juries must consist of 12 citizens. State juries need not resolve fact issues by a unanimous decision even in criminal cases. Margins of at least 9–3 are constitutionally permissible in state criminal cases, while unanimity is required if the jury is as small as 6. Unanimity is required in all federal criminal jury decisions. *See also* APODACA V. OREGON (406 U.S. 404: 1972), p. 256; GRAND JURY, p. 418; RISTAINO V. ROSS (424 U.S. 589: 1976), p. 254; SWAIN V. ALABAMA (380 U.S. 202: 1965), p. 251; WILLIAMS V. FLORIDA (399 U.S. 78: 1970), p. 255.

Significance   A jury is guaranteed in criminal cases by the Sixth Amendment. The jury system, like many other elements of the American legal process, was inherited from England. The expectation that selected citizens should participate in making judgments about other citizens is deeply ingrained in the legal traditions of both countries. Yet the quality of jury performance is frequently questioned. The options the Supreme Court has recently permitted states regarding jury size and unanimity will prompt further questions. The jury fosters citizen involvement in the justice system, and, specific case deviations notwithstanding, it brings a commonsense element into the legal process.

Justiciability   The appropriateness of an issue for resolution by judicial action. Justiciability refers to a question that may properly come before a court for decision. Justiciability differs from jurisdiction in that the latter involves the question of whether a court possesses the power to act. Justiciability presumes that the power to act exists, but it focuses on whether it is proper or reasonable to exercise that power. A court may have jurisdiction over a case, but it may find the question involved to be nonjusticiable. *See also* ADVISORY OPINION, p. 381; CASE OR CONTROVERSY, p. 389; JURISDICTION, p. 430; POLITICAL QUESTION, p. 442; STANDING, p. 452.

Significance   Justiciability considerations come in the form of real or bona fide cases as opposed to controversies raising abstract or hypothetical issues. A justiciable issue satisfies all requirements of standing, and it is not more appropriately resolved by the legislative or executive branches. Justiciability allows the courts to limit or expand the extent to which judicial power is exercised. It directly affects the functional relationship of the courts to the legislative and executive branches.

Libel   The use of false and malicious material that injures a person's status or reputation. Libel has consistently been held to be a category of unprotected speech. Relief from libel may be pursued through either civil or criminal proceedings. Libel laws may not inhibit debate on public issues, however, even if the debate includes vigorous and unpleasant attacks on the government and/or public officials. In such situations, statements must be made in print with reckless disregard of their falsehood and with actual malice before libel occurs. Plaintiffs in libel proceedings may inquire into the editorial processes of defendant publications as a means of establishing state of mind as an ingredient of malice. Oral defamation is called slander. *See also* EDITORIAL PRIVILEGE, p. 405; FREE PRESS CLAUSE, p. 416; *HERBERT* v. *LANDO* (441 U.S. 153: 1978), p. 123; *NEW YORK TIMES, INC.* v. *SULLIVAN* (376 U.S. 254: 1964), p. 121.

Significance   Libel actions afford private citizens much greater insulation from adverse comments than they do public officials. The category of public official has been expanded by the Supreme Court to include public figures. A public figure is a private citizen who may be in the midst of doing a public thing, or he or she may simply be a private person who attracts wide public attention.

Loyalty Oath   A declaration of allegiance to the state. A loyalty oath is usually not voluntary but is required for public employment. It may demand that persons offer a disclaimer of support for foreign governments or ideologies. *See also* KEYISHIAN V. BOARD OF REGENTS (385 U.S. 589: 1967), p. 151; OVERBREADTH DOCTRINE, p. 440.

Significance   The loyalty oath has not been categorically banned by the Supreme Court, but limits on its scope have been set. A loyalty oath cannot compel an individual to pledge that he or she will never become a member of a given organization at some time in the future. Neither may a loyalty oath be overbroad or vague. It is not generally regarded as an effective means of instilling allegiance in citizens.

Mandamus   An extraordinary writ issued by a court under its equity jurisdiction to require a public official to perform a specified official act. Mandamus is an affirmative command calling for an action to occur. A command preventing an action from occurring is an injunction.

Significance   A writ of mandamus can only be issued to compel performance of a nondiscretionary or ministerial function in an instance where the plaintiff has a legal right to the performance of the function. A mandamus may be directed by a higher court to a lower court to require an action that a party has a legal right to expect. Failure to comply with a command issued through a writ of mandamus constitutes contempt of court.

Mandatory Sentence   A punishment that is legislatively required and must be imposed by a sentencing judge. A mandatory sentence is set by statute, and the sentencing judge has no discretion. It is intended to promote incarceration of convicted criminals by precluding suspended sentences or probation. The policy does not permit consideration of the circumstances surrounding a particular offense or the background of the offender. For this reason the Supreme Court has invalidated mandatory death sentence statutes on cruel and unusual punishment grounds. Mandatory death sentences are flawed because they do not allow consideration of "compassion or mitigating factors." The Court's major objection is the undifferentiating character of the mandatory process. Statutes that mandate the death penalty treat all persons as "members of a faceless, undifferentiated mass to be subjected to the blind infliction of the death penalty." *See also* CRUEL AND UNUSUAL

PUNISHMENT, p. 401; *WOODSON V. NORTH CAROLINA* (428 U.S. 280: 1976), p. 297.

Significance   A mandatory sentence is used in many jurisdictions for noncapital offenses. It is often justified on two bases: (1) to warn the potential criminal that he or she will be incarcerated for certain kinds of criminal conduct, such as use of a gun while committing a crime; and (2) to discourage what may be perceived as judicial softness, thus promoting uniformity in sentencing. Mandatory sentencing is opposed by many judges and lawyers because it requires that unequal offenders and unequal situations be treated equally. Opponents argue that flexibility and discretion are at the heart of the sentencing process.

Mootness (Moot Question)   A case in which the courts can no longer provide a party any relief because the dispute has been resolved or has ceased to exist. A moot case is no longer a real controversy, and Article III of the Constitution requires that cases before courts be bona fide controversies. *See also* ADVISORY OPINION, p. 381; JUSTICIABILITY, p. 432; STANDING, p. 452.

Significance   Mootness is the absence of an active question. The matter is therefore nonjusticiable. When the Supreme Court refused to address the reverse discrimination issue in *DeFunis* v. *Odegaard* (416 U.S. 312: 1974) on grounds of mootness, it said the controversy was no longer definite and concrete. The case no longer touched "the legal relations of parties having adverse interests." Exceptions to the mootness threshold involve situations where time is too limited to litigate an issue fully, and where a likelihood exists that the question will reoccur. Abortion cases qualify for an exception to the mootness rule, for example, because no appellate court can ever get an abortion issue prior to a pregnancy running to full term. The Court observed in *Roe* v. *Wade* (410 U.S. 113: 1973) that appellate review would forever be foreclosed by mootness because a pregnancy would not last beyond the trial stage. Saying the law should not be that rigid, the Court acknowledged the need for the exception if issues are "capable of repetition, yet evading review." If the courts responded routinely to cases that had become moot, they would constantly be engaged in rendering advisory opinions.

Neutral Magistrate   A judicial officer with the power to issue a warrant based on probable cause. A neutral magistrate has no interest in the outcome of a case. He or she possesses sufficient training and qualifications to be able to make inferences from evidence presented, however, and may issue a warrant accordingly. *See also* COOLIDGE V. NEW HAMPSHIRE (403 U.S. 443: 1971), p. 162; PROBABLE CAUSE, p. 446; WARRANT, p. 460.

Significance   A neutral magistrate may be a judge, as in lower state courts, or a lawyer with at least five years' experience, as in federal courts. A federal magistrate is appointed by federal district judges and has wide judicial powers. The warrant-issuing role is an important one because the Supreme Court has said that Fourth Amendment protections are null if warrant judgments are made only by prosecutors or police officers. The Court has also ruled that searches are unreasonable if not authorized by a neutral magistrate.

Newsperson's Privilege   A rule that prevents journalists from having to disclose their news sources or the substance of information obtained from news sources. Newsperson's privilege means that journalists are free from the obligation to testify about their news sources in court because in testifying their press function would be impaired. *See also* BRANZBURG V. HAYES (408 U.S. 665: 1972), p. 125; EDITORIAL PRIVILEGE, p. 405; GRAND JURY, p. 418; PRIVILEGE, p. 445.

Significance   Newperson's privilege is based in the First Amendment. The doctrine was limited by the Supreme Court's holding in *Branzburg* v. *Hayes* (408 U.S. 665: 1972) that newspersons are obligated to disclose information and sources to grand juries. In response to *Branzburg*, a number of states passed shield laws that establish a special privilege for newspersons even before grand juries.

Obiter Dictum   Remarks contained in a court's opinion that are incidental to the disposition of the case. *Obiter dictum* or *obiter dicta*, sometimes simply called dictum or dicta, are normally directed at issues upon which no formal arguments have been heard. The positions represented by obiter dicta are therefore not binding on later cases. Dicta are not considered to be precedent and should be distinguished from the *ratio decidendi*, which provides the basis of the court's ruling.

Significance   Obiter dicta can be found in *Myers* v. *United States* (272 U.S. 52: 1926), for example, in which the Supreme Court held that Congress could not require Senate consent for presidential removal of postmasters. Postmasters are generally viewed as executive branch subordinates serving exclusively at the pleasure of the president. Chief Justice Taft offered the opinion, however, that removal power was incident to the power to appoint, as distinguished from the power to advise and consent. As a general proposition presidents could remove anyone appointed by them, including members of quasi-judicial agencies such as regulatory commissions. *Myers* did not require disposition of that question to settle the case. Thus the remarks of the chief justice went beyond those necessary to resolve a case or controversy and were therefore dicta.

Obscenity   Content that offends accepted standards of decency. Obscenity is not protected expression under the First Amendment because it is "utterly without redeeming social importance or value." Since it falls outside the scope of the First Amendment, a carefully constructed definition of obscenity is essential to distinguish between protected expression and unprotected obscenity. Central to the identification of obscenity is its appeal to what the Supreme Court has described as "prurient interest." It is material that prompts "lustful thoughts." *See also* COMMUNITY STANDARDS, p. 396; FREE PRESS CLAUSE, p. 415; *FREEDMAN* V. *MARYLAND* (380 U.S. 51: 1965), p. 141; *MILLER* V. *CALIFORNIA* (413 U.S. 95: 1973), p. 134; PRIOR RESTRAINT, p. 444; *ROTH* V. *UNITED STATES* (354 U.S. 476: 1957), p. 131; *STANLEY* V. *GEORGIA* (394 U.S. 557: 1969), p. 138.

Significance   Obscenity was first defined in *Roth* v. *United States* (354 U.S. 476: 1957). *Roth* dealt with the question of "whether to the average person, applying contemporary community standards, the dominant theme of the material taken as a whole appeals to prurient interest." Within a decade the Warren Court modified the *Roth* standard by refining elements within the definitions. In *Memoirs* v. *Massachusetts* (383 U.S. 413: 1966), the Court described obscenity in terms of "patent offensiveness," and elevated the role of the social value criterion. Obscenity was still seen as "utterly without redeeming social value," but the Court placed a severe burden on the prosecutors of obscene material by asking for proof of the absence of social value. The Court held in addition that each of the elements of the obscenity definition were to be applied independently. The social value dimension could not be weighed against nor cancelled by either the patent offensiveness or prurient appeal of obscene materials. The outcome of these changes was to put all but hardcore pornography outside the reach of obscenity statutes. The Burger Court modified the standard again in *Miller* v. *California* (413 U.S. 15: 1973), when it defined as obscene "works which, taken as a whole, appeal to prurient interest in sex," and which "portray sexual conduct in a patently offensive way." Obscenity must also lack "serious literary, artistic, political, or scientific value." The Burger Court removed the social value criterion as an insurmountable obstacle to prosecution, and it defined community standards in local terms. Obscenity may also be evaluated in contextual terms. Material may be found obscene if pandering is involved, for example. Pandering occurs when a person attempts commercially to exploit the sexual content of material offered for sale. Even if materials survive scrutiny under the *Miller* standards, they may become illicit through pandering. Under the provisions of *Miller,* many communities now attempt to regulate obscenity at the local level. The regulations frequently take the form of zoning ordinances or censorship techniques. While censorship is not inherently unconstitutional, it does suggest prior restraint, and is very carefully examined by the Court. Regulation of the commercial exhibition of obscenity has been allowed, even when the exhibition is confined to consenting adults. The Court has also held that privately possessed obscenity is beyond the control of government.

Offensive Speech   Expression that is objectionable and distasteful to a listener because it contains noxious language. Offensive speech is a form of pure speech in that no additional conduct is necessary. The Supreme Court has held that offensive speech is generally protected expression. In *Cohen* v. *California* (403 U.S. 15: 1971), the Court said that government cannot function as the guardian of public morality and excise epithets and other offensive speech from public discourse. A state does not possess the power "to cleanse public debate to the point where it is grammatically acceptable to the most squeamish among us." The Court said wide latitude must be afforded ostensibly offensive speech. *See also* COHEN V. *CALIFORNIA* (403 U.S. 15: 1971), p. 114; FREE SPEECH CLAUSE, p. 416; LIBEL, p. 433; OBSCENITY, p. 437; PURE SPEECH, p. 447.

Significance   Offensive speech standards are influenced by the fact that words are often chosen as much for their emotive as their cognitive value. Some offensive speech is not protected, as in the case of obscenity, libel, and "fighting words." Fighting words are words that are inherently insulting or likely to incite breach of the peace. Indeed, attempts to punish offensive speech typically take the form of prosecution for breach of the peace. Expressions of this kind are not protected by the First Amendment because they are of such slight value as to be outweighed by the public interest in maintaining order.

Opinion of the Court   The statement of a court that specifies its decision in a case and expresses the reasoning upon which the decision was based. The opinion of the court summarizes the principles of law that apply in a given case and represents the views of the majority of a court's members. Occasionally the opinion of a court may reflect the views of less than a majority of its members and is then called a plurality opinion. Trial courts also issue opinions, both written and oral.

Significance   The opinion of the court is the means by which the legal principles of a decision are transmitted. The opinion of the court contains the *ratio decidendi,* which is the rationale for the judgment and the principal item of precedent value. The opinion of the court is not the only statement that may be issued in a particular case, however. A *concurring opinion* may be issued by a member of a court who agrees with the outcome of a case but who uses different reasons for reaching a decision. In *Coker* v. *Georgia* (433 U.S. 584: 1977, p. 298), for example, the Supreme Court ruled that the death penalty could not be imposed for the offense of rape. The majority felt the death penalty was excessive for the specific crime involved. Justice Brennan agreed that Coker's sentence ought to be vacated but expressed in a concurring opinion that the death penalty is a cruel and unusual punishment under any circumstances. A *dissenting opinion,* on the other hand, is an opinion by a member of a court who disagrees with the majority opinion of the court. A dissent may be joined by other members of a court's minority. It may focus on only one element of a court's decision and may be a disagreement in part. A dissenting opinion that attracts other members of a court may serve as an encouragement to litigants to bring subsequent cases raising similar legal arguments. A court may also issue a *per curiam* opinion. *Per curiam* is a Latin term meaning "by the court." It is an opinion that is either unsigned or authored by the judges collectively. A *per curiam* opinion is sometimes used to announce a court's holding summarily without discussion of the rationale. Individual members of a court frequently enter individual concurring or dissenting opinions on such occasions. See, for example, *Furman* v. *Georgia* (408 U.S. 238: 1972,

p. 294), and *New York Times* v. *United States* (403 U.S. 713: 1971, p.119). Opinions are occasionally important for what they do not say. *Sub silentio* means "under silence" and refers to something that occurs without notice being taken of it. Sometimes an appeals court will overrule a precedent without explicitly acknowledging the precedent it overruled. The precedent is therefore replaced sub silentio.

Original Jurisdiction   The authority of a court initially to hear and determine a legal question. Original jurisdiction is vested with trial courts rather than appellate courts, although Article III of the Constitution extends limited original jurisdiction to the United States Supreme Court. Various trial courts are assigned specific original jurisdiction defined in terms of subject matter or party. Original jurisdiction in civil cases is often divided on the basis of the monetary value of the action. In criminal matters, certain courts may be assigned misdemeanor cases while others adjudicate felonies. A misdemeanor is a minor criminal offense generally punishable by imprisonment in local jails and/or a fine. A felony is a criminal offense for which punishment may be death or imprisonment for more than a year. Since the United States District Court is the only trial court of broad jurisdiction, it has original jurisdiction over both federal felonies and misdemeanors. *See also* APPEAL, p. 383; DIVERSITY JURIS-DICTION, p. 402; EQUITY JURISDICTION, p. 407; JURISDICTION, p. 430.

Significance   Original jurisdiction establishes which court will first respond to a case or controversy. Original jurisdiction is particularly important because comparatively few cases are appealed from courts of first instance.

Overbreadth Doctrine   A doctrine requiring that enactments proscribing certain activity must not touch conduct that is constitutionally protected. Overbreadth refers to a statute that may fail adequately to distinguish between those activities that may be regulated and those that may not. *See also* CHILLING EFFECT, p. 392; FREE SPEECH CLAUSE, p. 416; *VILLAGE OF SCHAUMBURG V. CITIZENS FOR A BETTER ENVIRONMENT* (444 U.S. 620: 1980), p. 116.

Significance   The overbreadth doctrine is illustrated in *Village of Schaumburg* v. *Citizens for a Better Environment* (444 U.S. 620: 1980), where the Supreme Court struck down a local ordinance that required all organizations soliciting contributions door-to-door to use at least 75 percent of their receipts for charitable purposes. The purpose of the ordinance was to prevent fraudulent solicitations. The Court objected to the approach because it imposed a direct and substantial limitation on organizations such as environmental education groups whose principal activities are research, advocacy, and public education. While such organizations obviously do not meet the ordinance definition of charitable, their activities are constitutionally permissible. The Village's ordinance in *Schaumburg* was simply too inclusive or overbroad. A similar ordinance was invalidated in *Coates* v. *Cincinnati* (402 U.S. 611: 1972) because the ordinance prohibited an assembly of three or more persons on public sidewalks. It subjected such assembled persons to arrest if their behavior annoyed a police officer or passerby. The ordinance made criminal what the Constitution says cannot be a crime. Neither may an enactment suffer from vagueness. Regulations must convey standards of conduct that persons of reasonable intelligence can understand. Enactments that do not clearly convey required or prohibited conduct may be invalidated as vague. Restrictions that are either overbroad or vague may have a chilling effect on expression or some other protected activity.

Plea Bargaining   A process whereby the prosecutor and the accused negotiate a mutually acceptable settlement in a criminal case. Plea bargaining usually involves a defendant's pleading guilty to a charge in exchange for a lessening of the charge, a reduction in the number of counts charged, and/or a favorable sentencing recommendation. A proposed settlement must be accepted by the trial judge assigned to the case. Plea bargaining accounts for the disposition of approximately 90 percent of all criminal cases in the United States. *See also* BORDENKIRCHER V. HAYES (434 U.S. 357: 1978), p. 275; BOYKIN V. ALABAMA (395 U.S. 238: 1969), p. 270; BRADY V. UNITED STATES (397 U.S. 742: 1970), p. 272; JURY, p. 431; SANTOBELLO V. NEW YORK (404 U.S. 257: 1971), p. 273.

Significance   Plea bargaining has been clearly endorsed by the Supreme Court. Benefits accrue to both prosecution and accused and produce a mutuality of advantage sufficient to prompt the high plea rate. In *Santobello* v. *New York* (404 U.S. 257: 1971), the Court spoke of plea bargaining as "an essential component of the administration of justice," and a practice to be encouraged if it is properly handled. Plea bargaining moves cases through the courts, relieving docket pressure that could not be handled through any other means. It is desirable because it produces prompt and largely final dispositions without lengthy pretrial confinement, with diminished chances of additional criminal conduct by those on pretrial release, and with enhanced rehabilitative prospects. The procedures by which pleas are made are carefully prescribed. The Federal Rules of Criminal Procedure set forth the steps by which pleas are to be entered in federal courts, and most states have established similar guidelines. At minimum, no plea can be taken without a trial judge inquiring into the voluntary nature of the plea. If a plea is determined to be freely and intelligently offered, all elements of the settlement agreement must be honored. The Supreme Court has determined that a plea to avoid the death penalty is not necessarily involuntary, nor is a prosecutorial threat to charge with a more serious or additional offense prohibited as long as the greater or supplementary charge is legally sufficient.

Police Power   Authority conveyed by the Reserve Clause of the Tenth Amendment to the effect that powers not delegated to the federal government or otherwise prohibited are "reserved to the States respectively, or the people." The police power gives the states broad authority to regulate private behavior in the interest of public health, safety, and general welfare. It enables states and their respective local units of government to enact and enforce policies deemed appropriate to serve the public good. Pursuit of these policies may include the creation of a police force. *See also* DUE PROCESS CLAUSES, p. 405; FEDERALISM, p. 30.

Significance   The police power is comprehensive, and substantial discretion is possessed by the states for its exercise. It is limited by various provisions of the United States Constitution and the constitutions of the states, however. It must conform to the expectations of due process.

Political Question   An issue that is not justiciable or that is not appropriate for judicial determination. A political question is one in which the substance of an issue is primarily political or involves a matter directed toward either the legislative or executive branch by constitutional language. *See also* BAKER V. CARR (369 U.S. 186: 1962), p. 343; JUSTICIABILITY, p. 432; SEPARATION OF POWERS, p. 58.

Significance   The political question doctrine is sometimes invoked by the Supreme Court not because the Court is without power or jurisdiction but because the Court adjudges the question inappropriate for judicial response. In the Court's view, to intervene or respond would be to encroach upon the functions and prerogatives of one of the other two branches of government. It would constitute a breach of the principle of separation of powers. In *Luther* v. *Borden* (7 Howard 1: 1849), the Court was asked to rule on the status of Dorr's Rebellion in Rhode Island. The Court refused to do so, holding that the Guaranty Clause of Article IV had committed the issue to Congress rather than the Supreme Court. Chief Justice Taney said it is the duty of the Court "not to pass beyond its appropriate sphere of action, and to take care not to involve itself in discussions which properly belong to other forums." Justice Brennan was more precise in characterizing a political question in *Baker* v. *Carr* (369 U.S. 186: 1962), the first case in which the Court held legislative apportionment to be a justiciable issue. Justice Brennan described a political question as one with "a textually demonstrable constitutional commitment of the issue to a coordinate political department; or a lack of judicially discoverable and manageable standards for resolving it." He added that such questions typically require "a policy determination of a kind clearly for nonjudicial discretion." On such matters the Court cannot undertake "independent resolution without expressing lack of respect due coordinate branches of the government."

Preemption Doctrine   Holds that federal laws supersede or preempt state laws in certain policy areas. The preemption doctrine is grounded in the Supremacy Clause of Article VI. *See also* FEDERALISM, p. 30; SMITH ACT, p. 451.

Significance   The preemption doctrine was said to have three criteria in *Pennsylvania* v. *Nelson* (350 U.S. 497: 1956). First, federal regulation must be so pervasive as to allow reasonable inference that no room is left to the states. Congress may state explicitly such a preemptive interest, or the courts may interpret the intent of Congress fully to occupy the field. Second, federal regulation must involve matters where the federal interest is so dominant as to preclude implementation of state laws in the field. Third, the administration of federal laws must be endangered by conflicting state laws. The policy area involved in *Nelson* was the regulation of seditious activity. Specifically the question was whether the federal Smith Act prohibited enforcement of the Pennsylvania Sedition Act, which proscribed the same conduct. On the basis of the criteria described, the Supreme Court concluded that Pennsylvania's statute had to give way.

Preferred Position Doctrine   Holds that legislative enactments that affect First Amendment rights must be scrutinized more carefully than legislation that does not. The preferred position doctrine says that certain legislative activity deserves priority consideration because it affects fundamental rights such as free speech. Any enactment that impinges on the First Amendment must serve a compelling state interest. The burden is clearly on the state to demonstrate justification for limiting a preferred position freedom. *See also* BALANCING TEST, p. 388; FREE SPEECH CLAUSE, p. 416.

Significance   The preferred position doctrine is attributed to Justice Harlan Fiske Stone, who said in a footnote to his opinion in *United States* v. *Carolene Products Company* (304 U.S. 144: 1938) that a lesser presumption of constitutionality exists when legislation "appears on its face to be within a specific prohibition such as those of the first ten amendments." Bolder articulation of the doctrine soon followed in such First Amendment cases as *Murdock* v. *Pennsylvania* (319 U.S. 105: 1943) and *Thomas* v. *Collins* (323 U.S. 516: 1945).

Prior Restraint   A restriction placed on a publication before it can be published or circulated. Prior restraint typically occurs through licensure or censorship or by a full prohibition on publication. Censorship requirements involve a review of materials by the state for objectionable content. The materials that satisfy the standards of the censor may be distributed or exhibited, while materials found unacceptable may be banned. *See also* FREE PRESS CLAUSE, p. 415; *FREEDMAN* V. *MARYLAND*(380 U.S. 51: 1965), p. 141; *KINGSLEY BOOKS, INC.* V. *BROWN* (354 U.S. 436: 1956), p. 139; *NEAR* V. *MINNESOTA* (283 U.S. 697: 1931), p. 118; *NEW YORK TIMES, INC.* V. *UNITED STATES* (403 U.S. 713: 1971), p. 119.

Significance   Prior restraint poses a greater threat to free expression than after-the-fact prosecution because government restrictions are imposed in a manner that precludes public scrutiny. The First Amendment therefore prohibits prior restraint in most instances. Prior restraint may be justified if the publication threatens national security, incites overthrow of the government, is obscene, or interferes with the private rights of others. Prior restraint is otherwise heavily suspect.

Privilege   A benefit possessed by a person or class having an advantage over other persons or classes by virtue of the benefit. A privilege may exempt a person from an obligation because, without the privilege, the person's office or function would be impaired. *See also* EDITORIAL PRIVILEGE, p. 405; NEWSPERSON'S PRIVILEGE, p. 436.

Significance   Privilege often refers to communications that are protected because they need to be confidential. Thus a lawyer cannot be compelled to disclose the substance of a conversation with a client unless the client waives the privilege. Executive privilege is protection afforded presidential communications, while newsperson's privilege protects against disclosure of news sources by reporters. A privilege may be waived by the person upon whom the law bestows it.

Privileges and Immunities Clauses   Clauses that protect benefits flowing from one's status as a citizen. A privilege is a benefit or an advantage. An immunity frees a person from an obligation. Certain privileges and immunities exist for a person by virtue of his or her citizenship. The United States Constitution contains two references to privileges and immunities. Article IV, Section 2, provides that the "Citizens of each State be entitled to the Privileges and Immunities of citizens in the several States." The purpose of this clause was to ensure that out-of-state citizens receive the same treatment as a state's own citizens. It protected parity across the states. The Fourteenth Amendment also provides that "No State shall make or enforce any law which shall abridge the privileges or immunities of the United States." This section of the Fourteenth Amendment was a specific response to the Black Codes, which in many southern states had the effect of restoring pre–Civil War conditions of slavery. *See also* CITIZENSHIP, p. 392; DUE PROCESS CLAUSES, p. 405; EQUAL PROTECTION CLAUSE, p. 313.

Significance   The Privileges and Immunities Clauses were severely limited by the *Slaughterhouse Cases* (16 Wallace 36: 1873), in which the Supreme Court distinguished between federal and state citizenship. The Court placed most key civil and political rights within the state citizenship category. That limited the privileges and immunities of federal citizenship to such rights as interstate travel, protection while abroad, and participation in federal elections. The protections afforded by federal citizenship through the Fourteenth Amendment have expanded substantially over the years since *Slaughterhouse,* but the expansion has taken place under the Due Process and Equal Protection Clauses rather than the Privileges and Immunities Clauses.

Probable Cause   The foremost element required in making a lawful arrest or conducting a legal search. Probable cause is a level of evidence required to convince a neutral third party, typically a judge or magistrate, to issue a warrant. The level of evidence needed for probable cause is not as substantial as that required to prove guilt. This is sometimes called making a prima facie case. *Prima facie* means "at first sight" and refers to a case or claim that may be sufficient without further support or evaluation. *See also* DRAPER V. UNITED *STATES* (385 U.S. 307: 1959), p. 160; WARRANT, p. 460.

Significance   Probable cause relates to reasonable inferences rather than technical judgments based on rigid requirements. In *Draper* v. *United States* (385 U.S. 307: 1959, p. 160), the Supreme Court spoke of "probabilities" that focus closely enough on a person or location to allow a neutral magistrate to authorize an arrest or search. The standard established in *Draper* holds that probable cause exists when trustworthy information known to authorities is sufficient to encourage a person of reasonable caution to believe that an offense has been or is being committed. The standard can be met by providing evidence such as direct observation of a criminal act by a law enforcement officer, indirect observation through informants, physical evidence, or accounts provided by witnesses.

Procedural Due Process   A procedural review that focuses on the means by which governmental actions are executed. Procedural due process guarantees fairness in the ways by which government imposes restrictions or punishments. It demands that before any deprivation of liberty or property can occur, a person must be formally notified and provided an opportunity for a fair hearing. *See also* DUE PROCESS CLAUSES, p. 405; SUBSTANTIVE DUE PROCESS, p. 456.

Significance   Procedural due process must be accorded persons accused of crimes. It includes access to legal counsel, the ability to confront witnesses against the accused, and a trial by jury.

Constitutional protection against loss of liberty or property is guaranteed in two constitutional amendments: the Fifth, which is directed at the federal government; and the Fourteenth, which is directed at the states.

Pure Speech   Expression or communication that occurs without any additional action or conduct on the part of the speaker. Pure speech is a conversation or a public address. Its content does not affect its character. *See also* FREE SPEECH CLAUSE, p. 416; OFFENSIVE SPEECH, p. 438; SPEECH PLUS, p. 451; SYMBOLIC SPEECH, p. 457.

Significance   Pure speech produces its effect, if any, only from the opinions, views, or positions communicated. It is the form of expression least subject to restriction. Pure speech is distinguished from speech plus or symbolic speech in that the latter two forms of speech require some kind of action beyond or instead of the language itself.

Reverse Discrimination   A policy based on a classification in which one class is disadvantaged in order to remedy past discrimination suffered by another class. Reverse discrimination policies aimed at remedial ends are often called affirmative action programs. The constitutional question raised by such policies is whether benevolent discrimination is permissible because of its compensatory character. *See also* BENEVOLENT CLASSIFICATION, p. 388; *REGENTS OF THE UNIVERSITY OF CALIFORNIA* V. *BAKKE* (438 U.S. 265: 1978), p. 337; EQUAL PROTECTION CLAUSE, p. 313; *FULLILOVE* V. *KLUTZNICK* (448 U.S. 448: 1980), p. 339.

Significance   Reverse discrimination was permitted by the Supreme Court in *Regents of the University of California* v. *Bakke* (438 U.S. 265: 1978). The Court upheld the use of race conscious admissions policies for a state university graduate program, although it disallowed the allocation of seats on a quota basis. The Court found that recruitment of a diverse or heterogeneous student body was a substantial enough interest to allow race-conscious admissions. More extensive reverse discrimination was permitted in *United Steelworkers of America* v. *Weber* (443 U.S. 193: 1979), in which the Court allowed a private employer to give preference to unskilled black employees over white employees for training programs designed to elevate the unskilled workers to craft levels. The Court permitted the preferential treatment because prior racial discrimination had demonstrably disadvantaged black workers in the past. The use of "set-asides" was upheld by the Court as a remedial solution in *Fullilove* v. *Klutznick* (448 U.S. 448: 1980). A set-aside reserves a certain percentage of federal funds for minority businesses. The Court determined that Congress may allow narrowly tailored corrective actions to redress historical disadvantages.

Right   A power or privilege to which a person is entitled. A right confers control of action upon an individual and provides protection for that action. *See also* BILL OF RIGHTS, p. 7; NATURAL LAW AND NATURAL RIGHTS, p. 51.

Significance   A right is legally conveyed by a constitution, statutes, or common law. It may be absolute, such as one's right to believe, or it may be conditional so that the acting out of one's beliefs will not injure other members of a political community. Rights within constitutional systems are called natural, civil, or political. A natural right is derived from the nature of man and flows from natural law. It is not dependent on manmade law. A civil right grows out of the political community, attaching to one's citizenship. Thus every person has the right to a jury trial or equal treatment before the law. A political right protects a person's capacity to participate in his or her own governance by voting and by seeking political office.

Self-Incrimination Clause   The Fifth Amendment provision that no person "shall be compelled in any criminal case to be a witness against himself." The Self-Incrimination Clause covers testimony at the trial of an accused person or statements made prior to the trial that may have the effect of implicating the person in a crime. It requires the prosecution to demonstrate guilt without assistance from the accused. *See also* CARTER V. KENTUCKY (450 U.S. 288: 1981), p. 226; ESTELLE V. SMITH (451 U.S. 454: 1981), p. 227; IDENTIFICATION PROCEDURES, p. 421; IMMUNITY, p. 422; KASTIGAR V. UNITED STATES (406 U.S. 441: 1972), p. 233; MIRANDA V. ARIZONA (384 U.S. 436: 1966), p. 219; NEIL V. BIGGERS (409 U.S. 188: 1972), p. 230; SCHMERBER V. CALIFORNIA (384 U.S. 757: 1966), p. 229.

Significance   The Self-Incrimination Clause was fully recognized in Great Britain by the early eighteenth century and was established in common law by the time the American Constitution was written. As the Supreme Court said in *Murphy* v. *Waterfront Commission of New York* (378 U.S. 52: 1964), the Self-Incrimination Clause reflects "many of our fundamental values and most noble aspirations." Those values and aspirations include "our unwillingness to subject those suspected of crime to the cruel trilemma of self-accusation, perjury or contempt." The privilege against self-incrimination represents a society's preference for an accusatorial rather than an inquisitorial system of criminal justice. It extends only to criminal prosecutions, however, and does not prevent compelled testimony that may damage a witness's reputation or create adverse economic or social consequences. The Supreme Court resisted early attempts to make the Self-Incrimination Clause applicable to the states through the Fourteenth Amendment. In *Twining* v. *New Jersey* (211 U.S. 78: 1908), the Court concluded that the privilege did not rank "among the fundamental and inalienable rights of mankind," but rather it constituted "a wise and beneficent rule of evidence." The Court said it may be "a just and useful principle of law," but it need not be required at the state level. The Warren Court reversed *Twining* in *Malloy* v. *Hogan* (378 U.S. 1: 1964). It declared "the *Twining* view of the privilege has been eroded," and that it was incongruous to have different standards dependent upon whether the right was asserted in a state or a federal court. The contemporary significance of the self-incrimination protection was underlined not only by the Warren Court's decision to apply the privilege to the states but by the Court's decision to extend the privilege to pretrial situations such as custodial interrogations. It did so in *Miranda* v. *Arizona* (384 U.S. 436: 1966). *Miranda* required that all detained persons be advised of their constitutional rights prior to interrogation. Voluntary confessions are not prohibited by *Miranda*. Even statements taken improperly may be used to impeach a defendant's trial testimony. The privilege against self-incrimination has been confined to communicative or testimonial evidence. Accordingly, it prohibits comment on a defendant's refusal to testify, but the prohibition does not extend to such defendant-derived evidence as blood samples or to involuntary identification procedures such as lineups. The Self-Incrimination Clause may be satisfied by granting immunity to a witness, thereby protecting the witness from having compelled testimony used in a subsequent prosecution against him or her.

Separate but Equal   The doctrine of a Supreme Court holding in *Plessy* v. *Ferguson* (163 U.S. 537: 1896) that a legal distinction between the black and white races does not destroy the legal equality of the two races. Separate but equal was a reaction to the Equal Protection

Clause of the Fourteenth Amendment, which prohibits discriminatory state conduct. Following ratification of the Amendment, many Southern states enacted statutes requiring racial segregation in a variety of situations. The states argued that such segregation did not constitute impermissible discrimination. In *Plessy,* the Supreme Court agreed and permitted state-mandated segregation as long as separate facilities were equal for both races. *See also* BROWN V. BOARD OF EDUCATION I (347 U.S. 483: 1954), p. 326; EQUAL PROTECTION CLAUSE, p. 313; PLESSY V. FERGUSON (163 U.S. 537: 1896), p. 322; STATE ACTION, p. 454.

Significance   The separate but equal formula was articulated in reference to a state statute that required all railroads operating in the state to provide "equal but separate accommodations." The Supreme Court said the separate but equal concept provided both races with equality under the law. For several decades following *Plessy,* the standard was maintained with little attention paid to the actual equivalence of facilities. Renunciation of the doctrine began in the mid-twentieth century with several graduate education decisions. Separate but equal was abandoned totally in the context of public education in *Brown* v. *Board of Education I* (347 U.S. 483: 1954). Soon after *Brown,* segregation was invalidated in transportation, public accommodations, and municipal facilities as well.

Sliding Scale Test   A standard for evaluating expression to determine if the expression is to be afforded First Amendment protection. The sliding scale test is a modification of the clear and present danger test. *See also* BALANCING TEST, p. 388; CLEAR AND PRESENT DANGER TEST, p. 395; DENNIS V. UNITED STATES (341 U.S. 494: 1951), p. 111.

Significance   The sliding scale test was first used by the Supreme Court in *Dennis* v. *United States* (341 U.S. 494: 1951). The Court held in *Dennis* that inquiry must be made into "whether the gravity of the evil, discounted by its improbability, justifies such invasion of free speech as is necessary to avoid the danger." If the threat posed is severe enough, such as the violent overthrow of the government, a response is required even if the attempted overthrow is doomed from the outset. If the evil is less grave, its probability of success must be greater. The sliding scale test is a comparative judgment determination applied on a case-by-case basis

Smith Act   The first federal legislative regulation of expression and association since the Alien and Sedition Acts of 1798. The Smith Act, formally known as the Alien Registration Act of 1940, required aliens living in the United States to register with the federal government. Any alien found to be associated with a subversive organization could be deported. The principal thrust of the statute, however, was its restriction on certain kinds of political expression by American citizens. The Smith Act prohibited advocacy of the violent overthrow of any government in the United States and the publication of any materials advocating forcible overthrow. It also prohibited the organization of any group dedicated to revolution. *See also* CLEAR AND PRESENT DANGER TEST, p. 395; *DENNIS* V. *UNITED STATES* (341 U.S. 494: 1951), p. 111; FIRST AMENDMENT, p. 77; SLIDING SCALE TEST, p. 450.

Significance   The Smith Act was upheld in *Dennis* v. *United States* (341 U.S. 494: 1951). The Supreme Court used a sliding scale test to determine that Congress had the authority to prevent an evil as extensive as forcible overthrow of the government. In the years following *Dennis,* successful prosecutions under the Smith Act became less and less likely as the Court further required that evidence of "knowing and active" participation in criminal conduct aimed at violent overthrow be demonstrated.

Speech Plus   Expression that requires additional action or conduct. Speech plus refers to such forms of expression as picketing, marching, demonstrating, and sitting in. These situations raise difficult First Amendment questions. While expression carries free speech protection, conduct associated with expression may be subject to regulation. *See also ADDERLEY* V. *FLORIDA* (385 U.S. 39: 1966), p. 142; FREE SPEECH CLAUSE, p. 416; *PRUNEYARD SHOPPING CENTER* V. *ROBINS* (447 U.S. 74: 1980), p. 144; PURE SPEECH, p. 447.

Significance   Speech plus takes normally protected speech out of bounds when it involves a demonstration in such places as the grounds of a county jail. If the conduct associated with speech is subject to regulation, the regulation comes at the expense of the expression. Cases that raise such First Amendment issues include access to private shopping malls, permit requirements, court injunctions, and time, place, and manner restrictions. Speech plus is distinguished from pure speech, which necessitates no additional conduct.

Speedy Trial   A safeguard of the Sixth Amendment, which provides a criminal defendant with the right to a "speedy and public trial." The speedy trial provision of the federal Constitution was made applicable to the states through the Fourteenth Amendment in *Klopfer* v. *North Carolina* (386 U.S. 213: 1967). Speedy trial is intended to keep an accused from protracted pretrial detention, and it protects against the diminution of a criminal defendant's ability to offer a defense. Speedy trial also ensures that the prosecutor's case will not erode because of delay, thus forming a two-edged constitutional sword. The speedy trial protection begins at the time a person is formally accused unless pre-charging delays aimed at gaining prosecutorial advantage occur. *See also* BARKER V. WINGO (407 U.S. 514: 1972), p. 245.

Significance   Speedy trial challenges that would establish fixed time limits for trials or would depend on a formal demand by the accused for a speedy trial have been rejected by the Supreme Court. The Court developed a balancing test for speedy trials in *Barker* v. *Wingo* (407 U.S. 514: 1972, p. 245). The four components are (1) length of delay; (2) sufficiency of reasons for the delay; (3) assertion of the right to a speedy trial by the accused; and (4) injury or prejudice suffered by the accused through pretrial incarceration, anxiety, and/or impairment of the ability to present a defense. In addition to these guidelines established by the Court, both federal and state legislation exists to govern the speed by which a criminal case progresses through the courts. Defense-initiated requests for postponements are not considered delays covered by the speedy trial protection.

Standing   The requirement that a real dispute exists between the prospective parties in a suit. Standing is necessary for a federal court to proceed with a case. The concept has several important components. Federal judicial power extends to cases or controversies through Article III of the Constitution. This has been interpreted to mean that bona fide disputes must exist if judicial resolution is to be sought. The federal courts are thus unable to respond to hypothetical or friendly suits, and they cannot render advisory opinions. The adversary system demands that litigants in a suit be true adversaries. Test cases have often been used to raise certain issues and satisfy the demands of the standing requirement. A test case is a legal action designed to obtain a court's judgment on a legal question and thereby have a principle or right established or clarified. Developing a test case is a common strategy of interest groups. The National

Association for the Advancement of Colored People (NAACP), for example, orchestrated various test cases involving different aspects of racial segregation in an effort to obtain favorable judgments in the courts. Standing means that the plaintiff bringing suit must have suffered direct injury, and the injury must be protected by constitutional or statutory provisions. This means suits cannot be brought by a third party or someone indirectly related to the legal injury. Further, each suit must specify the remedy being sought from the court. The burden rests with the plaintiff to define the relief the court might order. Standing also relates to the timing of a suit. A federal court must find a suit ripe, which means all other avenues of possible relief must have been exhausted. Similarly, a case cannot access federal courts if it has been resolved or if events have made pursuit of the original remedy inappropriate. A case that is too late is considered moot because there is no longer an adversarial situation. Exceptions will be made when the limited duration of a situation or condition interferes with the litigation of the issues. Abortion cases are examples of the need for such an exception.

Significance   Standing is discussed in several important Supreme Court decisions. The matter was first raised in *Frothingham* v. *Mellon* (262 U.S. 447: 1923). Plaintiff Frothingham attempted to enjoin the implementation of a federal program claiming injury by virtue of paying federal taxes. The Supreme Court denied standing and suggested that Frothingham's injury was shared by millions of others. The injury was therefore "comparatively minute and indeterminate." A plaintiff seeking judicial review of a federal statute must be able to show "direct injury as the result of its enforcement, and not merely that he suffers in some indefinite way in common with people generally." Inability to establish such injury will prevent consideration of the constitutional issue regardless of how real and pressing the issue may be. The *Frothingham* precedent lasted as an absolute barrier to judicial review of congressional spending legislation by taxpayers until *Flast* v. *Cohen* (392 U.S. 83: 1968). The Court held in *Flast* that a taxpayer could achieve standing by showing a nexus between the taxpayer and the challenged program. The case involved a challenge of federal aid to private elementary and secondary schools. The Warren Court found the relationship among the federal taxing power, the payment of federal taxes, and First Amendment protections adequate to produce standing. The decision immediately raised questions about judicial review of congressional spending initiatives. It distinguished between the *Frothingham* direct injury requirement and the litigant who might be acting on behalf of broader public rights. The Burger Court has shown, however, that access is still difficult. In *United States* v. *Richardson* (418 U.S. 166: 1974), the Court refused to allow a taxpayer to inquire into Central Intelligence Agency appropriations. The Court said that allowing "unrestricted taxpayer standing would significantly alter the allocation of power at the national level." A second case, *Schlesinger* v. *Reservist's Committee to Stop the War* (418 U.S. 208: 1974), challenged the military reserve status of more than a hundred members of Congress. The Court denied standing, saying that to allow such a challenge by someone who has no concrete injury would require the Court to respond to issues in the abstract. The Court said this would create the potential for abuse of the judicial process and distortion of the role of the judiciary. Standing too easily granted would open the courts to an arguable charge of government by the judiciary.

Stare Decisis   Latin for "let the decision stand." Stare decisis holds that once a principle of law is established for a particular fact situation, courts should adhere to that principle in similar cases in the future. The case in which the rule of law is established is called a precedent.

Significance   Stare decisis creates and maintains stability and predictability in the law. It creates a large body of settled usages that define common law. Precedents may be modified or abandoned if circumstances require, but the expectation is that rules from previously adjudicated cases will prevail.

State Action   A requirement that limits application of the Equal Protection Clause to situations where discriminatory conduct occurs under state authority. The state action requirement was first established by the Supreme Court in the *Civil Rights Cases* (109 U.S. 3: 1883). It placed private discrimination outside the reach of the Fourteenth Amendment. The Court held that the Amendment was intended to provide relief against state enactments rather than to empower Congress "to legislate upon subjects which are within the domain of state legislation" or "create a code of municipal law for the regulation of private rights." *See also* CIVIL RIGHTS CASES (109 U.S. 3: 1883), p. 321; CLASSIFICATION, p. 394; EQUAL PROTECTION CLAUSE, p. 313; SEPARATE BUT EQUAL, p. 449; *VILLAGE OF ARLINGTON HEIGHTS* V. *METROPOLITAN HOUSING DEVELOPMENT*

CORPORATION   (429 U.S. 258: 1977), p. 335; *WASHINGTON V. DAVIS* (426 U.S. 229: 1976), p. 333.

Significance   State action requires a judgment about whether certain kinds of conduct occur under color of state law. A court must determine if discriminatory action is situated closely enough to state authority to be treated as though it were an overt act of the state. A sufficient nexus between challenged action and state authority is generally not difficult to demonstrate, although some private discrimination remains insulated from regulation. While softening the distinctions between private and state-authorized discrimination, thus expanding the reach of the Equal Protection Clause, recent cases have required that discriminatory *intent* must be shown in addition to injurious impact in order to establish a constitutional violation.

Statute   A written law enacted by a legislative body. A statute declares, requires, or prohibits something. *See also* JUDICIAL REVIEW, p. 429.

Significance   A statute is the most common means by which conduct is governed. It must be enacted by a legislative body properly exercising the authority conveyed to it. A statute is inferior to constitutional provisions, and if a statute is incompatible with a constitutional command, the statute is void. Federal statutes are regularly compiled and found in the United States Code.

Stop and Frisk   A limited detention of a suspicious person accompanied by a cursory weapons search. A stop and frisk is a warrantless stop where probable cause to arrest does not exist. The stop, however, is based on an officer's reasonable suspicion that a crime is occurring or is about to occur. A stop and frisk is intended to be protective, but it is nonetheless "an intrusion upon the sanctity of the person," and is extensively circumscribed. *See also* BROWN V. *TEXAS* (443 U.S. 47: 1979), p. 190; PROBABLE CAUSE, p. 446; *TERRY* V. *OHIO* (392 U.S. 1: 1968), p. 188.

Significance   Stop and frisk is discussed at length in *Terry* v. *Ohio* (392 U.S. 1: 1968, p. 188), which held that the overriding consideration must be the discovery of weapons in suspicious situations. The major importance of *Terry* is that it distinguishes stops from arrests and frisks from full searches. Under *Terry,* even situations lacking probable cause may be subjected to the preventive action of a temporary stop and a cursory weapons search. Custodial arrest with a full search may follow if the frisk yields a weapon. Random stops to request identification are not permissible. The *Terry* rationale was used to extend stop and frisk to the passenger compartment of a stopped car. In *Michigan* v. *Long* (77 L.Ed.2d 1201: 1983), the Court held that *Terry* need not be restricted to a preventive search of the person of a detained suspect. A search of the passenger compartment is permitted if law enforcement agents have "an articulate and objectively reasonable belief that the suspect is potentially dangerous." *Long* allows a police officer to act upon reasonable suspicion to discover weapons that may be used to harm the officer or others.

Substantive Due Process   A substantive review focusing on the content of government policy and actions. Substantive due process is distinguished from procedural due process, which attends to the means by which policies are executed. Judicial review of the reasonableness of legislative enactments allows the Court actively to intervene in policy judgments more than it could if review were confined to procedural considerations. *See also* DUE PROCESS CLAUSES, p. 405; PROCEDURAL DUE PROCESS, p. 446.

Significance   Substantive due process represents considerable monitoring power in the hands of the courts. In *Meyer* v. *Nebraska* (262 U.S. 390: 1923), for example, the Supreme Court struck down a statute prohibiting the teaching of a foreign language to any pre–9th grade student, public or parochial. Justice McReynolds said the statute was "arbitrary and without reasonable relation to any end within the competency of the State." The use of substantive due process to invalidate economic regulations is illustrated by *Lochner* v. *New York* (198 U.S. 45: 1905). *Lochner* involved an attempt to limit the work week of bakers to 60 hours. The Court held that there is "no reasonable ground for interfering with the liberty of a person or the right of free contract by determining the hours of labor in the occupation of a baker." The Court made a substantive judgment that the regulation of work hours for bakers was sufficiently unreasonable to constitute a denial of due process of law. Substantive due process review also occurs when statutes are striken for reason of vagueness. When the Court voided a city ordinance in *Coates* v. *Cincinnati* (40 U.S. 611: 1971), an ordinance that prohibited public annoyance by assemblies of three or more persons standing on public sidewalks, it did so because the ordinance was arbitrary. It conveyed no discernible standard of conduct. Another example of substantive due process enforcement is the striking down of state statutes prohibiting abortion.

Symbolic Speech   The use of action or gesture as a surrogate or substitute for words. Symbolic speech is generally protected by the First Amendment because of its relationship to expression. It may be restricted, however, if the substituted action is not permitted. *See also* FREE SPEECH CLAUSE, p. 416; PURE SPEECH, p. 447; SPEECH PLUS, p. 451; *TINKER* V. *DES MOINES SCHOOL DISTRICT* (393 U.S. 503: 1969), p. 113.

Significance   Symbolic speech was protected in *Tinker* v. *Des Moines School District* (393 U.S. 503: 1969), when the Supreme Court upheld the wearing of armbands as a protest against American involvement in Vietnam. The Court found that the armbands were passive expression of opinion that closely resembled pure speech. Most restrictions on symbolic speech are invalidated in order to ensure free political debate, but limits have been applied. The Court upheld a conviction for draft card burning in *United States* v. *O'Brien* (391 U.S. 367: 1968), for example, saying that while the action was communicative, the Court could not accept a limitless variety of conduct labeled speech whenever a person intended to express an idea.

Third-Party Search   A search involving an indirectly affected third party offering consent to the search of a suspect's premises. Third-party consent may legally be granted even though the consenting party is not directly suspected of criminal conduct. The third party must share common authority over the place to be searched, but he or she may not give permission to search areas exclusively used by the nonconsenting party. *See also* CONSENT SEARCH, p. 398; PROBABLE CAUSE, p. 446; *UNITED STATES* V. *MATLOCK* (415 U.S. 164: 1974), p. 193; WARRANT, p. 460; *ZURCHER* V. *STANFORD DAILY* (436 U.S. 547: 1978), p. 167.

Significance   Third-party search consent is separable from a title to property. Landlords may not consent to the search of tenants' rooms, for example. The third party involved in a third-party search is frequently a spouse or a roommate. Another third-party situation involves the search of a location despite the fact the occupant is not a suspect. A warrant may be issued to search any premises as long as a neutral magistrate concludes there is probable cause to believe evidence pertaining to a crime is located there. In *Zurcher* v. *Stanford Daily* (436 U.S. 547: 1978, p. 167), the Supreme Court upheld a warrant-authorized third-party search of a newspaper office. Evidence germane to criminal investigations becomes more likely as computer-based record keeping by third parties develops. In *Zurcher* the Court rejected the policy option of using the subpoena to obtain evidence from third-party sources. Thus the premises of those not under active investigation are subject to search provided warrant conditions are met.

Thirteenth Amendment   A post–Civil War constitutional amendment providing that "Neither slavery nor involuntary servitude, except as a punishment for crime whereof the party shall have been duly convicted, shall exist within the United States, or any place subject to their jurisdiction." The Thirteenth Amendment gave legal effect to the Emancipation Proclamation. It also fundamentally altered the federal-state relationship in that it conferred on the federal government authority over a policy area previously residing exclusively in the states. A state could no longer permit slavery through the exercise of its own authority. The Thirteenth Amendment does not preclude military conscription, criminal sentences involving hard labor, or other similar requirements of involuntary service. The Amendment was designed to apply to black persons in the particular context of the Emancipation Proclamation. Section 2 of the Amendment empowered Congress "to enforce this article by appropriate legislation." *See also* FOURTEENTH AMENDMENT, p. 313; STATE ACTION, p. 454.

Significance   The Thirteenth Amendment gave Congress comprehensive power to legislate against racial discrimination and the denial of civil rights. Such power was incident to the power to outlaw slavery. Consistent with this view, Congress passed the Civil Rights Act of 1866, which clarified the citizenship status of freed slaves and protected certain rights such as entering into contracts and holding and conveying real property. Early Supreme Court construction of the Amendment defined slavery very narrowly, however, and placed private discrimination outside the amendment's reach. Congress therefore had no occasion to exercise the limited authority conferred by Section 2. In 1968 the Supreme Court substantially modified its previous interpretations and found that the Amendment empowered Congress to do more than simply abolish the institution of slavery. In the case of *Jones* v. *Alfred H. Mayer Company* (392 U.S. 409: 1968), a case in which a litigant attempted to utilize provisions of the Civil Rights Act of 1866 against a discriminatory housing developer, the Court said the Thirteenth Amendment had granted Congress power "to determine what are the badges and the incidents of slavery" and to respond accordingly. As construed in *Jones,* the Thirteenth Amendment became a foundation stone upon which civil-rights policy was established, particularly when the policy turns on what constitutes a badge or vestige of slavery. The correction of such badges and vestiges is now clearly located within the parameters of congressional power.

Tort   A private or civil injury to a person or property. A tort action must include the legal obligation of a defendant to a plaintiff, violation of that obligation, and a cause-and-effect relationship between the defendant's conduct and the injury suffered by the plaintiff.

Significance   A tort is any civil wrong except breach of contract. A lawsuit alleging the negligence of an automobile driver is a tort action, for example. An assault is a tort. So is a trespass. A constitutional tort involves an action or inaction that allegedly violates the Constitution of the United States.

Travel, Right to   A fundamental right drawn implicitly from the Constitution of the United States. The right to travel freely from state to state is spread among all American citizens. While several origins of the right have been suggested, the Supreme Court has settled on the Commerce Clause as the principal source. The Court has held that the power to regulate interstate commerce encompasses people as well as commodities. *See also* FUNDAMENTAL RIGHT, p. 417; SHAPIRO V. THOMPSON (394 U.S. 618: 1969), p. 349.

Significance   The right to travel not only precludes denial of movement from state to state, but it also prohibits state policies that may inhibit interstate travel. In *Shapiro* v. *Thompson* (394 U.S. 618: 1969), for example, the Court struck down a state residency requirement for welfare eligibility. The purpose of the enactment was to deter migration of welfare-eligible persons into a state. The Court categorically condemned any interference with the right to movement, saying that all citizens must be free to travel throughout the country. They must be "uninhibited by statutes, rules, or regulations which unreasonably burden or restrain this movement." A state must demonstrate a compelling interest before imposing any regulation that affects the right to travel.

Warrant   An order issued by a court authorizing the arrest of a person or the search of a specified location. The warrant requirement in criminal cases is found in the Fourth Amendment following the assertion of the people's right to be secure against unreasonable searches and seizures. *See also* COOLIDGE V. NEW HAMPSHIRE (403 U.S. 443: 1971), p. 162; DRAPER V. UNITED STATES (385 U.S. 307: 1959), p. 160; NEUTRAL MAGISTRATE, p. 435; PROBABLE CAUSE, p. 446; WARRANTLESS SEARCH, p. 460; YBARRA V. ILLINOIS (444 U.S. 85: 1979), p. 164.

Significance   A warrant authorizes an official government intrusion into personal security. It must be obtained from an appropriate authority, who is generally a neutral magistrate. A request for a warrant must establish probable cause that the person to be arrested is linked to a criminal act or that the location to be searched likely contains particular seizable items. The warrant must describe in detail the person to be arrested or the items to be sought in a search.

Warrantless Search   A search for evidence allowed if it is conducted incident to a lawful arrest. A warrantless search is permitted to allow removal of weapons from the arrestee or prevent the concealment or destruction of evidence. A search incident to arrest is confined to the area within the arrestee's immediate control. *See also* CHIMEL V. CALIFORNIA (395 U.S. 752: 1969), p. 175; CONSENT SEARCH, p. 398; EXIGENT CIRCUMSTANCE, p. 410; HOT PURSUIT, p. 421; STOP AND FRISK, p. 455; WARRANT, p. 460.

Significance   A warrantless search is an exception arising out of an exigent circumstance in which a police officer may be unable to seek a warrant. An exigency may be presented in an unforeseen stop and frisk situation, as in *Terry* v. *Ohio* (392 U.S. 1: 1968, p. 188). It may be presented in the search of an automobile, as in *Chambers* v. *Maroney* (399 U.S. 42: 1970, p. 182), or in hot pursuit. Items may be seized if they are in the plain view of the officer and if the seized items were discovered in a place where the officer was entitled to be. Finally, a warrantless search may occur when a person voluntarily waives his or her Fourth Amendment rights and consents to the search.

APPENDIX A: TABLES

TABLE A-1

Charters Granted to the Thirteen American Colonies

COLONY	FOUNDER(S)	DATE OF CHARTER	DATE OF FOUNDING	STATUS
Virginia	London Company	1606 (New charters were issued in 1609 and 1612.)	1607	Royal
New Hampshire	John Mason and others	1679	1623	Royal
Massachusetts (Plymouth Colony, settled in 1620 by the Pilgrims, was unchartered. It merged with Massachusetts in 1691.)	Puritans	1629	c1628	Royal
Maryland	Lord Baltimore	1632	1634	Proprietary
Connecticut (New Haven, settled by Massachusetts emigrants in 1638, was unchartered. It merged with Connecticut in 1662.)	Emigrants from Massachusetts	1662	1635	Self-Governing
Rhode Island	Roger Williams	1644 and 1663	1636	Self-Governing
North Carolina	Emigrants from Virginia	1663	1653	Royal
New York	Duke of York (after the Dutch)	1664	1664	Royal
New Jersey	Berkeley and Carteret	None	1664	Royal
South Carolina (The Carolinas were chartered as a single colony. They separated informally in 1691 and formally in 1712.)	Eight nobles	1663	1670	Royal
Pennsylvania	William Penn	1681	1681	Proprietary
Delaware	Sweden	None	1638	Proprietary
Georgia	Oglethorpe and others	1732	1732	Royal

Source: Adapted by Cynthia E. Brown, *State Constitutional Conventions from Independence to the Completion of the Present Union, 1776–1959* (Westport, Connecticut: The Greenwood Press, 1973), p. xvii; from Thomas A. Bailey, *The American Pageant*, 3d ed. (Boston: D.C. Heath, 1966), p. 17.

465

TABLE A-2

General Information on State Constitutions
(As of December 31, 1979)

STATE OR OTHER JURISDICTION	NUMBER OF CONSTITUTIONS	DATES OF ADOPTION	EFFECTIVE DATE OF PRESENT CONSTITUTION	ESTIMATED LENGTH (NUMBER OF WORDS)	NUMBER OF AMENDMENTS	
					SUBMITTED TO VOTERS	ADOPTED
Alabama	6	1819, 1861, 1865, 1868, 1875, 1901	November 28, 1901	129,000	566	383
Alaska	1	1956	January 3, 1959	12,880	19	16
Arizona	1	1911	February 14, 1912	28,779(a)	154	88
Arkansas	5	1836, 1861, 1864, 1868, 1874	October 30, 1874	38,654(a)	144	66(b)
California	2	1849, 1879	July 4, 1879	34,000	715	425
Colorado	1	1876	August 1, 1876	45,600	214	98
Connecticut	4	1818(c), 1965	December 30, 1965	7,900	13	12
Delaware	5	1776, 1792, 1831, 1853, 1897	June 10, 1897	18,700	(d)	101(c)
Florida	6	1839, 1861, 1865, 1868, 1886, 1968	January 7, 1969	25,000	41	21
Georgia	9	1777, 1789, 1798, 1861, 1865, 1868, 1877, 1945, 1976	January 1, 1977	600,000(f)	123	81
Hawaii	1(g)	1950	August 21, 1959	17,255(a)	76	71
Idaho	1	1889	July 3, 1890	21,323(a)	171	92
Illinois	4	1818, 1848, 1870, 1970	July 1, 1971	13,200	3	0
Indiana	2	1816, 1851	November 1, 1851	10,225(a)	63	34
Iowa	2	1846, 1857	September 3, 1857	12,500	45	43(h)
Kansas	1	1859	January 29, 1861	11,865	104	77(h)
Kentucky	4	1792, 1799, 1850, 1891	September 28, 1891	23,500	51	24
Louisiana	11	1812, 1845, 1852, 1861, 1865, 1868, 1879, 1898, 1913, 1921, 1974	January 1, 1975	35,387(a)	4	4
Maine	1	1819	March 15, 1820	13,500	164	140(i)
Maryland	4	1776, 1851, 1864, 1867	October 5, 1867	41,031	216	185

State						
Massachusetts	1	1780	October 25, 1780	34,000(j)	126	113
Michigan	4	1835, 1850, 1908, 1963	January 1, 1964	20,000	27	13
Minnesota	1	1857	May 11, 1858	9,491(a)	192	102
Mississippi	4	1817, 1832, 1869, 1890	November 1, 1890	23,500	117	48
Missouri	4	1820, 1865, 1875, 1945	March 30, 1945	40,134(a)	78	49
Montana	2	1889, 1972	July 1, 1973	11,363	11	6
Nebraska	2	1866, 1875	October 12, 1875	18,802(a)	259	173
Nevada	1	1864	October 31, 1864	19,735	113	86(h)
New Hampshire	2	1776, 1784(k)	June 2, 1784	9,450	165(k)	71(k)
New Jersey	3	1776, 1844, 1947	January 1, 1948	16,980	32	23
New Mexico	1	1911	January 6, 1912	27,066	199	95
New York	4	1777, 1822, 1846, 1894	January 1, 1895	41,000	267	195
North Carolina	3	1776, 1868, 1970	July 1, 1971	13,250	20	18
North Dakota	1	1889	November 2, 1889	30,000	182(l)	106(l)
Ohio	2	1802, 1851	September 1, 1851	36,300	234	129
Oklahoma	1	1907	November 16, 1907	68,500	217(m)	102(m)
Oregon	1	1857	February 14, 1859	24,700	325	163
Pennsylvania	5	1776, 1790, 1838, 1873, 1968(n)	1968	21,675	15(n)	12(n)
Rhode Island	2	1842(c)	April 2, 1843	19,026(a, j)	80	43
South Carolina	7	1776, 1778, 1790, 1861, 1865, 1868, 1895	January 1, 1896	22,500(o)	624(p)	441(p)
South Dakota	1	1889	November 2, 1889	23,250	168	87
Tennessee	3	1796, 1835, 1870	February 23, 1870	15,300	32	31
Texas	5	1845, 1861, 1866, 1869, 1876	February 15, 1876	61,000	375	235
Utah	1	1895	January 4, 1896	17,300	108	62
Vermont	3	1777, 1786, 1793	July 9, 1793	6,600	210	52
Virginia	6	1776, 1830, 1851, 1869, 1902, 1970	July 1, 1971	18,500	10	9
Washington	1	1889	November 11, 1889	29,350	126	70
West Virginia	2	1863, 1872	April 9, 1872	25,550(a)	85	51
Wisconsin	1	1848	May 29, 1848	13,435	155	112(h)
Wyoming	1	1889	July 10, 1890	27,600	83	46

Continued

TABLE A-2—*Continued*

General Information on State Constitutions
(As of December 31, 1979)

STATE OR OTHER JURISDICTION	NUMBER OF CONSTITUTIONS*	DATES OF ADOPTION	EFFECTIVE DATE OF PRESENT CONSTITUTION	ESTIMATED LENGTH (NUMBER OF WORDS)	NUMBER OF AMENDMENTS SUBMITTED TO VOTERS	NUMBER OF AMENDMENTS ADOPTED
American Samoa....	2	1960, 1967	July 1, 1967	6,000	13	7
Northern Mariana Is.	1	1977	October 24, 1977	...	...	...
Puerto Rico........	1	1952	July 25, 1952	9,281(a)	6	6

Source: Taken from Albert L. Sturm, "State Constitutions and Constitutional Revision: 1978–79 and the 1970's," in *The Book of the States, 1980–1981* Vol. 23 (Lexington, Kentucky: The Council of State Governments, 1980), p. 16.

*The constitutions in this table include those Civil War documents customarily listed by the individual states.

aActual word count.

bEight of the approved amendments have been superseded and are not printed in the current edition of the constitution. The total adopted does not include five amendments that were invalidated.

cColonial charters with some alterations served as the first constitutions in Connecticut (1638, 1662) and in Rhode Island (1663).

dProposed amendments are not submitted to the voters.

eVarious sections of the constitution have been amended 101 times by 56 acts of the legislature.

fEstimated length of the printed constitution, which includes only provisions of statewide applicability, is 48,000 words.

gAs a kingdom and a republic Hawaii had five constitutions.

hThe figure given includes amendments approved by the voters and later nullified by the state supreme court: in Iowa, 3; Kansas, 1; Nevada, 6; Wisconsin, 2.

iThe figure does not include one amendment approved by voters in 1967 that is inoperative until implemented by legislation.

jThe printed constitution includes many provisions that have been annulled. The length of effective provisions is: in Massachusetts, estimated 21,555 words (12,445 annulled); in Rhode Island, 11,399 words (7,627 annulled).

kThe constitution of 1784 was extensively revised in 1792. Figures show proposals and adoptions since 1792.

lThe figures do not include submission and approval of the constitution of 1889 itself and of Article XX; these are constitutional questions included in some counts of constitutional amendments, and would add 2 to the figure in each column.

mThe figures include one amendment submitted to and approved by the voters and subsequently ruled by the supreme court to have been illegally submitted.

nCertain sections of the constitution were revised by the limited constitutional convention of 1967–68. Amendments proposed and adopted are since 1968.

oOf the estimated length, approximately two thirds are of general statewide effect; the remaining are local amendments.

pOf the 624 proposed amendments submitted to the voters, 128 were of general statewide effect and 496 were local; the voters rejected 83 (12 statewide, 71 local); of the remaining 541, the legislature refused to approve 100 (22 statewide, 78 local); and 441 (94 statewide, 347 local) were finally added to the constitution.

APPENDIX B:
THE CONSTITUTION OF THE UNITED STATES

The Constitution of the United States

PREAMBLE

We the People of the United States, in Order to form a more perfect Union, establish Justice, insure domestic Tranquility, provide for the common defence, promote the general Welfare, and secure the Blessings of Liberty to ourselves and our Posterity, do ordain and establish this Constitution for the United States of America.

ARTICLE I

Section 1. All legislative Powers herein granted shall be vested in a Congress of the United States, which shall consist of a Senate and House of Representatives.

Section 2. The House of Representatives shall be composed of Members chosen every second Year by the People of the several States, and the Electors in each State shall have the Qualifications requisite for Electors of the most numerous Branch of the State Legislature.

No Person shall be a Representative who shall not have attained to the age of twenty five Years, and been seven Years a Citizen of the United States, and who shall not, when elected, be an Inhabitant of that State in which he shall be chosen.

Representatives and direct Taxes shall be apportioned among the several States which may be included within this Union, according to their respective Numbers, which shall be determined by adding to the whole Number of free Persons, including those bound to Service for a Term of Years, and excluding Indians not taxed, three fifths of all other Persons. The actual Enumeration shall be made within three Years after the first Meeting of the Congress of the United States, and within every subsequent Term of ten Years, in such Manner as they shall by Law direct. The Number of Representatives shall not exceed one for every thirty Thousand, but each State shall have at Least one Representative; and until such enumeration shall be made, the State of New Hampshire shall be entitled to chuse three, Massachusetts eight, Rhode-Island and Providence Plantations one, Connecticut five, New York six, New Jersey four, Pennsylvania eight, Delaware one, Maryland six, Virginia ten, North Carolina five, South Carolina five, and Georgia three.

When vacancies happen in the Representation from any State, the Executive Authority thereof shall issue Writs of Election to fill such Vacancies.

The House of Representatives shall chuse their Speaker and other Officers; and shall have the sole Power of Impeachment.

SECTION 3. The Senate of the United States shall be composed of two Senators from each State, chosen by the Legislature thereof, for six Years; and each Senator shall have one Vote.

Immediately after they shall be assembled in Consequence of the first Election, they shall be divided as equally as may be into three Classes. The seats of the Senators of the first Class shall be vacated at the Expiration of the second Year, of the second Class at the Expiration of the Fourth Year, and of the third Class at the Expiration of the sixth Year, so that one third may be chosen every second Year; and if Vacancies happen by Resignation, or otherwise, during the Recess of the Legislature of any State, the Executive thereof may make temporary Appointments until the next Meeting of the Legislature, which shall then fill such Vacancies.

No Person shall be a Senator who shall not have attained to the Age of thirty Years, and been nine Years a Citizen of the United States, and who shall not, when elected, be an Inhabitant of that State for which he shall be chosen.

The Vice President of the United States shall be President of the Senate, but shall have no Vote, unless they be equally divided.

The Senate shall chuse their other Officers, and also a President pro tempore, in the Absence of the Vice President, or when he shall exercise the Office of President of the United States.

The Senate shall have the sole Power to try all Impeachments. When sitting for that Purpose, they shall be on Oath or Affirmation. When the President of the United States is tried the Chief Justice shall preside: And no Person shall be convicted without the Concurrence of two thirds of the Members present.

Judgment in Cases of Impeachment shall not extend further than to removal from Office, and disqualification to hold and enjoy any Office of honor, Trust or Profit under the United States: but the Party convicted shall nevertheless be liable and subject to Indictment, Trial, Judgment and Punishment, according to Law.

SECTION 4. The Times, Places and Manner of holding Elections for Senators and Representatives, shall be prescribed in each State by the Legislature thereof; but the Congress may at any time by Law make or alter such Regulations, except as to the Places of chusing Senators.

The Congress shall assemble at least once in every Year, and such Meeting shall be on the first Monday in December unless they shall by Law appoint a different Day.

SECTION 5. Each House shall be the Judge of the Elections, Returns and Qualifications of its own Members, and a Majority of each shall constitute a Quorum to do Business; but a smaller Number may adjourn from day to day, and may be authorized to compel the Attendance of absent Members, in such Manner, and under such Penalties as each House may provide.

Each House may determine the Rules of its Proceedings, punish its Members for disorderly Behaviour, and, with the Concurrence of two thirds, expel a Member.

Each House shall keep a Journal of its Proceedings, and from time to time publish the same, excepting such Parts as may in their Judgment require Secrecy; and the Yeas and Nays of the Members of either House on any question shall, at the Desire of one fifth of those Present, be entered on the Journal.

Neither House, during the Session of Congress, shall, without the Consent of the other, adjourn for more than three days, nor to any other Place than that in which the two Houses shall be sitting.

SECTION 6. The Senators and Representatives shall receive a Compensation for their Services, to be ascertained by Law, and paid out of the Treasury of the United States. They shall in all Cases, except Treason, Felony and Breach of the Peace, be privileged from Arrest during their Attendance at the Session of their respective Houses, and in going to and returning from the same; and for any Speech or Debate in either House, they shall not be questioned in any other Place.

No Senator or Representative shall, during the Time for which he was elected, be appointed to any civil Office under the Authority of the United States, which shall have been created, or the Emoluments whereof shall have been encreased during such time; and no Person holding any Office under the United States, shall be a Member of either House during his Continuance in Office.

SECTION 7. All Bills for raising Revenue shall originate in the House of Representatives; but the Senate may propose or concur with amendments as on other Bills.

Every Bill which shall have passed the House of Representatives and the Senate, shall, before it becomes a Law, be presented to the President of the United States; If he approve he shall sign it, but if not he shall return it, with his Objections to that House in which it shall have originated, who shall enter the Objections at large on their Journal, and proceed to reconsider it. If after such Reconsideration two thirds of that House shall agree to pass the Bill, it shall be sent, together with the Objections, to the other House, by which it shall likewise be reconsidered, and if approved by two thirds of that House, it shall become a Law. But in all such Cases the Votes of both Houses shall be determined by Yeas and Nays, and the Names of the Persons voting for and against the Bill shall be entered on the Journal of each House respectively. If any Bill shall not be returned by the President within ten Days (Sunday excepted) after it shall have been presented to him, the Same shall be a Law, in like Manner as if he had signed it, unless the Congress by their Adjournment prevent its Return, in which Case it shall not be a Law.

Every Order, Resolution, or Vote to which the Concurrence of the Senate and House of Representatives may be necessary (except on a question of Adjournment) shall be presented to the President of the United States; and before the Same shall take Effect, shall be approved by him, or being disapproved by him, shall be repassed by two thirds of the Senate and House of Representatives, according to the Rules and Limitations prescribed in the Case of a Bill.

SECTION 8. The Congress shall have Power To lay and collect Taxes, Duties, Imposts and Excises, to pay the Debts and provide for the common Defence and general Welfare of the United States; but all Duties, Imposts and Excises shall be uniform throughout the United States;

To borrow Money on the credit of the United States;

To regulate Commerce with foreign Nations, and among the several States, and with the Indian Tribes;

To establish an uniform Rule of Naturalization, and uniform Laws on the subject of Bankruptcies throughout the United States;

To coin Money, regulate the Value thereof, and of foreign Coin, and fix the Standard of Weights and Measures;

To provide for the Punishment of counterfeiting the Securities and current

Coin of the United States;

To establish Post Offices and post Roads;

To promote the Progress of Science and useful Arts, by securing for limited Times to Authors and Inventors the exclusive Right to their respective Writings and Discoveries;

To constitute Tribunals inferior to the supreme Court;

To define and punish Piracies and Felonies commited on the high Seas, and Offences against the Law of Nations;

To declare War, grant letters of Marque and Reprisal, and make Rules concerning Captures on Land and Water;

To raise and support Armies, but no Appropriation of Money to that Use shall be for a longer Term than two Years;

To provide and maintain a Navy;

To make Rules for the Government and Regulation of the land and naval Forces;

To provide for calling forth the Militia to execute the Laws of the Union, suppress Insurrections and repel Invasions;

To provide for organizing, arming, and disciplining the Militia, and for governing such Part of them as may be employed in the Service of the United States, reserving to the States respectively, the Appointment of the Officers, and the Authority of training the Militia according to the discipline prescribed by Congress;

To exercise exclusive Legislation in all Cases whatsoever, over such District (not exceeding ten Miles square) as may, by Cession of Particular States, and the Acceptance of Congress, become the Seat of the Government of the United States, and to exercise like Authority over all Places purchased by the Consent of the Legislature of the State in which the Same shall be, for the Erection of Forts, Magazines, Arsenals, dock-Yards, and other needful Buildings;—

And

To make all Laws which shall be necessary and proper for carrying into Execution the foregoing Powers, and all other Powers vested by this Constitution in the Government of the United States, or in any Department or Officer thereof.

SECTION 9. The Migration or Importation of such Persons as any of the States now existing shall think proper to admit, shall not be prohibited by the Congress prior to the Year one thousand eight hundred and eight, but a Tax or duty may be imposed on such Importation, not exceeding ten dollars for each Person.

The Privilege of the Writ of Habeas Corpus shall not be suspended, unless when in Cases of Rebellion or Invasion the public Safety may require it.

No Bill of Attainder or ex post facto Law shall be passed.

No capitation, or other direct, Tax shall be laid, unless in Proportion to the Census of Enumeration herein before directed to be taken.

No Tax or Duty shall be laid on Articles exported from any State.

No Preference shall be given by any Regulation of Commerce or Revenue to the Ports of one State over those of another; nor shall Vessels bound to, or from, one State, be obliged to enter, clear or pay Duties in another.

No Money shall be drawn from the Treasury, but in Consequence of Appropriations made by Law; and a regular Statement and Account of the Receipts and Expenditures of all public Money shall be published from time to time.

No Title of Nobility shall be granted by the United States: And no Person holding any Office of Profit or Trust under them, shall, without the Consent of the Congress, accept of any present, Emolument, Office, or Title, of any kind whatever, from any King, Prince, or foreign State.

Section 10. No State shall enter into any Treaty, Alliance, or Confederation; grant Letters of Marque and Reprisal; coin Money; emit Bills of Credit; make any Thing but gold and silver Coin a Tender in Payment of Debts; pass any Bill of Attainder, ex post facto Law, or Law impairing the Obligation of Contracts, or grant any Title of Nobility.

No State shall, without the Consent of the Congress, lay any Imposts or Duties on Imports or Exports, except what may be absolutely necessary for executing it's inspection Laws: and the net Produce of all Duties and Imposts, laid by any State on Imports or Exports, shall be for the Use of the Treasury of the United States; and all such Laws shall be subject to the Revision and Controul of the Congress.

No State shall, without the Consent of Congress, lay any Duty of Tonnage, keep Troops, or Ships of War in time of Peace, enter into any Agreement or Compact with another State, or with a foreign Power, or engage in War, unless actually invaded, or in such imminent Danger as will not admit of delay.

ARTICLE II

Section 1. The executive Power shall be vested in a President of the United States of America. He shall hold his Office during the Term of four Years, and together with the Vice President, chosen for the same Term, be elected, as follows.

Each State shall appoint, in such Manner as the Legislature thereof may direct, a Number of Electors, equal to the whole Number of Senators and Representatives to which the State may be entitled in the Congress: but no Senator or Representative, or Person holding an Office of Trust or Profit under the United States, shall be appointed an Elector.

The Electors shall meet in their respective States, and vote by Ballot for two Persons, of whom one at least shall not be an Inhabitant of the same State with themselves. And they shall make a List of all the Persons voted for, and of the Number of Votes for each; which List they shall sign and certify, and transmit sealed to the Seat of the Government of the United States, directed to the President of the Senate. The President of the Senate shall, in the Presence of the Senate and House of Representatives, open all the Certificates, and the Votes shall then be counted. The Person having the greatest Number of Votes shall be the President, if such Number be a Majority of the whole Number of Electors appointed; and if there be more than one who have such Majority, and have an equal Number of Votes, then the House of Representatives shall immediately chuse by Ballot one of them for President; and if no Person have a Majority, then from the five highest on the list the said House shall in like Manner chuse the President. But in chusing the President, the Votes shall be taken by States, the Representation from each State having one Vote; a quorum for this Purpose shall consist of a Member or Members from two thirds of the States, and a Majority of all the States shall be necessary to a Choice. In every Case, after the Choice of the President, the Person having the greatest Number of Votes of the Electors shall be the Vice President. But if there should remain two or more who have equal Votes, the Senate shall chuse from them by Ballot the Vice President.

The Congress may determine the Time of chusing the Electors, and the Day on which they shall give their Votes; which Day shall be the same throughout the United States.

No Person except a natural born Citizen, or a Citizen of the United States, at the time of the Adoption of this Constitution, shall be eligible to the Office of President; neither shall any Person be eligible to that Office who shall not have attained to the Age of thirty five Years, and been fourteen Years a Resident within the United States.

In Case of the Removal of the President from Office, or of his Death, Resignation, or Inability to discharge the Powers and Duties of the said Office, the Same shall devolve on the Vice President, and the Congress may by Law provide for the Case of Removal, Death, Resignation or Inability, both of the President and Vice President, declaring what Officer shall then act as President, and such Officer shall act accordingly, until the Disability be removed, or a President shall be elected.

The President shall, at stated Times, receive for his Services, a Compensation, which shall neither be encreased nor diminished during the Period for which he shall have been elected, and he shall not receive within that Period any other Emolument from the United States, or any of them.

Before he enter on the Execution of his Office, he shall take the following Oath or Affirmation—"I do solemnly swear (or affirm) that I will faithfully execute the Office of President of the United States, and will to the best of my Ability, preserve, protect and defend the Constitution of the United States."

SECTION 2. The President shall be Commander in Chief of the Army and Navy of the United States, and of the Militia of the several States, when called into the actual Service of the United States; he may require the Opinion, in writing, of the principal Officer in each of the executive Departments, upon any Subject relating to the Duties of their respective Offices, and he shall have Power to grant Reprieves and Pardons for Offenses against the United States, except in Cases of Impeachment.

He shall have Power, by and with the Advice and Consent of the Senate, to make Treaties, provided two thirds of the Senators present concur; and he shall nominate, and by and with the Advice and Consent of the Senate, shall appoint Ambassadors, other public Ministers and Consuls, Judges of the supreme Court, and all other Officers of the United States, whose Appointments are not herein otherwise provided for, and which shall be established by Law: but the Congress may by Law vest the Appointment of such inferior Officers, as they think proper, in the President alone, in the Courts of Law, or in the Heads of Departments.

The President shall have Power to fill up all Vacancies that may happen during the Recess of the Senate, by granting Commissions which shall expire at the End of their next Session.

SECTION 3. He shall from time to time give to the Congress Information of the State of the Union, and recommend to their Consideration such Measures as he shall judge necessary and expedient; he may, on extraordinary Occasions, convene both Houses, or either of them, and in Case of Disagreement between them, with Respect to the Time of Adjournment, he may adjourn them to such Time as he shall think proper; he shall receive Ambassadors and other public Ministers; he shall take Care that the Laws be faithfully executed, and shall Commission all the Officers of the United States.

SECTION 4. The President, Vice President and all Civil Officers of the United States, shall be removed from office on Impeachment for, and Conviction of, Treason, Bribery, or other high Crimes and Misdemeanors.

ARTICLE III

SECTION 1. The judicial Power of the United States, shall be vested in one supreme Court, and in such inferior Courts as the Congress may from time to time ordain and establish. The Judges, both of the supreme and inferior Courts, shall hold their Offices during good Behaviour, and shall, at stated Times, receive for their Services, a Compensation, which shall not be diminished during their Continuance in Office.

SECTION 2. The judicial Power shall extend to all Cases, in Law and Equity, arising under this Constitution, the Laws of the United States, and Treaties made, or which shall be made, under their Authority;—to all Cases affecting Ambassadors, other public Ministers and Consuls;—to all Cases of admiralty and maritime Jurisdiction;—to Controversies to which the United States shall be a Party;—to Controversies between two or more States;—between a State and Citizens of another State;—between Citizens of different States;—between Citizens of the same State claiming Lands under Grants of different States, and between a State, or the Citizens thereof, and foreign States, Citizens or Subjects.

In all Cases affecting Ambassadors, other public Ministers and Consuls, and those in which a State shall be Party, the supreme Court shall have original Jurisdiction. In all the other Cases before mentioned, the supreme Court shall have appellate Jurisdiction, both as to Law and Fact, with such Exceptions, and under such Regulations as the Congress shall make.

The Trial of all Crimes, except in cases of Impeachment, shall be by Jury; and such Trial shall be held in the State where the said Crimes shall have been committed; but when not committed within any State, the Trial shall be at such Place or Places as the Congress may by Law have directed.

SECTION 3. Treason against the United States, shall consist only in levying War against them, or in adhering to their Enemies, giving them Aid and Comfort. No Person shall be convicted of Treason unless on the Testimony of two Witnesses to the same overt Act, or on Confession in open Court.

The Congress shall have Power to declare the Punishment of Treason, but no Attainder or Treason shall work Corruption of Blood, or Forfeiture except during the Life of the Person attainted.

ARTICLE IV

SECTION 1. Full Faith and Credit shall be given in each State to the public Acts, Records, and judicial Proceedings of every other State. And the Congress may by general Laws prescribe the Manner in which such Acts, Records and Proceedings shall be proved, and the Effect thereof.

SECTION 2. The Citizens of each State shall be entitled to all Privileges and Immunities of Citizens in the several States.

A Person charged in any State with Treason, Felony, or other Crime, who shall flee from Justice, and be found in another State, shall on Demand of the executive Authority of the State from which he fled, be delivered up, to be removed to the State having Jurisdiction of the Crime.

No Person held to Service or Labour in one State, under the Laws thereof, escaping into another, shall, in Consequence of any Law or Regulation therein, be discharged from such Service or Labour, but shall be delivered up on Claim of the Party to whom such Service or Labour may be due.

SECTION 3. New States may be admitted by the Congress into this Union; but no new State shall be formed or erected within the Jurisdiction of any other State; nor any State be formed by the Junction of two or more States, or

Parts of States, without the Consent of the Legislatures of the States concerned as well as of the Congress.

The Congress shall have Power to dispose of and make all needful Rules and Regulations respecting the Territory or other Property belonging to the United States; and nothing in this Constitution shall be so construed as to Prejudice any Claims of the United States, or of any particular State.

SECTION 4. The United States shall guarantee to every State in this Union a Republican Form of Government, and shall protect each of them against Invasion; and on Application of the Legislature, or of the Executive (when the Legislature cannot be convened) against domestic Violence.

ARTICLE V

The Congress, whenever two thirds of both Houses shall deem it necessary, shall propose Amendments to this Constitution, or, on the Application of the Legislatures of two thirds of the several States, shall call a Convention for proposing Amendments, which, in either Case, shall be valid to all Intents and Purposes, as Part of this Constitution, when ratified by the Legislatures of three fourths of the several States, or by Conventions in three fourths thereof, as the one or the other Mode of Ratification may be proposed by the Congress; Provided [that no Amendment which may be made prior to the Year One thousand eight hundred and eight shall in any Manner affect the first and fourth Clauses in the Ninth Section of the first Article; and] that no State, without its Consent, shall be deprived of its equal Suffrage in the Senate.

ARTICLE VI

All Debts contracted and Engagements entered into, before the Adoption of this Constitution, shall be as valid against the United States under this Constitution, as under the Confederation.

This Constitution, and the Laws of the United States which shall be made in Pursuance thereof; and all Treaties made, or which shall be made, under the Authority of the United States, shall be the supreme Law of the Land; and the Judges in every State shall be bound thereby, any Thing in the Constitution or Laws of any State to the Contrary notwithstanding.

The Senators and Representatives before mentioned, and the Members of the several State Legislatures, and all executive and judicial Officers, both of the United States and of the several States, shall be bound by Oath or Affirmation, to support this Constitution; but no religious Test shall ever be required as a Qualification to any Office or public Trust under the United States.

ARTICLE VII

The Ratification of the Conventions of nine States, shall be sufficient for the Establishment of this Constitution between the States so ratifying the Same.

AMENDMENT I

[First ten amendments ratified December 15, 1791]

Congress shall make no law respecting an establishment of religion, or prohibiting the free exercise thereof; or abridging the freedom of speech, or of the press; or the right of the people peaceably to assemble, and to petition the Government for a redress of grievances.

AMENDMENT II

A well regulated Militia, being necessary to the security of a free State, the right of the people to keep and bear Arms, shall not be infringed.

AMENDMENT III

No Soldier shall, in time of peace be quartered in any house, without the consent of the Owner, nor in time of war, but in a manner to be prescribed by law.

AMENDMENT IV

The right of the people to be secure in their persons, houses, papers, and effects, against unreasonable searches and seizures, shall not be violated, and no Warrants shall issue, but upon probable cause, supported by Oath or affirmation, and particularly describing the place to be searched, and the persons or things to be seized.

AMENDMENT V

No person shall be held to answer for a capital, or otherwise infamous crime, unless on a presentment or indictment of a Grand Jury, except in cases arising in the land or naval forces, or in the Militia, when in actual service in time of War or public danger; nor shall any person be subject for the same offence to be twice put in jeopardy of life or limb; nor shall be compelled in any criminal case to be a witness against himself, nor be deprived of life, liberty, or property, without due process of law; nor shall private property be taken for public use, without just compensation.

AMENDMENT VI

In all criminal prosecutions, the accused shall enjoy the right to a speedy and public trial, by an impartial jury of the State and district wherein the crime shall have been committed, which district shall have been previously ascertained by law, and to be informed of the nature and cause of the accusation; to be confronted with the witnesses against him; to have compulsory process for obtaining witnesses in his favor, and to have the Assistance of Counsel for his defence.

AMENDMENT VII

In Suits at common law, where the value in controversy shall exceed twenty dollars, the right of trial by jury shall be preserved, and no fact tried by a jury, shall be otherwise re-examined in any Court of the United States, than according to the rules of the common law.

AMENDMENT VIII

Excessive bail shall not be required, nor excessive fines imposed, nor cruel and unusual punishments inflicted.

AMENDMENT IX

The enumeration in the Constitution, of certain rights, shall not be construed to deny or disparage others retained by the people.

AMENDMENT X

The powers not delegated to the United States by the Constitution, nor prohibited by it to the States, are reserved to the States respectively, or to the people.

AMENDMENT XI *[Ratified February 7, 1795]*

The Judicial power of the United States shall not be construed to extend to any suit in law or equity, commenced or prosecuted against one of the United States by Citizens of another State, or by Citizens or Subjects of any Foreign State.

AMENDMENT XII *[Ratified June 15, 1804]*

The Electors shall meet in their respective states and vote by ballot for President and Vice-President, one of whom, at least, shall not be an inhabitant of the same state with themselves; they shall name in their ballots the person voted for as President, and in distinct ballots the person voted for as Vice-President, and they shall make distinct lists of all persons voted for as President, and of all persons voted for as Vice-President, and of the number of votes for each, which lists they shall sign and certify, and transmit sealed to the seat of the government of the United States, directed to the President of the Senate;—The President of the Senate shall, in the presence of the Senate and House of Representatives, open all the certificates and the votes shall then be counted;—The person having the greatest number of votes for President, shall be the President, if such number be a majority of the whole number of Electors appointed; and if no person have such majority, then from the persons having the highest numbers not exceeding three on the list of those voted for as President, the House of Representatives shall choose immediately, by ballot, the President. But in choosing the President, the votes shall be taken by states, the representation from each state having one vote; a quorum for this purpose shall consist of a member or members from two-thirds of the states, and a majority of all the states shall be necessary to a choice. And if the House of Representatives shall not choose a President whenever the right of choice shall devolve upon them, before the fourth day of March next following, then the Vice-President shall act as President, as in the case of the death or other constitutional disability of the President;—The person having the greatest number of votes as Vice-President, shall be the Vice-President, if such number be a majority of the whole number of Electors appointed, and if no person have a majority, then from the two highest numbers on the list, the Senate shall choose the Vice-President; a quorum for the purpose shall consist of two-thirds of the whole number of Senators, and a majority of the whole number shall be necessary to a choice. But no person constitutionally ineligible to the office of President shall be eligible to that of Vice-President of the United States.

AMENDMENT XIII *[Ratified December 6, 1865]*

SECTION 1. Neither slavery nor involuntary servitude, except as a punishment for crime whereof the party shall have been duly convicted, shall exist within the United States, or any place subject to their jurisdiction.

SECTION 2. Congress shall have power to enforce this article by appropriate legislation.

AMENDMENT XIV *[Ratified July 9, 1868]*

SECTION 1. All persons born or naturalized in the United States and subject to the jurisdiction thereof, are citizens of the United States and of the State wherein they reside. No State shall make or enforce any law which shall abridge the privileges or immunities of citizens of the United States; nor shall any State deprive any person of life, liberty, or property, without due process of law; nor deny to any person within its jurisdiction the equal protection of the laws.

SECTION 2. Representatives shall be apportioned among the several States according to their respective numbers, counting the whole number of persons in each State, excluding Indians not taxed. But when the right to vote at any election for the choice of electors for President and Vice President of the United States, Representatives in Congress, the Executive and Judicial officers of a State, or the members of the Legislature thereof, is denied to any of the male inhabitants of such State, being twenty-one years of age, and citizens of the United States, or in any way abridged, except for participation in rebellion, or other crime, the basis of representation therein shall be reduced in the proportion which the number of such male citizens shall bear to the whole number of male citizens twenty-one years of age in such State.

SECTION 3. No person shall be a Senator or Representative in Congress, or elector of President and Vice President, or hold any office, civil or military, under the United States, or under any State, who, having previously taken an oath, as a member of Congress, or as an officer of the United States, or as a member of any State legislature, or as an executive or judicial officer of any State, to support the Constitution of the United States, shall have engaged in insurrection or rebellion against the same, or given aid or comfort to the enemies thereof. But Congress may by a vote of two-thirds of each House, remove such disability.

SECTION 4. The validity of the public debt of the United States, authorized by law, including debts incurred for payment of pensions and bounties for services in suppressing insurrection or rebellion, shall not be questioned. But neither the United States nor any State shall assume or pay any debt or obligation incurred in aid of insurrection or rebellion against the United States, or any claim for the loss or emancipation of any slave; but all such debts, obligations and claims shall be held illegal and void.

SECTION 5. The Congress shall have power to enforce, by appropriate legislation, the provisions of this article.

AMENDMENT XV *[Ratified February 3, 1870]*

SECTION 1. The right of citizens of the United States to vote shall not be denied or abridged by the United States or by any State on account of race, color, or previous condition of servitude.

SECTION 2. The Congress shall have power to enforce this article by appropriate legislation.

AMENDMENT XVI *[Ratified February 3, 1913]*

The Congress shall have power to lay and collect taxes on incomes, from whatever source derived, without apportionment among the several States, and without regard to any census or enumeration.

AMENDMENT XVII *[Ratified April 8, 1913]*

The Senate of the United States shall be composed of two Senators from each State, elected by the people thereof, for six years; and each Senator shall have one vote. The electors in each State shall have the qualifications requisite for electors of the most numerous branch of the State legislatures.

When vacancies happen in the representation of any State in the Senate, the executive authority of such State shall issue writs of election to fill such vacancies: *Provided,* That the legislature of any State may empower the executive thereof to make temporary appointments until the people fill the vacancies by election as the legislature may direct.

This amendment shall not be so construed as to affect the election or term of any Senator chosen before it becomes valid as part of the Constitution.

AMENDMENT XVIII *[Ratified January 16, 1919]*

SECTION 1. After one year from the ratification of this article the manufacture, sale, or transportation of intoxicating liquors within, the importation thereof into, or the exportation thereof from the United States and all territory subject to the jurisdiction thereof for beverage purposes is hereby prohibited.

SECTION 2. The Congress and the several States shall have concurrent power to enforce this article by appropriate legislation.

SECTION 3. This article shall be inoperative unless it shall have been ratified as an amendment to the Constitution by the legislatures of the several States, as provided in the Constitution, within seven years from the date of the submission hereof to the States by the Congress.

AMENDMENT XIX *[Ratified August 18, 1920]*

The right of citizens of the United States to vote shall not be denied or abridged by the United States or by any State on account of sex.

Congress shall have power to enforce this article by appropriate legislation.

AMENDMENT XX *[Ratified January 23, 1933]*

SECTION 1. The terms of the President and Vice President shall end at noon on the 20th day of January, and the terms of Senators and Representatives at noon on the 3d day of January, of the years in which such terms would have ended if this article had not been ratified; and the terms of their successors shall then begin.

SECTION 2. The Congress shall assemble at least once in every year, and such meeting shall begin at noon on the 3d day of January, unless they shall by law appoint a different day.

SECTION 3. If, at the time fixed for the beginning of the term of the President, the President elect shall have died, the Vice President elect shall become President. If a President shall not have been chosen before the time fixed for the beginning of his term, or if the President elect shall have failed to qualify, then the Vice President elect shall act as President until a President shall have qualified; and the Congress may by law provide for the case wherein neither a President elect nor a Vice President elect shall have qualified, declaring who shall then act as President, or the manner in which one who is to act shall be selected, and such person shall act accordingly until a President or Vice President shall have qualified.

SECTION 4. The Congress may by law provide for the case of the death of any of the persons from whom the House of Representatives may choose a President whenever the right of choice shall have devolved upon them, and for the case of the death of any of the persons from whom the Senate may choose a Vice President whenever the right of choice shall have devolved upon them.

SECTION 5. Sections 1 and 2 shall take effect on the 15th day of October following the ratification of this article.

SECTION 6. This article shall be inoperative unless it shall have been ratified as an amendment to the Constitution by the legislatures of three-fourths of the several States within seven years from the date of its submission.

AMENDMENT XXI *[Ratified December 5, 1933]*

SECTION 1. The eighteenth article of amendment to the Constitution of the United States is hereby repealed.

SECTION 2. The transportation or importation into any State, Territory or possession of the United States for delivery or use therein of intoxicating liquors, in violation of the laws thereof, is hereby prohibited.

SECTION 3. This article shall be inoperative unless it shall have been ratified as an amendment to the Constitution by conventions in the several States, as provided in the Constitution, within seven years from the date of the submission hereof to the States by the Congress.

AMENDMENT XXII *[Ratified February 27, 1951]*

SECTION 1. No person shall be elected to the office of the President more than twice, and no person who has held the office of President, or acted as President, for more than two years of a term to which some other person was elected President shall be elected to the office of the President more than once. But this Article shall not apply to any person holding the office of President when this Article was proposed by the Congress, and shall not prevent any person who may be holding the office of President, or acting as President, during the term within which this Article become operative from holding the office of President or acting as President during the remainder of such term.

SECTION 2. This Article shall be inoperative unless it shall have been ratified as an amendment to the Constitution by the legislatures of three-fourths of the several States within seven years from the date of its submission to the States by the Congress.

AMENDMENT XXIII *[Ratified March 29, 1961]*

SECTION 1. The District constituting the seat of Government of the United States shall appoint in such manner as the Congress may direct:

A number of electors of President and Vice President equal to the whole number of Senators and Representatives in Congress to which the District would be entitled if it were a State, but in no event more than the least populous State; they shall be in addition to those appointed by the States, but they shall be considered, for the purposes of the election of President and Vice President, to be electors appointed by a State; and they shall meet in the District and perform such duties as provided by the twelfth article of amendment.

SECTION 2. The Congress shall have power to enforce this article by appropriate legislation.

AMENDMENT XXIV [Ratified January 23, 1964]

SECTION 1. The right of citizens of the United States to vote in any primary or other election for President or Vice President, for electors for President or Vice President, or for Senator or Representative in Congress, shall not be denied or abridged by the United States or any State by reason of failure to pay any poll tax or other tax.

SECTION 2. The Congress shall have power to enforce this article by appropriate legislation.

AMENDMENT XXV [Ratified February 10, 1967]

SECTION 1. In case of the removal of the President from office or of his death or resignation, the Vice President shall become President.

SECTION 2. Whenever there is a vacancy in the office of the Vice President, the President shall nominate a Vice President who shall take office upon confirmation by a majority vote of both Houses of Congress.

SECTION 3. Whenever the President transmits to the President pro tempore of the Senate and the Speaker of the House of Representatives his written declaration that he is unable to discharge the powers and duties of his office, and until he transmits to them a written declaration to the contrary, such powers and duties shall be discharged by the Vice President as Acting President.

SECTION 4. Whenever the Vice President and a majority of either the principal officers of the executive departments or of such other body as Congress may by law provide, transmit to the President pro tempore of the Senate and the Speaker of the House of Representatives their written declaration that the President is unable to discharge the powers and duties of his office, the Vice President shall immediately assume the powers and duties of the office as Acting President.

Thereafter, when the President transmits to the President pro tempore of the Senate and the Speaker of the House of Representatives his written declaration that no inability exists, he shall resume the powers and duties of his office unless the Vice President and a majority of either the principal officers of the executive department or of such other body as Congress may by law provide, transmit within four days to the President pro tempore of the Senate and the Speaker of the House of Representatives their written declaration that the President is unable to discharge the powers and duties of his office. Thereupon Congress shall decide the issue, assembling within forty-eight hours for that purpose if not in session. If the Congress, within twenty-one days after receipt of the latter written declaration, or, if Congress is not in session, within twenty-one days after Congress is required to assemble, determines by two-thirds vote of both houses that the President is unable to discharge the powers and duties of his office, the Vice President shall continue to discharge the same as Acting President; otherwise, the President shall resume the powers and duties of his office.

AMENDMENT XXVI *[Ratified July 1, 1971]*

SECTION 1. The right of citizens of the United States, who are eighteen years of age or older, to vote shall not be denied or abridged by the United States or by any State on account of age.

SECTION 2. The Congress shall have power to enforce this article by appropriate legislation.

APPENDIX C: JUSTICES OF THE SUPREME COURT

Justices of the Supreme Court

	TENURE	APPOINTED BY	REPLACED
JOHN JAY*	1789–1795	Washington	
John Rutledge	1789–1791	Washington	
William Cushing	1789–1810	Washington	
James Wilson	1789–1798	Washington	
John Blair	1789–1796	Washington	
James Iredell	1790–1799	Washington	
Thomas Johnson	1791–1793	Washington	Rutledge
William Paterson	1793–1806	Washington	Johnson
JOHN RUTLEDGE	1795	Washington	Jay
Samuel Chase	1796–1811	Washington	Blair
OLIVER ELLSWORTH	1796–1800	Washington	Rutledge
Bushrod Washington	1798–1829	John Adams	Wilson
Alfred Moore	1799–1804	John Adams	Iredell
JOHN MARSHALL	1801–1835	John Adams	Ellsworth
William Johnson	1804–1834	Jefferson	Moore
Brockholst Livingston	1806–1823	Jefferson	Paterson
Thomas Todd	1807–1826	Jefferson	(new judgeship)
Gabriel Duval	1811–1835	Madison	Chase
Joseph Story	1811–1845	Madison	Cushing
Smith Thompson	1823–1843	Monroe	Livingston
Robert Trimble	1826–1828	John Q. Adams	Todd
John McLean	1829–1861	Jackson	Trimble
Henry Baldwin	1830–1844	Jackson	Washington
James Wayne	1835–1867	Jackson	Johnson
ROGER B. TANEY	1836–1864	Jackson	Marshall
Phillip P. Barbour	1836–1841	Jackson	Duval
John Catron	1837–1865	Jackson	(new judgeship)
John McKinley	1837–1852	Van Buren	(new judgeship)
Peter V. Daniel	1841–1860	Van Buren	Barbour
Samuel Nelson	1845–1872	Tyler	Thompson
Levi Woodbury	1846–1851	Polk	Story
Robert C. Grier	1846–1870	Polk	Baldwin
Benjamin R. Curtis	1851–1857	Fillmore	Woodbury
John A. Campbell	1853–1861	Pierce	McKinley
Nathan Clifford	1858–1881	Buchanan	Curtis
Noah H. Swayne	1862–1881	Lincoln	McLean
Samuel F. Miller	1862–1890	Lincoln	Daniel
David Davis	1862–1877	Lincoln	Campbell
Stephen J. Field	1863–1897	Lincoln	(new judgeship)
SALMON CHASE	1864–1873	Lincoln	Taney
William Strong	1870–1880	Grant	Grier
Joseph P. Bradley	1870–1892	Grant	Wayne
Ward Hunt	1872–1882	Grant	Nelson
MORRISON R. WAITE	1874–1888	Grant	Chase
John Marshall Harlan	1877–1911	Hayes	Davis
William B. Woods	1880–1887	Hayes	Strong
Stanley Matthews	1881–1889	Garfield	Swayne
Horace Gray	1881–1902	Arthur	Clifford
Samuel Blatchford	1882–1893	Arthur	Hunt
Lucius Q. C. Lamar	1888–1893	Cleveland	Woods
MELVILLE W. FULLER	1888–1910	Cleveland	Waite
David J. Brewer	1889–1910	Harrison	Matthews

Chief justices capitalized

Continued

Justices of the Supreme Court – Continued

	TENURE	APPOINTED BY	REPLACED
Henry B. Brown	1890–1906	Harrison	Miller
George Shiras, Jr.	1892–1903	Harrison	Bradley
Howell E. Jackson	1893–1895	Harrison	Lamar
EDWARD D. WHITE	1894–1910	Cleveland	Blatchford
Rufus W. Peckham	1895–1909	Cleveland	Jackson
Joseph McKenna	1898–1925	McKinley	Field
Oliver Wendell Holmes	1902–1932	T. Roosevelt	Gray
William R. Day	1903–1922	T. Roosevelt	Shiras
William H. Moody	1906–1910	T. Roosevelt	Brown
Horace H. Lurton	1909–1914	Taft	Peckham
Charles Evans Hughes	1910–1916	Taft	Brewer
Edward D. White	1910–1921	Taft	Fuller
Willis Van Devanter	1910–1937	Taft	White
Joseph R. Lamar	1910–1916	Taft	Moody
Mahlon Pitney	1912–1922	Taft	Harlan
James McReynolds	1914–1941	Wilson	Lurton
Louis D. Brandeis	1916–1939	Wilson	Lamar
John H. Clark	1916–1922	Wilson	Hughes
WILLIAM H. TAFT	1921–1930	Harding	White
George Sutherland	1922–1938	Harding	Clarke
Pierce Butler	1922–1939	Harding	Day
Edward T. Sanford	1923–1930	Harding	Pitney
Harlan F. Stone	1925–1941	Coolidge	McKenna
CHARLES EVANS HUGHES	1930–1941	Hoover	Taft
Owen J. Roberts	1932–1945	Hoover	Sanford
Benjamin N. Cardozo	1932–1938	Hoover	Holmes
Hugo L. Black	1937–1971	F. Roosevelt	Van Devanter
Stanley F. Reed	1938–1957	F. Roosevelt	Sutherland
Felix Frankfurter	1939–1962	F. Roosevelt	Cardozo
William O. Douglas	1939–1975	F. Roosevelt	Brandeis
Frank Murphy	1940–1949	F. Roosevelt	Butler
James F. Byrnes	1941–1942	F. Roosevelt	McReynolds
HARLAN F. STONE	1941–1946	F. Roosevelt	Hughes
Robert H. Jackson	1941–1954	F. Roosevelt	Stone
Wiley B. Rutledge	1943–1949	F. Roosevelt	Byrnes
Harold H. Burton	1945–1958	Truman	Roberts
FRED M. VINSON	1946–1953	Truman	Stone
Tom C. Clark	1949–1967	Truman	Murphy
Sherman Minton	1949–1956	Truman	Rutledge
EARL WARREN	1954–1969	Eisenhower	Vinson
John M. Harlan	1955–1971	Eisenhower	Jackson
William J. Brennan	1957–	Eisenhower	Minton
Charles E. Whittaker	1957–1962	Eisenhower	Reed
Potter Stewart	1959–1981	Eisenhower	Burton
Byron R. White	1962–	Kennedy	Whittaker
Arthur J. Goldberg	1962–1965	Kennedy	Frankfurter
Abe Fortas	1965–1969	Johnson	Goldberg
Thurgood Marshall	1967–	Johnson	Clark
WARREN E. BURGER	1969–	Nixon	Warren
Harry A. Blackmun	1970–	Nixon	Fortas
Lewis F. Powell	1971–	Nixon	Black
William H. Rehnquist	1971–	Nixon	Harlan
John P. Stephens	1975–	Ford	Douglas
Sandra Day O'Connor	1981–	Reagan	Stewart

APPENDIX D:
COMPOSITION OF THE SUPREME COURT
SINCE 1900

Composition of the Supreme Court Since 1900

The table below represents the members of the Supreme Court since 1900. By locating the term in which a particular case was decided, the names of the justices on the Court at the time of the decision may be readily determined.

THE FULLER COURT (1900–1909 terms)

1900–01	Fuller	White	Gray	Peckham	Brown	Shiras	Harlan	Brewer	McKenna
1902	Fuller	White	Holmes	Peckham	Brown	Shiras	Harlan	Brewer	McKenna
1903–05	Fuller	White	Holmes	Peckham	Brown	Day	Harlan	Brewer	McKenna
1906–08	Fuller	White	Holmes	Peckham	Moody	Day	Harlan	Brewer	McKenna
1909	Fuller	White	Holmes	Lurton	Moody	Day	Harlan	Brewer	McKenna

THE WHITE COURT (1910–1920)

1910–11	White	VanDevanter	Holmes	Lurton	Lamar	Day	Harlan	Hughes	McKenna
1912–13	White	VanDevanter	Holmes	Lurton	Lamar	Day	Pitney	Hughes	McKenna
1914–15	White	VanDevanter	Holmes	McReynolds	Lamar	Day	Pitney	Hughes	McKenna
1916–20	White	VanDevanter	Holmes	McReynolds	Brandeis	Day	Pitney	Clarke	McKenna

THE TAFT COURT (1921–1929)

1921	Taft	VanDevanter	Holmes	McReynolds	Brandeis	Day	Pitney	Clarke	McKenna
1922	Taft	VanDevanter	Holmes	McReynolds	Brandeis	Butler	Pitney	Sutherland	McKenna
1923–24	Taft	VanDevanter	Holmes	McReynolds	Brandeis	Butler	Sanford	Sutherland	McKenna
1925–29	Taft	VanDevanter	Holmes	McReynolds	Brandeis	Butler	Sanford	Sutherland	Stone

THE HUGHES COURT (1930–1940)

1930–31	Hughes	VanDevanter	Holmes	McReynolds	Brandeis	Butler	Roberts	Sutherland	Stone
1932–36	Hughes	VanDevanter	Cardozo	McReynolds	Brandeis	Butler	Roberts	Sutherland	Stone
1937	Hughes	Black	Cardozo	McReynolds	Brandeis	Butler	Roberts	Sutherland	Stone
1938	Hughes	Black	Cardozo	McReynolds	Brandeis	Butler	Roberts	Reed	Stone
1939	Hughes	Black	Frankfurter	McReynolds	Douglas	Butler	Roberts	Reed	Stone
1940	Hughes	Black	Frankfurter	McReynolds	Douglas	Murphy	Roberts	Reed	Stone

continued

Composition of the Supreme Court Since 1900

THE STONE COURT (1941–1945)

1941–42	Stone	Black	Frankfurter	Byrnes	Douglas	Murphy	Reed	Roberts	Jackson
1943–44	Stone	Black	Frankfurter	Rutledge	Douglas	Murphy	Reed	Roberts	Jackson
1945	Stone	Black	Frankfurter	Rutledge	Douglas	Murphy	Reed	Burton	Jackson

THE VINSON COURT (1946–1952)

1946–48	Vinson	Black	Frankfurter	Rutledge	Douglas	Murphy	Reed	Burton	Jackson
1949–52	Vinson	Black	Frankfurter	Minton	Douglas	Clark	Reed	Burton	Jackson

THE WARREN COURT (1953–1968)

1953–54	Warren	Black	Frankfurter	Minton	Douglas	Clark	Reed	Burton	Jackson
1955	Warren	Black	Frankfurter	Minton	Douglas	Clark	Reed	Burton	Harlan
1956	Warren	Black	Frankfurter	Brennan	Douglas	Clark	Reed	Burton	Harlan
1957	Warren	Black	Frankfurter	Brennan	Douglas	Clark	Whittaker	Burton	Harlan
1958–61	Warren	Black	Frankfurter	Brennan	Douglas	Clark	Whittaker	Stewart	Harlan
1962–65	Warren	Black	Goldberg	Brennan	Douglas	Clark	White	Stewart	Harlan
1965–67	Warren	Black	Fortas	Brennan	Douglas	Clark	White	Stewart	Harlan
1967–69	Warren	Black	Fortas	Brennan	Douglas	Marshall	White	Stewart	Harlan

THE BURGER COURT (1969–)

1969	Burger	Black	Fortas	Brennan	Douglas	Marshall	White	Stewart	Harlan
1969–70	Burger	Black		Brennan	Douglas	Marshall	White	Stewart	Harlan
1970	Burger	Black	Blackmun	Brennan	Douglas	Marshall	Whtie	Stewart	Harlan
1971	Burger	Powell	Blackmun	Brennan	Douglas	Marshall	White	Stewart	Rehnquist
1975	Burger	Powell	Blackmun	Brennan	Stevens	Marshall	White	Stewart	Rehnquist
1981	Burger	Powell	Blackmun	Brennan	Stevens	Marshall	White	O'Connor	Rehnquist

INDEX

Cross-references to dictionary entries are located in the text at the end of each definition paragraph. Page references in BOLD type indicate dictionary entries.